Android Studio 3.0 Development Essentials

Android 8 Edition

Android Studio 3.0 Development Essentials – Android 8 Edition

Contents

Table of Contents

1. Introduction

Fully updated for Android Studio 3.0 and Android 8, the goal of this book is to teach the skills necessary to develop Android based applications using the Android Studio Integrated Development Environment (IDE), the Android 8 Software Development Kit (SDK) and the Java programming language.

Beginning with the basics, this book provides an outline of the steps necessary to set up an Android development and testing environment. An overview of Android Studio is included covering areas such as tool windows, the code editor and the Layout Editor tool. An introduction to the architecture of Android is followed by an in-depth look at the design of Android applications and user interfaces using the Android Studio environment. More advanced topics such as database management, content providers and intents are also covered, as are touch screen handling, gesture recognition, camera access and the playback and recording of both video and audio. This edition of the book also covers printing, transitions and cloud-based file storage.

The concepts of material design are also covered in detail, including the use of floating action buttons, Snackbars, tabbed interfaces, card views, navigation drawers and collapsing toolbars.

In addition to covering general Android development techniques, the book also includes Google Play specific topics such as implementing maps using the Google Maps Android API, and submitting apps to the Google Play Developer Console.

Other key features of Android Studio 3 and Android 8 are also covered in detail including the Layout Editor, the ConstraintLayout and ConstraintSet classes, constraint chains and barriers, direct reply notifications and multi-window support.

Chapters also cover advanced features of Android Studio such as App Links, Instant Apps, the Android Studio Profiler and Gradle build configuration.

Assuming you already have some Java programming experience, are ready to download Android Studio and the Android SDK, have access to a Windows, Mac or Linux system and ideas for some apps to develop, you are ready to get started.

1.1 Downloading the Code Samples

The source code and Android Studio project files for the examples contained in this book are available for download at:

http://www.ebookfrenzy.com/print/androidstudio30/index.php

The steps to load a project from the code samples into Android Studio are as follows:

1. From the Welcome to Android Studio dialog, select the Open an existing Android Studio project option.

2. In the project selection dialog, navigate to and select the folder containing the project to be imported and click on OK.

1.2 Firebase Essentials Book Now Available

Firebase Essentials - Android Edition, a companion book to Android Studio Development Essentials provides everything you need to successfully integrate Firebase cloud features into your Android apps.

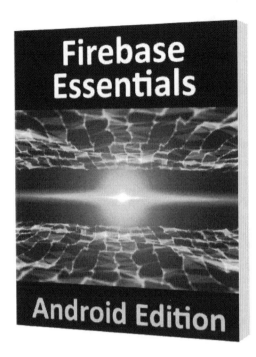

The Firebase Essentials book covers the key features of Android app development using Firebase including integration with Android Studio, User Authentication (including email, Twitter, Facebook and phone number sign-in), Realtime Database, Cloud Storage, Firebase Cloud Messaging (both upstream and downstream), Dynamic Links, Invites, App Indexing, Test Lab, Remote Configuration, Cloud Functions, Analytics and Performance Monitoring.

Find out more at *https://goo.gl/5F381e*.

1.3 Feedback

We want you to be satisfied with your purchase of this book. If you find any errors in the book, or have any comments, questions or concerns please contact us at *feedback@ebookfrenzy.com*.

1.4 Errata

While we make every effort to ensure the accuracy of the content of this book, it is inevitable that a book covering a subject area of this size and complexity may include some errors and oversights. Any known issues with the book will be outlined, together with solutions, at the following URL:

http://www.ebookfrenzy.com/errata/androidstudio30.html

In the event that you find an error not listed in the errata, please let us know by emailing our technical support team at *feedback@ebookfrenzy.com*. They are there to help you and will work to resolve any problems you may encounter.

1.5 Download the eBook

Thank you for purchasing the print edition of this book. If you would like to download the eBook version of this book, please email proof of purchase to *feedback@ebookfrenzy.com* and we will provide you with a download link for the book in PDF format.

2. Setting up an Android Studio Development Environment

Before any work can begin on the development of an Android application, the first step is to configure a computer system to act as the development platform. This involves a number of steps consisting of installing the Android Studio Integrated Development Environment (IDE) which also includes the Android Software Development Kit (SDK), the Kotlin plug-in and OpenJDK Java development environment.

This chapter will cover the steps necessary to install the requisite components for Android application development on Windows, macOS and Linux based systems.

2.1 System Requirements

Android application development may be performed on any of the following system types:

- Windows 7/8/10 (32-bit or 64-bit)

- macOS 10.10 or later (Intel based systems only)

- Linux systems with version 2.19 or later of GNU C Library (glibc)

- Minimum of 3GB of RAM (8GB is preferred)

- Approximately 4GB of available disk space

- 1280 x 800 minimum screen resolution

2.2 Downloading the Android Studio Package

Most of the work involved in developing applications for Android will be performed using the Android Studio environment. The content and examples in this book were created based on Android Studio version 3.0 which, at the time writing is the current version.

Android Studio is, however, subject to frequent updates so a newer version may have been released since this book was published.

The latest release of Android Studio may be downloaded from the primary download page which can be found at the following URL:

https://developer.android.com/studio/index.html

If this page provides instructions for downloading a newer version of Android Studio it is important to note that there may be some minor differences between this book and the software. A web search for Android Studio 3.0 should provide the option to download the older version in the event that these differences become a problem.

2.3 Installing Android Studio

Once downloaded, the exact steps to install Android Studio differ depending on the operating system on which the installation is being performed.

2.3.1 Installation on Windows

Locate the downloaded Android Studio installation executable file (named *android-studio-bundle-<version>.exe*) in a Windows Explorer window and double-click on it to start the installation process, clicking the *Yes* button in the User Account Control dialog if it appears.

Once the Android Studio setup wizard appears, work through the various screens to configure the installation to meet your requirements in terms of the file system location into which Android Studio should be installed and whether or not it should be made available to other users of the system. When prompted to select the components to install, make sure that the *Android Studio, Android SDK* and *Android Virtual Device* options are all selected.

Although there are no strict rules on where Android Studio should be installed on the system, the remainder of this book will assume that the installation was performed into *C:\Program Files\Android\Android Studio* and that the Android SDK packages have been installed into the user's *AppData\Local\Android\sdk* sub-folder. Once the options have been configured, click on the *Install* button to begin the installation process.

On versions of Windows with a Start menu, the newly installed Android Studio can be launched from the entry added to that menu during the installation. The executable may be pinned to the task bar for easy access by navigating to the *Android Studio\bin* directory, right-clicking on the executable and selecting the *Pin to Taskbar* menu option. Note that the executable is provided in 32-bit (*studio*) and 64-bit (*studio64*) executable versions. If you are running a 32-bit system be sure to use the *studio* executable.

2.3.2 Installation on macOS

Android Studio for macOS is downloaded in the form of a disk image (.dmg) file. Once the *android-studio-ide-<version>.dmg* file has been downloaded, locate it in a Finder window and double-click on it to open it as shown in Figure 2-1:

Figure 2-1

To install the package, simply drag the Android Studio icon and drop it onto the Applications folder. The Android Studio package will then be installed into the Applications folder of the system, a process which will typically take a few minutes to complete.

To launch Android Studio, locate the executable in the Applications folder using a Finder window and double-click on it.

For future easier access to the tool, drag the Android Studio icon from the Finder window and drop it onto the dock.

2.3.3 Installation on Linux

Having downloaded the Linux Android Studio package, open a terminal window, change directory to the location where Android Studio is to be installed and execute the following command:

```
unzip /<path to package>/android-studio-ide-<version>-linux.zip
```

Note that the Android Studio bundle will be installed into a sub-directory named *android-studio*. Assuming, therefore, that the above command was executed in */home/demo*, the software packages will be unpacked into */home/demo/android-studio*.

To launch Android Studio, open a terminal window, change directory to the *android-studio/bin* sub-directory and execute the following command:

```
./studio.sh
```

When running on a 64-bit Linux system, it will be necessary to install some 32-bit support libraries before Android Studio will run. On Ubuntu these libraries can be installed using the following command:

```
sudo apt-get install libc6:i386 libncurses5:i386 libstdc++6:i386 lib32z1 libbz2-1.0:i386
```

On RedHat and Fedora based 64-bit systems, use the following command:

```
sudo yum install zlib.i686 ncurses-libs.i686 bzip2-libs.i686
```

2.4 The Android Studio Setup Wizard

The first time that Android Studio is launched after being installed, a dialog will appear providing the option to import settings from a previous Android Studio version. If you have settings from a previous version and would like to import them into the latest installation, select the appropriate option and location. Alternatively, indicate that you do not need to import any previous settings and click on the OK button to proceed.

Next, the setup wizard may appear as shown in Figure 2-2 though this dialog does not appear on all platforms:

Figure 2-2

If the wizard appears, click on the Next button, choose the Standard installation option and click on Next once again.

Android Studio will proceed to download and configure the latest Android SDK and some additional components and packages. Once this process has completed, click on the *Finish* button in the *Downloading Components* dialog at which point the Welcome to Android Studio screen should then appear:

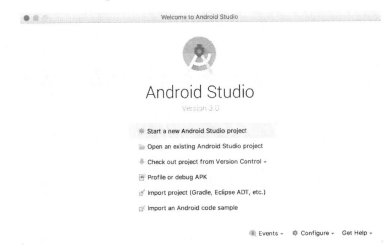

Figure 2-3

2.5 Installing Additional Android SDK Packages

The steps performed so far have installed Java, the Android Studio IDE and the current set of default Android SDK packages. Before proceeding, it is worth taking some time to verify which packages are installed and to install any missing or updated packages.

This task can be performed using the *Android SDK Settings* screen, which may be launched from within the Android Studio tool by selecting the *Configure -> SDK Manager* option from within the Android Studio welcome dialog. Once invoked, the *Android SDK* screen of the default settings dialog will appear as shown in Figure 2-4:

Figure 2-4

Immediately after installing Android Studio for the first time it is likely that only the latest released version of the Android SDK has been installed. To install older versions of the Android SDK simply select the checkboxes corresponding to the versions and click on the *Apply* button.

It is also possible that updates will be listed as being available for the latest SDK. To access detailed information about the packages that are available for update, enable the *Show Package Details* option located in the lower right-hand corner of the screen. This will display information similar to that shown in Figure 2-5:

Name	API Level	Revision	Status
Android TV Intel x86 Atom System Image	25	6	Not installed
Android Wear for China ARM EABI v7a System Image	25	3	Not installed
Android Wear for China Intel x86 Atom System Image	25	3	Not installed
Android Wear ARM EABI v7a System Image	25	3	Not installed
Android Wear Intel x86 Atom System Image	25	3	Not installed
Google APIs ARM 64 v8a System Image	25	8	Not installed
Google APIs ARM EABI v7a System Image	25	8	Not installed
Google APIs Intel x86 Atom System Image	25	8	Not installed
Google APIs Intel x86 Atom_64 System Image	25	6	Update Available: 8
Android 7.0 (Nougat)			
Google APIs	24	1	Not installed

Figure 2-5

The above figure highlights the availability of an update. To install the updates, enable the checkbox to the left of the item name and click on the *Apply* button.

In addition to the Android SDK packages, a number of tools are also installed for building Android applications. To view the currently installed packages and check for updates, remain within the SDK settings screen and select the SDK Tools tab as shown in Figure 2-6:

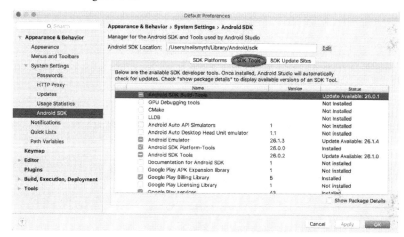

Figure 2-6

Within the Android SDK Tools screen, make sure that the following packages are listed as *Installed* in the Status column:

- Android SDK Build-tools

- Android Emulator

- Android SDK Platform-tools

- Android SDK Tools

- Google Play Services

- Instant Apps Development SDK

- Intel x86 Emulator Accelerator (HAXM installer)

- ConstraintLayout for Android

- Solver for ConstraintLayout

- Android Support Repository

- Google Repository

- Google USB Driver (Windows only)

In the event that any of the above packages are listed as *Not Installed* or requiring an update, simply select the checkboxes next to those packages and click on the *Apply* button to initiate the installation process.

Once the installation is complete, review the package list and make sure that the selected packages are now listed as *Installed* in the *Status* column. If any are listed as *Not installed,* make sure they are selected and click on the *Apply* button again.

2.6 Making the Android SDK Tools Command-line Accessible

Most of the time, the underlying tools of the Android SDK will be accessed from within the Android Studio environment. That being said, however, there will also be instances where it will be useful to be able to invoke those tools from a command prompt or terminal window. In order for the operating system on which you are developing to be able to find these tools, it will be necessary to add them to the system's *PATH* environment variable.

Regardless of operating system, the PATH variable needs to be configured to include the following paths (where *<path_to_android_sdk_installation>* represents the file system location into which the Android SDK was installed):

```
<path_to_android_sdk_installation>/sdk/tools
<path_to_android_sdk_installation>/sdk/tools/bin
<path_to_android_sdk_installation>/sdk/platform-tools
```

The location of the SDK on your system can be identified by launching the SDK Manager and referring to the *Android SDK Location:* field located at the top of the settings panel as highlighted in Figure 2-7:

Figure 2-7

Once the location of the SDK has been identified, the steps to add this to the PATH variable are operating system dependent:

2.6.1 Windows 7

1. Right-click on Computer in the desktop start menu and select Properties from the resulting menu.

2. In the properties panel, select the Advanced System Settings link and, in the resulting dialog, click on the Environment Variables… button.

3. In the Environment Variables dialog, locate the Path variable in the System variables list, select it and click on *Edit….* Locate the end of the current variable value string and append the path to the Android platform

tools to the end, using a semicolon to separate the path from the preceding values. For example, assuming the Android SDK was installed into C:\Users\demo\AppData\Local\Android\sdk, the following would be appended to the end of the current Path value:

```
;C:\Users\demo\AppData\Local\Android\sdk\platform-tools; C:\Users\demo\AppData\
Local\Android\sdk\tools; C:\Users\demo\AppData\Local\Android\sdk\tools\bin
```

4. Click on OK in each dialog box and close the system properties control panel.

Once the above steps are complete, verify that the path is correctly set by opening a *Command Prompt* window (*Start -> All Programs -> Accessories -> Command Prompt*) and at the prompt enter:

```
echo %Path%
```

The returned path variable value should include the paths to the Android SDK platform tools folders. Verify that the *platform-tools* value is correct by attempting to run the *adb* tool as follows:

```
adb
```

The tool should output a list of command line options when executed.

Similarly, check the *tools* path setting by attempting to launch the AVD Manager command line tool:

```
avdmanager
```

In the event that a message similar to the following message appears for one or both of the commands, it is most likely that an incorrect path was appended to the Path environment variable:

```
'adb' is not recognized as an internal or external command,
operable program or batch file.
```

2.6.2 Windows 8.1

1. On the start screen, move the mouse to the bottom right-hand corner of the screen and select Search from the resulting menu. In the search box, enter Control Panel. When the Control Panel icon appears in the results area, click on it to launch the tool on the desktop.

2. Within the Control Panel, use the Category menu to change the display to Large Icons. From the list of icons select the one labeled System.

3. Follow the steps outlined for Windows 7 starting from step 2 through to step 4.

Open the command prompt window (move the mouse to the bottom right-hand corner of the screen, select the Search option and enter *cmd* into the search box). Select *Command Prompt* from the search results.

Within the Command Prompt window, enter:

```
echo %Path%
```

The returned path variable value should include the paths to the Android SDK platform tools folders. Verify that the *platform-tools* value is correct by attempting to run the *adb* tool as follows:

```
adb
```

The tool should output a list of command line options when executed.

Similarly, check the *tools* path setting by attempting to run the AVD Manager command line tool:

```
avdmanager
```

In the event that a message similar to the following message appears for one or both of the commands, it is most likely that an incorrect path was appended to the Path environment variable:

```
'adb' is not recognized as an internal or external command,
```

```
operable program or batch file.
```

2.6.3 Windows 10

Right-click on the Start menu, select *System* from the resulting menu and click on the *Advanced system settings* option in the System window. Follow the steps outlined for Windows 7 starting from step 2 through to step 4.

2.6.4 Linux

On Linux, this configuration can typically be achieved by adding a command to the *.bashrc* file in your home directory (specifics may differ depending on the particular Linux distribution in use). Assuming that the Android SDK bundle package was installed into */home/demo/Android/sdk*, the export line in the *.bashrc* file would read as follows:

```
export PATH=/home/demo/Android/sdk/platform-tools:/home/demo/Android/sdk/tools:/
home/demo/Android/sdk/tools/bin:/home/demo/android-studio/bin:$PATH
```

Note also that the above command adds the *android-studio/bin* directory to the PATH variable. This will enable the *studio.sh* script to be executed regardless of the current directory within a terminal window.

2.6.5 macOS

A number of techniques may be employed to modify the $PATH environment variable on macOS. Arguably the cleanest method is to add a new file in the */etc/paths.d* directory containing the paths to be added to $PATH. Assuming an Android SDK installation location of */Users/demo/Library/Android/sdk*, the path may be configured by creating a new file named *android-sdk* in the */etc/paths.d* directory containing the following lines:

```
/Users/demo/Library/Android/sdk/tools
/Users/demo/Library/Android/sdk/tools/bin
/Users/demo/Library/Android/sdk/platform-tools
```

Note that since this is a system directory it will be necessary to use the *sudo* command when creating the file. For example:

```
sudo vi /etc/paths.d/android-sdk
```

2.7 Updating Android Studio and the SDK

From time to time new versions of Android Studio and the Android SDK are released. New versions of the SDK are installed using the Android SDK Manager. Android Studio will typically notify you when an update is ready to be installed.

To manually check for Android Studio updates, click on the *Configure -> Check for Update* menu option within the Android Studio welcome screen, or use the *Help -> Check for Update* menu option accessible from within the Android Studio main window.

2.8 Summary

Prior to beginning the development of Android based applications, the first step is to set up a suitable development environment. This consists of the Java Development Kit (JDK), Android SDKs, and Android Studio IDE. In this chapter, we have covered the steps necessary to install these packages on Windows, macOS and Linux.

3. Creating an Example Android App in Android Studio

The preceding chapters of this book have covered the steps necessary to configure an environment suitable for the development of Android applications using the Android Studio IDE. Before moving on to slightly more advanced topics, now is a good time to validate that all of the required development packages are installed and functioning correctly. The best way to achieve this goal is to create an Android application and compile and run it. This chapter will cover the creation of a simple Android application project using Android Studio. Once the project has been created, a later chapter will explore the use of the Android emulator environment to perform a test run of the application.

3.1 Creating a New Android Project

The first step in the application development process is to create a new project within the Android Studio environment. Begin, therefore, by launching Android Studio so that the "Welcome to Android Studio" screen appears as illustrated in Figure 3-1:

Figure 3-1

Once this window appears, Android Studio is ready for a new project to be created. To create the new project, simply click on the *Start a new Android Studio project* option to display the first screen of the *New Project* wizard as shown in Figure 3-2:

Figure 3-2

3.2 Defining the Project and SDK Settings

In the *New Project* window, set the *Application name* field to *AndroidSample*. The application name is the name by which the application will be referenced and identified within Android Studio and is also the name that will be used when the completed application goes on sale in the Google Play store.

The *Package Name* is used to uniquely identify the application within the Android application ecosystem. Although this can be set to any string that uniquely identifies your app, it is traditionally based on the reversed URL of your domain name followed by the name of the application. For example, if your domain is *www. mycompany.com*, and the application has been named *AndroidSample*, then the package name might be specified as follows:

```
com.mycompany.androidsample
```

If you do not have a domain name you can enter any other string into the Company Domain field, or you may use *example.com* for the purposes of testing, though this will need to be changed before an application can be published:

```
com.example.androidsample
```

The *Project location* setting will default to a location in the folder named *AndroidStudioProjects* located in your home directory and may be changed by clicking on the button to the right of the text field containing the current path setting.

Click Next to proceed. On the form factors screen, enable the *Phone and Tablet* option and set the minimum SDK setting to API 14: Android 4.0 (IceCreamSandwich). The reason for selecting an older SDK release is that this ensures that the finished application will be able to run on the widest possible range of Android devices. The higher the minimum SDK selection, the more the application will be restricted to newer Android devices. A useful chart (Figure 3-3) can be viewed by clicking on the *Help me choose* link. This outlines the various SDK versions and API levels available for use and the percentage of Android devices in the marketplace on which the application will run if that SDK is used as the minimum level. In general it should only be necessary to select a more recent SDK when that release contains a specific feature that is required for your application.

To help in the decision process, selecting an API level from the chart will display the features that are supported at that level.

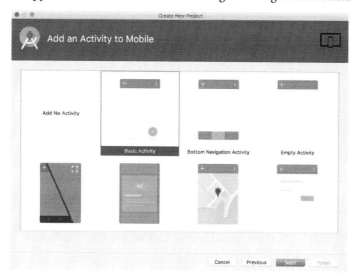

Figure 3-3

Since the project is not intended for Google TV, Android Auto or wearable devices, leave the remaining options disabled before clicking *Next*. Instant Apps will not be covered until later in this book so make sure that the *Include Android Instant App support* option is disabled.

3.3 Creating an Activity

The next step is to define the type of initial activity that is to be created for the application. A range of different activity types is available when developing Android applications. The *Empty, Master/Detail Flow, Google Maps* and *Navigation Drawer* options will be covered extensively in later chapters. For the purposes of this example, however, simply select the option to create a *Basic Activity*. The Basic Activity option creates a template user interface consisting of an app bar, menu, content area and a single floating action button.

Figure 3-4

Creating an Example Android App in Android Studio

With the Basic Activity option selected, click *Next*. On the final screen (Figure 3-5) name the activity and title *AndroidSampleActivity*. The activity will consist of a single user interface screen layout which, for the purposes of this example, should be named *activity_android_sample*. Finally, enter *My Android App* into the title field as shown in Figure 3-5:

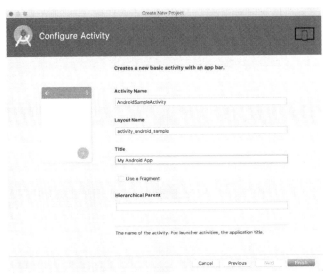

Figure 3-5

Since the AndroidSampleActivity is essentially the top level activity for the project and has no parent activity, there is no need to specify an activity for the Hierarchical parent (in other words AndroidSampleActivity does not need an "Up" button to return to another activity).

Click on *Finish* to initiate the project creation process.

3.4 Modifying the Example Application

At this point, Android Studio has created a minimal example application project and opened the main window.

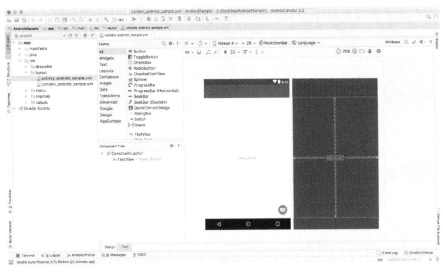

Figure 3-6

The newly created project and references to associated files are listed in the *Project* tool window located on the left-hand side of the main project window. The Project tool window has a number of modes in which information can be displayed. By default, this panel will be in *Android* mode. This setting is controlled by the menu at the top of the panel as highlighted in Figure 3-7. If the panel is not currently in Android mode, use the menu to switch mode:

Figure 3-7

The example project created for us when we selected the option to create an activity consists of a user interface containing a label that will read "Hello World!" when the application is executed.

The next step in this tutorial is to modify the user interface of our application so that it displays a larger text view object with a different message to the one provided for us by Android Studio.

The user interface design for our activity is stored in a file named *activity_android_sample.xml* which, in turn, is located under *app -> res -> layout* in the project file hierarchy. This layout file includes the app bar (also known as an action bar) that appears across the top of the device screen (marked A in Figure 3-8) and the floating action button (the email button marked B). In addition to these items, the *activity_android_sample.xml* layout file contains a reference to a second file containing the content layout (marked C):

Figure 3-8

Creating an Example Android App in Android Studio

By default, the content layout is contained within a file named *content_android_sample.xml* and it is within this file that changes to the layout of the activity are made. Using the Project tool window, locate this file as illustrated in Figure 3-9:

Figure 3-9

Once located, double-click on the file to load it into the user interface Layout Editor tool which will appear in the center panel of the Android Studio main window:

Figure 3-10

In the toolbar across the top of the Layout Editor window is a menu (currently set to *Nexus 4* in the above figure) which is reflected in the visual representation of the device within the Layout Editor panel. A wide range of other device options are available for selection by clicking on this menu.

To change the orientation of the device representation between landscape and portrait simply use the drop down menu immediately to the left of the device selection menu showing the ⬭ ▾ icon.

As can be seen in the device screen, the content layout already includes a label that displays a "Hello World!" message. Running down the left-hand side of the panel is a palette containing different categories of user interface components that may be used to construct a user interface, such as buttons, labels and text fields. It should be noted, however, that not all user interface components are obviously visible to the user. One such category consists of *layouts*. Android supports a variety of layouts that provide different levels of control over how visual user interface components are positioned and managed on the screen. Though it is difficult to tell from looking at the visual representation of the user interface, the current design has been created using a ConstraintLayout. This can be confirmed by reviewing the information in the *Component Tree* panel which, by default, is located in the lower left-hand corner of the Layout Editor panel and is shown in Figure 3-11:

Figure 3-11

As we can see from the component tree hierarchy, the user interface layout consists of a ConstraintLayout parent with a single child in the form of a TextView object.

Before proceeding, check that the Layout Editor's Autoconnect mode is enabled. This means that as components are added to the layout, the Layout Editor will automatically add constraints to make sure the components are correctly positioned for different screen sizes and device orientations (a topic that will be covered in much greater detail in future chapters). The Autoconnect button appears in the Layout Editor toolbar and is represented by a magnet icon. When disabled the magnet appears with a diagonal line through it (Figure 3-12). If necessary, re-enable Autoconnect mode by clicking on this button.

Figure 3-12

The next step in modifying the application is to delete the TextView component from the design. Begin by clicking on the TextView object within the user interface view so that it appears with a blue border around it. Once selected, press the Delete key on the keyboard to remove the object from the layout.

The Palette panel consists of two columns with the left-hand column containing a list of view component categories. The right-hand column lists the components contained within the currently selected category. In Figure 3-13, for example, the Button view is currently selected within the Widgets category:

Figure 3-13

Creating an Example Android App in Android Studio

Click and drag the *Button* object from the Widgets list and drop it in the center of the user interface design when the marker lines appear indicating the center of the display:

Figure 3-14

The next step is to change the text that is currently displayed by the Button component. The panel located to the right of the design area is the Attributes panel. This panel displays the attributes assigned to the currently selected component in the layout. Within this panel, locate the *text* property and change the current value from "Button" to "Demo" as shown in Figure 3-15:

Button

style	buttonStyle
background	
backgroundTint	
stateListAnimator	
elevation	
visibility	none
onClick	none

TextView

text	Demo
🔧 text	
contentDescription	

Figure 3-15

A useful shortcut to changing the text property of a component is to double-click on it in the layout. This will automatically locate the attribute in the attributes panel and select it ready for editing.

The second text property with a wrench next to it allows a text property to be set which only appears within the

18

Layout Editor tool but is not shown at runtime. This is useful for testing the way in which a visual component and the layout will behave with different settings without having to run the app repeatedly.

At this point it is important to explain the warning button located in the top right-hand corner of the Layout Editor tool as indicated in Figure 3-16. Obviously, this is indicating potential problems with the layout. For details on any problems, click on the button:

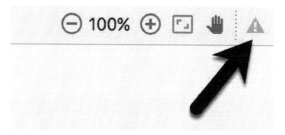

Figure 3-16

When clicked, a panel (Figure 3-17) will appear describing the nature of the problems and offering some possible corrective measures:

Figure 3-17

Currently, the only warning listed reads as follows:

```
Hardcoded string "Demo", should use '@string' resource
```

This I18N message is informing us that a potential issue exists with regard to the future internationalization of the project ("I18N" comes from the fact that the word "internationalization" begins with an "I", ends with an "N" and has 18 letters in between). The warning is reminding us that when developing Android applications, attributes and values such as text strings should be stored in the form of *resources* wherever possible. Doing so enables changes to the appearance of the application to be made by modifying resource files instead of changing the application source code. This can be especially valuable when translating a user interface to a different spoken language. If all of the text in a user interface is contained in a single resource file, for example, that file can be given to a translator who will then perform the translation work and return the translated file for inclusion in the application. This enables multiple languages to be targeted without the necessity for any source code changes to be made. In this instance, we are going to create a new resource named *demostring* and assign to it the string "Demo".

Click on the *Fix* button in the Issue Explanation panel to display the *Extract Resource* panel (Figure 3-18). Within this panel, change the resource name field to *demostring* and leave the resource value set to *Demo* before clicking on the OK button.

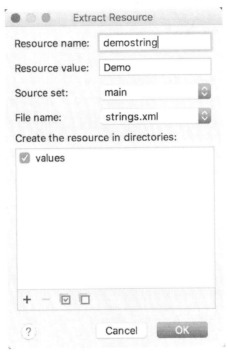

Figure 3-18

It is also worth noting that the string could also have been assigned to a resource when it was entered into the Attributes panel. This involves clicking on the button displaying three dots to the right of the property field in the Attributes panel and selecting the *Add new resource -> New String Value...* menu option from the resulting Resources dialog. In practice, however, it is often quicker to simply set values directly into the Attributes panel fields for any widgets in the layout, then work sequentially through the list in the warnings dialog to extract any necessary resources when the layout is complete.

3.5 Reviewing the Layout and Resource Files

Before moving on to the next chapter, we are going to look at some of the internal aspects of user interface design and resource handling. In the previous section, we made some changes to the user interface by modifying the *content_android_sample.xml* file using the Layout Editor tool. In fact, all that the Layout Editor was doing was providing a user-friendly way to edit the underlying XML content of the file. In practice, there is no reason why you cannot modify the XML directly in order to make user interface changes and, in some instances, this may actually be quicker than using the Layout Editor tool. At the bottom of the Layout Editor panel are two tabs labeled *Design* and *Text* respectively. To switch to the XML view simply select the *Text* tab as shown in Figure 3-19:

Figure 3-19

As can be seen from the structure of the XML file, the user interface consists of the ConstraintLayout component, which in turn, is the parent of the Button object. We can also see that the *text* property of the Button is set to our *demostring* resource. Although varying in complexity and content, all user interface layouts are structured in this hierarchical, XML based way.

One of the more powerful features of Android Studio can be found to the right-hand side of the XML editing panel. If the panel is not visible, display it by selecting the *Preview* button located along the right-hand edge of the Android Studio window. This is the Preview panel and shows the current visual state of the layout. As changes are made to the XML layout, these will be reflected in the preview panel. The layout may also be modified visually from within the Preview panel with the changes appearing in the XML listing. To see this in action, modify the XML layout to change the background color of the ConstraintLayout to a shade of red as follows:

```xml
<?xml version="1.0" encoding="utf-8"?>

<android.support.constraint.ConstraintLayout xmlns:android="http://schemas.
android.com/apk/res/android"

    xmlns:app="http://schemas.android.com/apk/res-auto"

    xmlns:tools="http://schemas.android.com/tools"

    android:layout_width="match_parent"

    android:layout_height="match_parent"

    app:layout_behavior="@string/appbar_scrolling_view_behavior"

  tools:context="com.ebookfrenzy.myapplication.AndroidSampleActivity"

    tools:showIn="@layout/activity_android_sample"

    android:background="#ff2438" >

    .

    .

</android.support.constraint.ConstraintLayout>
```

Note that the color of the preview changes in real-time to match the new setting in the XML file. Note also that a small red square appears in the left-hand margin (also referred to as the *gutter*) of the XML editor next to the line containing the color setting. This is a visual cue to the fact that the color red has been set on a property. Change the color value to #a0ff28 and note that both the small square in the margin and the preview change to green.

Finally, use the Project view to locate the *app -> res -> values -> strings.xml* file and double-click on it to load it into the editor. Currently the XML should read as follows:

```
<resources>
    <string name="app_name">AndroidSample</string>
    <string name="action_settings">Settings</string>
    <string name="demostring">Demo</string>
</resources>
```

As a demonstration of resources in action, change the string value currently assigned to the *demostring* resource to "Hello" and then return to the Layout Editor tool by selecting the tab for the layout file in the editor panel. Note that the layout has picked up the new resource value for the string.

There is also a quick way to access the value of a resource referenced in an XML file. With the Layout Editor tool in Text mode, click on the "@string/demostring" property setting so that it highlights and then press Ctrl-B on the keyboard (Cmd-B on macOS). Android Studio will subsequently open the *strings.xml* file and take you to the line in that file where this resource is declared. Use this opportunity to revert the string resource back to the original "Demo" text.

Resource strings may also be edited using the Android Studio Translations Editor. To open this editor, right-click on the *app -> res -> values -> strings.xml* file and select the *Open Editor* menu option. This will display the Translation Editor in the main panel of the Android Studio window:

Key	Resource Folder	Untranslata...	Default Value
app_name	app/src/main/res	☐	AndroidSample
action_settings	app/src/main/res	☐	Settings
demostring	app/src/main/res	☐	Demo

Figure 3-20

This editor allows the strings assigned to resource keys to be edited and for translations for multiple languages to be managed. The *Order a translation...* link may also be used to order a translation of the strings contained within the application to other languages. The cost of the translations will vary depending on the number of strings involved.

3.6 Summary

While not excessively complex, a number of steps are involved in setting up an Android development environment. Having performed those steps, it is worth working through a simple example to make sure the environment is correctly installed and configured. In this chapter, we have created a simple application and then used the Android Studio Layout Editor tool to modify the user interface layout. In doing so, we explored the importance of using resources wherever possible, particularly in the case of string values, and briefly touched on the topic of layouts. Finally, we looked at the underlying XML that is used to store the user interface designs of Android applications.

While it is useful to be able to preview a layout from within the Android Studio Layout Editor tool, there is no substitute for testing an application by compiling and running it. In a later chapter, the steps necessary to set up an emulator for testing purposes will be covered in detail. Before running the application, however, the next chapter will take a small detour to provide a guided tour of the Android Studio user interface.

4. A Tour of the Android Studio User Interface

While it is tempting to plunge into running the example application created in the previous chapter, doing so involves using aspects of the Android Studio user interface which are best described in advance.

Android Studio is a powerful and feature rich development environment that is, to a large extent, intuitive to use. That being said, taking the time now to gain familiarity with the layout and organization of the Android Studio user interface will considerably shorten the learning curve in later chapters of the book. With this in mind, this chapter will provide an initial overview of the various areas and components that make up the Android Studio environment.

4.1 The Welcome Screen

The welcome screen (Figure 4-1) is displayed any time that Android Studio is running with no projects currently open (open projects can be closed at any time by selecting the *File -> Close Project* menu option). If Android Studio was previously exited while a project was still open, the tool will by-pass the welcome screen next time it is launched, automatically opening the previously active project.

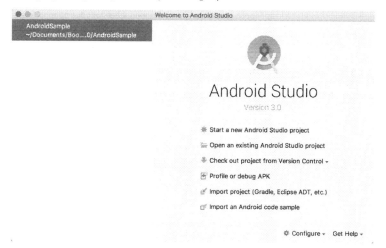

Figure 4-1

In addition to a list of recent projects, the Quick Start menu provides a range of options for performing tasks such as opening, creating and importing projects along with access to projects currently under version control. In addition, the *Configure* menu at the bottom of the window provides access to the SDK Manager along with a vast array of settings and configuration options. A review of these options will quickly reveal that there is almost no aspect of Android Studio that cannot be configured and tailored to your specific needs.

The Configure menu also includes an option to check if updates to Android Studio are available for download.

4.2 The Main Window

When a new project is created, or an existing one opened, the Android Studio *main window* will appear. When multiple projects are open simultaneously, each will be assigned its own main window. The precise configuration of the window will vary depending on which tools and panels were displayed the last time the project was open, but will typically resemble that of Figure 4-2.

Figure 4-2

The various elements of the main window can be summarized as follows:

A – Menu Bar – Contains a range of menus for performing tasks within the Android Studio environment.

B – Toolbar – A selection of shortcuts to frequently performed actions. The toolbar buttons provide quicker access to a select group of menu bar actions. The toolbar can be customized by right-clicking on the bar and selecting the *Customize Menus and Toolbars...* menu option.

C – Navigation Bar – The navigation bar provides a convenient way to move around the files and folders that make up the project. Clicking on an element in the navigation bar will drop down a menu listing the subfolders and files at that location ready for selection. This provides an alternative to the Project tool window.

D – Editor Window – The editor window displays the content of the file on which the developer is currently working. What gets displayed in this location, however, is subject to context. When editing code, for example, the code editor will appear. When working on a user interface layout file, on the other hand, the user interface Layout Editor tool will appear. When multiple files are open, each file is represented by a tab located along the top edge of the editor as shown in Figure 4-3.

Figure 4-3

E – Status Bar – The status bar displays informational messages about the project and the activities of Android Studio together with the tools menu button located in the far left corner. Hovering over items in the status bar will provide a description of that field. Many fields are interactive, allowing the user to click to perform tasks or obtain more detailed status information.

F – Project Tool Window – The project tool window provides a hierarchical overview of the project file structure allowing navigation to specific files and folders to be performed. The toolbar can be used to display the project in a number of different ways. The default setting is the *Android* view which is the mode primarily used in the remainder of this book.

The project tool window is just one of a number of tool windows available within the Android Studio environment.

4.3 The Tool Windows

In addition to the project view tool window, Android Studio also includes a number of other windows which, when enabled, are displayed along the bottom and sides of the main window. The tool window quick access menu can be accessed by hovering the mouse pointer over the button located in the far left-hand corner of the status bar (Figure 4-4) without clicking the mouse button.

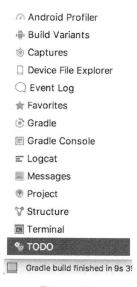

Figure 4-4

Selecting an item from the quick access menu will cause the corresponding tool window to appear within the main window.

Alternatively, a set of *tool window bars* can be displayed by clicking on the quick access menu icon in the status bar. These bars appear along the left, right and bottom edges of the main window (as indicated by the arrows in

Figure 4-5) and contain buttons for showing and hiding each of the tool windows. When the tool window bars are displayed, a second click on the button in the status bar will hide them.

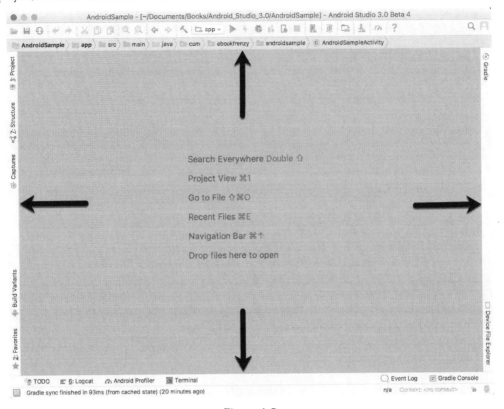

Figure 4-5

Clicking on a button will display the corresponding tool window while a second click will hide the window. Buttons prefixed with a number (for example 1: Project) indicate that the tool window may also be displayed by pressing the Alt key on the keyboard (or the Command key for macOS) together with the corresponding number.

The location of a button in a tool window bar indicates the side of the window against which the window will appear when displayed. These positions can be changed by clicking and dragging the buttons to different locations in other window tool bars.

Each tool window has its own toolbar along the top edge. The buttons within these toolbars vary from one tool to the next, though all tool windows contain a settings option, represented by the cog icon, which allows various aspects of the window to be changed. Figure 4-6 shows the settings menu for the project view tool window. Options are available, for example, to undock a window and to allow it to float outside of the boundaries of the Android Studio main window and to move and resize the tool panel.

Figure 4-6

All of the windows also include a far right button on the toolbar providing an additional way to hide the tool window from view. A search of the items within a tool window can be performed simply by giving that window focus by clicking in it and then typing the search term (for example the name of a file in the Project tool window). A search box will appear in the window's tool bar and items matching the search highlighted.

Android Studio offers a wide range of tool windows, the most commonly used of which are as follows:

Project – The project view provides an overview of the file structure that makes up the project allowing for quick navigation between files. Generally, double-clicking on a file in the project view will cause that file to be loaded into the appropriate editing tool.

Structure – The structure tool provides a high level view of the structure of the source file currently displayed in the editor. This information includes a list of items such as classes, methods and variables in the file. Selecting an item from the structure list will take you to that location in the source file in the editor window.

Captures – The captures tool window provides access to performance data files that have been generated by the monitoring tools contained within Android Studio.

Favorites – A variety of project items can be added to the favorites list. Right-clicking on a file in the project view, for example, provides access to an *Add to Favorites* menu option. Similarly, a method in a source file can be added as a favorite by right-clicking on it in the Structure tool window. Anything added to a Favorites list can be accessed through this Favorites tool window.

Build Variants – The build variants tool window provides a quick way to configure different build targets for the current application project (for example different builds for debugging and release versions of the application, or multiple builds to target different device categories).

TODO – As the name suggests, this tool provides a place to review items that have yet to be completed on the project. Android Studio compiles this list by scanning the source files that make up the project to look for comments that match specified TODO patterns. These patterns can be reviewed and changed by selecting the *File -> Settings…* menu option (*Android Studio -> Preferences…* on macOS) and navigating to the *TODO* page listed under *Editor*.

Messages – The messages tool window records output from the Gradle build system (Gradle is the underlying system used by Android Studio for building the various parts of projects into runnable applications) and can be useful for identifying the causes of build problems when compiling application projects.

Logcat – The Logcat tool window provides access to the monitoring log output from a running application in addition to options for taking screenshots and videos of the application and stopping and restarting a process.

Terminal – Provides access to a terminal window on the system on which Android Studio is running. On Windows systems this is the Command Prompt interface, while on Linux and macOS systems this takes the form of a Terminal prompt.

Run – The run tool window becomes available when an application is currently running and provides a view of the results of the run together with options to stop or restart a running process. If an application is failing to install and run on a device or emulator, this window will typically provide diagnostic information relating to the problem.

Event Log – The event log window displays messages relating to events and activities performed within Android Studio. The successful build of a project, for example, or the fact that an application is now running will be reported within this tool window.

Gradle Console – The Gradle console is used to display all output from the Gradle system as projects are built from within Android Studio. This will include information about the success or otherwise of the build process together with details of any errors or warnings.

Gradle – The Gradle tool window provides a view onto the Gradle tasks that make up the project build configuration. The window lists the tasks that are involved in compiling the various elements of the project into an executable application. Right-click on a top level Gradle task and select the *Open Gradle Config* menu option to load the Gradle build file for the current project into the editor. Gradle will be covered in greater detail later in this book.

Android Profiler – The Android Profiler tool window provides realtime monitoring and analysis tools for identifying performance issues within running apps, including CPU, memory and network usage.

Device File Explorer – The Device File Explorer tool window provides direct access to the filesystem of the currently connected Android device or emulator allowing the filesystem to be browsed and files copied to the local filesystem.

4.4 Android Studio Keyboard Shortcuts

Android Studio includes an abundance of keyboard shortcuts designed to save time when performing common tasks. A full keyboard shortcut keymap listing can be viewed and printed from within the Android Studio project window by selecting the *Help -> Keymap Reference* menu option.

4.5 Switcher and Recent Files Navigation

Another useful mechanism for navigating within the Android Studio main window involves the use of the *Switcher*. Accessed via the *Ctrl-Tab* keyboard shortcut, the switcher appears as a panel listing both the tool windows and currently open files (Figure 4-7).

Figure 4-7

Once displayed, the switcher will remain visible for as long as the Ctrl key remains depressed. Repeatedly tapping the Tab key while holding down the Ctrl key will cycle through the various selection options, while releasing the Ctrl key causes the currently highlighted item to be selected and displayed within the main window.

In addition to the switcher, navigation to recently opened files is provided by the Recent Files panel (Figure 4-8). This can be accessed using the Ctrl-E keyboard shortcut (Cmd-E on macOS). Once displayed, either the mouse pointer can be used to select an option or, alternatively, the keyboard arrow keys used to scroll through the file name and tool window options. Pressing the Enter key will select the currently highlighted item.

Figure 4-8

4.6 Changing the Android Studio Theme

The overall theme of the Android Studio environment may be changed either from the welcome screen using the *Configure -> Settings* option, or via the *File -> Settings…* menu option (*Android Studio -> Preferences…* on macOS) of the main window.

Once the settings dialog is displayed, select the *Appearance* option in the left-hand panel and then change the setting of the *Theme* menu before clicking on the *Apply* button. The themes available will depend on the platform but usually include options such as IntelliJ, Windows, Default and Darcula. Figure 4-9 shows an example of the main window with the Darcula theme selected:

Figure 4-9

4.7 Summary

The primary elements of the Android Studio environment consist of the welcome screen and main window. Each open project is assigned its own main window which, in turn, consists of a menu bar, toolbar, editing and design area, status bar and a collection of tool windows. Tool windows appear on the sides and bottom edges of the main window and can be accessed either using the quick access menu located in the status bar, or via the optional tool window bars.

There are very few actions within Android Studio which cannot be triggered via a keyboard shortcut. A keymap of default keyboard shortcuts can be accessed at any time from within the Android Studio main window.

5. Creating an Android Virtual Device (AVD) in Android Studio

In the course of developing Android apps in Android Studio it will be necessary to compile and run an application multiple times. An Android application may be tested by installing and running it either on a physical device or in an *Android Virtual Device (AVD)* emulator environment. Before an AVD can be used, it must first be created and configured to match the specifications of a particular device model. The goal of this chapter, therefore, is to work through the steps involved in creating such a virtual device using the Nexus 5X phone as a reference example.

5.1 About Android Virtual Devices

AVDs are essentially emulators that allow Android applications to be tested without the necessity to install the application on a physical Android based device. An AVD may be configured to emulate a variety of hardware features including options such as screen size, memory capacity and the presence or otherwise of features such as a camera, GPS navigation support or an accelerometer. As part of the standard Android Studio installation, a number of emulator templates are installed allowing AVDs to be configured for a range of different devices. Additional templates may be loaded or custom configurations created to match any physical Android device by specifying properties such as processor type, memory capacity and the size and pixel density of the screen. Check the online developer documentation for your device to find out if emulator definitions are available for download and installation into the AVD environment.

When launched, an AVD will appear as a window containing an emulated Android device environment. Figure 5-1, for example, shows an AVD session configured to emulate the Google Nexus 5X model.

New AVDs are created and managed using the Android Virtual Device Manager, which may be used either in command-line mode or with a more user-friendly graphical user interface.

Figure 5-1

5.2 Creating a New AVD

In order to test the behavior of an application in the absence of a physical device, it will be necessary to create an AVD for a specific Android device configuration.

To create a new AVD, the first step is to launch the AVD Manager. This can be achieved from within the Android Studio environment by selecting the *Tools -> Android -> AVD Manager* menu option from within the main window.

Once launched, the tool will appear as outlined in Figure 5-2 if existing AVD instances have been created:

Figure 5-2

To add an additional AVD, begin by clicking on the *Create Virtual Device* button in order to invoke the *Virtual Device Configuration* dialog:

Figure 5-3

Within the dialog, perform the following steps to create a Nexus 5X compatible emulator:

1. From the *Category* panel, select the *Phone* option to display the list of available Android tablet AVD

templates.

2. Select the *Nexus 5X* device option and click *Next*.

3. On the System Image screen, select the latest version of Android (at time of writing this is Oreo, API level 26, Android 8.0 with Google Play) for the *x86* ABI. Note that if the system image has not yet been installed a *Download* link will be provided next to the Release Name. Click this link to download and install the system image before selecting it. If the image you need is not listed, click on the *x86 images* and *Other images* tabs to view alternative lists.

4. Click *Next* to proceed and enter a descriptive name (for example *Nexus 5X API 26*) into the name field or simply accept the default name.

5. Click *Finish* to create the AVD.

6. With the AVD created, the AVD Manager may now be closed. If future modifications to the AVD are necessary, simply re-open the AVD Manager, select the AVD from the list and click on the pencil icon in the *Actions* column of the device row in the AVD Manager.

5.3 Starting the Emulator

To perform a test run of the newly created AVD emulator, simply select the emulator from the AVD Manager and click on the launch button (the green triangle in the Actions column). The emulator will appear in a new window and begin the startup process. The amount of time it takes for the emulator to start will depend on the configuration of both the AVD and the system on which it is running. In the event that the startup time on your system is considerable, do not hesitate to leave the emulator running. The system will detect that it is already running and attach to it when applications are launched, thereby saving considerable amounts of startup time.

The emulator probably defaulted to appearing in portrait orientation. It is useful to be aware that this and other default options can be changed. Within the AVD Manager, select the new Nexus 5X entry and click on the pencil icon in the *Actions* column of the device row. In the configuration screen locate the *Startup and orientation* section and change the orientation setting. Exit and restart the emulator session to see this change take effect. More details on the emulator are covered in the next chapter (*"Using and Configuring the Android Studio AVD Emulator"*).

To save time in the next section of this chapter, leave the emulator running before proceeding.

5.4 Running the Application in the AVD

With an AVD emulator configured, the example AndroidSample application created in the earlier chapter now can be compiled and run. With the AndroidSample project loaded into Android Studio, simply click on the run button represented by a green triangle located in the Android Studio toolbar as shown in Figure 5-4 below, select the *Run -> Run 'app'* menu option or use the Ctrl-R keyboard shortcut:

Figure 5-4

By default, Android Studio will respond to the run request by displaying the *Select Deployment Target* dialog. This provides the option to execute the application on an AVD instance that is already running, or to launch a new AVD session specifically for this application. Figure 5-5 lists the previously created Nexus 5X AVD as a running device as a result of the steps performed in the preceding section. With this device selected in the

Creating an Android Virtual Device (AVD) in Android Studio

dialog, click on *OK* to install and run the application on the emulator.

Figure 5-5

Once the application is installed and running, the user interface for the AndroidSampleActivity class will appear within the emulator:

Figure 5-6

In the event that the activity does not automatically launch, check to see if the launch icon has appeared among the apps on the emulator. If it has, simply click on it to launch the application. Once the run process begins, the Run and Logcat tool windows will become available. The Run tool window will display diagnostic information as the application package is installed and launched. Figure 5-7 shows the Run tool window output from a successful application launch:

```
Run     app                                                                                                    ⚙ ⌄ ⌄
   09/08 13:52:35: Launching app
   $ adb install-multiple -r -t -p com.ebookfrenzy.androidsample /Users/neilsmyth/Documents/Books/Android_Studio_3.0/AndroidSample/app/build/outputs/apk/
   Split APKs installed
   $ adb shell am start -n "com.ebookfrenzy.androidsample/com.ebookfrenzy.androidsample.AndroidSampleActivity" -a android.intent.action.MAIN -c android.i
   Client not ready yet..Waiting for process to come online
   Connected to process 15374 on device emulator-5554
   |
   4: Run   TODO   6: Logcat   Android Profiler   Terminal   0: Messages                          Event Log    Gradle Console
```

Figure 5-7

If problems are encountered during the launch process, the Run tool window will provide information that will hopefully help to isolate the cause of the problem.

Assuming that the application loads into the emulator and runs as expected, we have safely verified that the Android development environment is correctly installed and configured.

5.5 Run/Debug Configurations

A particular project can be configured such that a specific device or emulator is used automatically each time it is run from within Android Studio. This avoids the necessity to make a selection from the device chooser each time the application is executed. To review and modify the Run/Debug configuration, click on the button to the left of the run button in the Android Studio toolbar and select the *Edit Configurations...* option from the resulting menu:

Figure 5-8

In the *Run/Debug Configurations* dialog, the application may be configured to always use a preferred emulator by selecting *Emulator* from the *Target* menu located in the *Deployment Target Options* section and selecting the emulator from the drop down menu. Figure 5-9, for example, shows the AndroidSample application configured to run by default on the previously created Nexus 5X emulator:

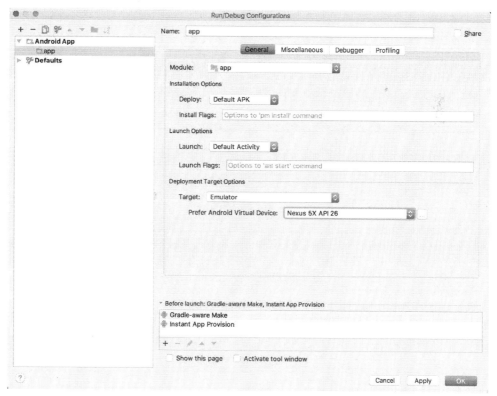

Figure 5-9

Be sure to switch the Target menu setting back to "Open Select Deployment Target Dialog" mode before moving on to the next chapter of the book.

5.6 Stopping a Running Application

To stop a running application, simply click on the stop button located in the main toolbar as shown in Figure 5-10:

Figure 5-10

An app may also be terminated using the Logcat tool window. Begin by displaying the *Logcat* tool window either using the window bar button, or via the quick access menu (invoked by moving the mouse pointer over the button in the left-hand corner of the status bar as shown in Figure 5-11).

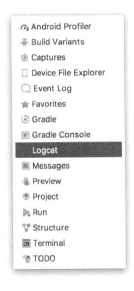

Figure 5-11

Once the Logcat tool window appears, select the *androidsample* app menu highlighted in Figure 5-12 below:

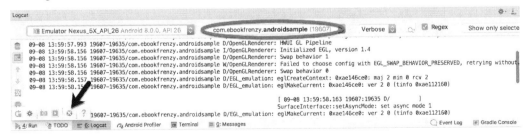

Figure 5-12

With the process selected, stop it by clicking on the red *Terminate Application* button in the toolbar to the left of the process list indicated by the arrow in the above figure.

An alternative to using the Android tool window is to open the Android Device Monitor. This can be launched via the *Tools -> Android -> Android Device Monitor* menu option. Once launched, the process may be selected from the list (Figure 5-13) and terminated by clicking on the red *Stop* button located in the toolbar above the list.

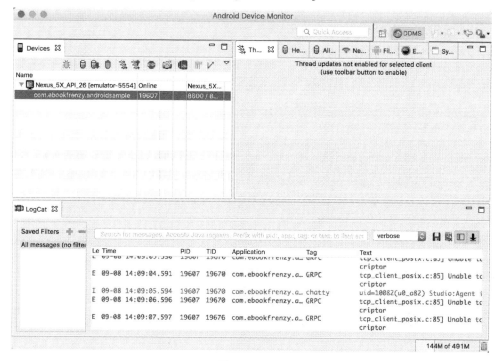

Figure 5-13

5.7 AVD Command-line Creation

As previously discussed, in addition to the graphical user interface it is also possible to create a new AVD directly from the command-line. This is achieved using the *avdmanager* tool in conjunction with some command-line options. Once initiated, the tool will prompt for additional information before creating the new AVD.

Assuming that the system has been configured such that the Android SDK *tools* directory is included in the PATH environment variable, a list of available targets for the new AVD may be obtained by issuing the following command in a terminal or command window:

```
avdmanager list targets
```

The resulting output from the above command will contain a list of Android SDK versions that are available on the system. For example:

```
Available Android targets:
----------
id: 1 or "android-25"
     Name: Android API 25
     Type: Platform
     API level: 25
     Revision: 3
----------
id: 2 or "android-26"
```

```
Name: Android API 26
Type: Platform
API level: 26
Revision: 1
```

The avdmanager tool also allows new AVD instances to be created from the command line. For example, to create a new AVD named *Nexus9* using the target ID for the Android API level 26 device using the x86 ABI, the following command may be used:

```
avdmanager create avd -n Nexus9 -k "system-images;android-26;google_apis;x86"
```

The android tool will create the new AVD to the specifications required for a basic Android 8 device, also providing the option to create a custom configuration to match the specification of a specific device if required. Once a new AVD has been created from the command line, it may not show up in the Android Device Manager tool until the *Refresh* button is clicked.

In addition to the creation of new AVDs, a number of other tasks may be performed from the command line. For example, a list of currently available AVDs may be obtained using the *list avd* command line arguments:

```
avdmanager list avd

Available Android Virtual Devices:
Name: Nexus_5X_API_26
  Device: Nexus 5X (Google)
    Path: /Users/neilsmyth/.android/avd/Nexus_5X_API_26.avd
  Target: Google Play (Google Inc.)
          Based on: Android 8.0 (Oreo) Tag/ABI: google_apis_playstore/x86
    Skin: nexus_5x
  Sdcard: 100M
```

Similarly, to delete an existing AVD, simply use the *delete* option as follows:

```
avdmanager delete avd -n <avd name>
```

5.8 Android Virtual Device Configuration Files

By default, the files associated with an AVD are stored in the *.android/avd* sub-directory of the user's home directory, the structure of which is as follows (where *<avd name>* is replaced by the name assigned to the AVD):

```
<avd name>.avd/config.ini
<avd name>.avd/userdata.img
<avd name>.ini
```

The *config.ini* file contains the device configuration settings such as display dimensions and memory specified during the AVD creation process. These settings may be changed directly within the configuration file and will be adopted by the AVD when it is next invoked.

The *<avd name>.ini* file contains a reference to the target Android SDK and the path to the AVD files. Note that a change to the *image.sysdir* value in the *config.ini* file will also need to be reflected in the *target* value of this file.

5.9 Moving and Renaming an Android Virtual Device

The current name or the location of the AVD files may be altered from the command line using the *avdmanager* tool's *move avd* argument. For example, to rename an AVD named Nexus9 to Nexus9B, the following command may be executed:

```
avdmanager move avd -n Nexus9 -r Nexus9B
```

To physically relocate the files associated with the AVD, the following command syntax should be used:

```
avdmanager move avd -n <avd name> -p <path to new location>
```

For example, to move an AVD from its current file system location to /tmp/Nexus9Test:

```
avdmanager move avd -n Nexus9 -p /tmp/Nexus9Test
```

Note that the destination directory must not already exist prior to executing the command to move an AVD.

5.10 Summary

A typical application development process follows a cycle of coding, compiling and running in a test environment. Android applications may be tested on either a physical Android device or using an Android Virtual Device (AVD) emulator. AVDs are created and managed using the Android AVD Manager tool which may be used either as a command line tool or using a graphical user interface. When creating an AVD to simulate a specific Android device model it is important that the virtual device be configured with a hardware specification that matches that of the physical device.

6. Using and Configuring the Android Studio AVD Emulator

The Android Virtual Device (AVD) emulator environment bundled with Android Studio 1.x was an uncharacteristically weak point in an otherwise reputable application development environment. Regarded by many developers as slow, inflexible and unreliable, the emulator was long overdue for an overhaul. Fortunately, Android Studio 2 introduced an enhanced emulator environment providing significant improvements in terms of configuration flexibility and overall performance and further enhancements have been made for Android Studio 3.

Before the next chapter explores testing on physical Android devices, this chapter will take some time to provide an overview of the Android Studio AVD emulator and highlight many of the configuration features that are available to customize the environment.

6.1 The Emulator Environment

When launched, the emulator displays an initial splash screen during the loading process. Once loaded, the main emulator window appears containing a representation of the chosen device type (in the case of Figure 6-1 this is a Nexus 5X device):

Figure 6-1

Positioned along the right-hand edge of the window is the toolbar providing quick access to the emulator controls and configuration options.

6.2 The Emulator Toolbar Options

The emulator toolbar (Figure 6-2) provides access to a range of options relating to the appearance and behavior of the emulator environment.

Figure 6-2

Each button in the toolbar has associated with it a keyboard accelerator which can be identified either by hovering the mouse pointer over the button and waiting for the tooltip to appear, or via the help option of the extended controls panel.

Though many of the options contained within the toolbar are self-explanatory, each option will be covered for the sake of completeness:

- **Exit / Minimize** – The uppermost 'x' button in the toolbar exits the emulator session when selected while the '-' option minimizes the entire window.

- **Power** – The Power button simulates the hardware power button on a physical Android device. Clicking and releasing this button will lock the device and turn off the screen. Clicking and holding this button will initiate the device "Power off" request sequence.

- **Volume Up / Down** – Two buttons that control the audio volume of playback within the simulator environment.

- **Rotate Left/Right** – Rotates the emulated device between portrait and landscape orientations.

- **Screenshot** – Takes a screenshot of the content currently displayed on the device screen. The captured image is stored at the location specified in the Settings screen of the extended controls panel as outlined later in this chapter.

- **Zoom Mode** – This button toggles in and out of zoom mode, details of which will be covered later in this chapter.

- **Back** – Simulates selection of the standard Android "Back" button. As with the Home and Overview buttons outlined below, the same results can be achieved by selecting the actual buttons on the emulator screen.

- **Home** – Simulates selection of the standard Android "Home" button.

- **Overview** – Simulates selection of the standard Android "Overview" button which displays the currently running apps on the device.

- **Extended Controls** – Displays the extended controls panel, allowing for the configuration of options such as simulated location and telephony activity, battery strength, cellular network type and fingerprint identification.

6.3 Working in Zoom Mode

The zoom button located in the emulator toolbar switches in and out of zoom mode. When zoom mode is active the toolbar button is depressed and the mouse pointer appears as a magnifying glass when hovering over the device screen. Clicking the left mouse button will cause the display to zoom in relative to the selected point on the screen, with repeated clicking increasing the zoom level. Conversely, clicking the right mouse button decreases the zoom level. Toggling the zoom button off reverts the display to the default size.

Clicking and dragging while in zoom mode will define a rectangular area into which the view will zoom when the mouse button is released.

While in zoom mode the visible area of the screen may be panned using the horizontal and vertical scrollbars located within the emulator window.

6.4 Resizing the Emulator Window

The size of the emulator window (and the corresponding representation of the device) can be changed at any time by clicking and dragging on any of the corners or sides of the window.

6.5 Extended Control Options

The extended controls toolbar button displays the panel illustrated in Figure 6-3. By default, the location settings will be displayed. Selecting a different category from the left-hand panel will display the corresponding group of controls:

Figure 6-3

6.5.1 Location

The location controls allow simulated location information to be sent to the emulator in the form of decimal or sexigesimal coordinates. Location information can take the form of a single location, or a sequence of points representing movement of the device, the latter being provided via a file in either GPS Exchange (GPX) or

Keyhole Markup Language (KML) format.

A single location is transmitted to the emulator when the *Send* button is clicked. The transmission of GPS data points begins once the "play" button located beneath the data table is selected. The speed at which the GPS data points are fed to the emulator can be controlled using the speed menu adjacent to the play button.

6.5.2 Cellular

The type of cellular connection being simulated can be changed within the cellular settings screen. Options are available to simulate different network types (CSM, EDGE, HSDPA etc) in addition to a range of voice and data scenarios such as roaming and denied access.

6.5.3 Battery

A variety of battery state and charging conditions can be simulated on this panel of the extended controls screen, including battery charge level, battery health and whether the AC charger is currently connected.

6.5.4 Phone

The phone extended controls provide two very simple but useful simulations within the emulator. The first option allows for the simulation of an incoming call from a designated phone number. This can be of particular use when testing the way in which an app handles high level interrupts of this nature.

The second option allows the receipt of text messages to be simulated within the emulator session. As in the real world, these messages appear within the Message app and trigger the standard notifications within the emulator.

6.5.5 Directional Pad

A directional pad (D-Pad) is an additional set of controls either built into an Android device or connected externally (such as a game controller) that provides directional controls (left, right, up, down). The directional pad settings allow D-Pad interaction to be simulated within the emulator.

6.5.6 Microphone

The microphone settings allow the microphone to be enabled and virtual headset and microphone connections to be simulated. A button is also provided to launch the Voice Assistant on the emulator.

6.5.7 Fingerprint

Many Android devices are now supplied with built-in fingerprint detection hardware. The AVD emulator makes it possible to test fingerprint authentication without the need to test apps on a physical device containing a fingerprint sensor. Details on how to configure fingerprint testing within the emulator will be covered in detail later in this chapter.

6.5.8 Virtual Sensors

The virtual sensors option allows the accelerometer and magnetometer to be simulated to emulate the effects of the physical motion of a device such as rotation, movement and tilting through yaw, pitch and roll settings.

6.5.9 Settings

The settings panel provides a small group of configuration options. Use this panel to choose a darker theme for the toolbar and extended controls panel, specify a file system location into which screenshots are to be saved, configure OpenGL support levels, and to configure the emulator window to appear on top of other windows on the desktop.

6.5.10 Help

The Help screen contains three sub-panels containing a list of keyboard shortcuts, links to access the emulator online documentation, file bugs and send feedback, and emulator version information.

6.6 Drag and Drop Support

An Android application is packaged into an APK file when it is built. When Android Studio built and ran the AndroidSample app created earlier in this book, for example, the application was compiled and packaged into an APK file. That APK file was then transferred to the emulator and launched.

The Android Studio emulator also supports installation of apps by dragging and dropping the corresponding APK file onto the emulator window. To experience this in action, start the emulator, open Settings and select the *Apps & notifications* option followed by the *App Info* option on the subsequent screen. Within the list of installed apps, locate and select the AndroidSample app and, in the app detail screen, uninstall the app from the emulator.

Open the file system navigation tool for your operating system (e.g. Windows Explorer for Windows or Finder for macOS) and navigate to the folder containing the AndroidSample project. Within this folder locate the *app/ build/outputs/apk/debug* subfolder. This folder should contain an APK file named *app-debug.apk*. Drag this file and drop it onto the emulator window. The dialog shown in (Figure 6-4) will subsequently appear as the APK file is installed.

Figure 6-4

Once the APK file installation has completed, locate the app on the device and click on it to launch it.

In addition to APK files, any other type of file such as image, video or data files can be installed onto the emulator using this drag and drop feature. Such files are added to the SD card storage area of the emulator where they may subsequently be accessed from within app code.

6.7 Configuring Fingerprint Emulation

The emulator allows up to 10 simulated fingerprints to be configured and used to test fingerprint authentication within Android apps. To configure simulated fingerprints begin by launching the emulator, opening the Settings app and selecting the *Security & Location* option.

Within the Security settings screen, select the *Use fingerprint* option. On the resulting information screen click on the *Next* button to proceed to the Fingerprint setup screen. Before fingerprint security can be enabled a backup screen unlocking method (such as a PIN number) must be configured. Click on the *Fingerprint + PIN* button and, when prompted, choose not to require the PIN on device startup. Enter and confirm a suitable PIN number and complete the PIN entry process by accepting the default notifications option.

Proceed through the remaining screens until the Settings app requests a fingerprint on the sensor. At this point display the extended controls dialog, select the *Fingerprint* category in the left-hand panel and make sure that *Finger 1* is selected in the main settings panel:

Figure 6-5

Click on the *Touch the Sensor* button to simulate Finger 1 touching the fingerprint sensor. The emulator will report the successful addition of the fingerprint:

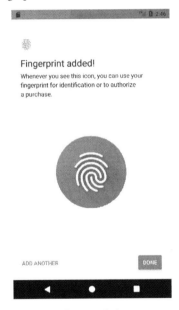

Figure 6-6

To add additional fingerprints click on the *Add Another* button and select another finger from the extended controls panel menu before clicking on the *Touch the Sensor* button once again. The topic of building fingerprint authentication into an Android app is covered in detail in the chapter entitled *"An Android Fingerprint Authentication Tutorial"*.

6.8 Summary

Android Studio 3 contains a new and improved Android Virtual Device emulator environment designed to make it easier to test applications without the need to run on a physical Android device. This chapter has provided a brief tour of the emulator and highlighted key features that are available to configure and customize the environment to simulate different testing conditions

7. Testing Android Studio Apps on a Physical Android Device

While much can be achieved by testing applications using an Android Virtual Device (AVD), there is no substitute for performing real world application testing on a physical Android device and there are a number of Android features that are only available on physical Android devices.

Communication with both AVD instances and connected Android devices is handled by the *Android Debug Bridge (ADB)*. In this chapter we will work through the steps to configure the adb environment to enable application testing on a physical Android device with macOS, Windows and Linux based systems.

7.1 An Overview of the Android Debug Bridge (ADB)

The primary purpose of the ADB is to facilitate interaction between a development system, in this case Android Studio, and both AVD emulators and physical Android devices for the purposes of running and debugging applications.

The ADB consists of a client, a server process running in the background on the development system and a daemon background process running in either AVDs or real Android devices such as phones and tablets.

The ADB client can take a variety of forms. For example, a client is provided in the form of a command-line tool named *adb* located in the Android SDK *platform-tools* sub-directory. Similarly, Android Studio also has a built-in client.

A variety of tasks may be performed using the *adb* command-line tool. For example, a listing of currently active virtual or physical devices may be obtained using the *devices* command-line argument. The following command output indicates the presence of an AVD on the system but no physical devices:

```
$ adb devices
List of devices attached
emulator-5554    device
```

7.2 Enabling ADB on Android based Devices

Before ADB can connect to an Android device, that device must first be configured to allow the connection. On phone and tablet devices running Android 6.0 or later, the steps to achieve this are as follows:

1. Open the Settings app on the device and select the *About tablet* or *About phone* option.

2. On the *About* screen, scroll down to the *Build number* field (Figure 7-1) and tap on it seven times until a message appears indicating that developer mode has been enabled.

Kernel version

3.10.103-ge912bb7
android-build@wped26.hot.corp.google.com #1
Fri Oct 21 17:15:52 UTC 2016

Build number

N4F26M

Figure 7-1

3. Return to the main Settings screen and note the appearance of a new option titled Developer options. Select this option and locate the setting on the developer screen entitled USB debugging. Enable the switch next to this item as illustrated in Figure 7-2:

Debugging

USB debugging
Debug mode when USB is connected

Figure 7-2

4. Swipe downward from the top of the screen to display the notifications panel (Figure 7-3) and note that the device is currently connected for debugging.

USB debugging connected
Touch to disable USB debugging.

Figure 7-3

At this point, the device is now configured to accept debugging connections from adb on the development system. All that remains is to configure the development system to detect the device when it is attached. While this is a relatively straightforward process, the steps involved differ depending on whether the development system is running Windows, macOS or Linux. Note that the following steps assume that the Android SDK *platform-tools* directory is included in the operating system PATH environment variable as described in the chapter entitled *"Setting up an Android Studio Development Environment"*.

7.2.1 macOS ADB Configuration

In order to configure the ADB environment on a macOS system, connect the device to the computer system using a USB cable, open a terminal window and execute the following command to restart the adb server:

```
$ adb kill-server
$ adb start-server
* daemon not running. starting it now on port 5037 *
* daemon started successfully *
```

Once the server is successfully running, execute the following command to verify that the device has been detected:

```
$ adb devices
List of devices attached
```

```
74CE000600000001          offline
```

If the device is listed as *offline*, go to the Android device and check for the presence of the dialog shown in Figure 7-4 seeking permission to *Allow USB debugging*. Enable the checkbox next to the option that reads *Always allow from this computer*, before clicking on *OK*. Repeating the *adb devices* command should now list the device as being available:

```
List of devices attached
015d41d4454bf80c          device
```

In the event that the device is not listed, try logging out and then back in to the macOS desktop and, if the problem persists, rebooting the system.

7.2.2 Windows ADB Configuration

The first step in configuring a Windows based development system to connect to an Android device using ADB is to install the appropriate USB drivers on the system. The USB drivers to install will depend on the model of Android Device. If you have a Google Nexus device, then it will be necessary to install and configure the Google USB Driver package on your Windows system. Detailed steps to achieve this are outlined on the following web page:

http://developer.android.com/sdk/win-usb.html

For Android devices not supported by the Google USB driver, it will be necessary to download the drivers provided by the device manufacturer. A listing of drivers together with download and installation information can be obtained online at:

http://developer.android.com/tools/extras/oem-usb.html

With the drivers installed and the device now being recognized as the correct device type, open a Command Prompt window and execute the following command:

```
adb devices
```

This command should output information about the connected device similar to the following:

```
List of devices attached
HT4CTJT01906          offline
```

If the device is listed as *offline* or *unauthorized*, go to the device display and check for the dialog shown in Figure 7-4 seeking permission to *Allow USB debugging*.

Figure 7-4

Enable the checkbox next to the option that reads *Always allow from this computer*, before clicking on *OK*. Repeating the *adb devices* command should now list the device as being ready:

```
List of devices attached
```

```
HT4CTJT01906      device
```

In the event that the device is not listed, execute the following commands to restart the ADB server:

```
adb kill-server
adb start-server
```

If the device is still not listed, try executing the following command:

```
android update adb
```

Note that it may also be necessary to reboot the system.

7.2.3 Linux adb Configuration

For the purposes of this chapter, we will once again use Ubuntu Linux as a reference example in terms of configuring adb on Linux to connect to a physical Android device for application testing.

Physical device testing on Ubuntu Linux requires the installation of a package named *android-tools-adb* which, in turn, requires that the Android Studio user be a member of the *plugdev* group. This is the default for user accounts on most Ubuntu versions and can be verified by running the *id* command. If plugdev group is not listed, run the following command to add your account to the group:

```
sudo usermod -aG plugdev $LOGNAME
```

After the group membership requirement has been met, the *android-tools-adb* package can be installed by executing the following command:

```
sudo apt-get install android-tools-adb
```

Once the above changes have been made, reboot the Ubuntu system. Once the system has restarted, open a Terminal window, start the adb server and check the list of attached devices:

```
$ adb start-server
* daemon not running. starting it now on port 5037 *
* daemon started successfully *
$ adb devices
List of devices attached
015d41d4454bf80c        offline
```

If the device is listed as *offline* or *unauthorized*, go to the Android device and check for the dialog shown in Figure 7-4 seeking permission to *Allow USB debugging*.

7.3 Testing the adb Connection

Assuming that the adb configuration has been successful on your chosen development platform, the next step is to try running the test application created in the chapter entitled *"Creating an Example Android App in Android Studio"* on the device.

Launch Android Studio, open the AndroidSample project and, once the project has loaded, click on the run button located in the Android Studio toolbar (Figure 7-5).

Figure 7-5

Assuming that the project has not previously been configured to run automatically in an emulator environment, the deployment target selection dialog will appear with the connected Android device listed as a currently running device. Figure 7-6, for example, lists a Nexus 9 device as a suitable target for installing and executing the application.

Figure 7-6

To make this the default device for testing, enable the *Use same device for future launches* option. With the device selected, click on the *OK* button to install and run the application on the device. As with the emulator environment, diagnostic output relating to the installation and launch of the application on the device will be logged in the Run tool window.

7.4 Summary

While the Android Virtual Device emulator provides an excellent testing environment, it is important to keep in mind that there is no real substitute for making sure an application functions correctly on a physical Android device. This, after all, is where the application will be used in the real world.

By default, however, the Android Studio environment is not configured to detect Android devices as a target testing device. It is necessary, therefore, to perform some steps in order to be able to load applications directly onto an Android device from within the Android Studio development environment. The exact steps to achieve this goal differ depending on the development platform being used. In this chapter, we have covered those steps for Linux, macOS and Windows based platforms.

8. The Basics of the Android Studio Code Editor

Developing applications for Android involves a considerable amount of programming work which, by definition, involves typing, reviewing and modifying lines of code. It should come as no surprise that the majority of a developer's time spent using Android Studio will typically involve editing code within the editor window.

The modern code editor needs to go far beyond the original basics of typing, deleting, cutting and pasting. Today the usefulness of a code editor is generally gauged by factors such as the amount by which it reduces the typing required by the programmer, ease of navigation through large source code files and the editor's ability to detect and highlight programming errors in real-time as the code is being written. As will become evident in this chapter, these are just a few of the areas in which the Android Studio editor excels.

While not an exhaustive overview of the features of the Android Studio editor, this chapter aims to provide a guide to the key features of the tool. Experienced programmers will find that some of these features are common to most code editors available today, while a number are unique to this particular editing environment.

8.1 The Android Studio Editor

The Android Studio editor appears in the center of the main window when a Java, Kotlin, XML or other text based file is selected for editing. Figure 8-1, for example, shows a typical editor session with a source code file loaded:

```java
package com.ebookfrenzy.androidsample;

import ...

public class AndroidSampleActivity extends AppCompatActivity {

    @Override
    protected void onCreate(Bundle savedInstanceState) {
        super.onCreate(savedInstanceState);
        setContentView(R.layout.activity_android_sample);
        Toolbar toolbar = (Toolbar) findViewById(R.id.toolbar);
        setSupportActionBar(toolbar);

        FloatingActionButton fab = (FloatingActionButton) findViewById(R.id.fab);
        fab.setOnClickListener((view) -> {
                Snackbar.make(view, text: "Replace with your own action", Snackbar.LENGTH_LONG)
                        .setAction( text: "Action", listener: null).show();
        });
    }

    @Override
    public boolean onCreateOptionsMenu(Menu menu) {
        // Inflate the menu; this adds items to the action bar if it is present.
        getMenuInflater().inflate(R.menu.menu_android_sample, menu);
        return true;
    }

    @Override
    public boolean onOptionsItemSelected(MenuItem item) {
```

Emulator: Process finished with exit code 0 (6 minutes ago)   18:28   LF ‡   UTF-8 ‡   Context: <no context>

Figure 8-1

The elements that comprise the editor window can be summarized as follows:

A – Document Tabs – Android Studio is capable of holding multiple files open for editing at any one time. As each file is opened, it is assigned a document tab displaying the file name in the tab bar located along the top edge of the editor window. A small dropdown menu will appear in the far right-hand corner of the tab bar when there is insufficient room to display all of the tabs. Clicking on this menu will drop down a list of additional open files. A wavy red line underneath a file name in a tab indicates that the code in the file contains one or more errors that need to be addressed before the project can be compiled and run.

Switching between files is simply a matter of clicking on the corresponding tab or using the *Alt-Left* and *Alt-Right* keyboard shortcuts. Navigation between files may also be performed using the Switcher mechanism (accessible via the *Ctrl-Tab* keyboard shortcut).

To detach an editor panel from the Android Studio main window so that it appears in a separate window, click on the tab and drag it to an area on the desktop outside of the main window. To return the editor to the main window, click on the file tab in the separated editor window and drag and drop it onto the original editor tab bar in the main window.

B – The Editor Gutter Area - The gutter area is used by the editor to display informational icons and controls. Some typical items, among others, which appear in this gutter area are debugging breakpoint markers, controls to fold and unfold blocks of code, bookmarks, change markers and line numbers. Line numbers are switched on by default but may be disabled by right-clicking in the gutter and selecting the *Show Line Numbers* menu option.

C – The Status Bar – Though the status bar is actually part of the main window, as opposed to the editor, it does contain some information about the currently active editing session. This information includes the current position of the cursor in terms of lines and characters and the encoding format of the file (UTF-8, ASCII etc.). Clicking on these values in the status bar allows the corresponding setting to be changed. Clicking on the line number, for example, displays the *Go to Line* dialog.

D – The Editor Area – This is the main area where the code is displayed, entered and edited by the user. Later sections of this chapter will cover the key features of the editing area in detail.

E – The Validation and Marker Sidebar – Android Studio incorporates a feature referred to as "on-the-fly code analysis". What this essentially means is that as you are typing code, the editor is analyzing the code to check for warnings and syntax errors. The indicator at the top of the validation sidebar will change from a green check mark (no warnings or errors detected) to a yellow square (warnings detected) or red alert icon (errors have been detected). Clicking on this indicator will display a popup containing a summary of the issues found with the code in the editor as illustrated in Figure 8-2:

Figure 8-2

The sidebar also displays markers at the locations where issues have been detected using the same color coding. Hovering the mouse pointer over a marker when the line of code is visible in the editor area will display a popup containing a description of the issue (Figure 8-3):

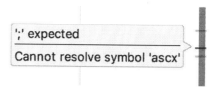

Figure 8-3

Hovering the mouse pointer over a marker for a line of code which is currently scrolled out of the viewing area of the editor will display a "lens" overlay containing the block of code where the problem is located (Figure 8-4) allowing it to be viewed without the necessity to scroll to that location in the editor:

```
12    public class AndroidSampleActivity extends AppCompatActivity {
13
14        @Override
15        protected void onCreate(Bundle savedInstanceState) {
16            super.onCreate(savedInstanceState);
17            setContentView(R.layout.activity_android_sample);
18            Toolbar toolbar = (Toolbar) findViewById(R.id.toolbar);    Casting 'findViewById(R.id.toolbar)' to 'Toolbar' is redund
19            setSupportActionBar(toolbar);
20            FloatingActionButton fab = (FloatingActionButton) findViewById(R.id.fab);    Casting 'findViewById(R.id.fab)' to '
21            fab.setOnClickListener((view) → {
```

Figure 8-4

It is also worth noting that the lens overlay is not limited to warnings and errors in the sidebar. Hovering over any part of the sidebar will result in a lens appearing containing the code present at that location within the source file.

Having provided an overview of the elements that comprise the Android Studio editor, the remainder of this chapter will explore the key features of the editing environment in more detail.

8.2 Splitting the Editor Window

By default, the editor will display a single panel showing the content of the currently selected file. A particularly useful feature when working simultaneously with multiple source code files is the ability to split the editor into multiple panes. To split the editor, right-click on a file tab within the editor window and select either the *Split Vertically* or *Split Horizontally* menu option. Figure 8-5, for example, shows the splitter in action with the editor split into three panels:

Figure 8-5

The orientation of a split panel may be changed at any time by right-clicking on the corresponding tab and selecting the *Change Splitter Orientation* menu option. Repeat these steps to unsplit a single panel, this time selecting the *Unsplit* option from the menu. All of the split panels may be removed by right-clicking on any tab and selecting the *Unsplit All* menu option.

Window splitting may be used to display different files, or to provide multiple windows onto the same file, allowing different areas of the same file to be viewed and edited concurrently.

8.3 Code Completion

The Android Studio editor has a considerable amount of built-in knowledge of programming syntax and the classes and methods that make up the Android SDK, as well as knowledge of your own code base. As code is typed, the editor scans what is being typed and, where appropriate, makes suggestions with regard to what might be needed to complete a statement or reference. When a completion suggestion is detected by the editor, a panel will appear containing a list of suggestions. In Figure 8-6, for example, the editor is suggesting possibilities for the beginning of a String declaration:

Figure 8-6

If none of the auto completion suggestions are correct, simply keep typing and the editor will continue to refine the suggestions where appropriate. To accept the top most suggestion, simply press the Enter or Tab key on the keyboard. To select a different suggestion, use the arrow keys to move up and down the list, once again using the Enter or Tab key to select the highlighted item.

Completion suggestions can be manually invoked using the *Ctrl-Space* keyboard sequence. This can be useful when changing a word or declaration in the editor. When the cursor is positioned over a word in the editor, that word will automatically highlight. Pressing *Ctrl-Space* will display a list of alternate suggestions. To replace the current word with the currently highlighted item in the suggestion list, simply press the Tab key.

In addition to the real-time auto completion feature, the Android Studio editor also offers a system referred to as *Smart Completion*. Smart completion is invoked using the *Shift-Ctrl-Space* keyboard sequence and, when selected, will provide more detailed suggestions based on the current context of the code. Pressing the *Shift-Ctrl-Space* shortcut sequence a second time will provide more suggestions from a wider range of possibilities.

Code completion can be a matter of personal preference for many programmers. In recognition of this fact, Android Studio provides a high level of control over the auto completion settings. These can be viewed and modified by selecting the *File -> Settings...* menu option (or *Android Studio -> Preferences...* on macOS) and choosing *Editor -> General -> Code Completion* from the settings panel as shown in Figure 8-7:

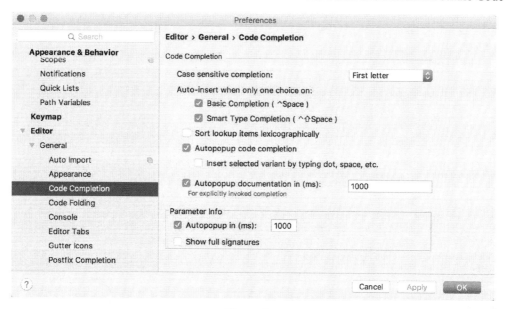

Figure 8-7

8.4 Statement Completion

Another form of auto completion provided by the Android Studio editor is statement completion. This can be used to automatically fill out the parentheses and braces for items such as methods and loop statements. Statement completion is invoked using the *Shift-Ctrl-Enter* (*Shift-Cmd-Enter* on macOS) keyboard sequence. Consider for example the following code:

```
protected void myMethod()
```

Having typed this code into the editor, triggering statement completion will cause the editor to automatically add the braces to the method:

```
protected void myMethod() {

}
```

8.5 Parameter Information

It is also possible to ask the editor to provide information about the argument parameters accepted by a method. With the cursor positioned between the brackets of a method call, the *Ctrl-P* (*Cmd-P* on macOS) keyboard sequence will display the parameters known to be accepted by that method, with the most likely suggestion highlighted in bold:

Figure 8-8

8.6 Parameter Name Hints

The code editor may be configured to display parameter name hints within method calls. Figure 8-9, for example, highlights the parameter name hints within the calls to the *make()* and *setAction()* methods of the *Snackbar* class:

```
FloatingActionButton fab = (FloatingActionButton) findViewById(R.id.fab);
fab.setOnClickListener((view) → {
        Snackbar.make(view, text: "Replace with your own action", Snackbar.LENGTH_LONG)
                .setAction( text: "Action", listener: null).show();
});
```

Figure 8-9

The settings for this mode may be configured by selecting the *File -> Settings* (*Android Studio -> Preferences* on macOS) menu option followed by *Editor -> Appearance* in the left-hand panel. On the Appearance screen, enable or disable the *Show parameter name hints* option. To adjust the hint settings, click on the *Configure...* button, select the programming language and make any necessary adjustments.

8.7 Code Generation

In addition to completing code as it is typed the editor can, under certain conditions, also generate code for you. The list of available code generation options shown in Figure 8-10 can be accessed using the *Alt-Insert* (*Cmd-N* on macOS) keyboard shortcut when the cursor is at the location in the file where the code is to be generated.

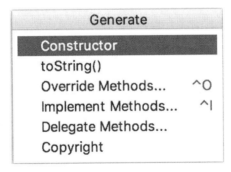

Figure 8-10

For the purposes of an example, consider a situation where we want to be notified when an Activity in our project is about to be destroyed by the operating system. As will be outlined in a later chapter of this book, this can be achieved by overriding the *onStop()* lifecycle method of the Activity superclass. To have Android Studio generate a stub method for this, simply select the *Override Methods...* option from the code generation list and select the *onStop()* method from the resulting list of available methods:

Figure 8-11

Having selected the method to override, clicking on *OK* will generate the stub method at the current cursor location in the source file as follows:

```
@Override
protected void onStop() {
    super.onStop();
}
```

8.8 Code Folding

Once a source code file reaches a certain size, even the most carefully formatted and well organized code can become overwhelming and difficult to navigate. Android Studio takes the view that it is not always necessary to have the content of every code block visible at all times. Code navigation can be made easier through the use of the *code folding* feature of the Android Studio editor. Code folding is controlled using markers appearing in the editor gutter at the beginning and end of each block of code in a source file. Figure 8-12, for example, highlights the start and end markers for a method declaration which is not currently folded:

```
override fun onCreateOptionsMenu(menu: Menu): Boolean {...}
```

Figure 8-12

Clicking on either of these markers will fold the statement such that only the signature line is visible as shown in Figure 8-13:

```
@Override
public boolean onCreateOptionsMenu(Menu menu) {...}
```

Figure 8-13

To unfold a collapsed section of code, simply click on the '+' marker in the editor gutter. To see the hidden code without unfolding it, hover the mouse pointer over the "{...}" indicator as shown in Figure 8-14. The editor will then display the lens overlay containing the folded code block:

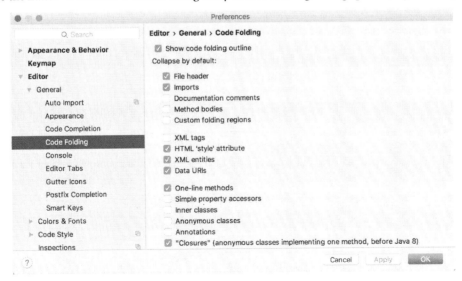

Figure 8-14

All of the code blocks in a file may be folded or unfolded using the *Ctrl-Shift-Plus* and *Ctrl-Shift-Minus* keyboard sequences.

By default, the Android Studio editor will automatically fold some code when a source file is opened. To configure the conditions under which this happens, select *File -> Settings…* (*Android Studio -> Preferences…* on macOS) and choose the *Editor -> General -> Code Folding* entry in the resulting settings panel (Figure 8-15):

Figure 8-15

8.9 Quick Documentation Lookup

Context sensitive and Android documentation can be accessed by placing the cursor over the declaration for which documentation is required and pressing the *Ctrl-Q* keyboard shortcut (*Ctrl-J* on macOS). This will display a popup containing the relevant reference documentation for the item. Figure 8-16, for example, shows the documentation for the Android Snackbar class.

Figure 8-16

Once displayed, the documentation popup can be moved around the screen as needed. Clicking on the push pin icon located in the right-hand corner of the popup title bar will ensure that the popup remains visible once focus moves back to the editor, leaving the documentation visible as a reference while typing code.

8.10 Code Reformatting

In general, the Android Studio editor will automatically format code in terms of indenting, spacing and nesting of statements and code blocks as they are added. In situations where lines of code need to be reformatted (a common occurrence, for example, when cutting and pasting sample code from a web site), the editor provides a source code reformatting feature which, when selected, will automatically reformat code to match the prevailing code style.

To reformat source code, press the *Ctrl-Alt-L* (*Cmd-Alt-L* on macOS) keyboard shortcut sequence. To display the *Reformat Code* dialog (Figure 8-17) use the *Ctrl-Alt-Shift-L* (*Cmd-Alt-Shift-L* on macOS). This dialog provides the option to reformat only the currently selected code, the entire source file currently active in the editor or only code that has changed as the result of a source code control update.

Figure 8-17

The full range of code style preferences can be changed from within the project settings dialog. Select the *File -> Settings* menu option (*Android Studio -> Preferences...* on macOS) and choose *Code Style* in the left-hand panel to access a list of supported programming and markup languages. Selecting a language will provide access to a vast array of formatting style options, all of which may be modified from the Android Studio default to match your preferred code style. To configure the settings for the *Rearrange code* option in the above dialog, for example, unfold the *Code Style* section, select and, from the settings, select the *Arrangement* tab.

8.11 Finding Sample Code

The Android Studio editor provides a way to access sample code relating to the currently highlighted entry within the code listing. This feature can be useful for learning how a particular Android class or method is used. To find sample code, highlight a method or class name in the editor, right-click on it and select the *Find Sample Code* menu option. The Find Sample Code panel (Figure 8-18) will appear beneath the editor with a list of matching samples. Selecting a sample from the list will load the corresponding code into the right-hand panel:

Figure 8-18

8.12 Summary

The Android Studio editor goes to great length to reduce the amount of typing needed to write code and to make that code easier to read and navigate. In this chapter we have covered a number of the key editor features including code completion, code generation, editor window splitting, code folding, reformatting and documentation lookup.

9. An Overview of the Android Architecture

So far in this book, steps have been taken to set up an environment suitable for the development of Android applications using Android Studio. An initial step has also been taken into the process of application development through the creation of a simple Android Studio application project.

Before delving further into the practical matters of Android application development, however, it is important to gain an understanding of some of the more abstract concepts of both the Android SDK and Android development in general. Gaining a clear understanding of these concepts now will provide a sound foundation on which to build further knowledge.

Starting with an overview of the Android architecture in this chapter, and continuing in the next few chapters of this book, the goal is to provide a detailed overview of the fundamentals of Android development.

9.1 The Android Software Stack

Android is structured in the form of a software stack comprising applications, an operating system, run-time environment, middleware, services and libraries. This architecture can, perhaps, best be represented visually as outlined in Figure 9-1. Each layer of the stack, and the corresponding elements within each layer, are tightly integrated and carefully tuned to provide the optimal application development and execution environment for mobile devices. The remainder of this chapter will work through the different layers of the Android stack, starting at the bottom with the Linux Kernel.

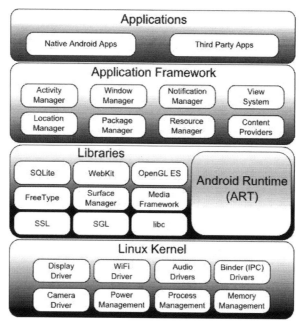

Figure 9-1

9.2 The Linux Kernel

Positioned at the bottom of the Android software stack, the Linux Kernel provides a level of abstraction between the device hardware and the upper layers of the Android software stack. Based on Linux version 2.6, the kernel provides preemptive multitasking, low-level core system services such as memory, process and power management in addition to providing a network stack and device drivers for hardware such as the device display, Wi-Fi and audio.

The original Linux kernel was developed in 1991 by Linus Torvalds and was combined with a set of tools, utilities and compilers developed by Richard Stallman at the Free Software Foundation to create a full operating system referred to as GNU/Linux. Various Linux distributions have been derived from these basic underpinnings such as Ubuntu and Red Hat Enterprise Linux.

It is important to note, however, that Android uses only the Linux kernel. That said, it is worth noting that the Linux kernel was originally developed for use in traditional computers in the form of desktops and servers. In fact, Linux is now most widely deployed in mission critical enterprise server environments. It is a testament to both the power of today's mobile devices and the efficiency and performance of the Linux kernel that we find this software at the heart of the Android software stack.

9.3 Android Runtime – ART

When an Android app is built within Android Studio it is compiled into an intermediate bytecode format (referred to as DEX format). When the application is subsequently loaded onto the device, the Android Runtime (ART) uses a process referred to as Ahead-of-Time (AOT) compilation to translate the bytecode down to the native instructions required by the device processor. This format is known as Executable and Linkable Format (ELF).

Each time the application is subsequently launched, the ELF executable version is run, resulting in faster application performance and improved battery life.

This contrasts with the Just-in-Time (JIT) compilation approach used in older Android implementations whereby the bytecode was translated within a virtual machine (VM) each time the application was launched.

9.4 Android Libraries

In addition to a set of standard Java development libraries (providing support for such general purpose tasks as string handling, networking and file manipulation), the Android development environment also includes the Android Libraries. These are a set of Java-based libraries that are specific to Android development. Examples of libraries in this category include the application framework libraries in addition to those that facilitate user interface building, graphics drawing and database access.

A summary of some key core Android libraries available to the Android developer is as follows:

- **android.app** – Provides access to the application model and is the cornerstone of all Android applications.

- **android.content** – Facilitates content access, publishing and messaging between applications and application components.

- **android.database** – Used to access data published by content providers and includes SQLite database management classes.

- **android.graphics** – A low-level 2D graphics drawing API including colors, points, filters, rectangles and canvases.

- **android.hardware** – Presents an API providing access to hardware such as the accelerometer and light sensor.

- **android.opengl** – A Java interface to the OpenGL ES 3D graphics rendering API.

- **android.os** – Provides applications with access to standard operating system services including messages, system services and inter-process communication.

- **android.media** – Provides classes to enable playback of audio and video.

- **android.net** – A set of APIs providing access to the network stack. Includes *android.net.wifi*, which provides access to the device's wireless stack.

- **android.print** – Includes a set of classes that enable content to be sent to configured printers from within Android applications.

- **android.provider** – A set of convenience classes that provide access to standard Android content provider databases such as those maintained by the calendar and contact applications.

- **android.text** – Used to render and manipulate text on a device display.

- **android.util** – A set of utility classes for performing tasks such as string and number conversion, XML handling and date and time manipulation.

- **android.view** – The fundamental building blocks of application user interfaces.

- **android.widget** - A rich collection of pre-built user interface components such as buttons, labels, list views, layout managers, radio buttons etc.

- **android.webkit** – A set of classes intended to allow web-browsing capabilities to be built into applications.

Having covered the Java-based libraries in the Android runtime, it is now time to turn our attention to the C/C++ based libraries contained in this layer of the Android software stack.

9.4.1 C/C++ Libraries

The Android runtime core libraries outlined in the preceding section are Java-based and provide the primary APIs for developers writing Android applications. It is important to note, however, that the core libraries do not perform much of the actual work and are, in fact, essentially Java "wrappers" around a set of C/C++ based libraries. When making calls, for example, to the *android.opengl* library to draw 3D graphics on the device display, the library actually ultimately makes calls to the *OpenGL ES* C++ library which, in turn, works with the underlying Linux kernel to perform the drawing tasks.

C/C++ libraries are included to fulfill a wide and diverse range of functions including 2D and 3D graphics drawing, Secure Sockets Layer (SSL) communication, SQLite database management, audio and video playback, bitmap and vector font rendering, display subsystem and graphic layer management and an implementation of the standard C system library (libc).

In practice, the typical Android application developer will access these libraries solely through the Java based Android core library APIs. In the event that direct access to these libraries is needed, this can be achieved using the Android Native Development Kit (NDK), the purpose of which is to call the native methods of non-Java or Kotlin programming languages (such as C and C++) from within Java code using the Java Native Interface (JNI).

9.5 Application Framework

The Application Framework is a set of services that collectively form the environment in which Android applications run and are managed. This framework implements the concept that Android applications are constructed from reusable, interchangeable and replaceable components. This concept is taken a step further in that an application is also able to *publish* its capabilities along with any corresponding data so that they can be found and reused by other applications.

The Android framework includes the following key services:

- **Activity Manager** – Controls all aspects of the application lifecycle and activity stack.

- **Content Providers** – Allows applications to publish and share data with other applications.

- **Resource Manager** – Provides access to non-code embedded resources such as strings, color settings and user interface layouts.

- **Notifications Manager** – Allows applications to display alerts and notifications to the user.

- **View System** – An extensible set of views used to create application user interfaces.

- **Package Manager** – The system by which applications are able to find out information about other applications currently installed on the device.

- **Telephony Manager** – Provides information to the application about the telephony services available on the device such as status and subscriber information.

- **Location Manager** – Provides access to the location services allowing an application to receive updates about location changes.

9.6 Applications

Located at the top of the Android software stack are the applications. These comprise both the native applications provided with the particular Android implementation (for example web browser and email applications) and the third party applications installed by the user after purchasing the device.

9.7 Summary

A good Android development knowledge foundation requires an understanding of the overall architecture of Android. Android is implemented in the form of a software stack architecture consisting of a Linux kernel, a runtime environment and corresponding libraries, an application framework and a set of applications. Applications are predominantly written in Java or Kotlin and compiled down to bytecode format within the Android Studio build environment. When the application is subsequently installed on a device, this bytecode is compiled down by the Android Runtime (ART) to the native format used by the CPU. The key goals of the Android architecture are performance and efficiency, both in application execution and in the implementation of reuse in application design.

10. The Anatomy of an Android Application

Regardless of your prior programming experiences, be it Windows, macOS, Linux or even iOS based, the chances are good that Android development is quite unlike anything you have encountered before.

The objective of this chapter, therefore, is to provide an understanding of the high-level concepts behind the architecture of Android applications. In doing so, we will explore in detail both the various components that can be used to construct an application and the mechanisms that allow these to work together to create a cohesive application.

10.1 Android Activities

Those familiar with object-oriented programming languages such as Java, Kotlin, C++ or C# will be familiar with the concept of encapsulating elements of application functionality into classes that are then instantiated as objects and manipulated to create an application. Since Android applications are written in Java and Kotlin, this is still very much the case. Android, however, also takes the concept of re-usable components to a higher level.

Android applications are created by bringing together one or more components known as *Activities*. An activity is a single, standalone module of application functionality that usually correlates directly to a single user interface screen and its corresponding functionality. An appointments application might, for example, have an activity screen that displays appointments set up for the current day. The application might also utilize a second activity consisting of a screen where new appointments may be entered by the user.

Activities are intended as fully reusable and interchangeable building blocks that can be shared amongst different applications. An existing email application, for example, might contain an activity specifically for composing and sending an email message. A developer might be writing an application that also has a requirement to send an email message. Rather than develop an email composition activity specifically for the new application, the developer can simply use the activity from the existing email application.

Activities are created as subclasses of the Android *Activity* class and must be implemented so as to be entirely independent of other activities in the application. In other words, a shared activity cannot rely on being called at a known point in a program flow (since other applications may make use of the activity in unanticipated ways) and one activity cannot directly call methods or access instance data of another activity. This, instead, is achieved using *Intents* and *Content Providers*.

By default, an activity cannot return results to the activity from which it was invoked. If this functionality is required, the activity must be specifically started as a *sub-activity* of the originating activity.

10.2 Android Intents

Intents are the mechanism by which one activity is able to launch another and implement the flow through the activities that make up an application. Intents consist of a description of the operation to be performed and, optionally, the data on which it is to be performed.

Intents can be *explicit*, in that they request the launch of a specific activity by referencing the activity by class name, or *implicit* by stating either the type of action to be performed or providing data of a specific type on which the action is to be performed. In the case of implicit intents, the Android runtime will select the activity to launch that most closely matches the criteria specified by the Intent using a process referred to as *Intent Resolution*.

10.3 Broadcast Intents

Another type of Intent, the *Broadcast Intent*, is a system wide intent that is sent out to all applications that have registered an "interested" *Broadcast Receiver*. The Android system, for example, will typically send out Broadcast Intents to indicate changes in device status such as the completion of system start up, connection of an external power source to the device or the screen being turned on or off.

A Broadcast Intent can be *normal* (asynchronous) in that it is sent to all interested Broadcast Receivers at more or less the same time, or *ordered* in that it is sent to one receiver at a time where it can be processed and then either aborted or allowed to be passed to the next Broadcast Receiver.

10.4 Broadcast Receivers

Broadcast Receivers are the mechanism by which applications are able to respond to Broadcast Intents. A Broadcast Receiver must be registered by an application and configured with an *Intent Filter* to indicate the types of broadcast in which it is interested. When a matching intent is broadcast, the receiver will be invoked by the Android runtime regardless of whether the application that registered the receiver is currently running. The receiver then has 5 seconds in which to complete any tasks required of it (such as launching a Service, making data updates or issuing a notification to the user) before returning. Broadcast Receivers operate in the background and do not have a user interface.

10.5 Android Services

Android Services are processes that run in the background and do not have a user interface. They can be started and subsequently managed from activities, Broadcast Receivers or other Services. Android Services are ideal for situations where an application needs to continue performing tasks but does not necessarily need a user interface to be visible to the user. Although Services lack a user interface, they can still notify the user of events using notifications and *toasts* (small notification messages that appear on the screen without interrupting the currently visible activity) and are also able to issue Intents.

Services are given a higher priority by the Android runtime than many other processes and will only be terminated as a last resort by the system in order to free up resources. In the event that the runtime does need to kill a Service, however, it will be automatically restarted as soon as adequate resources once again become available. A Service can reduce the risk of termination by declaring itself as needing to run in the *foreground*. This is achieved by making a call to *startForeground()*. This is only recommended for situations where termination would be detrimental to the user experience (for example, if the user is listening to audio being streamed by the Service).

Example situations where a Service might be a practical solution include, as previously mentioned, the streaming of audio that should continue when the application is no longer active, or a stock market tracking application that needs to notify the user when a share hits a specified price.

10.6 Content Providers

Content Providers implement a mechanism for the sharing of data between applications. Any application can provide other applications with access to its underlying data through the implementation of a Content Provider including the ability to add, remove and query the data (subject to permissions). Access to the data is provided via a Universal Resource Identifier (URI) defined by the Content Provider. Data can be shared in the form of a file or an entire SQLite database.

The native Android applications include a number of standard Content Providers allowing applications to access data such as contacts and media files.

The Content Providers currently available on an Android system may be located using a *Content Resolver*.

10.7 The Application Manifest

The glue that pulls together the various elements that comprise an application is the Application Manifest file. It is within this XML based file that the application outlines the activities, services, broadcast receivers, data providers and permissions that make up the complete application.

10.8 Application Resources

In addition to the manifest file and the Dex files that contain the byte code, an Android application package will also typically contain a collection of *resource files*. These files contain resources such as the strings, images, fonts and colors that appear in the user interface together with the XML representation of the user interface layouts. By default, these files are stored in the */res* sub-directory of the application project's hierarchy.

10.9 Application Context

When an application is compiled, a class named *R* is created that contains references to the application resources. The application manifest file and these resources combine to create what is known as the *Application Context*. This context, represented by the Android *Context* class, may be used in the application code to gain access to the application resources at runtime. In addition, a wide range of methods may be called on an application's context to gather information and make changes to the application's environment at runtime.

10.10 Summary

A number of different elements can be brought together in order to create an Android application. In this chapter, we have provided a high-level overview of Activities, Services, Intents and Broadcast Receivers together with an overview of the manifest file and application resources.

Maximum reuse and interoperability are promoted through the creation of individual, standalone modules of functionality in the form of activities and intents, while data sharing between applications is achieved by the implementation of content providers.

While activities are focused on areas where the user interacts with the application (an activity essentially equating to a single user interface screen), background processing is typically handled by Services and Broadcast Receivers.

The components that make up the application are outlined for the Android runtime system in a manifest file which, combined with the application's resources, represents the application's context.

Much has been covered in this chapter that is most likely new to the average developer. Rest assured, however, that extensive exploration and practical use of these concepts will be made in subsequent chapters to ensure a solid knowledge foundation on which to build your own applications.

11. Understanding Android Application and Activity Lifecycles

In the preceding few chapters we have learned that Android applications run within processes and that they are comprised of multiple components in the form of activities, Services and Broadcast Receivers. The goal of this chapter is to expand on this knowledge by looking at the lifecycle of applications and activities within the Android runtime system.

Regardless of the fanfare about how much memory and computing power resides in the mobile devices of today compared to the desktop systems of yesterday, it is important to keep in mind that these devices are still considered to be "resource constrained" by the standards of modern desktop and laptop based systems, particularly in terms of memory. As such, a key responsibility of the Android system is to ensure that these limited resources are managed effectively and that both the operating system and the applications running on it remain responsive to the user at all times. In order to achieve this, Android is given full control over the lifecycle and state of both the processes in which the applications run, and the individual components that comprise those applications.

An important factor in developing Android applications, therefore, is to gain an understanding of both the application and activity lifecycle management models of Android, and the ways in which an application can react to the state changes that are likely to be imposed upon it during its execution lifetime.

11.1 Android Applications and Resource Management

Each running Android application is viewed by the operating system as a separate process. If the system identifies that resources on the device are reaching capacity it will take steps to terminate processes to free up memory.

When making a determination as to which process to terminate in order to free up memory, the system takes into consideration both the *priority* and *state* of all currently running processes, combining these factors to create what is referred to by Google as an *importance hierarchy*. Processes are then terminated starting with the lowest priority and working up the hierarchy until sufficient resources have been liberated for the system to function.

11.2 Android Process States

Processes host applications and applications are made up of components. Within an Android system, the current state of a process is defined by the highest-ranking active component within the application that it hosts. As outlined in Figure 11-1, a process can be in one of the following five states at any given time:

Figure 11-1

11.2.1 Foreground Process

These processes are assigned the highest level of priority. At any one time, there are unlikely to be more than one or two foreground processes active and these are usually the last to be terminated by the system. A process must meet one or more of the following criteria to qualify for foreground status:

- Hosts an activity with which the user is currently interacting.

- Hosts a Service connected to the activity with which the user is interacting.

- Hosts a Service that has indicated, via a call to *startForeground()*, that termination would be disruptive to the user experience.

- Hosts a Service executing either its *onCreate()*, *onResume()* or *onStart()* callbacks.

- Hosts a Broadcast Receiver that is currently executing its *onReceive()* method.

11.2.2 Visible Process

A process containing an activity that is visible to the user but is not the activity with which the user is interacting is classified as a "visible process". This is typically the case when an activity in the process is visible to the user but another activity, such as a partial screen or dialog, is in the foreground. A process is also eligible for visible status if it hosts a Service that is, itself, bound to a visible or foreground activity.

11.2.3 Service Process

Processes that contain a Service that has already been started and is currently executing.

11.2.4 Background Process

A process that contains one or more activities that are not currently visible to the user, and does not host a Service that qualifies for *Service Process* status. Processes that fall into this category are at high risk of termination in the event that additional memory needs to be freed for higher priority processes. Android maintains a dynamic list of background processes, terminating processes in chronological order such that processes that were the least recently in the foreground are killed first.

11.2.5 Empty Process

Empty processes no longer contain any active applications and are held in memory ready to serve as hosts for newly launched applications. This is somewhat analogous to keeping the doors open and the engine running on a bus in anticipation of passengers arriving. Such processes are, obviously, considered the lowest priority and are the first to be killed to free up resources.

11.3 Inter-Process Dependencies

The situation with regard to determining the highest priority process is slightly more complex than outlined in the preceding section for the simple reason that processes can often be inter-dependent. As such, when making a determination as to the priority of a process, the Android system will also take into consideration whether the process is in some way serving another process of higher priority (for example, a service process acting as the content provider for a foreground process). As a basic rule, the Android documentation states that a process can never be ranked lower than another process that it is currently serving.

11.4 The Activity Lifecycle

As we have previously determined, the state of an Android process is determined largely by the status of the activities and components that make up the application that it hosts. It is important to understand, therefore, that these activities also transition through different states during the execution lifetime of an application. The current state of an activity is determined, in part, by its position in something called the *Activity Stack*.

11.5 The Activity Stack

For each application that is running on an Android device, the runtime system maintains an *Activity Stack*. When an application is launched, the first of the application's activities to be started is placed onto the stack. When a second activity is started, it is placed on the top of the stack and the previous activity is *pushed* down. The activity at the top of the stack is referred to as the *active (or running)* activity. When the active activity exits, it is *popped* off the stack by the runtime and the activity located immediately beneath it in the stack becomes the current active activity. The activity at the top of the stack might, for example, simply exit because the task for which it is responsible has been completed. Alternatively, the user may have selected a "Back" button on the screen to return to the previous activity, causing the current activity to be popped off the stack by the runtime system and therefore destroyed. A visual representation of the Android Activity Stack is illustrated in Figure 11-2.

As shown in the diagram, new activities are pushed on to the top of the stack when they are started. The current active activity is located at the top of the stack until it is either pushed down the stack by a new activity, or popped off the stack when it exits or the user navigates to the previous activity. In the event that resources become constrained, the runtime will kill activities, starting with those at the bottom of the stack.

The Activity Stack is what is referred to in programming terminology as a Last-In-First-Out (LIFO) stack in that the last item to be pushed onto the stack is the first to be popped off.

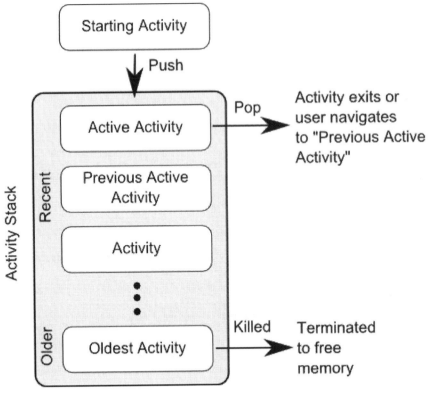

Figure 11-2

11.6 Activity States

An activity can be in one of a number of different states during the course of its execution within an application:

- **Active / Running** – The activity is at the top of the Activity Stack, is the foreground task visible on the device screen, has focus and is currently interacting with the user. This is the least likely activity to be terminated in the event of a resource shortage.

- **Paused** – The activity is visible to the user but does not currently have focus (typically because this activity is partially obscured by the current *active* activity). Paused activities are held in memory, remain attached to the window manager, retain all state information and can quickly be restored to active status when moved to the top of the Activity Stack.

- **Stopped** – The activity is currently not visible to the user (in other words it is totally obscured on the device display by other activities). As with paused activities, it retains all state and member information, but is at higher risk of termination in low memory situations.

- **Killed** – The activity has been terminated by the runtime system in order to free up memory and is no longer present on the Activity Stack. Such activities must be restarted if required by the application.

11.7 Configuration Changes

So far in this chapter, we have looked at two of the causes for the change in state of an Android activity, namely the movement of an activity between the foreground and background, and termination of an activity by the runtime system in order to free up memory. In fact, there is a third scenario in which the state of an activity can dramatically change and this involves a change to the device configuration.

By default, any configuration change that impacts the appearance of an activity (such as rotating the orientation of the device between portrait and landscape, or changing a system font setting) will cause the activity to be destroyed and recreated. The reasoning behind this is that such changes affect resources such as the layout of the user interface and simply destroying and recreating impacted activities is the quickest way for an activity to respond to the configuration change. It is, however, possible to configure an activity so that it is not restarted by the system in response to specific configuration changes.

11.8 Handling State Change

If nothing else, it should be clear from this chapter that an application and, by definition, the components contained therein will transition through many states during the course of its lifespan. Of particular importance is the fact that these state changes (up to and including complete termination) are imposed upon the application by the Android runtime subject to the actions of the user and the availability of resources on the device.

In practice, however, these state changes are not imposed entirely without notice and an application will, in most circumstances, be notified by the runtime system of the changes and given the opportunity to react accordingly. This will typically involve saving or restoring both internal data structures and user interface state, thereby allowing the user to switch seamlessly between applications and providing at least the appearance of multiple, concurrently running applications. The steps involved in gracefully handling state changes will be covered in detail in the next chapter entitled *"Handling Android Activity State Changes"*.

11.9 Summary

Mobile devices are typically considered to be resource constrained, particularly in terms of on-board memory capacity. Consequently, a prime responsibility of the Android operating system is to ensure that applications, and the operating system in general, remain responsive to the user.

Applications are hosted on Android within processes. Each application, in turn, is made up of components in the form of activities and Services.

The Android runtime system has the power to terminate both processes and individual activities in order to free up memory. Process state is taken into consideration by the runtime system when deciding whether a process is a suitable candidate for termination. The state of a process is largely dependent upon the status of the activities hosted by that process.

The key message of this chapter is that an application moves through a variety of states during its execution lifespan and has very little control over its destiny within the Android runtime environment. Those processes and activities that are not directly interacting with the user run a higher risk of termination by the runtime system. An essential element of Android application development, therefore, involves the ability of an application to respond to state change notifications from the operating system, a topic that is covered in the next chapter.

12. Handling Android Activity State Changes

Based on the information outlined in the chapter entitled *"Understanding Android Application and Activity Lifecycles"* it is now evident that the activities that make up an application pass through a variety of different states during the course of the application's lifespan. The change from one state to the other is imposed by the Android runtime system and is, therefore, largely beyond the control of the activity itself. That said, in most instances the runtime will provide the activity in question with a notification of the impending state change, thereby giving it time to react accordingly. In most cases, this will involve saving or restoring data relating to the state of the activity and its user interface.

The primary objective of this chapter is to provide a high-level overview of the ways in which an activity may be notified of a state change and to outline the areas where it is advisable to save or restore state information. Having covered this information, the chapter will then touch briefly on the subject of *activity lifetimes*.

12.1 The Activity Class

With few exceptions, activities in an application are created as subclasses of either the Android *Activity* class, or another class that is, itself, subclassed from the Activity class (for example the AppCompatActivity or FragmentActivity classes).

Consider, for example, the simple *AndroidSample* project created in *"Creating an Example Android App in Android Studio"*. Load this project into the Android Studio environment and locate the *AndroidSampleActvity. java* file (located in *app -> java -> com.<your domain>.androidsample*). Having located the file, double-click on it to load it into the editor where it should read as follows:

```
package com.ebookfrenzy.androidsample;

import android.os.Bundle;
import android.support.design.widget.FloatingActionButton;
import android.support.design.widget.Snackbar;
import android.support.v7.app.AppCompatActivity;
import android.support.v7.widget.Toolbar;
import android.view.View;
import android.view.Menu;
import android.view.MenuItem;

public class AndroidSampleActivity extends AppCompatActivity {

    @Override
    protected void onCreate(Bundle savedInstanceState) {
        super.onCreate(savedInstanceState);
        setContentView(R.layout.activity_android_sample);
        Toolbar toolbar = (Toolbar) findViewById(R.id.toolbar);
```

```
        setSupportActionBar(toolbar);

    FloatingActionButton fab =
            (FloatingActionButton) findViewById(R.id.fab);
    fab.setOnClickListener(new View.OnClickListener() {
        @Override
        public void onClick(View view) {
            Snackbar.make(view,
             "Replace with your own action", Snackbar.LENGTH_LONG)
                    .setAction("Action", null).show();
        }
    });
}

@Override
public boolean onCreateOptionsMenu(Menu menu) {
    // Inflate the menu; this adds items to the action bar if it is present.
    getMenuInflater().inflate(R.menu.menu_android_sample, menu);
    return true;
}

@Override
public boolean onOptionsItemSelected(MenuItem item) {
    // Handle action bar item clicks here. The action bar will
    // automatically handle clicks on the Home/Up button, so long
    // as you specify a parent activity in AndroidManifest.xml.
    int id = item.getItemId();

    //noinspection SimplifiableIfStatement
    if (id == R.id.action_settings) {
        return true;
    }

    return super.onOptionsItemSelected(item);
}
}
```

When the project was created, we instructed Android Studio also to create an initial activity named *AndroidSampleActivity*. As is evident from the above code, the AndroidSampleActivity class is a subclass of the AppCompatActivity class.

A review of the reference documentation for the AppCompatActivity class would reveal that it is itself a subclass of the Activity class. This can be verified within the Android Studio editor using the *Hierarchy* tool window. With the *AndroidSampleActivity.java* file loaded into the editor, click on AppCompatActivity in the *class* declaration line and press the *Ctrl-H* keyboard shortcut. The hierarchy tool window will subsequently appear displaying the class hierarchy for the selected class. As illustrated in Figure 12-1, AppCompatActivity is clearly subclassed from the FragmentActivity class which is itself ultimately a subclass of the Activity class:

Figure 12-1

The Activity class and its subclasses contain a range of methods that are intended to be called by the Android runtime to notify an activity that its state is changing. For the purposes of this chapter, we will refer to these as the *activity lifecycle methods*. An activity class simply needs to *override* these methods and implement the necessary functionality within them in order to react accordingly to state changes.

One such method is named *onCreate()* and, turning once again to the above code fragment, we can see that this method has already been overridden and implemented for us in the *AndroidSampleActivity* class. In a later section we will explore in detail both *onCreate()* and the other relevant lifecycle methods of the Activity class.

12.2 Dynamic State vs. Persistent State

A key objective of Activity lifecycle management is ensuring that the state of the activity is saved and restored at appropriate times. When talking about *state* in this context we mean the data that is currently being held within the activity and the appearance of the user interface. The activity might, for example, maintain a data model in memory that needs to be saved to a database, content provider or file. Such state information, because it persists from one invocation of the application to another, is referred to as the *persistent state*.

The appearance of the user interface (such as text entered into a text field but not yet committed to the application's internal data model) is referred to as the *dynamic state*, since it is typically only retained during a single invocation of the application (and also referred to as *user interface state* or *instance state*).

Understanding the differences between these two states is important because both the ways they are saved, and the reasons for doing so, differ.

The purpose of saving the persistent state is to avoid the loss of data that may result from an activity being killed by the runtime system while in the background. The dynamic state, on the other hand, is saved and restored for reasons that are slightly more complex.

Consider, for example, that an application contains an activity (which we will refer to as *Activity A*) containing a text field and some radio buttons. During the course of using the application, the user enters some text into the text field and makes a selection from the radio buttons. Before performing an action to save these changes, however, the user then switches to another activity causing *Activity A* to be pushed down the Activity Stack and placed into the background. After some time, the runtime system ascertains that memory is low and consequently kills *Activity A* to free up resources. As far as the user is concerned, however, *Activity A* was simply placed into the background and is ready to be moved to the foreground at any time. On returning *Activity A* to the foreground the user would, quite reasonably, expect the entered text and radio button selections to have been retained. In this scenario, however, a new instance of *Activity A* will have been created and, if the dynamic state was not saved and restored, the previous user input lost.

The main purpose of saving dynamic state, therefore, is to give the perception of seamless switching between foreground and background activities, regardless of the fact that activities may actually have been killed and restarted without the user's knowledge.

The mechanisms for saving persistent and dynamic state will become clearer in the following sections of this chapter.

12.3 The Android Activity Lifecycle Methods

As previously explained, the Activity class contains a number of lifecycle methods which act as event handlers when the state of an Activity changes. The primary methods supported by the Android Activity class are as follows:

- **onCreate(Bundle savedInstanceState)** – The method that is called when the activity is first created and the ideal location for most initialization tasks to be performed. The method is passed an argument in the form of a *Bundle* object that may contain dynamic state information (typically relating to the state of the user interface) from a prior invocation of the activity.

- **onRestart()** – Called when the activity is about to restart after having previously been stopped by the runtime system.

- **onStart()** – Always called immediately after the call to the *onCreate()* or *onRestart()* methods, this method indicates to the activity that it is about to become visible to the user. This call will be followed by a call to *onResume()* if the activity moves to the top of the activity stack, or *onStop()* in the event that it is pushed down the stack by another activity.

- **onResume()** – Indicates that the activity is now at the top of the activity stack and is the activity with which the user is currently interacting.

- **onPause()** – Indicates that a previous activity is about to become the foreground activity. This call will be followed by a call to either the *onResume()* or *onStop()* method depending on whether the activity moves back to the foreground or becomes invisible to the user. Steps may be taken within this method to store *persistent state* information not yet saved by the app. To avoid delays in switching between activities, time consuming operations such as storing data to a database or performing network operations should be avoided within this method. This method should also ensure that any CPU intensive tasks such as animation are stopped.

- **onStop()** – The activity is now no longer visible to the user. The two possible scenarios that may follow this call are a call to *onRestart()* in the event that the activity moves to the foreground again, or *onDestroy()* if the activity is being terminated.

- **onDestroy()** – The activity is about to be destroyed, either voluntarily because the activity has completed its tasks and has called the *finish()* method or because the runtime is terminating it either to release memory or due to a configuration change (such as the orientation of the device changing). It is important to note that a call will not always be made to *onDestroy()* when an activity is terminated.

- **onConfigurationChanged()** – Called when a configuration change occurs for which the activity has indicated it is not to be restarted. The method is passed a Configuration object outlining the new device configuration and it is then the responsibility of the activity to react to the change.

In addition to the lifecycle methods outlined above, there are two methods intended specifically for saving and restoring the *dynamic state* of an activity:

- **onRestoreInstanceState(Bundle savedInstanceState)** – This method is called immediately after a call to the *onStart()* method in the event that the activity is restarting from a previous invocation in which state was saved. As with *onCreate()*, this method is passed a Bundle object containing the previous state data. This method is typically used in situations where it makes more sense to restore a previous state after the initialization of the activity has been performed in *onCreate()* and *onStart()*.

- **onSaveInstanceState(Bundle outState)** – Called before an activity is destroyed so that the current *dynamic state* (usually relating to the user interface) can be saved. The method is passed the Bundle object into which the state should be saved and which is subsequently passed through to the *onCreate()* and *onRestoreInstanceState()* methods when the activity is restarted. Note that this method is only called in situations where the runtime ascertains that dynamic state needs to be saved.

When overriding the above methods in an activity, it is important to remember that, with the exception of *onRestoreInstanceState()* and *onSaveInstanceState()*, the method implementation must include a call to the corresponding method in the *Activity* super class. For example, the following method overrides the *onRestart()* method but also includes a call to the super class instance of the method:

```
protected void onRestart() {
        super.onRestart();
        Log.i(TAG, "onRestart");
}
```

Failure to make this super class call in method overrides will result in the runtime throwing an exception during execution of the activity. While calls to the super class in the *onRestoreInstanceState()* and *onSaveInstanceState()* methods are optional (they can, for example, be omitted when implementing custom save and restoration behavior) there are considerable benefits to using them, a subject that will be covered in the chapter entitled *"Saving and Restoring the State of an Android Activity"*.

12.4 Activity Lifetimes

The final topic to be covered involves an outline of the *entire*, *visible* and *foreground* lifetimes through which an activity will transition during execution:

- **Entire Lifetime** –The term "entire lifetime" is used to describe everything that takes place within an activity between the initial call to the *onCreate()* method and the call to *onDestroy()* prior to the activity terminating.

- **Visible Lifetime** – Covers the periods of execution of an activity between the call to *onStart()* and *onStop()*. During this period the activity is visible to the user though may not be the activity with which the user is currently interacting.

- **Foreground Lifetime** – Refers to the periods of execution between calls to the *onResume()* and *onPause()* methods.

It is important to note that an activity may pass through the *foreground* and *visible* lifetimes multiple times during the course of the *entire* lifetime.

The concepts of lifetimes and lifecycle methods are illustrated in Figure 12-2:

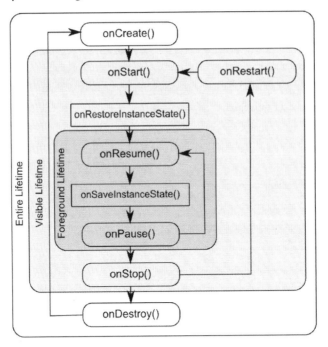

Figure 12-2

12.5 Disabling Configuration Change Restarts

As previously outlined, an activity may indicate that it is not to be restarted in the event of certain configuration changes. This is achieved by adding an *android:configChanges* directive to the activity element within the project manifest file. The following manifest file excerpt, for example, indicates that the activity should not be restarted in the event of configuration changes relating to orientation or device-wide font size:

```
<activity android:name=".DemoActivity"
          android:configChanges="orientation|fontScale"
          android:label="@string/app_name">
```

12.6 Summary

All activities are derived from the Android *Activity* class which, in turn, contains a number of event methods that are designed to be called by the runtime system when the state of an activity changes. By overriding these methods, an activity can respond to state changes and, where necessary, take steps to save and restore the current state of both the activity and the application. Activity state can be thought of as taking two forms. The persistent state refers to data that needs to be stored between application invocations (for example to a file or database). Dynamic state, on the other hand, relates instead to the current appearance of the user interface.

In this chapter, we have highlighted the lifecycle methods available to activities and covered the concept of activity lifetimes. In the next chapter, entitled *"Android Activity State Changes by Example"*, we will implement an example application that puts much of this theory into practice.

13. Android Activity State Changes by Example

The previous chapters have discussed in some detail the different states and lifecycles of the activities that comprise an Android application. In this chapter, we will put the theory of handling activity state changes into practice through the creation of an example application. The purpose of this example application is to provide a real world demonstration of an activity as it passes through a variety of different states within the Android runtime.

In the next chapter, entitled *"Saving and Restoring the State of an Android Activity"*, the example project constructed in this chapter will be extended to demonstrate the saving and restoration of dynamic activity state.

13.1 Creating the State Change Example Project

The first step in this exercise is to create the new project. Begin by launching Android Studio and, if necessary, closing any currently open projects using the *File -> Close Project* menu option so that the Welcome screen appears.

Select the *Start a new Android Studio project* quick start option from the welcome screen and, within the resulting new project dialog, enter *StateChange* into the Application name field and *ebookfrenzy.com* as the Company Domain setting before clicking on the *Next* button.

On the form factors screen, enable the *Phone and Tablet* option and set the minimum SDK setting to API 14: Android 4.0 (IceCreamSandwich). Continue to proceed through the screens, requesting the creation of a Basic Activity named *StateChangeActivity* with a corresponding layout named *activity_state_change*.

Upon completion of the project creation process, the *StateChange* project should be listed in the Project tool window located along the left-hand edge of the Android Studio main window with the *content_state_change.xml* layout file pre-loaded into the Layout Editor as illustrated in Figure 13-1.

The next action to take involves the design of the content area of the user interface for the activity. This is stored in a file named *content_state_change.xml* which should already be loaded into the Layout Editor tool. If it is not, navigate to it in the project tool window where it can be found in the *app -> res -> layout* folder. Once located, double-clicking on the file will load it into the Android Studio Layout Editor tool.

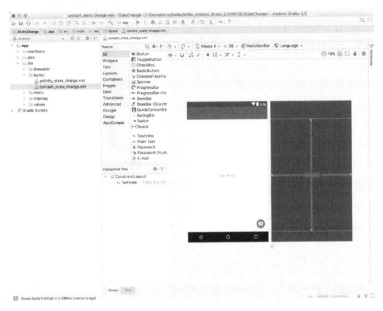

Figure 13-1

13.2 Designing the User Interface

With the user interface layout loaded into the Layout Editor tool, it is now time to design the user interface for the example application. Instead of the "Hello world!" TextView currently present in the user interface design, the activity actually requires an EditText view. Select the TextView object in the Layout Editor canvas and press the Delete key on the keyboard to remove it from the design.

From the Palette located on the left side of the Layout Editor, select the *Text* category and, from the list of text components, click and drag a *Plain Text* component over to the visual representation of the device screen. Move the component to the center of the display so that the center guidelines appear and drop it into place so that the layout resembles that of Figure 13-2.

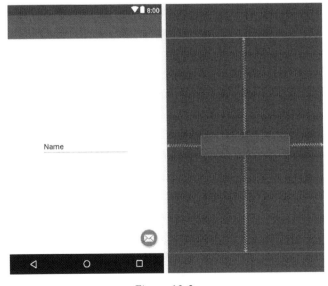

Figure 13-2

When using the EditText widget it is necessary to specify an *input type* for the view. This simply defines the type of text or data that will be entered by the user. For example, if the input type is set to *Phone*, the user will be restricted to entering numerical digits into the view. Alternatively, if the input type is set to *TextCapCharacters,* the input will default to upper case characters. Input type settings may also be combined.

For the purposes of this example, we will set the input type to support general text input. To do so, select the EditText widget in the layout and locate the *inputType* entry within the Attributes tool window. Click on the current setting to open the list of options and, within the list, switch off *textPersonName* and enable *text* before clicking on the OK button.

By default the EditText is displaying text which reads "Name". Remaining within the Attributes panel, delete this from the *text* property field so that the view is blank within the layout.

13.3 Overriding the Activity Lifecycle Methods

At this point, the project contains a single activity named *StateChangeActivity*, which is derived from the Android *AppCompatActivity* class. The source code for this activity is contained within the *StateChangeActivity.java* file which should already be open in an editor session and represented by a tab in the editor tab bar. In the event that the file is no longer open, navigate to it in the Project tool window panel (*app -> java -> com.ebookfrenzy. statechange -> StateChangeActivity*) and double-click on it to load the file into the editor. Once loaded the code should read as follows:

```
package com.ebookfrenzy.statechange;


import android.os.Bundle;
import android.support.design.widget.FloatingActionButton;
import android.support.design.widget.Snackbar;
import android.support.v7.app.AppCompatActivity;
import android.support.v7.widget.Toolbar;
import android.view.View;
import android.view.Menu;
import android.view.MenuItem;


public class StateChangeActivity extends AppCompatActivity {

    @Override
    protected void onCreate(Bundle savedInstanceState) {
        super.onCreate(savedInstanceState);
        setContentView(R.layout.activity_state_change);
        Toolbar toolbar = (Toolbar) findViewById(R.id.toolbar);
        setSupportActionBar(toolbar);

        FloatingActionButton fab =
                (FloatingActionButton) findViewById(R.id.fab);
        fab.setOnClickListener(new View.OnClickListener() {
            @Override
            public void onClick(View view) {
                Snackbar.make(view, "Replace with your own action",
                    Snackbar.LENGTH_LONG)
```

```
                              .setAction("Action", null).show();
            }
       });
   }


   @Override
   public boolean onCreateOptionsMenu(Menu menu) {
       // Inflate the menu; this adds items to the action bar if it is present.
       getMenuInflater().inflate(R.menu.menu_state_change, menu);
       return true;
   }


   @Override
   public boolean onOptionsItemSelected(MenuItem item) {
       // Handle action bar item clicks here. The action bar will
       // automatically handle clicks on the Home/Up button, so long
       // as you specify a parent activity in AndroidManifest.xml.
       int id = item.getItemId();

       //noinspection SimplifiableIfStatement
       if (id == R.id.action_settings) {
           return true;
       }

       return super.onOptionsItemSelected(item);
   }
}
```

So far the only lifecycle method overridden by the activity is the *onCreate()* method which has been implemented to call the super class instance of the method before setting up the user interface for the activity. We will now modify this method so that it outputs a diagnostic message in the Android Studio Logcat panel each time it executes. For this, we will use the *Log* class, which requires that we import *android.util.Log* and declare a tag that will enable us to filter these messages in the log output:

```
package com.ebookfrenzy.statechange;

import android.os.Bundle;
import android.support.design.widget.FloatingActionButton;
import android.support.design.widget.Snackbar;
import android.support.v7.app.AppCompatActivity;
import android.support.v7.widget.Toolbar;
import android.view.View;
import android.view.Menu;
import android.view.MenuItem;
import android.util.Log;

public class StateChangeActivity extends AppCompatActivity {
```

```
    private static final String TAG = "StateChange";

    @Override
    protected void onCreate(Bundle savedInstanceState) {
        super.onCreate(savedInstanceState);
        setContentView(R.layout.activity_state_change);
        Toolbar toolbar = (Toolbar) findViewById(R.id.toolbar);
        setSupportActionBar(toolbar);

        FloatingActionButton fab = (FloatingActionButton) findViewById(R.id.fab);
        fab.setOnClickListener(new View.OnClickListener() {
            @Override
            public void onClick(View view) {
                Snackbar.make(view, "Replace with your own action",
                    Snackbar.LENGTH_LONG)
                        .setAction("Action", null).show();
            }
        });

        Log.i(TAG, "onCreate");
    }
    .
    .
    .
}
```

The next task is to override some more methods, with each one containing a corresponding log call. These override methods may be added manually or generated using the *Alt-Insert* keyboard shortcut as outlined in the chapter entitled *"The Basics of the Android Studio Code Editor"*. Note that the Log calls will still need to be added manually if the methods are being auto-generated:

```
@Override
protected void onStart() {
    super.onStart();
    Log.i(TAG, "onStart");
}

@Override
protected void onResume() {
    super.onResume();
    Log.i(TAG, "onResume");
}

@Override
protected void onPause() {
    super.onPause();
    Log.i(TAG, "onPause");
```

```
}

@Override
protected void onStop() {
    super.onStop();
    Log.i(TAG, "onStop");
}

@Override
protected void onRestart() {
    super.onRestart();
    Log.i(TAG, "onRestart");
}

@Override
protected void onDestroy() {
    super.onDestroy();
    Log.i(TAG, "onDestroy");
}

@Override
protected void onSaveInstanceState(Bundle outState) {
    super.onSaveInstanceState(outState);
    Log.i(TAG, "onSaveInstanceState");
}

@Override
protected void onRestoreInstanceState(Bundle savedInstanceState) {
    super.onRestoreInstanceState(savedInstanceState);
    Log.i(TAG, "onRestoreInstanceState");
}
```

13.4 Filtering the Logcat Panel

The purpose of the code added to the overridden methods in *StateChangeActivity.java* is to output logging information to the *Logcat* tool window. This output can be configured to display all events relating to the device or emulator session, or restricted to those events that relate to the currently selected app. The output can also be further restricted to only those log events that match a specified filter.

Display the Logcat tool window and click on the filter menu (marked as B in Figure 13-3) to review the available options. When this menu is set to *Show only selected application*, only those messages relating to the app selected in the menu marked as A will be displayed in the Logcat panel. Choosing *No Filter*, on the other hand, will display all the messages generated by the device or emulator.

Figure 13-3

Before running the application, it is worth demonstrating the creation of a filter which, when selected, will further restrict the log output to ensure that only those log messages containing the tag declared in our activity are displayed.

From the filter menu (B), select the *Edit Filter Configuration* menu option. In the *Create New Logcat Filter* dialog (Figure 13-4), name the filter *Lifecycle* and, in the *Log Tag* field, enter the Tag value declared in *StateChangeActivity. java* (in the above code example this was *StateChange*).

Figure 13-4

Enter the package identifier in the *Package Name* field (clicking on the search icon in the text field will drop down a menu from which the package name may be selected) and, when the changes are complete, click on the *OK* button to create the filter and dismiss the dialog. Instead of listing *No Filters,* the newly created filter should now be selected in the Logcat tool window.

13.5 Running the Application

For optimal results, the application should be run on a physical Android device, details of which can be found in the chapter entitled *"Testing Android Studio Apps on a Physical Android Device"*. With the device configured and connected to the development computer, click on the run button represented by a green triangle located in the Android Studio toolbar as shown in Figure 13-5 below, select the *Run -> Run...* menu option or use the Shift+F10 keyboard shortcut:

Figure 13-5

Select the physical Android device from the *Choose Device* dialog if it appears (assuming that you have not already configured it to be the default target). After Android Studio has built the application and installed it on the device it should start up and be running in the foreground.

A review of the Logcat panel should indicate which methods have so far been triggered (taking care to ensure that the *Lifecycle* filter created in the preceding section is selected to filter out log events that are not currently of interest to us):

Figure 13-6

13.6 Experimenting with the Activity

With the diagnostics working, it is now time to exercise the application with a view to gaining an understanding of the activity lifecycle state changes. To begin with, consider the initial sequence of log events in the Logcat panel:

onCreate

onStart

onResume

Clearly, the initial state changes are exactly as outlined in *"Understanding Android Application and Activity Lifecycles"*. Note, however, that a call was not made to *onRestoreInstanceState()* since the Android runtime detected that there was no state to restore in this situation.

Tap on the Home icon in the bottom status bar on the device display and note the sequence of method calls reported in the log as follows:

onPause

onSaveInstanceState

onStop

In this case, the runtime has noticed that the activity is no longer in the foreground, is not visible to the user and has stopped the activity, but not without providing an opportunity for the activity to save the dynamic state. Depending on whether the runtime ultimately destroyed the activity or simply restarted it, the activity will either be notified it has been restarted via a call to *onRestart()* or will go through the creation sequence again when the user returns to the activity.

As outlined in *"Understanding Android Application and Activity Lifecycles"*, the destruction and recreation of an activity can be triggered by making a configuration change to the device, such as rotating from portrait to landscape. To see this in action, simply rotate the device while the *StateChange* application is in the foreground.

When using the emulator, device rotation may be simulated using the rotation button located in the emulator toolbar. The resulting sequence of method calls in the log should read as follows:

```
onPause
onSaveInstanceState
onStop
onDestroy
onCreate
onStart
onRestoreInstanceState
onResume
```

Clearly, the runtime system has given the activity an opportunity to save state before being destroyed and restarted.

13.7 Summary

The old adage that a picture is worth a thousand words holds just as true for examples when learning a new programming paradigm. In this chapter, we have created an example Android application for the purpose of demonstrating the different lifecycle states through which an activity is likely to pass. In the course of developing the project in this chapter, we also looked at a mechanism for generating diagnostic logging information from within an activity.

In the next chapter, we will extend the *StateChange* example project to demonstrate how to save and restore an activity's dynamic state.

14. Saving and Restoring the State of an Android Activity

If the previous few chapters have achieved their objective, it should now be a little clearer as to the importance of saving and restoring the state of a user interface at particular points in the lifetime of an activity.

In this chapter, we will extend the example application created in *"Android Activity State Changes by Example"* to demonstrate the steps involved in saving and restoring state when an activity is destroyed and recreated by the runtime system.

A key component of saving and restoring dynamic state involves the use of the Android SDK *Bundle* class, a topic that will also be covered in this chapter.

14.1 Saving Dynamic State

An activity, as we have already learned, is given the opportunity to save dynamic state information via a call from the runtime system to the activity's implementation of the *onSaveInstanceState()* method. Passed through as an argument to the method is a reference to a Bundle object into which the method will need to store any dynamic data that needs to be saved. The Bundle object is then stored by the runtime system on behalf of the activity and subsequently passed through as an argument to the activity's *onCreate()* and *onRestoreInstanceState()* methods if and when they are called. The data can then be retrieved from the Bundle object within these methods and used to restore the state of the activity.

14.2 Default Saving of User Interface State

In the previous chapter, the diagnostic output from the *StateChange* example application showed that an activity goes through a number of state changes when the device on which it is running is rotated sufficiently to trigger an orientation change.

Launch the *StateChange* application once again, this time entering some text into the EditText field prior to performing the device rotation. Having rotated the device, the following state change sequence should appear in the Logcat window:

```
onPause
onSaveInstanceState
onStop
onDestroy
onCreate
onStart
onRestoreInstanceState
onResume
```

Clearly this has resulted in the activity being destroyed and re-created. A review of the user interface of the running application, however, should show that the text entered into the EditText field has been preserved. Given that the activity was destroyed and recreated, and that we did not add any specific code to make sure the text was saved and restored, this behavior requires some explanation.

In actual fact most of the view widgets included with the Android SDK already implement the behavior necessary to automatically save and restore state when an activity is restarted. The only requirement to enable this behavior is for the *onSaveInstanceState()* and *onRestoreInstanceState()* override methods in the activity to include calls to the equivalent methods of the super class:

```
@Override
protected void onSaveInstanceState(Bundle outState) {
    super.onSaveInstanceState(outState);
}

@Override
protected void onRestoreInstanceState(Bundle savedInstanceState) {
    super.onRestoreInstanceState(savedInstanceState);
}
```

The automatic saving of state for a user interface view can be disabled in the XML layout file by setting the *android:saveEnabled* property to *false*. For the purposes of an example, we will disable the automatic state saving mechanism for the EditText view in the user interface layout and then add code to the application to manually save and restore the state of the view.

To configure the EditText view such that state will not be saved and restored in the event that the activity is restarted, edit the *content_state_change.xml* file so that the entry for the view reads as follows (note that the XML can be edited directly by clicking on the *Text* tab on the bottom edge of the Layout Editor panel):

```
<EditText
    android:id="@+id/editText"
    android:layout_width="wrap_content"
    android:layout_height="wrap_content"
    android:ems="10"
    android:inputType="text"
    android:saveEnabled="false"
    app:layout_constraintBottom_toBottomOf="parent"
    app:layout_constraintLeft_toLeftOf="parent"
    app:layout_constraintRight_toRightOf="parent"
    app:layout_constraintTop_toTopOf="parent" />
```

After making the change, run the application, enter text and rotate the device to verify that the text is no longer saved and restored before proceeding.

14.3 The Bundle Class

For situations where state needs to be saved beyond the default functionality provided by the user interface view components, the Bundle class provides a container for storing data using a *key-value pair* mechanism. The *keys* take the form of string values, while the *values* associated with those *keys* can be in the form of a primitive value or any object that implements the Android *Parcelable* interface. A wide range of classes already implements the Parcelable interface. Custom classes may be made "parcelable" by implementing the set of methods defined in the Parcelable interface, details of which can be found in the Android documentation at:

http://developer.android.com/reference/android/os/Parcelable.html

The Bundle class also contains a set of methods that can be used to get and set key-value pairs for a variety of data types including both primitive types (including Boolean, char, double and float values) and objects (such as Strings and CharSequences).

For the purposes of this example, and having disabled the automatic saving of text for the EditText view, we need to make sure that the text entered into the EditText field by the user is saved into the Bundle object and subsequently restored. This will serve as a demonstration of how to manually save and restore state within an Android application and will be achieved using the *putCharSequence()* and *getCharSequence()* methods of the Bundle class respectively.

14.4 Saving the State

The first step in extending the *StateChange* application is to make sure that the text entered by the user is extracted from the EditText component within the *onSaveInstanceState()* method of the *StateChangeActivity* activity, and then saved as a key-value pair into the Bundle object.

In order to extract the text from the EditText object we first need to identify that object in the user interface. Clearly, this involves bridging the gap between the Java code for the activity (contained in the *StateChangeActivity. java* source code file) and the XML representation of the user interface (contained within the *content_state_ change.xml* resource file). In order to extract the text entered into the EditText component we need to gain access to that user interface object.

Each component within a user interface has associated with it a unique identifier. By default, the Layout Editor tool constructs the ID for a newly added component from the object type. If more than one view of the same type is contained in the layout the type name is followed by a sequential number (though this can, and should, be changed to something more meaningful by the developer). As can be seen by checking the *Component Tree* panel within the Android Studio main window when the *content_state_change.xml* file is selected and the Layout Editor tool displayed, the EditText component has been assigned the ID *editText*:

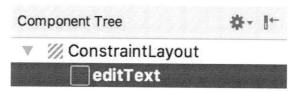

Figure 14-1

As outlined in the chapter entitled "*The Anatomy of an Android Application*", all of the resources that make up an application are compiled into a class named *R*. Amongst those resources are those that define layouts, including the layout for our current activity. Within the R class is a subclass named *layout*, which contains the layout resources, and within that subclass is our *content_state_change* layout. With this knowledge, we can make a call to the *findViewById()* method of our activity object to get a reference to the editText object as follows:

```
final EditText editText = (EditText) findViewById(R.id.editText);
```

Having either obtained a reference to the EditText object and assigned it to a variable, we can now obtain the text that it contains via the object's *getText()* method, which, in turn, returns the current text:

```
CharSequence userText = editText.getText();
```

Finally, we can save the text using the Bundle object's *putCharSequence()* method, passing through the key (this can be any string value but in this instance, we will declare it as "savedText") and the *userText* object as arguments:

```
outState.putCharSequence("savedText", userText);
```

Bringing this all together gives us a modified *onSaveInstanceState()* method in the *StateChangeActivity.java* file that reads as follows (noting also the additional import directive for *android.widget.EditText*):

```
package com.ebookfrenzy.statechange;

import android.os.Bundle;
import android.support.design.widget.FloatingActionButton;
import android.support.design.widget.Snackbar;
import android.support.v7.app.AppCompatActivity;
import android.support.v7.widget.Toolbar;
import android.view.View;
import android.view.Menu;
import android.view.MenuItem;
import android.util.Log;
import android.widget.EditText;

public class StateChangeActivity extends AppCompatActivity {
    .
    .
    .
        protected void onSaveInstanceState(Bundle outState) {
                super.onSaveInstanceState(outState);
                Log.i(TAG, "onSaveInstanceState");

                final EditText editText =
                        (EditText) findViewById(R.id.editText);
                CharSequence userText = editText.getText();
                outState.putCharSequence("savedText", userText);
        }
    .
    .
    .
```

Now that steps have been taken to save the state, the next phase is to ensure that it is restored when needed.

14.5 Restoring the State

The saved dynamic state can be restored in those lifecycle methods that are passed the Bundle object as an argument. This leaves the developer with the choice of using either *onCreate()* or *onRestoreInstanceState()*. The method to use will depend on the nature of the activity. In instances where state is best restored after the activity's initialization tasks have been performed, the *onRestoreInstanceState()* method is generally more suitable. For the purposes of this example we will add code to the *onRestoreInstanceState()* method to extract the saved state from the Bundle using the "savedText" key. We can then display the text on the editText component using the object's *setText()* method:

```
@Override
protected void onRestoreInstanceState(Bundle savedInstanceState) {
    super.onRestoreInstanceState(savedInstanceState);
    Log.i(TAG, "onRestoreInstanceState");
```

```
final EditText editText =
    (EditText) findViewById(R.id.editText);

CharSequence userText =
        savedInstanceState.getCharSequence("savedText");

editText.setText(userText);
}
```

14.6 Testing the Application

All that remains is once again to build and run the *StateChange* application. Once running and in the foreground, touch the EditText component and enter some text before rotating the device to another orientation. Whereas the text changes were previously lost, the new text is retained within the editText component thanks to the code we have added to the activity in this chapter.

Having verified that the code performs as expected, comment out the *super.onSaveInstanceState()* and *super. onRestoreInstanceState()* calls from the two methods, re-launch the app and note that the text is still preserved after a device rotation. The default save and restoration system has essentially been replaced by a custom implementation, thereby providing a way to dynamically and selectively save and restore state within an activity.

14.7 Summary

The saving and restoration of dynamic state in an Android application is simply a matter of implementing the appropriate code in the appropriate lifecycle methods. For most user interface views, this is handled automatically by the Activity super class. In other instances, this typically consists of extracting values and settings within the *onSaveInstanceState()* method and saving the data as key-value pairs within the Bundle object passed through to the activity by the runtime system.

State can be restored in either the *onCreate()* or the *onRestoreInstanceState()* methods of the activity by extracting values from the Bundle object and updating the activity based on the stored values.

In this chapter, we have used these techniques to update the *StateChange* project so that the Activity retains changes through the destruction and subsequent recreation of an activity.

15. Understanding Android Views, View Groups and Layouts

With the possible exception of listening to streaming audio, a user's interaction with an Android device is primarily visual and tactile in nature. All of this interaction takes place through the user interfaces of the applications installed on the device, including both the built-in applications and any third party applications installed by the user. It should come as no surprise, therefore, that a key element of developing Android applications involves the design and creation of user interfaces.

Within this chapter, the topic of Android user interface structure will be covered, together with an overview of the different elements that can be brought together to make up a user interface; namely Views, View Groups and Layouts.

15.1 Designing for Different Android Devices

The term "Android device" covers a vast array of tablet and smartphone products with different screen sizes and resolutions. As a result, application user interfaces must now be carefully designed to ensure correct presentation on as wide a range of display sizes as possible. A key part of this is ensuring that the user interface layouts resize correctly when run on different devices. This can largely be achieved through careful planning and the use of the layout managers outlined in this chapter.

It is also important to keep in mind that the majority of Android based smartphones and tablets can be held by the user in both portrait and landscape orientations. A well-designed user interface should be able to adapt to such changes and make sensible layout adjustments to utilize the available screen space in each orientation.

15.2 Views and View Groups

Every item in a user interface is a subclass of the Android *View* class (to be precise *android.view.View*). The Android SDK provides a set of pre-built views that can be used to construct a user interface. Typical examples include standard items such as the Button, CheckBox, ProgressBar and TextView classes. Such views are also referred to as *widgets* or *components*. For requirements that are not met by the widgets supplied with the SDK, new views may be created either by subclassing and extending an existing class, or creating an entirely new component by building directly on top of the View class.

A view can also be comprised of multiple other views (otherwise known as a *composite view*). Such views are subclassed from the Android *ViewGroup* class (*android.view.ViewGroup*) which is itself a subclass of *View*. An example of such a view is the RadioGroup, which is intended to contain multiple RadioButton objects such that only one can be in the "on" position at any one time. In terms of structure, composite views consist of a single parent view (derived from the ViewGroup class and otherwise known as a *container view* or *root element)* that is capable of containing other views (known as *child views*).

Another category of ViewGroup based container view is that of the layout manager.

15.3 Android Layout Managers

In addition to the widget style views discussed in the previous section, the SDK also includes a set of views referred to as *layouts*. Layouts are container views (and, therefore, subclassed from ViewGroup) designed for the sole purpose of controlling how child views are positioned on the screen.

The Android SDK includes the following layout views that may be used within an Android user interface design:

- **ConstraintLayout** – Introduced in Android 7, use of this layout manager is recommended for most layout requirements. ConstraintLayout allows the positioning and behavior of the views in a layout to be defined by simple constraint settings assigned to each child view. The flexibility of this layout allows complex layouts to be quickly and easily created without the necessity to nest other layout types inside each other, resulting in improved layout performance. ConstraintLayout is also tightly integrated into the Android Studio Layout Editor tool. Unless otherwise stated, this is the layout of choice for the majority of examples in this book.

- **LinearLayout** – Positions child views in a single row or column depending on the orientation selected. A *weight* value can be set on each child to specify how much of the layout space that child should occupy relative to other children.

- **TableLayout** – Arranges child views into a grid format of rows and columns. Each row within a table is represented by a *TableRow* object child, which, in turn, contains a view object for each cell.

- **FrameLayout** – The purpose of the FrameLayout is to allocate an area of screen, typically for the purposes of displaying a single view. If multiple child views are added they will, by default, appear on top of each other positioned in the top left-hand corner of the layout area. Alternate positioning of individual child views can be achieved by setting gravity values on each child. For example, setting a *center_vertical* gravity on a child will cause it to be positioned in the vertical center of the containing FrameLayout view.

- **RelativeLayout** – The RelativeLayout allows child views to be positioned relative both to each other and the containing layout view through the specification of alignments and margins on child views. For example, child *View A* may be configured to be positioned in the vertical and horizontal center of the containing RelativeLayout view. *View B*, on the other hand, might also be configured to be centered horizontally within the layout view, but positioned 30 pixels above the top edge of *View A*, thereby making the vertical position *relative* to that of *View A*. The RelativeLayout manager can be of particular use when designing a user interface that must work on a variety of screen sizes and orientations.

- **AbsoluteLayout** – Allows child views to be positioned at specific X and Y coordinates within the containing layout view. Use of this layout is discouraged since it lacks the flexibility to respond to changes in screen size and orientation.

- **GridLayout** – A GridLayout instance is divided by invisible lines that form a grid containing rows and columns of cells. Child views are then placed in cells and may be configured to cover multiple cells both horizontally and vertically allowing a wide range of layout options to be quickly and easily implemented. Gaps between components in a GridLayout may be implemented by placing a special type of view called a *Space* view into adjacent cells, or by setting margin parameters.

- **CoordinatorLayout** – Introduced as part of the Android Design Support Library with Android 5.0, the CoordinatorLayout is designed specifically for coordinating the appearance and behavior of the app bar across the top of an application screen with other view elements. When creating a new activity using the Basic Activity template, the parent view in the main layout will be implemented using a CoordinatorLayout instance. This layout manager will be covered in greater detail starting with the chapter entitled *"Working with the Floating Action Button and Snackbar"*.

When considering the use of layouts in the user interface for an Android application it is worth keeping in mind that, as will be outlined in the next section, these can be nested within each other to create a user interface design of just about any necessary level of complexity.

15.4 The View Hierarchy

Each view in a user interface represents a rectangular area of the display. A view is responsible for what is drawn in that rectangle and for responding to events that occur within that part of the screen (such as a touch event).

A user interface screen is comprised of a view hierarchy with a *root view* positioned at the top of the tree and child views positioned on branches below. The child of a container view appears on top of its parent view and is constrained to appear within the bounds of the parent view's display area. Consider, for example, the user interface illustrated in Figure 15-1:

Figure 15-1

In addition to the visible button and checkbox views, the user interface actually includes a number of layout views that control how the visible views are positioned. Figure 15-2 shows an alternative view of the user interface, this time highlighting the presence of the layout views in relation to the child views:

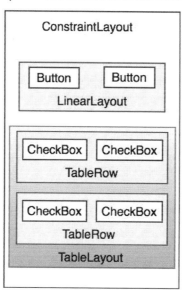

Figure 15-2

As was previously discussed, user interfaces are constructed in the form of a view hierarchy with a root view at the top. This being the case, we can also visualize the above user interface example in the form of the view tree illustrated in Figure 15-3:

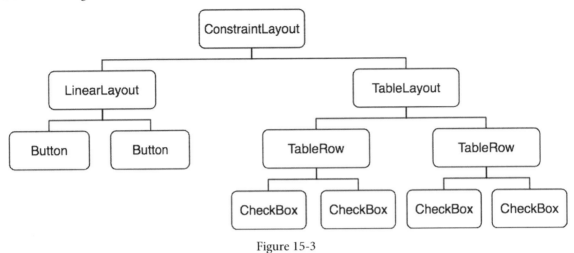

Figure 15-3

The view hierarchy diagram gives probably the clearest overview of the relationship between the various views that make up the user interface shown in Figure 15-1. When a user interface is displayed to the user, the Android runtime walks the view hierarchy, starting at the root view and working down the tree as it renders each view.

15.5 Creating User Interfaces

With a clearer understanding of the concepts of views, layouts and the view hierarchy, the following few chapters will focus on the steps involved in creating user interfaces for Android activities. In fact, there are three different approaches to user interface design: using the Android Studio Layout Editor tool, handwriting XML layout resource files or writing Java code, each of which will be covered.

15.6 Summary

Each element within a user interface screen of an Android application is a view that is ultimately subclassed from the *android.view.View* class. Each view represents a rectangular area of the device display and is responsible both for what appears in that rectangle and for handling events that take place within the view's bounds. Multiple views may be combined to create a single *composite view*. The views within a composite view are children of a *container view* which is generally a subclass of *android.view.ViewGroup* (which is itself a subclass of *android. view.View*). A user interface is comprised of views constructed in the form of a view hierarchy.

The Android SDK includes a range of pre-built views that can be used to create a user interface. These include basic components such as text fields and buttons, in addition to a range of layout managers that can be used to control the positioning of child views. In the event that the supplied views do not meet a specific requirement, custom views may be created, either by extending or combining existing views, or by subclassing *android.view. View* and creating an entirely new class of view.

User interfaces may be created using the Android Studio Layout Editor tool, handwriting XML layout resource files or by writing Java code. Each of these approaches will be covered in the chapters that follow.

16. A Guide to the Android Studio Layout Editor Tool

It is difficult to think of an Android application concept that does not require some form of user interface. Most Android devices come equipped with a touch screen and keyboard (either virtual or physical) and taps and swipes are the primary form of interaction between the user and application. Invariably these interactions take place through the application's user interface.

A well designed and implemented user interface, an important factor in creating a successful and popular Android application, can vary from simple to extremely complex, depending on the design requirements of the individual application. Regardless of the level of complexity, the Android Studio Layout Editor tool significantly simplifies the task of designing and implementing Android user interfaces.

16.1 Basic vs. Empty Activity Templates

As outlined in the chapter entitled *"The Anatomy of an Android Application"*, Android applications are made up of one or more activities. An activity is a standalone module of application functionality that usually correlates directly to a single user interface screen. As such, when working with the Android Studio Layout Editor we are invariably working on the layout for an activity.

When creating a new Android Studio project, a number of different templates are available to be used as the starting point for the user interface of the main activity. The most basic of these templates are the Basic Activity and Empty Activity templates. Although these seem similar at first glance, there are actually considerable differences between the two options.

The Empty Activity template creates a single layout file consisting of a ConstraintLayout manager instance containing a TextView object as shown in Figure 16-1:

Figure 16-1

The Basic Activity, on the other hand, consists of two layout files. The top level layout file has a CoordinatorLayout as the root view, a configurable app bar, a menu preconfigured with a single menu item (A in Figure 16-2), a floating action button (B) and a reference to the second layout file in which the layout for the content area of the activity user interface is declared:

Figure 16-2

Clearly the Empty Activity template is useful if you need neither a floating action button nor a menu in your activity and do not need the special app bar behavior provided by the CoordinatorLayout such as options to make the app bar and toolbar collapse from view during certain scrolling operations (a topic covered in the chapter entitled *"Working with the AppBar and Collapsing Toolbar Layouts"*). The Basic Activity is useful, however, in that it provides these elements by default. In fact, it is often quicker to create a new activity using the Basic Activity template and delete the elements you do not require than to use the Empty Activity template and manually implement behavior such as collapsing toolbars, a menu or floating action button.

Since not all of the examples in this book require the features of the Basic Activity template, however, most of the examples in this chapter will use the Empty Activity template unless the example requires one or other of the features provided by the Basic Activity template.

For future reference, if you need a menu but not a floating action button, use the Basic Activity and follow these steps to delete the floating action button:

1. Double-click on the main *activity* layout file located in the Project tool window under *app -> res -> layout* to load it into the Layout Editor. This will be the layout file prefixed with *activity_* and not the content file prefixed with *content_*.

2. With the layout loaded into the Layout Editor tool, select the floating action button and tap the keyboard *Delete* key to remove the object from the layout.

3. Locate and edit the Java code for the activity (located under *app -> java -> <package name> -> <activity class name>* and remove the floating action button code from the onCreate method as follows:

```
@Override
protected void onCreate(Bundle savedInstanceState) {
    super.onCreate(savedInstanceState);
```

```
setContentView(R.layout.activity_main);
Toolbar toolbar = (Toolbar) findViewById(R.id.toolbar);
setSupportActionBar(toolbar);

FloatingActionButton fab =
        (FloatingActionButton) findViewById(R.id.fab);
fab.setOnClickListener(new View.OnClickListener() {
    @Override
    public void onClick(View view) {
        Snackbar.make(view, "Replace with your own action",
                Snackbar.LENGTH_LONG)
                    .setAction("Action", null).show();
    }
});
}
```

If you need a floating action button but no menu, use the Basic Activity template and follow these steps:

1. Edit the activity class file and delete the *onCreateOptionsMenu* and *onOptionsItemSelected* methods.

2. Select the *res -> menu* item in the Project tool window and tap the keyboard *Delete* key to remove the folder and corresponding menu resource files from the project.

16.2 The Android Studio Layout Editor

As has been demonstrated in previous chapters, the Layout Editor tool provides a "what you see is what you get" (WYSIWYG) environment in which views can be selected from a palette and then placed onto a canvas representing the display of an Android device. Once a view has been placed on the canvas, it can be moved, deleted and resized (subject to the constraints of the parent view). Further, a wide variety of properties relating to the selected view may be modified using the Attributes tool window.

Under the surface, the Layout Editor tool actually constructs an XML resource file containing the definition of the user interface that is being designed. As such, the Layout Editor tool operates in two distinct modes referred to as *Design mode* and *Text mode*.

16.3 Design Mode

In design mode, the user interface can be visually manipulated by directly working with the view palette and the graphical representation of the layout. Figure 16-3 highlights the key areas of the Android Studio Layout Editor tool in design mode:

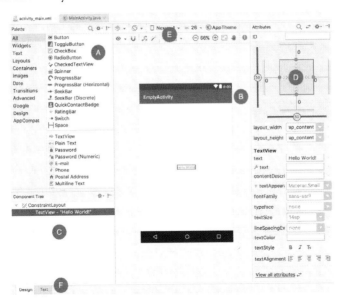

Figure 16-3

A – Palette – The palette provides access to the range of view components provided by the Android SDK. These are grouped into categories for easy navigation. Items may be added to the layout by dragging a view component from the palette and dropping it at the desired position on the layout.

B – Device Screen – The device screen provides a visual "what you see is what you get" representation of the user interface layout as it is being designed. This layout allows for direct manipulation of the design in terms of allowing views to be selected, deleted, moved and resized. The device model represented by the layout can be changed at any time using a menu located in the toolbar.

C – Component Tree – As outlined in the previous chapter (*"Understanding Android Views, View Groups and Layouts"*) user interfaces are constructed using a hierarchical structure. The component tree provides a visual overview of the hierarchy of the user interface design. Selecting an element from the component tree will cause the corresponding view in the layout to be selected. Similarly, selecting a view from the device screen layout will select that view in the component tree hierarchy.

D – Attributes – All of the component views listed in the palette have associated with them a set of attributes that can be used to adjust the behavior and appearance of that view. The Layout Editor's attributes panel provides access to the attributes of the currently selected view in the layout allowing changes to be made.

E – Toolbar – The Layout Editor toolbar provides quick access to a wide range of options including, amongst other options, the ability to zoom in and out of the device screen layout, change the device model currently displayed, rotate the layout between portrait and landscape and switch to a different Android SDK API level. The toolbar also has a set of context sensitive buttons which will appear when relevant view types are selected in the device screen layout.

F – Mode Switching Tabs – The tabs located along the lower edge of the Layout Editor provide a way to switch back and forth between the Layout Editor tool's text and design modes.

16.4 The Palette

The Layout Editor palette is organized into two panels designed to make it easy to locate and preview view components for addition to a layout design. The category panel (marked A in Figure 16-4) lists the different categories of view components supported by the Android SDK. When a category is selected from the list, the second panel (B) updates to display a list of the components that fall into that category:

Figure 16-4

To add a component from the palette onto the layout canvas, simply select the item either from the component list or the preview panel, drag it to the desired location on the canvas and drop it into place.

A search for a specific component within the currently selected category may be initiated by clicking on the search button (marked C in Figure 16-4 above) in the palette toolbar and typing in the component name. As characters are typed, matching results will appear in real-time within the component list panel. If you are unsure of the category in which the component resides, simply select the All category either before or during the search operation.

16.5 Pan and Zoom

When first opened, the Layout Editor will size the layout canvas so that it fits within the available space. Zooming in and out of the layout can be achieved using the plus and minus buttons located in the editor toolbar. When the view is zoomed in, it can be useful to pan around the layout to locate a particular area of the design. Although this can be achieved using the scrollbars, another option is to use the pan menu bar button highlighted in Figure 16-5. Once selected, a pan and zoom panel will appear containing a lens which can be moved to alter the currently visible area of the layout.

Figure 16-5

16.6 Design and Layout Views

When the Layout Editor tool is in Design mode, the layout can be viewed in two different ways. The view shown in Figure 16-3 above is the Design view and shows the layout and widgets as they will appear in the running app. A second mode, referred to as Layout or Blueprint view can be shown either instead of, or concurrently with the Design view. The toolbar menu shown in Figure 16-6 provides options to display the Design, Blueprint, or both views. A fourth option, *Force Refresh Layout*, causes the layout to rebuild and redraw. This can be useful when the layout enters an unexpected state or is not accurately reflecting the current design settings:

Figure 16-6

Whether to display the layout view, design view or both is a matter of personal preference. A good approach is to begin with both displayed as shown in Figure 16-7:

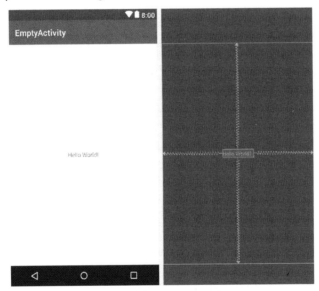

Figure 16-7

16.7 Text Mode

It is important to keep in mind when using the Android Studio Layout Editor tool that all it is really doing is providing a user friendly approach to creating XML layout resource files. At any time during the design process, the underlying XML can be viewed and directly edited simply by clicking on the *Text* tab located at the bottom of the Layout Editor tool panel. To return to design mode, simply click on the *Design* tab.

Figure 16-8 highlights the key areas of the Android Studio Layout Editor tool in text mode:

Figure 16-8

A – Editor – The editor panel displays the XML that makes up the current user interface layout design. This is the full Android Studio editor environment containing all of the features previously outlined in the *"The Basics of the Android Studio Code Editor"* chapter of this book.

B – Preview – As changes are made to the XML in the editor, these changes are visually reflected in the preview window. This provides instant visual feedback on the XML changes as they are made in the editor, thereby avoiding the need to switch back and forth between text and design mode to see changes. The preview also allows direct manipulation and design of the layout just as if the layout were in Design mode, with visual changes being reflected in the editor panel in real-time. As with Design mode, both the Design and Layout views may be displayed using the toolbar buttons highlighted in Figure 16-6 above.

C – Toolbar – The toolbar in text mode provides access to the same functions available in design mode.

D - Mode Switching Tabs – The tabs located along the lower edge of the Layout Editor provide a way to switch back and forth between the Layout Editor tool's Text and Design modes.

16.8 Setting Attributes

The Attributes panel provides access to all of the available settings for the currently selected component. By default, the attributes panel shows the most commonly changed attributes for the currently selected component in the layout. Figure 16-9, for example, shows this subset of attributes for the TextView widget:

Figure 16-9

To access all of the attributes for the currently selected widget, click on the button highlighted in Figure 16-10, or use the *View all attributes* link at the bottom of the attributes panel:

Figure 16-10

A search for a specific attribute may also be performed by selecting the search button in the toolbar of the attributes tool window and typing in the attribute name. Select the *View all attributes* button or link either before or during a search to ensure that all of the attributes for the currently selected component are included in the results.

Some attributes contain a button displaying three dots. This indicates that a settings dialog is available to assist in selecting a suitable property value. To display the dialog, simply click on the button. Attributes for which a finite number of valid options are available will present a drop down menu (Figure 16-11) from which a selection may be made.

Figure 16-11

16.9 Configuring Favorite Attributes

The attributes included on the initial subset attribute list may be extended by configuring *favorite attributes*. To add an attribute to the favorites list, display all the attributes for the currently selected component and hover the mouse pointer so that it is positioned to the far left of the attribute entry within the attributes tool window. A star icon will appear to the left of the attribute name which, when clicked, will add the property to the favorites list. Figure 16-12, for example, shows the autoText, background and backgroundTint attributes for a TextView widget configured as favorite attributes:

Figure 16-12

Once added as favorites, the attributes will be listed beneath the *Favorite Attributes* section in the subject attributes list:

textStyle	B *I* T̅ᴛ
textAlignment	⊫ ≡ ≡ ≡ ⊒

Favorite Attributes

autoText	⊖
background	[ ] ...
backgroundTint	[ ] ...

View all attributes ⇄

Figure 16-13

16.10 Creating a Custom Device Definition

The device menu in the Layout Editor toolbar (Figure 16-14) provides a list of preconfigured device types which, when selected, will appear as the device screen canvas. In addition to the pre-configured device types, any AVD instances that have previously been configured within the Android Studio environment will also be listed within the menu. To add additional device configurations, display the device menu, select the *Add Device Definition...* option and follow the steps outlined in the chapter entitled *"Creating an Android Virtual Device (AVD) in Android Studio"*.

Figure 16-14

16.11 Changing the Current Device

As an alternative to the device selection menu, the current device format may be changed by clicking on the resize handle located next to the bottom right-hand corner of the device screen (Figure 16-15) and dragging to select an alternate device display format. As the screen resizes, markers will appear indicating the various size options and orientations available for selection:

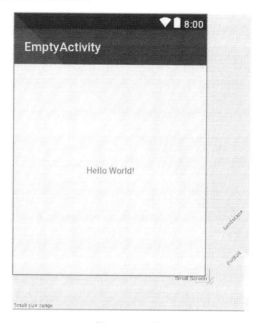

Figure 16-15

16.12 Summary

A key part of developing Android applications involves the creation of the user interface. Within the Android Studio environment, this is performed using the Layout Editor tool which operates in two modes. In design mode, view components are selected from a palette and positioned on a layout representing an Android device screen and configured using a list of attributes. In text mode, the underlying XML that represents the user interface layout can be directly edited, with changes reflected in a preview screen. These modes combine to provide an extensive and intuitive user interface design environment.

17. A Guide to the Android ConstraintLayout

As discussed in the chapter entitled *"A Guide to the Android ConstraintLayout"*, Android provides a number of layout managers for the purpose of designing user interfaces. With Android 7, Google has introduced a new layout that is intended to address many of the shortcomings of the older layout managers. This new layout, called ConstraintLayout, combines a simple, expressive and flexible layout system with powerful features built into the Android Studio Layout Editor tool to ease the creation of responsive user interface layouts that adapt automatically to different screen sizes and changes in device orientation.

This chapter will outline the basic concepts of ConstraintLayout while the next chapter will provide a detailed overview of how constraint-based layouts can be created using ConstraintLayout within the Android Studio Layout Editor tool.

17.1 How ConstraintLayout Works

In common with all other layouts, ConstraintLayout is responsible for managing the positioning and sizing behavior of the visual components (also referred to as widgets) it contains. It does this based on the constraint connections that are set on each child widget.

In order to fully understand and use ConstraintLayout, it is important to gain an appreciation of the following key concepts:

• Constraints

• Margins

• Opposing Constraints

• Constraint Bias

• Chains

• Chain Styles

• Barriers

17.1.1 Constraints

Constraints are essentially sets of rules that dictate the way in which a widget is aligned and distanced in relation to other widgets, the sides of the containing ConstraintLayout and special elements called *guidelines*. Constraints also dictate how the user interface layout of an activity will respond to changes in device orientation, or when displayed on devices of differing screen sizes. In order to be adequately configured, a widget must have sufficient constraint connections such that it's position can be resolved by the ConstraintLayout layout engine in both the horizontal and vertical planes.

17.1.2 Margins

A margin is a form of constraint that specifies a fixed distance. Consider a Button object that needs to be positioned near the top right-hand corner of the device screen. This might be achieved by implementing margin constraints from the top and right-hand edges of the Button connected to the corresponding sides of the parent ConstraintLayout as illustrated in Figure 17-1:

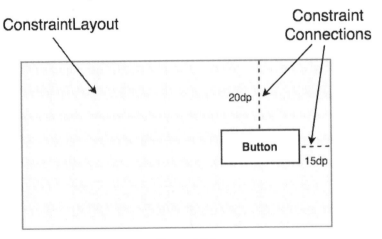

Figure 17-1

As indicated in the above diagram, each of these constraint connections has associated with it a margin value dictating the fixed distances of the widget from two sides of the parent layout. Under this configuration, regardless of screen size or the device orientation, the Button object will always be positioned 20 and 15 device-independent pixels (dp) from the top and right-hand edges of the parent ConstraintLayout respectively as specified by the two constraint connections.

While the above configuration will be acceptable for some situations, it does not provide any flexibility in terms of allowing the ConstraintLayout layout engine to adapt the position of the widget in order to respond to device rotation and to support screens of different sizes. To add this responsiveness to the layout it is necessary to implement opposing constraints.

17.1.3 Opposing Constraints

Two constraints operating along the same axis on a single widget are referred to as *opposing constraints*. In other words, a widget with constraints on both its left and right-hand sides is considered to have horizontally opposing constraints. Figure 17-2, for example, illustrates the addition of both horizontally and vertically opposing constraints to the previous layout:

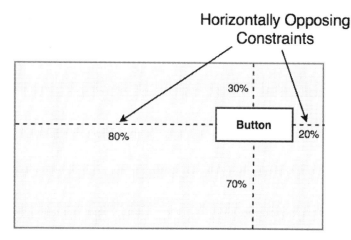

Figure 17-2

The key point to understand here is that once opposing constraints are implemented on a particular axis, the positioning of the widget becomes percentage rather than coordinate based. Instead of being fixed at 20dp from the top of the layout, for example, the widget is now positioned at a point 30% from the top of the layout. In different orientations and when running on larger or smaller screens, the Button will always be in the same location relative to the dimensions of the parent layout.

It is now important to understand that the layout outlined in Figure 17-2 has been implemented using not only opposing constraints, but also by applying *constraint bias*.

17.1.4 Constraint Bias

It has now been established that a widget in a ConstraintLayout can potentially be subject to opposing constraint connections. By default, opposing constraints are equal, resulting in the corresponding widget being centered along the axis of opposition. Figure 17-3, for example, shows a widget centered within the containing ConstraintLayout using opposing horizontal and vertical constraints:

Widget Centered by Opposing Constraints

Figure 17-3

To allow for the adjustment of widget position in the case of opposing constraints, the ConstraintLayout implements a feature known as *constraint bias*. Constraint bias allows the positioning of a widget along the axis of opposition to be biased by a specified percentage in favor of one constraint. Figure 17-4, for example, shows the previous constraint layout with a 75% horizontal bias and 10% vertical bias:

Widget Offset using Constraint Bias

Figure 17-4

The next chapter, entitled *"A Guide to using ConstraintLayout in Android Studio"*, will cover these concepts in greater detail and explain how these features have been integrated into the Android Studio Layout Editor tool. In the meantime, however, a few more areas of the ConstraintLayout class need to be covered.

17.1.5 Chains

ConstraintLayout chains provide a way for the layout behavior of two or more widgets to be defined as a group. Chains can be declared in either the vertical or horizontal axis and configured to define how the widgets in the chain are spaced and sized.

Widgets are chained when connected together by bi-directional constraints. Figure 17-5, for example, illustrates three widgets chained in this way:

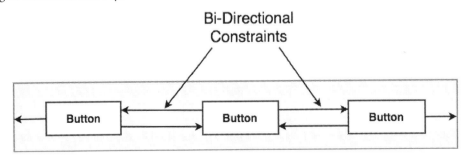

Figure 17-5

The first element in the chain is the *chain head* which translates to the top widget in a vertical chain or, in the case of a horizontal chain, the left-most widget. The layout behavior of the entire chain is primarily configured by setting attributes on the chain head widget.

17.1.6 Chain Styles

The layout behavior of a ConstraintLayout chain is dictated by the *chain style* setting applied to the chain head widget. The ConstraintLayout class currently supports the following chain layout styles:

- **Spread Chain** – The widgets contained within the chain are distributed evenly across the available space. This is the default behavior for chains.

Figure 17-6

- **Spread Inside Chain** – The widgets contained within the chain are spread evenly between the chain head and the last widget in the chain. The head and last widgets are not included in the distribution of spacing.

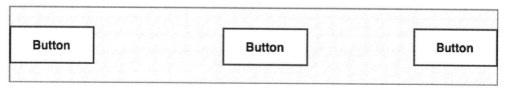

Figure 17-7

- **Weighted Chain** – Allows the space taken up by each widget in the chain to be defined via weighting properties.

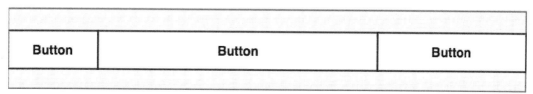

Figure 17-8

- **Packed Chain** – The widgets that make up the chain are packed together without any spacing. A bias may be applied to control the horizontal or vertical positioning of the chain in relation to the parent container.

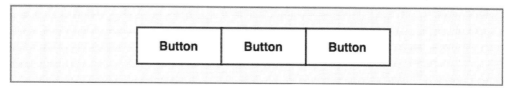

Figure 17-9

17.2 Baseline Alignment

So far, this chapter has only referred to constraints that dictate alignment relative to the sides of a widget (typically referred to as side constraints). A common requirement, however, is for a widget to be aligned relative to the content that it displays rather than the boundaries of the widget itself. To address this need, ConstraintLayout provides *baseline alignment* support.

As an example, assume that the previous theoretical layout from Figure 17-1 requires a TextView widget to be positioned 40dp to the left of the Button. In this case, the TextView needs to be *baseline aligned* with the Button view. This means that the text within the Button needs to be vertically aligned with the text within the TextView. The additional constraints for this layout would need to be connected as illustrated in Figure 17-10:

Figure 17-10

The TextView is now aligned vertically along the baseline of the Button and positioned 40dp horizontally from the Button object's left-hand edge.

17.3 Working with Guidelines

Guidelines are special elements available within the ConstraintLayout that provide an additional target to which constraints may be connected. Multiple guidelines may be added to a ConstraintLayout instance which may, in turn, be configured in horizontal or vertical orientations. Once added, constraint connections may be established from widgets in the layout to the guidelines. This is particularly useful when multiple widgets need to be aligned along an axis. In Figure 17-11, for example, three Button objects contained within a ConstraintLayout are constrained along a vertical guideline:

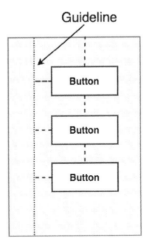

Figure 17-11

17.4 Configuring Widget Dimensions

Controlling the dimensions of a widget is a key element of the user interface design process. The ConstraintLayout provides three options which can be set on individual widgets to manage sizing behavior. These settings are configured individually for height and width dimensions:

- **Fixed** – The widget is fixed to specified dimensions.

- **Match Constraint** –Allows the widget to be resized by the layout engine to satisfy the prevailing constraints. Also referred to as the *AnySize* or MATCH_CONSTRAINT option.

• **Wrap Content** – The size of the widget is dictated by the content it contains (i.e. text or graphics).

17.5 Working with Barriers

Rather like guidelines, barriers are virtual views that can be used to constrain views within a layout. As with guidelines, a barrier can be vertical or horizontal and one or more views may be constrained to it (to avoid confusion, these will be referred to as *constrained views*). Unlike guidelines where the guideline remains at a fixed position within the layout, however, the position of a barrier is defined by a set of so called *reference views*. Barriers were introduced to address an issue that occurs with some frequency involving overlapping views. Consider, for example, the layout illustrated in Figure 17-12 below:

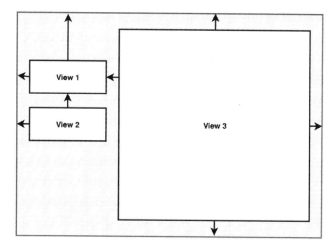

Figure 17-12

The key points to note about the above layout is that the width of View 3 is set to match constraint mode, and the left-hand edge of the view is connected to the right hand edge of View 1. As currently implemented, an increase in width of View 1 will have the desired effect of reducing the width of View 3:

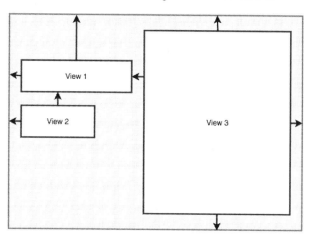

Figure 17-13

A problem arises, however, if View 2 increases in width instead of View 1:

Figure 17-14

Clearly because View 3 is only constrained by View 1, it does not resize to accommodate the increase in width of View 2 causing the views to overlap.

A solution to this problem is to add a vertical barrier and assign Views 1 and 2 as the barrier's *reference views* so that they control the barrier position. The left-hand edge of View 3 will then be constrained in relation to the barrier, making it a *constrained view*.

Now when either View 1 or View 2 increase in width, the barrier will move to accommodate the widest of the two views, causing the width of View 3 change in relation to the new barrier position:

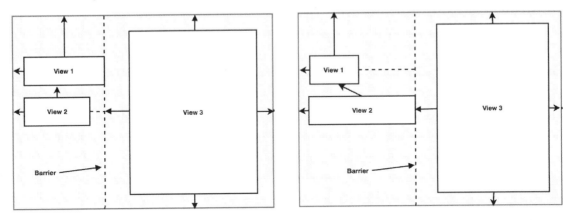

Figure 17-15

When working with barriers there is no limit to the number of reference views and constrained views that can be associated with a single barrier.

17.6 Ratios

The dimensions of a widget may be defined using ratio settings. A widget could, for example, be constrained using a ratio setting such that, regardless of any resizing behavior, the width is always twice the height dimension.

17.7 ConstraintLayout Advantages

ConstraintLayout provides a level of flexibility that allows many of the features of older layouts to be achieved with a single layout instance where it would previously have been necessary to nest multiple layouts. This has the benefit of avoiding the problems inherent in layout nesting by allowing so called "flat" or "shallow" layout hierarchies to be designed leading both to less complex layouts and improved user interface rendering performance at runtime.

ConstraintLayout was also implemented with a view to addressing the wide range of Android device screen sizes available on the market today. The flexibility of ConstraintLayout makes it easier for user interfaces to be designed that respond and adapt to the device on which the app is running.

Finally, as will be demonstrated in the chapter entitled *"A Guide to using ConstraintLayout in Android Studio"*, the Android Studio Layout Editor tool has been enhanced specifically for ConstraintLayout-based user interface design.

17.8 ConstraintLayout Availability

Although introduced with Android 7, ConstraintLayout is provided as a separate support library from the main Android SDK and is compatible with older Android versions as far back as API Level 9 (Gingerbread). This allows apps that make use of this new layout to run on devices running much older versions of Android.

17.9 Summary

ConstraintLayout is a layout manager introduced with Android 7. It is designed to ease the creation of flexible layouts that adapt to the size and orientation of the many Android devices now on the market. ConstraintLayout uses constraints to control the alignment and positioning of widgets in relation to the parent ConstraintLayout instance, guidelines, barriers and the other widgets in the layout. ConstraintLayout is the default layout for newly created Android Studio projects and is the recommended choice when designing user interface layouts. With this simple yet flexible approach to layout management, complex and responsive user interfaces can be implemented with surprising ease.

18. A Guide to using ConstraintLayout in Android Studio

As mentioned more than once in previous chapters, Google has made significant changes to the Android Studio Layout Editor tool, many of which were made solely to support user interface layout design using ConstraintLayout. Now that the basic concepts of ConstraintLayout have been outlined in the previous chapter, this chapter will explore these concepts in more detail while also outlining the ways in which the Layout Editor tool allows ConstraintLayout-based user interfaces to be designed and implemented.

18.1 Design and Layout Views

The chapter entitled *"A Guide to the Android Studio Layout Editor Tool"* explained that the Android Studio Layout Editor tool provides two ways to view the user interface layout of an activity in the form of Design and Layout (also known as blueprint) views. These views of the layout may be displayed individually or, as in Figure 18-1, side by side:

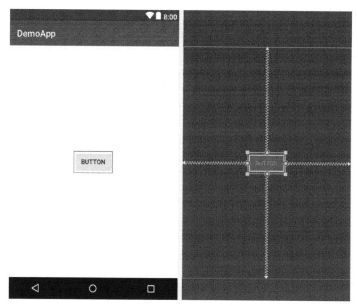

Figure 18-1

The Design view (positioned on the left in the above figure) presents a "what you see is what you get" representation of the layout, wherein the layout appears as it will within the running app. The Layout view, on the other hand, displays a blueprint style of view where the widgets are represented by shaded outlines. As can be seen in Figure 18-1 above, Layout view also displays the constraint connections (in this case opposing constraints used to center a button within the layout). These constraints are also overlaid onto the Design view when a specific widget in the layout is selected or when the mouse pointer hovers over the design area as illustrated in Figure 18-2:

Figure 18-2

The appearance of constraint connections in both views can be change using the toolbar menu shown in Figure 18-3:

Figure 18-3

In addition to the two modes of displaying the user interface layout, the Layout Editor tool also provides three different ways of establishing the constraints required for a specific layout design.

18.2 Autoconnect Mode

Autoconnect, as the name suggests, automatically establishes constraint connections as items are added to the layout. Autoconnect mode may be enabled and disabled using the toolbar button indicated in Figure 18-4:

Figure 18-4

Autoconnect mode uses algorithms to decide the best constraints to establish based on the position of the widget and the widget's proximity to both the sides of the parent layout and other elements in the layout. In the event that any of the automatic constraint connections fail to provide the desired behavior, these may be changed manually as outlined later in this chapter.

18.3 Inference Mode

Inference mode uses a heuristic approach involving algorithms and probabilities to automatically implement constraint connections after widgets have already been added to the layout. This mode is usually used when the Autoconnect feature has been turned off and objects have been added to the layout without any constraint connections. This allows the layout to be designed simply by dragging and dropping objects from the palette onto the layout canvas and making size and positioning changes until the layout appears as required. In essence this involves "painting" the layout without worrying about constraints. Inference mode may also be used at any time during the design process to fill in missing constraints within a layout.

Constraints are automatically added to a layout when the *Infer constraints* button (Figure 18-5) is clicked:

Figure 18-5

As with Autoconnect mode, there is always the possibility that the Layout Editor tool will infer incorrect constraints, though these may be modified and corrected manually.

18.4 Manipulating Constraints Manually

The third option for implementing constraint connections is to do so manually. When doing so, it will be helpful to understand the various handles that appear around a widget within the Layout Editor tool. Consider, for example, the widget shown in Figure 18-6:

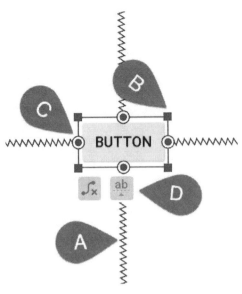

Figure 18-6

Clearly the spring-like lines (A) represent established constraint connections leading from the sides of the widget to the targets. The small square markers (B) in each corner of the object are resize handles which, when clicked and dragged, serve to resize the widget. The small circle handles (C) located on each side of the widget are the side constraint anchors. To create a constraint connection, click on the handle and drag the resulting line to the element to which the constraint is to be connected (such as a guideline or the side of either the parent layout or another widget) as outlined in Figure 18-7. When connecting to the side of another widget, simply drag the line to the side constraint handle of that widget and, when it turns green, release the line.

Figure 18-7

An additional marker indicates the anchor point for baseline constraints whereby the content within the widget (as opposed to outside edges) is used as the alignment point. To display this marker, simply click on the button displaying the letters 'ab' (referenced by marker D in Figure 18-6). To establish a constraint connection from a baseline constraint handle, simply hover the mouse pointer over the handle until it begins to flash before clicking and dragging to the target (such as the baseline anchor of another widget as shown in Figure 18-8). When the destination anchor begins to flash green, release the mouse button to make the constraint connection:

Figure 18-8

To hide the baseline anchors, simply click on the baseline button a second time.

18.5 Adding Constraints in the Inspector

Constraints may also be added to a view within the Android Studio Layout Editor tool using the *Inspector* panel located in the Attributes tool window as shown in Figure 18-9. The square in the center represents the currently selected view and the areas around the square the constraints, if any, applied to the corresponding sides of the view:

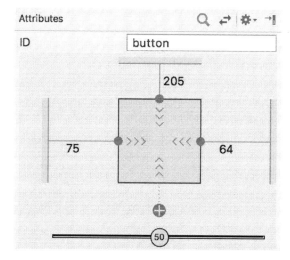

Figure 18-9

The absence of a constraint on a side of the view is represented by a dotted line leading to a blue circle containing a plus sign (as is the case with the bottom edge of the view in the above figure). To add a constraint, simply click on this blue circle and the layout editor will add a constraint connected to what it considers to be the most appropriate target within the layout.

18.6 Deleting Constraints

To delete an individual constraint, simply click within the anchor to which it is connected. The constraint will then be deleted from the layout (when hovering over the anchor it will glow red to indicate that clicking will perform a deletion):

Figure 18-10

Alternatively, remove all of the constraints on a widget by selecting it and clicking on the *Delete All Constraints* button which appears next to the widget when it is selected in the layout as highlighted in Figure 18-11:

Figure 18-11

To remove all of the constraints from every widget in a layout, use the toolbar button highlighted in Figure 18-12:

Figure 18-12

18.7 Adjusting Constraint Bias

In the previous chapter, the concept of using bias settings to favor one opposing constraint over another was outlined. Bias within the Android Studio Layout Editor tool is adjusted using the *Inspector* located in the Attributes tool window and shown in Figure 18-13. The two sliders indicated by the arrows in the figure are used to control the bias of the vertical and horizontal opposing constraints of the currently selected widget.

Figure 18-13

18.8 Understanding ConstraintLayout Margins

Constraints can be used in conjunction with margins to implement fixed gaps between a widget and another element (such as another widget, a guideline or the side of the parent layout). Consider, for example, the horizontal constraints applied to the Button object in Figure 18-14:

Figure 18-14

As currently configured, horizontal constraints run to the left and right edges of the parent ConstraintLayout. As such, the widget has opposing horizontal constraints indicating that the ConstraintLayout layout engine has some discretion in terms of the actual positioning of the widget at runtime. This allows the layout some flexibility to accommodate different screen sizes and device orientation. The horizontal bias setting is also able to control the position of the widget right up to the right-hand side of the layout. Figure 18-15, for example, shows the same button with 100% horizontal bias applied:

Figure 18-15

ConstraintLayout margins can appear at the end of constraint connections and represent a fixed gap into which the widget cannot be moved even when adjusting bias or in response to layout changes elsewhere in the activity. In Figure 18-16, the right-hand constraint now includes a 50dp margin into which the widget cannot be moved even though the bias is still set at 100%.

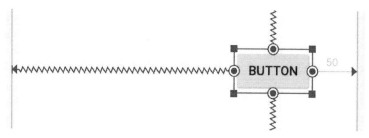

Figure 18-16

Existing margin values on a widget can be modified from within the Inspector. As can be seen in Figure 18-17, a dropdown menu is being used to change the right-hand margin on the currently selected widget to 16dp. Alternatively, clicking on the current value also allows a number to be typed into the field.

Figure 18-17

The default margin for new constraints can be changed at any time using the option in the toolbar highlighted in Figure 18-18:

Figure 18-18

18.9 The Importance of Opposing Constraints and Bias

As discussed in the previous chapter, opposing constraints, margins and bias form the cornerstone of responsive layout design in Android when using the ConstraintLayout. When a widget is constrained without opposing constraint connections, those constraints are essentially margin constraints. This is indicated visually within the Layout Editor tool by solid straight lines accompanied by margin measurements as shown in Figure 18-19.

Figure 18-19

The above constraints essentially fix the widget at that position. The result of this is that if the device is rotated to landscape orientation, the widget will no longer be visible since the vertical constraint pushes it beyond the top edge of the device screen (as is the case in Figure 18-20). A similar problem will arise if the app is run on a device with a smaller screen than that used during the design process.

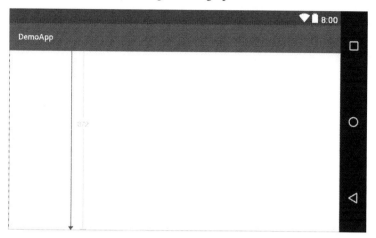

Figure 18-20

When opposing constraints are implemented, the constraint connection is represented by the spring-like jagged line (the spring metaphor is intended to indicate that the position of the widget is not fixed to absolute X and Y coordinates):

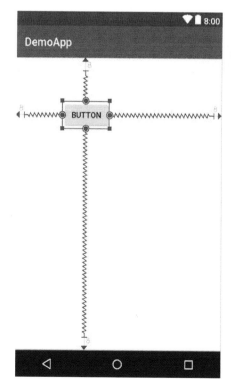

Figure 18-21

In the above layout, vertical and horizontal bias settings have been configured such that the widget will always be positioned 90% of the distance from the bottom and 35% from the left-hand edge of the parent layout. When rotated, therefore, the widget is still visible and positioned in the same location relative to the dimensions of the screen:

Figure 18-22

When designing a responsive and adaptable user interface layout, it is important to take into consideration both bias and opposing constraints when manually designing a user interface layout and making corrections to automatically created constraints.

18.10 Configuring Widget Dimensions

The inner dimensions of a widget within a ConstraintLayout can also be configured using the Inspector. As outlined in the previous chapter, widget dimensions can be set to wrap content, fixed or match constraint modes. The prevailing settings for each dimension on the currently selected widget are shown within the square representing the widget in the Inspector as illustrated in Figure 18-23:

Figure 18-23

In the above figure, both the horizontal and vertical dimensions are set to wrap content mode (indicated by the inward pointing chevrons). The inspector uses the following visual indicators to represent the three dimension modes:

Fixed Size	⊢─┤
Match Constraint	⊢/\/\/⊣
Wrap Content	〉〉〉

Table 18-1

To change the current setting, simply click on the indicator to cycle through the three different settings. When the dimension of a view within the layout editor is set to match constraint mode, the corresponding sides of the view are drawn with the spring-like line instead of the usual straight lines. In Figure 18-24, for example, only the width of the view has been set to match constraint:

TextView

Figure 18-24

In addition, the size of a widget can be expanded either horizontally or vertically to the maximum amount allowed by the constraints and other widgets in the layout using the *Expand horizontally* and *Expand vertically* options. These are accessible by right clicking on a widget within the layout and selecting the *Organize* option from the resulting menu (Figure 18-25). When used, the currently selected widget will increase in size horizontally or vertically to fill the available space around it.

Figure 18-25

18.11 Adding Guidelines

Guidelines provide additional elements to which constraints may be anchored. Guidelines are added by right-clicking on the layout and selecting either the *Add Vertical Guideline* or *Add Horizontal Guideline* menu option or using the toolbar menu options as shown in Figure 18-26:

Figure 18-26

Once added, a guideline will appear as a dashed line in the layout and may be moved simply by clicking and dragging the line. To establish a constraint connection to a guideline, click in the constraint handler of a widget and drag to the guideline before releasing. In Figure 18-27, the left sides of two Buttons are connected by constraints to a vertical guideline.

The position of a vertical guideline can be specified as an absolute distance from either the left or the right of the parent layout (or the top or bottom for a horizontal guideline). The vertical guideline in the above figure, for example, is positioned 96dp from the left-hand edge of the parent.

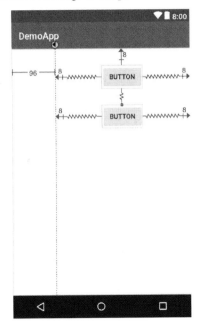

Figure 18-27

Alternatively, the guideline may be positioned as a percentage of overall width or height of the parent layout. To switch between these three modes, select the guideline and click on the circle at the top or start of the guideline (depending on whether the guideline is vertical or horizontal). Figure 18-28, for example, shows a guideline positioned based on percentage:

Figure 18-28

18.12 Adding Barriers

Barriers are added by right-clicking on the layout and selecting either the *Add Vertical Barrier* or *Add Horizontal Barrier* menu option, or using the toolbar menu options as shown in Figure 18-29:

Figure 18-29

Once a barrier has been added to the layout, it will appear as an entry in the Component Tree panel:

Figure 18-30

To add views as reference views (in other words, the views that control the position of the barrier), simply drag the widgets from within the Component Tree onto the barrier entry. In Figure 18-31, for example, widgets named textView1 and textView2 have been assigned as the reference widgets for barrier1:

Figure 18-31

After the reference views have been added, the barrier needs to be configured to specify the direction of the barrier in relation those views. This is the *barrier direction* setting and is defined within the Attributes tool window when the barrier is selected in the Component Tree panel:

Figure 18-32

The following figure shows a layout containing a barrier declared with textView1 and textView2 acting as the reference views and textview3 as the constrained view. Since the barrier is pushing from the end of the reference views towards the constrained view, the barrier direction has been set to *end*:

Figure 18-33

18.13 Widget Group Alignment

The Android Studio Layout Editor tool provides a range of alignment actions that can be performed when two or more widgets are selected in the layout. Simply shift-click on each of the widgets to be included in the action, right-click on the layout and make a selection from the many options displayed in the Align menu:

Figure 18-34

As shown in Figure 18-35 below, these options are also available as buttons in the Layout Editor toolbar:

Figure 18-35

18.14 Converting other Layouts to ConstraintLayout

For existing user interface layouts that make use of one or more of the other Android layout classes (such as RelativeLayout or LinearLayout), the Layout Editor tool provides an option to convert the user interface to use the ConstraintLayout.

When the Layout Editor tool is open and in Design mode, the Component Tree panel is displayed beneath the Palette. To convert a layout to ConstraintLayout, locate it within the Component Tree, right-click on it and select the *Convert <current layout> to Constraint Layout* menu option:

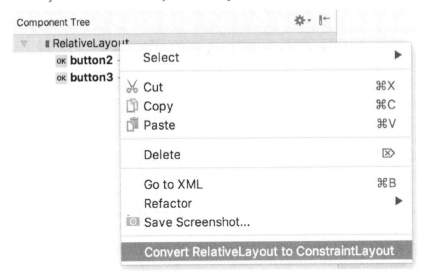

Figure 18-36

When this menu option is selected, Android Studio will convert the selected layout to a ConstraintLayout and use inference to establish constraints designed to match the layout behavior of the original layout type.

18.15 Summary

A redesigned Layout Editor tool combined with ConstraintLayout makes designing complex user interface layouts with Android Studio a relatively fast and intuitive process. This chapter has covered the concepts of constraints, margins and bias in more detail while also exploring the ways in which ConstraintLayout-based design has been integrated into the Layout Editor tool.

19. Working with ConstraintLayout Chains and Ratios in Android Studio

The previous chapters have introduced the key features of the ConstraintLayout class and outlined the best practices for ConstraintLayout-based user interface design within the Android Studio Layout Editor. Although the concepts of ConstraintLayout chains and ratios were outlined in the chapter entitled *"A Guide to the Android ConstraintLayout"*, we have not yet addressed how to make use of these features within the Layout Editor. The focus of this chapter, therefore, is to provide practical steps on how to create and manage chains and ratios when using the ConstraintLayout class.

19.1 Creating a Chain

Chains may be implemented either by adding a few lines to the XML layout resource file of an activity or by using some chain specific features of the Layout Editor.

Consider a layout consisting of three Button widgets constrained so as to be positioned in the top-left, top-center and top-right of the ConstraintLayout parent as illustrated in Figure 19-1:

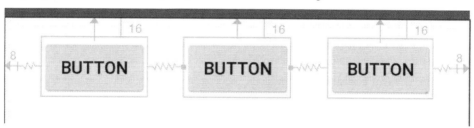

Figure 19-1

To represent such a layout, the XML resource layout file might contain the following entries for the button widgets:

```
<Button
    android:id="@+id/button1"
    android:layout_width="wrap_content"
    android:layout_height="wrap_content"
    android:layout_marginStart="8dp"
    android:layout_marginTop="16dp"
    android:text="Button"
    app:layout_constraintStart_toStartOf="parent"
    app:layout_constraintTop_toTopOf="parent" />

<Button
    android:id="@+id/button2"
    android:layout_width="wrap_content"
    android:layout_height="wrap_content"
```

```
    android:layout_marginEnd="8dp"
    android:layout_marginStart="8dp"
    android:layout_marginTop="16dp"
    android:text="Button"
    app:layout_constraintEnd_toStartOf="@+id/button3"
    app:layout_constraintStart_toEndOf="@+id/button1"
    app:layout_constraintTop_toTopOf="parent" />


<Button
    android:id="@+id/button3"
    android:layout_width="wrap_content"
    android:layout_height="wrap_content"
    android:layout_marginEnd="8dp"
    android:layout_marginTop="16dp"
    android:text="Button"
    app:layout_constraintEnd_toEndOf="parent"
    app:layout_constraintTop_toTopOf="parent" />
```

As currently configured, there are no bi-directional constraints to group these widgets into a chain. To address this, additional constraints need to be added from the right-hand side of button1 to the left side of button2, and from the left side of button3 to the right side of button2 as follows:

```
<Button
    android:id="@+id/button1"
    android:layout_width="wrap_content"
    android:layout_height="wrap_content"
    android:layout_marginStart="8dp"
    android:layout_marginTop="16dp"
    android:text="Button"
    app:layout_constraintStart_toStartOf="parent"
    app:layout_constraintTop_toTopOf="parent"
    app:layout_constraintRight_toLeftOf="@id/button2" />


<Button
    android:id="@+id/button2"
    android:layout_width="wrap_content"
    android:layout_height="wrap_content"
    android:layout_marginEnd="8dp"
    android:layout_marginStart="8dp"
    android:layout_marginTop="16dp"
    android:text="Button"
    app:layout_constraintEnd_toStartOf="@+id/button3"
    app:layout_constraintStart_toEndOf="@+id/button1"
    app:layout_constraintTop_toTopOf="parent" />


<Button
    android:id="@+id/button3"
```

```
android:layout_width="wrap_content"
android:layout_height="wrap_content"
android:layout_marginEnd="8dp"
android:layout_marginTop="16dp"
android:text="Button"
app:layout_constraintEnd_toEndOf="parent"
app:layout_constraintTop_toTopOf="parent"
app:layout_constraintLeft_toRightOf="@id/button2" />
```

With these changes, the widgets now have bi-directional horizontal constraints configured. This essentially constitutes a ConstraintLayout chain which is represented visually within the Layout Editor by chain connections as shown in Figure 19-2 below. Note that in this configuration the chain has defaulted to the spread chain style.

Figure 19-2

A chain may also be created by right-clicking on one of the views and selecting the *Chain -> Create Horizontal Chain* or *Chain -> Create Vertical Chain* menu options.

19.2 Changing the Chain Style

If no chain style is configured, the ConstraintLayout will default to the spread chain style. The chain style can be altered by selecting any of the widgets in the chain and clicking on the chain button as highlighted in Figure 19-3:

Figure 19-3

Each time the chain button is clicked the style will switch to another setting in the order of spread, spread inside and packed.

Alternatively, the style may be specified in the Attributes tool window by clicking on the *View all attributes* link, unfolding the *Constraints* section and changing either the *horizontal_chainStyle* or *vertical_chainStyle* property depending on the orientation of the chain:

Figure 19-4

19.3 Spread Inside Chain Style

Figure 19-5 illustrates the effect of changing the chain style to spread inside chain style using the above techniques:

Figure 19-5

19.4 Packed Chain Style

Using the same technique, changing the chain style property to *packed* causes the layout to change as shown in Figure 19-6:

Figure 19-6

19.5 Packed Chain Style with Bias

The positioning of the packed chain may be influenced by applying a bias value. The bias can be any value between 0.0 and 1.0, with 0.5 representing the center of the parent. Bias is controlled by selecting the chain head widget and assigning a value to the *horizontal_bias* or *vertical_bias* attribute in the Attributes panel. Figure 19-7 shows a packed chain with a horizontal bias setting of 0.2:

Figure 19-7

19.6 Weighted Chain

The final area of chains to explore involves weighting of the individual widgets to control how much space each widget in the chain occupies within the available space. A weighted chain may only be implemented using the *spread* chain style and any widget within the chain that is to respond to the weight property must have the corresponding dimension property (height for a vertical chain and width for a horizontal chain) configured for *match constraint* mode. Match constraint mode for a widget dimension may be configured by selecting the widget, displaying the Attributes panel and changing the dimension to *match_constraint*. In Figure 19-8, for example, the *layout_width* constraint for button1 has been set to *match_constraint* to indicate that the width of the widget is to be determined based on the prevailing constraint settings:

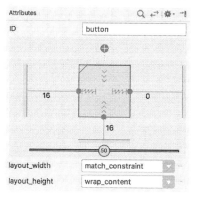

Figure 19-8

Assuming that the spread chain style has been selected, and all three buttons have been configured such that the width dimension is set to match the constraints, the widgets in the chain will expand equally to fill the available space:

Figure 19-9

The amount of space occupied by each widget relative to the other widgets in the chain can be controlled by adding weight properties to the widgets. Figure 19-10 shows the effect of setting the *horizontal_weight* property to 4 on button1, and to 2 on both button2 and button3:

Figure 19-10

As a result of these weighting values, button1 occupies half of the space (4/8), while button2 and button3 each occupy one quarter (2/8) of the space.

19.7 Working with Ratios

ConstraintLayout ratios allow one dimension of a widget to be sized relative to the widget's other dimension (otherwise known as aspect ratio). An aspect ratio setting could, for example, be applied to an ImageView to ensure that its width is always twice its height.

A dimension ratio constraint is configured by setting the constrained dimension to match constraint mode and configuring the *layout_constraintDimensionRatio* attribute on that widget to the required ratio. This ratio value may be specified either as a float value or a *width:height* ratio setting. The following XML excerpt, for example, configures a ratio of 2:1 on an ImageView widget:

```
<ImageView
        android:layout_width="0dp"
        android:layout_height="100dp"
        android:id="@+id/imageView"
        app:layout_constraintDimensionRatio="2:1" />
```

The above example demonstrates how to configure a ratio when only one dimension is set to match constraint. A ratio may also be applied when both dimensions are set to match constraint mode. This involves specifying the ratio preceded with either an H or a W to indicate which of the dimensions is constrained relative to the other.

Consider, for example, the following XML excerpt for an ImageView object:

```
<ImageView
        android:layout_width="0dp"
        android:layout_height="0dp"
        android:id="@+id/imageView"
        app:layout_constraintBottom_toBottomOf="parent"
        app:layout_constraintRight_toRightOf="parent"
        app:layout_constraintLeft_toLeftOf="parent"
        app:layout_constraintTop_toTopOf="parent"
        app:layout_constraintDimensionRatio="W,1:3" />
```

In the above example the height will be defined subject to the constraints applied to it. In this case constraints have been configured such that it is attached to the top and bottom of the parent view, essentially stretching the widget to fill the entire height of the parent. The width dimension, on the other hand, has been constrained to be one third of the ImageView's height dimension. Consequently, whatever size screen or orientation the layout appears on, the ImageView will always be the same height as the parent and the width one third of that height.

The same results may also be achieved without the need to manually edit the XML resource file. Whenever a widget dimension is set to match constraint mode, a ratio control toggle appears in the Inspector area of the property panel. Figure 19-11, for example, shows the layout width and height attributes of a button widget set to match constraint mode and 100dp respectively, and highlights the ratio control toggle in the widget sizing preview:

Figure 19-11

By default the ratio sizing control is toggled off. Clicking on the control enables the ratio constraint and displays an additional field where the ratio may be changed:

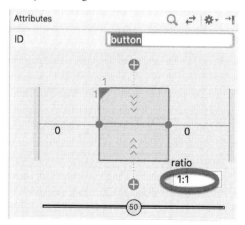

Figure 19-12

19.8 Summary

Both chains and ratios are powerful features of the ConstraintLayout class intended to provide additional options for designing flexible and responsive user interface layouts within Android applications. As outlined in this chapter, the Android Studio Layout Editor has been enhanced to make it easier to use these features during the user interface design process.

Chapter 20

20. An Android Studio Layout Editor ConstraintLayout Tutorial

By far the easiest and most productive way to design a user interface for an Android application is to make use of the Android Studio Layout Editor tool. The goal of this chapter is to provide an overview of how to create a ConstraintLayout-based user interface using this approach. The exercise included in this chapter will also be used as an opportunity to outline the creation of an activity starting with a "bare-bones" Android Studio project.

Having covered the use of the Android Studio Layout Editor, the chapter will also introduce the Layout Inspector tool.

20.1 An Android Studio Layout Editor Tool Example

The first step in this phase of the example is to create a new Android Studio project. Begin, therefore, by launching Android Studio and closing any previously opened projects by selecting the *File -> Close Project* menu option. Within the Android Studio welcome screen click on the *Start a new Android Studio project* quick start option to display the first screen of the new project dialog.

Enter *LayoutSample* into the Application name field and *ebookfrenzy.com* as the Company Domain setting before clicking on the *Next* button and setting the minimum SDK to API 14: Android 4.0 (IceCreamSandwich).

In previous examples, we have requested that Android Studio create a template activity for the project. We will, however, be using this tutorial to learn how to create an entirely new activity and corresponding layout resource file manually, so click *Next* once again and make sure that the *Add No Activity* option is selected before clicking on *Finish* to create the new project.

20.2 Creating a New Activity

Once the project creation process is complete, the Android Studio main window should appear with no tool windows open.

The next step in the project is to create a new activity. This will be a valuable learning exercise since there are many instances in the course of developing Android applications where new activities need to be created from the ground up.

Begin by displaying the Project tool window using the Alt-1/Cmd-1 keyboard shortcut. Once displayed, unfold the hierarchy by clicking on the right facing arrows next to the entries in the Project window. The objective here is to gain access to the *app -> java -> com.ebookfrenzy.layoutsample* folder in the project hierarchy. Once the package name is visible, right-click on it and select the *New -> Activity -> Empty Activity* menu option as illustrated in Figure 20-1:

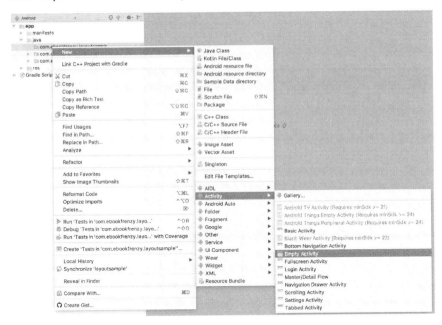

Figure 20-1

In the resulting *New Activity* dialog, name the new activity *LayoutSampleActivity* and the layout *activity_layout_ sample*. The activity will, of course, need a layout resource file so make sure that the *Generate Layout File* option is enabled.

In order for an application to be able to run on a device it needs to have an activity designated as the *launcher activity*. Without a launcher activity, the operating system will not know which activity to start up when the application first launches and the application will fail to start. Since this example only has one activity, it needs to be designated as the launcher activity for the application so make sure that the *Launcher Activity* option is enabled before clicking on the *Finish* button.

At this point Android Studio should have added two files to the project. The Java source code file for the activity should be located in the *app -> java -> com.ebookfrenzy.layoutsample* folder.

In addition, the XML layout file for the user interface should have been created in the *app -> res -> layout* folder. Note that the Empty Activity template was chosen for this activity so the layout is contained entirely within the *activity_layout_sample.xml* file and there is no separate content layout file.

Finally, the new activity should have been added to the *AndroidManifest.xml* file and designated as the launcher activity. The manifest file can be found in the project window under the *app -> manifests* folder and should contain the following XML:

```
<?xml version="1.0" encoding="utf-8"?>
<manifest xmlns:android="http://schemas.android.com/apk/res/android"
    package="com.ebookfrenzy.layoutsample">

    <application
        android:allowBackup="true"
        android:icon="@mipmap/ic_launcher"
        android:label="@string/app_name"
        android:roundIcon="@mipmap/ic_launcher_round"
```

```
        android:supportsRtl="true"
        android:theme="@style/AppTheme">
        <activity android:name=".LayoutSampleActivity">
            <intent-filter>
                <action android:name="android.intent.action.MAIN" />

                <category
    android:name="android.intent.category.LAUNCHER" />
            </intent-filter>
        </activity>
    </application>

</manifest>
```

20.3 Preparing the Layout Editor Environment

Locate and double-click on the *activity_layout_sample.xml* layout file located in the *app -> res -> layout* folder to load it into the Layout Editor tool. Since the purpose of this tutorial is to gain experience with the use of constraints, turn off the Autoconnect feature using the button located in the Layout Editor toolbar. Once disabled, the button will appear with a line through it as is the case in Figure 20-2:

Figure 20-2

The user interface design will also make use of the ImageView object to display an image. Before proceeding, this image should be added to the project ready for use later in the chapter. This file is named *galaxys6.png* and can be found in the *project_icons* folder of the sample code download available from the following URL:

http://www.ebookfrenzy.com/print/androidstudio30/index.php

Locate this image in the file system navigator for your operating system and copy the image file. Right-click on the *app -> res -> drawable* entry in the Project tool window and select Paste from the menu to add the file to the folder. When the copy dialog appears, click on OK to accept the default settings.

Figure 20-3

20.4 Adding the Widgets to the User Interface

From within the *Images* palette category, drag an ImageView object into the center of the display view. Note that horizontal and vertical dashed lines appear indicating the center axes of the display. When centered, release the mouse button to drop the view into position. Once placed within the layout, the Resources dialog will appear seeking the image to be displayed within the view. In the search bar located at the top of the dialog, enter "galaxy" to locate the *galaxys6.png* resource as illustrated in Figure 20-4.

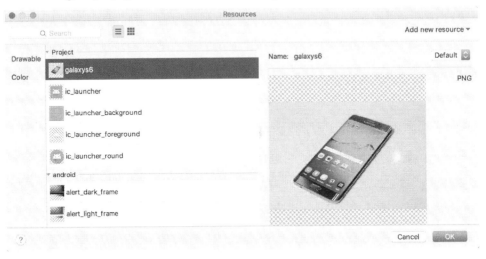

Figure 20-4

Select the image and click on OK to assign it to the ImageView object. If necessary, adjust the size of the ImageView using the resize handles and reposition it in the center of the layout. At this point the layout should match Figure 20-5:

Figure 20-5

Click and drag a TextView object from the Text section of the palette and position it so that it appears above the ImageView as illustrated in Figure 20-6.

Using the Attributes panel, change the *textSize* property to 24sp, the *textAlignment* setting to center and the text to "Samsung Galaxy S6".

Figure 20-6

Next, add three Button widgets along the bottom of the layout and set the text attributes of these views to "Buy Now", "Pricing" and "Details". The completed layout should now match Figure 20-7:

Figure 20-7

At this point, the widgets are not sufficiently constrained for the layout engine to be able to position and size the widgets at runtime. Were the app to run now, all of the widgets would be positioned in the top left-hand corner of the display.

With the widgets added to the layout, use the device rotation button located in the Layout Editor toolbar (indicated by the arrow in Figure 20-8) to view the user interface in landscape orientation:

Figure 20-8

The absence of constraints results in a layout that fails to adapt to the change in device orientation, leaving the content off center and with part of the image and all three buttons positioned beyond the viewable area of the screen. Clearly some work still needs to be done to make this into a responsive user interface.

20.5 Adding the Constraints

Constraints are the key to creating layouts that can adapt to device orientation changes and different screen sizes. Begin by rotating the layout back to portrait orientation and selecting the TextView widget located above the ImageView. With the widget selected, establish constraints from the left, right and top sides of the TextView to the corresponding sides of the parent ConstraintLayout as shown in Figure 20-9:

Figure 20-9

With the TextView widget constrained, select the ImageView instance and establish opposing constraints on the left and right-hand sides with each connected to the corresponding sides of the parent layout. Next, establish a constraint connection from the top of the ImageView to the bottom of the TextView and from the bottom of the ImageView to the top of the center Button widget. If necessary, click and drag the ImageView so that it is still positioned in the vertical center of the layout.

With the ImageView still selected, use the Inspector in the attributes panel to change the top and bottom margins on the ImageView to 24 and 8 respectively and to change both the widget height and width dimension properties to *match_constraint* so that the widget will resize to match the constraints. These settings will allow the layout engine to enlarge and reduce the size of the ImageView when necessary to accommodate layout changes:

Figure 20-10

Figure 20-11, shows the currently implemented constraints for the ImageView in relation to the other elements in the layout:

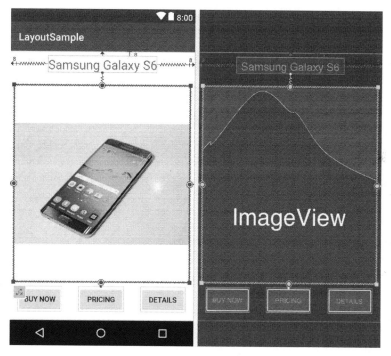

Figure 20-11

The final task is to add constraints to the three Button widgets. For this example, the buttons will be placed in a chain. Begin by turning on Autoconnect within the Layout Editor by clicking the toolbar button highlighted in Figure 20-2.

Next, click on the Buy Now button and then shift-click on the other two buttons so that all three are selected. Right-click on the Buy Now button and select the *Chain -> Create Horizontal Chain* menu option from the resulting menu. By default, the chain will be displayed using the spread style which is the correct behavior for this example.

Finally, establish a constraint between the bottom of the Buy Now button and the bottom of the layout. Repeat this step for the remaining buttons.

On completion of these steps the buttons should be constrained as outlined in Figure 20-12:

Figure 20-12

20.6 Testing the Layout

With the constraints added to the layout, rotate the screen into landscape orientation and verify that the layout adapts to accommodate the new screen dimensions.

While the Layout Editor tool provides a useful visual environment in which to design user interface layouts, when it comes to testing there is no substitute for testing the running app. Launch the app on a physical Android device or emulator session and verify that the user interface reflects the layout created in the Layout Editor. Figure 20-13, for example, shows the running app in landscape orientation:

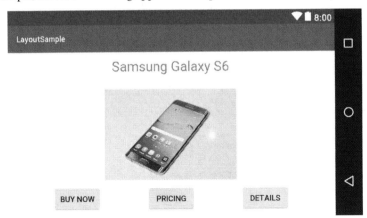

Figure 20-13

The very simple user interface design is now complete. Designing a more complex user interface layout is a continuation of the steps outlined above. Simply drag and drop views onto the display, position, constrain and set properties as needed.

20.7 Using the Layout Inspector

The hierarchy of components that make up a user interface layout may be viewed at any time using the Layout Inspector tool. In order to access this information the app must be running on a device or emulator. Once the app is running, select the *Tools -> Android -> Layout Inspector* menu option followed by the process to be inspected.

Once the inspector loads, the left most panel (A) shows the hierarchy of components that make up the user interface layout. The center panel (B) shows a visual representation of the layout design. Clicking on a widget in the visual layout will cause that item to highlight in the hierarchy list making it easy to find where a visual component is situated relative to the overall layout hierarchy.

Finally, the rightmost panel (marked C in Figure 20-14) contains all of the property settings for the currently selected component, allowing for in-depth analysis of the component's internal configuration.

Figure 20-14

20.8 Summary

The Layout Editor tool in Android Studio has been tightly integrated with the ConstraintLayout class. This chapter has worked through the creation of an example user interface intended to outline the ways in which a ConstraintLayout-based user interface can be implemented using the Layout Editor tool in terms of adding widgets and setting constraints. This chapter also introduced the Layout Inspector tool which is useful for analyzing the structural composition of a user interface layout.

21. Manual XML Layout Design in Android Studio

While the design of layouts using the Android Studio Layout Editor tool greatly improves productivity, it is still possible to create XML layouts by manually editing the underlying XML. This chapter will introduce the basics of the Android XML layout file format.

21.1 Manually Creating an XML Layout

The structure of an XML layout file is actually quite straightforward and follows the hierarchical approach of the view tree. The first line of an XML resource file should ideally include the following standard declaration:

```
<?xml version="1.0" encoding="utf-8"?>
```

This declaration should be followed by the root element of the layout, typically a container view such as a layout manager. This is represented by both opening and closing tags and any properties that need to be set on the view. The following XML, for example, declares a ConstraintLayout view as the root element, assigns the ID *activity_main* and sets *match_parent* attributes such that it fills all the available space of the device display:

```
<android.support.constraint.ConstraintLayout xmlns:android="http://schemas.
android.com/apk/res/android"
    xmlns:app="http://schemas.android.com/apk/res-auto"
    xmlns:tools="http://schemas.android.com/tools"
    android:id="@+id/main_activity"
    android:layout_width="match_parent"
    android:layout_height="match_parent"
    android:paddingLeft="16dp"
    android:paddingRight="16dp"
    android:paddingTop="16dp"
    android:paddingBottom="16dp"
    tools:context="com.ebookfrenzy.demoapp.MainActivity">

</android.support.constraint.ConstraintLayout>
```

Note that in the above example the layout element is also configured with padding on each side of 16dp (density independent pixels). Any specification of spacing in an Android layout must be specified using one of the following units of measurement:

• **in** – Inches.

• **mm** – Millimeters.

• **pt** – Points (1/72 of an inch).

• **dp** – Density-independent pixels. An abstract unit of measurement based on the physical density of the device display relative to a 160dpi display baseline.

- **sp** – Scale-independent pixels. Similar to dp but scaled based on the user's font preference.

- **px** – Actual screen pixels. Use is not recommended since different displays will have different pixels per inch. Use *dp* in preference to this unit.

Any children that need to be added to the ConstraintLayout parent must be *nested* within the opening and closing tags. In the following example a Button widget has been added as a child of the ConstraintLayout:

```
<?xml version="1.0" encoding="utf-8"?>
<android.support.constraint.ConstraintLayout xmlns:android="http://schemas.
android.com/apk/res/android"
    xmlns:app="http://schemas.android.com/apk/res-auto"
    xmlns:tools="http://schemas.android.com/tools"
    android:id="@+id/activity_main"
    android:layout_width="match_parent"
    android:layout_height="match_parent"
    android:paddingLeft="16dp"
    android:paddingRight="16dp"
    android:paddingTop="16dp"
    android:paddingBottom="16dp"
    tools:context="com.ebookfrenzy.demoapp.MainActivity">

    <Button
        android:text="Button"
        android:layout_width="wrap_content"
        android:layout_height="wrap_content"
        android:id="@+id/button" />

</android.support.constraint.ConstraintLayout>
```

As currently implemented, the button has no constraint connections. At runtime, therefore, the button will appear in the top left-hand corner of the screen (though indented 16dp by the padding assigned to the parent layout). If opposing constraints are added to the sides of the button, however, it will appear centered within the layout:

```
<Button
    android:text="Button"
    android:layout_width="wrap_content"
    android:layout_height="wrap_content"
    android:id="@+id/button"
    app:layout_constraintLeft_toLeftOf="@+id/activity_main"
    app:layout_constraintTop_toTopOf="@+id/activity_main"
    app:layout_constraintRight_toRightOf="@+id/activity_main"
    app:layout_constraintBottom_toBottomOf="@+id/activity_main" />
```

Note that each of the constraints is attached to the element named *activity_main* which is, in this case, the parent ConstraintLayout instance.

To add a second widget to the layout, simply embed it within the body of ConstraintLayout element. The following modification, for example, adds a TextView widget to the layout:

```
<?xml version="1.0" encoding="utf-8"?>
<android.support.constraint.ConstraintLayout
    xmlns:android="http://schemas.android.com/apk/res/android"
    xmlns:app="http://schemas.android.com/apk/res-auto"
    xmlns:tools="http://schemas.android.com/tools"
    android:id="@+id/activity_main"
    android:layout_width="match_parent"
    android:layout_height="match_parent"
    android:paddingLeft="16dp"
    android:paddingRight="16dp"
    android:paddingTop="16dp"
    android:paddingBottom="16dp"
    tools:context="com.ebookfrenzy.demoapp.MainActivity">

    <Button
        android:text="Button"
        android:layout_width="wrap_content"
        android:layout_height="wrap_content"
        android:id="@+id/button"
        app:layout_constraintLeft_toLeftOf="@+id/activity_main"
        app:layout_constraintTop_toTopOf="@+id/activity_main"
        app:layout_constraintRight_toRightOf="@+id/activity_main"
        app:layout_constraintBottom_toBottomOf="@+id/activity_main" />

    <TextView
        android:text="TextView"
        android:layout_width="wrap_content"
        android:layout_height="wrap_content"
        android:id="@+id/textView" />

</android.support.constraint.ConstraintLayout>
```

Once again, the absence of constraints on the newly added TextView will cause it to appear in the top left-hand corner of the layout at runtime. The following modifications add opposing constraints connected to the parent layout to center the widget horizontally, together with a constraint connecting the bottom of the TextView to the top of the button with a margin of 72dp:

```
<TextView
    android:text="TextView"
    android:layout_width="wrap_content"
    android:layout_height="wrap_content"
    android:id="@+id/textView"
    app:layout_constraintLeft_toLeftOf="@+id/activity_main"
    app:layout_constraintRight_toRightOf="@+id/activity_main"
    app:layout_constraintBottom_toTopOf="@+id/button"
    android:layout_marginBottom="72dp" />
```

Also, note that the Button and TextView views have a number of attributes declared. Both views have been

161

assigned IDs and configured to display text strings represented by string resources named *button_string* and *text_string* respectively. Additionally, the *wrap_content* height and width properties have been declared on both objects so that they are sized to accommodate the content (in this case the text referenced by the string resource value).

Viewed from within the Preview panel of the Layout Editor in Text mode, the above layout will be rendered as shown in Figure 21-1:

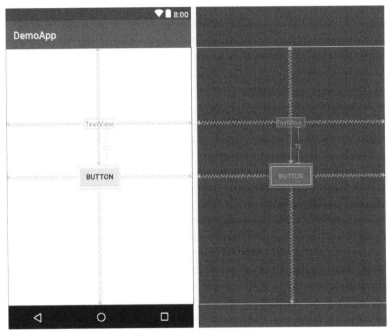

Figure 21-1

21.2 Manual XML vs. Visual Layout Design

When to write XML manually as opposed to using the Layout Editor tool in design mode is a matter of personal preference. There are, however, advantages to using design mode.

First, design mode will generally be quicker given that it avoids the necessity to type lines of XML. Additionally, design mode avoids the need to learn the intricacies of the various property values of the Android SDK view classes. Rather than continually refer to the Android documentation to find the correct keywords and values, most properties can be located by referring to the Attributes panel.

All the advantages of design mode aside, it is important to keep in mind that the two approaches to user interface design are in no way mutually exclusive. As an application developer, it is quite likely that you will end up creating user interfaces within design mode while performing fine-tuning and layout tweaks of the design by directly editing the generated XML resources. Both views of the interface design are, after all, displayed side by side within the Android Studio environment making it easy to work seamlessly on both the XML and the visual layout.

21.3 Summary

The Android Studio Layout Editor tool provides a visually intuitive method for designing user interfaces. Using a drag and drop paradigm combined with a set of property editors, the tool provides considerable productivity benefits to the application developer.

User interface designs may also be implemented by manually writing the XML layout resource files, the format of which is well structured and easily understood.

The fact that the Layout Editor tool generates XML resource files means that these two approaches to interface design can be combined to provide a "best of both worlds" approach to user interface development.

22. Managing Constraints using Constraint Sets

Up until this point in the book, all user interface design tasks have been performed using the Android Studio Layout Editor tool, either in text or design mode. An alternative to writing XML resource files or using the Android Studio Layout Editor is to write Java code to directly create, configure and manipulate the view objects that comprise the user interface of an Android activity. Within the context of this chapter, we will explore some of the advantages and disadvantages of writing Java code to create a user interface before describing some of the key concepts such as view properties and the creation and management of layout constraints.

In the next chapter, an example project will be created and used to demonstrate some of the typical steps involved in this approach to Android user interface creation.

22.1 Java Code vs. XML Layout Files

There are a number of key advantages to using XML resource files to design a user interface as opposed to writing Java code. In fact, Google goes to considerable lengths in the Android documentation to extol the virtues of XML resources over Java code. As discussed in the previous chapter, one key advantage to the XML approach includes the ability to use the Android Studio Layout Editor tool, which, itself, generates XML resources. A second advantage is that once an application has been created, changes to user interface screens can be made by simply modifying the XML file, thereby avoiding the necessity to recompile the application. Also, even when hand writing XML layouts, it is possible to get instant feedback on the appearance of the user interface using the preview feature of the Android Studio Layout Editor tool. In order to test the appearance of a Java created user interface the developer will, inevitably, repeatedly cycle through a loop of writing code, compiling and testing in order to complete the design work.

In terms of the strengths of the Java coding approach to layout creation, perhaps the most significant advantage that Java has over XML resource files comes into play when dealing with dynamic user interfaces. XML resource files are inherently most useful when defining static layouts, in other words layouts that are unlikely to change significantly from one invocation of an activity to the next. Java code, on the other hand, is ideal for creating user interfaces dynamically at run-time. This is particularly useful in situations where the user interface may appear differently each time the activity executes subject to external factors.

A knowledge of working with user interface components in Java code can also be useful when dynamic changes to a static XML resource based layout need to be performed in real-time as the activity is running.

Finally, some developers simply prefer to write Java code than to use layout tools and XML, regardless of the advantages offered by the latter approaches.

22.2 Creating Views

As previously established, the Android SDK includes a toolbox of view classes designed to meet most of the basic user interface design needs. The creation of a view in Java is simply a matter of creating instances of these classes, passing through as an argument a reference to the activity with which that view is to be associated.

The first view (typically a container view to which additional child views can be added) is displayed to the user via a call to the *setContentView()* method of the activity. Additional views may be added to the root view via calls to the object's *addView()* method.

When working with Java code to manipulate views contained in XML layout resource files, it is necessary to obtain the ID of the view. The same rule holds true for views created in Java. As such, it is necessary to assign an ID to any view for which certain types of access will be required in subsequent Java code. This is achieved via a call to the *setId()* method of the view object in question. In later code, the ID for a view may be obtained via the object's *getId()* method.

22.3 View Attributes

Each view class has associated with it a range of *attributes*. These property settings are set directly on the view instances and generally define how the view object will appear or behave. Examples of attributes are the text that appears on a Button object, or the background color of a ConstraintLayout view. Each view class within the Android SDK has a pre-defined set of methods that allow the user to *set* and *get* these property values. The Button class, for example, has a *setText()* method which can be called from within Java code to set the text displayed on the button to a specific string value. The background color of a *ConstraintLayout* object, on the other hand, can be set with a call to the object's *setBackgroundColor()* method.

22.4 Constraint Sets

While property settings are internal to view objects and dictate how a view appears and behaves, *constraint sets* are used to control how a view appears relative to its parent view and other sibling views. Every ConstraintLayout instance has associated with it a set of constraints that define how its child views are positioned and constrained.

The key to working with constraint sets in Java code is the *ConstraintSet* class. This class contains a range of methods that allow tasks such as creating, configuring and applying constraints to a ConstraintLayout instance. In addition, the current constraints for a ConstraintLayout instance may be copied into a ConstraintSet object and used to apply the same constraints to other layouts (with or without modifications).

A ConstraintSet instance is created just like any other Java object:

```
ConstraintSet set = new ConstraintSet();
```

Once a constraint set has been created, methods can be called on the instance to perform a wide range of tasks.

22.4.1 Establishing Connections

The *connect()* method of the ConstraintSet class is used to establish constraint connections between views. The following code configures a constraint set in which the left-hand side of a Button view is connected to the right-hand side of an EditText view with a margin of 70dp:

```
set.connect(button1.getId(), ConstraintSet.LEFT,
            editText1.getId(), ConstraintSet.RIGHT, 70);
```

22.4.2 Applying Constraints to a Layout

Once the constraint set is configured, it must be applied to a ConstraintLayout instance before it will take effect. A constraint set is applied via a call to the *applyTo()* method, passing through a reference to the layout object to which the settings are to be applied:

```
set.applyTo(myLayout);
```

22.4.3 Parent Constraint Connections

Connections may also be established between a child view and its parent ConstraintLayout by referencing the ConstraintSet.PARENT_ID constant. In the following example, the constraint set is configured to connect the top edge of a Button view to the top of the parent layout with a margin of 100dp:

```
set.connect(button1.getId(), ConstraintSet.TOP,
```

```
                    ConstraintSet.PARENT_ID, ConstraintSet.TOP, 100);
```

22.4.4 Sizing Constraints

A number of methods are available for controlling the sizing behavior of views. The following code, for example, sets the horizontal size of a Button view to *wrap_content* and the vertical size of an ImageView instance to a maximum of 250dp:

```
set.constrainWidth(button1.getId(), ConstraintSet.WRAP_CONTENT);
set.constrainMaxHeight(imageView1.getId(), 250);
```

22.4.5 Constraint Bias

As outlined in the chapter entitled *"A Guide to using ConstraintLayout in Android Studio"*, when a view has opposing constraints it is centered along the axis of the constraints (i.e. horizontally or vertically). This centering can be adjusted by applying a bias along the particular axis of constraint. When using the Android Studio Layout Editor, this is achieved using the controls in the Attributes tool window. When working with a constraint set, however, bias can be added using the *setHorizontalBias()* and *setVerticalBias()* methods, referencing the view ID and the bias as a floating point value between 0 and 1.

The following code, for example, constrains the left and right-hand sides of a Button to the corresponding sides of the parent layout before applying a 25% horizontal bias:

```
set.connect(button1.getId(), ConstraintSet.LEFT,
                ConstraintSet.PARENT_ID, ConstraintSet.LEFT, 0);
set.connect(button1.getId(), ConstraintSet.RIGHT,
                ConstraintSet.PARENT_ID, ConstraintSet.RIGHT, 0);
set.setHorizontalBias(button1.getId(), 0.25f);
```

22.4.6 Alignment Constraints

Alignments may also be applied using a constraint set. The full set of alignment options available with the Android Studio Layout Editor may also be configured using a constraint set via the *centerVertically()* and *centerHorizontally()* methods, both of which take a variety of arguments depending on the alignment being configured. In addition, the *center()* method may be used to center a view between two other views.

In the code below, button2 is positioned so that it is aligned horizontally with button1:

```
set.centerHorizontally(button2.getId(), button1.getId());
```

22.4.7 Copying and Applying Constraint Sets

The current constraint set for a ConstraintLayout instance may be copied into a constraint set object using the *clone()* method. The following line of code, for example, copies the constraint settings from a ConstraintLayout instance named *myLayout* into a constraint set object:

```
set.clone(myLayout);
```

Once copied, the constraint set may be applied directly to another layout or, as in the following example, modified before being applied to the second layout:

```
ConstraintSet set = new ConstraintSet();
set.clone(myLayout);
set.constrainWidth(button1.getId(), ConstraintSet.WRAP_CONTENT);
set.applyTo(mySecondLayout);
```

22.4.8 ConstraintLayout Chains

Vertical and horizontal chains may also be created within a constraint set using the *createHorizontalChain()* and *createVerticalChain()* methods. The syntax for using these methods is as follows:

```
createHorizontalChain(int leftId, int leftSide, int rightId,
     int rightSide, int[] chainIds, float[] weights, int style);
```

Based on the above syntax, the following example creates a horizontal spread chain that starts with button1 and ends with button4. In between these views are button2 and button3 with weighting set to zero for both:

```
int[] chainViews = {button2.getId(), button3.getId()};
float[] chainWeights = {0, 0};


set.createHorizontalChain(button1.getId(), ConstraintSet.LEFT,
                    button4.getId(), ConstraintSet.RIGHT,
                    chainViews, chainWeights,
                    ConstraintSet.CHAIN_SPREAD);
```

A view can be removed from a chain by passing the ID of the view to be removed through to either the *removeFromHorizontalChain()* or *removeFromVerticalChain()* methods. A view may be added to an existing chain using either the *addToHorizontalChain()* or *addToVerticalChain()* methods. In both cases the methods take as arguments the IDs of the views between which the new view is to be inserted as follows:

```
set.addToHorizontalChain(newViewId, leftViewId, rightViewId);
```

22.4.9 Guidelines

Guidelines are added to a constraint set using the *create()* method and then positioned using the *setGuidelineBegin()*, *setGuidelineEnd()* or *setGuidelinePercent()* methods. In the following code, a vertical guideline is created and positioned 50% across the width of the parent layout. The left side of a button view is then connected to the guideline with no margin:

```
set.create(R.id.myGuideline, ConstraintSet.VERTICAL_GUIDELINE);
set.setGuidelinePercent(R.id.myGuideline, 0.5f);


set.connect(button.getId(), ConstraintSet.LEFT,
          R.id.myGuideline, ConstraintSet.RIGHT, 0);


set.applyTo(layout);
```

22.4.10 Removing Constraints

A constraint may be removed from a view in a constraint set using the *clear()* method, passing through as arguments the view ID and the anchor point for which the constraint is to be removed:

```
set.clear(button.getId(), ConstraintSet.LEFT);
```

Similarly, all of the constraints on a view may be removed in a single step by referencing only the view in the *clear()* method call:

```
set.clear(button.getId());
```

22.4.11 Scaling

The scale of a view within a layout may be adjusted using the ConstraintSet *setScaleX()* and *setScaleY()* methods which take as arguments the view on which the operation is to be performed together with a float value indicating the scale. In the following code, a button object is scaled to twice its original width and half the height:

```
set.setScaleX(myButton.getId(), 2f);
set.setScaleY(myButton.getId(), 0.5f);
```

22.4.12 Rotation

A view may be rotated on either the X or Y axis using the *setRotationX()* and *setRotationY()* methods respectively both of which must be passed the ID of the view to be rotated and a float value representing the degree of rotation to be performed. The pivot point on which the rotation is to take place may be defined via a call to the *setTransformPivot()*, *setTransformPivotX()* and *setTransformPivotY()* methods. The following code rotates a button view 30 degrees on the Y axis using a pivot point located at point 500, 500:

```
set.setTransformPivot(button.getId(), 500, 500);
set.setRotationY(button.getId(), 30);
set.applyTo(layout);
```

Having covered the theory of constraint sets and user interface creation from within Java code, the next chapter will work through the creation of an example application with the objective of putting this theory into practice. For more details on the ConstraintSet class, refer to the reference guide at the following URL:

https://developer.android.com/reference/android/support/constraint/ConstraintSet.html

22.5 Summary

As an alternative to writing XML layout resource files or using the Android Studio Layout Editor tool, Android user interfaces may also be dynamically created in Java code.

Creating layouts in Java code consists of creating instances of view classes and setting attributes on those objects to define required appearance and behavior.

How a view is positioned and sized relative to its ConstraintLayout parent view and any sibling views is defined through the use of constraint sets. A constraint set is represented by an instance of the ConstraintSet class which, once created, can be configured using a wide range of method calls to perform tasks such as establishing constraint connections, controlling view sizing behavior and creating chains.

With the basics of the ConstraintSet class covered in this chapter, the next chapter will work through a tutorial that puts these features to practical use.

23. An Android ConstraintSet Tutorial

The previous chapter introduced the basic concepts of creating and modifying user interface layouts in Java code using the ConstraintLayout and ConstraintSet classes. This chapter will take these concepts and put them into practice through the creation of an example layout created entirely in Java code and without using the Android Studio Layout Editor tool.

23.1 Creating the Example Project in Android Studio

Launch Android Studio and select the *Start a new Android Studio project* option from the quick start menu in the welcome screen.

In the new project configuration dialog, enter *JavaLayout* into the Application name field and *ebookfrenzy.com* as the Company Domain setting before clicking on the *Next* button.

On the form factors screen, enable the *Phone and Tablet* option and set the minimum SDK setting to API 14: Android 4.0 (IceCreamSandwich). Continue to proceed through the screens, requesting the creation of an Empty Activity named *JavaLayoutActivity* with a corresponding layout named *activity_java_layout*.

Once the project has been created, the *JavaLayoutActivity.java* file should automatically load into the editing panel. As we have come to expect, Android Studio has created a template activity and overridden the *onCreate()* method, providing an ideal location for Java code to be added to create a user interface.

23.2 Adding Views to an Activity

The *onCreate()* method is currently designed to use a resource layout file for the user interface. Begin, therefore, by deleting this line from the method:

```
@Override
protected void onCreate(Bundle savedInstanceState) {
        super.onCreate(savedInstanceState);
        setContentView(R.layout.activity_java_layout);
}
```

The next modification is to add a ConstraintLayout object with a single Button view child to the activity. This involves the creation of new instances of the ConstraintLayout and Button classes. The Button view then needs to be added as a child to the ConstraintLayout view which, in turn, is displayed via a call to the *setContentView()* method of the activity instance:

```
package com.ebookfrenzy.javalayout;


import android.support.v7.app.AppCompatActivity;
import android.os.Bundle;
import android.support.constraint.ConstraintSet;
import android.support.constraint.ConstraintLayout;
import android.widget.Button;
```

```
import android.widget.EditText;

public class JavaLayoutActivity extends AppCompatActivity {

    @Override
    protected void onCreate(Bundle savedInstanceState) {
        super.onCreate(savedInstanceState);
        configureLayout();
    }

    private void configureLayout() {
        Button myButton = new Button(this);
        ConstraintLayout myLayout = new ConstraintLayout(this);
        myLayout.addView(myButton);
        setContentView(myLayout);
    }
}
```

When new instances of user interface objects are created in this way, the constructor methods must be passed the context within which the object is being created which, in this case, is the current activity. Since the above code resides within the activity class, the context is simply referenced by the standard *this* keyword:

```
Button myButton = new Button(this);
```

Once the above additions have been made, compile and run the application (either on a physical device or an emulator). Once launched, the visible result will be a button containing no text appearing in the top left-hand corner of the ConstraintLayout view as shown in Figure 23-1:

Figure 23-1

23.3 Setting View Attributes

For the purposes of this exercise, we need the background of the ConstraintLayout view to be blue and the Button view to display text that reads "Press Me" on a yellow background. Both of these tasks can be achieved by setting attributes on the views in the Java code as outlined in the following code fragment. In order to allow the text on the button to be easily translated to other languages it will be added as a String resource. Within the Project tool window, locate the *app -> res -> values -> strings.xml* file and modify it to add a resource value for the "Press Me" string:

```
<resources>
    <string name="app_name">JavaLayout</string>
```

```
<string name="press_me">Press Me</string>
</resources>
```

Although this is the recommended way to handle strings that are directly referenced in code, to avoid repetition of this step throughout the remainder of the book, many subsequent code samples will directly enter strings into the code.

Once the string is stored as a resource it can be accessed from within code as follows:

```
getString(R.string.press_me)
```

With the string resource created, add code to the *configureLayout()* method to set the button text and color attributes:

```
.
.
import android.graphics.Color;

public class JavaLayoutActivity extends AppCompatActivity {

    private void configureLayout() {
        Button myButton = new Button(this);
        myButton.setText(getString(R.string.press_me));
        myButton.setBackgroundColor(Color.YELLOW);

        ConstraintLayout myLayout = new ConstraintLayout(this);
        myLayout.setBackgroundColor(Color.BLUE);

        myLayout.addView(myButton);
        setContentView(myLayout);
}
```

When the application is now compiled and run, the layout will reflect the property settings such that the layout will appear with a blue background and the button will display the assigned text on a yellow background.

23.4 Creating View IDs

When the layout is complete it will consist of a Button and an EditText view. Before these views can be referenced within the methods of the ConstraintSet class, they must be assigned unique view IDs. The first step in this process is to create a new resource file containing these ID values.

Right click on the *app -> res -> values* folder, select the *New -> Values resource file* menu option and name the new resource file *id.xml*. With the resource file created, edit it so that it reads as follows:

```
<?xml version="1.0" encoding="utf-8"?>
<resources>
    <item name="myButton" type="id" />
    <item name="myEditText" type="id" />
</resources>
```

At this point in the tutorial, only the Button has been created, so edit the *createLayout()* method to assign the corresponding ID to the object:

```
private void configureLayout() {
```

```
Button myButton = new Button(this);
myButton.setText(getString(R.string.press_me));
myButton.setBackgroundColor(Color.YELLOW);
myButton.setId(R.id.myButton);
```

.

.

23.5 Configuring the Constraint Set

In the absence of any constraints, the ConstraintLayout view has placed the Button view in the top left corner of the display. In order to instruct the layout view to place the button in a different location, in this case centered both horizontally and vertically, it will be necessary to create a ConstraintSet instance, initialize it with the appropriate settings and apply it to the parent layout.

For this example, the button needs to be configured so that the width and height are constrained to the size of the text it is displaying and the view centered within the parent layout. Edit the *onCreate()* method once more to make these changes:

```
private void configureLayout() {
    Button myButton = new Button(this);
    myButton.setText(getString(R.string.press_me));
    myButton.setBackgroundColor(Color.YELLOW);
    myButton.setId(R.id.myButton);

    ConstraintLayout myLayout = new ConstraintLayout(this);
    myLayout.setBackgroundColor(Color.BLUE);

    myLayout.addView(myButton);
    setContentView(myLayout);

    ConstraintSet set = new ConstraintSet();

    set.constrainHeight(myButton.getId(),
            ConstraintSet.WRAP_CONTENT);
    set.constrainWidth(myButton.getId(),
            ConstraintSet.WRAP_CONTENT);

    set.connect(myButton.getId(), ConstraintSet.LEFT,
            ConstraintSet.PARENT_ID, ConstraintSet.LEFT, 0);
    set.connect(myButton.getId(), ConstraintSet.RIGHT,
            ConstraintSet.PARENT_ID, ConstraintSet.RIGHT, 0);
    set.connect(myButton.getId(), ConstraintSet.TOP,
            ConstraintSet.PARENT_ID, ConstraintSet.TOP, 0);
    set.connect(myButton.getId(), ConstraintSet.BOTTOM,
            ConstraintSet.PARENT_ID, ConstraintSet.BOTTOM, 0);

    set.applyTo(myLayout);
}
```

With the initial constraints configured, compile and run the application and verify that the Button view now appears in the center of the layout:

Figure 23-2

23.6 Adding the EditText View

The next item to be added to the layout is the EditText view. The first step is to create the EditText object, assign it the ID as declared in the *id.xml* resource file and add it to the layout. The code changes to achieve these steps now need to be made to the *onCreate()* method as follows:

```
private void configureLayout() {
    Button myButton = new Button(this);
    myButton.setText(getString(R.string.press_me));
    myButton.setBackgroundColor(Color.YELLOW);
    myButton.setId(R.id.myButton);

    EditText myEditText = new EditText(this);
    myEditText.setId(R.id.myEditText);

    ConstraintLayout myLayout = new ConstraintLayout(this);
    myLayout.setBackgroundColor(Color.BLUE);

    myLayout.addView(myButton);
    myLayout.addView(myEditText);

    setContentView(myLayout);
    .
    .
    .
}
```

The EditText widget is intended to be sized subject to the content it is displaying, centered horizontally within the layout and positioned 70dp above the existing Button view. Add code to the *onCreate()* method so that it reads as follows:

.

.

.

```
set.connect(myButton.getId(), ConstraintSet.LEFT,
                ConstraintSet.PARENT_ID, ConstraintSet.LEFT, 0);
set.connect(myButton.getId(), ConstraintSet.RIGHT,
                ConstraintSet.PARENT_ID, ConstraintSet.RIGHT, 0);
set.connect(myButton.getId(), ConstraintSet.TOP,
                ConstraintSet.PARENT_ID, ConstraintSet.TOP, 0);
set.connect(myButton.getId(), ConstraintSet.BOTTOM,
                ConstraintSet.PARENT_ID, ConstraintSet.BOTTOM, 0);

set.constrainHeight(myEditText.getId(),
                        ConstraintSet.WRAP_CONTENT);
set.constrainWidth(myEditText.getId(),
                        ConstraintSet.WRAP_CONTENT);

set.connect(myEditText.getId(), ConstraintSet.LEFT,
                ConstraintSet.PARENT_ID, ConstraintSet.LEFT, 0);
set.connect(myEditText.getId(), ConstraintSet.RIGHT,
                ConstraintSet.PARENT_ID, ConstraintSet.RIGHT, 0);
set.connect(myEditText.getId(), ConstraintSet.BOTTOM,
                myButton.getId(), ConstraintSet.TOP, 70);

set.applyTo(myLayout);
```

A test run of the application should show the EditText field centered above the button with a margin of 70dp.

23.7 Converting Density Independent Pixels (dp) to Pixels (px)

The next task in this exercise is to set the width of the EditText view to 200dp. As outlined in the chapter entitled *"An Android Studio Layout Editor ConstraintLayout Tutorial"* when setting sizes and positions in user interface layouts it is better to use density independent pixels (dp) rather than pixels (px). In order to set a position using dp it is necessary to convert a dp value to a px value at runtime, taking into consideration the density of the device display. In order, therefore, to set the width of the EditText view to 200dp, the following code needs to be added to the class:

```
package com.ebookfrenzy.javalayout;

import android.support.v7.app.AppCompatActivity;
import android.os.Bundle;
import android.support.constraint.ConstraintLayout;
import android.support.constraint.ConstraintSet;
import android.widget.Button;
import android.widget.EditText;
import android.graphics.Color;
import android.content.res.Resources;
import android.util.TypedValue;
```

```
public class JavaLayoutActivity extends AppCompatActivity {

    private int convertToPx(int value) {
        Resources r = getResources();
        int px = (int) TypedValue.applyDimension(
                TypedValue.COMPLEX_UNIT_DIP, value,
                r.getDisplayMetrics());
        return px;
    }

    private void configureLayout() {
        Button myButton = new Button(this);
        myButton.setText(getString(R.string.press_me));
        myButton.setBackgroundColor(Color.YELLOW);
        myButton.setId(R.id.myButton);

        EditText myEditText = new EditText(this);
        myEditText.setId(R.id.myEditText);

        int px = convertToPx(200);
        myEditText.setWidth(px);
.
.
}
```

Compile and run the application one more time and note that the width of the EditText view has changed as illustrated in Figure 23-3:

Figure 23-3

23.8 Summary

The example activity created in this chapter has, of course, created a similar user interface (the change in background color and view type notwithstanding) as that created in the earlier *"Manual XML Layout Design in Android Studio"* chapter. If nothing else, this chapter should have provided an appreciation of the level to which the Android Studio Layout Editor tool and XML resources shield the developer from many of the complexities of creating Android user interface layouts.

There are, however, instances where it makes sense to create a user interface in Java. This approach is most useful, for example, when creating dynamic user interface layouts.

24. A Guide to using Instant Run in Android Studio

Now that some of the basic concepts of Android development using Android Studio have been covered, now is a good time to introduce the Android Studio Instant Run feature. As all experienced developers know, every second spent waiting for an app to compile and run is time better spent writing and refining code.

24.1 Introducing Instant Run

Prior to the introduction of Instant Run, each time a change to a project needed to be tested Android Studio would recompile the code, convert it to Dex format, generate the APK package file and install it on the device or emulator. Having performed these steps the app would finally be launched ready for testing. Even on a fast development system this is a process that takes a considerable amount of time to complete. It is not uncommon for it to take a minute or more for this process to complete for a large application.

Instant Run, in contrast, allows many code and resource changes within a project to be reflected nearly instantaneously within the app while it is already running on a device or emulator session.

Consider, for the purposes of an example, an app being developed in Android Studio which has already been launched on a device or emulator. If changes are made to resource settings or the code within a method, Instant Run will push the updated code and resources to the running app and dynamically "swap" the changes. The changes are then reflected in the running app without the need to build, deploy and relaunch the entire app. In many cases, this allows changes to be tested in a fraction of the time it would take without Instant Run.

24.2 Understanding Instant Run Swapping Levels

Not all project changes are fully supported by Instant Run and different changes result in a different level of "swap" being performed. There are three levels of Instant Run support, referred to as hot, warm and cold swapping:

- **Hot Swapping** – Hot swapping occurs when the code within an existing method implementation is changed. The new method implementation is used next time it is called by the app. A hot swap occurs instantaneously and, if configured, is accompanied by a toast message on the device screen that reads "Applied code changes without activity restart".

- **Warm Swapping** – When a change is made to a resource file of the project (for example a layout change or the modification of a string or color resource setting) an Instant Run warm swap is performed. A warm swap involves the restarting of the currently running activity. Typically the screen will flicker as the activity restarts. A warm swap is reported on the device screen by a toast message that reads "Applied changes, restarted activity".

- **Cold Swapping** – Structural code changes such as the addition of a new method, a change to the signature of an existing method or a change to the class hierarchy of the project triggers a cold swap in which the entire app is restarted. In some conditions, such as the addition of new image resources to the project, the application package file (APK) will also be reinstalled during the swap.

24.3 Enabling and Disabling Instant Run

Instant Run is enabled and disabled via the Android Studio Settings screen. To view the current settings begin by selecting the *File -> Settings...* menu option (*Android Studio -> Preferences...* on macOS). Within the Settings dialog select the *Build, Execution, Deployment* entry in the left-hand panel followed by *Instant Run* as shown in Figure 24-1:

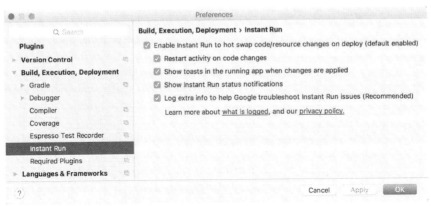

Figure 24-1

The options provided in the panel apply only to the current project. Each new project will start with the default settings. The first option controls whether or not Instant Run is enabled by default each time the project is opened in Android Studio. The *Restart activity on code changes* option forces Instant Run to restart the current activity every time a change is made, regardless of whether a hot swap could have been performed. The next option controls whether or not messages are displayed within Android Studio and the app indicating the type of Instant Run level performed. Finally, an option is provided to allow additional log information to be provided to Google to help in improving the reliability of the Instant Run feature.

24.4 Using Instant Run

When a project has been loaded into Android Studio, but is not yet running on a device or emulator, it can be launched as usual using either the run (marked A in Figure 24-2) or debug (B) button located in the toolbar:

Figure 24-2

After the app has launched and is running, Android Studio will indicate the availability of Instant Run by enabling the *Apply Changes* button located immediately to the right of the run button as highlighted in Figure 24-3:

Figure 24-3

When it is enabled, clicking on the Apply Changes button will use Instant Run to update the running app.

24.5 An Instant Run Tutorial

Begin by launching Android Studio and creating a new project. Within the *New Project* dialog, enter *InstantRunDemo* into the Application name field and *ebookfrenzy.com* as the Company Domain setting before clicking on the *Next* button.

On the form factors screen, enable the *Phone and Tablet* option and set the minimum SDK setting to API 23: Android 6.0 (Marshmallow). Continue to proceed through the screens, requesting the creation of a Basic Activity named *InstantRunDemoActivity* with a corresponding layout named *activity_instant_run_demo*.

Click on the *Finish* button to initiate the project creation process.

24.6 Triggering an Instant Run Hot Swap

Begin by clicking on the run button and selecting a suitable emulator or physical device as the run target. After clicking the run button, track the amount of time before the example app appears on the device or emulator.

Once running, click on the action button (the button displaying an envelope icon located in the lower right-hand corner of the screen). Note that a Snackbar instance appears displaying text which reads "Replace with your own action" as shown in Figure 24-4:

Figure 24-4

Once the app is running, the Apply Changes button should have been enabled indicating the availability of Instant Run. To see this in action, edit the *InstantRunDemoActivity.java* file, locate the *onCreate* method and modify the action code so that a different message is displayed when the action button is selected:

```
FloatingActionButton fab = (FloatingActionButton) findViewById(R.id.fab);
fab.setOnClickListener(new View.OnClickListener() {
    @Override
    public void onClick(View view) {
        Snackbar.make(view, "Instant Run is Amazing!",
                        Snackbar.LENGTH_LONG)
            .setAction("Action", null).show();
    }
});
```

With the code change implemented, click on the Apply Changes button and note that the toast message appears within a few seconds indicating the app has been updated. Tap the action button and note that the new message is now displayed in the Snackbar. Instant Run has successfully performed a hot swap.

24.7 Triggering an Instant Run Warm Swap

Any resource change should result in Instant Run performing a warm swap. Within Android Studio select the *app -> res -> layout -> content_instant_run_demo.xml* layout file. With the Layout Editor tool in Design mode, select the ConstraintLayout view within the Component Tree panel, switch the Attributes tool window to expert mode and locate the *background* property. Click on the button displaying three dots next to the background property text field, select a color from the Resources dialog and click on *OK*. With the background color of the activity content modified, click on the Apply Changes button once again. This time a warm swap will be performed and the currently running activity should quickly restart to adopt the new background color setting.

24.8 Triggering an Instant Run Cold Swap

As previously described, a cold swap triggers a complete restart of the running app. To experience an Instant Run cold swap, edit the *InstantRunDemoActivity.java* file and add a new method after the *onCreate* method as follows:

```
public void demoMethod() {


}
```

Click on the Apply Changes button and note that the app now has to terminate and restart to accommodate the addition of the new method. Within Android Studio a message will appear indicating that the app was restarted due to a method being added:

Figure 24-5

24.9 The Run Button

When no apps are running, the run button appears as shown in Figure 24-2. When an app is running, however, an additional green dot appears in the bottom right-hand corner of the button as shown in Figure 24-6 below:

Figure 24-6

Although the Instant Run feature has improved significantly since being introduced it can still occasionally produce unexpected results when performing hot or warm swaps. It is worth being aware, therefore, that clicking the run button when an app is currently running will force a cold swap to be performed regardless of the changes made to the project.

24.10 Summary

Instant Run is a feature of Android Studio designed to significantly accelerate the code, build and run cycle. Using a swapping mechanism, Instant Run is able to push updates to the running application, in many cases without the need to re-install or even restart the app. Instant Run provides a number of different levels of support depending on the nature of the modification being applied to the project. These levels are referred to as hot, warm and cold swapping. This chapter has introduced the concepts of Instant Run and worked through some demonstrations of the different levels of swapping.

25. An Overview and Example of Android Event Handling

Much has been covered in the previous chapters relating to the design of user interfaces for Android applications. An area that has yet to be covered, however, involves the way in which a user's interaction with the user interface triggers the underlying activity to perform a task. In other words, we know from the previous chapters how to create a user interface containing a button view, but not how to make something happen within the application when it is touched by the user.

The primary objective of this chapter, therefore, is to provide an overview of event handling in Android applications together with an Android Studio based example project.

25.1 Understanding Android Events

Events in Android can take a variety of different forms, but are usually generated in response to an external action. The most common form of events, particularly for devices such as tablets and smartphones, involve some form of interaction with the touch screen. Such events fall into the category of *input events*.

The Android framework maintains an *event queue* into which events are placed as they occur. Events are then removed from the queue on a first-in, first-out (FIFO) basis. In the case of an input event such as a touch on the screen, the event is passed to the view positioned at the location on the screen where the touch took place. In addition to the event notification, the view is also passed a range of information (depending on the event type) about the nature of the event such as the coordinates of the point of contact between the user's fingertip and the screen.

In order to be able to handle the event that it has been passed, the view must have in place an *event listener*. The Android View class, from which all user interface components are derived, contains a range of event listener interfaces, each of which contains an abstract declaration for a callback method. In order to be able to respond to an event of a particular type, a view must register the appropriate event listener and implement the corresponding callback. For example, if a button is to respond to a *click* event (the equivalent to the user touching and releasing the button view as though clicking on a physical button) it must both register the *View.onClickListener* event listener (via a call to the target view's *setOnClickListener()* method) and implement the corresponding *onClick()* callback method. In the event that a "click" event is detected on the screen at the location of the button view, the Android framework will call the *onClick()* method of that view when that event is removed from the event queue. It is, of course, within the implementation of the *onClick()* callback method that any tasks should be performed or other methods called in response to the button click.

25.2 Using the android:onClick Resource

Before exploring event listeners in more detail it is worth noting that a shortcut is available when all that is required is for a callback method to be called when a user "clicks" on a button view in the user interface. Consider a user interface layout containing a button view named *button1* with the requirement that when the user touches the button, a method called *buttonClick()* declared in the activity class is called. All that is required to implement this behavior is to write the *buttonClick()* method (which takes as an argument a reference to the view that triggered the click event) and add a single line to the declaration of the button view in the XML file. For example:

```
<Button
```

```
android:id="@+id/button1"
android:layout_width="wrap_content"
android:layout_height="wrap_content"
android:onClick="buttonClick"
android:text="Click me" />
```

This provides a simple way to capture click events. It does not, however, provide the range of options offered by event handlers, which are the topic of the rest of this chapter. When working within Android Studio Layout Editor, the onClick property can be found and configured in the Attributes panel when a suitable view type is selected in the device screen layout.

25.3 Event Listeners and Callback Methods

In the example activity outlined later in this chapter the steps involved in registering an event listener and implementing the callback method will be covered in detail. Before doing so, however, it is worth taking some time to outline the event listeners that are available in the Android framework and the callback methods associated with each one.

- **onClickListener** – Used to detect click style events whereby the user touches and then releases an area of the device display occupied by a view. Corresponds to the *onClick()* callback method which is passed a reference to the view that received the event as an argument.

- **onLongClickListener** – Used to detect when the user maintains the touch over a view for an extended period. Corresponds to the *onLongClick()* callback method which is passed as an argument the view that received the event.

- **onTouchListener** – Used to detect any form of contact with the touch screen including individual or multiple touches and gesture motions. Corresponding with the *onTouch()* callback, this topic will be covered in greater detail in the chapter entitled *"Android Touch and Multi-touch Event Handling"*. The callback method is passed as arguments the view that received the event and a MotionEvent object.

- **onCreateContextMenuListener** – Listens for the creation of a context menu as the result of a long click. Corresponds to the *onCreateContextMenu()* callback method. The callback is passed the menu, the view that received the event and a menu context object.

- **onFocusChangeListener** – Detects when focus moves away from the current view as the result of interaction with a track-ball or navigation key. Corresponds to the *onFocusChange()* callback method which is passed the view that received the event and a Boolean value to indicate whether focus was gained or lost.

- **onKeyListener** – Used to detect when a key on a device is pressed while a view has focus. Corresponds to the *onKey()* callback method. Passed as arguments are the view that received the event, the KeyCode of the physical key that was pressed and a KeyEvent object.

25.4 An Event Handling Example

In the remainder of this chapter, we will work through the creation of a simple Android Studio project designed to demonstrate the implementation of an event listener and corresponding callback method to detect when the user has clicked on a button. The code within the callback method will update a text view to indicate that the event has been processed.

Create a new project in Android Studio, entering *EventExample* into the Application name field and *ebookfrenzy. com* as the Company Domain setting before clicking on the *Next* button.

On the form factors screen, enable the *Phone and Tablet* option and set the minimum SDK setting to API 14: Android 4.0 (IceCreamSandwich). Continue to proceed through the screens, requesting the creation of an

Empty Activity named *EventExampleActivity* with a corresponding layout file named *activity_event_example*.

25.5 Designing the User Interface

The user interface layout for the *EventExampleActivity* class in this example is to consist of a ConstraintLayout, a Button and a TextView as illustrated in Figure 25-1.

Figure 25-1

Locate and select the *activity_event_example.xml* file created by Android Studio (located in the Project tool window under *app -> res -> layouts*) and double-click on it to load it into the Layout Editor tool.

Make sure that Autoconnect is enabled, then drag a Button widget from the palette and move it so that it is positioned in the horizontal center of the layout and beneath the existing TextView widget. When correctly positioned, drop the widget into place so that appropriate constraints are added by the autoconnect system. Add any missing constraints by clicking on the *Infer Constraints* button in the layout editor toolbar.

Figure 25-2

With the Button widget selected, use the Attributes panel to set the text property to Press Me. Using the yellow warning button located in the top right-hand corner of the Layout Editor (Figure 25-3), display the warnings list and click on the *Fix* button to extract the text string on the button to a resource named *press_me*:

Figure 25-3

Select the "Hello World!" TextView widget and use the Attributes panel to set the ID to *statusText*. Repeat this step to change the ID of the Button widget to *myButton*.

With the user interface layout now completed, the next step is to register the event listener and callback method.

25.6 The Event Listener and Callback Method

For the purposes of this example, an *onClickListener* needs to be registered for the *myButton* view. This is achieved by making a call to the *setOnClickListener()* method of the button view, passing through a new *onClickListener* object as an argument and implementing the *onClick()* callback method. Since this is a task that only needs to be performed when the activity is created, a good location is the *onCreate()* method of the EventExampleActivity class.

If the *EventExampleActivity.java* file is already open within an editor session, select it by clicking on the tab in the editor panel. Alternatively locate it within the Project tool window by navigating to (*app -> java -> com. ebookfrenzy.eventexample -> EventExampleActivity*) and double-click on it to load it into the code editor. Once loaded, locate the template *onCreate()* method and modify it to obtain a reference to the button view, register the event listener and implement the *onClick()* callback method:

```
package com.ebookfrenzy.eventexample;


import android.support.v7.app.AppCompatActivity;
import android.os.Bundle;
import android.view.View;
import android.widget.Button;
import android.widget.TextView;


public class EventExample extends AppCompatActivity {

    @Override
    protected void onCreate(Bundle savedInstanceState) {
        super.onCreate(savedInstanceState);
        setContentView(R.layout.activity_event_example);
        Button button = (Button)findViewById(R.id.myButton);

        button.setOnClickListener(
                new Button.OnClickListener() {
                    public void onClick(View v) {


                    }
                }
```

```
        );


    }
    .
    .
    .
}
```

The above code has now registered the event listener on the button and implemented the *onClick()* method. If the application were to be run at this point, however, there would be no indication that the event listener installed on the button was working since there is, as yet, no code implemented within the body of the *onClick()* callback method. The goal for the example is to have a message appear on the TextView when the button is clicked, so some further code changes need to be made:

```
@Override
protected void onCreate(Bundle savedInstanceState) {
        super.onCreate(savedInstanceState);
        setContentView(R.layout.activity_event_example);

        Button button = (Button)findViewById(R.id.myButton);

        button.setOnClickListener(
                new Button.OnClickListener() {
                        public void onClick(View v) {
                            TextView statusText =
                                (TextView)findViewById(R.id.statusText);
                            statusText.setText("Button clicked");
                        }
                }
        );
}
```

Complete this phase of the tutorial by compiling and running the application on either an AVD emulator or physical Android device. On touching and releasing the button view (otherwise known as "clicking") the text view should change to display the "Button clicked" text.

25.7 Consuming Events

The detection of standard clicks (as opposed to long clicks) on views is a very simple case of event handling. The example will now be extended to include the detection of long click events which occur when the user clicks and holds a view on the screen and, in doing so, cover the topic of event consumption.

Consider the code for the *onClick()* method in the above section of this chapter. The callback is declared as *void* and, as such, does not return a value to the Android framework after it has finished executing.

The code assigned to the *onLongClickListener*, on the other hand, is required to return a Boolean value to the Android framework. The purpose of this return value is to indicate to the Android runtime whether or not the callback has *consumed* the event. If the callback returns a *true* value, the event is discarded by the framework. If, on the other hand, the callback returns a *false* value the Android framework will consider the event still to be active and will consequently pass it along to the next matching event listener that is registered on the same view.

An Overview and Example of Android Event Handling

As with many programming concepts this is, perhaps, best demonstrated with an example. The first step is to add an event listener and callback method for long clicks to the button view in the example activity:

```
@Override
protected void onCreate(Bundle savedInstanceState) {
        super.onCreate(savedInstanceState);
        setContentView(R.layout.activity_event_example);


        Button button = (Button)findViewById(R.id.myButton);


        button.setOnClickListener(
                new Button.OnClickListener() {
                        public void onClick(View v) {
                            TextView statusText =
                        (TextView)findViewById(R.id.statusText);
                        statusText.setText("Button clicked");
                            }
                    }
            );


        button.setOnLongClickListener(
                new Button.OnLongClickListener() {
                        public boolean onLongClick(View v) {
                            TextView statusText =
                                (TextView)findViewById(R.id.statusText);
                            statusText.setText("Long button click");
                            return true;
                        }
                    }
            );
    }
```

Clearly, when a long click is detected, the *onLongClick()* callback method will display "Long button click" on the text view. Note, however, that the callback method also returns a value of *true* to indicate that it has consumed the event. Run the application and press and hold the Button view until the "Long button click" text appears in the text view. On releasing the button, the text view continues to display the "Long button click" text indicating that the onClick listener code was not called.

Next, modify the code such that the onLongClick listener now returns a *false* value:

```
button.setOnLongClickListener(
                        new Button.OnLongClickListener() {
                                public boolean onLongClick(View v) {
                                        TextView myTextView = (TextView)
findViewById(R.id.myTextView);
                                    myTextView.setText("Long button click");
                                    return false;
                                }
                        }
```

```
);
```

Once again, compile and run the application and perform a long click on the button until the long click message appears. Upon releasing the button this time, however, note that the *onClick* listener is also triggered and the text changes to "Button click". This is because the *false* value returned by the *onLongClick* listener code indicated to the Android framework that the event was not consumed by the method and was eligible to be passed on to the next registered listener on the view. In this case, the runtime ascertained that the onClickListener on the button was also interested in events of this type and subsequently called the *onClick* listener code.

25.8 Summary

A user interface is of little practical use if the views it contains do not do anything in response to user interaction. Android bridges the gap between the user interface and the back end code of the application through the concepts of event listeners and callback methods. The Android View class defines a set of event listeners, which can be registered on view objects. Each event listener also has associated with it a callback method.

When an event takes place on a view in a user interface, that event is placed into an event queue and handled on a first in, first out basis by the Android runtime. If the view on which the event took place has registered a listener that matches the type of event, the corresponding callback method is called. This code then performs any tasks required by the activity before returning. Some callback methods are required to return a Boolean value to indicate whether the event needs to be passed on to any other event listeners registered on the view or discarded by the system.

Having covered the basics of event handling, the next chapter will explore in some depth the topic of touch events with a particular emphasis on handling multiple touches.

26. Android Touch and Multi-touch Event Handling

Most Android based devices use a touch screen as the primary interface between user and device. The previous chapter introduced the mechanism by which a touch on the screen translates into an action within a running Android application. There is, however, much more to touch event handling than responding to a single finger tap on a view object. Most Android devices can, for example, detect more than one touch at a time. Nor are touches limited to a single point on the device display. Touches can, of course, be dynamic as the user slides one or more points of contact across the surface of the screen.

Touches can also be interpreted by an application as a *gesture*. Consider, for example, that a horizontal swipe is typically used to turn the page of an eBook, or how a pinching motion can be used to zoom in and out of an image displayed on the screen.

The objective of this chapter is to highlight the handling of touches that involve motion and to explore the concept of intercepting multiple concurrent touches. The topic of identifying distinct gestures will be covered in the next chapter.

26.1 Intercepting Touch Events

Touch events can be intercepted by a view object through the registration of an *onTouchListener* event listener and the implementation of the corresponding *onTouch()* callback method. The following code, for example, ensures that any touches on a ConstraintLayout view instance named *myLayout* result in a call to the *onTouch()* method:

```
myLayout.setOnTouchListener(
        new ConstraintLayout.OnTouchListener() {
                public boolean onTouch(View v, MotionEvent m) {
                        // Perform tasks here
                        return true;
                }
        }
);
```

As indicated in the code example, the *onTouch()* callback is required to return a Boolean value indicating to the Android runtime system whether or not the event should be passed on to other event listeners registered on the same view or discarded. The method is passed both a reference to the view on which the event was triggered and an object of type *MotionEvent*.

26.2 The MotionEvent Object

The MotionEvent object passed through to the *onTouch()* callback method is the key to obtaining information about the event. Information contained within the object includes the location of the touch within the view and the type of action performed. The MotionEvent object is also the key to handling multiple touches.

26.3 Understanding Touch Actions

An important aspect of touch event handling involves being able to identify the type of action performed by the user. The type of action associated with an event can be obtained by making a call to the *getActionMasked()* method of the MotionEvent object which was passed through to the *onTouch()* callback method. When the first touch on a view occurs, the MotionEvent object will contain an action type of ACTION_DOWN together with the coordinates of the touch. When that touch is lifted from the screen, an ACTION_UP event is generated. Any motion of the touch between the ACTION_DOWN and ACTION_UP events will be represented by ACTION_MOVE events.

When more than one touch is performed simultaneously on a view, the touches are referred to as *pointers*. In a multi-touch scenario, pointers begin and end with event actions of type ACTION_POINTER_DOWN and ACTION_POINTER_UP respectively. In order to identify the index of the pointer that triggered the event, the *getActionIndex()* callback method of the MotionEvent object must be called.

26.4 Handling Multiple Touches

The chapter entitled *"An Overview and Example of Android Event Handling"* began exploring event handling within the narrow context of a single touch event. In practice, most Android devices possess the ability to respond to multiple consecutive touches (though it is important to note that the number of simultaneous touches that can be detected varies depending on the device).

As previously discussed, each touch in a multi-touch situation is considered by the Android framework to be a *pointer*. Each pointer, in turn, is referenced by an *index* value and assigned an *ID*. The current number of pointers can be obtained via a call to the *getPointerCount()* method of the current MotionEvent object. The ID for a pointer at a particular index in the list of current pointers may be obtained via a call to the MotionEvent *getPointerId()* method. For example, the following code excerpt obtains a count of pointers and the ID of the pointer at index 0:

```
public boolean onTouch(View v, MotionEvent m) {
        int pointerCount = m.getPointerCount();
        int pointerId = m.getPointerId(0);
        return true;
}
```

Note that the pointer count will always be greater than or equal to 1 when the *onTouch* listener is triggered (since at least one touch must have occurred for the callback to be triggered).

A touch on a view, particularly one involving motion across the screen, will generate a stream of events before the point of contact with the screen is lifted. As such, it is likely that an application will need to track individual touches over multiple touch events. While the ID of a specific touch gesture will not change from one event to the next, it is important to keep in mind that the index value will change as other touch events come and go. When working with a touch gesture over multiple events, therefore, it is essential that the ID value be used as the touch reference in order to make sure the same touch is being tracked. When calling methods that require an index value, this should be obtained by converting the ID for a touch to the corresponding index value via a call to the *findPointerIndex()* method of the *MotionEvent* object.

26.5 An Example Multi-Touch Application

The example application created in the remainder of this chapter will track up to two touch gestures as they move across a layout view. As the events for each touch are triggered, the coordinates, index and ID for each touch will be displayed on the screen.

Create a new project in Android Studio, entering *MotionEvent* into the Application name field and *ebookfrenzy.*

com as the Company Domain setting before clicking on the *Next* button.

On the form factors screen, enable the *Phone and Tablet* option and set the minimum SDK setting to API 14: Android 4.0 (IceCreamSandwich). Continue to proceed through the screens, requesting the creation of an Empty Activity named *MotionEventActivity* with a corresponding layout file named *activity_motion_event*.

Click on the *Finish* button to initiate the project creation process.

26.6 Designing the Activity User Interface

The user interface for the application's sole activity is to consist of a ConstraintLayout view containing two TextView objects. Within the Project tool window, navigate to *app -> res -> layout* and double-click on the *activity_motion_event.xml* layout resource file to load it into the Android Studio Layout Editor tool.

Select and delete the default "Hello World!" TextView widget and then, with autoconnect enabled, drag and drop a new TextView widget so that it is centered horizontally and positioned at the 16dp margin line on the top edge of the layout:

Figure 26-1

Drag a second TextView widget and position and constrain it so that it is distanced by a 32dp margin from the bottom of the first widget:

Figure 26-2

Using the Attributes tool window, change the IDs for the TextView widgets to *textView1* and *textView2* respectively. Change the text displayed on the widgets to read "Touch One Status" and "Touch Two Status" and extract the strings to resources using the warning button in the top right-hand corner of the Layout Editor.

Select the ConstraintLayout entry in the Component Tree and use the Attributes panel to change the ID to *activity_motion_event*.

26.7 Implementing the Touch Event Listener

In order to receive touch event notifications it will be necessary to register a touch listener on the layout view within the *onCreate()* method of the *MotionEventActivity* activity class. Select the *MotionEventActivity.java* tab from the Android Studio editor panel to display the source code. Within the *onCreate()* method, add code to identify the ConstraintLayout view object, register the touch listener and implement code which, in this case, is going to call a second method named *handleTouch()* to which is passed the MotionEvent object:

```
package com.ebookfrenzy.motionevent;
```

```
import android.support.v7.app.AppCompatActivity;
import android.os.Bundle;
import android.view.MotionEvent;
import android.view.View;
import android.support.constraint.ConstraintLayout;
import android.widget.TextView;

public class MotionEventActivity extends AppCompatActivity {

    @Override
    protected void onCreate(Bundle savedInstanceState) {
        super.onCreate(savedInstanceState);
        setContentView(R.layout.activity_motion_event);

        ConstraintLayout myLayout =
          (ConstraintLayout)findViewById(R.id.activity_motion_event);

        myLayout.setOnTouchListener(
                new ConstraintLayout.OnTouchListener() {
                    public boolean onTouch(View v,
                                        MotionEvent m) {
                        handleTouch(m);
                        return true;
                    }
                }
        );
    }
    .
    .
    .
}
```

The final task before testing the application is to implement the *handleTouch()* method called by the listener. The code for this method reads as follows:

```
void handleTouch(MotionEvent m)
{
            TextView textView1 = (TextView)findViewById(R.id.textView1);
            TextView textView2 = (TextView)findViewById(R.id.textView2);

            int pointerCount = m.getPointerCount();

            for (int i = 0; i < pointerCount; i++)
            {
                    int x = (int) m.getX(i);
                    int y = (int) m.getY(i);
```

```
                int id = m.getPointerId(i);
                int action = m.getActionMasked();
                int actionIndex = m.getActionIndex();
                String actionString;


                switch (action)
                {
                        case MotionEvent.ACTION_DOWN:
                                actionString = "DOWN";
                                break;
                        case MotionEvent.ACTION_UP:
                                actionString = "UP";
                                break;
                        case MotionEvent.ACTION_POINTER_DOWN:
                                actionString = "PNTR DOWN";
                                break;
                        case MotionEvent.ACTION_POINTER_UP:
                            actionString = "PNTR UP";
                            break;
                        case MotionEvent.ACTION_MOVE:
                                actionString = "MOVE";
                                break;
                        default:
                                actionString = "";
                }

                String touchStatus = "Action: " + actionString + " Index: " +
actionIndex + " ID: " + id + " X: " + x + " Y: " + y;

                if (id == 0)
                        textView1.setText(touchStatus);
                else
                        textView2.setText(touchStatus);
        }
}
```

Before compiling and running the application, it is worth taking the time to walk through this code systematically to highlight the tasks that are being performed.

The code begins by obtaining references to the two TextView objects in the user interface and identifying how many pointers are currently active on the view:

```
TextView textView1 = (TextView)findViewById(R.id.textView1);
TextView textView2 = (TextView)findViewById(R.id.textView2);

int pointerCount = m.getPointerCount();
```

Next, the *pointerCount* variable is used to initiate a *for* loop which performs a set of tasks for each active pointer. The first few lines of the loop obtain the X and Y coordinates of the touch together with the corresponding event ID, action type and action index. Lastly, a string variable is declared:

```
for (int i = 0; i < pointerCount; i++)
{
                int x = (int) m.getX(i);
                int y = (int) m.getY(i);
                int id = m.getPointerId(i);
                int action = m.getActionMasked();
                int actionIndex = m.getActionIndex();
                String actionString;
```

Since action types equate to integer values, a *switch* statement is used to convert the action type to a more meaningful string value, which is stored in the previously declared *actionString* variable:

```
switch (action)
        {
            case MotionEvent.ACTION_DOWN:
                actionString = "DOWN";
                break;
            case MotionEvent.ACTION_UP:
                actionString = "UP";
                break;
            case MotionEvent.ACTION_POINTER_DOWN:
                actionString = "PNTR DOWN";
                break;
            case MotionEvent.ACTION_POINTER_UP:
                actionString = "PNTR UP";
                break;
            case MotionEvent.ACTION_MOVE:
                actionString = "MOVE";
                break;
            default:
                actionString = "";
        }
```

Finally, the string message is constructed using the *actionString* value, the action index, touch ID and X and Y coordinates. The ID value is then used to decide whether the string should be displayed on the first or second TextView object:

```
String touchStatus = "Action: " + actionString + " Index: "
        + actionIndex + " ID: " + id + " X: " + x + " Y: " + y;

                if (id == 0)
                        textView1.setText(touchStatus);
                else
                        textView2.setText(touchStatus);
```

26.8 Running the Example Application

Compile and run the application and, once launched, experiment with single and multiple touches on the screen and note that the text views update to reflect the events as illustrated in Figure 26-3. When running on an emulator, multiple touches may be simulated by holding down the Ctrl (Cmd on macOS) key while clicking the mouse button:

Action: PNTR UP Index: 0 ID: 0 X: 633 Y: 806

Action: UP Index: 0 ID: 1 X: 438 Y: 686

Figure 26-3

26.9 Summary

Activities receive notifications of touch events by registering an onTouchListener event listener and implementing the *onTouch()* callback method which, in turn, is passed a MotionEvent object when called by the Android runtime. This object contains information about the touch such as the type of touch event, the coordinates of the touch and a count of the number of touches currently in contact with the view.

When multiple touches are involved, each point of contact is referred to as a pointer with each assigned an index and an ID. While the index of a touch can change from one event to another, the ID will remain unchanged until the touch ends.

This chapter has worked through the creation of an example Android application designed to display the coordinates and action type of up to two simultaneous touches on a device display.

Having covered touches in general, the next chapter (entitled *"Detecting Common Gestures using the Android Gesture Detector Class"*) will look further at touch screen event handling through the implementation of gesture recognition.

27. Detecting Common Gestures using the Android Gesture Detector Class

The term "gesture" is used to define a contiguous sequence of interactions between the touch screen and the user. A typical gesture begins at the point that the screen is first touched and ends when the last finger or pointing device leaves the display surface. When correctly harnessed, gestures can be implemented as a form of communication between user and application. Swiping motions to turn the pages of an eBook, or a pinching movement involving two touches to zoom in or out of an image are prime examples of the ways in which gestures can be used to interact with an application.

The Android SDK provides mechanisms for the detection of both common and custom gestures within an application. Common gestures involve interactions such as a tap, double tap, long press or a swiping motion in either a horizontal or a vertical direction (referred to in Android nomenclature as a *fling*).

The goal of this chapter is to explore the use of the Android GestureDetector class to detect common gestures performed on the display of an Android device. The next chapter, entitled *"Implementing Custom Gesture and Pinch Recognition on Android"*, will cover the detection of more complex, custom gestures such as circular motions and pinches.

27.1 Implementing Common Gesture Detection

When a user interacts with the display of an Android device, the *onTouchEvent()* method of the currently active application is called by the system and passed MotionEvent objects containing data about the user's contact with the screen. This data can be interpreted to identify if the motion on the screen matches a common gesture such as a tap or a swipe. This can be achieved with very little programming effort by making use of the Android GestureDetectorCompat class. This class is designed specifically to receive motion event information from the application and to trigger method calls based on the type of common gesture, if any, detected.

The basic steps in detecting common gestures are as follows:

1. Declaration of a class which implements the GestureDetector.OnGestureListener interface including the required *onFling()*, *onDown()*, *onScroll()*, *onShowPress()*, *onSingleTapUp()* and *onLongPress()* callback methods. Note that this can be either an entirely new class, or the enclosing activity class. In the event that double tap gesture detection is required, the class must also implement the GestureDetector. OnDoubleTapListener interface and include the corresponding *onDoubleTap()* method.

2. Creation of an instance of the Android GestureDetectorCompat class, passing through an instance of the class created in step 1 as an argument.

3. An optional call to the *setOnDoubleTapListener()* method of the GestureDetectorCompat instance to enable double tap detection if required.

4. Implementation of the *onTouchEvent()* callback method on the enclosing activity which, in turn, must call the *onTouchEvent()* method of the GestureDetectorCompat instance, passing through the current motion

event object as an argument to the method.

Once implemented, the result is a set of methods within the application code that will be called when a gesture of a particular type is detected. The code within these methods can then be implemented to perform any tasks that need to be performed in response to the corresponding gesture.

In the remainder of this chapter, we will work through the creation of an example project intended to put the above steps into practice.

27.2 Creating an Example Gesture Detection Project

The goal of this project is to detect the full range of common gestures currently supported by the GestureDetectorCompat class and to display status information to the user indicating the type of gesture that has been detected.

Create a new project in Android Studio, entering *CommonGestures* into the Application name field and *ebookfrenzy.com* as the Company Domain setting before clicking on the *Next* button.

On the form factors screen, enable the *Phone and Tablet* option and set the minimum SDK setting to API 14: Android 4.0 (IceCreamSandwich). Continue to proceed through the screens, requesting the creation of an Empty Activity named *CommonGesturesActivity* with a corresponding layout resource file named *activity_common_gestures*.

Click on the *Finish* button to initiate the project creation process.

Once the new project has been created, navigate to the *app -> res -> layout -> activity_common_gestures.xml* file in the Project tool window and double-click on it to load it into the Layout Editor tool.

Within the Layout Editor tool, select the "Hello, World!" TextView component and, in the Attributes tool window, enter *gestureStatusText* as the ID.

27.3 Implementing the Listener Class

As previously outlined, it is necessary to create a class that implements the GestureDetector.OnGestureListener interface and, if double tap detection is required, the GestureDetector.OnDoubleTapListener interface. While this can be an entirely new class, it is also perfectly valid to implement this within the current activity class. For the purposes of this example, therefore, we will modify the CommonGesturesActivity class to implement these listener interfaces. Edit the *CommonGesturesActivity.java* file so that it reads as follows to declare the interfaces and to extract and store a reference to the TextView component in the user interface:

```
package com.ebookfrenzy.commongestures;

import android.support.v7.app.AppCompatActivity;
import android.os.Bundle;
import android.view.GestureDetector;
import android.widget.TextView;

public class CommonGesturesActivity extends AppCompatActivity
        implements GestureDetector.OnGestureListener,
        GestureDetector.OnDoubleTapListener
{
    private TextView gestureText;
```

```
@Override
protected void onCreate(Bundle savedInstanceState) {
    super.onCreate(savedInstanceState);
    setContentView(R.layout.activity_common_gestures);

    gestureText =
            (TextView)findViewById(R.id.gestureStatusText);


}
.
.
.
}
```

Declaring that the class implements the listener interfaces mandates that the corresponding methods also be implemented in the class:

```
package com.ebookfrenzy.commongestures;

import android.support.v7.app.AppCompatActivity;
import android.os.Bundle;
import android.view.GestureDetector;
import android.widget.TextView;
import android.view.MotionEvent;


public class CommonGesturesActivity extends AppCompatActivity
        implements GestureDetector.OnGestureListener,
        GestureDetector.OnDoubleTapListener {

    private TextView gestureText;

    @Override
    protected void onCreate(Bundle savedInstanceState) {
        super.onCreate(savedInstanceState);
        setContentView(R.layout.activity_common_gestures);
        gestureText =
                (TextView)findViewById(R.id.gestureStatusText);
    }

    @Override
    public boolean onDown(MotionEvent event) {
        gestureText.setText ("onDown");
        return true;
    }

    @Override
```

```java
    public boolean onFling(MotionEvent event1, MotionEvent event2,
                            float velocityX, float velocityY) {
        gestureText.setText("onFling");
        return true;
    }

    @Override
    public void onLongPress(MotionEvent event) {
        gestureText.setText("onLongPress");
    }

    @Override
    public boolean onScroll(MotionEvent e1, MotionEvent e2,
                            float distanceX, float distanceY) {
        gestureText.setText("onScroll");
        return true;
    }

    @Override
    public void onShowPress(MotionEvent event) {
        gestureText.setText("onShowPress");
    }

    @Override
    public boolean onSingleTapUp(MotionEvent event) {
        gestureText.setText("onSingleTapUp");
        return true;
    }

    @Override
    public boolean onDoubleTap(MotionEvent event) {
        gestureText.setText("onDoubleTap");
        return true;
    }

    @Override
    public boolean onDoubleTapEvent(MotionEvent event) {
        gestureText.setText("onDoubleTapEvent");
        return true;
    }

    @Override
    public boolean onSingleTapConfirmed(MotionEvent event) {
        gestureText.setText("onSingleTapConfirmed");
        return true;
```

```
        }
        .
        .
        .
}
```

Note that many of these methods return *true*. This indicates to the Android Framework that the event has been consumed by the method and does not need to be passed to the next event handler in the stack.

27.4 Creating the GestureDetectorCompat Instance

With the activity class now updated to implement the listener interfaces, the next step is to create an instance of the GestureDetectorCompat class. Since this only needs to be performed once at the point that the activity is created, the best place for this code is in the *onCreate()* method. Since we also want to detect double taps, the code also needs to call the *setOnDoubleTapListener()* method of the GestureDetectorCompat instance:

```
package com.ebookfrenzy.commongestures;

import android.support.v7.app.AppCompatActivity;
import android.os.Bundle;
import android.view.GestureDetector;
import android.widget.TextView;
import android.view.MotionEvent;
import android.support.v4.view.GestureDetectorCompat;

public class CommonGesturesActivity extends AppCompatActivity
        implements GestureDetector.OnGestureListener,
        GestureDetector.OnDoubleTapListener {

    private TextView gestureText;
    private GestureDetectorCompat gDetector;

    @Override
    protected void onCreate(Bundle savedInstanceState) {
        super.onCreate(savedInstanceState);
        setContentView(R.layout.activity_common_gestures);
        gestureText =
                (TextView)findViewById(R.id.gestureStatusText);

        this.gDetector = new GestureDetectorCompat(this,this);
        gDetector.setOnDoubleTapListener(this);
    }
    .
    .
    .
}
```

27.5 Implementing the onTouchEvent() Method

If the application were to be compiled and run at this point, nothing would happen if gestures were performed on the device display. This is because no code has been added to intercept touch events and to pass them through to the GestureDetectorCompat instance. In order to achieve this, it is necessary to override the *onTouchEvent()* method within the activity class and implement it such that it calls the *onTouchEvent()* method of the GestureDetectorCompat instance. Remaining in the *CommonGesturesActivity.java* file, therefore, implement this method so that it reads as follows:

```
@Override
public boolean onTouchEvent(MotionEvent event) {
        this.gDetector.onTouchEvent(event);
        // Be sure to call the superclass implementation
        return super.onTouchEvent(event);
}
```

27.6 Testing the Application

Compile and run the application on either a physical Android device or an AVD emulator. Once launched, experiment with swipes, presses, scrolling motions and double and single taps. Note that the text view updates to reflect the events as illustrated in Figure 27-1:

Figure 27-1

27.7 Summary

Any physical contact between the user and the touch screen display of a device can be considered a "gesture". Lacking the physical keyboard and mouse pointer of a traditional computer system, gestures are widely used as a method of interaction between user and application. While a gesture can be comprised of just about any sequence of motions, there is a widely used set of gestures with which users of touch screen devices have become familiar. A number of these so-called "common gestures" can be easily detected within an application by making use of the Android Gesture Detector classes. In this chapter, the use of this technique has been outlined both in theory and through the implementation of an example project.

Having covered common gestures in this chapter, the next chapter will look at detecting a wider range of gesture types including the ability to both design and detect your own gestures.

28. Implementing Custom Gesture and Pinch Recognition on Android

The previous chapter looked at the steps involved in detecting what are referred to as "common gestures" from within an Android application. In practice, however, a gesture can conceivably involve just about any sequence of touch motions on the display of an Android device. In recognition of this fact, the Android SDK allows custom gestures of just about any nature to be defined by the application developer and used to trigger events when performed by the user. This is a multistage process, the details of which are the topic of this chapter.

28.1 The Android Gesture Builder Application

The Android SDK allows developers to design custom gestures which are then stored in a gesture file bundled with an Android application package. These custom gesture files are most easily created using the *Gesture Builder* application which is bundled with the samples package supplied as part of the Android SDK. The creation of a gestures file involves launching the Gesture Builder application, either on a physical device or emulator, and "drawing" the gestures that will need to be detected by the application. Once the gestures have been designed, the file containing the gesture data can be pulled off the SD card of the device or emulator and added to the application project. Within the application code, the file is then loaded into an instance of the *GestureLibrary* class where it can be used to search for matches to any gestures performed by the user on the device display.

28.2 The GestureOverlayView Class

In order to facilitate the detection of gestures within an application, the Android SDK provides the GestureOverlayView class. This is a transparent view that can be placed over other views in the user interface for the sole purpose of detecting gestures.

28.3 Detecting Gestures

Gestures are detected by loading the gestures file created using the Gesture Builder app and then registering a *GesturePerformedListener* event listener on an instance of the GestureOverlayView class. The enclosing class is then declared to implement both the *OnGesturePerformedListener* interface and the corresponding *onGesturePerformed* callback method required by that interface. In the event that a gesture is detected by the listener, a call to the *onGesturePerformed* callback method is triggered by the Android runtime system.

28.4 Identifying Specific Gestures

When a gesture is detected, the *onGesturePerformed* callback method is called and passed as arguments a reference to the GestureOverlayView object on which the gesture was detected, together with a Gesture object containing information about the gesture.

With access to the Gesture object, the GestureLibrary can then be used to compare the detected gesture to those contained in the gestures file previously loaded into the application. The GestureLibrary reports the probability that the gesture performed by the user matches an entry in the gestures file by calculating a *prediction score* for each gesture. A prediction score of 1.0 or greater is generally accepted to be a good match between a gesture stored in the file and that performed by the user on the device display.

28.5 Building and Running the Gesture Builder Application

The Gesture Builder application is bundled by default with the AVD emulator profile for most versions of the SDK. It is not, however, pre-installed on most physical Android devices. If the utility is pre-installed, it will be listed along with the other apps installed in the device or AVD instance. In the event that it is not installed, the source code for the utility is included with the sample code provided with this book. If you have not already done so, download this now using the following link:

http://www.ebookfrenzy.com/print/androidstudio30/index.php

The source code for the Gesture Builder application is located within this archive in a folder named *GestureBuilder*.

The GestureBuilder project is based on Android 5.0.1 (API 21) so use the SDK Manager tool once again to ensure that this version of the Android SDK is installed before proceeding.

From the Android Studio welcome screen select the *Import project* option. Alternatively, from the Android Studio main window for an existing project, select the *File -> New -> Import Project…* menu option and, within the resulting dialog, navigate to and select the GestureBuilder folder within the samples directory and click on *OK*. At this point, Android Studio will import the project into the designated folder and convert it to match the Android Studio project file and build structure.

Once imported, install and run the GestureBuilder utility on an Android device attached to the development system.

28.6 Creating a Gestures File

Once the Gesture Builder application has loaded, it should indicate that no gestures have yet been created. To create a new gesture, click on the *Add gesture* button located at the bottom of the device screen, enter the name *Circle Gesture* into the *Name* text box and then "draw" a gesture using a circular motion on the screen as illustrated in Figure 28-1. Assuming that the gesture appears as required (represented by the yellow line on the device screen), click on the *Done* button to add the gesture to the gestures file:

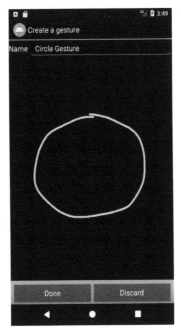

Figure 28-1

After the gesture has been saved, the Gesture Builder app will display a list of currently defined gestures, which, at this point, will consist solely of the new *Circle Gesture*.

Repeat the gesture creation process to add a further gesture to the file. This should involve a two-stroke gesture creating an X on the screen named *X Gesture*. When creating gestures involving multiple strokes, be sure to allow as little time as possible between each stroke so that the builder knows that the strokes are part of the same gesture. Once this gesture has been added, the list within the Gesture Builder application should resemble that outlined in Figure 28-2:

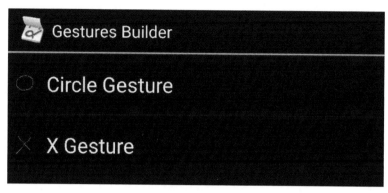

Figure 28-2

28.7 Creating the Example Project

Create a new project in Android Studio, entering *CustomGestures* into the Application name field and *ebookfrenzy. com* as the Company Domain setting before clicking on the *Next* button.

On the form factors screen, enable the *Phone and Tablet* option and set the minimum SDK setting to API 14: Android 4.0 (IceCreamSandwich). Continue to proceed through the screens, requesting the creation of an Empty Activity named *CustomGesturesActivity* with a corresponding layout file named *activity_custom_gestures*.

Click on the *Finish* button to initiate the project creation process.

28.8 Extracting the Gestures File from the SD Card

As each gesture was created within the Gesture Builder application, it was added to a file named *gestures* located on the SD Card of the emulator or device on which the app was running. Before this file can be added to an Android Studio project, however, it must first be pulled off the SD Card and saved to the local file system. This is most easily achieved by using the Android Studio Device File Explorer tool window. Display this tool using the *View -> Tool Windows -> Device File Explorer* menu option. Once displayed, select the device on which the gesture file was created from the dropdown menu, then navigate through the filesystem to the */sdcard* folder:

Name	Permissions	Date	Size
etc	lrwxrwxrwx	1969-12-31 19:00	11 B
▶ mnt	drwxr-xr-x	2017-07-24 13:16	220 B
▶ oem	drwxr-xr-x	1969-12-31 19:00	40 B
▶ proc	dr-xr-xr-x	2017-07-24 13:16	0 B
▶ root	drwx------	2017-04-18 20:57	40 B
▶ sbin	drwxr-x---	1969-12-31 19:00	120 B
▼ sdcard	lrwxrwxrwx	1969-12-31 19:00	21 B
▶ Alarms	drwxrwx--x	2017-07-13 10:57	4 KB
▶ Android	drwxrwx--x	2017-07-13 10:58	4 KB
▶ DCIM	drwxrwx--x	2017-07-13 10:57	4 KB
▶ Download	drwxrwx--x	2017-07-13 10:57	4 KB
▶ Movies	drwxrwx--x	2017-07-13 10:57	4 KB
▶ Music	drwxrwx--x	2017-07-13 10:57	4 KB
▶ Notifications	drwxrwx--x	2017-07-13 10:57	4 KB
▶ Pictures	drwxrwx--x	2017-07-13 10:57	4 KB
▶ Podcasts	drwxrwx--x	2017-07-13 10:57	4 KB
▶ Ringtones	drwxrwx--x	2017-07-13 10:57	4 KB
gestures	-rw-rw----	2017-07-24 13:21	1.1 KB
▶ storage	drwxr-xr-x	2017-07-24 13:17	100 B
▶ sys	dr-xr-xr-x	2017-07-24 13:16	0 B

Figure 28-3

Locate the *gestures* file in this folder, right click on it and select the *Save as…* menu and save the file to a temporary location.

Once the gestures file has been created and pulled off the SD Card, it is ready to be added to an Android Studio project as a resource file.

28.9 Adding the Gestures File to the Project

Within the Android Studio Project tool window, locate and right-click on the *res* folder (located under *app*) and select *New -> Directory* from the resulting menu. In the New Directory dialog, enter *raw* as the folder name and click on the *OK* button. Using the appropriate file explorer utility for your operating system type, locate the *gestures* file previously pulled from the SD Card and copy and paste it into the new *raw* folder in the Project tool window.

28.10 Designing the User Interface

This example application calls for a very simple user interface consisting of a LinearLayout view with a GestureOverlayView layered on top of it to intercept any gestures performed by the user. Locate the *app -> res -> layout -> activity_custom_gestures.xml* file and double-click on it to load it into the Layout Editor tool.

Once loaded, switch to Text mode and modify the XML so that it reads as follows:

```xml
<?xml version="1.0" encoding="utf-8"?>
<LinearLayout
    android:orientation="vertical"
    android:layout_width="match_parent"
    android:layout_height="match_parent"
    xmlns:android="http://schemas.android.com/apk/res/android">
```

```
<android.gesture.GestureOverlayView
    android:layout_width="match_parent"
    android:layout_height="match_parent"
    android:id="@+id/gOverlay"
    android:layout_gravity="center_horizontal">


</android.gesture.GestureOverlayView>
</LinearLayout>
```

28.11 Loading the Gestures File

Now that the gestures file has been added to the project, the next step is to write some code so that the file is loaded when the activity starts up. For the purposes of this project, the code to achieve this will be added to the *CustomGesturesActivity* class located in the *CustomGesturesActivity.java* source file as follows:

```
package com.ebookfrenzy.customgestures;

import android.support.v7.app.AppCompatActivity;
import android.os.Bundle;
import android.gesture.GestureLibraries;
import android.gesture.GestureLibrary;
import android.gesture.GestureOverlayView;
import android.gesture.GestureOverlayView.OnGesturePerformedListener;

public class CustomGesturesActivity extends AppCompatActivity
        implements OnGesturePerformedListener {

    private GestureLibrary gLibrary;

    @Override
    protected void onCreate(Bundle savedInstanceState) {
        super.onCreate(savedInstanceState);
        setContentView(R.layout.activity_custom_gestures);

        gestureSetup();
    }

    private void gestureSetup() {
        gLibrary =
                GestureLibraries.fromRawResource(this,
                        R.raw.gestures);
        if (!gLibrary.load()) {
            finish();
        }
    }
}
```

```
}
```

In addition to some necessary import directives, the above code also creates a *GestureLibrary* instance named *gLibrary* and then loads into it the contents of the gestures file located in the *raw* resources folder. The activity class has also been modified to implement the *OnGesturePerformedListener* interface, which requires the implementation of the *onGesturePerformed* callback method (which will be created in a later section of this chapter).

28.12 Registering the Event Listener

In order for the activity to receive notification that the user has performed a gesture on the screen, it is necessary to register the *OnGesturePerformedListener* event listener on the *gLayout* view, a reference to which can be obtained using the *findViewById* method as outlined in the following code fragment:

```
private void gestureSetup() {
    gLibrary =
            GestureLibraries.fromRawResource(this,
                    R.raw.gestures);
    if (!gLibrary.load()) {
        finish();
    }

    GestureOverlayView gOverlay = findViewById(R.id.gOverlay);
    gOverlay.addOnGesturePerformedListener(this);
}
```

28.13 Implementing the onGesturePerformed Method

All that remains before an initial test run of the application can be performed is to implement the *OnGesturePerformed* callback method. This is the method which will be called when a gesture is performed on the GestureOverlayView instance:

```
package com.ebookfrenzy.customgestures;

import android.support.v7.app.AppCompatActivity;
import android.os.Bundle;
import android.gesture.GestureLibraries;
import android.gesture.GestureLibrary;
import android.gesture.GestureOverlayView;
import android.gesture.GestureOverlayView.OnGesturePerformedListener;
import android.gesture.Prediction;
import android.widget.Toast;
import android.gesture.Gesture;
import java.util.ArrayList;

public class CustomGesturesActivity extends AppCompatActivity implements
OnGesturePerformedListener {

    private GestureLibrary gLibrary;
.
.
```

```
public void onGesturePerformed(GestureOverlayView overlay, Gesture
        gesture) {
    ArrayList<Prediction> predictions =
            gLibrary.recognize(gesture);

    if (predictions.size() > 0 && predictions.get(0).score > 1.0)
    {

        String action = predictions.get(0).name;

        Toast.makeText(this, action, Toast.LENGTH_SHORT).show();

    }
}
.
.
.
}
```

When a gesture on the gesture overlay view object is detected by the Android runtime, the *onGesturePerformed* method is called. Passed through as arguments are a reference to the GestureOverlayView object on which the gesture was detected together with an object of type *Gesture*. The Gesture class is designed to hold the information that defines a specific gesture (essentially a sequence of timed points on the screen depicting the path of the strokes that comprise a gesture).

The Gesture object is passed through to the *recognize()* method of our *gLibrary* instance, the purpose of which is to compare the current gesture with each gesture loaded from the gestures file. Once this task is complete, the *recognize()* method returns an ArrayList object containing a Prediction object for each comparison performed. The list is ranked in order from the best match (at position 0 in the array) to the worst. Contained within each prediction object is the name of the corresponding gesture from the gestures file and a prediction score indicating how closely it matches the current gesture.

The code in the above method, therefore, takes the prediction at position 0 (the closest match) makes sure it has a score of greater than 1.0 and then displays a Toast message (an Android class designed to display notification pop ups to the user) displaying the name of the matching gesture.

28.14 Testing the Application

Build and run the application on either an emulator or a physical Android device and perform the circle and swipe gestures on the display. When performed, the toast notification should appear containing the name of the gesture that was performed. Note that when a gesture is recognized, it is outlined on the display with a bright yellow line while gestures about which the overlay is uncertain appear as a faded yellow line. While useful during development, this is probably not ideal for a real world application. Clearly, therefore, there is still some more configuration work to do.

28.15 Configuring the GestureOverlayView

By default, the GestureOverlayView is configured to display yellow lines during gestures. The color used to draw recognized and unrecognized gestures can be defined via the *android:gestureColor* and *android:uncertainGestureColor* attributes. For example, to hide the gesture lines, modify the *activity_custom_ gestures.xml* file in the example project as follows:

```
<?xml version="1.0" encoding="utf-8"?>
```

```
<LinearLayout
    android:orientation="vertical"
    android:layout_width="match_parent"
    android:layout_height="match_parent"
    xmlns:android="http://schemas.android.com/apk/res/android">

    <android.gesture.GestureOverlayView
        android:layout_width="match_parent"
        android:layout_height="match_parent"
        android:id="@+id/gOverlay"
        android:layout_gravity="center_horizontal"
        android:gestureColor="#00000000"
        android:uncertainGestureColor="#00000000" >
    </android.gesture.GestureOverlayView>
</LinearLayout>
```

On re-running the application, gestures should now be invisible (since they are drawn in white on the white background of the LinearLayout view).

28.16 Intercepting Gestures

The GestureOverlayView is, as previously described, a transparent overlay that may be positioned over the top of other views. This leads to the question as to whether events intercepted by the gesture overlay should then be passed on to the underlying views when a gesture has been recognized. This is controlled via the *android:eventsInterceptionEnabled* property of the GestureOverlayView instance. When set to true, the gesture events are not passed to the underlying views when a gesture is recognized. This can be a particularly useful setting when gestures are being performed over a view that might be configured to scroll in response to certain gestures. Setting this property to *true* will avoid gestures also being interpreted as instructions to the underlying view to scroll in a particular direction.

28.17 Detecting Pinch Gestures

Before moving on from touch handling in general and gesture recognition in particular, the last topic of this chapter is that of handling pinch gestures. While it is possible to create and detect a wide range of gestures using the steps outlined in the previous sections of this chapter it is, in fact, not possible to detect a pinching gesture (where two fingers are used in a stretching and pinching motion, typically to zoom in and out of a view or image) using the techniques discussed so far.

The simplest method for detecting pinch gestures is to use the Android *ScaleGestureDetector* class. In general terms, detecting pinch gestures involves the following three steps:

1. Declaration of a new class which implements the SimpleOnScaleGestureListener interface including the required *onScale()*, *onScaleBegin()* and *onScaleEnd()* callback methods.

2. Creation of an instance of the ScaleGestureDetector class, passing through an instance of the class created in step 1 as an argument.

3. Implementing the *onTouchEvent()* callback method on the enclosing activity which, in turn, calls the *onTouchEvent()* method of the ScaleGestureDetector class.

In the remainder of this chapter, we will create a very simple example designed to demonstrate the implementation of pinch gesture recognition.

28.18 A Pinch Gesture Example Project

Create a new project in Android Studio, entering *PinchExample* into the Application name field and *ebookfrenzy. com* as the Company Domain setting before clicking on the *Next* button.

On the form factors screen, enable the *Phone and Tablet* option and set the minimum SDK setting to API 14: Android 4.0 (IceCreamSandwich). Continue to proceed through the screens, requesting the creation of an Empty Activity named *PinchExampleActivity* with a layout resource file named *activity_pinch_example*.

Within the *activity_pinch_example.xml* file, select the default TextView object and use the Attributes tool window to set the ID to *myTextView*.

Locate and load the *PinchExampleActivity.java* file into the Android Studio editor and modify the file as follows:

```
package com.ebookfrenzy.pinchexample;


import android.support.v7.app.AppCompatActivity;
import android.os.Bundle;
import android.view.MotionEvent;
import android.view.ScaleGestureDetector;
import android.view.ScaleGestureDetector.SimpleOnScaleGestureListener;
import android.widget.TextView;


public class PinchExampleActivity extends AppCompatActivity {

    TextView scaleText;
    ScaleGestureDetector scaleGestureDetector;

    @Override
    protected void onCreate(Bundle savedInstanceState) {
        super.onCreate(savedInstanceState);
        setContentView(R.layout.activity_pinch_example);

        scaleText = (TextView)findViewById(R.id.myTextView);

        scaleGestureDetector =
                new ScaleGestureDetector(this,
                        new MyOnScaleGestureListener());
    }

    @Override
    public boolean onTouchEvent(MotionEvent event) {
        scaleGestureDetector.onTouchEvent(event);
        return true;
    }

    public class MyOnScaleGestureListener extends
            SimpleOnScaleGestureListener {
```

```
    @Override
    public boolean onScale(ScaleGestureDetector detector) {

        float scaleFactor = detector.getScaleFactor();

        if (scaleFactor > 1) {
            scaleText.setText("Zooming Out");
        } else {
            scaleText.setText("Zooming In");
        }
        return true;
    }

    @Override
    public boolean onScaleBegin(ScaleGestureDetector detector) {
        return true;
    }

    @Override
    public void onScaleEnd(ScaleGestureDetector detector) {

    }
}
.
.
.
}
```

The code declares a new class named MyOnScaleGestureListener is which extends the Android SimpleOnScaleGestureListener class. This interface requires that three methods (*onScale()*, *onScaleBegin()* and *onScaleEnd()*) be implemented. In this instance the *onScale()* method identifies the scale factor and displays a message on the text view indicating the type of pinch gesture detected.

Within the *onCreate()* method, a reference to the text view object is obtained and assigned to the scaleText variable. Next, a new *ScaleGestureDetector* instance is created, passing through a reference to the enclosing activity and an instance of our new *MyOnScaleGestureListener* class as arguments. Finally, an *onTouchEvent()* callback method is implemented for the activity, which simply calls the corresponding *onTouchEvent()* method of the *ScaleGestureDetector* object, passing through the MotionEvent object as an argument.

Compile and run the application on an emulator or physical Android device and perform pinching gestures on the screen, noting that the text view displays either the zoom in or zoom out message depending on the pinching motion. Pinching gestures may be simulated within the emulator by holding down the Ctrl (or Cmd) key and clicking and dragging the mouse pointer as shown in Figure 28-4:

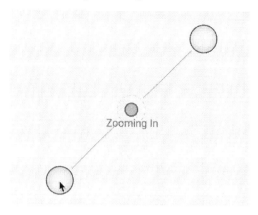

Figure 28-4

28.19 Summary

A gesture is essentially the motion of points of contact on a touch screen involving one or more strokes and can be used as a method of communication between user and application. Android allows gestures to be designed using the Gesture Builder application. Once created, gestures can be saved to a gestures file and loaded into an activity at application runtime using the GestureLibrary.

Gestures can be detected on areas of the display by overlaying existing views with instances of the transparent *GestureOverlayView* class and implementing an *OnGesturePerformedListener* event listener. Using the GestureLibrary, a ranked list of matches between a gesture performed by the user and the gestures stored in a gestures file may be generated, using a prediction score to decide whether a gesture is a close enough match.

Pinch gestures may be detected through the implementation of the ScaleGestureDetector class, an example of which was also provided in this chapter.

29. An Introduction to Android Fragments

As you progress through the chapters of this book it will become increasingly evident that many of the design concepts behind the Android system were conceived with the goal of promoting reuse of, and interaction between, the different elements that make up an application. One such area that will be explored in this chapter involves the use of Fragments.

This chapter will provide an overview of the basics of fragments in terms of what they are and how they can be created and used within applications. The next chapter will work through a tutorial designed to show fragments in action when developing applications in Android Studio, including the implementation of communication between fragments.

29.1 What is a Fragment?

A fragment is a self-contained, modular section of an application's user interface and corresponding behavior that can be embedded within an activity. Fragments can be assembled to create an activity during the application design phase, and added to or removed from an activity during application runtime to create a dynamically changing user interface.

Fragments may only be used as part of an activity and cannot be instantiated as standalone application elements. That being said, however, a fragment can be thought of as a functional "sub-activity" with its own lifecycle similar to that of a full activity.

Fragments are stored in the form of XML layout files and may be added to an activity either by placing appropriate <fragment> elements in the activity's layout file, or directly through code within the activity's class implementation.

Before starting to use Fragments in an Android application, it is important to be aware that Fragments were not introduced to Android until version 3.0 of the Android SDK. An application that uses Fragments must, therefore, make use of the *android-support-v4* Android Support Library in order to be compatible with older Android versions. The steps to achieve this will be covered in the next chapter, entitled *"Using Fragments in Android Studio - An Example"*.

29.2 Creating a Fragment

The two components that make up a fragment are an XML layout file and a corresponding Java class. The XML layout file for a fragment takes the same format as a layout for any other activity layout and can contain any combination and complexity of layout managers and views. The following XML layout, for example, is for a fragment consisting simply of a RelativeLayout with a red background containing a single TextView:

```xml
<?xml version="1.0" encoding="utf-8"?>
<RelativeLayout xmlns:android="http://schemas.android.com/apk/res/android"
    android:layout_width="match_parent"
    android:layout_height="match_parent"
    android:background="@color/red" >

    <TextView
        android:id="@+id/textView1"
        android:layout_width="wrap_content"
```

```
        android:layout_height="wrap_content"
        android:layout_centerHorizontal="true"
        android:layout_centerVertical="true"
        android:text="@string/fragone_label_text"
        android:textAppearance="?android:attr/textAppearanceLarge" />
</RelativeLayout>
```

The corresponding class to go with the layout must be a subclass of the Android *Fragment* class. If the application is to be compatible with devices running versions of Android predating version 3.0 then the class file must import *android.support.v4.app.Fragment*. The class should, at a minimum, override the *onCreateView()* method which is responsible for loading the fragment layout. For example:

```
package com.example.myfragmentdemo;


import android.os.Bundle;
import android.support.v4.app.Fragment;
import android.view.LayoutInflater;
import android.view.View;
import android.view.ViewGroup;


public class FragmentOne extends Fragment {

    @Override
    public View onCreateView(LayoutInflater inflater,
            ViewGroup container,
             Bundle savedInstanceState) {
        // Inflate the layout for this fragment
        return inflater.inflate(R.layout.fragment_one_layout,
                 container, false);
    }

}
```

In addition to the *onCreateView()* method, the class may also override the standard lifecycle methods.

Note that in order to make the above fragment compatible with Android versions prior to version 3.0, the Fragment class from the v4 support library has been imported.

Once the fragment layout and class have been created, the fragment is ready to be used within application activities.

29.3 Adding a Fragment to an Activity using the Layout XML File

Fragments may be incorporated into an activity either by writing Java code or by embedding the fragment into the activity's XML layout file. Regardless of the approach used, a key point to be aware of is that when the support library is being used for compatibility with older Android releases, any activities using fragments must be implemented as a subclass of *FragmentActivity* instead of the *AppCompatActivity* class:

```
package com.example.myfragmentdemo;


import android.os.Bundle;
import android.support.v4.app.FragmentActivity;
```

```
import android.view.Menu;

public class FragmentDemoActivity extends FragmentActivity {

        @Override
        protected void onCreate(Bundle savedInstanceState) {
                super.onCreate(savedInstanceState);
                setContentView(R.layout.activity_fragment_demo);
        }
}
```

Fragments are embedded into activity layout files using the <fragment> element. The following example layout embeds the fragment created in the previous section of this chapter into an activity layout:

```
<RelativeLayout xmlns:android="http://schemas.android.com/apk/res/android"
    xmlns:tools="http://schemas.android.com/tools"
    android:layout_width="match_parent"
    android:layout_height="match_parent"
    tools:context=".FragmentDemoActivity" >

    <fragment
        android:id="@+id/fragment_one"
        android:name="com.example.myfragmentdemo.myfragmentdemo.FragmentOne"
        android:layout_width="match_parent"
        android:layout_height="wrap_content"
        android:layout_alignParentLeft="true"
        android:layout_centerVertical="true"
        tools:layout="@layout/fragment_one_layout" />

</RelativeLayout>
```

The key properties within the <fragment> element are *android:name*, which must reference the class associated with the fragment, and *tools:layout*, which must reference the XML resource file containing the layout of the fragment.

Once added to the layout of an activity, fragments may be viewed and manipulated within the Android Studio Layout Editor tool. Figure 29-1, for example, shows the above layout with the embedded fragment within the Android Studio Layout Editor:

Figure 29-1

29.4 Adding and Managing Fragments in Code

The ease of adding a fragment to an activity via the activity's XML layout file comes at the cost of the activity not being able to remove the fragment at runtime. In order to achieve full dynamic control of fragments during runtime, those activities must be added via code. This has the advantage that the fragments can be added, removed and even made to replace one another dynamically while the application is running.

When using code to manage fragments, the fragment itself will still consist of an XML layout file and a corresponding class. The difference comes when working with the fragment within the hosting activity. There is a standard sequence of steps when adding a fragment to an activity using code:

1. Create an instance of the fragment's class.

2. Pass any additional intent arguments through to the class.

3. Obtain a reference to the fragment manager instance.

4. Call the beginTransaction() method on the fragment manager instance. This returns a fragment transaction instance.

5. Call the add() method of the fragment transaction instance, passing through as arguments the resource ID of the view that is to contain the fragment and the fragment class instance.

6. Call the commit() method of the fragment transaction.

The following code, for example, adds a fragment defined by the FragmentOne class so that it appears in the container view with an ID of LinearLayout1:

```
FragmentOne firstFragment = new FragmentOne();
firstFragment.setArguments(getIntent().getExtras());


FragmentManager fragManager = getSupportFragmentManager();
FragmentTransaction transaction = fragManager.beginTransaction();
```

```
transaction.add(R.id.LinearLayout1, firstFragment);
transaction.commit();
```

The above code breaks down each step into a separate statement for the purposes of clarity. The last four lines can, however, be abbreviated into a single line of code as follows:

```
getSupportFragmentManager().beginTransaction()
        .add(R.id.LinearLayout1, firstFragment).commit();
```

Once added to a container, a fragment may subsequently be removed via a call to the *remove()* method of the fragment transaction instance, passing through a reference to the fragment instance that is to be removed:

```
transaction.remove(firstFragment);
```

Similarly, one fragment may be replaced with another by a call to the *replace()* method of the fragment transaction instance. This takes as arguments the ID of the view containing the fragment and an instance of the new fragment. The replaced fragment may also be placed on what is referred to as the *back* stack so that it can be quickly restored in the event that the user navigates back to it. This is achieved by making a call to the *addToBackStack()* method of the fragment transaction object before making the *commit()* method call:

```
FragmentTwo secondFragment = new FragmentTwo();
transaction.replace(R.id.LinearLayout1, secondFragment);
transaction.addToBackStack(null);
transaction.commit();
```

29.5 Handling Fragment Events

As previously discussed, a fragment is very much like a sub-activity with its own layout, class and lifecycle. The view components (such as buttons and text views) within a fragment are able to generate events just like those in a regular activity. This raises the question as to which class receives an event from a view in a fragment; the fragment itself, or the activity in which the fragment is embedded. The answer to this question depends on how the event handler is declared.

In the chapter entitled *"An Overview and Example of Android Event Handling"*, two approaches to event handling were discussed. The first method involved configuring an event listener and callback method within the code of the activity. For example:

```
button.setOnClickListener(
        new Button.OnClickListener() {
                public void onClick(View v) {
                        // Code to be performed when
                        // the button is clicked
                }
        }
    );
```

In the case of intercepting click events, the second approach involved setting the *android:onClick* property within the XML layout file:

```
<Button
    android:id="@+id/button1"
    android:layout_width="wrap_content"
    android:layout_height="wrap_content"
    android:onClick="onClick"
```

```
android:text="Click me" />
```

The general rule for events generated by a view in a fragment is that if the event listener was declared in the fragment class using the event listener and callback method approach, then the event will be handled first by the fragment. If the *android:onClick* resource is used, however, the event will be passed directly to the activity containing the fragment.

29.6 Implementing Fragment Communication

Once one or more fragments are embedded within an activity, the chances are good that some form of communication will need to take place both between the fragments and the activity, and between one fragment and another. In fact, good practice dictates that fragments do not communicate directly with one another. All communication should take place via the encapsulating activity.

In order for an activity to communicate with a fragment, the activity must identify the fragment object via the ID assigned to it. Once this reference has been obtained, the activity can simply call the public methods of the fragment object.

Communicating in the other direction (from fragment to activity) is a little more complicated. In the first instance, the fragment must define a listener interface, which is then implemented within the activity class. For example, the following code declares an interface named ToolbarListener on a fragment class named ToolbarFragment. The code also declares a variable in which a reference to the activity will later be stored:

```
public class ToolbarFragment extends Fragment {

    ToolbarListener activityCallback;

    public interface ToolbarListener {
            public void onButtonClick(int position, String text);
    }
.
.
.
}
```

The above code dictates that any class that implements the ToolbarListener interface must also implement a callback method named *onButtonClick* which, in turn, accepts an integer and a String as arguments.

Next, the *onAttach()* method of the fragment class needs to be overridden and implemented. This method is called automatically by the Android system when the fragment has been initialized and associated with an activity. The method is passed a reference to the activity in which the fragment is contained. The method must store a local reference to this activity and verify that it implements the ToolbarListener interface:

```
@Override
public void onAttach(Context context) {
    super.onAttach(context);

    try {
        activityCallback = (ToolbarListener) activity;
    } catch (ClassCastException e) {
        throw new ClassCastException(activity.toString()
                + " must implement ToolbarListener");
    }
}
```

```
}
```

Upon execution of this example, a reference to the activity will be stored in the local *activityCallback* variable, and an exception will be thrown if that activity does not implement the ToolbarListener interface.

The next step is to call the callback method of the activity from within the fragment. When and how this happens is entirely dependent on the circumstances under which the activity needs to be contacted by the fragment. The following code, for example, calls the callback method on the activity when a button is clicked:

```
public void buttonClicked (View view) {
    activityCallback.onButtonClick(arg1, arg2);
}
```

All that remains is to modify the activity class so that it implements the ToolbarListener interface. For example:

```
public class FragmentExampleActivity extends FragmentActivity
                implements ToolbarFragment.ToolbarListener {


    public void onButtonClick(String arg1, int arg2) {
            // Implement code for callback method
    }
    .
    .
    .
}
```

As we can see from the above code, the activity declares that it implements the ToolbarListener interface of the ToolbarFragment class and then proceeds to implement the *onButtonClick()* method as required by the interface.

29.7 Summary

Fragments provide a powerful mechanism for creating re-usable modules of user interface layout and application behavior, which, once created, can be embedded in activities. A fragment consists of a user interface layout file and a class. Fragments may be utilized in an activity either by adding the fragment to the activity's layout file, or by writing code to manage the fragments at runtime. Fragments added to an activity in code can be removed and replaced dynamically at runtime. All communication between fragments should be performed via the activity within which the fragments are embedded.

Having covered the basics of fragments in this chapter, the next chapter will work through a tutorial designed to reinforce the techniques outlined in this chapter.

30. Using Fragments in Android Studio - An Example

As outlined in the previous chapter, fragments provide a convenient mechanism for creating reusable modules of application functionality consisting of both sections of a user interface and the corresponding behavior. Once created, fragments can be embedded within activities.

Having explored the overall theory of fragments in the previous chapter, the objective of this chapter is to create an example Android application using Android Studio designed to demonstrate the actual steps involved in both creating and using fragments, and also implementing communication between one fragment and another within an activity.

30.1 About the Example Fragment Application

The application created in this chapter will consist of a single activity and two fragments. The user interface for the first fragment will contain a toolbar of sorts consisting of an EditText view, a SeekBar and a Button, all contained within a RelativeLayout view. The second fragment will consist solely of a TextView object, also contained within a RelativeLayout view.

The two fragments will be embedded within the main activity of the application and communication implemented such that when the button in the first fragment is pressed, the text entered into the EditText view will appear on the TextView of the second fragment using a font size dictated by the position of the SeekBar in the first fragment.

Since this application is intended to work on earlier versions of Android, it will also be necessary to make use of the appropriate Android support library.

30.2 Creating the Example Project

Create a new project in Android Studio with , entering *FragmentExample* into the Application name field and *ebookfrenzy.com* as the Company Domain setting before clicking on the *Next* button.

On the form factors screen, enable the *Phone and Tablet* option and set the minimum SDK setting to API 14: Android 4.0 (IceCreamSandwich). Continue to proceed through the screens, requesting the creation of an Empty Activity named *FragmentExampleActivity* with a corresponding layout resource file named *activity_fragment_example*.

Click the *Finish* button to begin the project creation process.

30.3 Creating the First Fragment Layout

The next step is to create the user interface for the first fragment that will be used within our activity.

This user interface will, of course, reside in an XML layout file so begin by navigating to the *layout* folder located under *app -> res* in the Project tool window. Once located, right-click on the *layout* entry and select the *New -> Layout resource file* menu option as illustrated in Figure 30-1:

Figure 30-1

In the resulting dialog, name the layout *toolbar_fragment* and change the root element to RelativeLayout before clicking on OK to create the new resource file.

The new resource file will appear within the Layout Editor tool ready to be designed. Switch the Layout Editor to Text mode and modify the XML so that it reads as outlined in the following listing to add three new view elements to the layout:

```xml
<?xml version="1.0" encoding="utf-8"?>

<RelativeLayout
    xmlns:android="http://schemas.android.com/apk/res/android"
    android:layout_width="match_parent"
    android:layout_height="match_parent">

    <Button
        android:id="@+id/button1"
        android:layout_width="wrap_content"
        android:layout_height="wrap_content"
        android:layout_below="@+id/seekBar1"
        android:layout_centerHorizontal="true"
        android:layout_marginTop="17dp"
        android:text="Change Text" />

    <EditText
        android:id="@+id/editText1"
        android:layout_width="wrap_content"
        android:layout_height="wrap_content"
        android:layout_alignParentTop="true"
        android:layout_centerHorizontal="true"
        android:layout_marginTop="16dp"
        android:ems="10"
```

```
        android:inputType="text" >
        <requestFocus />
    </EditText>

    <SeekBar
        android:id="@+id/seekBar1"
        android:layout_width="match_parent"
        android:layout_height="wrap_content"
        android:layout_alignParentStart="true"
        android:layout_below="@+id/editText1"
        android:layout_marginTop="14dp"
        android:layout_alignParentLeft="true" />
```

```
</RelativeLayout>
```

Once the changes have been made, switch the Layout Editor tool back to Design mode and click on the warning button in the top right-hand corner of the design area. Select the hardcoded text warning, click the *Fix* button and assign the string to a resource named *change_text*.

Upon completion of these steps, the user interface layout should resemble that of Figure 30-2:

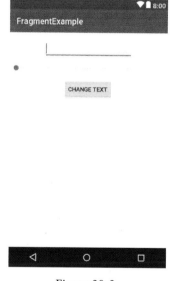

Figure 30-2

With the layout for the first fragment implemented, the next step is to create a class to go with it.

30.4 Creating the First Fragment Class

In addition to a user interface layout, a fragment also needs to have a class associated with it to do the actual work behind the scenes. Add a class for this purpose to the project by unfolding the *app -> java* folder in the Project tool window and right-clicking on the package name given to the project when it was created (in this instance *com.ebookfrenzy.fragmentexample*). From the resulting menu, select the *New -> Java Class* option. In the resulting *Create New Class* dialog, name the class *ToolbarFragment* and click on *OK* to create the new class.

Once the class has been created it should, by default, appear in the editing panel where it will read as follows:

```
package com.ebookfrenzy.fragmentexample;
```

```
/**
 * Created by <name> on <date>.
 */
public class ToolbarFragment {

}
```

For the time being, the only changes to this class are the addition of some import directives and the overriding of the *onCreateView()* method to make sure the layout file is inflated and displayed when the fragment is used within an activity. The class declaration also needs to indicate that the class extends the Android Fragment class:

```
package com.ebookfrenzy.fragmentexample;

import android.os.Bundle;
import android.support.v4.app.Fragment;
import android.view.LayoutInflater;
import android.view.View;
import android.view.ViewGroup;

public class ToolbarFragment extends Fragment {

    @Override
    public View onCreateView(LayoutInflater inflater,
                            ViewGroup container, Bundle
                            savedInstanceState) {

        // Inflate the layout for this fragment
        View view =  inflater.inflate(R.layout.toolbar_fragment,
                container, false);
        return view;
    }

}
```

Later in this chapter, more functionality will be added to this class. Before that, however, we need to create the second fragment.

30.5 Creating the Second Fragment Layout

Add a second new Android XML layout resource file to the project, once again selecting a RelativeLayout as the root element. Name the layout *text_fragment* and click *OK*. When the layout loads into the Layout Editor tool, change to Text mode and modify the XML to add a TextView to the fragment layout as follows:

```
<?xml version="1.0" encoding="utf-8"?>
<RelativeLayout xmlns:android="http://schemas.android.com/apk/res/android"
    android:layout_width="match_parent"
    android:layout_height="match_parent">
    <TextView
        android:id="@+id/textView1"
        android:layout_width="wrap_content"
```

```
    android:layout_height="wrap_content"
    android:layout_centerHorizontal="true"
    android:layout_centerVertical="true"
    android:text="Fragment Two"
    android:textAppearance="?android:attr/textAppearanceLarge" />
</RelativeLayout>
```

Once the XML changes have been made, switch back to Design mode and extract the string to a resource named *fragment_two*. Upon completion of these steps, the user interface layout for this second fragment should resemble that of Figure 30-3.

As with the first fragment, this one will also need to have a class associated with it. Right-click on *app -> java -> com.ebookfrenzy.fragmentexample* in the Project tool window. From the resulting menu, select the *New -> Java Class* option. Name the fragment *TextFragment* and click *OK* to create the class.

Figure 30-3

Edit the new *TextFragment.java* class file and modify it to implement the *onCreateView()* method and designate the class as extending the Android *Fragment* class:

```
package com.ebookfrenzy.fragmentexample;

import android.os.Bundle;
import android.support.v4.app.Fragment;
import android.view.LayoutInflater;
import android.view.View;
import android.view.ViewGroup;

public class TextFragment extends Fragment {

    @Override
    public View onCreateView(LayoutInflater inflater,
```

```
                            ViewGroup container,
                            Bundle savedInstanceState) {
        View view = inflater.inflate(R.layout.text_fragment,
                container, false);


        return view;
    }
}
```

Now that the basic structure of the two fragments has been implemented, they are ready to be embedded in the application's main activity.

30.6 Adding the Fragments to the Activity

The main activity for the application has associated with it an XML layout file named *activity_fragment_example. xml*. For the purposes of this example, the fragments will be added to the activity using the <fragment> element within this file. Using the Project tool window, navigate to the *app -> res -> layout* section of the *FragmentExample* project and double-click on the *activity_fragment_example.xml* file to load it into the Android Studio Layout Editor tool.

With the Layout Editor tool in Design mode, select and delete the default TextView object from the layout and select the *Layouts* category in the palette. Drag the *<fragment>* component from the list of layouts and drop it onto the layout so that it is centered horizontally and positioned such that the dashed line appears indicating the top layout margin:

Figure 30-4

On dropping the fragment onto the layout, a dialog will appear displaying a list of Fragments available within the current project as illustrated in Figure 30-5:

Figure 30-5

Select the ToolbarFragment entry from the list and click on the OK button to dismiss the Fragments dialog. Once added, click on the red warning button in the top right-hand corner of the layout editor to display the warnings panel. An *unknown fragments* message (Figure 30-6) will be listed indicating that the Layout Editor tool needs to know which fragment to display during the preview session. Display the ToolbarFragment fragment by clicking on the *Use @layout/toolbar_fragment* link within the message:

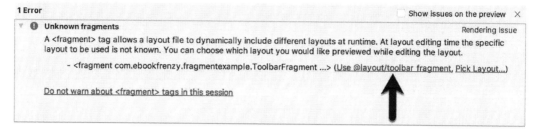

Figure 30-6

Click and drag another <fragment> entry from the panel and position it so that it is centered horizontally and positioned beneath the bottom edge of the first fragment. When prompted, select the *TextFragment* entry from the fragment dialog before clicking on the OK button. When the rendering message appears, click on the *Use @layout/text_fragment* option. Establish a constraint connection between the top edge of the TextFragment and the bottom edge of the ToolbarFragment.

Note that the fragments are now visible in the layout as demonstrated in Figure 30-7:

Figure 30-7

Before proceeding to the next step, select the TextFragment instance in the layout and, within the Attributes tool window, change the ID of the fragment to *text_fragment*.

30.7 Making the Toolbar Fragment Talk to the Activity

When the user touches the button in the toolbar fragment, the fragment class is going to need to get the text from the EditText view and the current value of the SeekBar and send them to the text fragment. As outlined in *"An Introduction to Android Fragments"*, fragments should not communicate with each other directly, instead using the activity in which they are embedded as an intermediary.

The first step in this process is to make sure that the toolbar fragment responds to the button being clicked. We also need to implement some code to keep track of the value of the SeekBar view. For the purposes of this example, we will implement these listeners within the ToolbarFragment class. Select the *ToolbarFragment.java* file and modify it so that it reads as shown in the following listing:

```
package com.ebookfrenzy.fragmentexample;
```

```java
import android.os.Bundle;
import android.support.v4.app.Fragment;
import android.view.LayoutInflater;
import android.view.View;
import android.view.ViewGroup;
import android.content.Context;
import android.widget.Button;
import android.widget.EditText;
import android.widget.SeekBar;
import android.widget.SeekBar.OnSeekBarChangeListener;

public class ToolbarFragment extends Fragment implements OnSeekBarChangeListener
{

    private static int seekvalue = 10;
    private static EditText edittext;

    @Override
    public View onCreateView(LayoutInflater inflater,
                            ViewGroup container, Bundle
                            savedInstanceState) {

        // Inflate the layout for this fragment
        View view = inflater.inflate(R.layout.toolbar_fragment,
                container, false);

        edittext = (EditText) view.findViewById(R.id.editText1);
        final SeekBar seekbar =
                (SeekBar) view.findViewById(R.id.seekBar1);

        seekbar.setOnSeekBarChangeListener(this);

        final Button button =
                (Button) view.findViewById(R.id.button1);

        button.setOnClickListener(new View.OnClickListener() {
            public void onClick(View v) {
                buttonClicked(v);
            }
        });

        return view;
    }

    public void buttonClicked (View view) {
```

```
    }

    @Override
    public void onProgressChanged(SeekBar seekBar, int progress,
                                  boolean fromUser) {
        seekvalue = progress;
    }

    @Override
    public void onStartTrackingTouch(SeekBar arg0) {

    }

    @Override
    public void onStopTrackingTouch(SeekBar arg0) {

    }
}
```

Before moving on, we need to take some time to explain the above code changes. First, the class is declared as implementing the OnSeekBarChangeListener interface. This is because the user interface contains a SeekBar instance and the fragment needs to receive notifications when the user slides the bar to change the font size. Implementation of the OnSeekBarChangeListener interface requires that the *onProgressChanged()*, *onStartTrackingTouch()* and *onStopTrackingTouch()* methods be implemented. These methods have been implemented but only the *onProgressChanged()* method is actually required to perform a task, in this case storing the new value in a variable named seekvalue which has been declared at the start of the class. Also declared is a variable in which to store a reference to the EditText object.

The *onCreateView()* method has been modified to obtain references to the EditText, SeekBar and Button views in the layout. Once a reference to the button has been obtained it is used to set up an onClickListener on the button which is configured to call a method named *buttonClicked()* when a click event is detected. This method is also then implemented, though at this point it does not do anything.

The next phase of this process is to set up the listener that will allow the fragment to call the activity when the button is clicked. This follows the mechanism outlined in the previous chapter:

```
public class ToolbarFragment extends Fragment
    implements OnSeekBarChangeListener {

        private static int seekvalue = 10;
        private static EditText edittext;

    ToolbarListener activityCallback;

    public interface ToolbarListener {
            public void onButtonClick(int position, String text);
    }
```

```java
@Override
public void onAttach(Context context) {
    super.onAttach(context);
    try {
        activityCallback = (ToolbarListener) context;
    } catch (ClassCastException e) {
        throw new ClassCastException(context.toString()
            + " must implement ToolbarListener");
    }
}


@Override
 public View onCreateView(LayoutInflater inflater,
    ViewGroup container, Bundle savedInstanceState) {
    // Inflate the layout for this fragment

    View view =
            inflater.inflate(R.layout.toolbar_fragment,
                    container, false);

    edittext = (EditText)
            view.findViewById(R.id.editText1);
    final SeekBar seekbar =
            (SeekBar) view.findViewById(R.id.seekBar1);

    seekbar.setOnSeekBarChangeListener(this);

    final Button button =
        (Button) view.findViewById(R.id.button1);
    button.setOnClickListener(new View.OnClickListener() {
        public void onClick(View v) {
            buttonClicked(v);
        }
    });

    return view;
}

public void buttonClicked (View view) {
    activityCallback.onButtonClick(seekvalue,
        edittext.getText().toString());
}
```

.

.

.

```
}
```

The above implementation will result in a method named *onButtonClick()* belonging to the activity class being called when the button is clicked by the user. All that remains, therefore, is to declare that the activity class implements the newly created ToolbarListener interface and to implement the *onButtonClick()* method.

Since the Android Support Library is being used for fragment support in earlier Android versions, the activity also needs to be changed to subclass from *FragmentActivity* instead of *AppCompatActivity*. Bringing these requirements together results in the following modified *FragmentExampleActivity.java* file:

```
package com.ebookfrenzy.fragmentexample;

import android.support.v7.app.AppCompatActivity;
import android.support.v4.app.FragmentActivity;
import android.os.Bundle;


public class FragmentExampleActivity extends FragmentActivity implements ToolbarFragment.ToolbarListener {

    @Override
    protected void onCreate(Bundle savedInstanceState) {
        super.onCreate(savedInstanceState);
        setContentView(R.layout.activity_fragment_example);
    }

    public void onButtonClick(int fontsize, String text) {

    }
}
```

With the code changes as they currently stand, the toolbar fragment will detect when the button is clicked by the user and call a method on the activity passing through the content of the EditText field and the current setting of the SeekBar view. It is now the job of the activity to communicate with the Text Fragment and to pass along these values so that the fragment can update the TextView object accordingly.

30.8 Making the Activity Talk to the Text Fragment

As outlined in *"An Introduction to Android Fragments"*, an activity can communicate with a fragment by obtaining a reference to the fragment class instance and then calling public methods on the object. As such, within the TextFragment class we will now implement a public method named *changeTextProperties()* which takes as arguments an integer for the font size and a string for the new text to be displayed. The method will then use these values to modify the TextView object. Within the Android Studio editing panel, locate and modify the *TextFragment.java* file to add this new method and to add code to the *onCreateView()* method to obtain the ID of the TextView object:

```
package com.ebookfrenzy.fragmentexample;

import android.os.Bundle;
import android.support.v4.app.Fragment;
import android.view.LayoutInflater;
import android.view.View;
```

```
import android.view.ViewGroup;
import android.widget.TextView;


public class TextFragment extends Fragment {

    private static TextView textview;

    @Override
    public View onCreateView(LayoutInflater inflater,
                             ViewGroup container,
                             Bundle savedInstanceState) {
        View view = inflater.inflate(R.layout.text_fragment,
                container, false);

        textview = (TextView) view.findViewById(R.id.textView1);

        return view;
    }

    public void changeTextProperties(int fontsize, String text)
    {
        textview.setTextSize(fontsize);
        textview.setText(text);
    }
}
```

When the TextFragment fragment was placed in the layout of the activity, it was given an ID of *text_fragment*. Using this ID, it is now possible for the activity to obtain a reference to the fragment instance and call the *changeTextProperties()* method on the object. Edit the *FragmentExampleActivity.java* file and modify the *onButtonClick()* method as follows:

```
public void onButtonClick(int fontsize, String text) {

    TextFragment textFragment =
      (TextFragment)
        getSupportFragmentManager().findFragmentById(R.id.text_fragment);

    textFragment.changeTextProperties(fontsize, text);
}
```

30.9 Testing the Application

With the coding for this project now complete, the last remaining task is to run the application. When the application is launched, the main activity will start and will, in turn, create and display the two fragments. When the user touches the button in the toolbar fragment, the *onButtonClick()* method of the activity will be called by the toolbar fragment and passed the text from the EditText view and the current value of the SeekBar. The activity will then call the *changeTextProperties()* method of the second fragment, which will modify the TextView to reflect the new text and font size:

Figure 30-8

30.10 Summary

The goal of this chapter was to work through the creation of an example project intended specifically to demonstrate the steps involved in using fragments within an Android application. Topics covered included the use of the Android Support Library for compatibility with Android versions predating the introduction of fragments, the inclusion of fragments within an activity layout and the implementation of inter-fragment communication.

31. Creating and Managing Overflow Menus on Android

An area of user interface design that has not yet been covered in this book relates to the concept of menus within an Android application. Menus provide a mechanism for offering additional choices to the user beyond the view components that are present in the user interface layout. While there are a number of different menu systems available to the Android application developer, this chapter will focus on the more commonly used Overflow menu. The chapter will cover the creation of menus both manually via XML and visually using the Android Studio Layout Editor tool.

31.1 The Overflow Menu

The overflow menu (also referred to as the options menu) is a menu that is accessible to the user from the device display and allows the developer to include other application options beyond those included in the user interface of the application. The location of the overflow menu is dependent upon the version of Android that is running on the device. With the Android 4.0 release and later, the overflow menu button is located in the top right-hand corner (Figure 31-1) in the action toolbar represented by the stack of three squares:

Figure 31-1

31.2 Creating an Overflow Menu

The items in a menu can be declared within an XML file, which is then inflated and displayed to the user on demand. This involves the use of the <menu> element, containing an <item> sub-element for each menu item. The following XML, for example, defines a menu consisting of two menu items relating to color choices:

```
<menu xmlns:android="http://schemas.android.com/apk/res/android"
    xmlns:app="http://schemas.android.com/apk/res-auto"
    xmlns:tools="http://schemas.android.com/tools"
    tools:context=
        ".MenuExampleActivity" >
    <item
        android:id="@+id/menu_red"
        android:orderInCategory="1"
        app:showAsAction="never"
        android:title="@string/red_string"/>
        <item
        android:id="@+id/menu_green"
```

```
            android:orderInCategory="2"
            app:showAsAction="never"
            android:title="@string/green_string"/>
</menu>
```

In the above XML, the *android:orderInCategory* property dictates the order in which the menu items will appear within the menu when it is displayed. The *app:showAsAction* property, on the other hand, controls the conditions under which the corresponding item appears as an item within the action bar itself. If set to *if Room*, for example, the item will appear in the action bar if there is enough room. Figure 31-2 shows the effect of setting this property to *ifRoom* for both menu items:

Figure 31-2

This property should be used sparingly to avoid over cluttering the action bar.

By default, a menu XML file is created by Android Studio when a new Android application project is created. This file is located in the *app -> res -> menu* project folder and contains a single menu item entitled "Settings":

```
<menu xmlns:android="http://schemas.android.com/apk/res/android"
    xmlns:app="http://schemas.android.com/apk/res-auto"
    xmlns:tools="http://schemas.android.com/tools"
    tools:context=".MainActivity">
        <item android:id="@+id/action_settings"
            android:title="@string/action_settings"
            android:orderInCategory="100"
            app:showAsAction="never" />
</menu>
```

This menu is already configured to be displayed when the user selects the overflow menu on the user interface when the app is running, so simply modify this one to meet your needs.

31.3 Displaying an Overflow Menu

An overflow menu is created by overriding the *onCreateOptionsMenu()* method of the corresponding activity and then inflating the menu's XML file. For example, the following code creates the menu contained within a menu XML file named *menu_menu_example*:

```
@Override
public boolean onCreateOptionsMenu(Menu menu) {
        getMenuInflater().inflate(R.menu.menu_menu_example, menu);
        return true;
}
```

As with the menu XML file, Android Studio will already have overridden this method in the main activity of a newly created Android application project. In the event that an overflow menu is not required in your activity, either remove or comment out this method.

31.4 Responding to Menu Item Selections

Once a menu has been implemented, the question arises as to how the application receives notification when the user makes menu item selections. All that an activity needs to do to receive menu selection notifications is to override the *onOptionsItemSelected()* method. Passed as an argument to this method is a reference to the selected menu item. The *getItemId()* method may then be called on the item to obtain the ID which may, in turn, be used to identify which item was selected. For example:

```
@Override
public boolean onOptionsItemSelected(MenuItem item) {

        switch (item.getItemId()) {
          case R.id.menu_red:
              // Red item was selected
              return true;
          case R.id.menu_green:
              // Green item was selected
              return true;
          default:
              return super.onOptionsItemSelected(item);
        }
}
```

31.5 Creating Checkable Item Groups

In addition to configuring independent menu items, it is also possible to create groups of menu items. This is of particular use when creating checkable menu items whereby only one out of a number of choices can be selected at any one time. Menu items can be assigned to a group by wrapping them in the *<group>* tag. The group is declared as checkable using the *android:checkableBehavior* property, setting the value to either *single, all or none*. The following XML declares that two menu items make up a group wherein only one item may be selected at any given time:

```
<menu xmlns:android="http://schemas.android.com/apk/res/android"
    xmlns:app="http://schemas.android.com/apk/res-auto">
    <group android:checkableBehavior="single">
        <item
            android:id="@+id/menu_red"
            android:title="@string/red_string"/>
        <item
            android:id="@+id/menu_green"
            android:title="@string/green_string"/>
    </group>
</menu>
```

When a menu group is configured to be checkable, a small circle appears next to the item in the menu as illustrated in Figure 31-3. It is important to be aware that the setting and unsetting of this indicator does not take place automatically. It is, therefore, the responsibility of the application to check and uncheck the menu item.

Figure 31-3

Continuing the color example used previously in this chapter, this would be implemented as follows:

```
@Override
public boolean onOptionsItemSelected(MenuItem item) {

        switch (item.getItemId()) {
            case R.id.menu_red:
                if (item.isChecked()) item.setChecked(false);
                else item.setChecked(true);
                return true;
            case R.id.menu_green:
                if (item.isChecked()) item.setChecked(false);
                else item.setChecked(true);
                return true;
            default:
                return super.onOptionsItemSelected(item);

        }

}
```

31.6 Menus and the Android Studio Menu Editor

Android Studio allows menus to be designed visually simply by loading the menu resource file into the Menu Editor tool, dragging and dropping menu elements from a palette and setting properties. This considerably eases the menu design process, though it is important to be aware that it is still necessary to write the code in the *onOptionsItemSelected()* method to implement the menu behavior.

To visually design a menu, locate the menu resource file and double-click on it to load it into the Menu Editor tool. Figure 31-4, for example, shows the default menu resource file for a basic activity loaded into the Menu Editor:

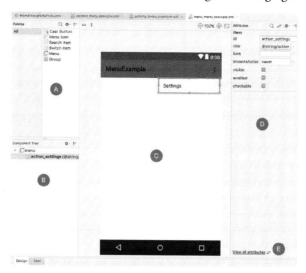

Figure 31-4

The palette (A) contains items that can be added to the menu contained in the design area (C). The Component Tree (B) is a useful tool for identifying the hierarchical structure of the menu. The Attributes panel (D) contains a subset of common attributes for the currently selected item. The view all attributes link (E) may be used to access the full list of attributes.

New elements may be added to the menu by dragging and dropping objects either onto the layout canvas or the Component Tree. When working with menus in the Layout Editor tool, it will sometimes be easier to drop the items onto the Component Tree since this provides greater control over where the item is placed within the tree. This is of particular use, for example, when adding items to a group.

Although the Menu Editor provides a visual approach to constructing menus, the underlying menu is still stored in XML format which may be viewed and edited manually by switching from Design to Text mode using the tab marked F in the above figure.

31.7 Creating the Example Project

To see the overflow menu in action, create a new project in Android Studio, entering *MenuExample* into the Application name field and *ebookfrenzy.com* as the Company Domain setting before clicking on the *Next* button.

On the form factors screen, enable the *Phone and Tablet* option and set the minimum SDK setting to API 14: Android 4.0 (IceCreamSandwich). Continue to proceed through the screens, requesting the creation of a basic activity named *MenuExampleActivity* with a corresponding layout file named *activity_menu_example*.

When the project has been created, navigate to the *app -> res -> layout* folder in the Project tool window and double-click on the *content_menu_example.xml* file to load it into the Android Studio Menu Editor tool. Switch the tool to Design mode, select the ConstraintLayout from the Component Tree panel and enter *layoutView* into the ID field of the Attributes panel.

31.8 Designing the Menu

Within the Project tool window, locate the project's *app -> res -> menu -> menu_menu_example.xml* file and double-click on it to load it into the Layout Editor tool. Select and delete the default Settings menu item added by Android Studio so that the menu currently has no items.

From the palette, click and drag a menu *group* object onto the title bar of the layout canvas as highlighted in

Figure 31-5:

Figure 31-5

Although the group item has been added, it will be invisible within the layout. To verify the presence of the element, refer to the Component Tree panel where the group will be listed as a child of the menu:

Figure 31-6

Select the *group* entry in the Component Tree and, referring to the Attributes panel, set the *checkableBehavior* property to *single* so that only one group menu item can be selected at any one time:

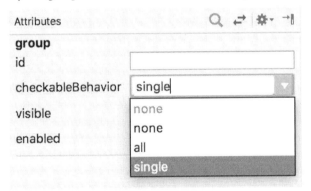

Figure 31-7

Next, drag four *Menu Item* elements from the palette and drop them onto the *group* element in the Component Tree. Select the first item and use the Attributes panel to change the title to "Red" and the ID to *menu_red*:

Figure 31-8

Repeat these steps for the remaining three menu items setting the titles to "Green", "Yellow" and "Blue" with matching IDs of *menu_green*, *menu_yellow* and *menu_blue*. Use the warning buttons to the right of the menu items in the Component Tree panel to extract the strings to resources:

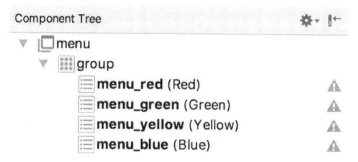

Figure 31-9

On completion of these steps, the menu layout should match that shown in Figure 31-10 below:

Figure 31-10

Switch the Layout Editor tool to Text mode and review the XML representation of the menu which should match the following listing:

```xml
<menu xmlns:android="http://schemas.android.com/apk/res/android"
    xmlns:app="http://schemas.android.com/apk/res-auto"
    xmlns:tools="http://schemas.android.com/tools"
    tools:context="com.ebookfrenzy.menuexample.MenuExampleActivity">

    <group android:checkableBehavior="single">
        <item android:title="@string/red_string"
            android:id="@+id/menu_red" />
        <item android:title="@string/green_string"
            android:id="@+id/menu_green" />
        <item android:title="@string/yellow_string"
            android:id="@+id/menu_yellow" />
        <item android:title="@string/blue_string"
            android:id="@+id/menu_blue" />
    </group>
</menu>
```

31.9 Modifying the onOptionsItemSelected() Method

When items are selected from the menu, the overridden *onOptionsItemsSelected()* method of the application's activity will be called. The role of this method will be to identify which item was selected and change the background color of the layout view to the corresponding color. Locate and double-click on the *app -> java -> com.ebookfrenzy.menuexample -> MenuExampleActivity* file and modify the method as follows:

```java
package com.ebookfrenzy.menuexample;

import android.os.Bundle;
import android.support.design.widget.FloatingActionButton;
import android.support.design.widget.Snackbar;
import android.support.v7.app.AppCompatActivity;
import android.support.v7.widget.Toolbar;
import android.view.View;
import android.view.Menu;
import android.view.MenuItem;
import android.support.constraint.ConstraintLayout;

public class MenuExampleActivity extends AppCompatActivity {
    .
    .
    .

    @Override
    public boolean onOptionsItemSelected(MenuItem item) {

        ConstraintLayout mainLayout =
                (ConstraintLayout) findViewById(R.id.layoutView);
```

```
switch (item.getItemId()) {
    case R.id.menu_red:
        if (item.isChecked()) item.setChecked(false);
        else item.setChecked(true);
        mainLayout.setBackgroundColor(android.graphics.Color.RED);
        return true;
    case R.id.menu_green:
        if (item.isChecked()) item.setChecked(false);
        else item.setChecked(true);
        mainLayout.setBackgroundColor(android.graphics.Color.GREEN);
        return true;
    case R.id.menu_yellow:
        if (item.isChecked()) item.setChecked(false);
        else item.setChecked(true);
        mainLayout.setBackgroundColor(android.graphics.Color.YELLOW);
        return true;
    case R.id.menu_blue:
        if (item.isChecked()) item.setChecked(false);
        else item.setChecked(true);
        mainLayout.setBackgroundColor(android.graphics.Color.BLUE);
        return true;
    default:
        return super.onOptionsItemSelected(item);
    }
}
    .
    .
}
```

31.10 Testing the Application

Build and run the application on either an emulator or physical Android device. Using the overflow menu, select menu items and verify that the layout background color changes appropriately. Note that the currently selected color is displayed as the checked item in the menu.

Figure 31-11

31.11 Summary

The Android overflow menu is accessed from the far right of the actions toolbar at the top of the display of the running app. This menu provides a location for applications to provide additional options to the user.

The structure of the menu is most easily defined within an XML file and the application activity receives notifications of menu item selections by overriding and implementing the *onOptionsItemSelected()* method.

32. Animating User Interfaces with the Android Transitions Framework

The Android Transitions framework was introduced as part of the Android 4.4 KitKat release and is designed to make it easy for you, as an Android developer, to add animation effects to the views that make up the screens of your applications. As will be outlined in both this and subsequent chapters, animated effects such as making the views in a user interface gently fade in and out of sight and glide smoothly to new positions on the screen can be implemented with just a few simple lines of code when using the Transitions framework in Android Studio.

32.1 Introducing Android Transitions and Scenes

Transitions allow the changes made to the layout and appearance of the views in a user interface to be animated during application runtime. While there are a number of different ways to implement Transitions from within application code, perhaps the most powerful mechanism involves the use of *Scenes*. A scene represents either the entire layout of a user interface screen, or a subset of the layout (represented by a ViewGroup).

To implement transitions using this approach, scenes are defined that reflect the two different user interface states (these can be thought of as the "before" and "after" scenes). One scene, for example, might consist of a EditText, Button and TextView positioned near the top of the screen. The second scene might remove the Button view and move the remaining EditText and TextView objects to the bottom of the screen to make room for the introduction of a MapView instance. Using the transition framework, the changes between these two scenes can be animated so that the Button fades from view, the EditText and TextView slide to the new locations and the map gently fades into view.

Scenes can be created in code from ViewGroups, or implemented in layout resource files that are loaded into Scene instances at application runtime.

Transitions can also be implemented dynamically from within application code. Using this approach, scenes are created by referencing collections of user interface views in the form of ViewGroups with transitions then being performed on those elements using the TransitionManager class, which provides a range of methods for triggering and managing the transitions between scenes.

Perhaps the simplest form of transition involves the use of the *beginDelayedTransition()* method of the TransitionManager class. When called and passed the ViewGroup representing a scene, any subsequent changes to any views within that scene (such as moving, resizing, adding or deleting views) will be animated by the Transition framework.

The actual animation is handled by the Transition framework via instances of the *Transition* class. Transition instances are responsible for detecting changes to the size, position and visibility of the views within a scene and animating those changes accordingly.

By default, transitions will be animated using a set of criteria defined by the AutoTransition class. Custom transitions can be created either via settings in XML transition files or directly within code. Multiple transitions can be combined together in a TransitionSet and configured to be performed either in parallel or sequentially.

32.2 Using Interpolators with Transitions

The Transitions framework makes extensive use of the Android Animation framework to implement animation effects. This fact is largely incidental when using transitions since most of this work happens behind the scenes, thereby shielding the developer from some of the complexities of the Animation framework. One area where some knowledge of the Animation framework is beneficial when using Transitions, however, involves the concept of interpolators.

Interpolators are a feature of the Android Animation framework that allow animations to be modified in a number of pre-defined ways. At present the Animation framework provides the following interpolators, all of which are available for use in customizing transitions:

- **AccelerateDecelerateInterpolator** – By default, animation is performed at a constant rate. The AccelerateDecelerateInterpolator can be used to cause the animation to begin slowly and then speed up in the middle before slowing down towards the end of the sequence.

- **AccelerateInterpolator** – As the name suggests, the AccelerateInterpolator begins the animation slowly and accelerates at a specified rate with no deceleration at the end.

- **AnticipateInterpolator** – The AnticipateInterpolator provides an effect similar to that of a sling shot. The animated view moves in the opposite direction to the configured animation for a short distance before being flung forward in the correct direction. The amount of backward force can be controlled through the specification of a tension value.

- **AnticipateOvershootInterpolator** – Combines the effect provided by the AnticipateInterpolator with the animated object overshooting and then returning to the destination position on the screen.

- **BounceInterpolator** – Causes the animated view to bounce on arrival at its destination position.

- **CycleInterpolator** – Configures the animation to be repeated a specified number of times.

- **DecelerateInterpolator** – The DecelerateInterpolator causes the animation to begin quickly and then decelerate by a specified factor as it nears the end.

- **LinearInterpolator** – Used to specify that the animation is to be performed at a constant rate.

- **OvershootInterpolator** – Causes the animated view to overshoot the specified destination position before returning. The overshoot can be configured by specifying a tension value.

As will be demonstrated in this and later chapters, interpolators can be specified both in code and XML files.

32.3 Working with Scene Transitions

Scenes can be represented by the content of an Android Studio XML layout file. The following XML, for example, could be used to represent a scene consisting of three button views within a RelativeLayout parent:

```xml
<?xml version="1.0" encoding="utf-8"?>
<RelativeLayout xmlns:android="http://schemas.android.com/apk/res/android"
    android:id="@+id/RelativeLayout1"
    android:layout_width="match_parent"
    android:layout_height="match_parent"
    android:orientation="vertical" >

    <Button
        android:id="@+id/button1"
```

```
        android:layout_width="wrap_content"
        android:layout_height="wrap_content"
        android:layout_alignParentLeft="true"
        android:layout_alignParentTop="true"
        android:onClick="goToScene2"
        android:text="@string/one_string" />

    <Button
        android:id="@+id/button2"
        android:layout_width="wrap_content"
        android:layout_height="wrap_content"
        android:layout_alignParentRight="true"
        android:layout_alignParentTop="true"
        android:onClick="goToScene1"
        android:text="@string/two_string" />

    <Button
        android:id="@+id/button3"
        android:layout_width="wrap_content"
        android:layout_height="wrap_content"
        android:layout_centerHorizontal="true"
        android:layout_centerVertical="true"
        android:text="@string/three_string" />

</RelativeLayout>
```

Assuming that the above layout resides in a file named *scene1_layout.xml* located in the *res/layout* folder of the project, the layout can be loaded into a scene using the *getSceneForLayout()* method of the Scene class. For example:

```
Scene scene1 = Scene.getSceneForLayout(rootContainer,
                R.layout.scene1_layout, this);
```

Note that the method call requires a reference to the root container. This is the view at the top of the view hierarchy in which the scene is to be displayed.

To display a scene to the user without any transition animation, the *enter()* method is called on the scene instance:

```
scene1.enter();
```

Transitions between two scenes using the default AutoTransition class can be triggered using the *go()* method of the TransitionManager class:

```
TransitionManager.go(scene2);
```

Scene instances can be created easily in code by bundling the view elements into one or more ViewGroups and then creating a scene from those groups. For example:

```
Scene scene1 = Scene(viewGroup1);
Scene scene2 = Scene(viewGroup2, viewGroup3);
```

32.4 Custom Transitions and TransitionSets in Code

The examples outlined so far in this chapter have used the default transition settings in which resizing, fading and motion are animated using pre-configured behavior. These can be modified by creating custom transitions which are then referenced during the transition process. Animations are categorized as either *change bounds* (relating to changes in the position and size of a view) and *fade* (relating to the visibility or otherwise of a view).

A single Transition can be created as follows:

```
Transition myChangeBounds = new ChangeBounds();
```

This new transition can then be used when performing a transition:

```
TransitionManager.go(scene2, myChangeBounds);
```

Multiple transitions may be bundled together into a TransitionSet instance. The following code, for example, creates a new TransitionSet object consisting of both change bounds and fade transition effects:

```
TransitionSet myTransition = new TransitionSet();
myTransition.addTransition(new ChangeBounds());
myTransition.addTransition(new Fade());
```

Transitions can be configured to target specific views (referenced by view ID). For example, the following code will configure the previous fade transition to target only the view with an ID that matches *myButton1*:

```
TransitionSet myTransition = new TransitionSet();
myTransition.addTransition(new ChangeBounds());
Transition fade = new Fade();
fade.addTarget(R.id.myButton1);
myTransition.addTransition(fade);
```

Additional aspects of the transition may also be customized, such as the duration of the animation. The following code specifies the duration over which the animation is to be performed:

```
Transition changeBounds = new ChangeBounds();
changeBounds.setDuration(2000);
```

As with Transition instances, once a TransitionSet instance has been created, it can be used in a transition via the TransitionManager class. For example:

```
TransitionManager.go(scene1, myTransition);
```

32.5 Custom Transitions and TransitionSets in XML

While custom transitions can be implemented in code, it is often easier to do so via XML transition files using the <fade> and <changeBounds> tags together with some additional options. The following XML includes a single changeBounds transition:

```
<?xml version="1.0" encoding="utf-8"?>
<changeBounds/>
```

As with the code based approach to working with transitions, each transition entry in a resource file may be customized. The XML below, for example, configures a duration for a change bounds transition:

```
<changeBounds android:duration="5000" >
```

Multiple transitions may be bundled together using the <transitionSet> element:

```
<?xml version="1.0" encoding="utf-8"?>
<transitionSet
  xmlns:android="http://schemas.android.com/apk/res/android" >
```

```
<fade
    android:duration="2000"
    android:fadingMode="fade_out" />

<changeBounds
    android:duration="5000" >

    <targets>
      <target android:targetId="@id/button2" />
    </targets>

</changeBounds>

<fade
    android:duration="2000"
    android:fadingMode="fade_in" />
</transitionSet>
```

Transitions contained within an XML resource file should be stored in the *res/transition* folder of the project in which they are being used and must be inflated before being referenced in the code of an application. The following code, for example, inflates the transition resources contained within a file named *transition.xml* and assigns the results to a reference named *myTransition*:

```
Transition myTransition = TransitionInflater.from(this)
        .inflateTransition(R.transition.transition);
```

Once inflated, the new transition can be referenced in the usual way:

```
TransitionManager.go(scene1, myTransition);
```

By default, transition effects within a TransitionSet are performed in parallel. To instruct the Transition framework to perform the animations sequentially, add the appropriate *android:transitionOrdering* property to the transitionSet element of the resource file:

```
<?xml version="1.0" encoding="utf-8"?>

<transitionSet
  xmlns:android="http://schemas.android.com/apk/res/android"
  android:transitionOrdering="sequential">

    <fade
      android:duration="2000"
      android:fadingMode="fade_out" />

    <changeBounds
      android:duration="5000" >
    </changeBounds>
</transitionSet>
```

Change the value from "sequential" to "together" to indicate that the animation sequences are to be performed in parallel.

32.6 Working with Interpolators

As previously discussed, interpolators can be used to modify the behavior of a transition in a variety of ways and may be specified either in code or via the settings within a transition XML resource file.

When working in code, new interpolator instances can be created by calling the constructor method of the required interpolator class and, where appropriate, passing through values to further modify the interpolator behavior:

- AccelerateDecelerateInterpolator()
- AccelerateInterpolator(float factor)
- AnticipateInterpolator(float tension)
- AnticipateOvershootInterpolator(float tension)
- BounceInterpolator()
- CycleInterpolator(float cycles)
- DecelerateInterpolator(float factor)
- LinearInterpolator()
- OvershootInterpolator(float tension)

Once created, an interpolator instance can be attached to a transition using the *setInterpolator()* method of the Transition class. The following code, for example, adds a bounce interpolator to a change bounds transition:

```
Transition changeBounds = new ChangeBounds();
changeBounds.setInterpolator(new BounceInterpolator());
```

Similarly, the following code adds an accelerate interpolator to the same transition, specifying an acceleration factor of 1.2:

```
changeBounds.setInterpolator(new AccelerateInterpolator(1.2f));
```

In the case of XML based transition resources, a default interpolator is declared using the following syntax:

```
android:interpolator="@android:anim/<interpolator_element>"
```

In the above syntax, *<interpolator_element>* must be replaced by the resource ID of the corresponding interpolator selected from the following list:

- accelerate_decelerate_interpolator
- accelerate_interpolator
- anticipate_interpolator
- anticipate_overshoot_interpolator
- bounce_interpolator
- cycle_interpolator
- decelerate_interpolator

- linear_interpolator

- overshoot_interpolator

The following XML fragment, for example, adds a bounce interpolator to a change bounds transition contained within a transition set:

```xml
<?xml version="1.0" encoding="utf-8"?>
<transitionSet
  xmlns:android="http://schemas.android.com/apk/res/android"
  android:transitionOrdering="sequential">

  <changeBounds
    android:interpolator="@android:anim/bounce_interpolator"
    android:duration="2000" />

  <fade
    android:duration="1000"
    android:fadingMode="fade_in" />
</transitionSet>
```

This approach to adding interpolators to transitions within XML resources works well when the default behavior of the interpolator is required. The task becomes a little more complex when the default behavior of an interpolator needs to be changed. Take, for example, the cycle interpolator. The purpose of this interpolator is to make an animation or transition repeat a specified number of times. In the absence of a *cycles* attribute setting, the cycle interpolator will perform only one cycle. Unfortunately, there is no way to directly specify the number of cycles (or any other interpolator attribute for that matter) when adding an interpolator using the above technique. Instead, a custom interpolator must be created and then referenced within the transition file.

32.7 Creating a Custom Interpolator

A custom interpolator must be declared in a separate XML file and stored within the *res/anim* folder of the project. The name of the XML file will be used by the Android system as the resource ID for the custom interpolator.

Within the custom interpolator XML resource file, the syntax should read as follows:

```xml
<?xml version="1.0" encoding="utf-8"?>
<interpolatorElement xmlns:android="http://schemas.android.com/apk/res/android" android:attribute="value" />
```

In the above syntax, *interpolatorElement* must be replaced with the element name of the required interpolator selected from the following list:

- accelerateDecelerateInterpolator

- accelerateInterpolator

- anticipateInterpolator

- anticipateOvershootInterpolator

- bounceInterpolator

- cycleInterpolator

- decelerateInterpolator

- linearInterpolator

- overshootInterpolator

The *attribute* keyword is replaced by the name attribute of the interpolator for which the value is to be changed (for example *tension* to change the tension attribute of an overshoot interpolator). Finally, *value* represents the value to be assigned to the specified attribute. The following XML, for example, contains a custom cycle interpolator configured to cycle 7 times:

```
<?xml version="1.0" encoding="utf-8"?>
<cycleInterpolator xmlns:android="http://schemas.android.com/apk/res/
android" android:cycles="7" />
```

Assuming that the above XML was stored in a resource file named *my_cycle.xml* stored in the *res/anim* project folder, the custom interpolator could be added to a transition resource file using the following XML syntax:

```
<changeBounds
    xmlns:android="http://schemas.android.com/apk/res/android"
    android:duration="5000"
    android:interpolator="@anim/my_cycle" >
```

32.8 Using the beginDelayedTransition Method

Perhaps the simplest form of Transition based user interface animation involves the use of the *beginDelayedTransition()* method of the TransitionManager class. This method is passed a reference to the root view of the viewgroup representing the scene for which animation is required. Subsequent changes to the views within that sub view will then be animated using the default transition settings:

```
myLayout = (ViewGroup) findViewById(R.id.myLayout);
TransitionManager.beginDelayedTransition(myLayout);
// Make changes to the scene here
```

If behavior other than the default animation behavior is required, simply pass a suitably configured Transition or TransitionSet instance through to the method call:

```
TransitionManager.beginDelayedTransition(myLayout, myTransition);
```

32.9 Summary

The Android 4.4 KitKat SDK release introduced the Transition Framework, the purpose of which is to simplify the task of adding animation to the views that make up the user interface of an Android application. With some simple configuration and a few lines of code, animation effects such as movement, visibility and resizing of views can be animated by making use of the Transition framework. A number of different approaches to implementing transitions are available involving a combination of Java code and XML resource files. The animation effects of transitions may also be enhanced through the use of a range of interpolators.

Having covered some of the theory of Transitions in Android, the next two chapters will put this theory into practice by working through some example Android Studio based transition implementations.

33. An Android Transition Tutorial using beginDelayedTransition

The previous chapter, entitled *"Animating User Interfaces with the Android Transitions Framework"*, provided an introduction to the animation of user interfaces using the Android Transitions framework. This chapter uses a tutorial based approach to demonstrate Android transitions in action using the *beginDelayedTransition()* method of the TransitionManager class.

The next chapter will create a more complex example that uses layout files and transition resource files to animate the transition from one scene to another within an application.

33.1 Creating the Android Studio TransitionDemo Project

Create a new project in Android Studio, entering *TransitionDemo* into the Application name field and *ebookfrenzy. com* as the Company Domain setting before clicking on the *Next* button.

On the form factors screen, enable the *Phone and Tablet* option and set the minimum SDK setting to API 19: Android 4.4 (KitKat). Continue to proceed through the screens, requesting the creation of an Empty Activity named *TransitionDemoActivity* with a layout resource file named *activity_transition_demo*.

33.2 Preparing the Project Files

The first example transition animation will be implemented through the use of the *beginDelayedTransition()* method of the TransitionManager class. If Android Studio does not automatically load the file, locate and double-click on the *app -> res -> layout -> activity_transition_demo.xml* file in the Project tool window panel to load it into the Layout Editor tool.

Switch the Layout Editor to Design mode, delete the "Hello World!" TextView, drag a Button from the Widget section of the Layout Editor palette and position it in the top left-hand corner of the device screen layout. Once positioned, select the button and use the Attributes tool window to specify an ID value of *myButton*.

Select the ConstraintLayout entry in the Component Tree tool window and use the Attributes window to set the ID to *myLayout*.

33.3 Implementing beginDelayedTransition Animation

The objective for the initial phase of this tutorial is to implement a touch handler so that when the user taps on the layout view the button view moves to the lower right-hand corner of the screen.

Open the *TransitionDemoActivity.java* file (located in the Project tool window under *app -> java -> com. ebookfrenzy.transitiondemo*) and modify the *onCreate()* method to implement the onTouch handler:

```
package com.ebookfrenzy.transitiondemo;


import android.support.v7.app.AppCompatActivity;
import android.os.Bundle;
import android.support.constraint.ConstraintLayout;
import android.support.constraint.ConstraintSet;
```

```
import android.view.MotionEvent;
import android.widget.Button;
import android.view.View;

public class TransitionDemoActivity extends AppCompatActivity {

    ConstraintLayout myLayout;

    @Override
    protected void onCreate(Bundle savedInstanceState) {
        super.onCreate(savedInstanceState);
        setContentView(R.layout.activity_transition_demo);

        myLayout = (ConstraintLayout) findViewById(R.id.myLayout);

        myLayout.setOnTouchListener(
                new ConstraintLayout.OnTouchListener() {
                    public boolean onTouch(View v,
                                                MotionEvent m) {
                        handleTouch();
                        return true;
                    }
                }
        );
    }
}
```

The above code simply sets up a touch listener on the ConstraintLayout container and configures it to call a method named *handleTouch()* when a touch is detected. The next task, therefore, is to implement the *handleTouch()* method as follows:

```
public void handleTouch() {
    Button button = (Button) findViewById(R.id.myButton);

    button.setMinimumWidth(500);
    button.setMinimumHeight(350);

    ConstraintSet set = new ConstraintSet();

    set.connect(R.id.myButton, ConstraintSet.BOTTOM,
            ConstraintSet.PARENT_ID, ConstraintSet.BOTTOM, 0);

    set.connect(R.id.myButton, ConstraintSet.RIGHT,
            ConstraintSet.PARENT_ID, ConstraintSet.RIGHT, 0);

    set.constrainWidth(R.id.myButton, ConstraintSet.WRAP_CONTENT);
```

```
        set.applyTo(myLayout);
    }
```

This method obtains a reference to the button view in the user interface layout and sets new minimum height and width attributes so that the button increases in size.

A ConstraintSet object is then created and configured with constraints that will position the button in the lower right-hand corner of the parent layout. This constraint set is then applied to the layout.

Test the code so far by compiling and running the application. Once launched, touch the background (not the button) and note that the button moves and resizes as illustrated in Figure 33-1:

Figure 33-1

Although the layout changes took effect, they did so instantly and without any form of animation. This is where the call to the *beginDelayedTransition()* method of the TransitionManager class comes in. All that is needed to add animation to this layout change is the addition of a single line of code before the layout changes are implemented. Remaining within the *TransitionDemoActivity.java* file, modify the code as follows:

```
.
.
import android.transition.TransitionManager;
.
.
    public void handleTouch() {
        Button button = (Button) findViewById(R.id.myButton);

        TransitionManager.beginDelayedTransition(myLayout);
```

```
        ConstraintSet set = new ConstraintSet();

        button.setMinimumWidth(500);
        button.setMinimumHeight(350);

        set.connect(R.id.myButton, ConstraintSet.BOTTOM,
                ConstraintSet.PARENT_ID, ConstraintSet.BOTTOM, 0);

        set.connect(R.id.myButton, ConstraintSet.RIGHT,
                ConstraintSet.PARENT_ID, ConstraintSet.RIGHT, 0);

        set.constrainWidth(R.id.myButton, ConstraintSet.WRAP_CONTENT);

        set.applyTo(myLayout);
    }
}
  .
  .
  .
  .
}
```

Compile and run the application once again and note that the transition is now animated.

33.4 Customizing the Transition

The final task in this example is to modify the changeBounds transition so that it is performed over a longer duration and incorporates a bounce effect when the view reaches its new screen location. This involves the creation of a Transition instance with appropriate duration interpolator settings which is, in turn, passed through as an argument to the *beginDelayedTransition()* method:

```
  .
  .
import android.transition.ChangeBounds;
import android.transition.Transition;
import android.view.animation.BounceInterpolator;
  .
  .
public void handleTouch() {
    Button button = (Button) findViewById(R.id.myButton);

    Transition changeBounds = new ChangeBounds();
    changeBounds.setDuration(3000);
    changeBounds.setInterpolator(new BounceInterpolator());

    TransitionManager.beginDelayedTransition(myLayout,
            changeBounds);
```

```
TransitionManager.beginDelayedTransition(myLayout);

ConstraintSet set = new ConstraintSet();

button.setMinimumWidth(500);
button.setMinimumHeight(350);

set.connect(R.id.myButton, ConstraintSet.BOTTOM,
        ConstraintSet.PARENT_ID, ConstraintSet.BOTTOM, 0);

set.connect(R.id.myButton, ConstraintSet.RIGHT,
        ConstraintSet.PARENT_ID, ConstraintSet.RIGHT, 0);

set.constrainWidth(R.id.myButton, ConstraintSet.WRAP_CONTENT);

set.applyTo(myLayout);
}
```

When the application is now executed, the animation will slow to match the new duration setting and the button will bounce on arrival at the bottom right-hand corner of the display.

33.5 Summary

The most basic form of transition animation involves the use of the *beginDelayedTransition()* method of the TransitionManager class. Once called, any changes in size and position of the views in the next user interface rendering frame, and within a defined view group, will be animated using the specified transitions. This chapter has worked through a simple Android Studio example that demonstrates the use of this approach to implementing transitions.

34. Implementing Android Scene Transitions – A Tutorial

This chapter will build on the theory outlined in the chapter entitled *"Animating User Interfaces with the Android Transitions Framework"* by working through the creation of a project designed to demonstrate transitioning from one scene to another using the Android Transition framework.

34.1 An Overview of the Scene Transition Project

The application created in this chapter will consist of two scenes, each represented by an XML layout resource file. A transition will then be used to animate the changes from one scene to another. The first scene will consist of three button views. The second scene will contain two of the buttons from the first scene positioned at different locations on the screen. The third button will be absent from the second scene. Once the transition has been implemented, movement of the first two buttons will be animated with a bounce effect. The third button will gently fade into view as the application transitions back to the first scene from the second.

34.2 Creating the Android Studio SceneTransitions Project

Create a new project in Android Studio, entering *SceneTransitions* into the Application name field and *ebookfrenzy.com* as the Company Domain setting before clicking on the *Next* button.

On the form factors screen, enable the *Phone and Tablet* option and set the minimum SDK setting to API 19: Android 4.4 (KitKat). Continue to proceed through the screens, requesting the creation of an Empty Activity named *SceneTransitionsActivity* with a corresponding layout file named *activity_scene_transitions*.

34.3 Identifying and Preparing the Root Container

When working with transitions it is important to identify the root container for the scenes. This is essentially the parent layout container into which the scenes are going to be displayed. When the project was created, Android Studio created a layout resource file in the *app -> res -> layout* folder named *activity_scene_transitions.xml* and containing a single layout container and TextView. When the application is launched, this is the first layout that will be displayed to the user on the device screen and for the purposes of this example, a RelativeLayout manager within this layout will act as the root container for the two scenes.

Begin by locating the *activity_scene_transitions.xml* layout resource file and loading it into the Android Studio Layout Editor tool. Switch to Text mode and replace the existing XML with the following to implement the RelativeLayout with an ID of *rootContainer*:

```
<?xml version="1.0" encoding="utf-8"?>
<RelativeLayout xmlns:android="http://schemas.android.com/apk/res/android"
    xmlns:app="http://schemas.android.com/apk/res-auto"
    xmlns:tools="http://schemas.android.com/tools"
    android:id="@+id/rootContainer"
    android:layout_width="match_parent"
    android:layout_height="match_parent"
tools:context="com.ebookfrenzy.scenetransitions.SceneTransitionsActivity">
```

`</RelativeLayout>`

34.4 Designing the First Scene

The first scene is going to consist of a layout containing three button views. Create this layout resource file by right-clicking on the *app -> res -> layout* entry in the Project tool window and selecting the *New -> Layout resource file...* menu option. In the resulting dialog, name the file *scene1_layout* and enter *android.support. constraint.ConstraintLayout* as the root element before clicking on *OK*.

When the newly created layout file has loaded into the Layout Editor tool, check that Autoconnect mode is enabled, drag a Button view from the Widgets section of the palette onto the layout canvas and position it in the top left-hand corner of the layout view so that the dashed margin guidelines appear as illustrated in Figure 34-1. Drop the Button view at this position, select it and change the text value in the Attributes tool window to "One".

Figure 34-1

Drag a second Button view from the palette and position it in the top right-hand corner of the layout view so that the margin guidelines appear. Repeating the steps for the first button, assign text that reads "Two" to the button.

Drag a third Button view and position it so that it is centered both horizontally and vertically within the layout, this time configuring the button text to read "Three".

Click on the warning button in the top right-hand corner of the Layout Editor and work through the list of I18N warnings, extracting the three button strings to resource values.

On completion of the above steps, the layout for the first scene should resemble that shown in Figure 34-2:

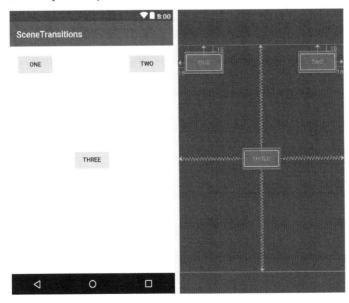

Figure 34-2

Select the "One" button and, using the Attributes tool window, configure the onClick attribute to call a method named *goToScene2*. Repeat this steps for the "Two" button, this time entering a method named *goToScene1* into the *onClick* field.

34.5 Designing the Second Scene

The second scene is simply a modified version of the first scene. The first and second buttons will still be present but will be located in the bottom right and left-hand corners of the layout respectively. The third button, on the other hand, will no longer be present in the second scene.

For the purposes of avoiding duplicated effort, the layout file for the second scene will be created by copying and modifying the *scene1_layout.xml* file. Within the Project tool window, locate the *app -> res -> layout -> scene1_layout.xml* file, right-click on it and select the *Copy* menu option. Right-click on the *layout* folder, this time selecting the *Paste* menu option and change the name of the file to *scene2_layout.xml* when prompted to do so.

Double-click on the new *scene2_layout.xml* file to load it into the Layout Editor tool and switch to Design mode if necessary. Use the *Clear all Constraints* button located in the toolbar to remove the current constraints from the layout.

Select and delete the "Three" button and move the first and second buttons to the bottom right and bottom left locations as illustrated in Figure 34-3:

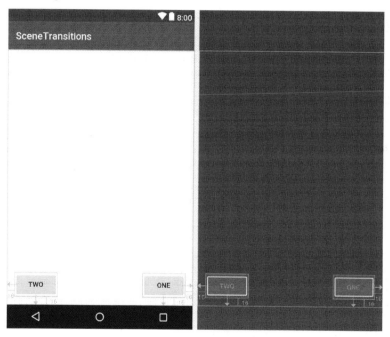

Figure 34-3

34.6 Entering the First Scene

If the application were to be run now, only the blank layout represented by the *activity_scene_transitions.xml* file would be displayed. Some code must, therefore, be added to the *onCreate()* method located in the *SceneTransitionsActivity.java* file so that the first scene is presented when the activity is created. This can be achieved as follows:

```
package com.ebookfrenzy.scenetransitions;
```

```
import android.support.v7.app.AppCompatActivity;
import android.os.Bundle;
import android.transition.Scene;
import android.transition.Transition;
import android.transition.TransitionManager;
import android.view.ViewGroup;
import android.view.View;

public class SceneTransitionsActivity extends AppCompatActivity {

    ViewGroup rootContainer;
    Scene scene1;

    @Override
    protected void onCreate(Bundle savedInstanceState) {
        super.onCreate(savedInstanceState);
        setContentView(R.layout.activity_scene_transitions);

        rootContainer =
                (ViewGroup) findViewById(R.id.rootContainer);

        scene1 = Scene.getSceneForLayout(rootContainer,
                R.layout.scene1_layout, this);

        scene1.enter();
    }
}
```

The code added to the activity class declares some variables in which to store references to the root container and first scene and obtains a reference to the root container view. The *getSceneForLayout()* method of the Scene class is then used to create a scene from the layout contained in the *scene1_layout.xml* file to convert that layout into a scene. The scene is then entered via the *enter()* method call so that it is displayed to the user.

Compile and run the application at this point and verify that scene 1 is displayed after the application has launched.

34.7 Loading Scene 2

Before implementing the transition between the first and second scene it is first necessary to add some code to load the layout from the *scene2_layout.xml* file into a Scene instance. Remaining in the *SceneTransitionsActivity.java* file, therefore, add this code as follows:

```
public class SceneTransitionsActivity extends AppCompatActivity {

    ViewGroup rootContainer;
    Scene scene1;
    Scene scene2;

    @Override
```

```
protected void onCreate(Bundle savedInstanceState) {
    super.onCreate(savedInstanceState);
    setContentView(R.layout.activity_scene_transitions);

    rootContainer =
            (ViewGroup) findViewById(R.id.rootContainer);

    scene1 = Scene.getSceneForLayout(rootContainer,
            R.layout.scene1_layout, this);

    scene2 = Scene.getSceneForLayout(rootContainer,
            R.layout.scene2_layout, this);

    scene1.enter();
}

    .

    .

}
```

34.8 Implementing the Transitions

The first and second buttons have been configured to call methods named *goToScene2* and *goToScene1* respectively when selected. As the method names suggest, it is the responsibility of these methods to trigger the transitions between the two scenes. Add these two methods within the *SceneTransitionsActivity.java* file so that they read as follows:

```
public void goToScene2 (View view)
{
        TransitionManager.go(scene2);
}

public void goToScene1 (View view)
{
        TransitionManager.go(scene1);
}
```

Run the application and note that selecting the first two buttons causes the layout to switch between the two scenes. Since we have yet to configure any transitions, these layout changes are not yet animated.

34.9 Adding the Transition File

All of the transition effects for this project will be implemented within a single transition XML resource file. As outlined in the chapter entitled *"Animating User Interfaces with the Android Transitions Framework"*, transition resource files must be placed in the *app -> res -> transition* folder of the project. Begin, therefore, by right-clicking on the *res* folder in the Project tool window and selecting the *New -> Directory* menu option. In the resulting dialog, name the new folder *transition* and click on the *OK* button. Right-click on the new transition folder, this time selecting the *New -> File* option and name the new file *transition.xml*.

With the newly created *transition.xml* file selected and loaded into the editing panel, add the following XML content to add a transition set that enables the change bounds transition animation with a duration attribute setting:

```xml
<?xml version="1.0" encoding="utf-8"?>

<transitionSet
  xmlns:android="http://schemas.android.com/apk/res/android">

    <changeBounds
        android:duration="2000">
    </changeBounds>


</transitionSet>
```

34.10 Loading and Using the Transition Set

Although a transition resource file has been created and populated with a change bounds transition, this will have no effect until some code is added to load the transitions into a TransitionManager instance and reference it in the scene changes. The changes to achieve this are as follows:

```java
package com.ebookfrenzy.scenetransitions;

import android.support.v7.app.AppCompatActivity;
import android.os.Bundle;
import android.transition.Scene;
import android.transition.Transition;
import android.transition.TransitionInflater;
import android.transition.TransitionManager;
import android.view.ViewGroup;
import android.view.View;

public class SceneTransitionsActivity extends AppCompatActivity {

    ViewGroup rootContainer;
    Scene scene1;
    Scene scene2;
    Transition transitionMgr;

    @Override
    protected void onCreate(Bundle savedInstanceState) {
        super.onCreate(savedInstanceState);
        setContentView(R.layout.activity_scene_transitions);

        rootContainer =
            (ViewGroup) findViewById(R.id.rootContainer);

        transitionMgr = TransitionInflater.from(this)
                .inflateTransition(R.transition.transition);

        scene1 = Scene.getSceneForLayout(rootContainer,
          R.layout.scene1_layout, this);
```

```
        scene2 = Scene.getSceneForLayout(rootContainer,
          R.layout.scene2_layout, this);

        scene1.enter();
    }

    public void goToScene2 (View view)
    {
        TransitionManager.go(scene2, transitionMgr);
    }

    public void goToScene1 (View view)
    {
        TransitionManager.go(scene1, transitionMgr);
    }
    .
    .
}
```

When the application is now run the two buttons will gently glide to their new positions during the transition.

34.11 Configuring Additional Transitions

With the transition file integrated into the project, any number of additional transitions may be added to the file without the need to make any further changes to the Java source code of the activity. Take, for example, the following changes to the *transition.xml* file to add a bounce interpolator to the change bounds transition, introduce a fade-in transition targeted at the third button and to change the transitions such that they are performed sequentially:

```xml
<?xml version="1.0" encoding="utf-8"?>

<transitionSet
  xmlns:android="http://schemas.android.com/apk/res/android"
  android:transitionOrdering="sequential" >



    <fade
      android:duration="2000"
      android:fadingMode="fade_in">

      <targets>
          <target android:targetId="@id/button3" />
      </targets>
    </fade>

  <changeBounds
      android:duration="2000"
```

```
        android:interpolator="@android:anim/bounce_interpolator">
    </changeBounds>
</transitionSet>
```

Buttons one and two will now bounce on arriving at the end destinations and button three will gently fade back into view when transitioning to scene 1 from scene 2.

Take some time to experiment with different transitions and interpolators by making changes to the *transition. xml* file and re-running the application.

34.12 Summary

Scene based transitions provide a flexible approach to animating user interface layout changes within an Android application. This chapter has demonstrated the steps involved in animating the transition between the scenes represented by two layout resource files. In addition, the example also used a transition XML resource file to configure the transition animation effects between the two scenes.

35. Working with the Floating Action Button and Snackbar

One of the objectives of this chapter is to provide an overview of the concepts of material design. Originally introduced as part of Android 5.0, material design is a set of design guidelines that dictate how the Android user interface, and that of the apps running on Android, appear and behave.

As part of the implementation of the material design concepts, Google also introduced the Android Design Support Library. This library contains a number of different components that allow many of the key features of material design to be built into Android applications. Two of these components, the floating action button and Snackbar, will also be covered in this chapter prior to introducing many of the other components in subsequent chapters.

35.1 The Material Design

The overall appearance of the Android environment is defined by the principles of material design. Material design was created by the Android team at Google and dictates that the elements that make up the user interface of Android and the apps that run on it appear and behave in a certain way in terms of behavior, shadowing, animation and style. One of the tenets of the material design is that the elements of a user interface appear to have physical depth and a sense that items are constructed in layers of physical material. A button, for example, appears to be raised above the surface of the layout in which it resides through the use of shadowing effects. Pressing the button causes the button to flex and lift as though made of a thin material that ripples when released.

Material design also dictates the layout and behavior of many standard user interface elements. A key example is the way in which the app bar located at the top of the screen should appear and the way in which it should behave in relation to scrolling activities taking place within the main content of the activity.

In fact, material design covers a wide range of areas from recommended color styles to the way in which objects are animated. A full description of the material design concepts and guidelines can be found online at the following link and is recommended reading for all Android developers:

https://www.google.com/design/spec/material-design/introduction.html

35.2 The Design Library

Many of the building blocks needed to implement Android applications that adopt the principles of material design are contained within the Android Design Support Library. This library contains a collection of user interface components that can be included in Android applications to implement much of the look, feel and behavior of material design. Two of the components from this library, the floating action button and Snackbar, will be covered in this chapter, while others will be introduced in later chapters.

35.3 The Floating Action Button (FAB)

The floating action button is a button which appears to float above the surface of the user interface of an app and is generally used to promote the most common action within a user interface screen. A floating action button might, for example, be placed on a screen to allow the user to add an entry to a list of contacts or to send an email from within the app. Figure 35-1, for example, highlights the floating action button that allows the user to add a new contact within the standard Android Contacts app:

Figure 35-1

To conform with the material design guidelines, there are a number of rules that should be followed when using floating action buttons. Floating action buttons must be circular and can be either 56 x 56dp (Default) or 40 x 40dp (Mini) in size. The button should be positioned a minimum of 16dp from the edge of the screen on phones and 24dp on desktops and tablet devices. Regardless of the size, the button must contain an interior icon that is 24x24dp in size and it is recommended that each user interface screen have only one floating action button.

Floating action buttons can be animated or designed to morph into other items when touched. A floating action button could, for example, rotate when tapped or morph into another element such as a toolbar or panel listing related actions.

35.4 The Snackbar

The Snackbar component provides a way to present the user with information in the form of a panel that appears at the bottom of the screen as shown in Figure 35-2. Snackbar instances contain a brief text message and an optional action button which will perform a task when tapped by the user. Once displayed, a Snackbar will either timeout automatically or can be removed manually by the user via a swiping action. During the appearance of the Snackbar the app will continue to function and respond to user interactions in the normal manner.

Figure 35-2

In the remainder of this chapter an example application will be created that makes use of the basic features of the floating action button and Snackbar to add entries to a list of items.

35.5 Creating the Example Project

Create a new project in Android Studio, entering *FabExample* into the Application name field and *ebookfrenzy. com* as the Company Domain setting before clicking on the *Next* button.

On the form factors screen, enable the *Phone and Tablet* option and set the minimum SDK setting to API 14: Android 4.0 (IceCreamSandwich).

Although it is possible to manually add a floating action button to an activity, it is much easier to use the Basic Activity template which includes a floating action button by default. Continue to proceed through the screens, therefore, requesting the creation of a Basic Activity named *FabExampleActivity* with corresponding layout and menu files named *activity_fab_example* and *menu_fab_example* respectively.

Click on the *Finish* button to initiate the project creation process.

35.6 Reviewing the Project

Since the Basic Activity template was selected, the activity contains two layout files. The *activity_fab_example. xml* file consists of a CoordinatorLayout manager containing entries for an app bar, a toolbar and a floating action button.

The *content_fab_example.xml* file represents the layout of the content area of the activity and contains a ConstraintLayout instance and a TextView. This file is embedded into the *activity_fab_example.xml* file via the following include directive:

```
<include layout="@layout/content_fab_example" />
```

The floating action button element within the *activity_fab_example.xml* file reads as follows:

```
<android.support.design.widget.FloatingActionButton
    android:id="@+id/fab"
    android:layout_width="wrap_content"
    android:layout_height="wrap_content"
    android:layout_gravity="bottom|end"
    android:layout_margin="@dimen/fab_margin"
    android:src="@android:drawable/ic_dialog_email" />
```

This declares that the button is to appear in the bottom right-hand corner of the screen with margins represented by the *fab_margin* identifier in the *values/dimens.xml* file (which in this case is set to 16dp). The XML further declares that the interior icon for the button is to take the form of the standard drawable built-in email icon.

The blank template has also configured the floating action button to display a Snackbar instance when tapped by the user. The code to implement this can be found in the *onCreate()* method of the *FabExampleActivity.java* file and reads as follows:

```
FloatingActionButton fab =
                (FloatingActionButton) findViewById(R.id.fab);

fab.setOnClickListener(new View.OnClickListener() {
    @Override
    public void onClick(View view) {
        Snackbar.make(view, "Replace with your own action",
                Snackbar.LENGTH_LONG)
                    .setAction("Action", null).show();
    }
```

```
});
```

The code obtains a reference to the floating action button via the button's ID and adds to it an onClickListener handler to be called when the button is tapped. This method simply displays a Snackbar instance configured with a message but no actions.

Finally, open the module level *build.gradle* file (*Gradle Scripts -> build.gradle (Module: App)*) and note that the Android design support library has been added as a dependency:

```
implementation 'com.android.support:design:26.1.0'
```

When the project is compiled and run the floating action button will appear at the bottom of the screen as shown in Figure 35-3:

Figure 35-3

Tapping the floating action button will trigger the onClickListener handler method causing the Snackbar to appear at the bottom of the screen:

Figure 35-4

When the Snackbar appears on a narrower device (as is the case in Figure 35-4 above) note that the floating action button is moved up to make room for the Snackbar to appear. This is handled for us automatically by the CoordinatorLayout container in the *activity_fab_example.xml* layout resource file.

35.7 Changing the Floating Action Button

Since the objective of this example is to configure the floating action button to add entries to a list, the email icon currently displayed on the button needs to be changed to something more indicative of the action being performed. The icon that will be used for the button is named *ic_add_entry.png* and can be found in the *project_icons* folder of the sample code download available from the following URL:

http://www.ebookfrenzy.com/print/androidstudio30/index.php

Locate this image in the file system navigator for your operating system and copy the image file. Right-click on the *app -> res -> drawable* entry in the Project tool window and select Paste from the menu to add the file to the folder:

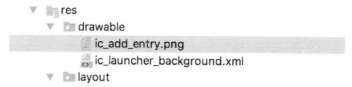

Figure 35-5

Next, edit the *activity_fab_example.xml* file and change the image source for the icon from *@android:drawable/ic_dialog_email* to *@drawable/ic_add_entry* as follows:

```
<android.support.design.widget.FloatingActionButton
    android:id="@+id/fab"
    android:layout_width="wrap_content"
    android:layout_height="wrap_content"
    android:layout_gravity="bottom|end"
    android:layout_margin="@dimen/fab_margin"
    android:src="@drawable/ic_add_entry" />
```

Within the layout preview, the interior icon for the button will have changed to a plus sign.

The background color of the floating action button is defined by the *accentColor* property of the prevailing theme used by the application. The color assigned to this value is declared in the *colors.xml* file located under *app -> res -> values* in the Project tool window. Instead of editing this XML file directly a better approach is to use the Android Studio Theme Editor.

Select the *Tools -> Android -> Theme Editor* menu option to display the Theme Editor as illustrated in Figure 35-6:

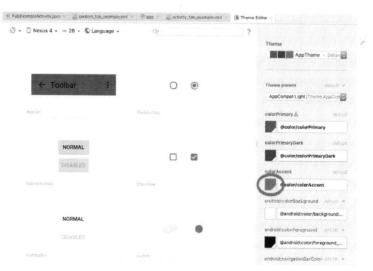

Figure 35-6

Click on the color swatch for the *colorAccent* setting (highlighted in the figure above) to display the color resource dialog. Within the color resource dialog, enter *holo_orange_light* into the search field and select the color from the list:

Figure 35-7

Click on the *OK* button to apply the new accentColor setting and return to the *activity_fab_example.xml* and verify that the floating action button now appears with an orange background.

35.8 Adding the ListView to the Content Layout

The next step in this tutorial is to add the ListView instance to the *content_fab_example.xml* file. The ListView class provides a way to display items in a list format and can be found in the *Containers* section of the Layout Editor tool palette.

Load the *content_fab_example.xml* file into the Layout Editor tool, select Design mode if necessary, and select and delete the default TextView object. Locate the ListView object in the Containers category of the palette and, with autoconnect mode enabled, drag and drop it onto the center of the layout canvas. Select the ListView object and change the ID to *listView* within the Attributes tool window. The Layout Editor should have sized the ListView to fill the entire container and established constraints on all four edges as illustrated in Figure 35-8:

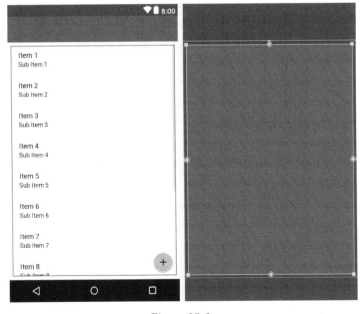

Figure 35-8

35.9 Adding Items to the ListView

Each time the floating action button is tapped by the user, a new item will be added to the ListView in the form of the prevailing time and date. To achieve this, some changes need to be made to the *FabExampleActivity.java* file.

Begin by modifying the *onCreate()* method to obtain a reference to the ListView instance and to initialize an adapter instance to allow us to add items to the list in the form of an array:

```java
import android.os.Bundle;
import android.support.design.widget.FloatingActionButton;
import android.support.design.widget.Snackbar;
import android.support.v7.app.AppCompatActivity;
import android.support.v7.widget.Toolbar;
import android.view.View;
import android.view.Menu;
import android.view.MenuItem;
import android.widget.ArrayAdapter;
import android.widget.ListView;

import java.util.ArrayList;

public class FabExampleActivity extends AppCompatActivity {

    ArrayList<String> listItems = new ArrayList<String>();
    ArrayAdapter<String> adapter;
    private ListView myListView;

    @Override
    protected void onCreate(Bundle savedInstanceState) {
        super.onCreate(savedInstanceState);
        setContentView(R.layout.activity_fab_example);
        Toolbar toolbar = (Toolbar) findViewById(R.id.toolbar);
        setSupportActionBar(toolbar);

        myListView = (ListView) findViewById(R.id.listView);

        adapter = new ArrayAdapter<String>(this,
                android.R.layout.simple_list_item_1,
                listItems);
        myListView.setAdapter(adapter);

        FloatingActionButton fab = (FloatingActionButton)
                        findViewById(R.id.fab);
        fab.setOnClickListener(new View.OnClickListener() {
            @Override
            public void onClick(View view) {
                Snackbar.make(view, "Replace with your own action",
```

```
                               Snackbar.LENGTH_LONG)
                                  .setAction("Action", null).show();

                  }
          });
     }

     .

     .

     .

}
```

The ListView needs an array of items to display, an adapter to manage the items in that array and a layout definition to dictate how items are to be presented to the user.

In the above code changes, the items are stored in an ArrayList instance assigned to an adapter that takes the form of an ArrayAdapter. The items added to the list will be displayed in the ListView using the *simple_list_item_1* layout, a built-in layout that is provided with Android to display simple string based items in a ListView instance.

Next, edit the onClickListener code for the floating action button to display a different message in the Snackbar and to call a method to add an item to the list:

```
FloatingActionButton fab = (FloatingActionButton)
                                 findViewById(R.id.fab);
fab.setOnClickListener(new View.OnClickListener() {
    @Override
    public void onClick(View view) {
        addListItem();
        Snackbar.make(view, "Item added to list",
             Snackbar.LENGTH_LONG)
                  .setAction("Action", null).show();

    }
});
```

Remaining within the *FabExampleActivity.java* file, add the *addListItem()* method as follows:

```
package com.ebookfrenzy.fabexample;

   .

   .

   .

import java.text.SimpleDateFormat;
import java.util.Date;
import java.util.Locale;

public class FabExampleActivity extends AppCompatActivity {

   .

   .

    private void addListItem() {

        SimpleDateFormat dateformat =
```

```
            new SimpleDateFormat("HH:mm:ss MM/dd/yyyy",
                    Locale.US);
        listItems.add(dateformat.format(new Date()));
        adapter.notifyDataSetChanged();
    }
    .
    .
    .
}
```

The code in the *addListItem()* method identifies and formats the current date and time and adds it to the list items array. The array adapter assigned to the ListView is then notified that the list data has changed, causing the ListView to update to display the latest list items.

Compile and run the app and test that tapping the floating action button adds new time and date entries to the ListView, displaying the Snackbar each time as shown in Figure 35-9:

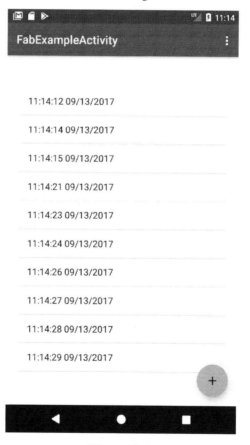

Figure 35-9

35.10 Adding an Action to the Snackbar

The final task in this project is to add an action to the Snackbar that allows the user to undo the most recent addition to the list. Edit the *FabExampleActivity.java* file and modify the Snackbar creation code to add an action titled "Undo" configured with an onClickListener named *undoOnClickListener*:

```
fab.setOnClickListener(new View.OnClickListener() {
```

```
    @Override
    public void onClick(View view) {
        addListItem();
        Snackbar.make(view, "Item added to list",
                Snackbar.LENGTH_LONG)
                    .setAction("Undo", undoOnClickListener).show();


    }
});
```

Within the *FabExampleActivity.java* file add the listener handler:

```
View.OnClickListener undoOnClickListener = new View.OnClickListener() {
    @Override
    public void onClick(View view) {
        listItems.remove(listItems.size() -1);
        adapter.notifyDataSetChanged();
        Snackbar.make(view, "Item removed", Snackbar.LENGTH_LONG)
                .setAction("Action", null).show();
    }
};
```

The code in the onClick method identifies the location of the last item in the list array and removes it from the list before triggering the list view to perform an update. A new Snackbar is then displayed indicating that the last item has been removed from the list.

Run the app once again and add some items to the list. On the final addition, tap the Undo button in the Snackbar (Figure 35-10) to remove the last item from the list:

Figure 35-10

It is also worth noting that the Undo button appears using the same color assigned to the accentColor property via the Theme Editor earlier in the chapter.

35.11 Summary

This chapter has provided a general overview of material design, the floating action button and Snackbar before working through an example project that makes use of these features

Both the floating action button and the Snackbar are part of the material design approach to user interface implementation in Android. The floating action button provides a way to promote the most common action within a particular screen of an Android application. The Snackbar provides a way for an application to both present information to the user and also allow the user to take action upon it.

36. Creating a Tabbed Interface using the TabLayout Component

The previous chapter outlined the concept of material design in Android and introduced two of the components provided by the design support library in the form of the floating action button and the Snackbar. This chapter will demonstrate how to use another of the design library components, the TabLayout, which can be combined with the ViewPager class to create a tab based interface within an Android activity.

36.1 An Introduction to the ViewPager

Although not part of the design support library, the ViewPager is a useful companion class when used in conjunction with the TabLayout component to implement a tabbed user interface. The primary role of the ViewPager is to allow the user to flip through different pages of information where each page is most typically represented by a layout fragment. The fragments that are associated with the ViewPager are managed by an instance of the FragmentPagerAdapter class.

At a minimum the pager adapter assigned to a ViewPager must implement two methods. The first, named *getCount()*, must return the total number of page fragments available to be displayed to the user. The second method, *getItem()*, is passed a page number and must return the corresponding fragment object ready to be presented to the user.

36.2 An Overview of the TabLayout Component

As previously discussed, TabLayout is one of the components introduced as part of material design and is included in the design support library. The purpose of the TabLayout is to present the user with a row of tabs which can be selected to display different pages to the user. The tabs can be fixed or scrollable, whereby the user can swipe left or right to view more tabs than will currently fit on the display. The information displayed on a tab can be text-based, an image or a combination of text and images. Figure 36-1, for example, shows the tab bar for the Android phone app consisting of three tabs displaying images:

Figure 36-1

Figure 36-2, on the other hand, shows a TabLayout configuration consisting of four tabs displaying text in a scrollable configuration:

Figure 36-2

The remainder of this chapter will work through the creation of an example project that demonstrates the use of the TabLayout component together with a ViewPager and four fragments.

36.3 Creating the TabLayoutDemo Project

Create a new project in Android Studio, entering *TabLayoutDemo* into the Application name field and *ebookfrenzy.com* as the Company Domain setting before clicking on the *Next* button.

On the form factors screen, enable the *Phone and Tablet* option and set the minimum SDK setting to API 14: Android 4.0 (IceCreamSandwich).

Continue through the configuration screens requesting the creation of a Basic Activity named *TabLayoutDemoActivity* with a corresponding layout file named *activity_tab_layout_demo*. Click on the *Finish* button to initiate the project creation process.

Once the project has been created, load the *content_tab_layout_demo.xml* file into the Layout Editor tool, select "Hello World" TextView object, and then delete it.

36.4 Creating the First Fragment

Each of the tabs on the TabLayout will display a different fragment when selected. Create the first of these fragments by right-clicking on the *app -> java -> com.ebookfrenzy.tablayoutdemo* entry in the Project tool window and selecting the *New -> Fragment -> Fragment (Blank)* option. In the resulting dialog, enter *Tab1Fragment* into the *Fragment Name:* field and *fragment_tab1* into the *Fragment Layout Name:* field. Enable the *Create layout XML?* option and disable both the *Include fragment factory methods?* and *Include interface callbacks?* options before clicking on the *Finish* button to create the new fragment:

Figure 36-3

Load the newly created *fragment_tab1.xml* file (located under *app -> res -> layout*) into the Layout Editor tool, right-click on the FrameLayout entry in the Component Tree panel and select the *Convert FrameLayout to ConstraintLayout* menu option. In the resulting dialog, verify that all conversion options are selected before clicking on OK.

Once the layout has been converted to a ConstraintLayout, delete the TextView from the layout. From the Palette, locate the TextView widget and drag and drop it so that it is positioned in the center of the layout. Edit the text property on the object so that it reads "Tab 1 Fragment" and extract the string to a resource named *tab_1_fragment*, at which point the layout should match that of Figure 36-4:

Figure 36-4

36.5 Duplicating the Fragments

So far, the project contains one of the four required fragments. Instead of creating the remaining three fragments using the previous steps it would be quicker to duplicate the first fragment. Each fragment consists of a layout XML file and a Java class file, each of which needs to be duplicated.

Right-click on the *fragment_tab1.xml* file in the Project tool window and select the Copy option from the resulting menu. Right-click on the *layout* entry, this time selecting the Paste option. In the resulting dialog, name the new layout file *fragment_tab2.xml* before clicking the *OK* button. Edit the new *fragment_tab2.xml* file and change the text on the Text View to "Tab 2 Fragment", following the usual steps to extract the string to a resource named *tab_2_fragment*.

To duplicate the Tab1Fragment class file, right-click on the class listed under *app -> java -> com.ebookfrenzy. tablayoutdemo* and select Copy. Right-click on the *com.ebookfrenzy.tablayoutdemo* entry and select Paste. In the Copy Class dialog, enter Tab2Fragment into the *New name:* field and click on OK. Edit the new *Tab2Fragment. java* file and change the *onCreateView()* method to inflate the *fragment_tab2* layout file:

```
@Override
public View onCreateView(LayoutInflater inflater, ViewGroup container,
                         Bundle savedInstanceState) {
    // Inflate the layout for this fragment
    return inflater.inflate(R.layout.fragment_tab2, container, false);
}
```

Perform the above duplication steps twice more to create the fragment layout and class files for the remaining two fragments. On completion of these steps the project structure should match that of Figure 36-5:

```
▼  java
   ▼  com.ebookfrenzy.tablayoutdemo
      ⓒ  Tab1Fragment
      ⓒ  Tab2Fragment
      ⓒ  Tab3Fragment
      ⓒ  Tab4Fragment
      ⓒ  TabLayoutDemoActivity
   ▶  com.ebookfrenzy.tablayoutdemo (androidTest)
   ▶  com.ebookfrenzy.tablayoutdemo (test)
▼  res
   ▶  drawable
   ▼  layout
      activity_tab_layout_demo.xml
      content_tab_layout_demo.xml
      fragment_tab1.xml
      fragment_tab2.xml
      fragment_tab3.xml
      fragment_tab4.xml
```

Figure 36-5

36.6 Adding the TabLayout and ViewPager

With the fragment creation process now complete, the next step is to add the TabLayout and ViewPager to the main activity layout file. Edit the *activity_tab_layout_demo.xml* file and add these elements as outlined in the following XML listing. Note that the TabLayout component is embedded into the AppBarLayout element while the ViewPager is placed after the AppBarLayout:

```xml
<?xml version="1.0" encoding="utf-8"?>
<android.support.design.widget.CoordinatorLayout
    xmlns:android="http://schemas.android.com/apk/res/android"
    xmlns:app="http://schemas.android.com/apk/res-auto"
    xmlns:tools="http://schemas.android.com/tools"
    android:layout_width="match_parent"
    android:layout_height="match_parent"
    android:fitsSystemWindows="true"
    tools:context=".TabLayoutDemoActivity">

    <android.support.design.widget.AppBarLayout
        android:layout_width="match_parent"
        android:layout_height="wrap_content"
        android:theme="@style/AppTheme.AppBarOverlay">

        <android.support.v7.widget.Toolbar
            android:id="@+id/toolbar"
            android:layout_width="match_parent"
            android:layout_height="?attr/actionBarSize"
            android:background="?attr/colorPrimary"
            app:popupTheme="@style/AppTheme.PopupOverlay" />

        <android.support.design.widget.TabLayout
            android:id="@+id/tab_layout"
```

```
        android:layout_width="match_parent"
        android:layout_height="wrap_content"
        app:tabMode="fixed"
        app:tabGravity="fill"/>

    </android.support.design.widget.AppBarLayout>

    <android.support.v4.view.ViewPager
        android:id="@+id/pager"
        android:layout_width="match_parent"
        android:layout_height="match_parent"
        app:layout_behavior="@string/appbar_scrolling_view_behavior"
    />

    <include layout="@layout/content_tab_layout_demo" />

    <android.support.design.widget.FloatingActionButton
        android:id="@+id/fab"
        android:layout_width="wrap_content"
        android:layout_height="wrap_content"
        android:layout_gravity="bottom|end"
        android:layout_margin="@dimen/fab_margin"
        android:src="@android:drawable/ic_dialog_email" />

</android.support.design.widget.CoordinatorLayout>
```

36.7 Creating the Pager Adapter

This example will use the ViewPager approach to handling the fragments assigned to the TabLayout tabs. With the ViewPager added to the layout resource file, a new class which subclasses FragmentPagerAdapter needs to be added to the project to manage the fragments that will be displayed when the tab items are selected by the user.

Add a new class to the project by right-clicking on the *com.ebookfrenzy.tablayoutdemo* entry in the Project tool window and selecting the *New -> Java Class* menu option. In the new class dialog, enter *TabPagerAdapter* into the *Name:* field and click *OK*.

Edit the *TabPagerAdapter.java* file so that it reads as follows:

```
package com.ebookfrenzy.tablayoutdemo;

import android.support.v4.app.Fragment;
import android.support.v4.app.FragmentManager;
import android.support.v4.app.FragmentPagerAdapter;

public class TabPagerAdapter extends FragmentPagerAdapter {

    int tabCount;

    public TabPagerAdapter(FragmentManager fm, int numberOfTabs) {
```

```java
            super(fm);
            this.tabCount = numberOfTabs;
    }


    @Override
    public Fragment getItem(int position) {

        switch (position) {
            case 0:
                return new Tab1Fragment();
            case 1:
                return new Tab2Fragment();
            case 2:
                return new Tab3Fragment();
            case 3:
                return new Tab4Fragment();
            default:
                return null;
        }
    }


    @Override
    public int getCount() {
        return tabCount;
    }
}
```

The class is declared as extending the FragmentPagerAdapter class and a constructor is implemented allowing the number of pages required to be passed to the class when an instance is created. The *getItem()* method will be called when a specific page is required. A switch statement is used to identify the page number being requested and to return a corresponding fragment instance. Finally, the *getCount()* method simply returns the count value passed through when the object instance was created.

36.8 Performing the Initialization Tasks

The remaining tasks involve initializing the TabLayout, ViewPager and TabPagerAdapter instances. All of these tasks will be performed in the *onCreate()* method of the *TabLayoutDemoActivity.java* file. Edit this file and modify the *onCreate()* method so that it reads as follows:

```java
package com.ebookfrenzy.tablayoutdemo;

import android.os.Bundle;
import android.support.design.widget.FloatingActionButton;
import android.support.design.widget.Snackbar;
import android.support.v7.app.AppCompatActivity;
import android.support.v7.widget.Toolbar;
import android.view.View;
import android.view.Menu;
import android.view.MenuItem;
```

```java
import android.support.design.widget.TabLayout;
import android.support.v4.view.PagerAdapter;
import android.support.v4.view.ViewPager;
.
.

    @Override
    protected void onCreate(Bundle savedInstanceState) {
        super.onCreate(savedInstanceState);
        setContentView(R.layout.activity_tab_layout_demo);
        Toolbar toolbar = (Toolbar) findViewById(R.id.toolbar);
        setSupportActionBar(toolbar);

        FloatingActionButton fab =
                FloatingActionButton) findViewById(R.id.fab);
        fab.setOnClickListener(new View.OnClickListener() {
            @Override
            public void onClick(View view) {
                Snackbar.make(view, "Replace with your own action",
                                Snackbar.LENGTH_LONG)
                        .setAction("Action", null).show();
            }
        });
        configureTabLayout();
    }

    private void configureTabLayout() {
            TabLayout tabLayout =
            (TabLayout) findViewById(R.id.tab_layout);

        tabLayout.addTab(tabLayout.newTab().setText("Tab 1 Item"));
        tabLayout.addTab(tabLayout.newTab().setText("Tab 2 Item"));
        tabLayout.addTab(tabLayout.newTab().setText("Tab 3 Item"));
        tabLayout.addTab(tabLayout.newTab().setText("Tab 4 Item"));

        final ViewPager viewPager =
                (ViewPager) findViewById(R.id.pager);
        final PagerAdapter adapter = new TabPagerAdapter
                (getSupportFragmentManager(),
                        tabLayout.getTabCount());
        viewPager.setAdapter(adapter);

        viewPager.addOnPageChangeListener(new
                TabLayout.TabLayoutOnPageChangeListener(tabLayout));
        tabLayout.addOnTabSelectedListener(new
                TabLayout.OnTabSelectedListener() {
```

```
        @Override
        public void onTabSelected(TabLayout.Tab tab) {
            viewPager.setCurrentItem(tab.getPosition());
        }

        @Override
        public void onTabUnselected(TabLayout.Tab tab) {


        }

        @Override
        public void onTabReselected(TabLayout.Tab tab) {


        }

    });
}

.

.

.

}
```

The code begins by obtaining a reference to the TabLayout object that was added to the *activity_tab_layout_ demo.xml* file and creating four tabs, assigning the text to appear on each:

```
tabLayout.addTab(tabLayout.newTab().setText("Tab 1 Item"));
tabLayout.addTab(tabLayout.newTab().setText("Tab 2 Item"));
tabLayout.addTab(tabLayout.newTab().setText("Tab 3 Item"));
tabLayout.addTab(tabLayout.newTab().setText("Tab 4 Item"));
```

A reference to the ViewPager instance in the layout file is then obtained and an instance of the TabPagerAdapter class created. Note that the code to create the TabPagerAdapter instance passes through the number of tabs that have been assigned to the TabLayout component. The TabPagerAdapter instance is then assigned as the adapter for the ViewPager and the TabLayout component added to the page change listener:

```
final ViewPager viewPager = (ViewPager) findViewById(R.id.pager);
final PagerAdapter adapter = new TabPagerAdapter
                (getSupportFragmentManager(),
                    tabLayout.getTabCount());
viewPager.setAdapter(adapter);

viewPager.addOnPageChangeListener(new
        TabLayout.TabLayoutOnPageChangeListener(tabLayout));
```

Finally, the onTabSelectedListener is configured on the TabLayout instance and the *onTabSelected()* method implemented to set the current page on the ViewPager based on the currently selected tab number. For the sake of completeness the other listener methods are added as stubs:

```
tabLayout.setOnTabSelectedListener(new
                TabLayout.OnTabSelectedListener()
```

```
{
        @Override
        public void onTabSelected(TabLayout.Tab tab) {
                viewPager.setCurrentItem(tab.getPosition());
        }

        @Override
        public void onTabUnselected(TabLayout.Tab tab) {

        }

        @Override
        public void onTabReselected(TabLayout.Tab tab) {

        }
});
```

36.9 Testing the Application

Compile and run the app on a device or emulator and make sure that selecting a tab causes the corresponding fragment to appear in the content area of the screen:

Figure 36-6

36.10 Customizing the TabLayout

The TabLayout in this example project is configured using *fixed* mode. This mode works well for a limited number of tabs with short titles. A greater number of tabs or longer titles can quickly become a problem when using fixed mode as illustrated by Figure 36-7:

Figure 36-7

In an effort to fit the tabs into the available display width the TabLayout has used multiple lines of text. Even so, the second line is clearly truncated making it impossible to see the full title. The best solution to this problem is to switch the TabLayout to *scrollable* mode. In this mode the titles appear in full length, single line format allowing the user to swipe to scroll horizontally through the available items as demonstrated in Figure 36-8:

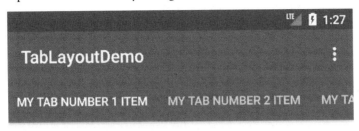

Figure 36-8

To switch a TabLayout to scrollable mode, simply change the *app:tabMode* property in the *activity_tab_layout_demo.xml* layout resource file from "fixed" to "scrollable":

```
<android.support.design.widget.TabLayout
    android:id="@+id/tab_layout"
    android:layout_width="match_parent"
    android:layout_height="wrap_content"
    app:tabMode="scrollable"
    app:tabGravity="fill"/>
</android.support.design.widget.AppBarLayout>
```

When in fixed mode, the TabLayout may be configured to control how the tab items are displayed to take up the available space on the screen. This is controlled via the *app:tabGravity* property, the results of which are more noticeable on wider displays such as tablets in landscape orientation. When set to "fill", for example, the items will be distributed evenly across the width of the TabLayout as shown in Figure 36-9:

Figure 36-9

Changing the property value to "center" will cause the items to be positioned relative to the center of the tab bar:

Figure 36-10

Before proceeding to the final step in this chapter, revert the tabMode and tabGravity attributes in the *activity_tab_layout_demo.xml* file to "fixed" and "fill" respectively.

36.11 Displaying Icon Tab Items

The last step in this tutorial is to replace the text based tabs with icons. To achieve this, modify the *onCreate()* method in the *TabLayoutDemoActivity.java* file to assign some built-in drawable icons to the tab items:

```
private void configureTabLayout() {

    TabLayout tabLayout = (TabLayout) findViewById(R.id.tab_layout);

    tabLayout.addTab(tabLayout.newTab().setIcon(
                    android.R.drawable.ic_dialog_email));
    tabLayout.addTab(tabLayout.newTab().setIcon(
                    android.R.drawable.ic_dialog_dialer));
    tabLayout.addTab(tabLayout.newTab().setIcon(
                    android.R.drawable.ic_dialog_map));
    tabLayout.addTab(tabLayout.newTab().setIcon(
                    android.R.drawable.ic_dialog_info));

    final ViewPager viewPager =
            (ViewPager) findViewById(R.id.pager);
.
.
.
}
```

Instead of using the *setText()* method of the tab item, the code is now calling the *setIcon()* method and passing through a drawable icon reference. When compiled and run, the tab bar should now appear as shown in Figure 36-11. Note if using Instant Run that it will be necessary to trigger a warm swap using Ctrl-Shift-R for the changes to take effect:

Figure 36-11

36.12 Summary

TabLayout is one of the components introduced as part of the Android material design implementation. The purpose of the TabLayout component is to present a series of tab items which, when selected, display different content to the user. The tab items can display text, images or a combination of both. When combined with the ViewPager class and fragments, tab layouts can be created with relative ease, with each tab item selection displaying a different fragment.

37. Working with the RecyclerView and CardView Widgets

The RecyclerView and CardView widgets work together to provide scrollable lists of information to the user in which the information is presented in the form of individual cards. Details of both classes will be covered in this chapter before working through the design and implementation of an example project.

37.1 An Overview of the RecyclerView

Much like the ListView class outlined in the chapter entitled *"Working with the Floating Action Button and Snackbar"*, the purpose of the RecyclerView is to allow information to be presented to the user in the form of a scrollable list. The RecyclerView, however, provides a number of advantages over the ListView. In particular, the RecyclerView is significantly more efficient in the way it manages the views that make up a list, essentially reusing existing views that make up list items as they scroll off the screen instead if creating new ones (hence the name "recycler"). This both increases the performance and reduces the resources used by a list, a feature that is of particular benefit when presenting large amounts of data to the user.

Unlike the ListView, the RecyclerView also provides a choice of three built-in layout managers to control the way in which the list items are presented to the user:

• **LinearLayoutManager** – The list items are presented as either a horizontal or vertical scrolling list.

Figure 37-1

• **GridLayoutManager** – The list items are presented in grid format. This manager is best used when the list items of are of uniform size.

Figure 37-2

- **StaggeredGridLayoutManager** - The list items are presented in a staggered grid format. This manager is best used when the list items are not of uniform size.

Figure 37-3

For situations where none of the three built-in managers provide the necessary layout, custom layout managers may be implemented by subclassing the RecyclerView.LayoutManager class.

Each list item displayed in a RecyclerView is created as an instance of the ViewHolder class. The ViewHolder instance contains everything necessary for the RecyclerView to display the list item, including the information to be displayed and the view layout used to display the item.

As with the ListView, the RecyclerView depends on an adapter to act as the intermediary between the RecyclerView instance and the data that is to be displayed to the user. The adapter is created as a subclass of the RecyclerView.Adapter class and must, at a minimum, implement the following methods, which will be called at various points by the RecyclerView object to which the adapter is assigned:

- **getItemCount()** – This method must return a count of the number of items that are to be displayed in the list.

- **onCreateViewHolder()** – This method creates and returns a ViewHolder object initialized with the view that is to be used to display the data. This view is typically created by inflating the XML layout file.

- **onBindViewHolder()** – This method is passed the ViewHolder object created by the *onCreateViewHolder()* method together with an integer value indicating the list item that is about to be displayed. Contained within the ViewHolder object is the layout assigned by the *onCreateViewHolder()* method. It is the responsibility of the *onBindViewHolder()* method to populate the views in the layout with the text and graphics corresponding to the specified item and to return the object to the RecyclerView where it will be presented to the user.

Adding a RecyclerView to a layout is simply a matter of adding the appropriate element to the XML layout file of the activity in which it is to appear. For example:

```
<?xml version="1.0" encoding="utf-8"?>
<android.support.design.widget.CoordinatorLayout
    xmlns:android="http://schemas.android.com/apk/res/android"
    xmlns:app="http://schemas.android.com/apk/res-auto"
    xmlns:tools="http://schemas.android.com/tools"
            android:layout_width="match_parent"
    android:layout_height="match_parent" android:fitsSystemWindows="true"
    tools:context=".CardStuffActivity">

    <android.support.v7.widget.RecyclerView
        android:id="@+id/recycler_view"
        android:layout_width="match_parent"
        android:layout_height="match_parent"
        app:layout_behavior="@string/appbar_scrolling_view_behavior"/>

    <android.support.design.widget.AppBarLayout
            android:layout_height="wrap_content"
        android:layout_width="match_parent"
            android:theme="@style/AppTheme.AppBarOverlay">

        <android.support.v7.widget.Toolbar android:id="@+id/toolbar"
            android:layout_width="match_parent"
              android:layout_height="?attr/actionBarSize"
            android:background="?attr/colorPrimary"
              app:popupTheme="@style/AppTheme.PopupOverlay" />

    </android.support.design.widget.AppBarLayout>
        .
        .
        .
}
```

In the above example the RecyclerView has been embedded into the CoordinatorLayout of a main activity layout file along with the AppBar and Toolbar. This provides some additional features, such as configuring the Toolbar and AppBar to scroll off the screen when the user scrolls up within the RecyclerView (a topic covered in more detail in the chapter entitled *"Working with the AppBar and Collapsing Toolbar Layouts"*).

37.2 An Overview of the CardView

The CardView class is a user interface view that allows information to be presented in groups using a card metaphor. Cards are usually presented in lists using a RecyclerView instance and may be configured to appear with shadow effects and rounded corners. Figure 37-4, for example, shows three CardView instances configured to display a layout consisting of an ImageView and two TextViews:

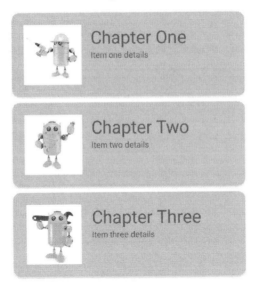

Figure 37-4

The user interface layout to be presented with a CardView instance is defined within an XML layout resource file and loaded into the CardView at runtime. The CardView layout can contain a layout of any complexity using the standard layout managers such as RelativeLayout and LinearLayout. The following XML layout file represents a card view layout consisting of a RelativeLayout and a single ImageView. The card is configured to be elevated to create shadowing effect and to appear with rounded corners:

```xml
<?xml version="1.0" encoding="utf-8"?>
    <android.support.v7.widget.CardView
        xmlns:card_view="http://schemas.android.com/apk/res-auto"
        xmlns:android="http://schemas.android.com/apk/res/android"
        android:id="@+id/card_view"
        android:layout_width="match_parent"
        android:layout_height="wrap_content"
        android:layout_margin="5dp"
        card_view:cardCornerRadius="12dp"
        card_view:cardElevation="3dp"
        card_view:contentPadding="4dp">

        <RelativeLayout
            android:layout_width="match_parent"
            android:layout_height="wrap_content"
            android:padding="16dp" >

            <ImageView
                android:layout_width="100dp"
                android:layout_height="100dp"
                android:id="@+id/item_image"
                android:layout_alignParentLeft="true"
                android:layout_alignParentTop="true"
```

```
        android:layout_marginRight="16dp" />
    </RelativeLayout>
</android.support.v7.widget.CardView>
```

When combined with the RecyclerView to create a scrollable list of cards, the *onCreateViewHolder()* method of the recycler view inflates the layout resource file for the card, assigns it to the ViewHolder instance and returns it to the RecyclerView instance.

37.3 Adding the Libraries to the Project

In order to use the RecyclerView and CardView components, the corresponding libraries must be added to the Gradle build dependencies for the project. Within the module level *build.gradle* file, therefore, the following lines need to be added to the *dependencies* section:

```
dependencies {
   .

   .

    implementation 'com.android.support:recyclerview-v7:26.1.0'
    implementation 'com.android.support:cardview-v7:26.1.0'
}
```

37.4 Summary

This chapter has introduced the Android RecyclerView and CardView components. The RecyclerView provides a resource efficient way to display scrollable lists of views within an Android app. The CardView is useful when presenting groups of data (such as a list of names and addresses) in the form of cards. As previously outlined, and demonstrated in the tutorial contained in the next chapter, the RecyclerView and CardView are particularly useful when combined.

38. An Android RecyclerView and CardView Tutorial

In this chapter an example project will be created that makes use of both the CardView and RecyclerView components to create a scrollable list of cards. The completed app will display a list of cards containing images and text. In addition to displaying the list of cards, the project will be implemented such that selecting a card causes a messages to be displayed to the user indicating which card was tapped.

38.1 Creating the CardDemo Project

Create a new project in Android Studio, entering *CardDemo* into the Application name field and *ebookfrenzy. com* as the Company Domain setting before clicking on the *Next* button.

On the form factors screen, enable the *Phone and Tablet* option and set the minimum SDK setting to API 14: Android 4.0 (IceCreamSandwich) and continue to proceed through the screens.

In the next chapter, the scroll handling features of the AppBar, Toolbar and CoordinatorLayout layout will be demonstrated using this project. On the activity selection screen, therefore, request the creation of a Basic Activity named *CardDemoActivity* with a corresponding layout file named *activity_card_demo*. Click on the *Finish* button to initiate the project creation process.

Once the project has been created, load the *content_card_demo.xml* file into the Layout Editor tool and select and delete the "Hello World" TextView object.

38.2 Removing the Floating Action Button

Since the Basic Activity was selected, the layout includes a floating action button which is not required for this project. Load the *activity_card_demo.xml* layout file into the Layout Editor tool, select the floating action button and tap the keyboard delete key to remove the object from the layout. Edit the *CardDemoActivity.java* file and remove the floating action button code from the onCreate method as follows:

```
@Override
protected void onCreate(Bundle savedInstanceState) {
    super.onCreate(savedInstanceState);
    setContentView(R.layout.activity_card_demo);
    Toolbar toolbar = (Toolbar) findViewById(R.id.toolbar);
    setSupportActionBar(toolbar);

    FloatingActionButton fab =
        (FloatingActionButton) findViewById(R.id.fab);
    fab.setOnClickListener(new View.OnClickListener() {
        @Override
        public void onClick(View view) {
            Snackbar.make(view, "Replace with your own action",
                Snackbar.LENGTH_LONG)
```

```
                                  .setAction("Action", null).show();
                    }
                });
}
```

38.3 Adding the RecyclerView and CardView Libraries

Within the Project tool window locate and select the module level *build.gradle* file and modify the dependencies section of the file to add the support library dependencies for the RecyclerView and CardView:

```
dependencies {
    implementation fileTree(dir: 'libs', include: ['*.jar'])
    implementation 'com.android.support:appcompat-v7:26.1.0'
    implementation 'com.android.support.constraint:constraint-layout:1.0.2'
    implementation 'com.android.support:design:26.1.0'
    implementation 'com.android.support:recyclerview-v7:26.1.0'
    implementation 'com.android.support:cardview-v7:26.1.0'
  .
  .
  .
}
```

When prompted to do so, resync the new Gradle build configuration by clicking on the *Sync Now* link in the warning bar.

38.4 Designing the CardView Layout

The layout of the views contained within the cards will be defined within a separate XML layout file. Within the Project tool window right click on the *app -> res -> layout* entry and select the *New -> Layout resource file* menu option. In the New Resource Dialog enter *card_layout* into the *File name:* field and *android.support.v7.widget.CardView* into the root element field before clicking on the *OK* button.

Load the *card_layout.xml* file into the Layout Editor tool, switch to Text mode and modify the layout so that it reads as follows:

```
<?xml version="1.0" encoding="utf-8"?>
<android.support.v7.widget.CardView
    xmlns:android="http://schemas.android.com/apk/res/android"
    xmlns:card_view="http://schemas.android.com/apk/res-auto"
    android:layout_width="match_parent"
    android:layout_height="wrap_content"
    android:id="@+id/card_view"
    android:layout_margin="5dp"
    card_view:cardBackgroundColor="#81C784"
    card_view:cardCornerRadius="12dp"
    card_view:cardElevation="3dp"
    card_view:contentPadding="4dp" >

    <RelativeLayout
        android:layout_width="match_parent"
        android:layout_height="wrap_content"
        android:padding="16dp" >
```

```xml
    <ImageView
        android:layout_width="100dp"
        android:layout_height="100dp"
        android:id="@+id/item_image"
        android:layout_alignParentStart="true"
        android:layout_alignParentLeft="true"
        android:layout_alignParentTop="true"
        android:layout_marginEnd="16dp"
        android:layout_marginRight="16dp" />

    <TextView
        android:layout_width="wrap_content"
        android:layout_height="wrap_content"
        android:id="@+id/item_title"
        android:layout_toEndOf="@+id/item_image"
        android:layout_toRightOf="@+id/item_image"
        android:layout_alignParentTop="true"
        android:textSize="30sp" />

    <TextView
        android:layout_width="wrap_content"
        android:layout_height="wrap_content"
        android:id="@+id/item_detail"
        android:layout_toEndOf="@+id/item_image"
        android:layout_toRightOf="@+id/item_image"
        android:layout_below="@+id/item_title" />

</RelativeLayout>
</android.support.v7.widget.CardView>
```

38.5 Adding the RecyclerView

Select the *activity_card_demo.xml* layout file and modify it to add the RecyclerView component immediately before the AppBarLayout:

```xml
<?xml version="1.0" encoding="utf-8"?>
<android.support.design.widget.CoordinatorLayout
    xmlns:android="http://schemas.android.com/apk/res/android"
    xmlns:app="http://schemas.android.com/apk/res-auto"
    xmlns:tools="http://schemas.android.com/tools"
    android:layout_width="match_parent"
    android:layout_height="match_parent"
    android:fitsSystemWindows="true"
    tools:contextcom.ebookfrenzy.carddemo.CardDemoActivity">

    <android.support.v7.widget.RecyclerView
        android:id="@+id/recycler_view"
```

```
        android:layout_width="match_parent"
        android:layout_height="match_parent"
    app:layout_behavior="@string/appbar_scrolling_view_behavior" />


    <android.support.design.widget.AppBarLayout
        android:layout_height="wrap_content"
        android:layout_width="match_parent"
        android:theme="@style/AppTheme.AppBarOverlay">
```
.
.
.

38.6 Creating the RecyclerView Adapter

As outlined in the previous chapter, the RecyclerView needs to have an adapter to handle the creation of the list items. Add this new class to the project by right-clicking on the *app -> java -> com.ebookfrenzy.carddemo* entry in the Project tool window and selecting the *New -> Java Class* menu option. In the Create New Class dialog, enter *RecyclerAdapter* into the *Name:* field before clicking on the *OK* button to create the new Java class file.

Edit the new *RecyclerAdapter.java* file to add some import directives and to declare that the class now extends RecyclerView.Adapter. Rather than create a separate class to provide the data to be displayed, some basic arrays will also be added to the adapter to act as the data for the app:

```
package com.ebookfrenzy.carddemo;


import android.support.v7.widget.RecyclerView;
import android.view.LayoutInflater;
import android.view.View;
import android.view.ViewGroup;
import android.widget.ImageView;
import android.widget.TextView;


public class RecyclerAdapter extends RecyclerView.Adapter<RecyclerAdapter.
ViewHolder> {

    private String[] titles = {"Chapter One",
            "Chapter Two",
            "Chapter Three",
            "Chapter Four",
            "Chapter Five",
            "Chapter Six",
            "Chapter Seven",
            "Chapter Eight"};

    private String[] details = {"Item one details",
            "Item two details", "Item three details",
            "Item four details", "Item file details",
            "Item six details", "Item seven details",
            "Item eight details"};
```

```
        private int[] images = { R.drawable.android_image_1,
                                 R.drawable.android_image_2,
                                 R.drawable.android_image_3,
                                 R.drawable.android_image_4,
                                 R.drawable.android_image_5,
                                 R.drawable.android_image_6,
                                 R.drawable.android_image_7,
                                 R.drawable.android_image_8 };
}
```

Within the RecyclerAdapter class we now need our own implementation of the ViewHolder class configured to reference the view elements in the *card_layout.xml* file. Remaining within the *RecyclerAdapter.java* file implement this class as follows:

```
    .
    .
public class RecyclerAdapter extends RecyclerView.Adapter<RecyclerAdapter.
ViewHolder> {
    .
    .

    class ViewHolder extends RecyclerView.ViewHolder {

        public ImageView itemImage;
        public TextView itemTitle;
        public TextView itemDetail;

        public ViewHolder(View itemView) {
            super(itemView);
            itemImage =
                (ImageView)itemView.findViewById(R.id.item_image);
            itemTitle =
                (TextView)itemView.findViewById(R.id.item_title);
            itemDetail =
                (TextView)itemView.findViewById(R.id.item_detail);
        }
    }
    .
    .
}
```

The ViewHolder class contains an ImageView and two TextView variables together with a constructor method that initializes those variables with references to the three view items in the *card_layout.xml* file.

The next item to be added to the *RecyclerAdapter.java* file is the implementation of the *onCreateViewHolder()* method:

```
@Override
public ViewHolder onCreateViewHolder(ViewGroup viewGroup, int i) {
```

```
View v = LayoutInflater.from(viewGroup.getContext())
            .inflate(R.layout.card_layout, viewGroup, false);
ViewHolder viewHolder = new ViewHolder(v);
return viewHolder;
}
```

This method will be called by the RecyclerView to obtain a ViewHolder object. It inflates the view hierarchy *card_layout.xml* file and creates an instance of our ViewHolder class initialized with the view hierarchy before returning it to the RecyclerView.

The purpose of the *onBindViewHolder()* method is to populate the view hierarchy within the ViewHolder object with the data to be displayed. It is passed the ViewHolder object and an integer value indicating the list item that is to be displayed. This method should now be added, using the item number as an index into the data arrays. This data is then displayed on the layout views using the references created in the constructor method of the ViewHolder class:

```
@Override
public void onBindViewHolder(ViewHolder viewHolder, int i) {
    viewHolder.itemTitle.setText(titles[i]);
    viewHolder.itemDetail.setText(details[i]);
    viewHolder.itemImage.setImageResource(images[i]);
}
```

The final requirement for the adapter class is an implementation of the *getItem()* method which, in this case, simply returns the number of items in the *titles* array:

```
@Override
public int getItemCount() {
    return titles.length;
}
```

38.7 Adding the Image Files

In addition to the two TextViews, the card layout also contains an ImageView on which the Recycler adapter has been configured to display images. Before the project can be tested these images must be added. The images that will be used for the project are named *android_image_<n>.jpg* and can be found in the *project_icons* folder of the sample code download available from the following URL:

http://www.ebookfrenzy.com/print/androidstudio30/index.php

Locate these images in the file system navigator for your operating system and select and copy the eight images. Right click on the *app -> res -> drawable* entry in the Project tool window and select Paste to add the files to the folder:

Figure 38-1

38.8 Initializing the RecyclerView Component

At this point the project consists of a RecyclerView instance, an XML layout file for the CardView instances and an adapter for the RecyclerView. The last step before testing the progress so far is to initialize the RecyclerView with a layout manager, create an instance of the adapter and assign that instance to the RecyclerView object. For the purposes of this example, the RecyclerView will be configured to use the LinearLayoutManager layout option. Edit the *CardDemoActivity.java* file and modify the *onCreate()* method to implement this initialization code:

```
package com.ebookfrenzy.carddemo;

import android.os.Bundle;
import android.support.v7.app.AppCompatActivity;
import android.support.v7.widget.Toolbar;
import android.view.Menu;
import android.view.MenuItem;
import android.support.v7.widget.LinearLayoutManager;
import android.support.v7.widget.RecyclerView;

public class CardDemoActivity extends AppCompatActivity {

    RecyclerView recyclerView;
    RecyclerView.LayoutManager layoutManager;
    RecyclerView.Adapter adapter;

    @Override
    protected void onCreate(Bundle savedInstanceState) {
        super.onCreate(savedInstanceState);
        setContentView(R.layout.activity_card_demo);
        Toolbar toolbar = (Toolbar) findViewById(R.id.toolbar);
        setSupportActionBar(toolbar);

        recyclerView =
                (RecyclerView) findViewById(R.id.recycler_view);

        layoutManager = new LinearLayoutManager(this);
```

```
        recyclerView.setLayoutManager(layoutManager);

        adapter = new RecyclerAdapter();
        recyclerView.setAdapter(adapter);
    }
    .
    .
    .
}
```

38.9 Testing the Application

Compile and run the app on a physical device or emulator session and scroll through the different card items in the list:

Figure 38-2

38.10 Responding to Card Selections

The last phase of this project is to make the cards in the list selectable so that clicking on a card triggers an event within the app. For this example, the cards will be configured to present a message on the display when tapped by the user. To respond to clicks, the ViewHolder class needs to be modified to assign an onClickListener on each item view. Edit the *RecyclerAdapter.java* file and modify the ViewHolder class declaration so that it reads as follows:

```
import android.support.design.widget.Snackbar;
.
.
.
class ViewHolder extends RecyclerView.ViewHolder{
```

```
public ImageView itemImage;
public TextView itemTitle;
public TextView itemDetail;

public ViewHolder(View itemView) {
    super(itemView);
    itemImage = (ImageView)itemView.findViewById(R.id.item_image);
    itemTitle = (TextView)itemView.findViewById(R.id.item_title);
    itemDetail =
            (TextView)itemView.findViewById(R.id.item_detail);

    itemView.setOnClickListener(new View.OnClickListener() {
        @Override public void onClick(View v) {


        }
    });
    }
}
```

Within the body of the onClick handler, code can now be added to display a message indicating that the card has been clicked. Given that the actions performed as a result of a click will likely depend on which card was tapped it is also important to identify the selected card. This information can be obtained via a call to the *getAdapterPosition()* method of the *RecyclerView.ViewHolder* class. Remaining within the *RecyclerAdapter.java* file, add code to the *onClick* handler so it reads as follows:

```
@override
public void onClick(View v) {

    int position = getAdapterPosition();

    Snackbar.make(v, "Click detected on item " + position,
            Snackbar.LENGTH_LONG)
            .setAction("Action", null).show();
    }
});
```

The last task is to enable the material design ripple effect that appears when items are tapped within Android applications. This simply involves the addition of some properties to the declaration of the CardView instance in the *card_layout.xml* file as follows:

```
<?xml version="1.0" encoding="utf-8"?>
<android.support.v7.widget.CardView
    xmlns:android="http://schemas.android.com/apk/res/android"
    xmlns:card_view="http://schemas.android.com/apk/res-auto"
    android:layout_width="match_parent"
    android:layout_height="match_parent"
    android:id="@+id/card_view"
    android:layout_margin="5dp"
    card_view:cardBackgroundColor="#81C784"
```

```
card_view:cardCornerRadius="12dp"
card_view:cardElevation="3dp"
card_view:contentPadding="4dp"
android:foreground="?selectableItemBackground"
android:clickable="true" >
```

Run the app once again and verify that tapping a card in the list triggers both the standard ripple effect at the point of contact and the appearance of a Snackbar reporting the number of the selected item.

38.11 Summary

This chapter has worked through the steps involved in combining the CardView and RecyclerView components to display a scrollable list of card based items. The example also covered the detection of clicks on list items, including the identification of the selected item and the enabling of the ripple effect visual feedback on the tapped CardView instance.

39. Working with the AppBar and Collapsing Toolbar Layouts

In this chapter we will be exploring the ways in which the app bar within an activity layout can be customized and made to react to the scrolling events taking place within other views on the screen. By making use of the CoordinatorLayout in conjunction with the AppBarLayout and CollapsingToolbarLayout containers, the app bar can be configured to display an image and to animate in and out of view. An upward scrolling motion on a list, for example, can be configured so that the app bar recedes from view and then reappears when a downward scrolling motion is performed.

Beginning with an overview of the elements that can comprise an app bar, this chapter will then work through a variety of examples of app bar configuration.

39.1 The Anatomy of an AppBar

The app bar is the area that appears at the top of the display when an app is running and can be configured to contain a variety of different items including the status bar, toolbar, tab bar and a flexible space area. Figure 39-1, for example, shows an app bar containing a status bar, toolbar and tab bar:

Figure 39-1

The flexible space area can be filled by a blank background color, or as shown in Figure 39-2, an image displayed on an ImageView object:

Figure 39-2

As will be demonstrated in the remainder of this chapter, if the main content area of the activity user interface layout contains scrollable content, the elements of the app bar can be configured to expand and contract as the content on the screen is scrolled.

39.2 The Example Project

For the purposes of this example, changes will be made to the CardDemo project created in the previous chapter entitled *"An Android RecyclerView and CardView Tutorial"*. Begin by launching Android Studio and loading this project.

Once the project has loaded, run the app and note when scrolling the list upwards that the toolbar remains visible as shown in Figure 39-3:

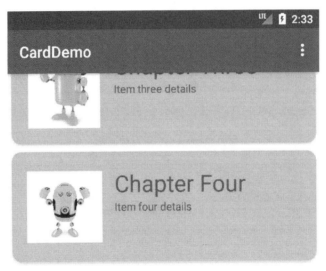

Figure 39-3

The first step is to make some configuration changes so that the toolbar contracts during an upward scrolling motion, and then expands on a downward scroll.

39.3 Coordinating the RecyclerView and Toolbar

Load the *activity_card_demo.xml* file into the Layout Editor tool, switch to text mode and review the XML layout design, the hierarchy of which is represented by the diagram in Figure 39-4:

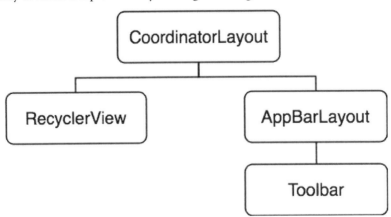

Figure 39-4

At the top level of the hierarchy is the CoordinatorLayout which, as the name suggests, coordinates the interactions between the various child view elements it contains. As highlighted in *"Working with the Floating*

Action Button and Snackbar" for example, the CoordinatorLayout automatically slides the floating action button upwards to accommodate the appearance of a Snackbar when it appears, then moves the button back down after the bar is dismissed.

The CoordinatorLayout can similarly be used to cause elements of the app bar to slide in and out of view based on the scrolling action of certain views within the view hierarchy. One such element within the layout hierarchy shown in Figure 39-4 is the RecyclerView. To achieve this coordinated behavior, it is necessary to set properties on both the element on which scrolling takes place and the elements with which the scrolling is to be coordinated.

On the scrolling element (in this case the RecyclerView) the *android:layout_behavior* property must be set to *appbar_scrolling_view_behavior*. Within the *activity_card_demo.xml* file, locate the RecyclerView element and note that this property was already set in the previous chapter:

```
<android.support.v7.widget.RecyclerView
    android:id="@+id/recycler_view"
    android:layout_width="match_parent"
    android:layout_height="match_parent"
    app:layout_behavior="@string/appbar_scrolling_view_behavior" />
```

The only child of AppBarLayout in the view hierarchy is the Toolbar. To make the toolbar react to the scroll events taking place in the RecyclerView the *app:layout_scrollFlags* property must be set on this element. The value assigned to this property will depend on the nature of the interaction required and must consist of one or more of the following:

- **scroll** – Indicates that the view is to be scrolled off the screen. If this is not set the view will remain pinned at the top of the screen during scrolling events.

- **enterAlways** – When used in conjunction with the scroll option, an upward scrolling motion will cause the view to retract. Any downward scrolling motion in this mode will cause the view to re-appear.

- **enterAlwaysCollapsed** – When set on a view, that view will not expand from the collapsed state until the downward scrolling motion reaches the limit of the list. If the minHeight property is set, the view will appear during the initial scrolling motion but only until the minimum height is reached. It will then remain at that height and will not expand fully until the top of the list is reached. Note this option only works when used in conjunction with both the enterAlways and scroll options. For example:

```
app:layout_scrollFlags="scroll|enterAlways|enterAlwaysCollapsed"
android:minHeight="20dp"
```

- **exitUntilCollapsed** – When set, the view will collapse during an upward scrolling motion until the minHeight threshold is met, at which point it will remain at that height until the scroll direction changes.

For the purposes of this example, the *scroll* and *enterAlways* options will be set on the Toolbar as follows:

```
<android.support.v7.widget.Toolbar
    android:id="@+id/toolbar"
    android:layout_width="match_parent"
    android:layout_height="?attr/actionBarSize"
    android:background="?attr/colorPrimary"
    app:popupTheme="@style/AppTheme.PopupOverlay"
    app:layout_scrollFlags="scroll|enterAlways" />
```

With the appropriate properties set, run the app once again and make an upward scrolling motion in the RecyclerView list. This should cause the toolbar to collapse out of view (Figure 39-5). A downward scrolling motion should cause the toolbar to re-appear.

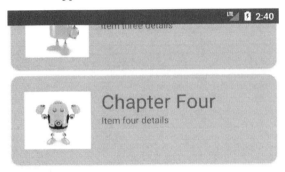

Figure 39-5

39.4 Introducing the Collapsing Toolbar Layout

The CollapsingToolbarLayout container enhances the standard toolbar by providing a greater range of options and level of control over the collapsing of the app bar and its children in response to coordinated scrolling actions. The CollapsingToolbarLayout class is intended to be added as a child of the AppBarLayout and provides features such as automatically adjusting the font size of the toolbar title as the toolbar collapses and expands. A *parallax* mode allows designated content in the app bar to fade from view as it collapses while a *pin* mode allows elements of the app bar to remain in fixed position during the contraction.

A *scrim* option is also available to designate the color to which the toolbar should transition during the collapse sequence.

To see these features in action, the app bar contained in the *activity_card_demo.xml* file will be modified to use the CollapsingToolbarLayout class together with the addition of an ImageView to better demonstrate the effect of parallax mode. The new view hierarchy that makes use of the CollapsingToolbarLayout is represented by the diagram in Figure 39-6:

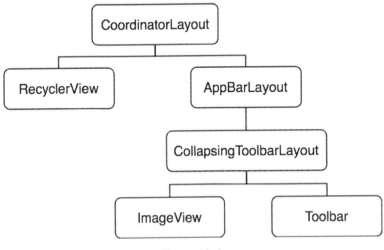

Figure 39-6

Load the *activity_card_demo.xml* file into the Layout Editor tool in Text mode and modify the layout so that it reads as follows:

```
<?xml version="1.0" encoding="utf-8"?>
```

```xml
<android.support.design.widget.CoordinatorLayout
    xmlns:android="http://schemas.android.com/apk/res/android"
    xmlns:app="http://schemas.android.com/apk/res-auto"
    xmlns:tools="http://schemas.android.com/tools"
    android:layout_width="match_parent"
    android:layout_height="match_parent"
    android:fitsSystemWindows="true"
    tools:context=".CardDemoActivity">

    <android.support.v7.widget.RecyclerView
        android:id="@+id/recycler_view"
        android:layout_width="match_parent"
        android:layout_height="match_parent"
        app:layout_behavior="@string/appbar_scrolling_view_behavior"/>

    <android.support.design.widget.AppBarLayout
        android:layout_height="200dp"
        android:layout_width="match_parent"
        android:theme="@style/AppTheme.AppBarOverlay">

        <android.support.design.widget.CollapsingToolbarLayout
            android:id="@+id/collapsing_toolbar"
            android:layout_width="match_parent"
            android:layout_height="match_parent"
            app:layout_scrollFlags="scroll|enterAlways"
            android:fitsSystemWindows="true"
            app:contentScrim="?attr/colorPrimary"
            app:expandedTitleMarginStart="48dp"
            app:expandedTitleMarginEnd="64dp">

            <ImageView
                android:id="@+id/backdrop"
                android:layout_width="match_parent"
                android:layout_height="200dp"
                android:scaleType="centerCrop"
                android:fitsSystemWindows="true"
                app:layout_collapseMode="parallax"
                android:src="@drawable/appbar_image" />

        <android.support.v7.widget.Toolbar
            android:id="@+id/toolbar"
            android:layout_width="match_parent"
            android:layout_height="?attr/actionBarSize"
            android:background="?attr/colorPrimary"
            app:popupTheme="@style/AppTheme.PopupOverlay"
```

```
                app:layout_scrollFlags="scroll|enterAlways"
                app:layout_collapseMode="pin" />


        </android.support.design.widget.CollapsingToolbarLayout>
    </android.support.design.widget.AppBarLayout>

    <include layout="@layout/content_card_demo" />

</android.support.design.widget.CoordinatorLayout>
```

In addition to adding the new elements to the layout above, the background color property setting has been removed. This change has the advantage of providing a transparent toolbar allowing more of the image to be visible in the app bar.

Using the file system navigator for your operating system, locate the *appbar_image.jpg* image file in the *project_icons* folder of the code sample download for the book and copy it. Right-click on the *app -> res -> drawable* entry in the Project tool window and select *Paste* from the resulting menu.

When run, the app bar should appear as illustrated in Figure 39-7:

Figure 39-7

Scrolling the list upwards will cause the app bar to gradually collapse. During the contraction, the image will fade to the color defined by the scrim property while the title text font size reduces at a corresponding rate until only the toolbar is visible:

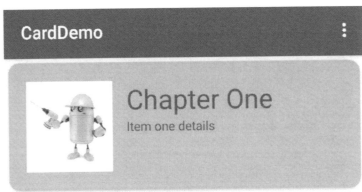

Figure 39-8

The toolbar has remained visible during the initial stages of the scrolling motion (the toolbar will also recede from view if the upward scrolling motion continues) as the flexible area collapses because the toolbar element in the *activity_card_demo.xml* file was configured to use pin mode:

```
app:layout_collapseMode="pin"
```

Had the collapse mode been set to parallax the toolbar would have retracted along with the image view.

Continuing the upward scrolling motion will cause the toolbar to also collapse leaving only the status bar visible:

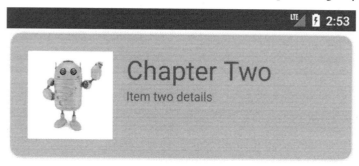

Figure 39-9

Since the scroll flags property for the CollapsingToolbarLayout element includes the enterAlways option, a downward scrolling motion will cause the app bar to expand once again.

To fix the toolbar in place so that it no longer recedes from view during the upward scrolling motion, replace *enterAlways* with *exitUntilCollapsed* in the *layout_scrollFlags* property of the CollapsingToolbarLayout element in the *activity_card_demo.xml* file as follows:

```
<android.support.design.widget.CollapsingToolbarLayout
    android:id="@+id/collapsing_toolbar"
    android:layout_width="match_parent"
    android:layout_height="match_parent"
    app:layout_scrollFlags="scroll|exitUntilCollapsed"
    android:fitsSystemWindows="true"
    app:contentScrim="?attr/colorPrimary"
    app:expandedTitleMarginStart="48dp"
    app:expandedTitleMarginEnd="64dp">
```

39.5 Changing the Title and Scrim Color

As a final task, edit the *CardDemoActivity.java* file and add some code to the *onCreate()* method to change the title text on the collapsing layout manager instance and to set a different scrim color (note that the scrim color may also be set within the layout resource file):

```
package com.ebookfrenzy.carddemo;

import android.graphics.Color;
import android.os.Bundle;
import android.support.v7.widget.LinearLayoutManager;
import android.support.v7.app.AppCompatActivity;
import android.support.v7.widget.RecyclerView;
import android.support.v7.widget.Toolbar;
import android.view.Menu;
```

```
import android.view.MenuItem;
import android.support.design.widget.CollapsingToolbarLayout;
import android.graphics.Color;

    .
    .
    .

    @Override
    protected void onCreate(Bundle savedInstanceState) {
        super.onCreate(savedInstanceState);
        setContentView(R.layout.activity_card_demo);
        Toolbar toolbar = (Toolbar) findViewById(R.id.toolbar);
        setSupportActionBar(toolbar);

        CollapsingToolbarLayout collapsingToolbarLayout =
    (CollapsingToolbarLayout) findViewById(R.id.collapsing_toolbar);

        collapsingToolbarLayout.setTitle("My Toolbar Title");
        collapsingToolbarLayout.setContentScrimColor(Color.GREEN);

        recyclerView =
            (RecyclerView) findViewById(R.id.recycler_view);

        layoutManager = new LinearLayoutManager(this);
        recyclerView.setLayoutManager(layoutManager);

        adapter = new RecyclerAdapter();
        recyclerView.setAdapter(adapter);
    }
```

Run the app one last time and note that the new title appears in the app bar and that scrolling now causes the toolbar to transition to green as it retracts from view.

39.6 Summary

The app bar that appears at the top of most Android apps can consist of a number of different elements including a toolbar, tab layout and even an image view. When embedded in a CoordinatorLayout parent, a number of different options are available to control the way in which the app bar behaves in response to scrolling events in the main content of the activity. For greater control over this behavior, the CollapsingToolbarLayout manager provides a range of additional levels of control over the way the app bar content expands and contracts in relation to scrolling activity.

40. Implementing an Android Navigation Drawer

In this, the final of this series of chapters dedicated to the Android material design components, the topic of the navigation drawer will be covered. Comprising the DrawerLayout, NavigationView and ActionBarDrawerToggle classes, a navigation drawer takes the form of a panel appearing from the left-hand edge of screen when selected by the user and containing a range of options and sub-options which can be selected to perform tasks within the application.

40.1 An Overview of the Navigation Drawer

The navigation drawer is a panel that slides out from the left of the screen and contains a range of options available for selection by the user, typically intended to facilitate navigation to some other part of the application. Figure 40-1, for example, shows the navigation drawer built into the Google Play app:

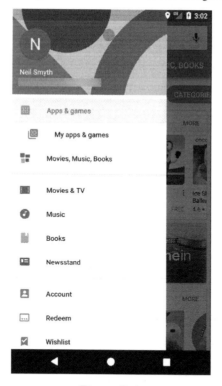

Figure 40-1

A navigation drawer is made up of the following components:

• An instance of the DrawerLayout component.

• An instance of the NavigationView component embedded as a child of the DrawerLayout.

- A menu resource file containing the options to be displayed within the navigation drawer.

- An optional layout resource file containing the content to appear in the header section of the navigation drawer.

- A listener assigned to the NavigationView to detect when an item has been selected by the user.

- An ActionBarDrawerToggle instance to connect and synchronize the navigation drawer to the app bar. The ActionBarDrawerToggle also displays the drawer indicator in the app bar which presents the drawer when tapped.

The following XML listing shows an example navigation drawer implementation which also contains an include directive for a second layout file containing the standard app bar layout.

```xml
<?xml version="1.0" encoding="utf-8"?>
<android.support.v4.widget.DrawerLayout xmlns:android="http://schemas.android.
com/apk/res/android"
    xmlns:app="http://schemas.android.com/apk/res-auto"
    xmlns:tools="http://schemas.android.com/tools"
    android:id="@+id/drawer_layout"
    android:layout_width="match_parent"
    android:layout_height="match_parent"
    android:fitsSystemWindows="true"
    tools:openDrawer="start">

    <include
        layout="@layout/app_bar_main"
        android:layout_width="match_parent"
        android:layout_height="match_parent" />

    <android.support.design.widget.NavigationView
        android:id="@+id/nav_view"
        android:layout_width="wrap_content"
        android:layout_height="match_parent"
        android:layout_gravity="start"
        android:fitsSystemWindows="true"
        app:headerLayout="@layout/nav_header_main"
        app:menu="@menu/activity_main_drawer" />

</android.support.v4.widget.DrawerLayout>
```

40.2 Opening and Closing the Drawer

When the user taps the drawer indicator in the app bar, the drawer will automatically appear. Whether the drawer is currently open may be identified via a call to the *isDrawerOpen()* method of the DrawerLayout object passing through a gravity setting:

```
if (drawer.isDrawerOpen(GravityCompat.START)) {
    // Drawer is open
}
```

The GravityCompat.START setting indicates a drawer open along the x-axis of the layout. An open drawer may be closed via a call to the *closeDrawer()* method:

```
drawer.closeDrawer(GravityCompat.START);
```

Conversely, the drawer may be opened using the *openDrawer()* method:

```
drawer.openDrawer(GravityCompat.START);
```

40.3 Responding to Drawer Item Selections

Handling selections within a navigation drawer is a two-step process. The first step is to specify an object to act as the item selection listener. This is achieved by obtaining a reference to the NavigationView instance in the layout and making a call to its *setNavigationItemSelectedListener()* method, passing through a reference to the object that is to act as the listener. Typically the listener will be configured to be the current activity, for example:

```
NavigationView navigationView =
                (NavigationView) findViewById(R.id.nav_view);
navigationView.setNavigationItemSelectedListener(this);
```

The second step is to implement the *onNavigationItemSelected()* method within the designated listener. This method is called each time a selection is made within the navigation drawer and is passed a reference to the selected menu item as an argument which can then be used to extract and identify the selected item id:

```
@Override
public boolean onNavigationItemSelected(MenuItem item) {
    // Handle navigation view item clicks here.
    int id = item.getItemId();

    } else if (id == R.id.nav_slideshow) {

    } else if (id == R.id.nav_manage) {

    } else if (id == R.id.nav_share) {

    } else if (id == R.id.nav_send) {

    }

    DrawerLayout drawer =
                (DrawerLayout) findViewById(R.id.drawer_layout);
    drawer.closeDrawer(GravityCompat.START);
    return true;
}
```

If it is appropriate to do so, and as outlined in the above example, it is also important to close the drawer after the item has been selected.

40.4 Using the Navigation Drawer Activity Template

While it is possible to implement a navigation drawer within any activity, the easiest approach is to select the Navigation Drawer Activity template when creating a new project or adding a new activity to an existing project:

Figure 40-2

This template creates all of the components and requirements necessary to implement a navigation drawer, requiring only that the default settings be adjusted where necessary.

40.5 Creating the Navigation Drawer Template Project

Create a new project in Android Studio, entering *NavDrawerDemo* into the Application name field and *ebookfrenzy.com* as the Company Domain setting before clicking on the *Next* button.

On the form factors screen, enable the *Phone and Tablet* option and set the minimum SDK setting to API 14: Android 4.0 (IceCreamSandwich). Continue to proceed through the screens, requesting the creation of a Navigation Drawer Activity named *NavDrawerActivity* with a corresponding layout file named *activity_nav_drawer*. Click on the *Finish* button to initiate the project creation process.

40.6 The Template Layout Resource Files

Once the project has been created, it will contain the following XML resource files located under *app -> res -> layout* in the Project tool window:

- **activity_nav_drawer.xml** – This is the top level layout resource file. It contains the DrawerLayout container and the NavigationView child. The NavigationView declaration in this file indicates that the layout for the drawer header is contained within the *nav_header_nav_drawer.xml* file and that the menu options for the drawer are located in the *activity_nav_drawer_drawer.xml* file. In addition, it includes a reference to the *app_bar_nav_drawer.xml* file.

- **app_bar_nav_drawer.xml** – This layout resource file is included by the *activity_nav_drawer.xml* file and is the standard app bar layout file built within a CoordinatorLayout container as covered in the preceding chapters. As with previous examples this file also contains a directive to include the content file which, in this case, is named *content_nav_drawer.xml*.

- **content_nav_drawer.xml** – The standard layout for the content area of the activity layout. This layout consists of a ConstraintLayout container and a "Hello World!" TextView.

- **nav_header_nav_drawer.xml** – Referenced by the NavigationView element in the *activity_nav_drawer.xml* file this is a placeholder header layout for the drawer.

40.7 The Header Coloring Resource File

In addition to the layout resource files, the *side_nav_bar.xml* file located under *app -> drawable* may be modified to change the colors applied to the drawer header. By default, this file declares a rectangular color gradient transitioning horizontally from dark to light green.

40.8 The Template Menu Resource File

The menu options presented within the navigation drawer can be found in the *activity_nav_drawer_drawer.xml* file located under *app -> res -> menu* in the project tool window. By default, the menu consists of a range of text based titles with accompanying icons (the files for which are all located in the *drawable* folder). For more details on menu resource files, refer to the chapter entitled *"Creating and Managing Overflow Menus on Android"*.

40.9 The Template Code

The *onCreate()* method located in the *NavDrawerActivity.java* file performs much of the initialization work required for the navigation drawer:

```
DrawerLayout drawer = (DrawerLayout) findViewById(R.id.drawer_layout);

ActionBarDrawerToggle toggle = new ActionBarDrawerToggle(
                    this, drawer, toolbar,
                    R.string.navigation_drawer_open,
                    R.string.navigation_drawer_close);

drawer.setDrawerListener(toggle);
toggle.syncState();

NavigationView navigationView = (NavigationView)
                    findViewById(R.id.nav_view);

navigationView.setNavigationItemSelectedListener(this);
```

The code obtains a reference to the DrawerLayout object and then creates an ActionBarDrawerToggle object, initializing it with a reference to the current activity, the DrawerLayout object, the toolbar contained within the app bar and two strings describing the drawer opening and closing actions for accessibility purposes. The ActionBarDrawerToggle object is then assigned as the listener for the drawer and synchronized.

The code then obtains a reference to the NavigationView instance before declaring the current activity as the listener for any item selections made within the navigation drawer.

Since the current activity is now declared as the drawer listener, the *onNavigationItemSelected()* method is also implemented in the *NavDrawerActivity.java* file. The implementation of this method in the activity matches that outlined earlier in this chapter.

Finally, an additional method named *onBackPressed()* has been added to the activity by Android Studio. This method is added to handle situations whereby the activity has a "back" button to return to a previous activity screen. The code in this method ensures that the drawer is closed before the app switches back to the previous activity screen:

```
@Override
public void onBackPressed() {
```

```
DrawerLayout drawer =
            (DrawerLayout) findViewById(R.id.drawer_layout);
if (drawer.isDrawerOpen(GravityCompat.START)) {
    drawer.closeDrawer(GravityCompat.START);
} else {
    super.onBackPressed();
}
}
```

40.10 Running the App

Compile and run the project and note the appearance of the drawer indicator as highlighted in Figure 40-3:

Figure 40-3

Tap the indicator and note that the icon rotates as the navigation drawer appears:

Figure 40-4

40.11 Summary

The navigation drawer is a panel that extends from the left-hand edge of an activity screen when an indicator is selected by the user. The drawer contains menu options available for selection and serves as a useful application navigation tool that conforms to the material design guidelines. Although it is possible to add a navigation drawer to any activity, the quickest technique is to use the Android Studio Navigation Drawer Activity template and then customize it for specific requirements. This chapter has outlined the components that make up a navigation drawer and highlighted how these are implemented within the template.

41. An Android Studio Master/Detail Flow Tutorial

This chapter will explain the concept of the Master/Detail user interface design before exploring, in detail, the elements that make up the Master/Detail Flow template included with Android Studio. An example application will then be created that demonstrates the steps involved in modifying the template to meet the specific needs of the application developer.

41.1 The Master/Detail Flow

A master/detail flow is an interface design concept whereby a list of items (referred to as the *master list*) is displayed to the user. On selecting an item from the list, additional information relating to that item is then presented to the user within a *detail* pane. An email application might, for example, consist of a master list of received messages consisting of the address of the sender and the subject of the message. Upon selection of a message from the master list, the body of the email message would appear within the detail pane.

On tablet sized Android device displays in landscape orientation, the master list appears in a narrow vertical panel along the left-hand edge of the screen. The remainder of the display is devoted to the detail pane in an arrangement referred to as *two-pane mode*. Figure 41-1, for example, shows the master/detail, two-pane arrangement with master items listed and the content of item one displayed in the detail pane:

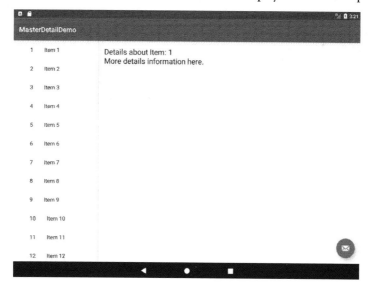

Figure 41-1

On smaller, phone sized Android devices, the master list takes up the entire screen and the detail pane appears on a separate screen which appears when a selection is made from the master list. In this mode, the detail screen includes an action bar entry to return to the master list. Figure 41-2 for example, illustrates both the master and detail screens for the same item list on a 4" phone screen:

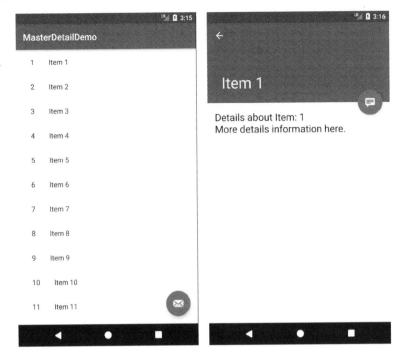

Figure 41-2

41.2 Creating a Master/Detail Flow Activity

In the next section of this chapter, the different elements that comprise the Master/Detail Flow template will be covered in some detail. This is best achieved by creating a project using the Master/Detail Flow template to use while working through the information. This project will subsequently be used as the basis for the tutorial at the end of the chapter.

Create a new project in Android Studio, entering *MasterDetailFlow* into the Application name field and *ebookfrenzy.com* as the Company Domain setting before clicking on the *Next* button.

On the form factors screen, enable the *Phone and Tablet* option and set the minimum SDK setting to API 14: Android 4.0 (IceCreamSandwich). When selecting a minimum SDK of less than API 14, Android Studio creates a Master/Detail Flow project template that uses an outdated and less efficient approach to handling the list of items displayed in the master panel. After the project has been created, the *minSdkVersion* setting in the *build. gradle (module: app)* file located under *Gradle Scripts* in the Project tool window may be changed to target older Android versions if required.

When the activity configuration screen of the New Project dialog appears, select the *Master/Detail Flow* option as illustrated in Figure 41-3 before clicking on *Next* once again:

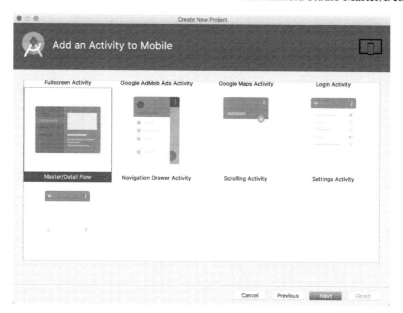

Figure 41-3

The next screen (Figure 41-4) provides the opportunity to configure the objects that will be displayed within the master/detail activity. In the tutorial later in this chapter, the master list will contain a number of web site names which, when selected, will load the chosen web site into a web view within the detail pane. With these requirements in mind, set the *Object Kind* field to "Website", and the *Object Kind Plural* and *Title* settings to "Websites".

Figure 41-4

Finally, click Finish to create the new Master/Detail Flow based application project.

41.3 The Anatomy of the Master/Detail Flow Template

Once a new project has been created using the Master/Detail Flow template, a number of Java and XML layout resource files will have been created automatically. It is important to gain an understanding of these different files in order to be able to adapt the template to specific requirements. A review of the project within the Android Studio Project tool window will reveal the following files, where *<item>* is replaced by the Object Kind name that was specified when the project was created (this being "Website" in the case of the *MasterDetailFlow* example project):

- **activity_<item>_list.xml** – The top level layout file for the master list, this file is loaded by the *<item>ListActivity* class. This layout contains a toolbar, a floating action button and includes the *<item>_list.xml* file.

- **<item>ListActivity.java** – The activity class responsible for displaying and managing the master list (declared in the *activity_<item>_list.xml* file) and for both displaying and responding to the selection of items within that list.

- **<item>_list.xml** – The layout file used to display the master list of items in single-pane mode where the master list and detail pane appear on different screens. This file consists of a RecyclerView object configured to use the LinearLayoutManager. The RecyclerView element declares that each item in the master list is to be displayed using the layout declared within the *<item>_list_content.xml* file.

- **<item>_list.xml (w900dp)** – The layout file for the master list in the two-pane mode used on tablets in landscape (where the master list and detail pane appear side by side). This file contains a horizontal LinearLayout parent within which resides a RecyclerView to display the master list, and a FrameLayout to contain the content of the detail pane. As with the single-pane variant of this file, the RecyclerView element declares that each item in the list be displayed using the layout contained within the *<item>_list_content.xml* file.

- **<item>_content_list.xml** – This file contains the layout to be used for each item in the master list. By default, this consists of two TextView objects embedded in a horizontal LinearLayout but may be changed to meet specific application needs.

- **activity_<item>_detail.xml** – The top level layout file used for the detail pane when running in single-pane mode. This layout contains an app bar, collapsing toolbar, scrolling view and a floating action button. At runtime this layout file is loaded and displayed by the *<item>DetailActivity* class.

- **<item>DetailActivity.java** – This class displays the layout defined in the *activity_<item>_detail.xml* file. The class also initializes and displays the fragment containing the detail content defined in the *item_detail.xml* and *<item>DetailFragment.java* files.

- **<item>_detail.xml** – The layout file that accompanies the *<item>DetailFragment* class and contains the layout for the content area of the detail pane. By default, this contains a single TextView object, but may be changed to meet your specific application needs. In single-pane mode, this fragment is loaded into the layout defined by the *activity_<item>_detail.xml* file. In two-pane mode, this layout is loaded into the FrameLayout area of the *<item>_list.xml (w900dp)* file so that it appears adjacent to the master list.

- **<item>DetailFragment.java** – The fragment class file responsible for displaying the *<item>_detail.xml* layout and populating it with the content to be displayed in the detail pane. This fragment is initialized and displayed within the *<item>DetailActivity.java* file to provide the content displayed within the *activity_<item>_detail.xml* layout for single-pane mode and the *<item>_list.xml (w900dp)* layout for two-pane mode.

- **DummyContent.java** – A class file intended to provide sample data for the template. This class can either be modified to meet application needs, or replaced entirely. By default, the content provided by this class simply consists of a number of string items.

41.4 Modifying the Master/Detail Flow Template

While the structure of the Master/Detail Flow template can appear confusing at first, the concepts will become clearer as the default template is modified in the remainder of this chapter. As will become evident, much of the functionality provided by the template can remain unchanged for many master/detail implementation requirements.

In the rest of this chapter, the *MasterDetailFlow* project will be modified such that the master list displays a list of web site names and the detail pane altered to contain a WebView object instead of the current TextView. When a web site is selected by the user, the corresponding web page will subsequently load and display in the detail pane.

41.5 Changing the Content Model

The content for the example as it currently stands is defined by the *DummyContent* class file. Begin, therefore, by selecting the *DummyContent.java* file (located in the Project tool window in the *app -> java -> com.ebookfrenzy. masterdetailflow -> dummy* folder) and reviewing the code. At the bottom of the file is a declaration for a class named *DummyItem* which is currently able to store two String objects representing a content string and an ID. The updated project, on the other hand, will need each item object to contain an ID string, a string for the web site name, and a string for the corresponding URL of the web site. To add these features, modify the *DummyItem* class so that it reads as follows:

```java
public static class DummyItem {
        public String id;
        public String website_name;
        public String website_url;

        public DummyItem(String id, String website_name,
              String website_url)
        {
              this.id = id;
              this.website_name = website_name;
              this.website_url = website_url;
        }

        @Override
        public String toString() {
              return website_name;
        }
}
```

Note that the encapsulating DummyContent class currently contains a *for* loop that adds 25 items by making multiple calls to methods named *createDummyItem()* and *makeDetails()*. Much of this code will no longer be required and should be deleted from the class as follows:

```
public static Map<String, DummyItem> ITEM_MAP = new HashMap<String, DummyItem>();

private static final int COUNT = 25;

static {
    // Add some sample items.
    for (int i = 1; i <= COUNT; i++) {
        addItem(createDummyItem(i));
    }
}

private static void addItem(DummyItem item) {
    ITEMS.add(item);
    ITEM_MAP.put(item.id, item);
}

private static DummyItem createDummyItem(int position) {
    return new DummyItem(String.valueOf(position), "Item " + position,
makeDetails(position));
}

private static String makeDetails(int position) {
    StringBuilder builder = new StringBuilder();
    builder.append("Details about Item: ").append(position);
    for (int i = 0; i < position; i++) {
        builder.append("\nMore details information here.");
    }
    return builder.toString();
}
```

This code needs to be modified to initialize the data model with the required web site data:

```
public static final Map<String, DummyItem> ITEM_MAP =
        new HashMap<String, DummyItem>();


static {
    // Add 3 sample items.
    addItem(new DummyItem("1", "eBookFrenzy",
            "http://www.ebookfrenzy.com"));
    addItem(new DummyItem("2", "Amazon",
            "http://www.amazon.com"));
    addItem(new DummyItem("3", "New York Times",
            "http://www.nytimes.com"));
}
```

The code now takes advantage of the modified DummyItem class to store an ID, web site name and URL for each item.

41.6 Changing the Detail Pane

The detail information shown to the user when an item is selected from the master list is currently displayed via the layout contained in the *website_detail.xml* file. By default, this contains a single view in the form of a TextView. Since the TextView class is not capable of displaying a web page, this needs to be changed to a WebView object for this tutorial. To achieve this, navigate to the *app -> res -> layout -> website_detail.xml* file in the Project tool window and double-click on it to load it into the Layout Editor tool. Switch to Text mode and delete the current XML content from the file. Replace this content with the following XML:

```xml
<WebView xmlns:android="http://schemas.android.com/apk/res/android"
    xmlns:tools="http://schemas.android.com/tools"
    android:layout_width="match_parent"
    android:layout_height="match_parent"
    android:id="@+id/website_detail"
    tools:context=
        "com.ebookfrenzy.masterdetailflow.WebsiteDetailFragment">
</WebView>
```

Switch to Design mode and verify that the layout now matches that shown in Figure 41-5:

Figure 41-5

41.7 Modifying the WebsiteDetailFragment Class

At this point the user interface detail pane has been modified but the corresponding Java class is still designed for working with a TextView object instead of a WebView. Load the source code for this class by double-clicking on the *WebsiteDetailFragment.java* file in the Project tool window.

In order to load the web page URL corresponding to the currently selected item only a few lines of code need to be changed. Once this change has been made, the code should read as follows:

```
package com.ebookfrenzy.masterdetailflow;

import android.app.Activity;
import android.support.design.widget.CollapsingToolbarLayout;
import android.os.Bundle;
import android.support.v4.app.Fragment;
import android.view.LayoutInflater;
import android.view.View;
import android.view.ViewGroup;
import android.widget.TextView;
import android.webkit.WebViewClient;
import android.webkit.WebView;
import android.webkit.WebResourceRequest;

import com.ebookfrenzy.masterdetailflow.dummy.DummyContent;

public class WebSiteDetailFragment extends Fragment {

    .
    .
    .

    public void onCreate(Bundle savedInstanceState) {
        super.onCreate(savedInstanceState);

        if (getArguments().containsKey(ARG_ITEM_ID)) {
            // Load the dummy content specified by the fragment
            // arguments. In a real-world scenario, use a Loader
            // to load content from a content provider.
            mItem = DummyContent.ITEM_MAP.get(getArguments().getString(ARG_ITEM_
ID));

            Activity activity = this.getActivity();
            CollapsingToolbarLayout appBarLayout = (CollapsingToolbarLayout)
activity.findViewById(R.id.toolbar_layout);
            if (appBarLayout != null) {
                appBarLayout.setTitle(mItem.website_name);
            }
        }
    }

    @Override
    public View onCreateView(LayoutInflater inflater,
                ViewGroup container, Bundle savedInstanceState) {
        View rootView = inflater.inflate(
            R.layout.fragment_website_detail, container, false);

        // Show the dummy content as text in a TextView.
        if (mItem != null) {
```

```
((WebView) rootView.findViewById(R.id.website_detail))
        .loadUrl(mItem.website_url);
WebView webView = (WebView)
    rootView.findViewById(R.id.website_detail);
webView.setWebViewClient(new WebViewClient(){
    @Override
    public boolean shouldOverrideUrlLoading(
        WebView view, WebResourceRequest request) {
        return super.shouldOverrideUrlLoading(
                    view, request);
    }
});
webView.getSettings().setJavaScriptEnabled(true);
webView.loadUrl(mItem.website_url);
}


    return rootView;
}
}
```

The above changes modify the *onCreate()* method to display the web site name on the app bar:

```
appBarLayout.setTitle(mItem.website_name);
```

The *onCreateView()* method is then modified to find the view with the ID of *website_detail* (this was formally the TextView but is now a WebView) and extract the URL of the web site from the selected item. An instance of the WebViewClient class is created and assigned the *shouldOverrideUrlLoading()* callback method. This method is implemented so as to force the system to use the WebView instance to load the page instead of the Chrome browser. Finally, JavaScript support is enabled on the webView instance and the web page loaded.

41.8 Modifying the WebsiteListActivity Class

A minor change also needs to be made to the *WebsiteListActivity.java* file to make sure that the web site names appear in the master list. Edit this file, locate the *onBindViewHolder()* method and modify the *setText()* method call to reference the web site name as follows:

```
public void onBindViewHolder(final ViewHolder holder, int position) {
    holder.mItem = mValues.get(position);
    holder.mIdView.setText(mValues.get(position).id);
    holder.mContentView.setText(mValues.get(position).website_name);
.
.
.
}
```

41.9 Adding Manifest Permissions

The final step is to add internet permission to the application via the manifest file. This will enable the WebView object to access the internet and download web pages. Navigate to, and load the *AndroidManifest.xml* file in the Project tool window (*app -> manifests*), and double-click on it to load it into the editor. Once loaded, add the appropriate permission line to the file:

```
<?xml version="1.0" encoding="utf-8"?>
```

```
<manifest xmlns:android="http://schemas.android.com/apk/res/android"
    package="com.example.masterdetailflow" >

    <uses-permission android:name="android.permission.INTERNET" />

    <application
        android:allowBackup="true"
        android:icon="@mipmap/ic_launcher"
        android:label="@string/app_name"
        android:theme="@style/AppTheme" >.
```

.

.

41.10 Running the Application

Compile and run the application on a suitably configured emulator or an attached Android device. Depending on the size of the display, the application will appear either in small screen or two-pane mode. Regardless, the master list should appear primed with the names of the three web sites defined in the content model. Selecting an item should cause the corresponding web site to appear in the detail pane as illustrated in two-pane mode in Figure 41-6:

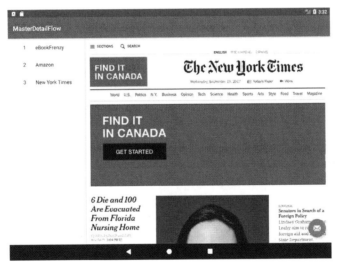

Figure 41-6

41.11 Summary

A master/detail user interface consists of a master list of items which, when selected, displays additional information about that selection within a detail pane. The Master/Detail Flow is a template provided with Android Studio that allows a master/detail arrangement to be created quickly and with relative ease. As demonstrated in this chapter, with minor modifications to the default template files, a wide range of master/detail based functionality can be implemented with minimal coding and design effort.

42. An Overview of Android Intents

By this stage of the book, it should be clear that Android applications are comprised, among other things, of one or more activities. An area that has yet to be covered in extensive detail, however, is the mechanism by which one activity can trigger the launch of another activity. As outlined briefly in the chapter entitled *"The Anatomy of an Android Application"*, this is achieved primarily by using *Intents*.

Prior to working through some Android Studio based example implementations of intents in the following chapters, the goal of this chapter is to provide an overview of intents in the form of *explicit intents* and *implicit intents* together with an introduction to *intent filters*.

42.1 An Overview of Intents

Intents (*android.content.Intent*) are the messaging system by which one activity is able to launch another activity. An activity can, for example, issue an intent to request the launch of another activity contained within the same application. Intents also, however, go beyond this concept by allowing an activity to request the services of any other appropriately registered activity on the device for which permissions are configured. Consider, for example, an activity contained within an application that requires a web page to be loaded and displayed to the user. Rather than the application having to contain a second activity to perform this task, the code can simply send an intent to the Android runtime requesting the services of any activity that has registered the ability to display a web page. The runtime system will match the request to available activities on the device and either launch the activity that matches or, in the event of multiple matches, allow the user to decide which activity to use.

Intents also allow for the transfer of data from the sending activity to the receiving activity. In the previously outlined scenario, for example, the sending activity would need to send the URL of the web page to be displayed to the second activity. Similarly, the receiving activity may also be configured to return data to the sending activity when the required tasks are completed.

Though not covered until later chapters, it is also worth highlighting the fact that, in addition to launching activities, intents are also used to launch and communicate with services and broadcast receivers.

Intents are categorized as either *explicit* or *implicit*.

42.2 Explicit Intents

An *explicit intent* requests the launch of a specific activity by referencing the *component name* (which is actually the class name) of the target activity. This approach is most common when launching an activity residing in the same application as the sending activity (since the class name is known to the application developer).

An explicit intent is issued by creating an instance of the Intent class, passing through the activity context and the component name of the activity to be launched. A call is then made to the *startActivity()* method, passing the intent object as an argument. For example, the following code fragment issues an intent for the activity with the class name ActivityB to be launched:

```
Intent i = new Intent(this, ActivityB.class);
startActivity(i);
```

Data may be transmitted to the receiving activity by adding it to the intent object before it is started via calls to the *putExtra()* method of the intent object. Data must be added in the form of key-value pairs. The following code extends the previous example to add String and integer values with the keys "myString" and "myInt" respectively to the intent:

```
Intent i = new Intent(this, ActivityB.class);
i.putExtra("myString", "This is a message for ActivityB");
i.putExtra("myInt", 100);

startActivity(i);
```

The data is received by the target activity as part of a Bundle object which can be obtained via a call to *getIntent()*. *getExtras()*. The *getIntent()* method of the Activity class returns the intent that started the activity, while the *getExtras()* method (of the Intent class) returns a Bundle object containing the data. For example, to extract the data values passed to ActivityB:

```
Bundle extras = getIntent().getExtras();

if (extras != null) {
    String myString = extras.getString("myString");
    int myInt = extras.getInt("myInt");
}
```

When using intents to launch other activities within the same application, it is essential that those activities be listed in the application manifest file. The following *AndroidManifest.xml* contents are correctly configured for an application containing activities named ActivityA and ActivityB:

```
<?xml version="1.0" encoding="utf-8"?>
<manifest xmlns:android="http://schemas.android.com/apk/res/android"
        package="com.ebookfrenzy.intent1.intent1" >

    <application
        android:icon="@mipmap/ic_launcher"
        android:label="@string/app_name" >
        <activity
            android:label="@string/app_name"
            android:name="com.ebookfrenzy.intent1.intent1.ActivityA" >
            <intent-filter>
                <action android:name="android.intent.action.MAIN" />
                <category android:name="android.intent.category.LAUNCHER" />
            </intent-filter>
        </activity>
        <activity
            android:name="ActivityB"
            android:label="ActivityB" >
        </activity>
    </application>
</manifest>
```

42.3 Returning Data from an Activity

As the example in the previous section stands, while data is transferred to ActivityB, there is no way for data to be returned to the first activity (which we will call ActivityA). This can, however, be achieved by launching

ActivityB as a *sub-activity* of ActivityA. An activity is started as a sub-activity by starting the intent with a call to the *startActivityForResult()* method instead of using *startActivity()*. In addition to the intent object, this method is also passed a *request code* value which can be used to identify the return data when the sub-activity returns. For example:

```
startActivityForResult(i, REQUEST_CODE);
```

In order to return data to the parent activity, the sub-activity must implement the *finish()* method, the purpose of which is to create a new intent object containing the data to be returned, and then calling the *setResult()* method of the enclosing activity, passing through a *result code* and the intent containing the return data. The result code is typically *RESULT_OK*, or *RESULT_CANCELED*, but may also be a custom value subject to the requirements of the developer. In the event that a sub-activity crashes, the parent activity will receive a *RESULT_CANCELED* result code.

The following code, for example, illustrates the code for a typical sub-activity *finish()* method:

```
public void finish() {
        Intent data = new Intent();

        data.putExtra("returnString1", "Message to parent activity");
        setResult(RESULT_OK, data);
        super.finish();
}
```

In order to obtain and extract the returned data, the parent activity must implement the *onActivityResult()* method, for example:

```
protected void onActivityResult(int requestCode, int resultCode, Intent data)
{
    String returnString;
    if (requestCode == REQUEST_CODE && resultCode == RESULT_OK) {
        if (data.hasExtra("returnString1")) {
                returnString = data.getExtras().getString("returnString1");
        }
    }
}
```

Note that the above method checks the returned request code value to make sure that it matches that passed through to the *startActivityForResult()* method. When starting multiple sub-activities it is especially important to use the request code to track which activity is currently returning results, since all will call the same *onActivityResult()* method on exit.

42.4 Implicit Intents

Unlike explicit intents, which reference the class name of the activity to be launched, implicit intents identify the activity to be launched by specifying the action to be performed and the type of data to be handled by the receiving activity. For example, an action type of ACTION_VIEW accompanied by the URL of a web page in the form of a URI object will instruct the Android system to search for, and subsequently launch, a web browser capable activity. The following implicit intent will, when executed on an Android device, result in the designated web page appearing in a web browser activity:

```
Intent intent = new Intent(Intent.ACTION_VIEW,
        Uri.parse("http://www.ebookfrenzy.com"));
```

```
startActivity(intent);
```

When the above implicit intent is issued by an activity, the Android system will search for activities on the device that have registered the ability to handle ACTION_VIEW requests on *http* scheme data using a process referred to as *intent resolution*. In the event that a single match is found, that activity will be launched. If more than one match is found, the user will be prompted to choose from the available activity options.

42.5 Using Intent Filters

Intent filters are the mechanism by which activities "advertise" supported actions and data handling capabilities to the Android intent resolution process. Continuing the example in the previous section, an activity capable of displaying web pages would include an intent filter section in its manifest file indicating support for the ACTION_VIEW type of intent requests on http scheme data.

It is important to note that both the sending and receiving activities must have requested permission for the type of action to be performed. This is achieved by adding *<uses-permission>* tags to the manifest files of both activities. For example, the following manifest lines request permission to access the internet and contacts database:

```
<uses-permission android:name="android.permission.READ_CONTACTS" />
<uses-permission android:name="android.permission.INTERNET"/>
```

The following *AndroidManifest.xml* file illustrates a configuration for an activity named *WebViewActivity* with intent filters and permissions enabled for internet access:

```
<?xml version="1.0" encoding="utf-8"?>
<manifest xmlns:android="http://schemas.android.com/apk/res/android"
    package="com.ebookfreny.WebView"
    android:versionCode="1"
    android:versionName="1.0" >

    <uses-sdk android:minSdkVersion="10" />

    <uses-permission android:name="android.permission.INTERNET" />

    <application
        android:icon="@mipmap/ic_launcher"
        android:label="@string/app_name" >
        <activity
            android:label="@string/app_name"
            android:name=".WebViewActivity" >
            <intent-filter>
                <action android:name="android.intent.action.VIEW" />
                <category android:name="android.intent.category.DEFAULT" />
                <data android:scheme="http" />
            </intent-filter>
        </activity>
    </application>

</manifest>
```

42.6 Checking Intent Availability

It is generally unwise to assume that an activity will be available for a particular intent, especially since the absence of a matching action will typically result in the application crashing. Fortunately, it is possible to identify the availability of an activity for a specific intent before it is sent to the runtime system. The following method can be used to identify the availability of an activity for a specified intent action type:

```
public static boolean isIntentAvailable(Context context, String action) {
    final PackageManager packageManager = context.getPackageManager();
    final Intent intent = new Intent(action);
    List<ResolveInfo> list =
            packageManager.queryIntentActivities(intent,
                    PackageManager.MATCH_DEFAULT_ONLY);
    return list.size() > 0;
}
```

42.7 Summary

Intents are the messaging mechanism by which one Android activity can launch another. An explicit intent references a specific activity to be launched by referencing the receiving activity by class name. Explicit intents are typically, though not exclusively, used when launching activities contained within the same application. An implicit intent specifies the action to be performed and the type of data to be handled, and lets the Android runtime find a matching activity to launch. Implicit intents are generally used when launching activities that reside in different applications.

An activity can send data to the receiving activity by bundling data into the intent object in the form of key-value pairs. Data can only be returned from an activity if it is started as a *sub-activity* of the sending activity.

Activities advertise capabilities to the Android intent resolution process through the specification of intent-filters in the application manifest file. Both sending and receiving activities must also request appropriate permissions to perform tasks such as accessing the device contact database or the internet.

Having covered the theory of intents, the next few chapters will work through the creation of some examples in Android Studio that put both explicit and implicit intents into action.

43. Android Explicit Intents – A Worked Example

The chapter entitled *"An Overview of Android Intents"* covered the theory of using intents to launch activities. This chapter will put that theory into practice through the creation of an example application.

The example Android Studio application project created in this chapter will demonstrate the use of an explicit intent to launch an activity, including the transfer of data between sending and receiving activities. The next chapter (*"Android Implicit Intents – A Worked Example"*) will demonstrate the use of implicit intents.

43.1 Creating the Explicit Intent Example Application

Launch Android Studio and create a new project, entering *ExplicitIntent* into the Application name field and *ebookfrenzy.com* as the Company Domain setting before clicking on the *Next* button.

On the form factors screen, enable the *Phone and Tablet* option and set the minimum SDK setting to API 14: Android 4.0 (IceCreamSandwich). Continue to proceed through the screens, requesting the creation of an Empty Activity named *ActivityA* with a corresponding layout named *activity_a*.

Click *Finish* to create the new project.

43.2 Designing the User Interface Layout for ActivityA

The user interface for ActivityA will consist of a ConstraintLayout view containing EditText (Plain Text), TextView and Button views named *editText1*, *textView1* and *button1* respectively. Using the Project tool window, locate the *activity_a.xml* resource file for ActivityA (located under *app -> res -> layout*) and double-click on it to load it into the Android Studio Layout Editor tool. Select and delete the default "Hello World!" TextView.

For this tutorial, Inference mode will be used to add constraints after the layout has been designed. Begin, therefore, by turning off the Autoconnect feature of the Layout Editor using the toolbar button indicated in Figure 43-1:

Figure 43-1

Drag a TextView widget from the palette and drop it so that it is centered within the layout and use the Attributes tool window to assign an ID of *textView1*.

Drag a Button object from the palette and position it so that it is centered horizontally and located beneath the bottom edge of the TextView. Change the text property so that it reads "Ask Question" and configure the *onClick* property to call a method named *onClick()*.

Next, add an Plain Text object so that it is centered horizontally and positioned above the top edge of the TextView. Using the Attributes tool window, remove the "Name" string assigned to the text property and set the ID to *editText1*. With the layout completed, click on the toolbar *Infer constraints* button to add appropriate constraints:

Figure 43-2

Finally, click on the red warning button in the top right-hand corner of the Layout Editor window and use the resulting panel to extract the "Ask Question" string to a resource named *ask_question*.

Once the layout is complete, the user interface should resemble that illustrated in Figure 43-3:

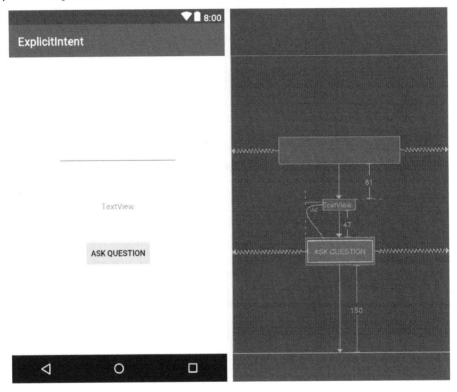

Figure 43-3

43.3 Creating the Second Activity Class

When the "Ask Question" button is touched by the user, an intent will be issued requesting that a second activity be launched into which an answer can be entered by the user. The next step, therefore, is to create the second activity. Within the Project tool window, right-click on the *com.ebookfrenzy.explicitintent* package name located in *app -> java* and select the *New -> Activity -> Empty Activity* menu option to display the *New Android Activity* dialog as shown in Figure 43-4:

Figure 43-4

Enter *ActivityB* into the Activity Name and Title fields and name the layout file *activity_b*. Since this activity will not be started when the application is launched (it will instead be launched via an intent by ActivityA when the button is pressed), it is important to make sure that the *Launcher Activity* option is disabled before clicking on the Finish button.

43.4 Designing the User Interface Layout for ActivityB

The elements that are required for the user interface of the second activity are a Plain Text EditText, TextView and Button view. With these requirements in mind, load the *activity_b.xml* layout into the Layout Editor tool, turn off Autoconnect mode in the Layout Editor toolbar and add the views.

During the design process, note that the *onClick* property on the button view has been configured to call a method named *onClick()*, and the TextView and EditText views have been assigned IDs *textView1* and *editText1* respectively. Once completed, the layout should resemble that illustrated in Figure 43-5. Note that the text on the button (which reads "Answer Question") has been extracted to a string resource named *answer_question*.

With the layout complete, click on the Infer constraints toolbar button to add the necessary constraints to the layout:

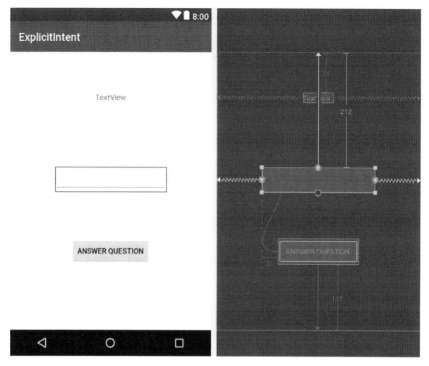

Figure 43-5

43.5 Reviewing the Application Manifest File

In order for ActivityA to be able to launch ActivityB using an intent, it is necessary that an entry for ActivityB be present in the *AndroidManifest.xml* file. Locate this file within the Project tool window (*app -> manifests*), double-click on it to load it into the editor and verify that Android Studio has automatically added an entry for the activity:

```
<?xml version="1.0" encoding="utf-8"?>
<manifest xmlns:android="http://schemas.android.com/apk/res/android"
    package="com.ebookfrenzy.explicitintent">

    <application
        android:allowBackup="true"
        android:icon="@mipmap/ic_launcher"
        android:label="@string/app_name"
        android:supportsRtl="true"
        android:theme="@style/AppTheme">
        <activity android:name=".ActivityA">
            <intent-filter>
                <action android:name="android.intent.action.MAIN" />

                <category
     android:name="android.intent.category.LAUNCHER" />
            </intent-filter>
        </activity>
```

```
        <activity android:name=".ActivityB"></activity>
    </application>
```

```
</manifest>
```

With the second activity created and listed in the manifest file, it is now time to write some code in the ActivityA class to issue the intent.

43.6 Creating the Intent

The objective for ActivityA is to create and start an intent when the user touches the "Ask Question" button. As part of the intent creation process, the question string entered by the user into the EditText view will be added to the intent object as a key-value pair. When the user interface layout was created for ActivityA, the button object was configured to call a method named *onClick()* when "clicked" by the user. This method now needs to be added to the ActivityA class *ActivityA.java* source file as follows:

```java
package com.ebookfrenzy.explicitintent;


import android.support.v7.app.AppCompatActivity;
import android.os.Bundle;
import android.content.Intent;
import android.view.View;
import android.widget.EditText;
import android.widget.TextView;


public class ActivityA extends AppCompatActivity {

    @Override
    protected void onCreate(Bundle savedInstanceState) {
        super.onCreate(savedInstanceState);
        setContentView(R.layout.activity_a);
    }

    public void onClick(View view) {

        Intent i = new Intent(this, ActivityB.class);

        final EditText editText1 = (EditText)
                findViewById(R.id.editText1);
        String myString = editText1.getText().toString();
        i.putExtra("qString", myString);
        startActivity(i);
    }
}
```

The code for the *onClick()* method follows the techniques outlined in *"An Overview of Android Intents"*. First, a new Intent instance is created, passing through the current activity and the class name of ActivityB as arguments. Next, the text entered into the EditText object is added to the intent object as a key-value pair and the intent started via a call to *startActivity()*, passing through the intent object as an argument.

Compile and run the application and touch the "Ask Question" button to launch ActivityB and the back button (located in the toolbar along the bottom of the display) to return to ActivityA.

43.7 Extracting Intent Data

Now that ActivityB is being launched from ActivityA, the next step is to extract the String data value included in the intent and assign it to the TextView object in the ActivityB user interface. This involves adding some code to the *onCreate()* method of ActivityB in the *ActivityB.java* source file:

```
package com.ebookfrenzy.explicitintent;

import android.support.v7.app.AppCompatActivity;
import android.os.Bundle;
import android.content.Intent;
import android.view.View;
import android.widget.TextView;
import android.widget.EditText;

public class ActivityB extends AppCompatActivity {

        public void onCreate(Bundle savedInstanceState) {
          super.onCreate(savedInstanceState);
          setContentView(R.layout.activityb);

        Bundle extras = getIntent().getExtras();
            if (extras == null) {
                    return;
            }

            String qString = extras.getString("qString");

            final TextView textView = (TextView)
              findViewById(R.id.textView1);
            textView.setText(qString);
    }
}
```

Compile and run the application either within an emulator or on a physical Android device. Enter a question into the text box in ActivityA before touching the "Ask Question" button. The question should now appear on the TextView component in the ActivityB user interface.

43.8 Launching ActivityB as a Sub-Activity

In order for ActivityB to be able to return data to ActivityA, ActivityB must be started as a *sub-activity* of ActivityA. This means that the call to *startActivity()* in the ActivityA *onClick()* method needs to be replaced with a call to *startActivityForResult()*. Unlike the *startActivity()* method, which takes only the intent object as an argument, *startActivityForResult()* requires that a request code also be passed through. The request code can be any number value and is used to identify which sub-activity is associated with which set of return data. For the purposes of this example, a request code of 5 will be used, giving us a modified ActivityA class that reads as follows:

```
public class ActivityA extends AppCompatActivity {

    private static final int request_code = 5;

    @Override
    public void onCreate(Bundle savedInstanceState) {
        super.onCreate(savedInstanceState);
        setContentView(R.layout.main);
    }

    public void onClick(View view) {

            Intent i = new Intent(this, ActivityB.class);

            final EditText editText1 = (EditText)
                    findViewById(R.id.editText1);
            String myString = editText1.getText().toString();
            i.putExtra("qString", myString);
            startActivityForResult(i, request_code);

    }
}
```

When the sub-activity exits, the *onActivityResult()* method of the parent activity is called and passed as arguments the request code associated with the intent, a result code indicating the success or otherwise of the sub-activity and an intent object containing any data returned by the sub-activity. Remaining within the ActivityA class source file, implement this method as follows:

```
protected void onActivityResult(int requestCode, int resultCode, Intent data) {
        if ((requestCode == request_code) &&
                    (resultCode == RESULT_OK)) {

            TextView textView1 =
                    (TextView) findViewById(R.id.textView1);

            String returnString =
                    data.getExtras().getString("returnData");

            textView.setText(returnString);

        }
}
```

The code in the above method begins by checking that the request code matches the one used when the intent was issued and ensuring that the activity was successful. The return data is then extracted from the intent and displayed on the TextView object.

43.9 Returning Data from a Sub-Activity

ActivityB is now launched as a sub-activity of ActivityA, which has, in turn, been modified to handle data returned from ActivityB. All that remains is to modify *ActivityB.java* to implement the *finish()* method and to add code for the *onClick()* method, which is called when the "Answer Question" button is touched. The *finish()* method is triggered when an activity exits (for example when the user selects the back button on the device):

```
public void onClick(View view) {
            finish();
}


@Override
public void finish() {
        Intent data = new Intent();

        EditText editText1 = (EditText) findViewById(R.id.editText1);

        String returnString = editText1.getText().toString();
        data.putExtra("returnData", returnString);

        setResult(RESULT_OK, data);
        super.finish();
}
```

All that the *finish()* method needs to do is create a new intent, add the return data as a key-value pair and then call the *setResult()* method, passing through a result code and the intent object. The *onClick()* method simply calls the *finish()* method.

43.10 Testing the Application

Compile and run the application, enter a question into the text field on ActivityA and touch the "Ask Question" button. When ActivityB appears, enter the answer to the question and use either the back button or the "Submit Answer" button to return to ActivityA where the answer should appear in the text view object.

43.11 Summary

Having covered the basics of intents in the previous chapter, the goal of this chapter was to work through the creation of an application project in Android Studio designed to demonstrate the use of explicit intents together with the concepts of data transfer between a parent activity and sub-activity.

The next chapter will work through an example designed to demonstrate implicit intents in action.

44. Android Implicit Intents – A Worked Example

In this chapter, an example application will be created in Android Studio designed to demonstrate a practical implementation of implicit intents. The goal will be to create and send an intent requesting that the content of a particular web page be loaded and displayed to the user. Since the example application itself will not contain an activity capable of performing this task, an implicit intent will be issued so that the Android intent resolution algorithm can be engaged to identify and launch a suitable activity from another application. This is most likely to be an activity from the Chrome web browser bundled with the Android operating system.

Having successfully launched the built-in browser, a new project will be created that also contains an activity capable of displaying web pages. This will be installed onto the device or emulator and used to demonstrate what happens when two activities match the criteria for an implicit intent.

44.1 Creating the Android Studio Implicit Intent Example Project

Launch Android Studio and create a new project, entering *ImplicitIntent* into the Application name field and *ebookfrenzy.com* as the Company Domain setting before clicking on the *Next* button.

On the form factors screen, enable the *Phone and Tablet* option and set the minimum SDK to API 14: Android 4.0 (IceCreamSandwich). Continue to proceed through the screens, requesting the creation of an Empty Activity named *ImplicitIntentActivity* with a corresponding layout resource file named *activity_implicit_intent*.

Click *Finish* to create the new project.

44.2 Designing the User Interface

The user interface for the *ImplicitIntentActivity* class is very simple, consisting solely of a ConstraintLayout and a Button object. Within the Project tool window, locate the *app -> res -> layout -> activity_implicit_intent.xml* file and double-click on it to load it into the Layout Editor tool.

Delete the default TextView and, with Autoconnect mode enabled, position a Button widget so that it is centered within the layout. Note that the text on the button ("Show Web Page") has been extracted to a string resource named *show_web_page*.

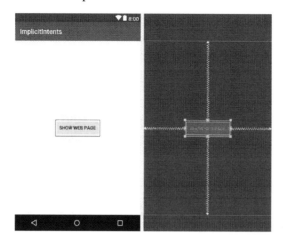

Figure 44-1

With the Button selected use the Attributes tool window to configure the *onClick* property to call a method named *showWebPage()*.

44.3 Creating the Implicit Intent

As outlined above, the implicit intent will be created and issued from within a method named *showWebPage()* which, in turn, needs to be implemented in the *ImplicitIntentActivity* class, the code for which resides in the *ImplicitIntentActivity.java* source file. Locate this file in the Project tool window and double-click on it to load it into an editing pane. Once loaded, modify the code to add the *showWebPage()* method together with a few requisite imports:

```java
package com.ebookfrenzy.implicitintent;

import android.support.v7.app.AppCompatActivity;
import android.os.Bundle;
import android.net.Uri;
import android.content.Intent;
import android.view.View;

public class ImplicitIntentActivity extends AppCompatActivity {

    @Override
    protected void onCreate(Bundle savedInstanceState) {
        super.onCreate(savedInstanceState);
        setContentView(R.layout.activity_implicit_intent);
    }

    public void showWebPage(View view) {
        Intent intent = new Intent(Intent.ACTION_VIEW,
                Uri.parse("http://www.ebookfrenzy.com"));

        startActivity(intent);
    }
}
```

}

The tasks performed by this method are actually very simple. First, a new intent object is created. Instead of specifying the class name of the intent, however, the code simply indicates the nature of the intent (to display something to the user) using the ACTION_VIEW option. The intent object also includes a URI containing the URL to be displayed. This indicates to the Android intent resolution system that the activity is requesting that a web page be displayed. The intent is then issued via a call to the *startActivity()* method.

Compile and run the application on either an emulator or a physical Android device and, once running, touch the *Show Web Page* button. When touched, a web browser view should appear and load the web page designated by the URL. A successful implicit intent has now been executed.

44.4 Adding a Second Matching Activity

The remainder of this chapter will be used to demonstrate the effect of the presence of more than one activity installed on the device matching the requirements for an implicit intent. To achieve this, a second application will be created and installed on the device or emulator. Begin, therefore, by creating a new project within Android Studio with the application name set to *MyWebView*, using the same SDK configuration options used when creating the ImplicitIntent project earlier in this chapter. Select an Empty Activity and, when prompted, name the activity *MyWebViewActivity* and the layout and resource file *activity_my_web_view*.

44.5 Adding the Web View to the UI

The user interface for the sole activity contained within the new *MyWebView* project is going to consist of an instance of the Android WebView widget. Within the Project tool window, locate the *activity_my_web_view.xml* file, which contains the user interface description for the activity, and double-click on it to load it into the Layout Editor tool.

With the Layout Editor tool in Design mode, select the default TextView widget and remove it from the layout by using the keyboard delete key.

Drag and drop a WebView object from the *Containers* section of the palette onto the existing ConstraintLayout view as illustrated in Figure 44-2:

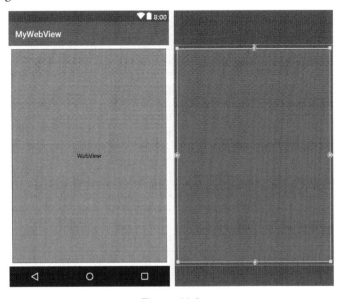

Figure 44-2

Before continuing, change the ID of the WebView instance to *webView1*.

44.6 Obtaining the Intent URL

When the implicit intent object is created to display a web browser window, the URL of the web page to be displayed will be bundled into the intent object within a Uri object. The task of the *onCreate()* method within the *MyWebViewActivity* class is to extract this Uri from the intent object, convert it into a URL string and assign it to the WebView object. To implement this functionality, modify the *MyWebViewActivity.java* file so that it reads as follows:

```
package com.ebookfrenzy.mywebview;

import android.support.v7.app.AppCompatActivity;
import android.os.Bundle;
import java.net.URL;
import android.net.Uri;
import android.content.Intent;
import android.webkit.WebView;

public class MyWebViewActivity extends AppCompatActivity {

    @Override
    protected void onCreate(Bundle savedInstanceState) {
        super.onCreate(savedInstanceState);
        setContentView(R.layout.activity_my_web_view);

        handleIntent();
    }

    private void handleIntent() {
        Intent intent = getIntent();

        Uri data = intent.getData();
        URL url = null;

        try {
            url = new URL(data.getScheme(),
                    data.getHost(),
                    data.getPath());
        } catch (Exception e) {
            e.printStackTrace();
        }

        WebView webView = (WebView) findViewById(R.id.webView1);
        webView.loadUrl(url.toString());
    }
}
```

The new code added to the *onCreate()* method performs the following tasks:

- Obtains a reference to the intent which caused this activity to be launched

- Extracts the Uri data from the intent object

- Converts the Uri data to a URL object

- Obtains a reference to the WebView object in the user interface

- Loads the URL into the web view, converting the URL to a String in the process

The coding part of the MyWebView project is now complete. All that remains is to modify the manifest file.

44.7 Modifying the MyWebView Project Manifest File

There are a number of changes that must be made to the MyWebView manifest file before it can be tested. In the first instance, the activity will need to seek permission to access the internet (since it will be required to load a web page). This is achieved by adding the appropriate permission line to the manifest file:

```
<uses-permission android:name="android.permission.INTERNET" />
```

Further, a review of the contents of the intent filter section of the *AndroidManifest.xml* file for the MyWebView project will reveal the following settings:

```
<intent-filter>
        <action android:name="android.intent.action.MAIN" />
        <category android:name="android.intent.category.LAUNCHER" />
</intent-filter>
```

In the above XML, the *android.intent.action.MAIN* entry indicates that this activity is the point of entry for the application when it is launched without any data input. The *android.intent.category.LAUNCHER* directive, on the other hand, indicates that the activity should be listed within the application launcher screen of the device.

Since the activity is not required to be launched as the entry point to an application, cannot be run without data input (in this case a URL) and is not required to appear in the launcher, neither the MAIN nor LAUNCHER directives are required in the manifest file for this activity.

The intent filter for the *MyWebViewActivity* activity does, however, need to be modified to indicate that it is capable of handling ACTION_VIEW intent actions for http data schemes.

Android also requires that any activities capable of handling implicit intents that do not include MAIN and LAUNCHER entries, also include the so-called *default category* in the intent filter. The modified intent filter section should therefore read as follows:

```
<intent-filter>
        <action android:name="android.intent.action.VIEW" />
        <category android:name="android.intent.category.DEFAULT" />
        <data android:scheme="http" />
</intent-filter>
```

Bringing these requirements together results in the following complete *AndroidManifest.xml* file:

```
<?xml version="1.0" encoding="utf-8"?>
<manifest xmlns:android="http://schemas.android.com/apk/res/android"
    package="com.ebookfrenzy.mywebview" >
```

```
<uses-permission android:name="android.permission.INTERNET" />

<application
    android:allowBackup="true"
    android:icon="@mipmap/ic_launcher"
    android:label="@string/app_name"
    android:theme="@style/AppTheme" >
    <activity
        android:name=".MyWebViewActivity"
        android:label="@string/app_name" >
        <intent-filter>
            <action android:name="android.intent.action.VIEW" />
            <category
                android:name="android.intent.category.DEFAULT" />
            <data android:scheme="http" />
        </intent-filter>

    </activity>
</application>

</manifest>
```

Load the *AndroidManifest.xml* file into the manifest editor by double-clicking on the file name in the Project tool window. Once loaded, modify the XML to match the above changes.

Having made the appropriate modifications to the manifest file, the new activity is ready to be installed on the device.

44.8 Installing the MyWebView Package on a Device

Before the MyWebViewActivity can be used as the recipient of an implicit intent, it must first be installed onto the device. This is achieved by running the application in the normal manner. Because the manifest file contains neither the *android.intent.action.MAIN* nor the *android.intent.category.LAUNCHER* Android Studio needs to be instructed to install, but not launch, the app. To configure this behavior, select the *app -> Edit configurations…* menu from the toolbar as illustrated in Figure 44-3:

Figure 44-3

Within the Run/Debug Configurations dialog, change the Launch option located in the *Launch Options* section of the panel to *Nothing* and click on Apply followed by OK:

Figure 44-4

With this setting configured run the app as usual. Note that the app is installed on the device, but not launched.

44.9 Testing the Application

In order to test MyWebView, simply re-launch the *ImplicitIntent* application created earlier in this chapter and touch the *Show Web Page* button. This time, however, the intent resolution process will find two activities with intent filters matching the implicit intent. As such, the system will display a dialog (Figure 44-5) providing the user with the choice of activity to launch.

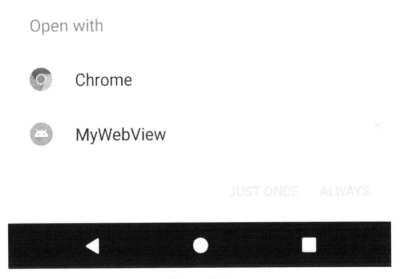

Figure 44-5

Selecting the *MyWebView* option followed by the *Just once* button should cause the intent to be handled by our new *MyWebViewActivity*, which will subsequently appear and display the designated web page.

If the web page loads into the Chrome browser without the above selection dialog appearing, it may be that Chrome has been configured as the default browser on the device. This can be changed by going to *Settings -> Apps & notifications* on the device followed *by App info*. Scroll down the list of apps and select *Chrome*. On the Chrome app info screen, tap the *Open by default* option followed by the *Clear Defaults* button.

44.10 Summary

Implicit intents provide a mechanism by which one activity can request the service of another, simply by specifying an action type and, optionally, the data on which that action is to be performed. In order to be eligible as a target candidate for an implicit intent, however, an activity must be configured to extract the appropriate data from the inbound intent object and be included in a correctly configured manifest file, including appropriate permissions and intent filters. When more than one matching activity for an implicit intent is found during an intent resolution search, the user is prompted to make a choice as to which to use.

Within this chapter an example was created to demonstrate both the issuing of an implicit intent, and the creation of an example activity capable of handling such an intent.

45. Android Broadcast Intents and Broadcast Receivers

In addition to providing a mechanism for launching application activities, intents are also used as a way to broadcast system wide messages to other components on the system. This involves the implementation of Broadcast Intents and Broadcast Receivers, both of which are the topic of this chapter.

45.1 An Overview of Broadcast Intents

Broadcast intents are Intent objects that are broadcast via a call to the *sendBroadcast()*, *sendStickyBroadcast()* or *sendOrderedBroadcast()* methods of the Activity class (the latter being used when results are required from the broadcast). In addition to providing a messaging and event system between application components, broadcast intents are also used by the Android system to notify interested applications about key system events (such as the external power supply or headphones being connected or disconnected).

When a broadcast intent is created, it must include an *action string* in addition to optional data and a category string. As with standard intents, data is added to a broadcast intent using key-value pairs in conjunction with the *putExtra()* method of the intent object. The optional category string may be assigned to a broadcast intent via a call to the *addCategory()* method.

The action string, which identifies the broadcast event, must be unique and typically uses the application's package name syntax. For example, the following code fragment creates and sends a broadcast intent including a unique action string and data:

```
Intent intent = new Intent();
intent.setAction("com.example.Broadcast");
intent.putExtra("MyData", 1000);
sendBroadcast(intent);
```

The above code would successfully launch the corresponding broadcast receiver on a device running an Android version earlier than 3.0. On more recent versions of Android, however, the intent would not be received by the broadcast receiver. This is because Android 3.0 introduced a launch control security measure that prevents components of *stopped* applications from being launched via an intent. An application is considered to be in a stopped state if the application has either just been installed and not previously launched, or been manually stopped by the user using the application manager on the device. To get around this, however, a flag can be added to the intent before it is sent to indicate that the intent is to be allowed to start a component of a stopped application. This flag is FLAG_INCLUDE_STOPPED_PACKAGES and would be used as outlined in the following adaptation of the previous code fragment:

```
Intent intent = new Intent();
intent.addFlags(Intent.FLAG_INCLUDE_STOPPED_PACKAGES);
intent.setAction("com.example.Broadcast");
intent.putExtra("MyData", 1000);
sendBroadcast(intent);
```

45.2 An Overview of Broadcast Receivers

An application listens for specific broadcast intents by registering a *broadcast receiver*. Broadcast receivers are implemented by extending the Android BroadcastReceiver class and overriding the *onReceive()* method. The broadcast receiver may then be registered, either within code (for example within an activity), or within a manifest file. Part of the registration implementation involves the creation of intent filters to indicate the specific broadcast intents the receiver is required to listen for. This is achieved by referencing the *action string* of the broadcast intent. When a matching broadcast is detected, the *onReceive()* method of the broadcast receiver is called, at which point the method has 5 seconds within which to perform any necessary tasks before returning. It is important to note that a broadcast receiver does not need to be running all the time. In the event that a matching intent is detected, the Android runtime system will automatically start up the broadcast receiver before calling the *onReceive()* method.

The following code outlines a template Broadcast Receiver subclass:

```
package com.example.broadcastdetector;

import android.content.BroadcastReceiver;
import android.content.Context;
import android.content.Intent;

public class MyReceiver extends BroadcastReceiver {

    public MyReceiver() {
    }

    @Override
    public void onReceive(Context context, Intent intent) {
        // Implement code here to be performed when
        // broadcast is detected
    }
}
```

When registering a broadcast receiver within a manifest file, a *<receiver>* entry must be added for the receiver.

The following example manifest file registers the above example broadcast receiver:

```
<?xml version="1.0" encoding="utf-8"?>
<manifest xmlns:android="http://schemas.android.com/apk/res/android"
    package="com.example.broadcastdetector.broadcastdetector"
    android:versionCode="1"
    android:versionName="1.0" >

    <uses-sdk android:minSdkVersion="17" />

    <application
        android:icon="@mipmap/ic_launcher"
        android:label="@string/app_name" >
        <receiver android:name="MyReceiver" >
        </receiver>
```

```
    </application>
</manifest>
```

When running on versions of Android older than Android 8.0, the intent filters associated with a receiver can be placed within the receiver element of the manifest file as follows:

```
<receiver android:name="MyReceiver" >
    <intent-filter>
        <action android:name="com.example.Broadcast" >
        </action>
    </intent-filter>
</receiver>
```

On Android 8.0 or later, the receiver must be registered in code using the *registerReceiver()* method of the Activity class together with an appropriately configured IntentFilter object:

```
IntentFilter filter = new IntentFilter("com.example.Broadcast");

MyReceiver receiver = new MyReceiver();
registerReceiver(receiver, filter);
```

When a broadcast receiver registered in code is no longer required, it may be unregistered via a call to the *unregisterReceiver()* method of the activity class, passing through a reference to the receiver object as an argument. For example, the following code will unregister the above broadcast receiver:

```
unregisterReceiver(receiver);
```

It is important to keep in mind that some system broadcast intents can only be detected by a broadcast receiver if it is registered in code rather than in the manifest file. Check the Android Intent class documentation for a detailed overview of the system broadcast intents and corresponding requirements online at:

http://developer.android.com/reference/android/content/Intent.html

45.3 Obtaining Results from a Broadcast

When a broadcast intent is sent using the *sendBroadcast()* method, there is no way for the initiating activity to receive results from any broadcast receivers that pick up the broadcast. In the event that return results are required, it is necessary to use the *sendOrderedBroadcast()* method instead. When a broadcast intent is sent using this method, it is delivered in sequential order to each broadcast receiver with a registered interest.

The *sendOrderedBroadcast()* method is called with a number of arguments including a reference to another broadcast receiver (known as the *result receiver*) which is to be notified when all other broadcast receivers have handled the intent, together with a set of data references into which those receivers can place result data. When all broadcast receivers have been given the opportunity to handle the broadcast, the *onReceive()* method of the *result receiver* is called and passed the result data.

45.4 Sticky Broadcast Intents

By default, broadcast intents disappear once they have been sent and handled by any interested broadcast receivers. A broadcast intent can, however, be defined as being "sticky". A sticky intent, and the data contained therein, remains present in the system after it has completed. The data stored within a sticky broadcast intent can be obtained via the return value of a call to the *registerReceiver()* method, using the usual arguments (references to the broadcast receiver and intent filter object). Many of the Android system broadcasts are sticky, a prime example being those broadcasts relating to battery level status.

A sticky broadcast may be removed at any time via a call to the *removeStickyBroadcast()* method, passing through as an argument a reference to the broadcast intent to be removed.

45.5 The Broadcast Intent Example

The remainder of this chapter will work through the creation of an Android Studio based example of broadcast intents in action. In the first instance, a simple application will be created for the purpose of issuing a custom broadcast intent. A corresponding broadcast receiver will then be created that will display a message on the display of the Android device when the broadcast is detected. Finally, the broadcast receiver will be modified to detect notification by the system that external power has been disconnected from the device.

45.6 Creating the Example Application

Launch Android Studio and create a new project, entering *SendBroadcast* into the Application name field and *ebookfrenzy.com* as the Company Domain setting before clicking on the *Next* button.

On the form factors screen, enable the *Phone and Tablet* option and set the minimum SDK setting to API 14: Android 4.0 (IceCreamSandwich). Continue to proceed through the screens, requesting the creation of an Empty Activity named *SendBroadcastActivity* with a corresponding layout resource file named *activity_send_broadcast*.

Once the new project has been created, locate and load the *activity_send_broadcast.xml* layout file located in the Project tool window under *app -> res -> layout* and, with the Layout Editor tool in Design mode, replace the TextView object with a Button view and set the text property so that it reads "Send Broadcast". Once the text value has been set, follow the usual steps to extract the string to a resource named *send_broadcast*.

With the button still selected in the layout, locate the *onClick* property in the Attributes panel and configure it to call a method named *broadcastIntent*.

45.7 Creating and Sending the Broadcast Intent

Having created the framework for the *SendBroadcast* application, it is now time to implement the code to send the broadcast intent. This involves implementing the *broadcastIntent()* method specified previously as the *onClick* target of the Button view in the user interface. Locate and double-click on the *SendBroadcastActivity. java* file and modify it to add the code to create and send the broadcast intent. Once modified, the source code for this class should read as follows:

```
package com.ebookfrenzy.sendbroadcast;

import android.support.v7.app.AppCompatActivity;
import android.os.Bundle;
import android.content.Intent;
import android.view.View;

public class SendBroadcastActivity extends AppCompatActivity {

    @Override
    protected void onCreate(Bundle savedInstanceState) {
        super.onCreate(savedInstanceState);
        setContentView(R.layout.activity_send_broadcast);
    }

    public void broadcastIntent(View view)
    {
        Intent intent = new Intent();
```

```
        intent.setAction("com.ebookfrenzy.sendbroadcast");
        intent.addFlags(Intent.FLAG_INCLUDE_STOPPED_PACKAGES);
        sendBroadcast(intent);
    }
}
```

Note that in this instance the action string for the intent is *com.ebookfrenzy.sendbroadcast*. When the broadcast receiver class is created in later sections of this chapter, it is essential that the intent filter declaration match this action string.

This concludes the creation of the application to send the broadcast intent. All that remains is to build a matching broadcast receiver.

45.8 Creating the Broadcast Receiver

In order to create the broadcast receiver, a new class needs to be created which subclasses the BroadcastReceiver superclass. Within the Project tool window, navigate to *app -> java* and right-click on the package name. From the resulting menu, select the *New -> Other -> Broadcast Receiver* menu option, name the class *MyReceiver* and make sure the *Exported* and *Enabled* options are selected. These settings allow the Android system to launch the receiver when needed and ensure that the class can receive messages sent by other applications on the device. With the class configured, click on *Finish*.

Once created, Android Studio will automatically load the new *MyReceiver.java* class file into the editor where it should read as follows:

```
package com.ebookfrenzy.sendbroadcast;

import android.content.BroadcastReceiver;
import android.content.Context;
import android.content.Intent;

public class MyReceiver extends BroadcastReceiver {

    public MyReceiver() {
    }

    @Override
    public void onReceive(Context context, Intent intent) {
        // TODO: This method is called when the BroadcastReceiver is receiving
        // an Intent broadcast.
        throw new UnsupportedOperationException("Not yet implemented");
    }
}
```

As can be seen in the code, Android Studio has generated a template for the new class and generated a stub for the *onReceive()* method. A number of changes now need to be made to the class to implement the required behavior. Remaining in the *MyReceiver.java* file, therefore, modify the code so that it reads as follows:

```
package com.ebookfrenzy.sendbroadcast;

import android.content.BroadcastReceiver;
import android.content.Context;
```

```
import android.content.Intent;
import android.widget.Toast;

public class MyReceiver extends BroadcastReceiver {

    public MyReceiver() {
    }

    @Override
    public void onReceive(Context context, Intent intent) {
        // TODO: This method is called when the BroadcastReceiver is receiving
        // an Intent broadcast.
        throw new UnsupportedOperationException("Not yet implemented");

        Toast.makeText(context, "Broadcast Intent Detected.",
                Toast.LENGTH_LONG).show();

    }
}
```

The code for the broadcast receiver is now complete.

45.9 Registering the Broadcast Receiver

The file needs to publicize the presence of the broadcast receiver and must include an intent filter to specify the broadcast intents in which the receiver is interested. When the BroadcastReceiver class was created in the previous section, Android Studio automatically added a <receiver> element to the manifest file. All that remains, therefore, is to add code within the *SendBroadcastActivity.java* file to create an intent filter and to register the receiver:

```
package com.ebookfrenzy.sendbroadcast;
.
.
import android.content.BroadcastReceiver;
import android.content.IntentFilter;
.
.
public class SendBroadcastActivity extends AppCompatActivity {

    BroadcastReceiver receiver;

    @Override
    protected void onCreate(Bundle savedInstanceState) {
        super.onCreate(savedInstanceState);
        setContentView(R.layout.activity_send_broadcast);

        configureReceiver();
    }
```

```
    private void configureReceiver() {
        IntentFilter filter = new IntentFilter();
        filter.addAction("com.ebookfrenzy.sendbroadcast");
        receiver = new MyReceiver();
        registerReceiver(receiver, filter);
    }
    .
    .
}
```

It is also important to unregister the broadcast receiver when it is no longer needed:

```
@Override
protected void onDestroy() {
    super.onDestroy();
    unregisterReceiver(receiver);
}
```

45.10 Testing the Broadcast Example

In order to test the broadcast sender and receiver, run the SendBroadcast app on a device or AVD and wait for it to appear on the display. Once running, touch the button, at which point the toast message reading "Broadcast Intent Detected." should pop up for a few seconds before fading away.

45.11 Listening for System Broadcasts

The final stage of this example is to modify the intent filter for the broadcast receiver to listen also for the system intent that is broadcast when external power is disconnected from the device. That action is *android.intent. action.ACTION_POWER_DISCONNECTED*. Modify the *onCreate()* method in the *SendBroadcastActivity.java* file to add this additional filter:

```
private void configureReceiver() {
    IntentFilter filter = new IntentFilter();
    filter.addAction("com.ebookfrenzy.sendbroadcast");
    filter.addAction(
            "android.intent.action.ACTION_POWER_DISCONNECTED");

    receiver = new MyReceiver();
    registerReceiver(receiver, filter);
}
```

Since the *onReceive()* method is now going to be listening for two types of broadcast intent, it is worthwhile to modify the code so that the action string of the current intent is also displayed in the toast message. This string can be obtained via a call to the *getAction()* method of the intent object passed as an argument to the *onReceive()* method:

```
public void onReceive(Context context, Intent intent) {
    String message = "Broadcast intent detected "
                    + intent.getAction();

    Toast.makeText(context, message,
            Toast.LENGTH_LONG).show();
```

```
}
```

Test the receiver by re-installing the modified *BroadcastReceiver* package. Touching the button in the *SendBroadcast* application should now result in a new message containing the custom action string:

```
Broadcast intent detected com.ebookfrenzy.sendbroadcast
```

Next, remove the USB connector that is currently supplying power to the Android device, at which point the receiver should report the following in the toast message. If the app is running on an emulator, display the extended controls, select the *Battery* option and change the *Charger connection* setting to *None*.

```
Broadcast intent detected android.intent.action.ACTION_POWER_DISCONNECTED
```

To avoid this message appearing every time the device is disconnected from a power supply launch the Settings app on the device and select the Apps option. Select the BroadcastReceiver app from the resulting list and taps the *Uninstall* button.

45.12 Summary

Broadcast intents are a mechanism by which an intent can be issued for consumption by multiple components on an Android system. Broadcasts are detected by registering a Broadcast Receiver which, in turn, is configured to listen for intents that match particular action strings. In general, broadcast receivers remain dormant until woken up by the system when a matching intent is detected. Broadcast intents are also used by the Android system to issue notifications of events such as a low battery warning or the connection or disconnection of external power to the device.

In addition to providing an overview of Broadcast intents and receivers, this chapter has also worked through an example of sending broadcast intents and the implementation of a broadcast receiver to listen for both custom and system broadcast intents.

46. A Basic Overview of Threads and AsyncTasks

The next chapter will be the first in a series of chapters intended to introduce the use of Android Services to perform application tasks in the background. It is impossible, however, to understand the steps involved in implementing services without first gaining a basic understanding of the concept of threading in Android applications. Threads and the AsyncTask class are, therefore, the topic of this chapter.

46.1 An Overview of Threads

Threads are the cornerstone of any multitasking operating system and can be thought of as mini-processes running within a main process, the purpose of which is to enable at least the appearance of parallel execution paths within applications.

46.2 The Application Main Thread

When an Android application is first started, the runtime system creates a single thread in which all application components will run by default. This thread is generally referred to as the *main thread*. The primary role of the main thread is to handle the user interface in terms of event handling and interaction with views in the user interface. Any additional components that are started within the application will, by default, also run on the main thread.

Any component within an application that performs a time consuming task using the main thread will cause the entire application to appear to lock up until the task is completed. This will typically result in the operating system displaying an "Application is not responding" warning to the user. Clearly, this is far from the desired behavior for any application. This can be avoided simply by launching the task to be performed in a separate thread, allowing the main thread to continue unhindered with other tasks.

46.3 Thread Handlers

Clearly, one of the key rules of Android development is to never perform time-consuming operations on the main thread of an application. The second, equally important, rule is that the code within a separate thread must never, under any circumstances, directly update any aspect of the user interface. Any changes to the user interface must always be performed from within the main thread. The reason for this is that the Android UI toolkit is not *thread-safe*. Attempts to work with non-thread-safe code from within multiple threads will typically result in intermittent problems and unpredictable application behavior.

If a time consuming task needs to run in a background thread and also update the user interface the best approach is to implement an asynchronous task by subclassing the AsyncTask class.

46.4 A Basic AsyncTask Example

The remainder of this chapter will work through some simple examples intended to provide a basic introduction to threads and the use of the AsyncTask class. The first step will be to highlight the importance of performing time-consuming tasks in a separate thread from the main thread. Begin, therefore, by creating a new project in Android Studio, entering *AsyncDemo* into the Application name field and *ebookfrenzy.com* as the Company Domain setting before clicking on the *Next* button.

A Basic Overview of Threads and AsyncTasks

On the form factors screen, enable the *Phone and Tablet* option and set the minimum SDK setting to API 14: Android 4.0 (IceCreamSandwich). Continue to proceed through the screens, requesting the creation of an Empty Activity named *AsyncDemoActivity*, using the default for the layout resource files.

Click *Finish* to create the new project.

Load the *activity_async_demo.xml* file for the project into the Layout Editor tool. Select the default TextView component and change the ID for the view to *myTextView* in the Attributes tool window.

With autoconnect mode disabled, add a Button view to the user interface, positioned directly beneath the existing TextView object as illustrated in Figure 46-1. Once the button has been added, click on the Infer Constraints button in the toolbar to add the missing constraints.

Change the text to "Press Me" and extract the string to a resource named *press_me*. With the button view still selected in the layout locate the *onClick* property and enter *buttonClick* as the method name.

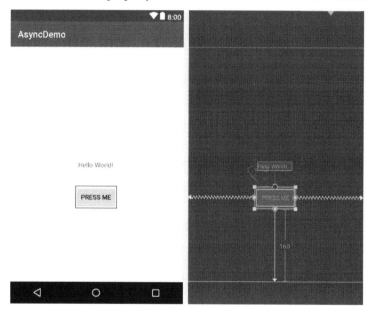

Figure 46-1

Next, load the *AsyncDemoActivity.java* file into an editing panel and add code to implement the *buttonClick()* method which will be called when the Button view is touched by the user. Since the goal here is to demonstrate the problem of performing lengthy tasks on the main thread, the code will simply pause for 20 seconds before displaying different text on the TextView object:

```
package com.ebookfrenzy.asyncdemo;

import android.support.v7.app.AppCompatActivity;
import android.os.Bundle;
import android.view.View;
import android.widget.TextView;

public class AsyncDemoActivity extends AppCompatActivity {

    private TextView myTextView;
```

```java
    @Override
    protected void onCreate(Bundle savedInstanceState) {
        super.onCreate(savedInstanceState);
        setContentView(R.layout.activity_thread_example);

        myTextView =
                (TextView)findViewById(R.id.myTextView);
    }


    public void buttonClick(View view)
    {
        int i = 0;
        while (i <= 20) {
            try {
                Thread.sleep(1000);
                i++;
            }
            catch (Exception e) {
            }
        }
        myTextView.setText("Button Pressed");
    }
}
```

With the code changes complete, run the application on either a physical device or an emulator. Once the application is running, touch the Button, at which point the application will appear to freeze. It will, for example, not be possible to touch the button a second time and in some situations the operating system will, as demonstrated in Figure 46-2, report the application as being unresponsive:

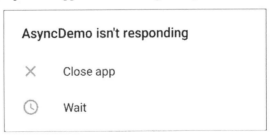

Figure 46-2

Clearly, anything that is going to take time to complete within the *buttonClick()* method needs to be performed within a separate thread.

46.5 Subclassing AsyncTask

In order to create a new thread, the code to be executed in that thread needs to be performed within an AsyncTask instance. The first step is to subclass AsyncTask in the *AsyncDemoActivity.java* file as follows:

.
.
.

A Basic Overview of Threads and AsyncTasks

```java
import android.os.AsyncTask;
.
.

public class AsyncDemoActivity extends AppCompatActivity {
.
.

    private class MyTask extends AsyncTask<String, Void, String> {

        @Override
        protected void onPreExecute() {
        }

        @Override
        protected String doInBackground(String... params) {
        }

        @Override
        protected void onProgressUpdate(Void... values) {
        }

        @Override
        protected void onPostExecute(String result) {
        }
    }
.
.
.
}
```

The AsyncTask class uses three different types which are declared in the class signature line as follows:

```java
private class MyTask extends AsyncTask<Type 1, Type 2, Type 3> {
.
.
```

These three types correspond to the argument types for the *doInBackground()*, *onProgressUpdate()* and *onPostExecute()* methods respectively. If a method does not expect an argument then Void is used, as is the case for the *onProgressUpdate()* in the above code. To change the argument type for a method, change the type declaration both in the class declaration and in the method signature. For this example, the *onProgressUpdate()* method will be passed an Integer, so modify the class declaration as follows:

```java
private class MyTask extends AsyncTask<String, Integer, String> {
.
.

        @Override
        protected void onProgressUpdate(Integer... values) {
        }
.
.
}
```

The *onPreExecute()* is called before the background tasks are initiated and can be used to perform initialization steps. This method runs on the main thread so may be used to update the user interface.

The code to be performed in the background on a different thread from the main thread resides in the *doInBackground()* method. This method does not have access to the main thread so cannot make user interface changes. The *onProgressUpdate()* method, however, is called each time a call is made to the *publishProgress()* method from within the *doInBackground()* method and can be used to update the user interface with progress information.

The *onPostExecute()* method is called when the tasks performed within the *doInBackground()* method complete. This method is passed the value returned by the *doInBackground()* method and runs within the main thread allowing user interface updates to be made.

Modify the code to move the timer code from the *buttonClick()* method to the *doInBackground()* method as follows:

```
@Override
protected String doInBackground(String... params) {

    int i = 0;
    while (i <= 20) {
        try {
            Thread.sleep(1000);
            publishProgress(i);
            i++;
        }
        catch (Exception e) {
            return(e.getLocalizedMessage());
        }
    }
    return "Button Pressed";
}
```

Next, move the TextView update code to the *onPostExecute()* method where it will display the text returned by the *doInBackground()* method:

```
@Override
protected void onPostExecute(String result) {
    myTextView.setText(result);
}
```

To provide regular updates via the *onProgressUpdate()* method, modify the class to add a call to the *publishProgress()* method in the timer loop code (passing through the current loop counter) and to display the current count value in the *onProgressUpdate()* method:

```
@Override
protected String doInBackground(String... params) {

    int i = 0;
    while (i <= 20) {
        publishProgress(i);
```

```
        try {
            Thread.sleep(1000);
            publishProgress(i);
            i++;
        }
        catch (Exception e) {
            return(e.getLocalizedMessage());
        }
    }
    return "Button Pressed";
}
```

```
@Override
protected void onProgressUpdate(Integer... values) {
    myTextView.setText("Counter = " + values[0]);
}
```

Finally, modify the *buttonClicked()* method to begin the asynchronous task execution:

```
public void buttonClick(View view)
{
    AsyncTask task = new MyTask().execute();
}
```

By default, asynchronous tasks are performed serially. In other words, if an app executes more than one task, only the first task begins execution. The remaining tasks are placed in a queue and executed in sequence as each one finishes. To execute asynchronous tasks in parallel, those tasks must be executed using the AsyncTask *thread pool executor* as follows:

```
AsyncTask task = new
        MyTask().executeOnExecutor(AsyncTask.THREAD_POOL_EXECUTOR);
```

The number of tasks that can be executed in parallel using this approach is limited by the core pool size on the device which, in turn, is dictated by the number of CPU cores available. The number of CPU cores available on a device can be identified from with app using the following code:

```
int cpu_cores = Runtime.getRuntime().availableProcessors();
```

Android uses an algorithm to calculate the default number of pool threads. The minimum number of threads is 2 while the maximum default value is equal to either 4, or the number of CPU core count minus 1 (whichever is smallest). The maximum possible number of threads available to the pool on any device is calculated by doubling the CPU core count and adding one.

46.6 Testing the App

When the application is now run, touching the button causes the delay to be performed in a new thread leaving the main thread to continue handling the user interface, including responding to additional button presses. During the delay, the user interface will be updated every second showing the counter value. On completion of the timeout, the TextView will display the "Button Pressed" message.

46.7 Canceling a Task

A running task may be canceled by calling the *cancel()* method of the task object passing through a Boolean value indicating whether the task can be interrupted before the in-progress task completes:

```
AsyncTask task = new MyTask().execute();
.
.
task.cancel(true);
```

46.8 Summary

The goal of this chapter was to provide an overview of threading within Android applications. When an application is first launched in a process, the runtime system creates a *main thread* in which all subsequently launched application components run by default. The primary role of the main thread is to handle the user interface, so any time consuming tasks performed in that thread will give the appearance that the application has locked up. It is essential, therefore, that tasks likely to take time to complete be started in a separate thread.

Because the Android user interface toolkit is not thread-safe, changes to the user interface should not be made in any thread other than the main thread. Background tasks may be performed in separate thread by subclassing the AsyncTask class and implementing the class methods to perform the task and update the user interface.

47. An Overview of Android Started and Bound Services

The Android Service class is designed specifically to allow applications to initiate and perform background tasks. Unlike broadcast receivers, which are intended to perform a task quickly and then exit, services are designed to perform tasks that take a long time to complete (such as downloading a file over an internet connection or streaming music to the user) but do not require a user interface.

In this chapter, an overview of the different types of services available will be covered, including *started services*, *bound services* and *intent services*. Once these basics have been covered, subsequent chapters will work through a number of examples of services in action.

47.1 Started Services

Started services are launched by other application components (such as an activity or even a broadcast receiver) and potentially run indefinitely in the background until the service is stopped, or is destroyed by the Android runtime system in order to free up resources. A service will continue to run if the application that started it is no longer in the foreground, and even in the event that the component that originally started the service is destroyed.

By default, a service will run within the same main thread as the application process from which it was launched (referred to as a *local service*). It is important, therefore, that any CPU intensive tasks be performed in a new thread within the service. Instructing a service to run within a separate process (and therefore known as a *remote service*) requires a configuration change within the manifest file.

Unless a service is specifically configured to be private (once again via a setting in the manifest file), that service can be started by other components on the same Android device. This is achieved using the Intent mechanism in the same way that one activity can launch another, as outlined in preceding chapters.

Started services are launched via a call to the *startService()* method, passing through as an argument an Intent object identifying the service to be started. When a started service has completed its tasks, it should stop itself via a call to *stopSelf()*. Alternatively, a running service may be stopped by another component via a call to the *stopService()* method, passing through as an argument the matching Intent for the service to be stopped.

Services are given a high priority by the Android system and are typically among the last to be terminated in order to free up resources.

47.2 Intent Service

As previously outlined, services run by default within the same main thread as the component from which they are launched. As such, any CPU intensive tasks that need to be performed by the service should take place within a new thread, thereby avoiding impacting the performance of the calling application.

The *IntentService* class is a convenience class (subclassed from the Service class) that sets up a worker thread for handling background tasks and handles each request in an asynchronous manner. Once the service has handled all queued requests, it simply exits. All that is required when using the IntentService class is that the *onHandleIntent()* method be implemented containing the code to be executed for each request.

For services that do not require synchronous processing of requests, IntentService is the recommended option. Services requiring synchronous handling of requests will, however, need to subclass from the Service class and manually implement and manage threading to handle any CPU intensive tasks efficiently.

47.3 Bound Service

A *bound service* is similar to a started service with the exception that a started service does not generally return results or permit interaction with the component that launched it. A bound service, on the other hand, allows the launching component to interact with, and receive results from, the service. Through the implementation of interprocess communication (IPC), this interaction can also take place across process boundaries. An activity might, for example, start a service to handle audio playback. The activity will, in all probability, include a user interface providing controls to the user for the purpose of pausing playback or skipping to the next track. Similarly, the service will quite likely need to communicate information to the calling activity to indicate that the current audio track has completed and to provide details of the next track that is about to start playing.

A component (also referred to in this context as a *client*) starts and *binds* to a bound service via a call to the *bindService()* method. Also, multiple components may bind to a service simultaneously. When the service binding is no longer required by a client, a call should be made to the *unbindService()* method. When the last bound client unbinds from a service, the service will be terminated by the Android runtime system. It is important to keep in mind that a bound service may also be started via a call to *startService()*. Once started, components may then bind to it via *bindService()* calls. When a bound service is launched via a call to *startService()* it will continue to run even after the last client unbinds from it.

A bound service must include an implementation of the *onBind()* method which is called both when the service is initially created and when other clients subsequently bind to the running service. The purpose of this method is to return to binding clients an object of type *IBinder* containing the information needed by the client to communicate with the service.

In terms of implementing the communication between a client and a bound service, the recommended technique depends on whether the client and service reside in the same or different processes and whether or not the service is private to the client. Local communication can be achieved by extending the Binder class and returning an instance from the *onBind()* method. Interprocess communication, on the other hand, requires Messenger and Handler implementation. Details of both of these approaches will be covered in later chapters.

47.4 The Anatomy of a Service

A service must, as has already been mentioned, be created as a subclass of the Android Service class (more specifically *android.app.Service*) or a sub-class thereof (such as *android.app.IntentService*). As part of the subclassing procedure, one or more of the following superclass callback methods must be overridden, depending on the exact nature of the service being created:

- **onStartCommand()** – This is the method that is called when the service is started by another component via a call to the *startService()* method. This method does not need to be implemented for bound services.

- **onBind()** – Called when a component binds to the service via a call to the *bindService()* method. When implementing a bound service, this method must return an *IBinder* object facilitating communication with the client. In the case of *started services*, this method must be implemented to return a NULL value.

- **onCreate()** – Intended as a location to perform initialization tasks, this method is called immediately before the call to either *onStartCommand()* or the *first* call to the *onBind()* method.

- **onDestroy()** – Called when the service is being destroyed.

- **onHandleIntent()** – Applies only to IntentService subclasses. This method is called to handle the processing for the service. It is executed in a separate thread from the main application.

Note that the IntentService class includes its own implementations of the *onStartCommand()* and *onBind()* callback methods so these do not need to be implemented in subclasses.

47.5 Controlling Destroyed Service Restart Options

The *onStartCommand()* callback method is required to return an integer value to define what should happen with regard to the service in the event that it is destroyed by the Android runtime system. Possible return values for these methods are as follows:

- **START_NOT_STICKY** – Indicates to the system that the service should not be restarted in the event that it is destroyed unless there are pending intents awaiting delivery.

- **START_STICKY** – Indicates that the service should be restarted as soon as possible after it has been destroyed if the destruction occurred after the *onStartCommand()* method returned. In the event that no pending intents are waiting to be delivered, the *onStartCommand()* callback method is called with a NULL intent value. The intent being processed at the time that the service was destroyed is discarded.

- **START_REDELIVER_INTENT** – Indicates that, if the service was destroyed after returning from the *onStartCommand()* callback method, the service should be restarted with the current intent redelivered to the *onStartCommand()* method followed by any pending intents.

47.6 Declaring a Service in the Manifest File

In order for a service to be useable, it must first be declared within a manifest file. This involves embedding an appropriately configured *<service>* element into an existing *<application>* entry. At a minimum, the <service> element must contain a property declaring the class name of the service as illustrated in the following XML fragment:

.

.

```
    <application
        android:icon="@mipmap/ic_launcher"
        android:label="@string/app_name" >
        <activity
            android:label="@string/app_name"
            android:name=".TestActivity" >
            <intent-filter>
              <action android:name="android.intent.action.MAIN" />
              <category android:name="android.intent.category.LAUNCHER" />
            </intent-filter>
        </activity>
        <service android:name="MyService>
            </service>
    </application>
</manifest>
```

By default, services are declared as public, in that they can be accessed by components outside of the application package in which they reside. In order to make a service private, the *android:exported* property must be declared as *false* within the <service> element of the manifest file. For example:

```
<service android:name="MyService"
```

```
android:exported="false">
</service>
```

As previously discussed, services run within the same process as the calling component by default. In order to force a service to run within its own process, add an *android:process* property to the <service> element, declaring a name for the process prefixed with a colon (:):

```
<service android:name="MyService"
android:exported="false"
android:process=":myprocess">
</service>
```

The colon prefix indicates that the new process is private to the local application. If the process name begins with a lower case letter instead of a colon, however, the process will be global and available for use by other components.

Finally, using the same intent filter mechanisms outlined for activities, a service may also advertise capabilities to other applications running on the device. For more details on intent filters, refer to the chapter entitled *"An Overview of Android Intents"*.

47.7 Starting a Service Running on System Startup

Given the background nature of services, it is not uncommon for a service to need to be started when an Android based system first boots up. This can be achieved by creating a broadcast receiver with an intent filter configured to listen for the system *android.intent.action.BOOT_COMPLETED* intent. When such an intent is detected, the broadcast receiver would simply invoke the necessary service and then return. Note that, in order to function, such a broadcast receiver will need to request the *android.permission.RECEIVE_BOOT_COMPLETED* permission.

47.8 Summary

Android services are a powerful mechanism that allows applications to perform tasks in the background. A service, once launched, will continue to run regardless of whether the calling application is the foreground task or not, and even in the event that the component that initiated the service is destroyed.

Services are subclassed from the Android Service class and fall into the category of either *started services* or *bound services*. Started services run until they are stopped or destroyed and do not inherently provide a mechanism for interaction or data exchange with other components. Bound services, on the other hand, provide a communication interface to other client components and generally run until the last client unbinds from the service.

By default, services run locally within the same process and main thread as the calling application. A new thread should, therefore, be created within the service for the purpose of handling CPU intensive tasks. Remote services may be started within a separate process by making a minor configuration change to the corresponding <service> entry in the application manifest file.

The IntentService class (itself a subclass of the Android Service class) provides a convenient mechanism for handling asynchronous service requests within a separate worker thread.

48. Implementing an Android Started Service – A Worked Example

The previous chapter covered a considerable amount of information relating to Android services and, at this point, the concept of services may seem somewhat overwhelming. In order to reinforce the information in the previous chapter, this chapter will work through an Android Studio tutorial intended to gradually introduce the concepts of started service implementation.

Within this chapter, a sample application will be created and used as the basis for implementing an Android service. In the first instance, the service will be created using the *IntentService* class. This example will subsequently be extended to demonstrate the use of the *Service* class. Finally, the steps involved in performing tasks within a separate thread when using the Service class will be implemented. Having covered started services in this chapter, the next chapter, entitled *"Android Local Bound Services – A Worked Example"*, will focus on the implementation of bound services and client-service communication.

48.1 Creating the Example Project

Launch Android Studio and follow the usual steps to create a new project, entering *ServiceExample* into the Application name field and *ebookfrenzy.com* as the Company Domain setting before clicking on the *Next* button.

On the form factors screen, enable the *Phone and Tablet* option and set the minimum SDK setting to API 14: Android 4.0 (IceCreamSandwich). Continue to proceed through the screens, requesting the creation of an Empty Activity named *ServiceExampleActivity* using the default values for the remaining options.

48.2 Creating the Service Class

Before writing any code, the first step is to add a new class to the project to contain the service. The first type of service to be demonstrated in this tutorial is to be based on the IntentService class. As outlined in the preceding chapter (*"An Overview of Android Started and Bound Services"*), the purpose of the IntentService class is to provide the developer with a convenient mechanism for creating services that perform tasks asynchronously within a separate thread from the calling application.

Add a new class to the project by right-clicking on the *com.ebookfrenzy.serviceexample* package name located under *app -> java* in the Project tool window and selecting the *New -> Java Class* menu option. Within the resulting *Create New Class* dialog, name the new class *MyIntentService*. Finally, click on the *OK* button to create the new class.

Review the new *MyIntentService.java* file in the Android Studio editor where it should read as follows:

```
package com.ebookfrenzy.serviceexample;


/**
 * Created by <name> on <date>.
 */
public class MyIntentService {
}
```

The class needs to be modified so that it subclasses the IntentService class. When subclassing the IntentService class, there are two rules that must be followed. First, a constructor for the class must be implemented which calls the superclass constructor, passing through the class name of the service. Second, the class must override the *onHandleIntent()* method. Modify the code in the *MyIntentService.java* file, therefore, so that it reads as follows:

```java
package com.ebookfrenzy.serviceexample;

import android.app.IntentService;
import android.content.Intent;

public class MyIntentService extends IntentService {

    @Override
    protected void onHandleIntent(Intent arg0) {

    }

    public MyIntentService() {
        super("MyIntentService");
    }
}
```

All that remains at this point is to implement some code within the *onHandleIntent()* method so that the service actually does something when invoked. Ordinarily this would involve performing a task that takes some time to complete such as downloading a large file or playing audio. For the purposes of this example, however, the handler will simply output a message to the Android Studio Logcat panel:

```java
package com.ebookfrenzy.serviceexample;

import android.app.IntentService;
import android.content.Intent;
import android.util.Log;

public class MyIntentService extends IntentService {

    private static final String TAG =
                "ServiceExample";

    @Override
    protected void onHandleIntent(Intent arg0) {
        Log.i(TAG, "Intent Service started");
    }

    public MyIntentService() {
        super("MyIntentService");
    }
}
```

48.3 Adding the Service to the Manifest File

Before a service can be invoked, it must first be added to the manifest file of the application to which it belongs. At a minimum, this involves adding a <service> element together with the class name of the service.

Double-click on the *AndroidManifest.xml* file (*app -> manifests*) for the current project to load it into the editor and modify the XML to add the service element as shown in the following listing:

```xml
<?xml version="1.0" encoding="utf-8"?>
<manifest xmlns:android="http://schemas.android.com/apk/res/android"
    package="com.ebookfrenzy.serviceexample">

    <application
        android:allowBackup="true"
        android:icon="@mipmap/ic_launcher"
        android:label="@string/app_name"
        android:supportsRtl="true"
        android:theme="@style/AppTheme">
        <activity android:name=".ServiceExampleActivity">
            <intent-filter>
                <action android:name="android.intent.action.MAIN" />

                <category android:name="android.intent.category.LAUNCHER" />
            </intent-filter>
        </activity>
        <service android:name=".MyIntentService" />
    </application>

</manifest>
```

48.4 Starting the Service

Now that the service has been implemented and declared in the manifest file, the next step is to add code to start the service when the application launches. As is typically the case, the ideal location for such code is the *onCreate()* callback method of the activity class (which, in this case, can be found in the *ServiceExampleActivity. java* file). Locate and load this file into the editor and modify the *onCreate()* method to add the code to start the service:

```java
package com.ebookfrenzy.serviceexample;

import android.support.v7.app.AppCompatActivity;
import android.os.Bundle;
import android.content.Intent;

public class ServiceExampleActivity extends AppCompatActivity {

    @Override
    protected void onCreate(Bundle savedInstanceState) {
        super.onCreate(savedInstanceState);
        setContentView(R.layout.activity_service_example);
```

```
        Intent intent = new Intent(this, MyIntentService.class);
        startService(intent);
    }
}
```

All that the added code needs to do is to create a new Intent object primed with the class name of the service to start and then use it as an argument to the *startService()* method.

48.5 Testing the IntentService Example

The example IntentService based service is now complete and ready to be tested. Since the message displayed by the service will appear in the Logcat panel, it is important that this is configured in the Android Studio environment.

Begin by displaying the Logcat tool window before clicking on the menu in the upper right-hand corner of the panel (which will probably currently read *Show only selected application*). From this menu, select the *Edit Filter Configuration* menu option.

In the *Create New Logcat Filter* dialog name the filter *ServiceExample* and, in the *by Log Tag* field, enter the TAG value declared in *ServiceExampleActivity.java* (in the above code example this was *ServiceExample*).

When the changes are complete, click on the *OK* button to create the filter and dismiss the dialog. The newly created filter should now be selected in the Android tool window.

With the filter configured, run the application on a physical device or AVD emulator session and note that the "Intent Service Started" message appears in the Logcat panel. Note that it may be necessary to change the filter menu setting back to ServiceExample after the application has launched:

```
06-29 09:05:16.887 3389-3948/com.ebookfrenzy.serviceexample I/ServiceExample: Int
ent Service started
```

Had the service been tasked with a long-term activity, the service would have continued to run in the background in a separate thread until the task was completed, allowing the application to continue functioning and responding to the user. Since all our service did was log a message, it will have simply stopped upon completion.

48.6 Using the Service Class

While the IntentService class allows a service to be implemented with minimal coding, there are situations where the flexibility and synchronous nature of the Service class will be required. As will become evident in this chapter, this involves some additional programming work to implement.

In order to avoid introducing too many concepts at once, and as a demonstration of the risks inherent in performing time-consuming service tasks in the same thread as the calling application, the example service created here will not run the service task within a new thread, instead relying on the main thread of the application. Creation and management of a new thread within a service will be covered in the next phase of the tutorial.

48.7 Creating the New Service

For the purposes of this example, a new class will be added to the project that will subclass from the Service class. Right-click, therefore, on the package name listed under *app -> java* in the Project tool window and select the *New -> Service -> Service* menu option. Create a new class named *MyService* with both the *Exported* and *Enabled* options selected.

The minimal requirement in order to create an operational service is to implement the *onStartCommand()* callback method which will be called when the service is starting up. In addition, the *onBind()* method must return a null value to indicate to the Android system that this is not a bound service. For the purposes of this example, the *onStartCommand()* method will loop 3 times sleeping for 10 seconds on each loop iteration. For the sake of completeness, stub versions of the *onCreate()* and *onDestroy()* methods will also be implemented in the new *MyService.java* file as follows:

```
package com.ebookfrenzy.serviceexample;

import android.app.Service;
import android.content.Intent;
import android.os.IBinder;
import android.util.Log;

public class MyService extends Service {

    public MyService() {
    }

    private static final String TAG =
            "ServiceExample";

    @Override
    public void onCreate() {
        Log.i(TAG, "Service onCreate");
    }

    @Override
    public int onStartCommand(Intent intent, int flags, int startId) {

        Log.i(TAG, "Service onStartCommand " + startId);

        int i = 0;
        while (i <= 3) {

            try {
                Thread.sleep(10000);
                i++;
            } catch (Exception e) {
            }
            Log.i(TAG, "Service running");
        }
        return Service.START_STICKY;
    }

    @Override
    public IBinder onBind(Intent arg0) {
        Log.i(TAG, "Service onBind");
```

```
            return null;
    }


    @Override
    public void onDestroy() {
        Log.i(TAG, "Service onDestroy");
    }
}
```

With the service implemented, load the *AndroidManifest.xml* file into the editor and verify that Android Studio has added an appropriate entry for the new service which should read as follows:

```
<service
 android:name=".MyService"
            android:enabled="true"
            android:exported="true" >
</service>
```

48.8 Modifying the User Interface

As will become evident when the application runs, failing to create a new thread for the service to perform tasks creates a serious usability problem. In order to be able to appreciate fully the magnitude of this issue, it is going to be necessary to add a Button view to the user interface of the *ServiceExampleActivity* activity and configure it to call a method when "clicked" by the user.

Locate and load the *activity_service_example.xml* file in the Project tool window (*app -> res -> layout -> activity_service_example.xml*). Delete the TextView and add a Button view to the layout. Select the new button, change the text to read "Start Service" and extract the string to a resource named *start_service*.

With the new Button still selected, locate the *onClick* property in the Attributes panel and assign to it a method named *buttonClick*.

Next, edit the *ServiceExampleActivity.java* file to add the *buttonClick()* method and remove the code from the *onCreate()* method that was previously added to launch the MyIntentService service:

```
package com.ebookfrenzy.serviceexample;


import android.support.v7.app.AppCompatActivity;
import android.os.Bundle;
import android.content.Intent;
import android.view.View;


public class ServiceExampleActivity extends AppCompatActivity {

    @Override
    protected void onCreate(Bundle savedInstanceState) {
        super.onCreate(savedInstanceState);
        setContentView(R.layout.activity_service_example);
        Intent intent = new Intent(this, MyIntentService.class);
        startService(intent);
    }
}
```

```
public void buttonClick(View view)
{
    Intent intent = new Intent(this, MyService.class);
    startService(intent);
}
}
```

All that the *buttonClick()* method does is create an intent object for the new service and then start it running.

48.9 Running the Application

Run the application and, once loaded, touch the *Start Service* button. Within the Logcat tool window (using the *ServiceExample* filter created previously) the log messages will appear indicating that the *onCreate()* method was called and that the loop in the *onStartCommand()* method is executing.

Before the final loop message appears, attempt to touch the *Start Service* button a second time. Note that the button is unresponsive. After approximately 20 seconds, the system may display a warning dialog containing the message "ServiceExample isn't responding". The reason for this is that the main thread of the application is currently being held up by the service while it performs the looping task. Not only does this prevent the application from responding to the user, but also to the system, which eventually assumes that the application has locked up in some way.

Clearly, the code for the service needs to be modified to perform tasks in a separate thread from the main thread.

48.10 Creating an AsyncTask for Service Tasks

As outlined in *"A Basic Overview of Threads and AsyncTasks"*, when an Android application is first started, the runtime system creates a single thread in which all application components will run by default. This thread is generally referred to as the *main thread*. The primary role of the main thread is to handle the user interface in terms of event handling and interaction with views in the user interface. Any additional components that are started within the application will, by default, also run on the main thread.

As demonstrated in the previous section, any component that undertakes a time consuming operation on the main thread will cause the application to become unresponsive until that task is complete. It is not surprising, therefore, that Android provides an API that allows applications to create and use additional threads. Any tasks performed in a separate thread from the main thread are essentially performed in the background. Such threads are typically referred to as *background* or *worker* threads.

A very simple solution to this problem involves performing the service task within an AsyncTask instance. To add this support to the app, modify the *MyService.java* file create an AsyncTask subclass containing the timer code from the *onStartCommand()* method:

```
.
.
import android.os.AsyncTask;
.
.
private class SrvTask extends AsyncTask<Integer, Integer, String> {

    @Override
    protected String doInBackground(Integer... params) {
```

```
        int startId = params[0];
        int i = 0;
        while (i <= 3) {

            publishProgress(params[0]);
            try {
                Thread.sleep(10000);
                i++;
            } catch (Exception e) {

            }
        }
        return("Service complete " + startId);
    }


    @Override
    protected void onPostExecute(String result) {
        Log.i(TAG, result);
    }


    @Override
    protected void onPreExecute() {


    }


    @Override
    protected void onProgressUpdate(Integer... values) {
        Log.i(TAG, "Service Running " + values[0]);
    }
}
```

Next, modify the *onStartCommand()* method to execute the task in the background, this time using the thread pool executor to allow multiple instances of the task to run in parallel:

```
@Override
public int onStartCommand(Intent intent, int flags, int startId) {

    AsyncTask task = new SrvTask().executeOnExecutor(
                    AsyncTask.THREAD_POOL_EXECUTOR, startId);


    return Service.START_STICKY;
}
```

When the application is now run, it should be possible to touch the *Start Service* button multiple times. When doing so, the Logcat output should indicate more than one task running simultaneously (subject to CPU core limitations):

```
I/ServiceExample: Service Running 1
I/ServiceExample: Service Running 2
I/ServiceExample: Service Running 1
```

```
I/ServiceExample: Service Running 2
I/ServiceExample: Service Running 1
I/ServiceExample: Service Running 2
I/ServiceExample: Service Running 1
I/ServiceExample: Service Running 2
I/ServiceExample: Service complete 1
I/ServiceExample: Service complete 2
```

With the service now handling requests outside of the main thread, the application remains responsive to both the user and the Android system.

48.11 Summary

This chapter has worked through an example implementation of an Android started service using the *IntentService* and *Service* classes. The example also demonstrated the use of asynchronous tasks within a service to avoid making the main thread of the application unresponsive.

49. Android Local Bound Services – A Worked Example

As outlined in some detail in the previous chapters, bound services, unlike started services, provide a mechanism for implementing communication between an Android service and one or more client components. The objective of this chapter is to build on the overview of bound services provided in *"An Overview of Android Started and Bound Services"* before embarking on an example implementation of a *local* bound service in action.

49.1 Understanding Bound Services

In common with started services, bound services are provided to allow applications to perform tasks in the background. Unlike started services, however, multiple client components may *bind* to a bound service and, once bound, interact with that service using a variety of different mechanisms.

Bound services are created as sub-classes of the Android Service class and must, at a minimum, implement the *onBind()* method. Client components bind to a service via a call to the *bindService()* method. The first bind request to a bound service will result in a call to that service's *onBind()* method (subsequent bind requests do not trigger an *onBind()* call). Clients wishing to bind to a service must also implement a ServiceConnection subclass containing *onServiceConnected()* and *onServiceDisconnected()* methods which will be called once the client-server connection has been established or disconnected, respectively. In the case of the *onServiceConnected()* method, this will be passed an IBinder object containing the information needed by the client to interact with the service.

49.2 Bound Service Interaction Options

There are two recommended mechanisms for implementing interaction between client components and a bound service. In the event that the bound service is local and private to the same application as the client component (in other words it runs within the same process and is not available to components in other applications), the recommended method is to create a subclass of the Binder class and extend it to provide an interface to the service. An instance of this Binder object is then returned by the *onBind()* method and subsequently used by the client component to directly access methods and data held within the service.

In situations where the bound service is not local to the application (in other words, it is running in a different process from the client component), interaction is best achieved using a Messenger/Handler implementation.

In the remainder of this chapter, an example will be created with the aim of demonstrating the steps involved in creating, starting and interacting with a local, private bound service.

49.3 An Android Studio Local Bound Service Example

The example application created in the remainder of this chapter will consist of a single activity and a bound service. The purpose of the bound service is to obtain the current time from the system and return that information to the activity where it will be displayed to the user. The bound service will be local and private to the same application as the activity.

Launch Android Studio and follow the usual steps to create a new project, entering *LocalBound* into the Application name field and *ebookfrenzy.com* as the Company Domain setting before clicking on the *Next* button.

On the form factors screen, enable the *Phone and Tablet* option and set the minimum SDK setting to API 14: Android 4.0 (IceCreamSandwich). Continue to proceed through the screens, requesting the creation of an Empty Activity named *LocalBoundActivity* with the remaining fields set to the default values.

Once the project has been created, the next step is to add a new class to act as the bound service.

49.4 Adding a Bound Service to the Project

To add a new class to the project, right-click on the package name (located under *app -> java -> com.ebookfrenzy. localbound*) within the Project tool window and select the *New -> Service -> Service* menu option. Specify *BoundService* as the class name and make sure that both the *Exported* and *Enabled* options are selected before clicking on *Finish* to create the class. By default, Android Studio will load the *BoundService.java* file into the editor where it will read as follows:

```
package com.ebookfrenzy.localbound;


import android.app.Service;
import android.content.Intent;
import android.os.IBinder;


public class BoundService extends Service {
    public BoundService() {
    }

    @Override
    public IBinder onBind(Intent intent) {
        // TODO: Return the communication channel to the service.
        throw new UnsupportedOperationException("Not yet implemented");
    }
}
```

49.5 Implementing the Binder

As previously outlined, local bound services can communicate with bound clients by passing an appropriately configured Binder object to the client. This is achieved by creating a Binder subclass within the bound service class and extending it by adding one or more new methods that can be called by the client. In most cases, this simply involves implementing a method that returns a reference to the bound service instance. With a reference to this instance, the client can then access data and call methods within the bound service directly.

For the purposes of this example, therefore, some changes are needed to the template *BoundService* class created in the preceding section. In the first instance, a Binder subclass needs to be declared. This class will contain a single method named *getService()* which will simply return a reference to the current service object instance (represented by the *this* keyword). With these requirements in mind, edit the *BoundService.java* file and modify it as follows:

```
package com.ebookfrenzy.localbound;


import android.app.Service;
import android.content.Intent;
import android.os.IBinder;
import android.os.Binder;
```

```
public class BoundService extends Service {

    private final IBinder myBinder = new MyLocalBinder();

    public BoundService() {
    }

    @Override
    public IBinder onBind(Intent intent) {
        // TODO: Return the communication channel to the service.
        throw new UnsupportedOperationException("Not yet implemented");
    }

    public class MyLocalBinder extends Binder {
        BoundService getService() {
            return BoundService.this;
        }
    }
}
```

Having made the changes to the class, it is worth taking a moment to recap the steps performed here. First, a new subclass of Binder (named *MyLocalBinder*) is declared. This class contains a single method for the sole purpose of returning a reference to the current instance of the *BoundService* class. A new instance of the *MyLocalBinder* class is created and assigned to the *myBinder* IBinder reference (since Binder is a subclass of IBinder there is no type mismatch in this assignment).

Next, the *onBind()* method needs to be modified to return a reference to the *myBinder* object and a new public method implemented to return the current time when called by any clients that bind to the service:

```
package com.ebookfrenzy.localbound;

import java.text.SimpleDateFormat;
import java.util.Date;
import java.util.Locale;

import android.app.Service;
import android.content.Intent;
import android.os.IBinder;
import android.os.Binder;

public class BoundService extends Service {

    private final IBinder myBinder = new MyLocalBinder();

    public BoundService() {
    }

    @Override
```

```
public IBinder onBind(Intent intent) {
    return myBinder;
}


public String getCurrentTime() {
    SimpleDateFormat dateformat =
            new SimpleDateFormat("HH:mm:ss MM/dd/yyyy",
                    Locale.US);
    return (dateformat.format(new Date()));
}


public class MyLocalBinder extends Binder {
    BoundService getService() {
        return BoundService.this;
    }
}

}
```

At this point, the bound service is complete and is ready to be added to the project manifest file. Locate and double-click on the *AndroidManifest.xml* file for the *LocalBound* project in the Project tool window and, once loaded into the Manifest Editor, verify that Android Studio has already added a <service> entry for the service as follows:

```
<?xml version="1.0" encoding="utf-8"?>
<manifest xmlns:android="http://schemas.android.com/apk/res/android"
    package="com.ebookfrenzy.localbound.localbound" >

    <application
        android:allowBackup="true"
        android:icon="@mipmap/ic_launcher"
        android:label="@string/app_name"
        android:theme="@style/AppTheme" >
        <activity
            android:name=" .LocalBoundActivity" >
            <intent-filter>
                <action android:name="android.intent.action.MAIN" />

                <category android:name="android.intent.category.LAUNCHER" />
            </intent-filter>
        </activity>

        <service
            android:name=".BoundService"
            android:enabled="true"
            android:exported="true" >
        </service>
    </application>
```

```
</manifest>
```

The next phase is to implement the necessary code within the activity to bind to the service and call the *getCurrentTime()* method.

49.6 Binding the Client to the Service

For the purposes of this tutorial, the client is the *LocalBoundActivity* instance of the running application. As previously noted, in order to successfully bind to a service and receive the IBinder object returned by the service's *onBind()* method, it is necessary to create a ServiceConnection subclass and implement *onServiceConnected()* and *onServiceDisconnected()* callback methods. Edit the *LocalBoundActivity.java* file and modify it as follows:

```
package com.ebookfrenzy.localbound;

import android.support.v7.app.AppCompatActivity;
import android.os.Bundle;
import android.os.IBinder;
import android.content.Context;
import android.content.Intent;
import android.content.ComponentName;
import android.content.ServiceConnection;
import com.ebookfrenzy.localbound.BoundService.MyLocalBinder;

public class LocalBoundActivity extends AppCompatActivity {

    BoundService myService;
    boolean isBound = false;

    @Override
    protected void onCreate(Bundle savedInstanceState) {
        super.onCreate(savedInstanceState);
        setContentView(R.layout.activity_local_bound);
    }

    private ServiceConnection myConnection = new ServiceConnection()
    {
        @Override
        public void onServiceConnected(ComponentName className,
                                        IBinder service) {
            MyLocalBinder binder = (MyLocalBinder) service;
            myService = binder.getService();
            isBound = true;
        }

        @Override
        public void onServiceDisconnected(ComponentName name) {
            isBound = false;
```

```
            }
      };
}
```

The *onServiceConnected()* method will be called when the client binds successfully to the service. The method is passed as an argument the IBinder object returned by the *onBind()* method of the service. This argument is cast to an object of type MyLocalBinder and then the *getService()* method of the binder object is called to obtain a reference to the service instance, which, in turn, is assigned to *myService*. A Boolean flag is used to indicate that the connection has been successfully established.

The *onServiceDisconnected()* method is called when the connection ends and simply sets the Boolean flag to false.

Having established the connection, the next step is to modify the activity to bind to the service. This involves the creation of an intent and a call to the *bindService()* method, which can be performed in the *onCreate()* method of the activity:

```
@Override
    public void onCreate(Bundle savedInstanceState) {
        super.onCreate(savedInstanceState);
        setContentView(R.layout.activity_local_bound);
        Intent intent = new Intent(this, BoundService.class);
        bindService(intent, myConnection, Context.BIND_AUTO_CREATE);
}
```

49.7 Completing the Example

All that remains is to implement a mechanism for calling the *getCurrentTime()* method and displaying the result to the user. As is now customary, Android Studio will have created a template *activity_local_bound.xml* file for the activity containing only a TextView. Load this file into the Layout Editor tool and, using Design mode, select the TextView component and change the ID to *myTextView*. Add a Button view beneath the TextView and change the text on the button to read "Show Time", extracting the text to a string resource named *show_time*. On completion of these changes, the layout should resemble that illustrated in Figure 49-1. If any constraints are missing, click on the Infer Constraints button in the Layout Editor toolbar.

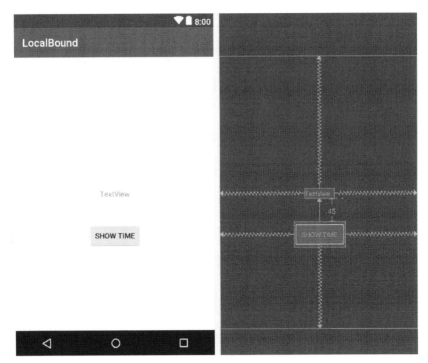

Figure 49-1

Complete the user interface design by selecting the Button and configuring the *onClick* property to call a method named *showTime*.

Finally, edit the code in the *LocalBoundActivity.java* file to implement the *showTime()* method. This method simply calls the *getCurrentTime()* method of the service (which, thanks to the *onServiceConnected()* method, is now available from within the activity via the *myService* reference) and assigns the resulting string to the TextView:

```
package com.ebookfrenzy.localbound;


import android.support.v7.app.AppCompatActivity;
import android.os.Bundle;
import android.os.IBinder;
import android.content.Context;
import android.content.Intent;
import android.content.ComponentName;
import android.content.ServiceConnection;
import com.ebookfrenzy.localbound.BoundService.MyLocalBinder;
import android.view.View;
import android.widget.TextView;


public class LocalBoundActivity extends AppCompatActivity {

    BoundService myService;
    boolean isBound = false;
```

```
public void showTime(View view)
{
    String currentTime = myService.getCurrentTime();
    TextView myTextView =
            (TextView)findViewById(R.id.myTextView);
    myTextView.setText(currentTime);
}
 .
 .
 .
}
```

49.8 Testing the Application

With the code changes complete, perform a test run of the application. Once visible, touch the button and note that the text view changes to display the current date and time. The example has successfully started and bound to a service and then called a method of that service to cause a task to be performed and results returned to the activity.

49.9 Summary

When a bound service is local and private to an application, components within that application can interact with the service without the need to resort to inter-process communication (IPC). In general terms, the service's *onBind()* method returns an IBinder object containing a reference to the instance of the running service. The client component implements a ServiceConnection subclass containing callback methods that are called when the service is connected and disconnected. The former method is passed the IBinder object returned by the *onBind()* method allowing public methods within the service to be called.

Having covered the implementation of local bound services, the next chapter will focus on using IPC to interact with remote bound services.

50. Android Remote Bound Services – A Worked Example

In this, the final chapter dedicated to Android services, an example application will be developed to demonstrate the use of a messenger and handler configuration to facilitate interaction between a client and remote bound service.

50.1 Client to Remote Service Communication

As outlined in the previous chapter, interaction between a client and a local service can be implemented by returning to the client an IBinder object containing a reference to the service object. In the case of remote services, however, this approach does not work because the remote service is running in a different process and, as such, cannot be reached directly from the client.

In the case of remote services, a Messenger and Handler configuration must be created which allows messages to be passed across process boundaries between client and service.

Specifically, the service creates a Handler instance that will be called when a message is received from the client. In terms of initialization, it is the job of the Handler to create a Messenger object which, in turn, creates an IBinder object to be returned to the client in the *onBind()* method. This IBinder object is used by the client to create an instance of the Messenger object and, subsequently, to send messages to the service handler. Each time a message is sent by the client, the *handleMessage()* method of the handler is called, passing through the message object.

The simple example created in this chapter will consist of an activity and a bound service running in separate processes. The Messenger/Handler mechanism will be used to send a string to the service, which will then display that string in a Toast message.

50.2 Creating the Example Application

Launch Android Studio and follow the steps to create a new project, entering *RemoteBound* into the Application name field and *ebookfrenzy.com* as the Company Domain setting before clicking on the *Next* button.

On the form factors screen, enable the *Phone and Tablet* option and set the minimum SDK setting to API 14: Android 4.0 (IceCreamSandwich). Continue to proceed through the screens, requesting the creation of an Empty Activity named *RemoteBoundActivity* with a corresponding layout resource file named *activity_remote_bound*.

50.3 Designing the User Interface

Locate the *activity_remote_bound.xml* file in the Project tool window and double-click on it to load it into the Layout Editor tool. With the Layout Editor tool in Design mode, delete the default TextView instance and drag and drop a Button widget from the palette so that it is positioned in the center of the layout. Change the text property of the button to read "Send Message" and extract the string to a new resource named *send_message*.

Finally, configure the *onClick* property to call a method named *sendMessage*.

50.4 Implementing the Remote Bound Service

In order to implement the remote bound service for this example, add a new class to the project by right-clicking on the package name (located under *app -> java*) within the Project tool window and select the *New -> Service -> Service* menu option. Specify *RemoteService* as the class name and make sure that both the *Exported* and *Enabled* options are selected before clicking on *Finish* to create the class.

The next step is to implement the handler class for the new service. This is achieved by extending the Handler class and implementing the *handleMessage()* method. This method will be called when a message is received from the client. It will be passed a Message object as an argument containing any data that the client needs to pass to the service. In this instance, this will be a Bundle object containing a string to be displayed to the user. The modified class in the *RemoteService.java* file should read as follows once this has been implemented:

```
package com.ebookfrenzy.remotebound;

import android.app.Service;
import android.content.Intent;
import android.os.IBinder;
import android.os.Bundle;
import android.os.Handler;
import android.os.Message;
import android.widget.Toast;
import android.os.Messenger;

public class RemoteService extends Service {

    public RemoteService() {
    }

    class IncomingHandler extends Handler {
        @Override
        public void handleMessage(Message msg) {

            Bundle data = msg.getData();
            String dataString = data.getString("MyString");
            Toast.makeText(getApplicationContext(),
                    dataString, Toast.LENGTH_SHORT).show();
        }
    }

    @Override
    public IBinder onBind(Intent intent) {
        // TODO: Return the communication channel to the service.
        throw new UnsupportedOperationException("Not yet implemented");
    }
}
```

With the handler implemented, the only remaining task in terms of the service code is to modify the *onBind()*

method such that it returns an IBinder object containing a Messenger object which, in turn, contains a reference to the handler:

```
final Messenger myMessenger = new Messenger(new IncomingHandler());


@Override
public IBinder onBind(Intent intent) {
        return myMessenger.getBinder();
}
```

The first line of the above code fragment creates a new instance of our handler class and passes it through to the constructor of a new Messenger object. Within the *onBind()* method, the *getBinder()* method of the messenger object is called to return the messenger's IBinder object.

50.5 Configuring a Remote Service in the Manifest File

In order to portray the communication between a client and remote service accurately, it will be necessary to configure the service to run in a separate process from the rest of the application. This is achieved by adding an *android:process* property within the <service> tag for the service in the manifest file. In order to launch a remote service it is also necessary to provide an intent filter for the service. To implement these changes, modify the *AndroidManifest.xml* file to add the required entries:

```xml
<?xml version="1.0" encoding="utf-8"?>
<manifest xmlns:android="http://schemas.android.com/apk/res/android"
    package="com.ebookfrenzy.remotebound" >

    <application
        android:allowBackup="true"
        android:icon="@mipmap/ic_launcher"
        android:label="@string/app_name"
        android:supportsRtl="true"
        android:theme="@style/AppTheme" >
        <activity
            android:name=".RemoteBoundActivity" >
            <intent-filter>
                <action android:name="android.intent.action.MAIN" />

                <category android:name="android.intent.category.LAUNCHER" />
            </intent-filter>
        </activity>

        <service
            android:name=".RemoteService"
            android:enabled="true"
            android:exported="true"
            android:process=":my_process" >
        </service>
    </service>
    </application>
```

```
</manifest>
```

50.6 Launching and Binding to the Remote Service

As with a local bound service, the client component needs to implement an instance of the ServiceConnection class with *onServiceConnected()* and *onServiceDisconnected()* methods. Also, in common with local services, the *onServiceConnected()* method will be passed the IBinder object returned by the *onBind()* method of the remote service which will be used to send messages to the server handler. In the case of this example, the client is *RemoteBoundActivity*, the code for which is located in *RemoteBoundActivity.java*. Load this file and modify it to add the ServiceConnection class and a variable to store a reference to the received Messenger object together with a Boolean flag to indicate whether or not the connection is established:

```
package com.ebookfrenzy.remotebound;

import android.support.v7.app.AppCompatActivity;
import android.os.Bundle;
import android.os.IBinder;
import android.os.Message;
import android.os.Messenger;
import android.os.RemoteException;
import android.content.ComponentName;
import android.content.Context;
import android.content.Intent;
import android.content.ServiceConnection;
import android.view.View;

public class RemoteBoundActivity extends AppCompatActivity {

    Messenger myService = null;
    boolean isBound;

    @Override
    protected void onCreate(Bundle savedInstanceState) {
        super.onCreate(savedInstanceState);
        setContentView(R.layout.activity_remote_bound);
    }

    private ServiceConnection myConnection =
            new ServiceConnection() {
                public void onServiceConnected(
                        ComponentName className,
                                        IBinder service) {
                    myService = new Messenger(service);
                    isBound = true;
                }

                public void onServiceDisconnected(
```

```
                             ComponentName className) {
                myService = null;
                isBound = false;
            }
        };
}
```

Next, some code needs to be added to bind to the remote service. This involves creating an intent that matches the intent filter for the service as declared in the manifest file and then making a call to the *bindService()* method, providing the intent and a reference to the ServiceConnection instance as arguments. For the purposes of this example, this code will be implemented in the activity's *onCreate()* method:

```
@Override
protected void onCreate(Bundle savedInstanceState) {
        super.onCreate(savedInstanceState);
        setContentView(R.layout.activity_remote_bound);

        Intent intent = new Intent(getApplicationContext(),
                        RemoteService.class);

        bindService(intent, myConnection, Context.BIND_AUTO_CREATE);
}
```

50.7 Sending a Message to the Remote Service

All that remains before testing the application is to implement the *sendMessage()* method in the *RemoteBoundActivity* class which is configured to be called when the button in the user interface is touched by the user. This method needs to check that the service is connected, create a bundle object containing the string to be displayed by the server, add it to a Message object and send it to the server:

```
public void sendMessage(View view)
{
        if (!isBound) return;

     Message msg = Message.obtain();

     Bundle bundle = new Bundle();
     bundle.putString("MyString", "Message Received");

     msg.setData(bundle);

     try {
         myService.send(msg);
     } catch (RemoteException e) {
         e.printStackTrace();
     }
}
```

With the code changes complete, compile and run the application. Once loaded, touch the button in the user interface, at which point a Toast message should appear that reads "Message Received".

50.8 Summary

In order to implement interaction between a client and remote bound service it is necessary to implement a handler/message communication framework. The basic concepts behind this technique have been covered in this chapter together with the implementation of an example application designed to demonstrate communication between a client and a bound service, each running in a separate process.

51. An Android 8 Notifications Tutorial

Notifications provide a way for an app to convey a message to the user when the app is either not running or is currently in the background. A messaging app might, for example, issue a notification to let the user know that a new message has arrived from a contact. Notifications can be categorized as being either local or remote. A local notification is triggered by the app itself on the device on which it is running. Remote notifications, on the other hand, are initiated by a remote server and delivered to the device for presentation to the user.

Notifications appear in the notification drawer that is pulled down from the status bar of the screen and each notification can include actions such as a button to open the app that sent the notification. Android 7 has also introduced Direct Reply, a feature that allows the user to type in and submit a response to a notification from within the notification panel.

The goal of this chapter is to outline and demonstrate the implementation of local notifications within an Android app. The next chapter (*"An Android 8 Direct Reply Notification Tutorial"*) will cover the implementation of direct reply notifications.

Although outside the scope of this book, the use of Firebase to initiate and send remote notifications is covered in detail in a companion book titled *Firebase Essentials – Android Edition*.

51.1 An Overview of Notifications

When a notification is initiated on an Android device, it appears as an icon in the status bar. Figure 51-1, for example, shows a status bar with a number of notification icons:

Figure 51-1

To view the notifications, the user makes a downward swiping motion starting at the status bar to pull down the notification drawer as shown in Figure 51-2:

Figure 51-2

In devices running Android 8 or newer, performing a long press on an app launcher icon will display any pending notifications associated with that app as shown in Figure 51-3:

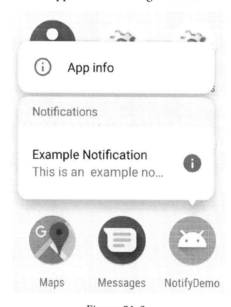

Figure 51-3

Android 8 also supports notification badges that appear on app launcher icons when a notification is waiting to be seen by the user.

A typical notification will simply display a message and, when tapped, launch the app responsible for issuing the notification. Notifications may also contain action buttons which perform a task specific to the corresponding app when tapped. Figure 51-4, for example, shows a notification containing two action buttons allowing the user to either delete or save an incoming message.

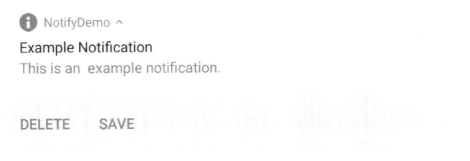

Figure 51-4

It is also possible for the user to enter an in-line text reply into the notification and send it to the app, as is the case in Figure 51-5 below. This allows the user to respond to a notification without having to launch the corresponding app into the foreground.

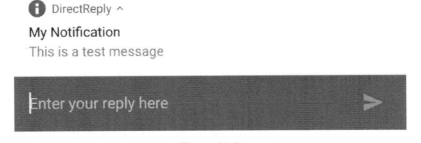

Figure 51-5

The remainder of this chapter will work through the steps involved in creating and issuing a simple notification containing actions. The topic of direct reply support will then be covered in the next chapter entitled *"An Android 8 Direct Reply Notification Tutorial"*.

51.2 Creating the NotifyDemo Project

Start Android Studio and create a new project, entering *NotifyDemo* into the Application name field and *ebookfrenzy.com* as the Company Domain setting before clicking on the *Next* button.

On the form factors screen, enable the *Phone and Tablet* option and set the minimum SDK setting to API 26: Android 8.0 (Oreo). Continue through the screens, requesting the creation of an Empty Activity named *NotifyDemoActivity* with a corresponding layout file named *activity_notify_demo*.

51.3 Designing the User Interface

The main activity will contain a single button, the purpose of which is to create and issue an intent. Locate and load the *activity_notify_demo.xml* file into the Layout Editor tool and delete the default TextView widget.

With Autoconnect enabled, drag and drop a Button object from the panel onto the center of the layout canvas as illustrated in Figure 51-6.

With the Button widget selected in the layout, use the Attributes panel to configure the onClick property to call a method named *sendNotification*.

Figure 51-6

51.4 Creating the Second Activity

For the purposes of this example, the app will contain a second activity which will be launched by the user from within the notification. Add this new activity to the project by right-clicking on the *com.ebookfrenzy.notifydemo* package name located in *app -> java* and select the *New -> Activity -> Empty Activity* menu option to display the *New Android Activity* dialog.

Enter *ResultActivity* into the Activity Name field and name the layout file *activity_result*. Since this activity will not be started when the application is launched (it will instead be launched via an intent from within the notification), it is important to make sure that the *Launcher Activity* option is disabled before clicking on the Finish button.

Open the layout for the second activity (*app -> res -> layout -> activity_result.xml*) and drag and drop a TextView widget so that it is positioned in the center of the layout. Edit the text of the TextView so that it reads "Result Activity" and extract the property value to a string resource.

51.5 Creating a Notification Channel

Before an app can send a notification, it must first create a notification channel. A notification channel consists of an ID that uniquely identifies the channel within the app, a channel name and a channel description (only the latter two of which will be seen by the user). Channels are created by configuring a NotificationChannel instance and then passing that object through to the *createNotificationChannel()* method of the NotificationManager class. For this example, the app will contain a single notification channel named "NotifyDemo News". Edit the *NotifyDemoActivty.java* file and implement code to create the channel when the app starts:

.

.

```
import android.app.NotificationManager;
```

```java
import android.app.NotificationChannel;
import android.content.Context;
import android.graphics.Color;

public class NotifyDemoActivity extends AppCompatActivity {

    NotificationManager notificationManager;

    @Override
    protected void onCreate(Bundle savedInstanceState) {
        super.onCreate(savedInstanceState);
        setContentView(R.layout.activity_notify_demo);

        notificationManager =
                (NotificationManager)
                  getSystemService(Context.NOTIFICATION_SERVICE);

        createNotificationChannel(
                "com.ebookfrenzy.notifydemo.news",
                "NotifyDemo News",
                "Example News Channel");
    }

    protected void createNotificationChannel(String id, String name,
                String description) {

        int importance = NotificationManager.IMPORTANCE_LOW;
        NotificationChannel channel =
                new NotificationChannel(id, name, importance);

        channel.setDescription(description);
        channel.enableLights(true);
        channel.setLightColor(Color.RED);
        channel.enableVibration(true);
        channel.setVibrationPattern(
          new long[]{100, 200, 300, 400, 500, 400, 300, 200, 400});
        notificationManager.createNotificationChannel(channel);
    }
    .
    .
}
```

The code declares and initializes a NotificationManager instance and then creates the new channel with a low important level (other options are high, low, max, min and none) with the name and description properties configured. A range of optional settings are also added to the channel to customize the way in which the user is alerted to the arrival of a notification. These settings apply to all notifications sent to this channel. Finally, the channel is created by passing the notification channel object through to the *createNotificationChannel()* method of the notification manager instance.

With the code changes complete, compile and run the app on a device or emulator running Android 8. After the app has launched, place it into the background and open the Setting app. Within the Settings app, select the *Apps & notifications* option followed by *App info*. On the App info screen locate and select the NotifyDemo project and, on the subsequent screen, tap the *App notifications* entry. The notification screen should list the NotifyDemo News category as being active for the user:

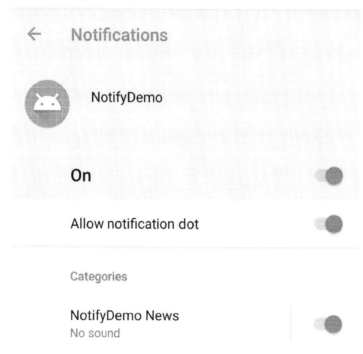

Figure 51-7

Although not a requirement for this example, it is worth noting that a channel can be deleted from with the app via a call to the *deleteNotificationChannel()* method of the notification manager, passing through the ID of the channel to be deleted:

```
String channelID = "com.ebookfrenzy.notifydemo.news";
notificationManager.deleteNotificationChannel(channelID);
```

51.6 Creating and Issuing a Basic Notification

Notifications are created using the Notification.Builder class and must contain an icon, title and content. Open the *NotifyDemoActivity.java* file and implement the *sendNotification()* method as follows to build a basic notification:

```
.
.
import android.app.Notification;
import android.view.View;
.
.
protected void sendNotification(View view) {
```

```
String channelID = "com.ebookfrenzy.notifydemo.news";

Notification notification =
        new Notification.Builder(NotifyDemoActivity.this,
                                    channelID)
    .setContentTitle("Example Notification")
    .setContentText("This is an  example notification.")
    .setSmallIcon(android.R.drawable.ic_dialog_info)
    .setChannelId(channelID)
    .build();
}
```

Once a notification has been built, it needs to be issued using the *notify()* method of the NotificationManager instance. The code to access the NotificationManager and issue the notification needs to be added to the *sendNotification()* method as follows:

```
protected void sendNotification(View view) {

    int notificationID = 101;

    String channelID = "com.ebookfrenzy.notifydemo.news";

    Notification notification =
            new Notification.Builder(NotifyDemoActivity.this,
                        channelID)
        .setContentTitle("New Message")
        .setContentText("You've received new messages.")
        .setSmallIcon(android.R.drawable.ic_dialog_info)
        .setChannelId(channelID)
        .build();

    notificationManager.notify(notificationID, notification);
}
```

Note that when the notification is issued, it is assigned a notification ID. This can be any integer and may be used later when updating the notification.

Compile and run the app and tap the button on the main activity. When the notification icon appears in the status bar, touch and drag down from the status bar to view the full notification:

 NotifyDemo

Example Notification
This is an example notification.

Figure 51-8

Click and slide right on the notification, then select the settings gear icon to view additional information about the notification:

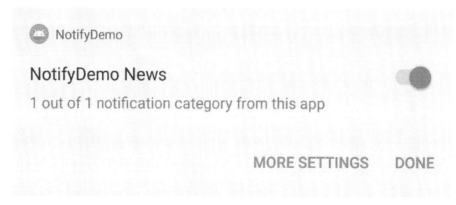

Figure 51-9

Next, place the app in the background, navigate to the home screen displaying the launcher icons for all of the apps and note that a notification badge has appeared on the NotifyDemo launcher icon as indicated by the arrow in Figure 51-10:

Figure 51-10

Performing a long press over the launcher icon will display a popup containing the notification:

Figure 51-11

If more than one notification is pending for an app, the long press menu popup will contain a count of the number of notifications (highlighted in the above figure). This number may be configured from within the app by making a call to the *setNumber()* method when building the notification:

```
Notification notification = new Notification.Builder(NotifyDemoActivity.this,
CHANNEL_ID)
        .setContentTitle("Example Notification")
        .setContentText("This is an  example notification.")
        .setSmallIcon(android.R.drawable.ic_dilaog_info)
        .setChannelId(CHANNEL_ID)
        .setNumber(10)
        .build();
```

As currently implemented, tapping on the notification has no effect regardless of where it is accessed. The next step is to configure the notification to launch an activity when tapped.

51.7 Launching an Activity from a Notification

A notification should ideally allow the user to perform some form of action, such as launching the corresponding app, or taking some other form of action in response to the notification. A common requirement is to simply launch an activity belonging to the app when the user taps the notification.

This approach requires an activity to be launched and an Intent configured to launch that activity. Assuming an app that contains an activity named ResultActivity, the intent would be created as follows:

```
Intent resultIntent = new Intent(this, ResultActivity.class);
```

This intent needs to then be wrapped in a PendingIntent instance. PendingIntent objects are designed to allow an intent to be passed to other applications, essentially granting those applications permission to perform the intent at some point in the future. In this case, the PendingIntent object is being used to provide the Notification system with a way to launch the ResultActivity activity when the user taps the notification panel:

```
PendingIntent pendingIntent =
    PendingIntent.getActivity(
    this,
    0,
    resultIntent,
    PendingIntent.FLAG_UPDATE_CURRENT
);
```

All that remains is to assign the PendingIntent object during the notification build process using the *setContentIntent()* method.

Bringing these changes together results in a modified *sendNotification()* method which reads as follows:

```
.
.
import android.app.PendingIntent;
import android.content.Intent;
import android.graphics.drawable.Icon;

.
.
protected void sendNotification(View view) {
```

```
    int notificationId = 101;

    Intent resultIntent = new Intent(this, ResultActivity.class);

    PendingIntent pendingIntent =
            PendingIntent.getActivity(
                    this,
                    0,
                    resultIntent,
                    PendingIntent.FLAG_UPDATE_CURRENT
            );

    String CHANNEL_ID = "com.ebookfrenzy.notifydemo.news";

    Notification notification = new Notification.Builder(NotifyDemoActivity.this,
CHANNEL_ID)
            .setContentTitle("Example Notification")
            .setContentText("This is an  example notification.")
            .setSmallIcon(android.R.drawable.ic_dialog_info)
            .setChannelId(CHANNEL_ID)
            .setContentIntent(pendingIntent)
            .build();

    notificationManager.notify(notificationId, notification);
}
```

Compile and run the app once again, tap the button and display the notification drawer. This time, however, tapping the notification will cause the ResultActivity to launch.

51.8 Adding Actions to a Notification

Another way to add interactivity to a notification is to create actions. These appear as buttons beneath the notification message and are programmed to trigger specific intents when tapped by the user. The following code, if added to the *sendNotification()* method, will add an action button labeled "Open" which launches the referenced pending intent when selected:

```
final Icon icon = Icon.createWithResource(NotifyDemoActivity.this,
            android.R.drawable.ic_dialog_info);

Notification.Action action =
        new Notification.Action.Builder(icon, "Open", pendingIntent)
                .build();

Notification notification = new Notification.Builder(NotifyDemoActivity.this,
CHANNEL_ID)
        .setContentTitle("Example Notification")
        .setContentText("This is an  example notification.")
        .setSmallIcon(R.drawable.ic_info_24dp)
        .setChannelId(CHANNEL_ID)
```

```
    .setContentIntent(pendingIntent)
    .setActions(action)
    .build();
```

`notificationManager.notify(notificationId, notification);`

Add the above code to the method and run the app. Issue the notification and note the appearance of the Open action within the notification:

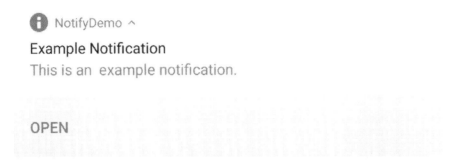

Figure 51-12

Tapping the action will trigger the pending intend and launch the ResultActivity.

51.9 Bundled Notifications

If an app has a tendency to regularly issue notifications there is a danger that those notifications will rapidly clutter both the status bar and the notification drawer providing a less than optimal experience for the user. This can be particularly true of news or messaging apps that send a notification every time there is either a breaking news story or a new message arrives from a contact. Consider, for example, the notifications in Figure 51-13:

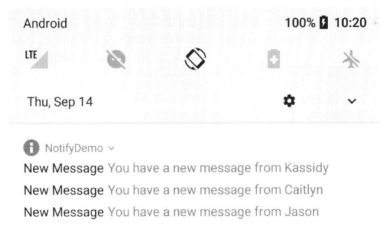

Figure 51-13

Now imagine if ten or even twenty new messages had arrived. To avoid this kind of problem Android 7 allows notifications to be bundled together into groups.

To bundle notifications, each notification must be designated as belonging to the same group via the *setGroup()* method, and an additional notification must be issued and configured as being the *summary notification*. The following code, for example, creates and issues the three notifications shown in Figure 51-13 above, but bundles them into the same group. The code also issues a notification to act as the summary:

```
final String GROUP_KEY_NOTIFY = "group_key_notify";

Notification.Builder builderSummary =
        new Notification.Builder(this, channelID)
                .setSmallIcon(android.R.drawable.ic_dialog_info)
                .setContentTitle("A Bundle Example")
                .setContentText("You have 3 new messages")
                .setGroup(GROUP_KEY_NOTIFY)
                .setGroupSummary(true);

Notification.Builder builder1 =
        new Notification.Builder(this, channelID)
                .setSmallIcon(android.R.drawable.ic_dialog_info)
                .setContentTitle("New Message")
                .setContentText("You have a new message from Kassidy")
                .setGroup(GROUP_KEY_NOTIFY);

Notification.Builder builder2 =
        new Notification.Builder(this, channelID)
                .setSmallIcon(android.R.drawable.ic_dialog_info)
                .setContentTitle("New Message")
                .setContentText("You have a new message from Caitlyn")
                .setGroup(GROUP_KEY_NOTIFY);

Notification.Builder builder3 =
        new Notification.Builder(this, channelID)
                .setSmallIcon(android.R.drawable.ic_dialog_info)
                .setContentTitle("New Message")
                .setContentText("You have a new message from Jason")
                .setGroup(GROUP_KEY_NOTIFY);

int notificationId0 = 100;
int notificationId1 = 101;
int notificationId2 = 102;
int notificationId3 = 103;

notificationManager.notify(notificationId1, builder1.build());
notificationManager.notify(notificationId2, builder2.build());
notificationManager.notify(notificationId3, builder3.build());
notificationManager.notify(notificationId0, builderSummary.build());
```

When the code is executed, a single notification icon will appear in the status bar even though four notifications have actually been issued by the app. Within the notification drawer, a single summary notification is displayed listing the information in each of the bundled notifications:

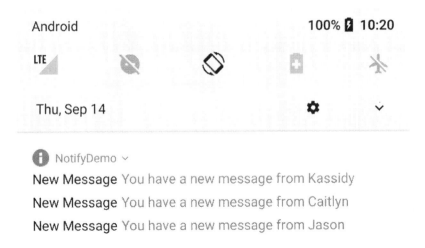

Figure 51-14

Pulling further downward on the notification entry expands the panel to show the details of each of the bundled notifications:

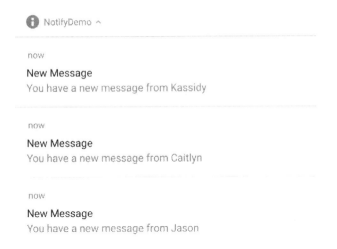

Figure 51-15

51.10 Summary

Notifications provide a way for an app to deliver a message to the user when the app is not running, or is currently in the background. Notifications appear in the status bar and notification drawer. Local notifications are triggered on the device by the running app while remote notifications are initiated by a remote server and delivered to the device. Local notifications are created using the NotificationCompat.Builder class and issued using the NotificationManager service.

As demonstrated in this chapter, notifications can be configured to provide the user with options (such as launching an activity or saving a message) by making use of actions, intents and the PendingIntent class. Notification bundling provides a mechanism for grouping together notifications to provide an improved experience for apps that issue a greater number of notifications.

52. An Android 8 Direct Reply Notification Tutorial

Direct reply is a feature introduced in Android 7 that allows the user to enter text into a notification and send it to the app associated with that notification. This allows the user to reply to a message in the notification without the need to launch an activity within the app. This chapter will build on the knowledge gained in the previous chapter to create an example app that makes use of this notification feature.

52.1 Creating the DirectReply Project

Start Android Studio and create a new project, entering *DirectReply* into the Application name field and *ebookfrenzy.com* as the Company Domain setting before clicking on the *Next* button.

On the form factors screen, enable the *Phone and Tablet* option and set the minimum SDK setting to API 26: Android 8.0 (Oreo). Continue through the setup screens, requesting the creation of an Empty Activity named *DirectReplyActivity* with a corresponding layout file named *activity_direct_reply*.

52.2 Designing the User Interface

Load the *activity_direct_reply.xml* layout file into the layout tool. With Autoconnect enabled, add a Button object beneath the existing "Hello World!" label. With the Button widget selected in the layout, use the Attributes tool window to set the onClick property to call a method named *sendNotification*. If necessary, use the Infer Constraints button to add any missing constraints to the layout.

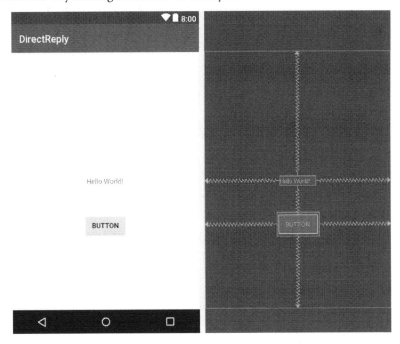

Figure 52-1

Before continuing, select the "Hello World!" TextView and change ID attribute to *textView*.

52.3 Creating the Notification Channel

As with the example in the previous chapter, a channel must be created before a notification can be sent. Edit the *DirectReplyActivity.java* file and add code to create a new channel as follows:

```
.
.
import android.app.NotificationChannel;
import android.app.NotificationManager;
import android.content.Context;
import android.graphics.Color;
.
.
public class DirectReplyActivity extends AppCompatActivity {

    NotificationManager notificationManager;
    private String channelID = "com.ebookfrenzy.directreply.news";

    @Override
    protected void onCreate(Bundle savedInstanceState) {
        super.onCreate(savedInstanceState);
        setContentView(R.layout.activity_direct_reply);

        notificationManager =
                (NotificationManager)
                    getSystemService(Context.NOTIFICATION_SERVICE);

        createNotificationChannel(channelID,
                "DirectReply News", "Example News Channel");
    }

    protected void createNotificationChannel(String id,
            String name, String description) {

        int importance = NotificationManager.IMPORTANCE_HIGH;
        NotificationChannel channel =
                new NotificationChannel(id, name, importance);

        channel.setDescription(description);
        channel.enableLights(true);
        channel.setLightColor(Color.RED);
        channel.enableVibration(true);
        channel.setVibrationPattern(new long[]{100, 200, 300, 400,
                        500, 400, 300, 200, 400});
```

```
        notificationManager.createNotificationChannel(channel);
    }
    .
    .
}
```

52.4 Building the RemoteInput Object

The key element that makes direct reply in-line text possible within a notification is the RemoteInput class. The previous chapters introduced the PendingIntent class and explained the way in which it allows one application to create an intent and then grant other applications or services the ability to launch that intent from outside the original app. In that chapter, entitled *"An Android 8 Notifications Tutorial"*, a pending intent was created that allowed an activity in the original app to be launched from within a notification. The RemoteInput class allows a request for user input to be included in the PendingIntent object along with the intent. When the intent within the PendingIntent object is triggered, for example launching an activity, that activity is also passed any input provided by the user.

The first step in implementing direct reply within a notification is to create the RemoteInput object. This is achieved using the *RemoteInput.Builder()* method. To build a RemoteInput object, a key string is required that will be used to extract the input from the resulting intent. The object also needs a label string that will appear within the text input field of the notification. Edit the *DirectReplyAction.java* file and begin implementing the *sendNotification()* method. Note also the addition of some import directives and variables that will be used later as the chapter progresses:

```
package com.ebookfrenzy.directreply;
    .
    .
import android.view.View;
import android.app.PendingIntent;
import android.app.RemoteInput;
import android.content.Intent;
    .
    .
public class DirectReplyActivity extends AppCompatActivity {

    private static int notificationId = 101;
    private static String KEY_TEXT_REPLY = "key_text_reply";
    private static String channelID =
                    "com.ebookfrenzy.directreply.news";


    NotificationManager notificationManager;
    .
    .
    .

    public void sendNotification(View view) {

        String replyLabel = "Enter your reply here";
        RemoteInput remoteInput =
```

```
            new RemoteInput.Builder(KEY_TEXT_REPLY)
                .setLabel(replyLabel)
                .build();
    }
    .
    .
    .
}
```

Now that the RemoteInput object has been created and initialized with a key and a label string it will need to be placed inside a notification action object. Before that step can be performed, however, the PendingIntent instance needs to be created.

52.5 Creating the PendingIntent

The steps to creating the PendingIntent are the same as those outlined in the *"An Android 8 Notifications Tutorial"* chapter, with the exception that the intent will be configured to launch the main DirectReplyActivity activity. Remaining within the *DirectReplyActivity.java* file, add the code to create the PendingIntent as follows:

```
public void sendNotification(View view) {

    String replyLabel = "Enter your reply here";
    RemoteInput remoteInput =
            new RemoteInput.Builder(KEY_TEXT_REPLY)
            .setLabel(replyLabel)
            .build();

    Intent resultIntent = new Intent(this, DirectReplyActivity.class);

    PendingIntent resultPendingIntent =
            PendingIntent.getActivity(
                    this,
                    0,
                    resultIntent,
                    PendingIntent.FLAG_UPDATE_CURRENT
            );
    }
}
```

52.6 Creating the Reply Action

The in-line reply will be accessible within the notification via an action button. This action now needs to be created and configured with an icon, a label to appear on the button, the PendingIntent object and the RemoteInput object. Modify the *sendNotification()* method to add the code to create this action:

```
    .
    .
    .
import android.graphics.drawable.Icon;
import android.app.Notification;
import android.graphics.Color;
import android.support.v4.content.ContextCompat;
```

```
public void sendNotification(View view) {

    String replyLabel = "Enter your reply here";
    RemoteInput remoteInput =
            new RemoteInput.Builder(KEY_TEXT_REPLY)
            .setLabel(replyLabel)
            .build();

    Intent resultIntent = new Intent(this, DirectReplyActivity.class);

    PendingIntent resultPendingIntent =
            PendingIntent.getActivity(
                    this,
                    0,
                    resultIntent,
                    PendingIntent.FLAG_UPDATE_CURRENT
            );

    final Icon icon =
                Icon.createWithResource(DirectReplyActivity.this,
                    android.R.drawable.ic_dialog_info);

    Notification.Action replyAction =
                new Notification.Action.Builder(
                        icon,
                        "Reply", resultPendingIntent)
                        .addRemoteInput(remoteInput)
                        .build();
    }
```

At this stage in the tutorial we have the RemoteInput, PendingIntent and Notification Action objects built and ready to be used. The next stage is to build the notification and issue it:

```
public void sendNotification(View view) {

    String replyLabel = "Enter your reply here";
    RemoteInput remoteInput =
            new RemoteInput.Builder(KEY_TEXT_REPLY)
                    .setLabel(replyLabel)
                    .build();

    Intent resultIntent = new Intent(this, DirectReplyActivity.class);
```

```
PendingIntent resultPendingIntent =
        PendingIntent.getActivity(
                this,
                0,
                resultIntent,
                PendingIntent.FLAG_UPDATE_CURRENT
        );

final Icon icon =
    Icon.createWithResource(DirectReplyActivity.this,
        android.R.drawable.ic_dialog_info);

Notification.Action replyAction =
        new Notification.Action.Builder(
                icon,
                "Reply", resultPendingIntent)
                .addRemoteInput(remoteInput)
                .build();

Notification newMessageNotification =
        new Notification.Builder(this, channelID)
                .setColor(ContextCompat.getColor(this,
                        R.color.colorPrimary))
                .setSmallIcon(
                        android.R.drawable.ic_dialog_info)
                .setContentTitle("My Notification")
                .setContentText("This is a test message")
                .addAction(replyAction).build();

NotificationManager notificationManager =
        (NotificationManager)
                getSystemService(Context.NOTIFICATION_SERVICE);

notificationManager.notify(notificationId,
        newMessageNotification);
}
```

With the changes made, compile and run the app and test that tapping the button successfully issues the notification. When viewing the notification drawer, the notification should appear as shown in Figure 52-2:

Figure 52-2

Tap the Reply action button so that the text input field appears displaying the reply label that was embedded into the RemoteInput object when it was created.

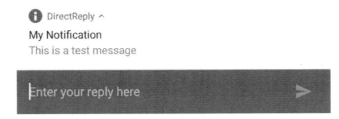

Figure 52-3

Enter some text, tap the send arrow button located at the end of the input field.

52.7 Receiving Direct Reply Input

Now that the notification is successfully seeking input from the user, the app needs to do something with that input. The goal of this particular tutorial is to have the text entered by the user into the notification appear on the TextView widget in the activity user interface.

When the user enters text and taps the send button the DirectReplyActivity activity is launched via the intent contained in the PendingIntent object. Embedded in this intent is the text entered by the user via the notification. Within the *onCreate()* method of the activity, a call to the *getIntent()* method will return a copy of the intent that launched the activity. Passing this through to the *RemoteInput.getResultsFromIntent()* method will, in turn, return a Bundle object containing the reply text which can be extracted and assigned to the TextView widget. This results in a modified *onCreate()* method within the *DirectReplyActivity.java* file which reads as follows:

```
.
.
import android.widget.TextView;
.
.
@Override
protected void onCreate(Bundle savedInstanceState) {
    super.onCreate(savedInstanceState);
    setContentView(R.layout.activity_direct_reply);

    notificationManager =
            (NotificationManager)
              getSystemService(Context.NOTIFICATION_SERVICE);
```

```
        createNotificationChannel(channelID, "DirectReply News",
                            Example News Channel");


    handleIntent();


}


private void handleIntent() {

    Intent intent = this.getIntent();

    Bundle remoteInput = RemoteInput.getResultsFromIntent(intent);

    if (remoteInput != null) {

        TextView myTextView = (TextView) findViewById(R.id.textView);
        String inputString = remoteInput.getCharSequence(
            KEY_TEXT_REPLY).toString();

        myTextView.setText(inputString);
    }
}
.
.
```

After making these code changes build and run the app once again. Click the button to issue the notification and enter and send some text from within the notification panel. Note that the TextView widget in the DirectReplyActivity activity is updated to display the in-line text that was entered.

52.8 Updating the Notification

After sending the reply within the notification you may have noticed that the progress indicator continues to spin within the notification panel as highlighted in Figure 52-4:

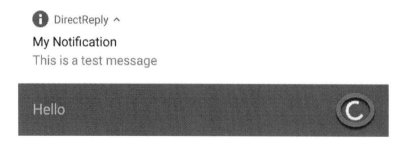

Figure 52-4

The notification is showing this indicator because it is waiting for a response from the activity confirming receipt of the sent text. The recommended approach to performing this task is to update the notification with a new message indicating that the reply has been received and handled. Since the original notification was assigned an ID when it was issued, this can be used once again to perform an update. Add the following code to the *onCreate()* method to perform this task:

```
private void handleIntent() {

    Intent intent = this.getIntent();

    Bundle remoteInput = RemoteInput.getResultsFromIntent(intent);

    if (remoteInput != null) {

        TextView myTextView = (TextView) findViewById(R.id.textView);
        String inputString = remoteInput.getCharSequence(
                KEY_TEXT_REPLY).toString();

        myTextView.setText(inputString);

        Notification repliedNotification =
                new Notification.Builder(this, channelID)
                        .setSmallIcon(
                                android.R.drawable.ic_dialog_info)
                        .setContentText("Reply received")
                        .build();

        notificationManager.notify(notificationId,
                repliedNotification);
    }
}
```

Test the app one last time and verify that the progress indicator goes away after the in-line reply text has been sent and that a new panel appears indicating that the reply has been received:

Figure 52-5

52.9 Summary

The direct reply notification feature allows text to be entered by the user within a notification and passed via an intent to an activity of the corresponding application. Direct reply is made possible by the RemoteInput class, an instance of which can be embedded within an action and bundled with the notification. When working with direct reply notifications, it is important to let the NotificationManager service know that the reply has been received and processed. The best way to achieve this is to simply update the notification message using the notification ID provided when the notification was first issued.

53. An Introduction to Android Multi-Window Support

Android 7 introduced a new feature in the form of multi-window support. Unlike previous versions of Android, multi-window support in Android 7 allowed more than one activity to be displayed on the device screen at one time. In this chapter, an overview of Android multi-window modes will be provided from both user and app developer perspectives.

Once the basics of multi-window support have been covered, the next chapter will work through a tutorial outlining the practical steps involved in working with multi-window mode when developing Android apps.

53.1 Split-Screen, Freeform and Picture-in-Picture Modes

Multi-window support in Android provides three different forms of window support. Split-screen mode, available on most phone and tablet devices, provides a split screen environment where two activities appear either side by side or one above the other. A moveable divider is provided which, when dragged by the user, adjusts the percentage of the screen assigned to each of the adjacent activities:

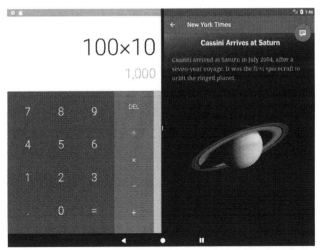

Figure 53-1

Freeform mode provides a windowing environment on devices with larger screens and is currently enabled at the discretion of the device manufacturer. Freeform differs from split-screen mode in that it allows each activity to appear in a separate, resizable window and is not limited to two activities being displayed concurrently. Figure 53-2, for example, shows a device in freeform mode with the Calculator and Contacts apps displayed in separate windows:

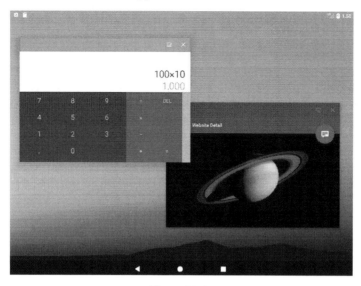

Figure 53-2

Picture-in-picture support, as the name suggests, allows video playback to continue in a smaller window while the user performs other tasks. At present this feature is only available on Android TV and, as such, is outside the scope of this book.

53.2 Entering Multi-Window Mode

Split-screen mode can be entered by pressing and holding the square Overview button until the display switches mode. Once in split-screen mode, the Overview button will change to display two rectangles as shown in Figure 53-3 and the current activity will fill one half of the screen. The Overview screen will appear in the adjacent half of the screen allowing the second activity to be selected for display:

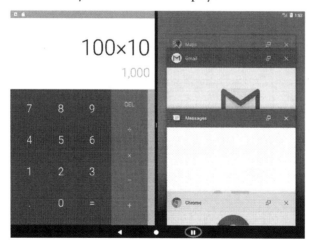

Figure 53-3

Alternatively, an app may be placed in split-screen mode by displaying the Overview screen, pressing and holding the title bar of a listed app and then dragging and dropping the app onto the highlighted section of the screen.

To exit split-screen mode, simply drag the divider separating the two activities to a far edge so that only one activity fills the screen, or press and hold the Overview button until it reverts to a single square.

In the case of freeform mode, an additional button appears within the title bar of the apps when listed in the Overview screen. When selected, this button (highlighted in Figure 53-4) causes the activity to appear in a freeform window:

Figure 53-4

The additional button located in the title bar of a freeform activity (shown in Figure 53-5) may be pressed to return the activity to full screen mode:

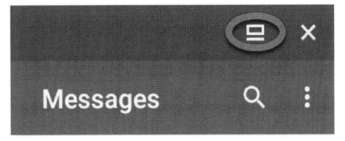

Figure 53-5

53.3 Enabling Freeform Support

Although not officially supported on all devices, it is possible to enable freeform multi-window mode on large screen devices and emulators. To enable this mode, run the following adb command while the emulator is running, or the device is connected:

```
adb shell settings put global enable_freeform_support 1
```

After making this change, it may be necessary to reboot the device before the setting takes effect.

53.4 Checking for Freeform Support

As outlined earlier in the chapter, Google is leaving the choice of whether to enable freeform multi-window mode to the individual Android device manufacturers. Since it only makes sense to use freeform on larger devices, there is no guarantee that freeform will be available on every device on which an app is likely to run. Fortunately all of the freeform specific methods and attributes are ignored by the system if freeform mode is not available on a device, so using these will not cause the app to crash on a non-freeform device. Situations might arise, however, where it may be useful to be able to detect if a device supports freeform multi-window mode. Fortunately, this can be achieved by checking for the freeform window management feature in the package manager. The following code example checks for freeform multi-window support and returns a Boolean value based on the result of the test:

```
public Boolean checkFreeform() {
    return getPackageManager().hasSystemFeature(
            PackageManager.FEATURE_FREEFORM_WINDOW_MANAGEMENT);
}
```

53.5 Enabling Multi-Window Support in an App

The *android:resizableActivity* manifest file setting controls whether multi-window behavior is supported by an app. This setting can be made at either the application or individual activity levels. The following fragment, for example, configures the activity named MainActivity to support both split-screen and freeform multi-window modes:

```
<activity
    android:name=".MainActivity"
    android:resizeableActivity="true"
    android:label="@string/app_name"
    android:theme="@style/AppTheme.NoActionBar">
    <intent-filter>
        <action android:name="android.intent.action.MAIN" />

        <category android:name="android.intent.category.LAUNCHER" />
    </intent-filter>
</activity>
```

Setting the property to false will prevent the activity from appearing in split-screen or freeform mode. Launching an activity for which multi-window support is disabled will result in a message appearing indicating that the app does not support multi-window mode and the activity filling the entire screen. When a device is in multi-window mode, the title bar of such activities will also display a message within the Overview screen indicating that multi-window mode is not supported by the activity (Figure 53-6):

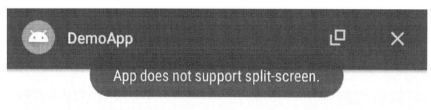

Figure 53-6

53.6 Specifying Multi-Window Attributes

A number of attributes are available as part of the <layout> element for specifying the size and placement of an activity when it is launched into a multi-window mode. The initial height, width and position of an activity when launched in freeform mode may be specified using the following attributes:

- **android:defaultWidth** – Specifies the default width of the activity.

- **android:defaultHeight** – Specifies the default height of the activity.

- **android:gravity** – Specifies the initial position of the activity (start, end, left, right, top etc.).

Note that the above attributes apply to the activity only when it is displayed in freeform mode. The following example configures an activity to appear with a specific height and width at the top of the starting edge of the screen:

```
<activity android:name=".MainActivity ">
    <layout android:defaultHeight="350dp"
            android:defaultWidth="450dp"
```

```
        android:gravity="start|end" />
</activity>
```

The following <layout> attributes may be used to specify the minimum width and height to which an activity may be reduced in either split-view or freeform modes:

- **android:minimalHeight** – Specifies the minimum height to which the activity may be reduced while in split-screen or freeform mode.

- **android:minimalWidth** - Specifies the minimum width to which the activity may be reduced while in split-screen or freeform mode.

When the user slides the split-screen divider beyond the minimal height or width boundaries, the system will stop resizing the layout of the shrinking activity and simply clip the user interface to make room for the adjacent activity.

The following manifest file fragment implements the minimal width and height attributes for an activity:

```
<activity android:name=".MainActivity ">
    <layout android:minimalHeight="400dp"
            android:minimalWidth="290dp" />
</activity>
```

53.7 Detecting Multi-Window Mode in an Activity

Situations may arise where an activity needs to detect whether it is currently being displayed to the user in multi-window mode. The current status can be obtained via a call to the *isInMultiWindowMode()* method of the Activity class. When called, this method returns a true or false value depending on whether or not the activity is currently full screen:

```
if (this.isInMultiWindowMode()) {
    // Activity is running in Multi-Window mode
} else {
    // Activity is not in Multi-Window mode
}
```

53.8 Receiving Multi-Window Notifications

An activity will receive notification that it is entering or exiting multi-window mode if it overrides the *onMultiWindowModeChanged()* callback method. The first argument passed to this method is true on entering multi-window mode, and false when the activity exits the mode. The new configuration settings are contained within the Configuration object passed as the second argument:

```
@Override
public void onMultiWindowModeChanged(boolean isInMultiWindowMode,
                                     Configuration newConfig) {
    super.onMultiWindowModeChanged(isInMultiWindowMode, newConfig);

    if (isInMultiWindowMode) {
        // Activity has entered multi-window mode
    } else {
        // Activity has exited multi-window mode
    }
}
```

53.9 Launching an Activity in Multi-Window Mode

In the *"Android Explicit Intents – A Worked Example"* chapter of this book, an example app was created in which an activity uses an intent to launch a second activity. By default, activities launched via an intent are considered to reside in the same *task stack* as the originating activity. An activity can, however, be launched into a new task stack by passing through the appropriate flags with the intent.

When an activity in multi-window mode launches another activity within the same task stack, the new activity replaces the originating activity within the split-screen or freeform window (the user returns to the original activity via the back button).

When launched into a new task stack in split-screen mode, however, the second activity will appear in the window adjacent to the original activity, allowing both activities to be viewed simultaneously. In the case of freeform mode, the launched activity will appear in a separate window from the original activity.

In order to launch an activity into a new task stack, the following flags must be set on the intent before it is started:

- Intent.FLAG_ACTIVITY_LAUNCH_ADJACENT

- Intent.FLAG_ACTIVITY_MULTIPLE_TASK

- Intent.FLAG_ACTIVITY_NEW_TASK

The following code, for example, configures and launches a second activity designed to appear in a separate window:

```
Intent i = new Intent(this, SecondActivity.class);

i.addFlags(Intent.FLAG_ACTIVITY_LAUNCH_ADJACENT|
           Intent.FLAG_ACTIVITY_MULTIPLE_TASK|
           Intent.FLAG_ACTIVITY_NEW_TASK);

startActivity(i);
```

53.10 Configuring Freeform Activity Size and Position

By default, an activity launched into a different task stack while in freeform mode will be positioned in the center of the screen at a size dictated by the system. The location and dimensions of this window can be controlled by passing *launch bounds* settings to the intent via the *ActivityOptions* class. The first step in this process is to create a *Rect* object configured with the left (X), top (Y), right (X) and bottom (Y) coordinates of the rectangle representing the activity window. The following code, for example, creates a Rect object in which the top-left corner is positioned at coordinate (100, 800) and the bottom-right at (900, 700):

```
Rect rect = new Rect(100, 800, 900, 700);
```

The next step is to create a basic instance of the ActivityOptions class and initialize it with the Rect settings via the *setLaunchBounds()* method:

```
ActivityOptions options = ActivityOptions.makeBasic();
ActivityOptions bounds = options.setLaunchBounds(rect);
```

Finally, the ActivityOptions instance is converted to a Bundle object and passed to the *startActivity()* method along with the Intent object:

```
startActivity(i, bounds.toBundle());
```

Combining these steps results in a code sequence that reads as follows:

```
Intent i = new Intent(this, SecondActivity.class);
i.addFlags(Intent.FLAG_ACTIVITY_LAUNCH_ADJACENT|
          Intent.FLAG_ACTIVITY_MULTIPLE_TASK|
          Intent.FLAG_ACTIVITY_NEW_TASK);

Rect rect = new Rect(100, 800, 900, 700);

ActivityOptions options = ActivityOptions.makeBasic();
ActivityOptions bounds = options.setLaunchBounds(rect);

startActivity(i, bounds.toBundle());
```

When the second activity is launched by the intent while the originating activity is in freeform mode, the new activity window will appear with the location and dimensions defined in the Rect object.

53.11 Summary

Android 7 introduced multi-window support, a system whereby more than one activity is displayed on the screen at any one time. The three modes provided by multi-window support are split-screen, freeform and picture-in-picture. In split-screen mode, the screen is split either horizontally or vertically into two panes with an activity displayed in each pane. Freeform mode, which is only supported on certain Android devices, allows each activity to appear in a separate, movable and resizable window. Picture-in-picture mode is only available on Android TV and allows video playback to continue in a small window while the user is performing other tasks.

As outlined in this chapter, a number of methods and property settings are available within the Android SDK to detect, respond to and control multi-window behavior within an app.

54. An Android Studio Multi-Window Split-Screen and Freeform Tutorial

With the basics of Android multi-window support covered in the previous chapter, this chapter will work through the steps involved in implementing multi-window support within an Android app. This project will be used to demonstrate the steps involved in configuring and managing both split-screen and freeform behavior within a multi-activity app.

54.1 Creating the Multi-Window Project

Start Android Studio and create a new project, entering *MultiWindow* into the Application name field and *ebookfrenzy.com* as the Company Domain setting before clicking on the *Next* button.

On the form factors screen, enable the *Phone and Tablet* option and set the minimum SDK setting to API 24: Android 7.0 (Nougat). Continue through the remaining setup screens, requesting the creation of an Empty Activity named *FirstActivity* with a corresponding layout file named *activity_first*.

54.2 Designing the FirstActivity User Interface

The user interface will need to be comprised of a single Button and a TextView. Within the Project tool window, navigate to the *activity_first.xml* layout file located in *app -> res -> layout* and double-click on it to load it into the Layout Editor tool. With the tool in Design mode, select and delete the *Hello World!* TextView object.

With Autoconnect mode enabled in the Layout Editor toolbar, drag a TextView widget from the palette and position it in the center of the layout. Next, drag a Button object and position it beneath the TextView. Edit the text on the Button so that it reads "Launch". If any constraints are missing from the layout, simply click on the Infer Constraints button in the Layout Editor toolbar to add them. On completion of these steps, the layout should resemble that shown in Figure 54-1:

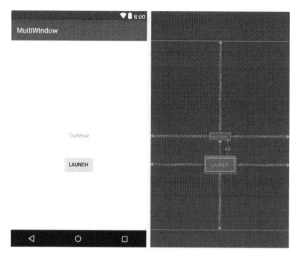

Figure 54-1

In the attributes panel, change the widget ID for the TextView to *myTextView* and assign an *onClick* property to the button so that it calls a method named *launchIntent* when selected by the user.

54.3 Adding the Second Activity

The second activity will be launched when the user clicks on the button in the first activity. Add this new activity by right-clicking on the *com.ebookfrenzy.multiwindow* package name located in *app -> java* and select the *New -> Activity -> Empty Activity* menu option to display the *New Android Activity* dialog.

Enter *SecondActivity* into the Activity Name and Title fields and name the layout file *activity_second*. Since this activity will not be started when the application is launched (it will instead be launched via an intent by FirstActivity when the button is pressed), it is important to make sure that the *Launcher Activity* option is disabled before clicking on the Finish button.

Open the layout for the second activity (*app -> res -> layout -> activity_second.xml*) and drag and drop a TextView widget so that it is positioned in the center of the layout. Edit the text of the TextView so that it reads "Second Activity":

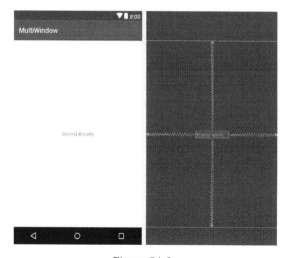

Figure 54-2

54.4 Launching the Second Activity

The next step is to add some code to the *FirstActivity.java* class file to implement the *launchIntent()* method. Edit the *FirstActivity.java* file and implement this method as follows:

```
package com.ebookfrenzy.multiwindow;

import android.support.v7.app.AppCompatActivity;
import android.os.Bundle;
import android.view.View;
import android.content.Intent;

public class FirstActivity extends AppCompatActivity {

    @Override
    protected void onCreate(Bundle savedInstanceState) {
        super.onCreate(savedInstanceState);
        setContentView(R.layout.activity_first);
    }

    public void launchIntent(View view) {
        Intent i = new Intent(this, SecondActivity.class);
        startActivity(i);
    }
}
```

Compile and run the app and verify that the second activity is launched when the Launch button is clicked.

54.5 Enabling Multi-Window Mode

Edit the *AndroidManifest.xml* file and add the directive to enable multi-window support for the app as follows:

```
<?xml version="1.0" encoding="utf-8"?>
<manifest xmlns:android="http://schemas.android.com/apk/res/android"
    package="com.ebookfrenzy.multiwindow">

    <application
        android:allowBackup="true"
        android:icon="@mipmap/ic_launcher"
        android:label="@string/app_name"
        android:supportsRtl="true"
        android:theme="@style/AppTheme">
        <activity
            android:name=".FirstActivity"
            android:resizeableActivity="true">
            <intent-filter>
                <action android:name="android.intent.action.MAIN" />

                <category
```

```
                    android:name="android.intent.category.LAUNCHER" />
        </intent-filter>
    </activity>
    <activity android:name=".SecondActivity"></activity>
</application>

</manifest>
```

Note that, at the time of writing, multi-window support is enabled by default. The above step, however, is recommended for the purposes of completeness and to defend against the possibility that this default behavior may change in the future.

54.6 Testing Multi-Window Support

Build and run the app once again and, once running, press and hold the Overview button as outlined in the previous chapter to switch to split-screen mode. From the Overview screen in the second half of the screen, choose an app to appear in the adjacent panel:

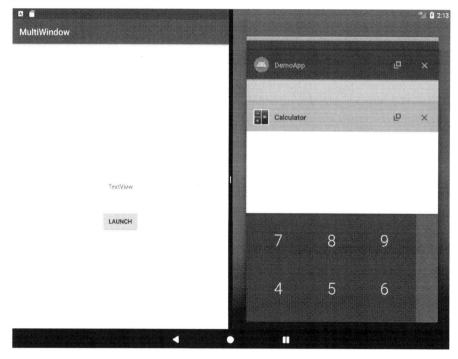

Figure 54-3

Click on the Launch button and note that the second activity appears in the same panel as the first activity.

If the app is running on a device or emulator session that supports freeform mode, or on which freeform mode has been enabled as outlined in the previous chapter, press and hold the Overview button a second time until multi-window mode exits. Click in the Overview button once again and, in the resulting Overview screen, select the freeform button located in the title bar of the MultiWindow app as outlined in Figure 54-4:

Figure 54-4

Once selected, the activity should appear in freeform mode as illustrated in Figure 54-5:

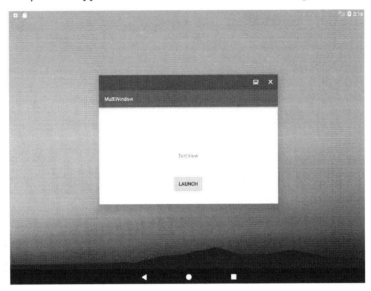

Figure 54-5

Click on the Launch button and note that, once again, the second activity appears in place of the first rather than in a separate window.

In order for the second activity to appear in a different split-screen panel or freeform window, the intent must be launched with the appropriate flags set.

54.7 Launching the Second Activity in a Different Window

To prevent the second activity from replacing the first activity the *launchIntent()* method needs to be modified to launch the second activity in a different task stack as follows:

```
public void launchIntent(View view) {
    Intent i = new Intent(this, SecondActivity.class);

    i.addFlags(Intent.FLAG_ACTIVITY_LAUNCH_ADJACENT|
            Intent.FLAG_ACTIVITY_MULTIPLE_TASK|
            Intent.FLAG_ACTIVITY_NEW_TASK);

    startActivity(i);
}
```

After making this change, rerun the app, enter split-screen mode and launch the second activity. The second activity should now appear in the panel adjacent to the first activity:

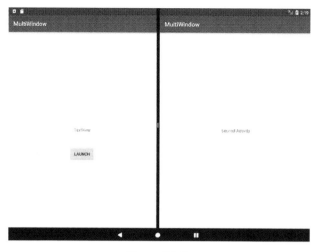

Figure 54-6

Repeat the steps from the previous section to enter freeform mode and verify that the second activity appears in a separate window from the first as shown in Figure 54-7:

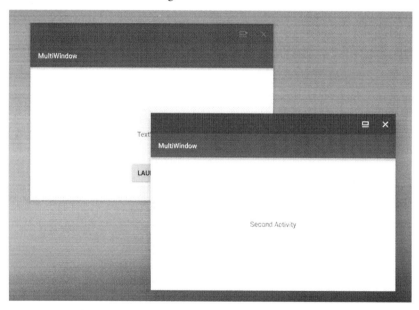

Figure 54-7

54.8 Summary

This chapter has demonstrated some of the basics of enabling and working with multi-window support within an Android app through the implementation of an example project. In particular, this example has focused on enabling multi-window support and launching a second activity into a new task stack.

55. An Overview of Android SQLite Databases

Mobile applications that do not need to store at least some amount of persistent data are few and far between. The use of databases is an essential aspect of most applications, ranging from applications that are almost entirely data driven, to those that simply need to store small amounts of data such as the prevailing score of a game.

The importance of persistent data storage becomes even more evident when taking into consideration the somewhat transient lifecycle of the typical Android application. With the ever-present risk that the Android runtime system will terminate an application component to free up resources, a comprehensive data storage strategy to avoid data loss is a key factor in the design and implementation of any application development strategy.

This chapter will provide an overview of the SQLite database management system bundled with the Android operating system, together with an outline of the Android SDK classes that are provided to facilitate persistent SQLite based database storage from within an Android application. Before delving into the specifics of SQLite in the context of Android development, however, a brief overview of databases and SQL will be covered.

55.1 Understanding Database Tables

Database *Tables* provide the most basic level of data structure in a database. Each database can contain multiple tables and each table is designed to hold information of a specific type. For example, a database may contain a *customer* table that contains the name, address and telephone number for each of the customers of a particular business. The same database may also include a *products* table used to store the product descriptions with associated product codes for the items sold by the business.

Each table in a database is assigned a name that must be unique within that particular database. A table name, once assigned to a table in one database, may not be used for another table except within the context of another database.

55.2 Introducing Database Schema

Database Schemas define the characteristics of the data stored in a database table. For example, the table schema for a customer database table might define that the customer name is a string of no more than 20 characters in length, and that the customer phone number is a numerical data field of a certain format.

Schemas are also used to define the structure of entire databases and the relationship between the various tables contained in each database.

55.3 Columns and Data Types

It is helpful at this stage to begin to view a database table as being similar to a spreadsheet where data is stored in rows and columns.

Each column represents a data field in the corresponding table. For example, the name, address and telephone data fields of a table are all *columns*.

Each column, in turn, is defined to contain a certain type of data. A column designed to store numbers would, therefore, be defined as containing numerical data.

55.4 Database Rows

Each new record that is saved to a table is stored in a row. Each row, in turn, consists of the columns of data associated with the saved record.

Once again, consider the spreadsheet analogy described earlier in this chapter. Each entry in a customer table is equivalent to a row in a spreadsheet and each column contains the data for each customer (name, address, telephone etc). When a new customer is added to the table, a new row is created and the data for that customer stored in the corresponding columns of the new row.

Rows are also sometimes referred to as *records* or *entries* and these terms can generally be used interchangeably.

55.5 Introducing Primary Keys

Each database table should contain one or more columns that can be used to identify each row in the table uniquely. This is known in database terminology as the *Primary Key*. For example, a table may use a bank account number column as the primary key. Alternatively, a customer table may use the customer's social security number as the primary key.

Primary keys allow the database management system to identify a specific row in a table uniquely. Without a primary key it would not be possible to retrieve or delete a specific row in a table because there can be no certainty that the correct row has been selected. For example, suppose a table existed where the customer's last name had been defined as the primary key. Imagine then the problem that might arise if more than one customer named "Smith" were recorded in the database. Without some guaranteed way to identify a specific row uniquely, it would be impossible to ensure the correct data was being accessed at any given time.

Primary keys can comprise a single column or multiple columns in a table. To qualify as a single column primary key, no two rows can contain matching primary key values. When using multiple columns to construct a primary key, individual column values do not need to be unique, but all the columns' values combined together must be unique.

55.6 What is SQLite?

SQLite is an embedded, relational database management system (RDBMS). Most relational databases (Oracle, SQL Server and MySQL being prime examples) are standalone server processes that run independently, and in cooperation with, applications that require database access. SQLite is referred to as *embedded* because it is provided in the form of a library that is linked into applications. As such, there is no standalone database server running in the background. All database operations are handled internally within the application through calls to functions contained in the SQLite library.

The developers of SQLite have placed the technology into the public domain with the result that it is now a widely deployed database solution.

SQLite is written in the C programming language and as such, the Android SDK provides a Java based "wrapper" around the underlying database interface. This essentially consists of a set of classes that may be utilized within the Java or Kotlin code of an application to create and manage SQLite based databases.

For additional information about SQLite refer to *http://www.sqlite.org*.

55.7 Structured Query Language (SQL)

Data is accessed in SQLite databases using a high-level language known as Structured Query Language. This is usually abbreviated to SQL and pronounced *sequel*. SQL is a standard language used by most relational database management systems. SQLite conforms mostly to the SQL-92 standard.

SQL is essentially a very simple and easy to use language designed specifically to enable the reading and writing of database data. Because SQL contains a small set of keywords, it can be learned quickly. In addition, SQL syntax is more or less identical between most DBMS implementations, so having learned SQL for one system, it is likely that your skills will transfer to other database management systems.

While some basic SQL statements will be used within this chapter, a detailed overview of SQL is beyond the scope of this book. There are, however, many other resources that provide a far better overview of SQL than we could ever hope to provide in a single chapter here.

55.8 Trying SQLite on an Android Virtual Device (AVD)

For readers unfamiliar with databases in general and SQLite in particular, diving right into creating an Android application that uses SQLite may seem a little intimidating. Fortunately, Android is shipped with SQLite pre-installed, including an interactive environment for issuing SQL commands from within an *adb shell* session connected to a running Android AVD emulator instance. This is both a useful way to learn about SQLite and SQL, and also an invaluable tool for identifying problems with databases created by applications running in an emulator.

To launch an interactive SQLite session, begin by running an AVD session. This can be achieved from within Android Studio by launching the Android Virtual Device Manager (*Tools -> Android -> AVD Manager*), selecting a previously configured AVD and clicking on the start button.

Once the AVD is up and running, open a Terminal or Command-Prompt window and connect to the emulator using the *adb* command-line tool as follows (note that the –e flag directs the tool to look for an emulator with which to connect, rather than a physical device):

```
adb -e shell
```

Once connected, the shell environment will provide a command prompt at which commands may be entered. Begin by obtaining super user privileges using the *su* command:

```
Generic_x86:/ su
root@android:/ #
```

If a message appears indicating that super user privileges are not allowed, it is likely that the AVD instance includes Google Play support. To resolve this create a new AVD and, on the "Choose a device definition" screen, select a device that does not have a marker in the "Play Store" column.

Data stored in SQLite databases are actually stored in database files on the file system of the Android device on which the application is running. By default, the file system path for these database files is as follows:

```
/data/data/<package name>/databases/<database filename>.db
```

For example, if an application with the package name *com.example.MyDBApp* creates a database named *mydatabase.db*, the path to the file on the device would read as follows:

```
/data/data/com.example.MyDBApp/databases/mydatabase.db
```

For the purposes of this exercise, therefore, change directory to /data/data within the adb shell and create a sub-directory hierarchy suitable for some SQLite experimentation:

```
cd /data/data
mkdir com.example.dbexample
cd com.example.dbexample
mkdir databases
cd databases
```

With a suitable location created for the database file, launch the interactive SQLite tool as follows:

An Overview of Android SQLite Databases

```
root@android:/data/data/databases # sqlite3 ./mydatabase.db
sqlite3 ./mydatabase.db
SQLite version 3.8.10.2 2015-05-20 18:17:19
Enter ".help" for usage hints.
sqlite>
```

At the *sqlite>* prompt, commands may be entered to perform tasks such as creating tables and inserting and retrieving data. For example, to create a new table in our database with fields to hold ID, name, address and phone number fields the following statement is required:

```
create table contacts (_id integer primary key autoincrement, name text, address
text, phone text);
```

Note that each row in a table should have a *primary key* that is unique to that row. In the above example, we have designated the ID field as the primary key, declared it as being of type *integer* and asked SQLite to increment the number automatically each time a row is added. This is a common way to make sure that each row has a unique primary key. On most other platforms, the choice of name for the primary key is arbitrary. In the case of Android, however, it is essential that the key be named *_id* in order for the database to be fully accessible using all of the Android database related classes. The remaining fields are each declared as being of type *text*.

To list the tables in the currently selected database, use the *.tables* statement:

```
sqlite> .tables
contacts
```

To insert records into the table:

```
sqlite> insert into contacts (name, address, phone) values ("Bill Smith", "123
Main Street, California", "123-555-2323");
sqlite> insert into contacts (name, address, phone) values ("Mike Parks", "10
Upping Street, Idaho", "444-444-1212");
```

To retrieve all rows from a table:

```
sqlite> select * from contacts;
1|Bill Smith|123 Main Street, California|123-555-2323
2|Mike Parks|10 Upping Street, Idaho|444-444-1212
```

To extract a row that meets specific criteria:

```
sqlite> select * from contacts where name="Mike Parks";
2|Mike Parks|10 Upping Street, Idaho|444-444-1212
```

To exit from the sqlite3 interactive environment:

```
sqlite> .exit
```

When running an Android application in the emulator environment, any database files will be created on the file system of the emulator using the previously discussed path convention. This has the advantage that you can connect with adb, navigate to the location of the database file, load it into the sqlite3 interactive tool and perform tasks on the data to identify possible problems occurring in the application code.

It is also important to note that, while it is possible to connect with an adb shell to a physical Android device, the shell is not granted sufficient privileges by default to create and manage SQLite databases. Debugging of database problems is, therefore, best performed using an AVD session.

55.9 Android SQLite Classes

SQLite is, as previously mentioned, written in the C programming language while Android applications are primarily developed using Java. To bridge this "language gap", the Android SDK includes a set of classes that provide a Java layer on top of the SQLite database management system. The remainder of this chapter will provide a basic overview of each of the major classes within this category. More details on each class can be found in the online Android documentation.

55.9.1 Cursor

A class provided specifically to provide access to the results of a database query. For example, a SQL SELECT operation performed on a database will potentially return multiple matching rows from the database. A Cursor instance can be used to step through these results, which may then be accessed from within the application code using a variety of methods. Some key methods of this class are as follows:

- **close()** – Releases all resources used by the cursor and closes it.

- **getCount()** – Returns the number of rows contained within the result set.

- **moveToFirst()** – Moves to the first row within the result set.

- **moveToLast()** – Moves to the last row in the result set.

- **moveToNext()** – Moves to the next row in the result set.

- **move()** – Moves by a specified offset from the current position in the result set.

- **get<type>()** – Returns the value of the specified *<type>* contained at the specified column index of the row at the current cursor position (variations consist of *getString(), getInt(), getShort(), getFloat()* and *getDouble()*).

55.9.2 SQLiteDatabase

This class provides the primary interface between the application code and underlying SQLite databases including the ability to create, delete and perform SQL based operations on databases. Some key methods of this class are as follows:

- **insert()** – Inserts a new row into a database table.

- **delete()** – Deletes rows from a database table.

- **query()** – Performs a specified database query and returns matching results via a Cursor object.

- **execSQL()** – Executes a single SQL statement that does not return result data.

- **rawQuery()** – Executes a SQL query statement and returns matching results in the form of a Cursor object.

55.9.3 SQLiteOpenHelper

A helper class designed to make it easier to create and update databases. This class must be subclassed within the code of the application seeking database access and the following callback methods implemented within that subclass:

- **onCreate()** – Called when the database is created for the first time. This method is passed the SQLiteDatabase object as an argument for the newly created database. This is the ideal location to initialize the database in terms of creating a table and inserting any initial data rows.

- **onUpgrade()** – Called in the event that the application code contains a more recent database version number reference. This is typically used when an application is updated on the device and requires that the database schema also be updated to handle storage of additional data.

In addition to the above mandatory callback methods, the *onOpen()* method, called when the database is opened, may also be implemented within the subclass.

The constructor for the subclass must also be implemented to call the super class, passing through the application context, the name of the database and the database version.

Notable methods of the SQLiteOpenHelper class include:

- **getWritableDatabase()** – Opens or creates a database for reading and writing. Returns a reference to the database in the form of a SQLiteDatabase object.

- **getReadableDatabase()** – Creates or opens a database for reading only. Returns a reference to the database in the form of a SQLiteDatabase object.

- **close**() – Closes the database.

55.9.4 ContentValues

ContentValues is a convenience class that allows key/value pairs to be declared consisting of table column identifiers and the values to be stored in each column. This class is of particular use when inserting or updating entries in a database table.

55.10 Summary

SQLite is a lightweight, embedded relational database management system that is included as part of the Android framework and provides a mechanism for implementing organized persistent data storage for Android applications. In addition to the SQLite database, the Android framework also includes a range of Java classes that may be used to create and manage SQLite based databases and tables.

The goal of this chapter was to provide an overview of databases in general and SQLite in particular within the context of Android application development. The next chapters will work through the creation of an example application intended to put this theory into practice in the form of a step-by-step tutorial. Since the user interface for the example application will require a forms based layout, the first chapter, entitled *"An Android TableLayout and TableRow Tutorial"*, will detour slightly from the core topic by introducing the basics of the TableLayout and TableRow views.

56. An Android TableLayout and TableRow Tutorial

When the work began on the next chapter of this book (*"An Android SQLite Database Tutorial"*) it was originally intended that it would include the steps to design the user interface layout for the database example application. It quickly became evident, however, that the best way to implement the user interface was to make use of the Android TableLayout and TableRow views and that this topic area deserved a self-contained chapter. As a result, this chapter will focus solely on the user interface design of the database application completed in the next chapter, and in doing so, take some time to introduce the basic concepts of table layouts in Android Studio.

56.1 The TableLayout and TableRow Layout Views

The purpose of the TableLayout container view is to allow user interface elements to be organized on the screen in a table format consisting of rows and columns. Each row within a TableLayout is occupied by a TableRow instance, which, in turn, is divided into cells, with each cell containing a single child view (which may itself be a container with multiple view children).

The number of columns in a table is dictated by the row with the most columns and, by default, the width of each column is defined by the widest cell in that column. Columns may be configured to be shrinkable or stretchable (or both) such that they change in size relative to the parent TableLayout. In addition, a single cell may be configured to span multiple columns.

Consider the user interface layout shown in Figure 56-1:

Figure 56-1

From the visual appearance of the layout, it is difficult to identify the TableLayout structure used to design the interface. The hierarchical tree illustrated in Figure 56-2, however, makes the structure a little easier to understand:

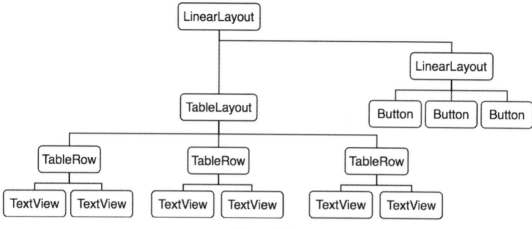

Figure 56-2

Clearly, the layout consists of a parent LinearLayout view with TableLayout and LinearLayout children. The TableLayout contains three TableRow children representing three rows in the table. The TableRows contain two child views, with each child representing the contents of a column cell. The LinearLayout child view contains three Button children.

The layout shown in Figure 56-2 is the exact layout that is required for the database example that will be completed in the next chapter. The remainder of this chapter, therefore, will be used to work step by step through the design of this user interface using the Android Studio Layout Editor tool.

56.2 Creating the Database Project

Start Android Studio and create a new project, entering *Database* into the Application name field and *ebookfrenzy. com* as the Company Domain setting before clicking on the *Next* button.

On the form factors screen, enable the *Phone and Tablet* option and set the minimum SDK setting to API 14: Android 4.0 (IceCreamSandwich). Continue to proceed through the screens, requesting the creation of an Empty Activity named *DatabaseActivity* with a corresponding layout file named *activity_database*.

56.3 Adding the TableLayout to the User Interface

Locate the *activity_database.xml* file in the Project tool window (*app -> res -> layout*) and double-click on it to load it into the Layout Editor tool. By default, Android Studio has used a ConstraintLayout as the root layout element in the user interface. This needs to be replaced by a vertically oriented LinearLayout. With the Layout Editor tool in Text mode, replace the XML with the following:

```xml
<?xml version="1.0" encoding="utf-8"?>
<LinearLayout
    android:orientation="vertical"
    android:layout_width="match_parent"
    android:layout_height="match_parent"
    xmlns:android="http://schemas.android.com/apk/res/android">
</LinearLayout>
```

Switch to Design mode and, referring to the Layouts category of the Palette, drag and drop a TableLayout view so that it is positioned at the top of the LinearLayout canvas area. With the LinearLayout component selected, use the Attributes tool window to set the layout_height property to *wrap_content*.

Once these initial steps are complete, the Component Tree for the layout should resemble that shown in Figure 56-3.

Figure 56-3

Clearly, Android Studio has automatically added four TableRow instances to the TableLayout. Since only three rows are required for this example, select and delete the fourth TableRow instance. Additional rows may be added to the TableLayout at any time by dragging the TableRow object from the palette and dropping it onto the TableLayout entry in the Component Tree tool window.

56.4 Configuring the TableRows

From within the *Text* section of the palette, drag and drop two TextView objects onto the uppermost TableRow entry in the Component Tree (Figure 56-4):

Figure 56-4

Select the left most TextView within the screen layout and, in the Attributes tool window, change the *text* property to "Product ID". Repeat this step for the right most TextView, this time changing the text to "Not assigned" and specifying an *ID* value of *productID*.

Drag and drop another TextView widget onto the second TableRow entry in the Component Tree and change the text on the view to read "Product Name". Locate the Plain Text object in the palette and drag and drop it so that it is positioned beneath the Product Name TextView within the Component Tree as outlined in Figure 56-5.

With the TextView selected, change the inputType property from textPersonName to None, delete the "Name" string from the text property and set the ID to *productName*.

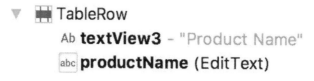

Figure 56-5

Drag and drop another TextView and a Number (Decimal) Text Field onto the third TableRow so that the TextView is positioned above the Text Field in the hierarchy. Change the text on the TextView to *Product Quantity* and the ID of the Text Field object to *productQuantity*.

Shift-click to select all of the widgets in the layout as shown in Figure 56-6 below, and use the Attributes tool window to set the textSize property on all of the objects to 18sp:

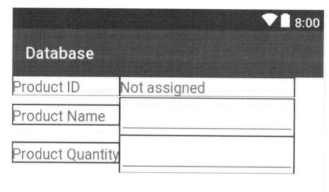

Figure 56-6

Before proceeding, be sure to extract all of the text properties added in the above steps to string resources.

56.5 Adding the Button Bar to the Layout

The next step is to add a LinearLayout (Horizontal) view to the parent LinearLayout view, positioned immediately below the TableLayout view. Begin by clicking on the small arrow to the left of the TableLayout entry in the Component Tree so that the TableRows are folded away from view. Drag a *LinearLayout (Horizontal)* instance from the *Layouts* section of the Layout Editor palette, drop it immediately beneath the TableLayout entry in the Component Tree panel and change the layout_height property to *wrap_content*:

Figure 56-7

Drag and drop three Button objects onto the new LinearLayout and assign string resources for each button that read "Add", "Find" and "Delete" respectively. Buttons in this type of button bar arrangement should generally be displayed with a borderless style. For each button, use the Attributes tool window to change the style setting to

Widget.AppCompat.Button.Borderless.

With the new horizontal Linear Layout view selected in the Component Tree change the gravity property to *center_horizontal* (Figure 56-8) so that the buttons are centered horizontally within the display:

Figure 56-8

Before proceeding, check the hierarchy of the layout in the Component Tree panel, taking extra care to ensure the view ID names match those in the following figure:

Figure 56-9

56.6 Adjusting the Layout Margins

All that remains is to adjust some of the layout settings. Begin by clicking on the first TableRow entry in the Component Tree panel so that it is selected. Hold down the Cmd/Ctrl-key on the keyboard and click in the second and third TableRows so that all three items are selected. In the Attributes panel, list all attributes, locate the *layout_margins* attributes category and, once located, change all the *all* value to 10dp as shown in Figure 56-10:

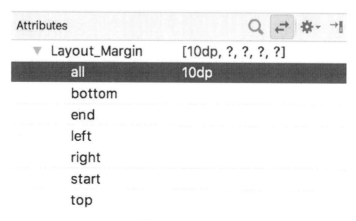

Figure 56-10

With margins set on all three TableRows, the user interface should appear as illustrated in Figure 56-1.

56.7 Summary

The Android TableLayout container view provides a way to arrange view components in a row and column configuration. While the TableLayout view provides the overall container, each row and the cells contained therein are implemented via instances of the TableRow view. In this chapter, a user interface has been designed in Android Studio using the TableLayout and TableRow containers. The next chapter will add the functionality behind this user interface to implement the SQLite database capabilities.

57. An Android SQLite Database Tutorial

The chapter entitled *"An Overview of Android SQLite Databases"* covered the basic principles of integrating relational database storage into Android applications using the SQLite database management system. The previous chapter took a minor detour into the territory of designing TableLayouts within the Android Studio Layout Editor tool, in the course of which, the user interface for an example database application was created. In this chapter, work on the *Database* application project will be continued with the ultimate objective of completing the database example.

57.1 About the Database Example

As is probably evident from the user interface layout designed in the preceding chapter, the example project is a simple data entry and retrieval application designed to allow the user to add, query and delete database entries. The idea behind this application is to allow the tracking of product inventory.

The name of the database will be *productID.db* which, in turn, will contain a single table named *products*. Each record in the database table will contain a unique product ID, a product description and the quantity of that product item currently in stock, corresponding to column names of "productid", "productname" and "productquantity", respectively. The productid column will act as the primary key and will be automatically assigned and incremented by the database management system.

The database schema for the *products* table is outlined in Table 57-2:

Column	Data Type
productid	Integer / Primary Key / Auto Increment
productname	Text
productquantity	Integer

Table 57-2

57.2 Creating the Data Model

Once completed, the application will consist of an activity and a database handler class. The database handler will be a subclass of SQLiteOpenHelper and will provide an abstract layer between the underlying SQLite database and the activity class, with the activity calling on the database handler to interact with the database (adding, removing and querying database entries). In order to implement this interaction in a structured way, a third class will need to be implemented to hold the database entry data as it is passed between the activity and the handler. This is actually a very simple class capable of holding product ID, product name and product quantity values, together with getter and setter methods for accessing these values. Instances of this class can then be created within the activity and database handler and passed back and forth as needed. Essentially, this class can be thought of as representing the database model.

An Android SQLite Database Tutorial

Within Android Studio, navigate within the Project tool window to *app -> java* and right-click on the package name. From the popup menu, choose the *New -> Java Class* option and, in the *Create New Class* dialog, name the class *Product* before clicking on the *OK* button.

Once created the *Product.java* source file will automatically load into the Android Studio editor. Once loaded, modify the code to add the appropriate data members and methods:

```java
package com.ebookfrenzy.database;


public class Product {

    private int _id;
    private String _productname;
    private int _quantity;

    public Product() {

    }

    public Product(int id, String productname, int quantity) {
        this._id = id;
        this._productname = productname;
        this._quantity = quantity;
    }

    public Product(String productname, int quantity) {
        this._productname = productname;
        this._quantity = quantity;
    }

    public void setID(int id) {
        this._id = id;
    }

    public int getID() {
        return this._id;
    }

    public void setProductName(String productname) {
        this._productname = productname;
    }

    public String getProductName() {
        return this._productname;
    }

    public void setQuantity(int quantity) {
```

```
        this._quantity = quantity;
    }


    public int getQuantity() {
        return this._quantity;
    }
}
```

The completed class contains private data members for the internal storage of data columns from database entries and a set of methods to get and set those values.

57.3 Implementing the Data Handler

The data handler will be implemented by subclassing from the Android SQLiteOpenHelper class and, as outlined in *"An Overview of Android SQLite Databases"*, adding the constructor, *onCreate()* and *onUpgrade()* methods. Since the handler will be required to add, query and delete data on behalf of the activity component, corresponding methods will also need to be added to the class.

Begin by adding a second new class to the project to act as the handler, this time named *MyDBHandler*. Once the new class has been created, modify it so that it reads as follows:

```
package com.ebookfrenzy.database;


import android.database.sqlite.SQLiteDatabase;
import android.database.sqlite.SQLiteOpenHelper;


public class MyDBHandler extends SQLiteOpenHelper {


    @Override
    public void onCreate(SQLiteDatabase db) {


    }


    @Override
    public void onUpgrade(SQLiteDatabase db, int oldVersion,
                          int newVersion) {


    }
}
```

Having now pre-populated the source file with template *onCreate()* and *onUpgrade()* methods, the next task is to add a constructor method. Modify the code to declare constants for the database name, table name, table columns and database version and to add the constructor method as follows:

```
package com.ebookfrenzy.database;


import android.database.sqlite.SQLiteDatabase;
import android.database.sqlite.SQLiteOpenHelper;
import android.content.Context;
import android.content.ContentValues;
import android.database.Cursor;
```

```
public class MyDBHandler extends SQLiteOpenHelper {

    private static final int DATABASE_VERSION = 1;
    private static final String DATABASE_NAME = "productDB.db";
    public static final String TABLE_PRODUCTS = "products";

    public static final String COLUMN_ID = "_id";
    public static final String COLUMN_PRODUCTNAME = "productname";
    public static final String COLUMN_QUANTITY = "quantity";

    public MyDBHandler(Context context, String name,
        SQLiteDatabase.CursorFactory factory, int version) {
            super(context, DATABASE_NAME, factory, DATABASE_VERSION);
    }

    @Override
    public void onCreate(SQLiteDatabase db) {

    }

    @Override
    public void onUpgrade(SQLiteDatabase db, int oldVersion,
                int newVersion) {

    }
}
```

Next, the *onCreate()* method needs to be implemented so that the *products* table is created when the database is first initialized. This involves constructing a SQL CREATE statement containing instructions to create a new table with the appropriate columns and then passing that through to the *execSQL()* method of the SQLiteDatabase object passed as an argument to *onCreate()*:

```
@Override
public void onCreate(SQLiteDatabase db) {
        String CREATE_PRODUCTS_TABLE = "CREATE TABLE " +
                TABLE_PRODUCTS + "("
                + COLUMN_ID + " INTEGER PRIMARY KEY," +
                    COLUMN_PRODUCTNAME
                + " TEXT," + COLUMN_QUANTITY + " INTEGER" + ")";
        db.execSQL(CREATE_PRODUCTS_TABLE);
}
```

The *onUpgrade()* method is called when the handler is invoked with a greater database version number from the one previously used. The exact steps to be performed in this instance will be application specific, so for the purposes of this example, we will simply remove the old database and create a new one:

```
@Override
public void onUpgrade(SQLiteDatabase db, int oldVersion,
```

```
                                        int newVersion) {
    db.execSQL("DROP TABLE IF EXISTS " + TABLE_PRODUCTS);
    onCreate(db);
}
```

All that now remains to be implemented in the *MyDBHandler.java* handler class are the methods to add, query and remove database table entries.

57.3.1 The Add Handler Method

The method to insert database records will be named *addProduct()* and will take as an argument an instance of our Product data model class. A ContentValues object will be created in the body of the method and primed with key-value pairs for the data columns extracted from the Product object. Next, a reference to the database will be obtained via a call to *getWritableDatabase()* followed by a call to the *insert()* method of the returned database object. Finally, once the insertion has been performed, the database needs to be closed:

```
public void addProduct(Product product) {

        ContentValues values = new ContentValues();
        values.put(COLUMN_PRODUCTNAME, product.getProductName());
        values.put(COLUMN_QUANTITY, product.getQuantity());

        SQLiteDatabase db = this.getWritableDatabase();

        db.insert(TABLE_PRODUCTS, null, values);
        db.close();
}
```

57.3.2 The Query Handler Method

The method to query the database will be named *findProduct()* and will take as an argument a String object containing the name of the product to be located. Using this string, a SQL SELECT statement will be constructed to find all matching records in the table. For the purposes of this example, only the first match will then be returned, contained within a new instance of our Product data model class:

```
public Product findProduct(String productname) {
        String query = "SELECT * FROM " + TABLE_PRODUCTS + " WHERE " + COLUMN_
PRODUCTNAME + " =  \"" + productname + "\"";

        SQLiteDatabase db = this.getWritableDatabase();

        Cursor cursor = db.rawQuery(query, null);

        Product product = new Product();

        if (cursor.moveToFirst()) {
                cursor.moveToFirst();
                product.setID(Integer.parseInt(cursor.getString(0)));
                product.setProductName(cursor.getString(1));
                product.setQuantity(Integer.parseInt(cursor.getString(2)));
                cursor.close();
```

```
    } else {
            product = null;
    }
    db.close();
    return product;
}
```

57.3.3 The Delete Handler Method

The deletion method will be named *deleteProduct()* and will accept as an argument the entry to be deleted in the form of a Product object. The method will use a SQL SELECT statement to search for the entry based on the product name and, if located, delete it from the table. The success or otherwise of the deletion will be reflected in a Boolean return value:

```
public boolean deleteProduct (String productname) {

    boolean result = false;

    String query = "SELECT * FROM " + TABLE_PRODUCTS + " WHERE " + COLUMN_
PRODUCTNAME + " = \"" + productname + "\"";

    SQLiteDatabase db = this.getWritableDatabase();

    Cursor cursor = db.rawQuery(query, null);

    Product product = new Product();

    if (cursor.moveToFirst()) {
            product.setID(Integer.parseInt(cursor.getString(0)));
            db.delete(TABLE_PRODUCTS, COLUMN_ID + " = ?",
                new String[] { String.valueOf(product.getID()) });
            cursor.close();
            result = true;
    }
    db.close();
    return result;
}
```

57.4 Implementing the Activity Event Methods

The final task prior to testing the application is to wire up *onClick* event handlers on the three buttons in the user interface and to implement corresponding methods for those events. Locate and load the *activity_database.xml* file into the Layout Editor tool, switch to Text mode and locate and modify the three button elements to add *onClick* properties:

```
<Button
    android:text="@string/add"
    android:layout_width="wrap_content"
    android:layout_height="wrap_content"
    android:id="@+id/button3"
    android:layout_weight="1"
```

```
            style="@style/Widget.AppCompat.Button.Borderless"
            android:onClick="newProduct" />


<Button
        android:text="@string/find"
        android:layout_width="wrap_content"
        android:layout_height="wrap_content"
        android:id="@+id/button2"
        android:layout_weight="1"
        style="@style/Widget.AppCompat.Button.Borderless"
        android:onClick="lookupProduct" />


<Button
        android:text="@string/delete"
        android:layout_width="wrap_content"
        android:layout_height="wrap_content"
        android:id="@+id/button"
        android:layout_weight="1"
        style="@style/Widget.AppCompat.Button.Borderless"
        android:onClick="removeProduct" />
```

Load the *DatabaseActivity.java* source file into the editor and implement the code to identify the views in the user interface and to implement the three "onClick" target methods:

```
package com.ebookfrenzy.database;


import android.support.v7.app.AppCompatActivity;
import android.os.Bundle;
import android.view.View;
import android.widget.EditText;
import android.widget.TextView;


public class DatabaseActivity extends AppCompatActivity {

    TextView idView;
    EditText productBox;
    EditText quantityBox;

    @Override
    protected void onCreate(Bundle savedInstanceState) {
        super.onCreate(savedInstanceState);
        setContentView(R.layout.activity_database);

        idView = (TextView) findViewById(R.id.productID);
        productBox = (EditText) findViewById(R.id.productName);
        quantityBox =
                (EditText) findViewById(R.id.productQuantity);
```

```
    }

    public void newProduct (View view) {
        MyDBHandler dbHandler = new MyDBHandler(this, null, null, 1);

        int quantity =
                Integer.parseInt(quantityBox.getText().toString());

        Product product =
                new Product(productBox.getText().toString(),
                            quantity);

        dbHandler.addProduct(product);
        productBox.setText("");
        quantityBox.setText("");
    }

    public void lookupProduct (View view) {
        MyDBHandler dbHandler = new MyDBHandler(this, null, null, 1);

        Product product = dbHandler.findProduct(
                productBox.getText().toString());

        if (product != null) {
            idView.setText(String.valueOf(product.getID()));

            quantityBox.setText(
                    String.valueOf(product.getQuantity()));
        } else {
            idView.setText("No Match Found");
        }
    }

    public void removeProduct (View view) {
        MyDBHandler dbHandler = new MyDBHandler(this, null,
                null, 1);

        boolean result = dbHandler.deleteProduct(
                productBox.getText().toString());

        if (result)
        {
            idView.setText("Record Deleted");
            productBox.setText("");
            quantityBox.setText("");
```

```
        }
        else
            idView.setText("No Match Found");
    }
}
```

57.5 Testing the Application

With the coding changes completed, compile and run the application either in an AVD session or on a physical Android device. Once the application is running, enter a product name and quantity value into the user interface form and touch the *Add* button. Once the record has been added the text boxes will clear. Repeat these steps to add a second product to the database. Next, enter the name of one of the newly added products into the product name field and touch the *Find* button. The form should update with the product ID and quantity for the selected product. Touch the *Delete* button to delete the selected record. A subsequent search by product name should indicate that the record no longer exists.

57.6 Summary

The purpose of this chapter has been to work step by step through a practical application of SQLite based database storage in Android applications. As an exercise to develop your new database skill set further, consider extending the example to include the ability to update existing records in the database table.

58. Understanding Android Content Providers

The previous chapter worked through the creation of an example application designed to store data using a SQLite database. When implemented in this way, the data is private to the application and, as such, inaccessible to other applications running on the same device. While this may be the desired behavior for many types of application, situations will inevitably arise whereby the data stored on behalf of an application could be of benefit to other applications. A prime example of this is the data stored by the built-in Contacts application on an Android device. While the Contacts application is primarily responsible for the management of the user's address book details, this data is also made accessible to any other applications that might need access to this data. This sharing of data between Android applications is achieved through the implementation of *content providers*.

58.1 What is a Content Provider?

A content provider provides access to structured data between different Android applications. This data is exposed to applications either as tables of data (in much the same way as a SQLite database) or as a handle to a file. This essentially involves the implementation of a client/server arrangement whereby the application seeking access to the data is the client and the content provider is the server, performing actions and returning results on behalf of the client.

A successful content provider implementation involves a number of different elements, each of which will be covered in detail in the remainder of this chapter.

58.2 The Content Provider

A content provider is created as a subclass of the *android.content.ContentProvider* class. Typically, the application responsible for managing the data to be shared will implement a content provider to facilitate the sharing of that data with other applications.

The creation of a content provider involves the implementation of a set of methods to manage the data on behalf of other, client applications. These methods are as follows:

58.2.1 onCreate()

This method is called when the content provider is first created and should be used to perform any initialization tasks required by the content provider.

58.2.2 query()

This method will be called when a client requests that data be retrieved from the content provider. It is the responsibility of this method to identify the data to be retrieved (either single or multiple rows), perform the data extraction and return the results wrapped in a Cursor object.

58.2.3 insert()

This method is called when a new row needs to be inserted into the provider database. This method must identify the destination for the data, perform the insertion and return the full URI of the newly added row.

58.2.4 update()

The method called when existing rows need to be updated on behalf of the client. The method uses the arguments passed through to update the appropriate table rows and return the number of rows updated as a result of the operation.

58.2.5 delete()

Called when rows are to be deleted from a table. This method deletes the designated rows and returns a count of the number of rows deleted.

58.2.6 getType()

Returns the MIME type of the data stored by the content provider.

It is important when implementing these methods in a content provider to keep in mind that, with the exception of the *onCreate()* method, they can be called from many processes simultaneously and must, therefore, be thread safe.

Once a content provider has been implemented, the issue that then arises is how the provider is identified within the Android system. This is where the *content URI* comes into play.

58.3 The Content URI

An Android device will potentially contain a number of content providers. The system must, therefore, provide some way of identifying one provider from another. Similarly, a single content provider may provide access to multiple forms of content (typically in the form of database tables). Client applications, therefore, need a way to specify the underlying data for which access is required. This is achieved through the use of content URIs.

The content URI is essentially used to identify specific data within a specific content provider. The *Authority* section of the URI identifies the content provider and usually takes the form of the package name of the content provider. For example:

```
com.example.mydbapp.myprovider
```

A specific database table within the provider data structure may be referenced by appending the table name to the authority. For example, the following URI references a table named *products* within the content provider:

```
com.example.mydbapp.myprovider/products
```

Similarly, a specific row within the specified table may be referenced by appending the row ID to the URI. The following URI, for example, references the row in the products table in which the value stored in the _ID column equals 3:

```
com.example.mydbapp.myprovider/products/3
```

When implementing the insert, query, update and delete methods in the content provider, it will be the responsibility of these methods to identify whether the incoming URI is targeting a specific row in a table, or references multiple rows, and act accordingly. This can potentially be a complex task given that a URI can extend to multiple levels. This process can, however, be eased significantly by making use of the *UriMatcher* class as will be outlined in the next chapter.

58.4 The Content Resolver

Access to a content provider is achieved via a ContentResolver object. An application can obtain a reference to its content resolver by making a call to the *getContentResolver()* method of the application context.

The content resolver object contains a set of methods that mirror those of the content provider (insert, query, delete etc.). The application simply makes calls to the methods, specifying the URI of the content on which the operation is to be performed. The content resolver and content provider objects then communicate to perform the requested task on behalf of the application.

58.5 The <provider> Manifest Element

In order for a content provider to be visible within an Android system, it must be declared within the Android manifest file for the application in which it resides. This is achieved using the *<provider>* element, which must contain the following items:

- **android:authority** – The full authority URI of the content provider. For example com.example.mydbapp. mydbapp.myprovider.

- **android:name** – The name of the class that implements the content provider. In most cases, this will use the same value as the authority.

Similarly, the <provider> element may be used to define the permissions that must be held by client applications in order to qualify for access to the underlying data. If no permissions are declared, the default behavior is for permission to be allowed for all applications.

Permissions can be set to cover the entire content provider, or limited to specific tables and records.

58.6 Summary

The data belonging to an application is typically private to the application and inaccessible to other applications. In situations where the data needs to be shared, it is necessary to set up a content provider. This chapter has covered the basic elements that combine to enable data sharing between applications, and outlined the concepts of the content provider, content URI and content resolver.

In the next chapter, the Android Studio Database example application created previously will be extended to make the underlying product data available via a content provider.

59. Implementing an Android Content Provider in Android Studio

As outlined in the previous chapter, content providers provide a mechanism through which the data stored by one Android application can be made accessible to other applications. Having provided a theoretical overview of content providers, this chapter will continue the coverage of content providers by extending the Database project created in the chapter entitled *"An Android TableLayout and TableRow Tutorial"* to implement content provider based access to the database.

59.1 Copying the Database Project

In order to keep the original Database project intact, we will make a backup copy of the project before modifying it to implement content provider support for the application. If the Database project is currently open within Android Studio, close it using the *File -> Close Project* menu option.

Using the file system explorer for your operating system type, navigate to the directory containing your Android Studio projects (typically this will be a folder named *AndroidStudioProjects* located in your home directory). Within this folder, copy the Database project folder to a new folder named *DatabaseOriginal*.

Within the Android Studio welcome screen, select the *Open an existing Android Studio project* option from the Quick Start list and navigate to and select the original *Database* project so that it loads into the main window.

59.2 Adding the Content Provider Package

The next step is to add a new package to the Database project into which the content provider class will be created. Add this new package by navigating within the Project tool window to *app -> java,* right-clicking on the *java* entry and selecting the *New -> Package* menu option. When the *Choose Destination Directory* dialog appears, select the *..\app\src\main\java* option from the *Directory Structure* panel and click on OK.

In the *New Package* dialog, enter the following package name into the name field before clicking on the *OK* button:

```
com.ebookfrenzy.database.provider
```

The new package should now be listed within the Project tool window as illustrated in Figure 59-1:

Figure 59-1

59.3 Creating the Content Provider Class

As discussed in *"Understanding Android Content Providers"*, content providers are created by subclassing the *android.content.ContentProvider* class. Consequently, the next step is to add a class to the new *provider* package to serve as the content provider for this application. Locate the new package in the Project tool window, right-click on it and select the *New -> Other -> Content Provider* menu option. In the *Configure Component* dialog, enter *MyContentProvider* into the *Class Name* field and the following into the *URI Authorities* field:

```
com.ebookfrenzy.database.provider.MyContentProvider
```

Make sure that the new content provider class is both exported and enabled before clicking on *Finish* to create the new class.

Once the new class has been created, the *MyContentProvider.java* file should be listed beneath the *provider* package in the Project tool window and automatically loaded into the editor where it should appear as outlined in the following listing:

```java
package com.ebookfrenzy.database.provider;

import android.content.ContentProvider;
import android.content.ContentValues;
import android.database.Cursor;
import android.net.Uri;

public class MyContentProvider extends ContentProvider {
    public MyContentProvider() {
    }

    @Override
    public int delete(Uri uri, String selection, String[] selectionArgs) {
        // Implement this to handle requests to delete one or more rows.
        throw new UnsupportedOperationException("Not yet implemented");
    }

    @Override
    public String getType(Uri uri) {
        // TODO: Implement this to handle requests for the MIME type of the data
        // at the given URI.
        throw new UnsupportedOperationException("Not yet implemented");
    }

    @Override
    public Uri insert(Uri uri, ContentValues values) {
        // TODO: Implement this to handle requests to insert a new row.
        throw new UnsupportedOperationException("Not yet implemented");
    }

    @Override
    public boolean onCreate() {
```

```
        // TODO: Implement this to initialize your content provider on startup.
        return false;
    }


    @Override
    public Cursor query(Uri uri, String[] projection, String selection,
            String[] selectionArgs, String sortOrder) {
        // TODO: Implement this to handle query requests from clients.
        throw new UnsupportedOperationException("Not yet implemented");
    }


    @Override
    public int update(Uri uri, ContentValues values, String selection,
            String[] selectionArgs) {
        // TODO: Implement this to handle requests to update one or more rows.
        throw new UnsupportedOperationException("Not yet implemented");
    }
}
}
```

As is evident from a quick review of the code in this file, Android Studio has already populated the class with stubs for each of the methods that a subclass of ContentProvider is required to implement. It will soon be necessary to begin implementing these methods, but first some constants relating to the provider's content authority and URI need to be declared.

59.4 Constructing the Authority and Content URI

As outlined in the previous chapter, all content providers must have associated with them an *authority* and a *content uri*. In practice, the authority is typically the full package name of the content provider class itself, in this case *com.ebookfrenzy.database.database.provider.MyContentProvider* as declared when the new Content Provider class was created in the previous section.

The content URI will vary depending on application requirements, but for the purposes of this example it will comprise the authority with the name of the database table appended at the end. Within the *MyContentProvider. java* file, make the following modifications:

```
package com.ebookfrenzy.database.provider;

import android.content.ContentProvider;
import android.content.ContentValues;
import android.database.Cursor;
import android.net.Uri;
import android.content.UriMatcher;

public class MyContentProvider extends ContentProvider {

    private static final String AUTHORITY =
        "com.ebookfrenzy.database.provider.MyContentProvider";
    private static final String PRODUCTS_TABLE = "products";
    public static final Uri CONTENT_URI =
```

```
        Uri.parse("content://" + AUTHORITY + "/" +
                PRODUCTS_TABLE);


    public MyContentProvider() {
    }
    .
    .
    .
}
```

The above statements begin by creating a new String object named *AUTHORITY* and assigning the authority string to it. Similarly, a second String object named *PRODUCTS_TABLE* is created and initialized with the name of our database table (products).

Finally, these two string elements are combined, prefixed with *content://* and converted to a Uri object using the *parse()* method of the Uri class. The result is assigned to a variable named *CONTENT_URI*.

59.5 Implementing URI Matching in the Content Provider

When the methods of the content provider are called, they will be passed as an argument a URI indicating the data on which the operation is to be performed. This URI may take the form of a reference to a specific row in a specific table. It is also possible that the URI will be more general, for example specifying only the database table. It is the responsibility of each method to identify the *Uri type* and to act accordingly. This task can be eased considerably by making use of a UriMatcher instance. Once a UriMatcher instance has been created, it can be configured to return a specific integer value corresponding to the type of URI it detects when asked to do so. For the purposes of this tutorial, we will be configuring our UriMatcher instance to return a value of 1 when the URI references the entire products table, and a value of 2 when the URI references the ID of a specific row in the products table. Before working on creating the URIMatcher instance, we will first create two integer variables to represent the two URI types:

```
package com.ebookfrenzy.database.provider;


import android.content.ContentProvider;
import android.content.ContentValues;
import android.database.Cursor;
import android.net.Uri;
import android.content.UriMatcher;


public class MyContentProvider extends ContentProvider {

    private static final String AUTHORITY =
      "com.ebookfrenzy.database.provider.MyContentProvider";
    private static final String PRODUCTS_TABLE = "products";
    public static final Uri CONTENT_URI =
            Uri.parse("content://" + AUTHORITY + "/" +
                    PRODUCTS_TABLE);

    public static final int PRODUCTS = 1;
    public static final int PRODUCTS_ID = 2;
    .
    .
```

```
}
```

With the Uri type variables declared, it is now time to add code to create a UriMatcher instance and configure it to return the appropriate variables:

```
public class MyContentProvider extends ContentProvider {

    private static final String AUTHORITY =
      "com.ebookfrenzy.database.provider.MyContentProvider";
    private static final String PRODUCTS_TABLE = "products";
    public static final Uri CONTENT_URI =
            Uri.parse("content://" + AUTHORITY + "/" +
                    PRODUCTS_TABLE);

    public static final int PRODUCTS = 1;
    public static final int PRODUCTS_ID = 2;

    private static final UriMatcher sURIMatcher =
                            new UriMatcher(UriMatcher.NO_MATCH);

    static {
            sURIMatcher.addURI(AUTHORITY, PRODUCTS_TABLE, PRODUCTS);
            sURIMatcher.addURI(AUTHORITY, PRODUCTS_TABLE + "/#",
                                            PRODUCTS_ID);
    }
    .
    .
    .
}
```

The UriMatcher instance (named sURIMatcher) is now primed to return the value of PRODUCTS when just the products table is referenced in a URI, and PRODUCTS_ID when the URI includes the ID of a specific row in the table.

59.6 Implementing the Content Provider onCreate() Method

When the content provider class is created and initialized, a call will be made to the *onCreate()* method of the class. It is within this method that any initialization tasks for the class need to be performed. For the purposes of this example, all that needs to be performed is for an instance of the MyDBHandler class implemented in *"An Android SQLite Database Tutorial"* to be created. Once this instance has been created, it will need to be accessible from the other methods in the class, so a declaration for the database handler also needs to be declared, resulting in the following code changes to the *MyContentProvider.java* file:

```
package com.ebookfrenzy.database.provider;

import com.ebookfrenzy.database.MyDBHandler;

import android.content.ContentProvider;
import android.content.ContentValues;
import android.database.Cursor;
import android.net.Uri;
import android.content.UriMatcher;
```

```java
import android.database.sqlite.SQLiteDatabase;
import android.database.sqlite.SQLiteQueryBuilder;
import android.text.TextUtils;


public class MyContentProvider extends ContentProvider {


    private MyDBHandler myDB;
.

.

.

    @Override
    public boolean onCreate() {
        myDB = new MyDBHandler(getContext(), null, null, 1);
        return false;
    }

}
```

59.7 Implementing the Content Provider insert() Method

When a client application or activity requests that data be inserted into the underlying database, the *insert()* method of the content provider class will be called. At this point, however, all that exists in the *MyContentProvider. java* file of the project is a stub method, which reads as follows:

```java
@Override
public Uri insert(Uri uri, ContentValues values) {
    // TODO: Implement this to handle requests to insert a new row.
    throw new UnsupportedOperationException("Not yet implemented");
}
```

Passed as arguments to the method are a URI specifying the destination of the insertion and a ContentValues object containing the data to be inserted.

This method now needs to be modified to perform the following tasks:

- Use the sUriMatcher object to identify the URI type.

- Throw an exception if the URI is not valid.

- Obtain a reference to a writable instance of the underlying SQLite database.

- Perform a SQL insert operation to insert the data into the database table.

- Notify the corresponding content resolver that the database has been modified.

- Return the URI of the newly added table row.

Bringing these requirements together results in a modified *insert()* method, which reads as follows:

```java
@Override
public Uri insert(Uri uri, ContentValues values) {

    int uriType = sURIMatcher.match(uri);
```

```
        SQLiteDatabase sqlDB = myDB.getWritableDatabase();


        long id = 0;
        switch (uriType) {
            case PRODUCTS:
                id = sqlDB.insert(MyDBHandler.TABLE_PRODUCTS,
                        null, values);
                break;
            default:
                throw new IllegalArgumentException("Unknown URI: "
                        + uri);
        }
        getContext().getContentResolver().notifyChange(uri, null);
        return Uri.parse(PRODUCTS_TABLE + "/" + id);
}
```

59.8 Implementing the Content Provider query() Method

When a content provider is called upon to return data, the *query()* method of the provider class will be called. When called, this method is passed some or all of the following arguments:

- **URI** – The URI specifying the data source on which the query is to be performed. This can take the form of a general query with multiple results, or a specific query targeting the ID of a single table row.

- **Projection** – A row within a database table can comprise multiple columns of data. In the case of this application, for example, these correspond to the ID, product name and product quantity. The projection argument is simply a String array containing the name for each of the columns that is to be returned in the result data set.

- **Selection** – The "where" element of the selection to be performed as part of the query. This argument controls which rows are selected from the specified database. For example, if the query was required to select only products named "Cat Food" then the selection string passed to the query() method would read *productname = "Cat Food"*.

- **Selection Args** – Any additional arguments that need to be passed to the SQL query operation to perform the selection.

- **Sort Order** – The sort order for the selected rows.

When called, the *query()* method is required to perform the following operations:

- Use the sUriMatcher to identify the Uri type.

- Throw an exception if the URI is not valid.

- Construct a SQL query based on the criteria passed to the method. For convenience, the SQLiteQueryBuilder class can be used in construction of the query.

- Execute the query operation on the database.

- Notify the content resolver of the operation.

- Return a Cursor object containing the results of the query.

With these requirements in mind, the code for the *query()* method in the *MyContentProvider.java* file should now read as outlined in the following listing:

```
@Override
public Cursor query(Uri uri, String[] projection, String selection,
        String[] selectionArgs, String sortOrder) {

    SQLiteQueryBuilder queryBuilder = new SQLiteQueryBuilder();
    queryBuilder.setTables(MyDBHandler.TABLE_PRODUCTS);

    int uriType = sURIMatcher.match(uri);

    switch (uriType) {
        case PRODUCTS_ID:
            queryBuilder.appendWhere(MyDBHandler.COLUMN_ID + "="
                    + uri.getLastPathSegment());
            break;
        case PRODUCTS:
            break;
        default:
            throw new IllegalArgumentException("Unknown URI");
    }

    Cursor cursor = queryBuilder.query(myDB.getReadableDatabase(),
                projection, selection, selectionArgs, null, null,
                sortOrder);
    cursor.setNotificationUri(getContext().getContentResolver(),
                uri);
    return cursor;
}
```

59.9 Implementing the Content Provider update() Method

The *update()* method of the content provider is called when changes are being requested to existing database table rows. The method is passed a URI with the new values in the form of a ContentValues object and the usual selection argument strings.

When called, the *update()* method would typically perform the following steps:

- Use the sUriMatcher to identify the URI type.

- Throw an exception if the URI is not valid.

- Obtain a reference to a writable instance of the underlying SQLite database.

- Perform the appropriate update operation on the database, depending on the selection criteria and the URI type.

- Notify the content resolver of the database change.

- Return a count of the number of rows that were changed as a result of the update operation.

A general-purpose *update()* method, and the one we will use for this project, would read as follows:

```
@Override
public int update(Uri uri, ContentValues values, String selection,
        String[] selectionArgs) {

    int uriType = sURIMatcher.match(uri);
    SQLiteDatabase sqlDB = myDB.getWritableDatabase();
    int rowsUpdated = 0;

    switch (uriType) {
        case PRODUCTS:
            rowsUpdated =
                    sqlDB.update(MyDBHandler.TABLE_PRODUCTS,
                            values,
                            selection,
                            selectionArgs);
            break;
        case PRODUCTS_ID:
            String id = uri.getLastPathSegment();
            if (TextUtils.isEmpty(selection)) {
                rowsUpdated =
                        sqlDB.update(MyDBHandler.TABLE_PRODUCTS,
                                values,
                                MyDBHandler.COLUMN_ID + "=" + id,
                                null);
            } else {
                rowsUpdated =
                        sqlDB.update(MyDBHandler.TABLE_PRODUCTS,
                                values,
                                MyDBHandler.COLUMN_ID + "=" + id
                                        + " and "
                                        + selection,
                                selectionArgs);
            }
            break;
        default:
            throw new IllegalArgumentException("Unknown URI: "
                    + uri);
    }
    getContext().getContentResolver().notifyChange(uri,
            null);
    return rowsUpdated;

}
```

59.10 Implementing the Content Provider delete() Method

In common with a number of other content provider methods, the *delete()* method is passed a URI, a selection string and an optional set of selection arguments. A typical *delete()* method will also perform the following, and by now largely familiar, tasks when called:

- Use the sUriMatcher to identify the URI type.

- Throw an exception if the URI is not valid.

- Obtain a reference to a writable instance of the underlying SQLite database.

- Perform the appropriate delete operation on the database depending on the selection criteria and the Uri type.

- Notify the content resolver of the database change.

- Return the number of rows deleted as a result of the operation.

A typical *delete()* method is in many ways similar to the *update()* method and may be implemented as follows:

```
@Override
public int delete(Uri uri, String selection, String[] selectionArgs) {
    int uriType = sURIMatcher.match(uri);
    SQLiteDatabase sqlDB = myDB.getWritableDatabase();
    int rowsDeleted = 0;

    switch (uriType) {
        case PRODUCTS:
            rowsDeleted = sqlDB.delete(MyDBHandler.TABLE_PRODUCTS,
                    selection,
                    selectionArgs);
            break;

        case PRODUCTS_ID:
            String id = uri.getLastPathSegment();
            if (TextUtils.isEmpty(selection)) {
                rowsDeleted = sqlDB.delete(MyDBHandler.TABLE_PRODUCTS,
                        MyDBHandler.COLUMN_ID + "=" + id,
                        null);
            } else {
                rowsDeleted = sqlDB.delete(MyDBHandler.TABLE_PRODUCTS,
                        MyDBHandler.COLUMN_ID + "=" + id
                                + " and " + selection,
                        selectionArgs);
            }
            break;
        default:
            throw new IllegalArgumentException("Unknown URI: " +
                    uri);
    }
```

```
getContext().getContentResolver().notifyChange(uri, null);
return rowsDeleted;
}
```

With these methods implemented, the content provider class, in terms of the requirements for this example at least, is complete. The next step is to make sure that the content provider is declared in the project manifest file so that it is visible to any content resolvers seeking access to it.

59.11 Declaring the Content Provider in the Manifest File

Unless a content provider is declared in the manifest file of the application to which it belongs, it will not be possible for a content resolver to locate and access it. As outlined, content providers are declared using the <provider> tag and the manifest entry must correctly reference the content provider authority and content URI.

For the purposes of this project, therefore, locate the *AndroidManifest.xml* file for the DatabaseProvider project within the Project tool window and double-click on it to load it into the editing panel. Within the editing panel, make sure that the content provider declaration has already been added by Android Studio when the MyContentProvider class was added to the project:

```xml
<?xml version="1.0" encoding="utf-8"?>
<manifest xmlns:android="http://schemas.android.com/apk/res/android"
    package="com.ebookfrenzy.database" >

    <application
        android:allowBackup="true"
        android:icon="@mipmap/ic_launcher"
        android:label="@string/app_name"
        android:theme="@style/AppTheme" >
        <activity
            android:name=".DatabaseActivity"
            android:label="@string/app_name" >
            <intent-filter>
                <action android:name="android.intent.action.MAIN" />

                <category android:name="android.intent.category.LAUNCHER" />
            </intent-filter>
        </activity>

        <provider android:name=".provider.MyContentProvider"
            android:authorities=
                "com.ebookfrenzy.database.provider.MyContentProvider"
            android:enabled="true"
            android:exported="true" >
        </provider>
    </application>

</manifest>
```

All that remains before testing the application is to modify the database handler class to use the content provider instead of directly accessing the database.

59.12 Modifying the Database Handler

When this application was originally created, it was designed to use a database handler to access the underlying database directly. Now that a content provider has been implemented, the database handler needs to be modified so that all database operations are performed using the content provider via a content resolver.

The first step is to modify the *MyDBHandler.java* class so that it obtains a reference to a ContentResolver instance. This can be achieved in the constructor method of the class:

```
package com.ebookfrenzy.database;

import com.ebookfrenzy.database.provider.MyContentProvider;

import android.database.sqlite.SQLiteDatabase;
import android.database.sqlite.SQLiteOpenHelper;
import android.content.Context;
import android.content.ContentValues;
import android.database.Cursor;
import android.content.ContentResolver;

public class MyDBHandler extends SQLiteOpenHelper {

    private ContentResolver myCR;

    private static final int DATABASE_VERSION = 1;
    private static final String DATABASE_NAME = "productDB.db";
    public static final String TABLE_PRODUCTS = "products";

    public static final String COLUMN_ID = "_id";
    public static final String COLUMN_PRODUCTNAME = "productname";
    public static final String COLUMN_QUANTITY = "quantity";

    public MyDBHandler(Context context, String name,
                SQLiteDatabase.CursorFactory factory, int version) {
        super(context, DATABASE_NAME, factory, DATABASE_VERSION);
        myCR = context.getContentResolver();
    }
.
.
.
}
```

Next, the *addProduct()*, *findProduct()* and *removeProduct()* methods need to be rewritten to use the content resolver and content provider for data management purposes:

```
public void addProduct(Product product) {

        ContentValues values = new ContentValues();
        values.put(COLUMN_PRODUCTNAME, product.getProductName());
```

```
        values.put(COLUMN_QUANTITY, product.getQuantity());

        myCR.insert(MyContentProvider.CONTENT_URI, values);
}


public Product findProduct(String productname) {
        String[] projection = {COLUMN_ID,
            COLUMN_PRODUCTNAME, COLUMN_QUANTITY };

        String selection = "productname = \"" + productname + "\"";

        Cursor cursor = myCR.query(MyContentProvider.CONTENT_URI,
            projection, selection, null,
                null);

    Product product = new Product();

    if (cursor.moveToFirst()) {
            cursor.moveToFirst();
            product.setID(Integer.parseInt(cursor.getString(0)));
            product.setProductName(cursor.getString(1));
            product.setQuantity(
                    Integer.parseInt(cursor.getString(2)));
            cursor.close();
    } else {
            product = null;
    }
    return product;
}


public boolean deleteProduct(String productname) {

    boolean result = false;

        String selection = "productname = \"" + productname + "\"";

        int rowsDeleted = myCR.delete(MyContentProvider.CONTENT_URI,
                selection, null);

        if (rowsDeleted > 0)
                result = true;

        return result;
}
```

With the database handler class updated to use a content resolver and content provider, the application is now ready to be tested. Compile and run the application and perform some operations to add, find and remove product entries. In terms of operation and functionality, the application should behave exactly as it did when directly accessing the database, except that it is now using the content provider.

With the content provider now implemented and declared in the manifest file, any other applications can potentially access that data (since no permissions were declared, the default full access is in effect). The only information that the other applications need to know to gain access is the content URI and the names of the columns in the products table.

59.13 Summary

The goal of this chapter was to provide a more detailed overview of the exact steps involved in implementing an Android content provider with a particular emphasis on the structure and implementation of the query, insert, delete and update methods of the content provider class. Practical use of the content resolver class to access data in the content provider was also covered, and the Database project was modified to make use of both a content provider and content resolver.

60. Accessing Cloud Storage using the Android Storage Access Framework

Recent years have seen the wide adoption of remote storage services (otherwise known as "cloud storage") to store user files and data. Driving this growth are two key factors. One is that most mobile devices now provide continuous, high speed internet connectivity, thereby making the transfer of data fast and affordable. The second factor is that, relative to traditional computer systems (such as desktops and laptops) these mobile devices are constrained in terms of internal storage resources. A high specification Android tablet today, for example, typically comes with 128Gb of storage capacity. When compared with a mid-range laptop system with a 750Gb disk drive, the need for the seamless remote storage of files is a key requirement for many mobile applications today.

In recognition of this fact, Google introduced the Storage Access Framework as part of the Android 4.4 SDK. This chapter will provide a high level overview of the storage access framework in preparation for the more detail oriented tutorial contained in the next chapter, entitled *"An Android Storage Access Framework Example"*.

60.1 The Storage Access Framework

From the perspective of the user, the Storage Access Framework provides an intuitive user interface that allows the user to browse, select, delete and create files hosted by storage services (also referred to as *document providers*) from within Android applications. Using this browsing interface (also referred to as the *picker*), users can, for example, browse through the files (such as documents, audio, images and videos) hosted by their chosen document providers. Figure 60-1, for example, shows the picker user interface displaying a collection of files hosted by a document provider service:

Figure 60-1

Document providers can range from cloud-based services to local document providers running on the same device as the client application. At the time of writing, the most prominent document providers compatible with the Storage Access Framework are Box and, unsurprisingly, Google Drive. It is highly likely that other cloud storage providers and application developers will soon also provide services that conform to the Android Storage Access Framework.

In addition to cloud based document providers the picker also provides access to internal storage on the device, providing a range of file storage options to the application user.

Through a set of Intents included with Android 4.4, Android application developers can incorporate these storage capabilities into applications with just a few lines of code. A particularly compelling aspect of the Storage Access Framework from the point of view of the developer is that the underlying document provider selected by the user is completely transparent to the application. Once the storage functionality has been implemented using the framework within an application, it will work with all document providers without any code modifications.

60.2 Working with the Storage Access Framework

Android 4.4 introduced a new set of Intents designed to integrate the features of the Storage Access Framework into Android applications. These intents display the Storage Access Framework picker user interface to the user and return the results of the interaction to the application via a call to the *onActivityResult()* method of the activity that launched the intent. When the *onActivityResult()* method is called, it is passed the Uri of the selected file together with a value indicating the success or otherwise of the operation.

The Storage Access Framework intents can be summarized as follows:

- **ACTION_OPEN_DOCUMENT** – Provides the user with access to the picker user interface so that files may be selected from the document providers configured on the device. Selected files are passed back to the application in the form of Uri objects.

- **ACTION_CREATE_DOCUMENT** – Allows the user to select a document provider, a location on that provider's storage and a file name for a new file. Once selected, the file is created by the Storage Access Framework and the Uri of that file returned to the application for further processing.

60.3 Filtering Picker File Listings

The files listed within the picker user interface when an intent is started may be filtered using a variety of options. Consider, for example, the following code to start an ACTION_OPEN_DOCUMENT intent:

```
private static final int OPEN_REQUEST_CODE = 41;


Intent intent = new Intent(Intent.ACTION_OPEN_DOCUMENT);
startActivityForResult(intent, OPEN_REQUEST_CODE);
```

When executed, the above code will cause the picker user interface to be displayed, allowing the user to browse and select any files hosted by available document providers. Once a file has been selected by the user, a reference to that file will be provided to the application in the form of a Uri object. The application can then open the file using the *openFileDescriptor(Uri, String)* method. There is some risk, however, that not all files listed by a document provider can be opened in this way. The exclusion of such files within the picker can be achieved by modifying the intent using the *CATEGORY_OPENABLE* option. For example:

```
private static final int OPEN_REQUEST_CODE = 41;


Intent intent = new Intent(Intent.ACTION_OPEN_DOCUMENT);
intent.addCategory(Intent.CATEGORY_OPENABLE);
startActivityForResult(intent, OPEN_REQUEST_CODE);
```

When the picker is now displayed, files which cannot be opened using the *openFileDescriptor()* method will be listed but not selectable by the user.

Another useful approach to filtering allows the files available for selection to be restricted by file type. This involves specifying the types of the files the application is able to handle. An image editing application might, for example, only want to provide the user with the option of selecting image files from the document providers. This is achieved by configuring the intent object with the MIME types of the files that are to be selectable by the user. The following code, for example, specifies that only image files are suitable for selection in the picker:

```
Intent intent = new Intent(Intent.ACTION_OPEN_DOCUMENT);


intent.addCategory(Intent.CATEGORY_OPENABLE);
intent.setType("image/*");
startActivityForResult(intent, OPEN_REQUEST_CODE);
```

This could be further refined to limit selection to JPEG images:

```
intent.setType("image/jpeg");
```

Alternatively, an audio player app might only be able to handle audio files:

```
intent.setType("audio/*");
```

The audio app might be limited even further in only supporting the playback of MP4 based audio files:

```
intent.setType("audio/mp4");
```

A wide range of MIME type settings are available for use when working with the Storage Access Framework, the more common of which can be found listed online at:

http://en.wikipedia.org/wiki/Internet_media_type#List_of_common_media_types

60.4 Handling Intent Results

When an intent returns control to the application, it does so by calling the *onActivityResult()* method of the activity which started the intent. This method is passed the request code that was handed to the intent at launch time, a result code indicating whether or not the intent was successful and a result data object containing the Uri of the selected file. The following code, for example, might be used as the basis for handling the results from the ACTION_OPEN_DOCUMENT intent outlined in the previous section:

```
public void onActivityResult(int requestCode, int resultCode,
        Intent resultData) {


    Uri currentUri = null;


    if (resultCode == Activity.RESULT_OK)
    {
            if (requestCode == OPEN_REQUEST_CODE)
            {
                    if (resultData != null) {
                            currentUri = resultData.getData();
                                readFileContent(currentUri);
                    }
            }
    }
}
```

The above method verifies that the intent was successful, checks that the request code matches that for a file open request and then extracts the Uri from the intent data. The Uri can then be used to read the content of the file.

60.5 Reading the Content of a File

The exact steps required to read the content of a file hosted by a document provider will depend to a large extent on the type of the file. The steps to read lines from a text file, for example, differ from those for image or audio files.

An image file can be assigned to a Bitmap object by extracting the file descriptor from the Uri object and then decoding the image into a BitmapFactory instance. For example:

```
ParcelFileDescriptor pFileDescriptor =
            getContentResolver().openFileDescriptor(uri, "r");

FileDescriptor fileDescriptor =
            pFileDescriptor.getFileDescriptor();

Bitmap image = BitmapFactory.decodeFileDescriptor(fileDescriptor);

pFileDescriptor.close();

myImageView.setImageBitmap(image);
```

Note that the file descriptor is opened in "r" mode. This indicates that the file is to be opened for reading. Other options are "w" for write access and "rwt" for read and write access, where existing content in the file is truncated by the new content.

Reading the content of a text file requires slightly more work and the use of an InputStream object. The following code, for example, reads the lines from a text file:

```
InputStream inputStream = getContentResolver().openInputStream(uri);

BufferedReader reader = new BufferedReader(new InputStreamReader(
                        inputStream));
String readline;

while ((readline = reader.readLine()) != null) {
        // Do something with each line in the file
}
inputStream.close();
```

60.6 Writing Content to a File

Writing to an open file hosted by a document provider is similar to reading with the exception that an output stream is used instead of an input stream. The following code, for example, writes text to the output stream of the storage based file referenced by the specified Uri:

```
try{
        ParcelFileDescriptor pFileDescriptor = this.getContentResolver().
                openFileDescriptor(uri, "w");

        FileOutputStream fileOutputStream =
```

```
new FileOutputStream(pFileDescriptor.getFileDescriptor());

        String textContent = "Some sample text";
        fileOutputStream.write(textContent.getBytes());
        fileOutputStream.close();
        pFileDescriptor.close();
} catch (FileNotFoundException e) {
        e.printStackTrace();
} catch (IOException e) {
        e.printStackTrace();
}
```

First, the file descriptor is extracted from the Uri, this time requesting write permission to the target file. The file descriptor is subsequently used to obtain a reference to the file's output stream. The content (in this example, some text) is then written to the output stream before the file descriptor and output stream are closed.

60.7 Deleting a File

Whether a file can be deleted from storage depends on whether or not the file's document provider supports deletion of the file. Assuming deletion is permitted, it may be performed on a designated Uri as follows:

```
if (DocumentsContract.deleteDocument(getContentResolver(), uri))
        // Deletion was successful
else
        // Deletion failed
```

60.8 Gaining Persistent Access to a File

When an application gains access to a file via the Storage Access Framework, the access will remain valid until the Android device on which the application is running is restarted. Persistent access to a specific file can be obtained by "taking" the necessary permissions for the Uri. The following code, for example, persists read and write permissions for the file referenced by the *fileUri* Uri instance:

```
final int takeFlags = intent.getFlags()
                & (Intent.FLAG_GRANT_READ_URI_PERMISSION
                | Intent.FLAG_GRANT_WRITE_URI_PERMISSION);

getContentResolver().takePersistableUriPermission(fileUri, takeFlags);
```

Once the permissions for the file have been taken by the application, and assuming the Uri has been saved by the application, the user should be able to continue accessing the file after a device restart without the user having to reselect the file from the picker interface.

If, at any time, the persistent permissions are no longer required, they can be released via a call to the *releasePersistableUriPermission()* method of the content resolver:

```
final int releaseFlags = intent.getFlags()
                & (Intent.FLAG_GRANT_READ_URI_PERMISSION
                | Intent.FLAG_GRANT_WRITE_URI_PERMISSION);

getContentResolver().releasePersistableUriPermission(fileUri,
                        releaseFlags);
```

60.9 Summary

It is interesting to consider how perceptions of storage have changed in recent years. Once synonymous with high capacity internal hard disk drives, the term "storage" is now just as likely to refer to storage space hosted remotely in the cloud and accessed over an internet connection. This is increasingly the case with the wide adoption of resource constrained, "always-connected" mobile devices with minimal internal storage capacity.

The Android Storage Access Framework provides a simple mechanism for both users and application developers to seamlessly gain access to files stored in the cloud. Through the use of a set of intents introduced into Android 4.4 and a built-in user interface for selecting document providers and files, comprehensive cloud based storage can now be integrated into Android applications with a minimal amount of coding.

61. An Android Storage Access Framework Example

As previously discussed, the Storage Access Framework considerably eases the process of integrating cloud based storage access into Android applications. Consisting of a picker user interface and a set of new intents, access to files stored on document providers such as Google Drive and Box can now be built into Android applications with relative ease. With the basics of the Android Storage Access Framework covered in the preceding chapter, this chapter will work through the creation of an example application which uses the Storage Access Framework to store and manage files.

61.1 About the Storage Access Framework Example

The Android application created in this chapter will take the form of a rudimentary text editor designed to create and store text files remotely onto a cloud based storage service. In practice, the example will work with any cloud based document storage provider that is compatible with the Storage Access Framework, though for the purpose of this example the use of Google Drive is assumed.

In functional terms, the application will present the user with a multi-line text view into which text may be entered and edited, together with a set of buttons allowing storage based text files to be created, opened and saved.

61.2 Creating the Storage Access Framework Example

Create a new project in Android Studio, entering *StorageDemo* into the Application name field and *ebookfrenzy. com* as the Company Domain setting before clicking on the *Next* button.

On the form factors screen, enable the *Phone and Tablet* option and set the minimum SDK setting to API 19: Android 4.4 (KitKat). Continue to proceed through the screens, requesting the creation of an Empty Activity named *StorageDemoActivity* with a corresponding layout named *activity_storage_demo*.

61.3 Designing the User Interface

The user interface will need to be comprised of three Button views and a single EditText view. Within the Project tool window, navigate to the *activity_storage_demo.xml* layout file located in *app -> res -> layout* and double-click on it to load it into the Layout Editor tool. With the tool in Design mode, select and delete the *Hello World!* TextView object.

Drag and position a Button widget in the top left-hand corner of the layout so that both the left and top dotted margin guidelines appear before dropping the widget in place. Position a second Button such that the center and top margin guidelines appear. The third Button widget should then be placed so that the top and right-hand margin guidelines appear.

Change the text attributes on the three buttons to "New", "Open" and "Save" respectively. Next, position a Plain Text widget so that it is centered horizontally and positioned beneath the center Button so that the user interface layout matches that shown in Figure 61-1. Use the Infer Constraints button in the Layout Editor toolbar to add any missing constraints.

Select the Plain Text widget in the layout, delete the current text property setting so that the field is initially blank and set the ID to *fileText*, remembering to extract all the string attributes to resource values:

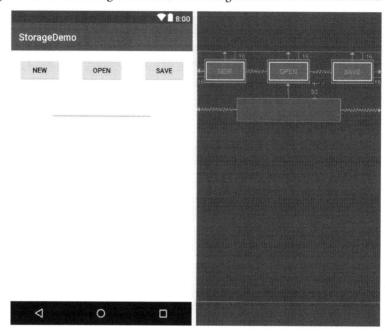

Figure 61-1

Using the Attributes tool window, configure the onClick property on the Button widgets to call methods named *newFile, openFile* and *saveFile* respectively.

61.4 Declaring Request Codes

Working with files in the Storage Access Framework involves triggering a variety of intents depending on the specific action to be performed. Invariably this will result in the framework displaying the storage picker user interface so that the user can specify the storage location (such as a directory on Google Drive and the name of a file). When the work of the intent is complete, the application will be notified by a call to a method named *onActivityResult()*.

Since all intents from a single activity will result in a call to the same *onActivityResult()* method, a mechanism is required to identify which intent triggered the call. This can be achieved by passing a request code through to the intent when it is launched. This code is then passed on to the *onActivityResult()* method by the intents, enabling the method to identify which action has been requested by the user. Before implementing the onClick handlers to create, save and open files, the first step is to declare some request codes for these three actions.

Locate and load the *StorageDemoActivity.java* file into the editor and declare constant values for the three actions to be performed by the application. Also, add some code to obtain a reference to the multi-line EditText object which will be referenced in later methods:

```
package com.ebookfrenzy.storagedemo;

import android.support.v7.app.AppCompatActivity;
import android.os.Bundle;
import android.widget.EditText;

public class StorageDemoActivity extends AppCompatActivity {
```

```
private static EditText textView;


private static final int CREATE_REQUEST_CODE = 40;
private static final int OPEN_REQUEST_CODE = 41;
private static final int SAVE_REQUEST_CODE = 42;


@Override
protected void onCreate(Bundle savedInstanceState) {
    super.onCreate(savedInstanceState);
    setContentView(R.layout.activity_storage_demo);

    textView = (EditText) findViewById(R.id.fileText);
}
}
```

61.5 Creating a New Storage File

When the New button is selected, the application will need to trigger an *ACTION_CREATE_DOCUMENT* intent configured to create a file with a plain-text MIME type. When the user interface was designed, the New button was configured to call a method named *newFile()*. It is within this method that the appropriate intent needs to be launched.

Remaining in the *StorageDemoActivity.java* file, implement this method as follows:

```
package com.ebookfrenzy.storagedemo;

import android.app.Activity;
import android.support.v7.app.AppCompatActivity;
import android.os.Bundle;
import android.widget.EditText;
import android.content.Intent;
import android.view.View;

public class StorageDemoActivity extends AppCompatActivity {

public class StorageDemoActivity extends Activity {

    private static EditText textView;

    private static final int CREATE_REQUEST_CODE = 40;
    private static final int OPEN_REQUEST_CODE = 41;
    private static final int SAVE_REQUEST_CODE = 42;

.
.
.

    public void newFile(View view)
    {
```

```
        Intent intent = new Intent(Intent.ACTION_CREATE_DOCUMENT);

        intent.addCategory(Intent.CATEGORY_OPENABLE);
        intent.setType("text/plain");
        intent.putExtra(Intent.EXTRA_TITLE, "newfile.txt");

        startActivityForResult(intent, CREATE_REQUEST_CODE);
    }
    .
    .
}
```

This code creates a new ACTION_CREATE_INTENT Intent object. This intent is then configured so that only files that can be opened with a file descriptor are returned (via the Intent.CATEGORY_OPENABLE category setting).

Next the code specifies that the file to be opened is to have a plain text MIME type and a placeholder filename is provided (which can be changed by the user in the picker interface). Finally, the intent is started, passing through the previously declared *CREATE_REQUEST_CODE*.

When this method is executed and the intent has completed the assigned task, a call will be made to the application's *onActivityResult()* method and passed, amongst other arguments, the Uri of the newly created document and the request code that was used when the intent was started. Now is an ideal opportunity to begin to implement this method.

61.6 The onActivityResult() Method

The *onActivityResult()* method will be shared by all of the intents that will be called during the lifecycle of the application. In each case, the method will be passed a request code, a result code and a set of result data which contains the Uri of the storage file. The method will need to be implemented such that it checks for the success of the intent action, identifies the type of action performed and extracts the file Uri from the results data. At this point in the tutorial, the method only needs to handle the creation of a new file on the selected document provider, so modify the *StorageDemoActivity.java* file to add this method as follows:

```
public void onActivityResult(int requestCode, int resultCode,
        Intent resultData) {

    if (resultCode == Activity.RESULT_OK)
    {
        if (requestCode == CREATE_REQUEST_CODE)
        {
            if (resultData != null) {
                textView.setText("");
            }
        }

    }
}
```

The code in this method is largely straightforward. The result of the activity is checked and, if successful, the request code is compared to the CREATE_REQUEST_CODE value to verify that the user is creating a new file.

That being the case, the edit text view is cleared of any previous text to signify the creation of a new file.

Compile and run the application and select the New button. The Storage Access Framework should subsequently display the "Save to" storage picker user interface as illustrated in Figure 61-2.

From this menu, select the *Drive* option followed by *My Drive* and navigate to a suitable location on your Google Drive storage into which to save the file. In the text field at the bottom of the picker interface, change the name from "newfile.txt" to a suitable name (but keeping the *.txt* extension) before selecting the *Save* option.

Figure 61-2

Once the new file has been created, the app should return to the main activity and a notification will appear within the notifications panel which reads "1 file uploaded".

Figure 61-3

At this point, it should be possible to log into your Google Drive account in a browser window and find the newly created file in the requested location. In the event that the file is missing, make sure that the Android device on which the application is running has an active internet connection. Access to Google Drive on the device may also be verified by running the Google *Drive* app, which is installed by default on many Android devices, and available for download from the Google Play store.

61.7 Saving to a Storage File

Now that the application is able to create new storage based files, the next step is to add the ability to save any text entered by the user to a file. The user interface is configured to call the *saveFile()* method when the Save button is selected by the user. This method will be responsible for starting a new intent of type *ACTION_OPEN_DOCUMENT* which will result in the picker user interface appearing so that the user can choose the file to which the text is to be stored. Since we are only working with plain text files, the intent needs to be configured to restrict the user's selection options to existing files that match the text/plain MIME type. Having identified the actions to be performed by the *saveFile()* method, this can now be added to the *StorageDemoActivity.java* class file as follows:

```java
public void saveFile(View view)
{
        Intent intent = new Intent(Intent.ACTION_OPEN_DOCUMENT);
        intent.addCategory(Intent.CATEGORY_OPENABLE);
        intent.setType("text/plain");

        startActivityForResult(intent, SAVE_REQUEST_CODE);
}
```

Since the SAVE_REQUEST_CODE was passed through to the intent, the *onActivityResult()* method must now be extended to handle save actions:

```java
package com.ebookfrenzy.storagedemo;

import android.app.Activity;
import android.support.v7.app.AppCompatActivity;
import android.os.Bundle;
import android.widget.EditText;
import android.content.Intent;
import android.view.View;
import android.net.Uri;

public class StorageDemoActivity extends AppCompatActivity {
.
.
        public void onActivityResult(int requestCode, int resultCode,
                Intent resultData) {

                Uri currentUri = null;

                if (resultCode == Activity.RESULT_OK)
                {
                        if (requestCode == CREATE_REQUEST_CODE)
                        {
                                if (resultData != null) {
                                        textView.setText("");
                                }
                        } else if (requestCode == SAVE_REQUEST_CODE) {
```

```
                        if (resultData != null) {
                            currentUri =
                                    resultData.getData();
                            writeFileContent(currentUri);
                        }
                    }
                }
            }
        }
```

The method now checks for the save request code, extracts the Uri of the file selected by the user in the storage picker and calls a method named *writeFileContent()*, passing through the Uri of the file to which the text is to be written. Remaining in the *StorageDemoActivity.java* file, implement this method now so that it reads as follows:

```java
package com.ebookfrenzy.storagedemo;

import java.io.FileNotFoundException;
import java.io.FileOutputStream;
import java.io.IOException;

import android.app.Activity;
import android.support.v7.app.AppCompatActivity;
import android.os.Bundle;
import android.widget.EditText;
import android.content.Intent;
import android.view.View;
import android.net.Uri;
import android.os.ParcelFileDescriptor;

public class StorageDemoActivity extends AppCompatActivity {
.
.

    private void writeFileContent(Uri uri)
    {
        try{
            ParcelFileDescriptor pfd =
                    this.getContentResolver().
                        openFileDescriptor(uri, "w");

            FileOutputStream fileOutputStream =
                    new FileOutputStream(
                        pfd.getFileDescriptor());

            String textContent =
                    textView.getText().toString();
```

```
                    fileOutputStream.write(textContent.getBytes());

                    fileOutputStream.close();
                    pfd.close();
        } catch (FileNotFoundException e) {
                    e.printStackTrace();
        } catch (IOException e) {
                    e.printStackTrace();
        }
    }
.
.
}
```

The method begins by obtaining and opening the file descriptor from the Uri of the file selected by the user. Since the code will need to write to the file, the descriptor is opened in write mode ("w"). The file descriptor is then used as the basis for creating an output stream that will enable the application to write to the file.

The text entered by the user is extracted from the edit text object and written to the output stream before both the file descriptor and stream are closed. Code is also added to handle any IO exceptions encountered during the file writing process.

With the new method added, compile and run the application, enter some text into the text view and select the *Save* button. From the picker interface, locate the previously created file from the Google Drive storage to save the text to that file. Return to your Google Drive account in a browser window and select the text file to display the contents. The file should now contain the text entered within the StorageDemo application on the Android device.

61.8 Opening and Reading a Storage File

Having written the code to create and save text files, the final task is to add some functionality to open and read a file from the storage. This will involve writing the *openFile()* onClick event handler method and implementing it so that it starts an ACTION_OPEN_DOCUMENT intent:

```
public void openFile(View view)
{
        Intent intent = new Intent(Intent.ACTION_OPEN_DOCUMENT);
        intent.addCategory(Intent.CATEGORY_OPENABLE);
        intent.setType("text/plain");
        startActivityForResult(intent, OPEN_REQUEST_CODE);
}
```

In this code, the intent is configured to filter selection to files which can be opened by the application. When the activity is started, it is passed the open request code constant which will now need to be handled within the *onActivityResult()* method:

```
public void onActivityResult(int requestCode, int resultCode,
        Intent resultData) {

        Uri currentUri = null;

        if (resultCode == Activity.RESULT_OK)
```

```
        {
                if (requestCode == CREATE_REQUEST_CODE)
                {
                        if (resultData != null) {
                                textView.setText("");
                        }
                } else if (requestCode == SAVE_REQUEST_CODE) {

                        if (resultData != null) {
                                currentUri = resultData.getData();
                                writeFileContent(currentUri);
                        }
                } else if (requestCode == OPEN_REQUEST_CODE) {

                        if (resultData != null) {
                                currentUri = resultData.getData();

                            try {
                                String content =
                                                readFileContent(currentUri);
                                        textView.setText(content);
                            } catch (IOException e) {
                                        // Handle error here
                                }
                        }
                }
        }
}
```

The new code added above to handle the open request obtains the Uri of the file selected by the user from the picker user interface and passes it through to a method named *readFileContent()* which is expected to return the content of the selected file in the form of a String object. The resulting string is then assigned to the text property of the edit text view. Clearly, the next task is to implement the *readFileContent()* method:

```
package com.ebookfrenzy.storagedemo;

import java.io.FileNotFoundException;
import java.io.FileOutputStream;
import java.io.IOException;
import java.io.BufferedReader;
import java.io.InputStream;
import java.io.InputStreamReader;

import android.app.Activity;
import android.support.v7.app.AppCompatActivity;
import android.os.Bundle;
```

An Android Storage Access Framework Example

```java
import android.widget.EditText;
import android.content.Intent;
import android.view.View;
import android.net.Uri;
import android.os.ParcelFileDescriptor;

public class StorageDemoActivity extends AppCompatActivity {
.
.
.
        private String readFileContent(Uri uri) throws IOException {

            InputStream inputStream =
                        getContentResolver().openInputStream(uri);
            BufferedReader reader =
                    new BufferedReader(new InputStreamReader(
                            inputStream));
            StringBuilder stringBuilder = new StringBuilder();
            String currentline;
            while ((currentline = reader.readLine()) != null) {
                    stringBuilder.append(currentline + "\n");
            }
            inputStream.close();
            return stringBuilder.toString();
        }
.
.
.
}
```

This method begins by extracting the file descriptor for the selected text file and opening it for reading. The input stream associated with the Uri is then opened and used as the input source for a BufferedReader instance. Each line within the file is then read and stored in a StringBuilder object. Once all the lines have been read, the input stream and file descriptor are both closed, and the file content is returned as a String object.

61.9 Testing the Storage Access Application

With the coding phase complete the application is now ready to be fully tested. Begin by launching the application on a physical Android device and selecting the "New" button. Within the resulting storage picker interface, select a Google Drive location and name the text file *storagedemo.txt* before selecting the Save option located to the right of the file name field.

When control returns to your application look for the file uploading notification, then enter some text into the text area before selecting the "Save" button. Select the previously created *storagedemo.txt* file from the picker to save the content to the file. On returning to the application, delete the text and select the "Open" button, once again choosing the *storagedemo.txt* file. When control is returned to the application, the text view should have been populated with the content of the text file.

It is important to note that the Storage Access Framework will cache storage files locally in the event that the Android device lacks an active internet connection. Once connectivity is re-established, however, any cached data will be synchronized with the remote storage service. As a final test of the application, therefore, log into your Google Drive account in a browser window, navigate to the *storagedemo.txt* file and click on it to view the content which should, all being well, contain the text saved by the application.

61.10 Summary

This chapter has worked through the creation of an example Android Studio application in the form of a very rudimentary text editor designed to use cloud based storage to create, save and open files using the Android Storage Access Framework.

62. Implementing Video Playback on Android using the VideoView and MediaController Classes

One of the primary uses for smartphones and tablets is to enable the user to access and consume content. One key form of content widely used, especially in the case of tablet devices, is video.

The Android SDK includes two classes that make the implementation of video playback on Android devices extremely easy to implement when developing applications. This chapter will provide an overview of these two classes, VideoView and MediaController, before working through the creation of a simple video playback application.

62.1 Introducing the Android VideoView Class

By far the simplest way to display video within an Android application is to use the VideoView class. This is a visual component which, when added to the layout of an activity, provides a surface onto which a video may be played. Android currently supports the following video formats:

- H.263

- H.264 AVC

- H.265 HEVC

- MPEG-4 SP

- VP8

- VP9

The VideoView class has a wide range of methods that may be called in order to manage the playback of video. Some of the more commonly used methods are as follows:

- **setVideoPath(String path)** – Specifies the path (as a string) of the video media to be played. This can be either the URL of a remote video file or a video file local to the device.

- **setVideoUri(Uri uri)** – Performs the same task as the setVideoPath() method but takes a Uri object as an argument instead of a string.

- **start()** – Starts video playback.

- **stopPlayback()** – Stops the video playback.

- **pause()** – Pauses video playback.

- **isPlaying()** – Returns a Boolean value indicating whether a video is currently playing.

- **setOnPreparedListener(MediaPlayer.OnPreparedListener)** – Allows a callback method to be called when the video is ready to play.

- **setOnErrorListener(MediaPlayer.OnErrorListener)** - Allows a callback method to be called when an error occurs during the video playback.

- **setOnCompletionListener(MediaPlayer.OnCompletionListener)** - Allows a callback method to be called when the end of the video is reached.

- **getDuration()** – Returns the duration of the video. Will typically return -1 unless called from within the OnPreparedListener() callback method.

- **getCurrentPosition()** – Returns an integer value indicating the current position of playback.

- **setMediaController(MediaController)** – Designates a MediaController instance allowing playback controls to be displayed to the user.

62.2 Introducing the Android MediaController Class

If a video is simply played using the VideoView class, the user will not be given any control over the playback, which will run until the end of the video is reached. This issue can be addressed by attaching an instance of the MediaController class to the VideoView instance. The MediaController will then provide a set of controls allowing the user to manage the playback (such as pausing and seeking backwards/forwards in the video time-line).

The position of the controls is designated by anchoring the controller instance to a specific view in the user interface layout. Once attached and anchored, the controls will appear briefly when playback starts and may subsequently be restored at any point by the user tapping on the view to which the instance is anchored.

Some of the key methods of this class are as follows:

- **setAnchorView(View view)** – Designates the view to which the controller is to be anchored. This controls the location of the controls on the screen.

- **show()** – Displays the controls.

- **show(int timeout)** – Controls are displayed for the designated duration (in milliseconds).

- **hide()** – Hides the controller from the user.

- **isShowing()** – Returns a Boolean value indicating whether the controls are currently visible to the user.

62.3 Creating the Video Playback Example

The remainder of this chapter is dedicated to working through an example application intended to use the VideoView and MediaController classes to play a web based MPEG-4 video file.

Create a new project in Android Studio, entering *VideoPlayer* into the Application name field and *ebookfrenzy. com* as the Company Domain setting before clicking on the *Next* button.

On the form factors screen, enable the *Phone and Tablet* option and set the minimum SDK setting to API 14: Android 4.0 (IceCreamSandwich). Continue to proceed through the screens, requesting the creation of an Empty Activity named *VideoPlayerActivity* with a corresponding layout named *activity_video_player*.

62.4 Designing the VideoPlayer Layout

The user interface for the main activity will consist solely of an instance of the VideoView class. Use the Project tool window to locate the *app -> res -> layout -> activity_video_player.xml* file, double-click on it, switch the

Layout Editor tool to Design mode and delete the default TextView widget.

From the Images category of the Palette panel, drag and drop a VideoView instance onto the layout so that it fills the available canvas area as shown in Figure 62-1. Using the Attributes panel, change the layout_width and layout_height attributes to *match_constraint* and *wrap_content* respectively. Also, remove the constraint connecting the bottom of the VideoView to the bottom of the parent ConstraintLayout. Finally, change the ID of the component to *videoView1*.

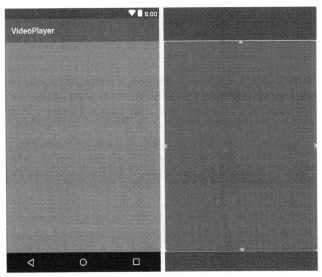

Figure 62-1

On completion of the layout design, the XML resources for the layout should read as follows:

```xml
<?xml version="1.0" encoding="utf-8"?>
<android.support.constraint.ConstraintLayout xmlns:android="http://schemas.
android.com/apk/res/android"
    xmlns:app="http://schemas.android.com/apk/res-auto"
    xmlns:tools="http://schemas.android.com/tools"
    android:layout_width="match_parent"
    android:layout_height="match_parent"
    tools:context="com.ebookfrenzy.videoplayer.VideoPlayerActivity"
    tools:layout_editor_absoluteX="0dp"
    tools:layout_editor_absoluteY="81dp">

    <VideoView
        android:id="@+id/videoView1"
        android:layout_width="0dp"
        android:layout_height="wrap_content"
        app:layout_constraintBottom_toBottomOf="parent"
        app:layout_constraintLeft_toLeftOf="parent"
        app:layout_constraintRight_toRightOf="parent"
        app:layout_constraintTop_toTopOf="parent" />
</android.support.constraint.ConstraintLayout>
```

62.5 Configuring the VideoView

The next step is to configure the VideoView with the path of the video to be played and then start the playback. This will be performed when the main activity has initialized, so load the *VideoPlayerActivity.java* file into the editor and modify the it as outlined in the following listing:

```
package com.ebookfrenzy.videoplayer;

import android.support.v7.app.AppCompatActivity;
import android.os.Bundle;
import android.widget.VideoView;

public class VideoPlayerActivity extends AppCompatActivity {

    private VideoView videoView;

    @Override
    protected void onCreate(Bundle savedInstanceState) {
        super.onCreate(savedInstanceState);
        setContentView(R.layout.activity_video_player);
        configureVideoView();
    }

    private void configureVideoView() {

        videoView =
                findViewById(R.id.videoView1);

        videoView.setVideoPath(
                "http://www.ebookfrenzy.com/android_book/movie.mp4");

        videoView.start();
    }
}
```

All that this code does is obtain a reference to the VideoView instance in the layout, set the video path on it to point to an MPEG-4 file hosted on a web site and then start the video playing.

62.6 Adding Internet Permission

An attempt to run the application at this point would result in the application failing to launch with an error dialog appearing on the Android device that reads "Unable to Play Video. Sorry, this video cannot be played". This is not because of an error in the code or an incorrect video file format. The issue would be that the application is attempting to access a file over the internet, but has failed to request appropriate permissions to do so. To resolve this, edit the *AndroidManifest.xml* file for the project and add a line to request internet access:

```
<?xml version="1.0" encoding="utf-8"?>
<manifest xmlns:android="http://schemas.android.com/apk/res/android"
    package="com.ebookfrenzy.videoplayer" >
```

```
<uses-permission android:name="android.permission.INTERNET" />

    <application
        android:allowBackup="true"
        android:icon="@mipmap/ic_launcher"
        android:label="@string/app_name"
        android:supportsRtl="true"
        android:theme="@style/AppTheme" >
        .
        .
        .

</manifest>
```

Test the application by running it on a physical Android device. After the application launches there may be a short delay while video content is buffered before the playback begins (Figure 62-2).

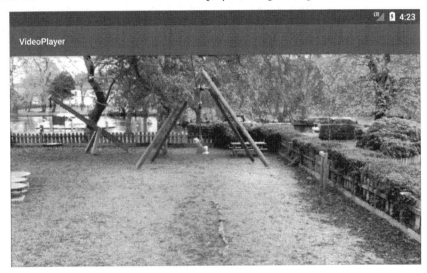

Figure 62-2

This provides an indication of how easy it can be to integrate video playback into an Android application. Everything so far in this example has been achieved using a VideoView instance and three lines of code.

62.7 Adding the MediaController to the Video View

As the VideoPlayer application currently stands, there is no way for the user to control playback. As previously outlined, this can be achieved using the MediaController class. To add a controller to the VideoView, modify the *configureVideoView()* method once again:

```
package com.ebookfrenzy.videoplayer;

import android.support.v7.app.AppCompatActivity;
import android.os.Bundle;
import android.widget.VideoView;
import android.widget.MediaController;
```

```
public class VideoPlayerActivity extends AppCompatActivity {

        private VideoView videoView;
        private MediaController mediaController;
.

.

    private void configureVideoView() {

        final VideoView videoView =
                findViewById(R.id.videoView1);

        videoView.setVideoPath(
                "http://www.ebookfrenzy.com/android_book/movie.mp4");

        mediaController = new MediaController(this);
        mediaController.setAnchorView(videoView);
        videoView.setMediaController(mediaController);

        videoView.start();


    }
}
```

When the application is launched with these changes implemented, tapping the VideoView canvas will cause the media controls will appear over the video playback. These controls should include a seekbar together with fast forward, rewind and play/pause buttons. After the controls recede from view, they can be restored at any time by tapping on the VideoView canvas once again. With just three more lines of code, our video player application now has media controls as shown in Figure 62-3:

Figure 62-3

62.8 Setting up the onPreparedListener

As a final example of working with video based media, the activity will now be extended further to demonstrate the mechanism for configuring a listener. In this case, a listener will be implemented that is intended to output the duration of the video as a message in the Android Studio Logcat panel. The listener will also configure video playback to loop continuously:

```
package com.ebookfrenzy.videoplayer;

import android.support.v7.app.AppCompatActivity;
import android.os.Bundle;
import android.widget.VideoView;
import android.widget.MediaController;
import android.util.Log;
```

```
import android.media.MediaPlayer;

public class VideoPlayerActivity extends AppCompatActivity {

    private VideoView videoView;
    private MediaController mediaController;
    String TAG = "VideoPlayer";

    private void configureVideoView() {

        final VideoView videoView =
                findViewById(R.id.videoView1);

        videoView.setVideoPath(
                "http://www.ebookfrenzy.com/android_book/movie.mp4");

        MediaController mediaController = new
                MediaController(this);
        mediaController.setAnchorView(videoView);
        videoView.setMediaController(mediaController);

        videoView.setOnPreparedListener(new
                    MediaPlayer.OnPreparedListener()  {
                        @Override
                        public void onPrepared(MediaPlayer mp) {
                            mp.setLooping(true);
                            Log.i(TAG, "Duration = " +
                                    videoView.getDuration());
                        }
                    });
        videoView.start();
    }
}
```

Now just before the video playback begins, a message will appear in the Android Studio Logcat panel that reads along the lines of the following and the video will restart after playback ends:

```
11-05 10:27:52.256 12542-12542/com.ebookfrenzy.videoplayer I/
VideoPlayer: Duration = 6874
```

62.9 Summary

Tablet based Android devices make excellent platforms for the delivery of content to users, particularly in the form of video media. As outlined in this chapter, the Android SDK provides two classes, namely VideoView and MediaController, which combine to make the integration of video playback into Android applications quick and easy, often involving just a few lines of Java code.

63. Android Picture-in-Picture Mode

When multi-tasking in Android was covered in earlier chapters, Picture-in-picture (PiP) mode was mentioned briefly but not covered in any detail. Intended primarily for video playback, PiP mode allows an activity screen to be reduced in size and positioned at any location on the screen. While in this state, the activity continues to run and the window remains visible regardless of any other activities running on the device. This allows the user to, for example, continue watching video playback while performing tasks such as checking email or working on a spreadsheet.

This chapter will provide an overview of Picture-in-Picture mode before Picture-in-Picture support is added to the VideoPlayer project in the next chapter.

63.1 Picture-in-Picture Features

As will be explained later in the chapter, and demonstrated in the next chapter, an activity is placed into PiP mode via an API call from within the running app. When placed into PiP mode, configuration options may be specified that control the aspect ratio of the PiP window and also to define the area of the activity screen that is to be included in the window. Figure 63-1, for example, shows a video playback activity in PiP mode:

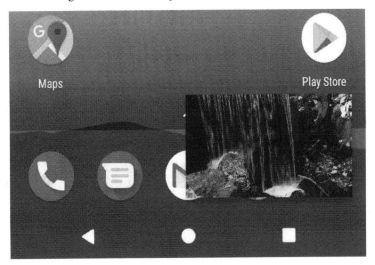

Figure 63-1

Figure 63-2 shows a PiP mode window after it has been tapped by the user. When in this mode, the window appears larger and includes a full screen action in the center which, when tapped, restores the window to full screen mode and an exit button in the top right-hand corner to close the window and place the app in the background. Any custom actions added to the PiP window will also appear on the screen when it is displayed in this mode. In the case of Figure 63-2, the PiP window includes custom play and pause action buttons:

Figure 63-2

The remainder of this chapter will outline how PiP mode is enabled and managed from within an Android app.

63.2 Enabling Picture-in-Picture Mode

PiP mode is currently only supported on devices running Android 8.0 (API 26) or newer. The first step in implementing PiP mode is to enable it within the project's manifest file. PiP mode is configured on a per activity basis by adding the following lines to each activity element for which PiP support is required:

```
<activity android:name=".MyActivity"
    android:supportsPictureInPicture="true"
    android:configChanges=
        "screenSize|smallestScreenSize|screenLayout|orientation"
    <intent-filter>
        <action android:name="android.intent.action.MAIN" />
        <category android:name="android.intent.category.LAUNCHER" />
    </intent-filter>
</activity>
```

The *android:supportsPictureInPicture* entry enables PiP for the activity while the *android:configChanges* property notifies Android that the activity is able to handle layout configuration changes. Without this setting, each time the activity moves in and out of PiP mode the activity will be restarted resulting in playback restarting from the beginning of the video during the transition.

63.3 Configuring Picture-in-Picture Parameters

PiP behavior is defined through the use of the PictureInPictureParams class, instances of which can be created using the Builder class as follows:

```
PictureInPictureParams params =
                new PictureInPictureParams.Builder().build();
```

The above code creates a default PictureInPictureParams instance with special parameters defined. The following optional method calls may also be used to customize the parameters:

- **setActions()** – Used to define actions that can be performed from within the PiP window while the activity is in PiP mode. Actions will be covered in more detail later in this chapter.

- **setAspectRatio()** – Declares the preferred aspect ratio for appearance of the PiP window. This method takes as an argument a Rational object containing the height width / height ratio.

- **setSourceRectHint()** – Takes as an argument a Rect object defining the area of the activity screen to be displayed within the PiP window.

The following code, for example, configures aspect ratio and action parameters within a PictureInPictureParams object. In the case of the aspect ratio, this is defined using the width and height dimensions of a VideoView instance:

```
Rational rational = new Rational(videoView.getWidth(),
                                 videoView.getHeight());


PictureInPictureParams params =
        new PictureInPictureParams.Builder()
                .setAspectRatio(rational)
                .setActions(actions)
                .build();
```

Once defined, PiP parameters may be set at any time using the *setPictureInPictureParams()* method as follows:

```
setPictureInPictureParams(params);
```

Parameters may also be specified when entering PiP mode.

63.4 Entering Picture-in-Picture Mode

An activity is placed into Picture-in-Picture mode via a call to the *enterPictureInPictureMode()* method, passing through a PictureInPictureParams object:

```
enterPictureInPictureMode(params);
```

If no parameters are required, simply create a default PictureInPictureParams object as outlined in the previous section. If parameters have previously been set using the *setPictureInPictureParams()* method, these parameters are combined with those specified during the *enterPictureInPictureMode()* method call.

63.5 Detecting Picture-in-Picture Mode Changes

When an activity enters PiP mode, it is important to hide any unnecessary views so that only the video playback is visible within the PiP window. When the activity re-enters full screen mode, any hidden user interface components need to be re-instated. These and any other app specific tasks can be performed by overriding the *onPictureInPictureModeChanged()* method. When added to the activity, this method is called each time the activity transitions between PiP and full screen modes and is passed a Boolean value indicating whether the activity is currently in PiP mode:

```
@Override
public void onPictureInPictureModeChanged(
                    boolean isInPictureInPictureMode) {

    super.onPictureInPictureModeChanged(isInPictureInPictureMode);

    if (isInPictureInPictureMode) {
        // Acitivity entered Picture-in-Picture mode
    } else {
        // Activity entered full screen mode
    }
```

```
}
```

63.6 Adding Picture-in-Picture Actions

Picture-in-Picture actions appear as icons within the PiP window when it is tapped by the user. Implementation of PiP actions is a multi-step process that begins with implementing a way for the PiP window to notify the activity that an action has been selected. This is achieved by setting up a broadcast receiver within the activity, and then creating a pending intent within the PiP action which, in turn, is configured to broadcast an intent for which the broadcast receiver is listening. When the broadcast receiver is triggered by the intent, the data stored in the intent can be used to identify the action performed and to take the necessary action within the activity.

PiP actions are declared using the RemoteAction instances which are initialized with an icon, a title, a description and the PendingIntent object. Once one or more actions have been created, they are added to an ArrayList and passed through to the *setActions()* method while building a PictureInPictureParams object.

The following code fragment demonstrates the creation of the Intent, PendingIntent and RemoteAction objects together with a PictureInPictureParams instance which is then applied to the activity's PiP settings:

```
final ArrayList<RemoteAction> actions = new ArrayList<>();

Intent actionIntent = new Intent("MY_PIP_ACTION");

final PendingIntent pendingIntent =
            PendingIntent.getBroadcast(MyActivity.this,
                        REQUEST_CODE, actionIntent, 0);

final Icon icon = Icon.createWithResource(MyActivity.this,
                        R.drawable.action_icon);

RemoteAction remoteAction = new RemoteAction(icon,
                        "My Action Title",
                        "My Action Description",
                        pendingIntent);

actions.add(remoteAction);

PictureInPictureParams params =
        new PictureInPictureParams.Builder()
                .setActions(actions)
                .build();

setPictureInPictureParams(params);
```

63.7 Summary

Picture-in-Picture mode is a multitasking feature introduced with Android 8.0 designed specifically to allow video playback to continue in a small window while the user performs tasks in other apps and activities. Before PiP mode can be used, it must first be enabled within the manifest file for those activities that require PiP support.

PiP mode behavior is configured using instances of the PictureInPictureParams class and initiated via a call to the *enterPictureInPictureMode()* method from within the activity. When in PiP mode, only the video playback should be visible, requiring that any other user interface elements be hidden until full screen mode is selected. These and other mode transition related tasks can be performed by overriding the *onPictureInPictureModeChanged()* method.

PiP actions appear as icons overlaid onto the PiP window when it is tapped by the user. When selected, these actions trigger behavior within the activity. The activity is notified of an action by the PiP window using broadcast receivers and pending intents.

64. An Android Picture-in-Picture Tutorial

Following on from the previous chapters, this chapter will take the existing VideoPlayer project and enhance it to add Picture-in-Picture support, including detecting PiP mode changes and the addition of a PiP action designed to display information about the currently running video.

64.1 Changing the Minimum SDK Setting

Picture-in-Picture support is only available on Android 8 API 26 or later. When the VideoPlayer project was originally created, it was configured with a minimum SDK of Android 4.0 API 14 which will prevent the PiP code added in this chapter from compiling. To modify the SDK setting, locate the *Gradle Scripts -> build.gradle (Module: app)* file and increase the *minSdkVersion* setting from 14 to 26:

```
pply plugin: 'com.android.application'

android {
    compileSdkVersion 26
    buildToolsVersion "26.0.0"
    defaultConfig {
        applicationId "com.ebookfrenzy.videoplayer"
        minSdkVersion 26
        targetSdkVersion 26
        versionCode 1
        versionName "1.0"
```

Once the change has been made, click on the *Sync Now* link in the yellow warning bar located across the top of the code editor.

64.2 Adding Picture-in-Picture Support to the Manifest

The first step in adding PiP support to an Android app project is to enable it within the project Manifest file. Open the *manifests -> AndroidManifest.xml* file and modify the activity element to enable PiP support:

```
    .
    .
<activity android:name=".VideoPlayerActivity"
    android:supportsPictureInPicture="true"
    android:configChanges="screenSize|smallestScreenSize|
            screenLayout|orientation">
    <intent-filter>
        <action android:name="android.intent.action.MAIN" />
        <category android:name="android.intent.category.LAUNCHER" />
    </intent-filter>
</activity>
```

.

.

64.3 Adding a Picture-in-Picture Button

As currently designed, the layout for the VideoPlayer activity consists solely of a VideoView instance. A button will now be added to the layout for the purpose of switching into PiP mode. Load the *activity_video_player.xml* file into the layout editor and drag a Button object from the palette onto the layout so that it is positioned as shown in Figure 64-1:

Figure 64-1

Change the text on the button so that it reads "Enter PiP Mode" and extract the string to a resource named *enter_pip_mode*. Before moving on to the next step, change the ID of the button to *pipButton* and configure the button to call a method named *enterPipMode*.

64.4 Entering Picture-in-Picture Mode

The *enterPipMode* onClick callback method now needs to be added to the *VideoPlayerActivity.java* class file. Locate this file, open it in the code editor and add this method as follows:

.

.

```
import android.view.View;
import android.app.PictureInPictureParams;
import android.util.Rational;
import android.widget.Button;

.

.

public void enterPipMode(View view) {

    Button pipButton = (Button) findViewById(R.id.pipButton);

    Rational rational = new Rational(videoView.getWidth(),
            videoView.getHeight());


    PictureInPictureParams params =
            new PictureInPictureParams.Builder()
                    .setAspectRatio(rational)
                    .build();

    pipButton.setVisibility(View.INVISIBLE);
    videoView.setMediaController(null);
```

```
    enterPictureInPictureMode(params);
}
```

The method begins by obtaining a reference to the Button view, then creates a Rational object containing the width and height of the VideoView. A set of Picture-in-Picture parameters is then created using the PictureInPictureParams Builder, passing through the Rational object as the aspect ratio for the video playback. Since the button does not need to be visible while the video is in PiP mode it is made invisible. The video playback controls are also hidden from view so that the video view will be unobstructed while in PiP mode.

Compile and run the app on a device or emulator running Android 8 and wait for video playback to begin before clicking on the PiP mode button. The video playback should minimize and appear in the PiP window as shown in Figure 64-2:

Figure 64-2

Although the video is now playing the PiP window, much of the view is obscured by the standard Android action bar. To remove this requires a change to the application theme style of the activity. Within Android Studio, locate and edit the *app -> res -> styles.xml* file and modify the AppTheme element to use the *NoActionBar* theme:

```xml
<resources>

    <!-- Base application theme. -->
    <style name="AppTheme" parent="Theme.AppCompat.Light.NoActionBar">
        <!-- Customize your theme here. -->
        <item name="colorPrimary">@color/colorPrimary</item>
        <item name="colorPrimaryDark">@color/colorPrimaryDark</item>
        <item name="colorAccent">@color/colorAccent</item>
    </style>
</resources>
```

Compile and run the app, place the video playback into PiP mode and note that the action bar no longer appears in the window:

Figure 64-3

Click in the PiP window so that it increases in size, then click within the full screen mode markers that appear in the center of the window. Although the activity returns to full screen mode, note the button and media playback controls remain hidden.

Clearly some code needs to be added to the project to detect when PiP mode changes take place within the activity.

64.5 Detecting Picture-in-Picture Mode Changes

As discussed in the previous chapter, PiP mode changes are detected by overriding the *onPictureInPictureModeChanged()* method within the affected activity. In this case, the method needs to be written such that it can detect whether the activity is entering or exiting PiP mode and to take appropriate action to re-activate the PiP button and the playback controls. Remaining within the *VideoPlayerActivity.java* file, add this method now:

```
@Override
public void onPictureInPictureModeChanged(boolean isInPictureInPictureMode) {
    super.onPictureInPictureModeChanged(isInPictureInPictureMode);

    Button pipButton = (Button) findViewById(R.id.pipButton);

    if (isInPictureInPictureMode) {

    } else {
        pipButton.setVisibility(View.VISIBLE);
        videoView.setMediaController(mediaController);
    }
}
```

When the method is called, it is passed a Boolean value indicating whether the activity is now in PiP mode. The code in the above method simply checks this value to decide whether to show the PiP button and to re-activate the playback controls.

64.6 Adding a Broadcast Receiver

The final step in the project is to add an action to the PiP window. The purpose of this action is to display a Toast message containing the name of the currently playing video. This will require some communication between the PiP window and the activity. One of the simplest ways to achieve this is to implement a broadcast receiver within the activity, and the use of a pending intent to broadcast a message from the PiP window to the activity. These steps will need to be performed each time the activity enters PiP mode so code will need to be added to the *onPictureInPictureModeChanged()* method. Locate this method now and begin by adding some code to create an intent filter and initialize the broadcast receiver:

```
.
.
import android.content.BroadcastReceiver;
import android.content.Context;
import android.content.Intent;
import android.content.IntentFilter;
import android.widget.Toast;
.
.
```

```java
public class VideoPlayerActivity extends AppCompatActivity {

    private BroadcastReceiver receiver;
    private VideoView videoView;
    private MediaController mediaController;
    String TAG = "VideoPlayer";
.

.
@Override
    public void onPictureInPictureModeChanged(
                    boolean isInPictureInPictureMode) {
        super.onPictureInPictureModeChanged(isInPictureInPictureMode);

        Button pipButton = (Button) findViewById(R.id.pipButton);

        if (isInPictureInPictureMode) {
            IntentFilter filter = new IntentFilter();
            filter.addAction(
              "com.ebookfrenzy.videoplayer.VIDEO_INFO");

            receiver = new BroadcastReceiver() {
                @Override
                public void onReceive(Context context,
                                        Intent intent) {
                    Toast.makeText(context,
                      "Favorite Home Movie Clips",
                            Toast.LENGTH_LONG).show();
                }
            };

            registerReceiver(receiver, filter);

        } else {
            pipButton.setVisibility(View.VISIBLE);
            videoView.setMediaController(mediaController);

            if (receiver != null) {
                unregisterReceiver(receiver);
            }
        }
    }
.

.

}
```

64.7 Adding the PiP Action

With the broadcast receiver implemented, the next step is to create a RemoteAction object configured with an image to represent the action within the PiP window. For the purposes of this example, an image icon file named *ic_info_24dp.xml* will be used. This file can be found in the *project_icons* folder of the source code download archive available from the following URL:

http://www.ebookfrenzy.com/print/androidstudio30/index.php

Locate this icon file and copy and paste it into the *app -> res -> drawables* folder within the Project tool window:

Figure 64-4

The next step is to create an Intent that will be sent to the broadcast receiver. This intent then needs to be wrapped up within a PendingIntent object, allowing the intent to be triggered later when the user taps the action button in the PiP window.

Edit the *VideoPlayerActivity.java* file to add a method to create the Intent and PendingIntent objects as follows:

```
.

.

import android.app.PendingIntent;

.

.

public class VideoPlayerActivity extends AppCompatActivity {

    private static final int REQUEST_CODE = 101;

.

.

.

    private void createPipAction() {
        Intent actionIntent =
            new Intent("com.ebookfrenzy.videoplayer.VIDEO_INFO");

        final PendingIntent pendingIntent =
            PendingIntent.getBroadcast(VideoPlayerActivity.this,
                REQUEST_CODE, actionIntent, 0);
    }

.

.
```

```
}
```

Now that both the Intent object, and the PendingIntent instance in which it is contained have been created, a RemoteAction object needs to created containing the icon to appear in the PiP window, and the PendingIntent object. Remaining with the *createPipAction()* method, add this code as follows:

```
.

.
import android.app.RemoteAction;
import android.graphics.drawable.Icon;
.

.
private void createPipAction() {

    final ArrayList<RemoteAction> actions = new ArrayList<>();

    Intent actionIntent =
            new Intent("com.ebookfrenzy.videoplayer.VIDEO_INFO");

    final PendingIntent pendingIntent = PendingIntent.getBroadcast(VideoPlayerActi
vity.this,
            REQUEST_CODE, actionIntent, 0);

    final Icon icon =
            Icon.createWithResource(VideoPlayerActivity.this,
                    R.drawable.ic_info_24dp);
    RemoteAction remoteAction = new RemoteAction(icon, "Info",
            "Video Info", pendingIntent);

    actions.add(remoteAction);
}
```

Now a PictureInPictureParams object containing the action needs to be created and the parameters applied so that the action appears within the PiP window:

```
private void createPipAction() {

    final ArrayList<RemoteAction> actions = new ArrayList<>();

    Intent actionIntent =
            new Intent("com.ebookfrenzy.videoplayer.VIDEO_INFO");

    final PendingIntent pendingIntent =
        PendingIntent.getBroadcast(VideoPlayerActivity.this,
            REQUEST_CODE, actionIntent, 0);

    final Icon icon =
            Icon.createWithResource(VideoPlayerActivity.this,
                    R.drawable.ic_info_24dp);
```

```
RemoteAction remoteAction = new RemoteAction(icon, "Info",
        "Video Info", pendingIntent);


actions.add(remoteAction);

PictureInPictureParams params =
            new PictureInPictureParams.Builder()
                    .setActions(actions)
                    .build();

setPictureInPictureParams(params);
}
```

The final task before testing the action is to make a call to the *createPipAction()* method when the activity enter PiP mode:

```
@Override
public void onPictureInPictureModeChanged(boolean isInPictureInPictureMode) {
    super.onPictureInPictureModeChanged(isInPictureInPictureMode);
.
.

    registerReceiver(receiver, filter);
    createPipAction();
} else {
    pipButton.setVisibility(View.VISIBLE);
    videoView.setMediaController(mediaController);
.
.
}
```

64.8 Testing the Picture-in-Picture Action

Build and run the app once again and place the activity into PiP mode. Tap on the PiP window so that the new action button appears as shown in Figure 64-5:

Figure 64-5

Click on the action button and wait for the Toast message to appear displaying the name of the video:

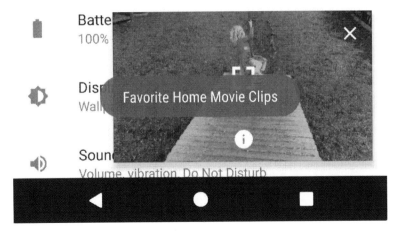

Figure 64-6

64.9 Summary

This chapter has demonstrated addition of Picture-in-Picture support to an Android Studio app project including enabling and entering PiP mode and the implementation of a PiP action. This included the use of a broadcast receiver and pending intents to implement communication between the PiP window and the activity.

65. Video Recording and Image Capture on Android using Camera Intents

Many Android devices are equipped with at least one camera. There are a number of ways to allow the user to record video from within an Android application via these built-in cameras, but by far the easiest approach is to make use of a camera intent included with the Android operating system. This allows an application to invoke the standard Android video recording interface. When the user has finished recording, the intent will return to the application, passing through a reference to the media file containing the recorded video.

As will be demonstrated in this chapter, this approach allows video recording capabilities to be added to applications with just a few lines of code.

65.1 Checking for Camera Support

Before attempting to access the camera on an Android device, it is essential that defensive code be implemented to verify the presence of camera hardware. This is of particular importance since not all Android devices include a camera.

The presence or otherwise of a camera can be identified via a call to the *PackageManager.hasSystemFeature()* method. In order to check for the presence of a front-facing camera, the code needs to check for the presence of the *PackageManager.FEATURE_CAMERA_FRONT* feature. This can be encapsulated into the following convenience method:

```
private boolean hasCamera() {
        return (getPackageManager().hasSystemFeature(
            PackageManager.FEATURE_CAMERA_FRONT));
}
```

The presence of a camera facing away from the device screen can be similarly verified using the *PackageManager. FEATURE_CAMERA* constant. A test for whether a device has any camera can be performed by referencing *PackageManager.FEATURE_CAMERA_ANY.*

65.2 Calling the Video Capture Intent

Use of the video capture intent involves, at a minimum, the implementation of code to call the intent activity and a method to handle the return from the activity. The Android built-in video recording intent is represented by *MediaStore.ACTION_VIDEO_CAPTURE* and may be launched as follows:

```
private static final int VIDEO_CAPTURE = 101;

Intent intent = new Intent(MediaStore.ACTION_VIDEO_CAPTURE);
startActivityForResult(intent, VIDEO_CAPTURE);
```

When invoked in this way, the intent will place the recorded video into a file using a default location and file name.

Video Recording and Image Capture on Android using Camera Intents

When the user either completes or cancels the video recording session, the *onActivityResult()* method of the calling activity will be called. This method needs to check that the request code passed through as an argument matches that specified when the intent was launched, verify that the recording session was successful and extract the path of the video media file. The corresponding *onActivityResult()* method for the above intent launch code might, therefore, be implemented as follows:

```
@Override
protected void onActivityResult(int requestCode, int resultCode, Intent data) {
    Uri videoUri = data.getData();

    if (requestCode == VIDEO_CAPTURE) {
        if (resultCode == RESULT_OK) {
            Toast.makeText(this, "Video saved to:\n" +
                    videoUri, Toast.LENGTH_LONG).show();
        } else if (resultCode == RESULT_CANCELED) {
            Toast.makeText(this, "Video recording cancelled.",
                    Toast.LENGTH_LONG).show();
        } else {
            Toast.makeText(this, "Failed to record video",
                    Toast.LENGTH_LONG).show();
        }
    }
}
```

The above code example simply displays a toast message indicating the success of the recording intent session. In the event of a successful recording, the path to the stored video file is displayed.

When executed, the video capture intent (Figure 65-1) will launch and provide the user the opportunity to record video.

Figure 65-1

65.3 Calling the Image Capture Intent

In addition to the video capture intent, Android also includes an intent designed for taking still photos using the built-in camera, launched by referencing *MediaStore.ACTION_IMAGE_CAPTURE*:

```
private static final int IMAGE_CAPTURE = 102;


Intent intent = new Intent(MediaStore.ACTION_IMAGE_CAPTURE);
startActivityForResult(intent, IMAGE_CAPTURE);
```

As with video capture, the intent may be passed the location and file name into which the image is to be stored, or left to use the default location and naming convention.

65.4 Creating an Android Studio Video Recording Project

In the remainder of this chapter, a very simple application will be created to demonstrate the use of the video capture intent. The application will consist of a single button which will launch the video capture intent. Once video has been recorded and the video capture intent dismissed, the application will simply display the path to the video file as a Toast message. The VideoPlayer application created in the previous chapter may then be modified to play back the recorded video.

Create a new project in Android Studio, entering *CameraApp* into the Application name field and *ebookfrenzy. com* as the Company Domain setting before clicking on the *Next* button.

On the form factors screen, enable the *Phone and Tablet* option and set the minimum SDK setting to API 14: Android 4.0 (IceCreamSandwich). Continue to proceed through the screens, requesting the creation of an Empty Activity named *CameraAppActivity* with a layout file named *activity_camera_app*.

65.5 Designing the User Interface Layout

Navigate to *app -> res -> layout* and double-click on the *activity_camera_app.xml* layout file to load it into the Layout Editor tool.

With the Layout Editor tool in Design mode, delete the default "Hello World!" text view and replace it with a Button view positioned in the center of the layout canvas. Change the text on the button to read "Record Video" and extract the text to a string resource. Also, assign an *onClick* property to the button so that it calls a method named *startRecording* when selected by the user:

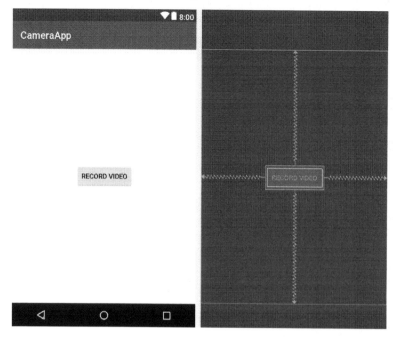

Figure 65-2

Remaining within the Attributes tool window, change the ID to *recordButton*.

65.6 Checking for the Camera

Before attempting to launch the video capture intent, the application first needs to verify that the device on which it is running actually has a camera. For the purposes of this example, we will simply make use of the previously outlined *hasCamera()* method, this time checking for any camera type. In the event that a camera is not present, the Record Video button will be disabled.

Edit the *CameraAppActivity.java* file and modify it as follows:

```
package com.ebookfrenzy.cameraapp;
import android.support.v7.app.AppCompatActivity;
import android.os.Bundle;
import android.content.pm.PackageManager;
import android.widget.Button;

public class CameraAppActivity extends AppCompatActivity {

    @Override
    protected void onCreate(Bundle savedInstanceState) {
        super.onCreate(savedInstanceState);
        setContentView(R.layout.activity_camera_app);

        Button recordButton =
            (Button) findViewById(R.id.recordButton);

        if (!hasCamera())
```

```
                        recordButton.setEnabled(false);
    }


    private boolean hasCamera() {
        return (getPackageManager().hasSystemFeature(
                    PackageManager.FEATURE_CAMERA_ANY));
    }
}
```

65.7 Launching the Video Capture Intent

The objective is for the video capture intent to launch when the user selects the *Record Video* button. Since this is now configured to call a method named *startRecording()*, the next logical step is to implement this method within the *CameraAppActivity.java* source file:

```
package com.ebookfrenzy.cameraapp;
import android.support.v7.app.AppCompatActivity;
import android.os.Bundle;
import android.content.pm.PackageManager;
import android.widget.Button;
import android.net.Uri;
import android.os.Environment;
import android.provider.MediaStore;
import android.content.Intent;
import android.view.View;

public class CameraAppActivity extends AppCompatActivity {

    private static final int VIDEO_CAPTURE = 101;

    public void startRecording(View view)
    {
        Intent intent = new Intent(MediaStore.ACTION_VIDEO_CAPTURE);
        startActivityForResult(intent, VIDEO_CAPTURE);
    }
    .
    .
    .
}
```

65.8 Handling the Intent Return

When control returns back from the intent to the application's main activity, the *onActivityResult()* method will be called. All that this method needs to do for this example is verify the success of the video capture and display the path of the file into which the video has been stored:

.
.

```
import android.widget.Toast;
```

.
.
.

```
public class CameraAppActivity extends AppCompatActivity {

.
.

    protected void onActivityResult(int requestCode,
            int resultCode, Intent data) {

        Uri videoUri = data.getData();

        if (requestCode == VIDEO_CAPTURE) {
            if (resultCode == RESULT_OK) {
                Toast.makeText(this, "Video saved to:\n" +
                        videoUri, Toast.LENGTH_LONG).show();
            } else if (resultCode == RESULT_CANCELED) {
                Toast.makeText(this, "Video recording cancelled.",
                        Toast.LENGTH_LONG).show();
            } else {
                Toast.makeText(this, "Failed to record video",
                        Toast.LENGTH_LONG).show();
            }
        }
    }

.
.
.

}
```

65.9 Testing the Application

Compile and run the application on a physical Android device or emulator session, touch the record button and use the video capture intent to record some video. Once completed, stop the video recording. Play back the recording by selecting the play button on the screen. Finally, touch the *Done* (sometimes represented by a check mark) button on the screen to return to the CameraApp application. On returning, a Toast message should appear stating that the video has been stored in a specific location on the device (the exact location will differ from one device type to another) from where it can be moved, stored or played back depending on the requirements of the app.

65.10 Summary

Most Android tablet and smartphone devices include a camera that can be accessed by applications. While there are a number of different approaches to adding camera support to applications, the Android video and image capture intents provide a simple and easy solution to capturing video and images.

66. Making Runtime Permission Requests in Android

In a number of the example projects created in preceding chapters, changes have been made to the AndroidManifest.xml file to request permission for the app to perform a specific task. In a couple of instances, for example, internet access permission has been requested in order to allow the app to download and display web pages. In each case up until this point, the addition of the request to the manifest was all that is required in order for the app to obtain permission from the user to perform the designated task.

There are, however, a number of permissions for which additional steps are required in order for the app to function when running on Android 6.0 or later. The first of these so-called "dangerous" permissions will be encountered in the next chapter. Before reaching that point, however, this chapter will outline the steps involved in requesting such permissions when running on the latest generations of Android.

66.1 Understanding Normal and Dangerous Permissions

Android enforces security by requiring the user to grant permission for an app to perform certain tasks. Prior to the introduction of Android 6, permission was always sought at the point that the app was installed on the device. Figure 66-1, for example, shows a typical screen seeking a variety of permissions during the installation of an app via Google Play.

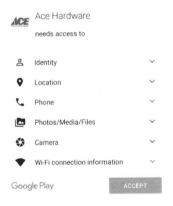

Figure 66-1

For many types of permissions this scenario still applies for apps on Android 6.0 or later. These permissions are referred to as *normal permissions* and are still required to be accepted by the user at the point of installation. A second type of permission, referred to as *dangerous permissions* must also be declared within the manifest file in the same way as a normal permission, but must also be requested from the user when the application is first launched. When such a request is made, it appears in the form of a dialog box as illustrated in Figure 66-2:

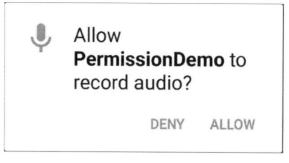

Figure 66-2

The full list of permissions that fall into the dangerous category is contained in Table 66-3:

Permission Group	Permission
Calendar	READ_CALENDAR
	WRITE_CALENDAR
Camera	CAMERA
Contacts	READ_CONTACTS
	WRITE_CONTACTS
	GET_ACCOUNTS
Location	ACCESS_FINE_LOCATION
	ACCESS_COARSE_LOCATION
Microphone	RECORD_AUDIO
Phone	READ_PHONE_STATE
	CALL_PHONE
	READ_CALL_LOG
	WRITE_CALL_LOG
	ADD_VOICEMAIL
	USE_SIP
	PROCESS_OUTGOING_CALLS
Sensors	BODY_SENSORS
SMS	SEND_SMS
	RECEIVE_SMS
	READ_SMS
	RECEIVE_WAP_PUSH
	RECEIVE_MMS

Storage	READ_EXTERNAL_STORAGE
	WRITE_EXTERNAL_STORAGE

Table 66-3

66.2 Creating the Permissions Example Project

Create a new project in Android Studio, entering *PermissionDemo* into the Application name field and *com. ebookfrenzy* as the Company Domain setting before clicking on the *Next* button.

On the form factors screen, enable the *Phone and Tablet* option and set the minimum SDK setting to API 19: Android 4.4 (KitKat). Continue to proceed through the screens, requesting the creation of an Empty Activity named *PermissionDemoActivity* with a corresponding layout named *activity_permission_demo*.

66.3 Checking for a Permission

The Android Support Library contains a number of methods that can be used to seek and manage dangerous permissions within the code of an Android app. These API calls can be made safely regardless of the version of Android on which the app is running, but will only perform meaningful tasks when executed on Android 6.0 or later.

Before an app attempts to make use of a feature that requires approval of a dangerous permission, and regardless of whether or not permission was previously granted, the code must check that the permission has been granted. This can be achieved via a call to the *checkSelfPermission()* method of the ContextCompat class, passing through as arguments a reference to the current activity and the permission being requested. The method will check whether the permission has been previously granted and return an integer value matching *PackageManager. PERMISSION_GRANTED* or *PackageManager.PERMISSION_DENIED*.

Within the *PermissionDemoActivity.java* file of the example project, modify the code to check whether permission has been granted for the app to record audio:

```
package com.ebookfrenzy.permissiondemoactivity;


import android.support.v7.app.AppCompatActivity;
import android.os.Bundle;
import android.Manifest;
import android.content.pm.PackageManager;
import android.support.v4.content.ContextCompat;
import android.util.Log;


public class PermissionDemoActivity extends AppCompatActivity {

    private static String TAG = "PermissionDemo";

    @Override
    protected void onCreate(Bundle savedInstanceState) {
        super.onCreate(savedInstanceState);
        setContentView(R.layout.activity_permission_demo);

        setupPermissions();
    }
```

```
    private void setupPermissions() {
        int permission = ContextCompat.checkSelfPermission(this,
                Manifest.permission.RECORD_AUDIO);

        if (permission != PackageManager.PERMISSION_GRANTED) {
            Log.i(TAG, "Permission to record denied");
        }
    }
}
```

Run the app on a device or emulator running a version of Android that predates Android 6.0 and check the log cat output within Android Studio. After the app has launched, the Logcat output should include the "Permission to record denied" message.

Edit the *AndroidManifest.xml* file (located in the Project tool window under *app -> manifests*) and add a line to request recording permission as follows:

```
<?xml version="1.0" encoding="utf-8"?>
<manifest xmlns:android="http://schemas.android.com/apk/res/android"
    package="com.ebookfrenzy.permissiondemoactivity" >

    <uses-permission android:name="android.permission.RECORD_AUDIO" />

    <application
        android:allowBackup="true"
        android:icon="@mipmap/ic_launcher"
        android:label="@string/app_name"
        android:supportsRtl="true"
        android:theme="@style/AppTheme" >
        <activity android:name=".PermissionDemoActivity" >
            <intent-filter>
                <action android:name="android.intent.action.MAIN" />

                <category
                    android:name="android.intent.category.LAUNCHER" />
            </intent-filter>
        </activity>
    </application>

</manifest>
```

Compile and run the app once again and note that this time the permission denial message does not appear. Clearly, everything that needs to be done to request this permission on older versions of Android has been done. Run the app on a device or emulator running Android 6.0 or later, however, and note that even though permission has been added to the manifest file, the check still reports that permission has been denied. This is because Android version 6 or later requires that the app also request dangerous permissions at runtime.

66.4 Requesting Permission at Runtime

A permission request is made via a call to the *requestPermissions()* method of the ActivityCompat class. When this method is called, the permission request is handled asynchronously and a method named *onRequestPermissionsResult()* is called when the task is completed.

The *requestPermissions()* method takes as arguments a reference to the current activity, together with the identifier of the permission being requested and a request code. The request code can be any integer value and will be used to identify which request has triggered the call to the *onRequestPermissionsResult()* method. Modify the *PermissionDemoActivity.java* file to declare a request code and request recording permission in the event that the permission check failed:

```
package com.ebookfrenzy.permissiondemoactivity;

import android.Manifest;
import android.content.pm.PackageManager;
import android.support.v4.content.ContextCompat;
import android.support.v7.app.AppCompatActivity;
import android.os.Bundle;
import android.util.Log;
import android.support.v4.app.ActivityCompat;

public class PermissionDemoActivity extends AppCompatActivity {

    private static String TAG = "PermissionDemo";
    private static final int RECORD_REQUEST_CODE = 101;
    .
    .
    @Override
    private void setupPermissions() {

        int permission = ContextCompat.checkSelfPermission(this,
                Manifest.permission.RECORD_AUDIO);

        if (permission != PackageManager.PERMISSION_GRANTED) {
            Log.i(TAG, "Permission to record denied");
            makeRequest();
        }
    }

    protected void makeRequest() {
        ActivityCompat.requestPermissions(this,
                new String[]{Manifest.permission.RECORD_AUDIO},
                RECORD_REQUEST_CODE);
    }
}
```

Next, implement the *onRequestPermissionsResult()* method so that it reads as follows:

```
@Override
public void onRequestPermissionsResult(int requestCode,
                                    String permissions[], int[] grantResults)
{
    switch (requestCode) {
        case RECORD_REQUEST_CODE: {

            if (grantResults.length == 0
                    || grantResults[0] !=
                    PackageManager.PERMISSION_GRANTED) {

                Log.i(TAG, "Permission has been denied by user");
            } else {
                Log.i(TAG, "Permission has been granted by user");
            }
        }
    }
}
```

Compile and run the app on an Android 6 or later emulator or device and note that a dialog seeking permission to record audio appears as shown in Figure 66-3:

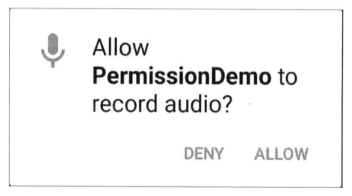

Figure 66-3

Tap the Allow button and check that the "Permission has been granted by user" message appears in the Logcat panel.

Once the user has granted the requested permission, the *checkSelfPermission()* method call will return a PERMISSION_GRANTED result on future app invocations until the user uninstalls and re-installs the app or changes the permissions for the app in Settings.

66.5 Providing a Rationale for the Permission Request

As is evident from Figure 66-3, the user has the option to deny the requested permission. In this case, the app will continue to request the permission each time that it is launched by the user unless the user selected the "Never ask again" option prior to clicking on the Deny button. Repeated denials by the user may indicate that the user doesn't understand why the permission is required by the app. The user might, therefore, be more likely to grant permission if the reason for the requirements is explained when the request is made. Unfortunately, it is not possible to change the content of the request dialog to include such an explanation.

An explanation is best included in a separate dialog which can be displayed before the request dialog is presented to the user. This raises the question as to when to display this explanation dialog. The Android documentation recommends that an explanation dialog only be shown in the event that the user has previously denied the permission and provides a method to identify when this is the case.

A call to the *shouldShowRequestPermissionRationale()* method of the ActivityCompat class will return a true result if the user has previously denied a request for the specified permission, and a false result if the request has not previously been made. In the case of a true result, the app should display a dialog containing a rationale for needing the permission and, once the dialog has been read and dismissed by the user, the permission request should be repeated.

To add this functionality to the example app, modify the *onCreate()* method so that it reads as follows:

```
.
.
import android.app.AlertDialog;
import android.content.DialogInterface;
.
.
private void setupPermissions() {

    int permission = ContextCompat.checkSelfPermission(this,
            Manifest.permission.RECORD_AUDIO);

    if (permission != PackageManager.PERMISSION_GRANTED) {
        Log.i(TAG, "Permission to record denied");

        if (ActivityCompat.shouldShowRequestPermissionRationale(this,
                Manifest.permission.RECORD_AUDIO)) {
            AlertDialog.Builder builder =
                    new AlertDialog.Builder(this);
            builder.setMessage("Permission to access the microphone is required
for this app to record audio.")
                    .setTitle("Permission required");

            builder.setPositiveButton("OK",
                    new DialogInterface.OnClickListener() {

                public void onClick(DialogInterface dialog, int id) {
                    Log.i(TAG, "Clicked");
                    makeRequest();
                }
            });

            AlertDialog dialog = builder.create();
            dialog.show();
        } else {
            makeRequest();
```

```
        }
    }
}
```

The method still checks whether or not the permission has been granted, but now also identifies whether a rationale needs to be displayed. If the user has previously denied the request, a dialog is displayed containing an explanation and an OK button on which a listener is configured to call the *makeRequest()* method when the button is tapped. In the event that the permission request has not previously been made, the code moves directly to seeking permission.

66.6 Testing the Permissions App

On the Android 6 or later device or emulator session on which testing is being performed, launch the Settings app, select the Apps option and scroll to and select the PermissionDemo app. On the app settings screen, tap the uninstall button to remove the app from the device.

Run the app once again and, when the permission request dialog appears, click on the Deny button. Terminate the app, run it a second time and verify that the rationale dialog appears. Tap the OK button and, when the permission request dialog appears, tap the Allow button.

Return to the Settings app, select the Apps option and select the PermissionDemo app once again from the list. Once the settings for the app are listed, verify that the Permissions section lists the *Microphone* permission:

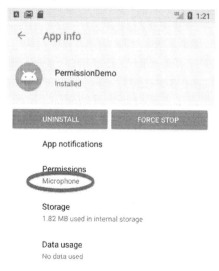

Figure 66-4

66.7 Summary

Prior to the introduction of Android 6.0 the only step necessary for an app to request permission to access certain functionality was to add an appropriate line to the application's manifest file. The user would then be prompted to approve the permission at the point that the app was installed. This is still the case for most permissions, with the exception of a set of permissions that are considered dangerous. Permissions that are considered dangerous usually have the potential to allow an app to violate the user's privacy such as allowing access to the microphone, contacts list or external storage.

As outlined in this chapter, apps based on Android 6 or later must now request dangerous permission approval from the user when the app launches in addition to including the permission request in the manifest file.

67. Android Audio Recording and Playback using MediaPlayer and MediaRecorder

This chapter will provide an overview of the MediaRecorder class and explain the basics of how this class can be used to record audio or video. The use of the MediaPlayer class to play back audio will also be covered. Having covered the basics, an example application will be created to demonstrate these techniques in action. In addition to looking at audio and video handling, this chapter will also touch on the subject of saving files to the SD card.

67.1 Playing Audio

In terms of audio playback, most implementations of Android support AAC LC/LTP, HE-AACv1 (AAC+), HE-AACv2 (enhanced AAC+), AMR-NB, AMR-WB, MP3, MIDI, Ogg Vorbis, and PCM/WAVE formats.

Audio playback can be performed using either the MediaPlayer or the AudioTrack classes. AudioTrack is a more advanced option that uses streaming audio buffers and provides greater control over the audio. The MediaPlayer class, on the other hand, provides an easier programming interface for implementing audio playback and will meet the needs of most audio requirements.

The MediaPlayer class has associated with it a range of methods that can be called by an application to perform certain tasks. A subset of some of the key methods of this class is as follows:

- **create()** – Called to create a new instance of the class, passing through the Uri of the audio to be played.

- **setDataSource()** – Sets the source from which the audio is to play.

- **prepare()** – Instructs the player to prepare to begin playback.

- **start()** – Starts the playback.

- **pause()** – Pauses the playback. Playback may be resumed via a call to the *resume()* method.

- **stop()** – Stops playback.

- **setVolume()** – Takes two floating-point arguments specifying the playback volume for the left and right channels.

- **resume()** – Resumes a previously paused playback session.

- **reset()** – Resets the state of the media player instance. Essentially sets the instance back to the uninitialized state. At a minimum, a reset player will need to have the data source set again and the *prepare()* method called.

- **release()** – To be called when the player instance is no longer needed. This method ensures that any resources held by the player are released.

In a typical implementation, an application will instantiate an instance of the MediaPlayer class, set the source of the audio to be played and then call *prepare()* followed by *start()*. For example:

```
MediaPlayer mediaPlayer = new MediaPlayer();

mediaPlayer.setDataSource("http://www.yourcompany.com/myaudio.mp3");
mediaPlayer.prepare();
mediaPlayer.start();
```

67.2 Recording Audio and Video using the MediaRecorder Class

As with audio playback, recording can be performed using a number of different techniques. One option is to use the MediaRecorder class, which, as with the MediaPlayer class, provides a number of methods that are used to record audio:

- **setAudioSource()** – Specifies the source of the audio to be recorded (typically this will be MediaRecorder. AudioSource.MIC for the device microphone).

- **setVideoSource()** – Specifies the source of the video to be recorded (for example MediaRecorder.VideoSource. CAMERA).

- **setOutputFormat()** – Specifies the format into which the recorded audio or video is to be stored (for example MediaRecorder.OutputFormat.AAC_ADTS).

- **setAudioEncoder()** – Specifies the audio encoder to be used for the recorded audio (for example MediaRecorder.AudioEncoder.AAC).

- **setOutputFile()** – Configures the path to the file into which the recorded audio or video is to be stored.

- **prepare()** – Prepares the MediaRecorder instance to begin recording.

- **start()** - Begins the recording process.

- **stop()** – Stops the recording process. Once a recorder has been stopped, it will need to be completely reconfigured and prepared before being restarted.

- **reset()** – Resets the recorder. The instance will need to be completely reconfigured and prepared before being restarted.

- **release()** – Should be called when the recorder instance is no longer needed. This method ensures all resources held by the instance are released.

A typical implementation using this class will set the source, output and encoding format and output file. Calls will then be made to the *prepare()* and *start()* methods. The *stop()* method will then be called when recording is to end, followed by the *reset()* method. When the application no longer needs the recorder instance, a call to the *release()* method is recommended:

```
MediaRecorder mediaRecorder = new MediaRecorder();

mediaRecorder.setAudioSource(MediaRecorder.AudioSource.MIC);
mediaRecorder.setOutputFormat(MediaRecorder.OutputFormat.AAC_ADTS);
mediaRecorder.setAudioEncoder(MediaRecorder.AudioEncoder.AAC);
mediaRecorder.setOutputFile(audioFilePath);

mediaRecorder.prepare();
mediaRecorder.start();
```

.

```
mediaRecorder.stop();
mediaRecorder.reset();
mediaRecorder.release();
```

In order to record audio, the manifest file for the application must include the android.permission.RECORD_AUDIO permission:

```
<uses-permission android:name="android.permission.RECORD_AUDIO" />
```

As outlined in the chapter entitled *"Making Runtime Permission Requests in Android"*, access to the microphone falls into the category of dangerous permissions. To support Android 6, therefore, a specific request for microphone access must also be made when the application launches, the steps for which will be covered later in this chapter.

67.3 About the Example Project

The remainder of this chapter will work through the creation of an example application intended to demonstrate the use of the MediaPlayer and MediaRecorder classes to implement the recording and playback of audio on an Android device.

When developing applications that make use of specific hardware features, the microphone being a case in point, it is important to check the availability of the feature before attempting to access it in the application code. The application created in this chapter will, therefore, also demonstrate the steps involved in detecting the presence of a microphone on the device.

Once completed, this application will provide a very simple interface intended to allow the user to record and playback audio. The recorded audio will need to be stored within an audio file on the device. That being the case, this tutorial will also briefly explore the mechanism for using SD Card storage.

67.4 Creating the AudioApp Project

Create a new project in Android Studio, entering *AudioApp* into the Application name field and *ebookfrenzy.com* as the Company Domain setting before clicking on the *Next* button.

On the form factors screen, enable the *Phone and Tablet* option and set the minimum SDK setting to API 14: Android 4.0 (IceCreamSandwich). Continue to proceed through the screens, requesting the creation of an Empty Activity named *AudioAppActivity* with a corresponding layout resource file named *activity_audio_app*.

67.5 Designing the User Interface

Once the new project has been created, select the *activity_audio_app.xml* file from the Project tool window and with the Layout Editor tool in Design mode, select the "Hello World!" TextView and delete it from the layout.

Drag and drop three Button views onto the layout. The positioning of the buttons is not of paramount importance to this example, though Figure 67-1 shows a suggested layout using a vertical chain.

Configure the buttons to display string resources that read *Play, Record* and *Stop* and give them view IDs of *playButton, recordButton,* and *stopButton* respectively.

Select the Play button and, within the Attributes panel, configure the *onClick* property to call a method named *playAudio* when selected by the user. Repeat these steps to configure the remaining buttons to call methods named *recordAudio* and *stopAudio* respectively.

Figure 67-1

67.6 Checking for Microphone Availability

Attempting to record audio on a device without a microphone will cause the Android system to throw an exception. It is vital, therefore, that the code check for the presence of a microphone before making such an attempt. There are a number of ways of doing this, including checking for the physical presence of the device. An easier approach, and one that is more likely to work on different Android devices, is to ask the Android system if it has a package installed for a particular *feature*. This involves creating an instance of the Android PackageManager class and then making a call to the object's *hasSystemFeature()* method. *PackageManager. FEATURE_MICROPHONE* is the feature of interest in this case.

For the purposes of this example, we will create a method named *hasMicrophone()* that may be called upon to check for the presence of a microphone. Within the Project tool window, locate and double-click on the *AudioAppActivity.java* file and modify it to add this method:

```
package com.ebookfrenzy.audioapp;

import android.support.v7.app.AppCompatActivity;
import android.os.Bundle;
import android.content.pm.PackageManager;

public class AudioAppActivity extends AppCompatActivity {

    @Override
    protected void onCreate(Bundle savedInstanceState) {
        super.onCreate(savedInstanceState);
        setContentView(R.layout.activity_audio_app);
    }

    protected boolean hasMicrophone() {
        PackageManager pmanager = this.getPackageManager();
```

```
    return pmanager.hasSystemFeature(
            PackageManager.FEATURE_MICROPHONE);
    }
}
```

67.7 Performing the Activity Initialization

The next step is to modify the activity to perform a number of initialization tasks. Remaining within the *AudioAppActivity.java* file, modify the code as follows:

```
package com.ebookfrenzy.audioapp;

import java.io.IOException;

import android.support.v7.app.AppCompatActivity;
import android.os.Bundle;
import android.content.pm.PackageManager;
import android.media.MediaRecorder;
import android.os.Environment;
import android.widget.Button;
import android.view.View;
import android.media.MediaPlayer;

public class AudioAppActivity extends AppCompatActivity {

    private static MediaRecorder mediaRecorder;
    private static MediaPlayer mediaPlayer;

    private static String audioFilePath;
    private static Button stopButton;
    private static Button playButton;
    private static Button recordButton;

    private boolean isRecording = false;

    @Override
    protected void onCreate(Bundle savedInstanceState) {
        super.onCreate(savedInstanceState);
        setContentView(R.layout.activity_audio_app);
        audioSetup();
    }

    private void audioSetup()
    {
        recordButton =
                (Button) findViewById(R.id.recordButton);
        playButton = (Button) findViewById(R.id.playButton);
        stopButton = (Button) findViewById(R.id.stopButton);
```

```
        if (!hasMicrophone())
        {
            stopButton.setEnabled(false);
            playButton.setEnabled(false);
            recordButton.setEnabled(false);
        } else {
            playButton.setEnabled(false);
            stopButton.setEnabled(false);
        }

        audioFilePath =
                Environment.getExternalStorageDirectory()
                    .getAbsolutePath()
                        + "/myaudio.3gp";
    }
    .
    .
}
```

The added code begins by obtaining references to the three button views in the user interface. Next, the previously implemented *hasMicrophone()* method is called to ascertain whether the device includes a microphone. If it does not, all the buttons are disabled, otherwise only the Stop and Play buttons are disabled.

The next line of code needs a little more explanation:

```
audioFilePath =
        Environment.getExternalStorageDirectory().getAbsolutePath()
            + "/myaudio.3gp";
```

The purpose of this code is to identify the location of the SD card storage on the device and to use that to create a path to a file named *myaudio.3gp* into which the audio recording will be stored. The path of the SD card (which is referred to as external storage even though it is internal to the device on many Android devices) is obtained via a call to the *getExternalStorageDirectory()* method of the Android Environment class.

When working with external storage it is important to be aware that such activity by an application requires permission to be requested in the application manifest file. For example:

```
<uses-permission android:name="android.permission.WRITE_EXTERNAL_STORAGE" />
```

67.8 Implementing the recordAudio() Method

When the user touches the Record button, the *recordAudio()* method will be called. This method will need to enable and disable the appropriate buttons and configure the MediaRecorder instance with information about the source of the audio, the output format and encoding, and the location of the file into which the audio is to be stored. Finally, the *prepare()* and *start()* methods of the MediaRecorder object will need to be called. Combined, these requirements result in the following method implementation in the *AudioAppActivity.java* file:

```
public void recordAudio (View view) throws IOException
{
    isRecording = true;
    stopButton.setEnabled(true);
```

```
    playButton.setEnabled(false);
    recordButton.setEnabled(false);

    try {
      mediaRecorder = new MediaRecorder();
      mediaRecorder.setAudioSource(MediaRecorder.AudioSource.MIC);
      mediaRecorder.setOutputFormat(
            MediaRecorder.OutputFormat.THREE_GPP);
      mediaRecorder.setOutputFile(audioFilePath);
      mediaRecorder.setAudioEncoder(MediaRecorder.AudioEncoder.AMR_NB);
      mediaRecorder.prepare();
    } catch (Exception e) {
            e.printStackTrace();
    }
    mediaRecorder.start();
}
```

67.9 Implementing the stopAudio() Method

The *stopAudio()* method is responsible for enabling the Play button, disabling the Stop button and then stopping and resetting the MediaRecorder instance. The code to achieve this reads as outlined in the following listing and should be added to the *AudioAppActivity.java* file:

```
public void stopAudio (View view)
{

        stopButton.setEnabled(false);
        playButton.setEnabled(true);

        if (isRecording)
        {
                recordButton.setEnabled(false);
                mediaRecorder.stop();
                mediaRecorder.release();
                mediaRecorder = null;
                isRecording = false;
        } else {
                mediaPlayer.release();
                 mediaPlayer = null;
                recordButton.setEnabled(true);
        }
}
```

67.10 Implementing the playAudio() method

The *playAudio()* method will simply create a new MediaPlayer instance, assign the audio file located on the SD card as the data source and then prepare and start the playback:

```
public void playAudio (View view) throws IOException
{
```

```
        playButton.setEnabled(false);
        recordButton.setEnabled(false);
        stopButton.setEnabled(true);

        mediaPlayer = new MediaPlayer();
        mediaPlayer.setDataSource(audioFilePath);
        mediaPlayer.prepare();
        mediaPlayer.start();
}
```

67.11 Configuring and Requesting Permissions

Before testing the application, it is essential that the appropriate permissions be requested within the manifest file for the application. Specifically, the application will require permission to record audio and to access the external storage (SD card). Within the Project tool window, locate and double-click on the *AndroidManifest.xml* file to load it into the editor and modify the XML to add the two permission tags:

```xml
<?xml version="1.0" encoding="utf-8"?>
<manifest xmlns:android="http://schemas.android.com/apk/res/android"
    package="com.ebookfrenzy.audioapp" >

    <uses-permission android:name=
                "android.permission.WRITE_EXTERNAL_STORAGE" />
    <uses-permission android:name="android.permission.RECORD_AUDIO" />

    <application
        android:allowBackup="true"
        android:icon="@mipmap/ic_launcher"
        android:label="@string/app_name"
        android:theme="@style/AppTheme" >
        <activity android:name=".AudioAppActivity"
            android:label="@string/app_name" >
            <intent-filter>
                <action android:name="android.intent.action.MAIN" />

                <category android:name=
                    "android.intent.category.LAUNCHER" />
            </intent-filter>
        </activity>
    </application>
</manifest>
```

The above steps will be adequate to ensure that the user enables these permissions when the app is installed on devices running versions of Android pre-dating Android 6.0. Both microphone and external storage access are categorized in Android as being dangerous permissions because they give the app the potential to compromise the user's privacy. In order for the example app to function on Android 6 or later devices, therefore, code needs to be added to specifically request these two permissions at app runtime.

Edit the *AudioAppActivity.java* file and begin by adding some additional import directives and constants to act as request identification codes for the permissions being requested:

.

.

```
import android.widget.Toast;
import android.support.v4.content.ContextCompat;
import android.Manifest;
import android.support.v4.app.ActivityCompat;
```

.

.

```
public class AudioAppActivity extends AppCompatActivity {

    private static final int RECORD_REQUEST_CODE = 101;
    private static final int STORAGE_REQUEST_CODE = 102;
```

.

.

Next, a method needs to be added to the class, the purpose of which is to take as arguments the permission to be requested and the corresponding request identification code. Remaining with the *AudioAppActivity.java* class file, implement this method as follows:

```
protected void requestPermission(String permissionType, int requestCode) {
    int permission = ContextCompat.checkSelfPermission(this,
                permissionType);

    if (permission != PackageManager.PERMISSION_GRANTED) {
        ActivityCompat.requestPermissions(this,
                new String[]{permissionType}, requestCode
        );
    }
}
```

Using the steps outlined in the *"Making Runtime Permission Requests in Android"* chapter of this book, the above method verifies that the specified permission has not already been granted before making the request, passing through the identification code as an argument.

When the request has been handled, the *onRequestPermissionsResult()* method will be called on the activity, passing through the identification code and the results of the request. The next step, therefore, is to implement this method within the *AudioAppActivity.java* file as follows:

```
@Override
public void onRequestPermissionsResult(int requestCode,
                     String permissions[], int[] grantResults) {
    switch (requestCode) {
        case RECORD_REQUEST_CODE: {

            if (grantResults.length == 0
                || grantResults[0] !=
                    PackageManager.PERMISSION_GRANTED) {
```

```
                    recordButton.setEnabled(false);

                    Toast.makeText(this,
                            "Record permission required",
                                    Toast.LENGTH_LONG).show();
                } else {
                    requestPermission(
                            Manifest.permission.WRITE_EXTERNAL_STORAGE,
                                STORAGE_REQUEST_CODE);
                }
                return;
            }
            case STORAGE_REQUEST_CODE: {

                if (grantResults.length == 0
                        || grantResults[0] !=
                        PackageManager.PERMISSION_GRANTED) {
                    recordButton.setEnabled(false);
                    Toast.makeText(this,
                            "External Storage permission required",
                            Toast.LENGTH_LONG).show();
                }
                return;
            }
        }
    }
}
```

The above code checks the request identifier code to identify which permission request has returned before checking whether or not the corresponding permission was granted. If the user grants permission to access the microphone the code then proceeds to request access to the external storage. In the event that either permission was denied, a message is displayed to the user indicating the app will not function. In both instances, the record button is also disabled.

All that remains prior to testing the app is to call the newly added *requestPermission()* method for microphone access when the app launches. Remaining in the *AudioAppActivity.java* file, modify the *audioSetup()* method as follows:

```
private void audioSetup(){
    recordButton =
            (Button) findViewById(R.id.recordButton);
    playButton = (Button) findViewById(R.id.playButton);
    stopButton = (Button) findViewById(R.id.stopButton);

    if (!hasMicrophone())
    {
        stopButton.setEnabled(false);
        playButton.setEnabled(false);
        recordButton.setEnabled(false);
```

```
    } else {
        playButton.setEnabled(false);
        stopButton.setEnabled(false);
    }


    audioFilePath =
            Environment.getExternalStorageDirectory()
                .getAbsolutePath()
                    + "/myaudio.3gp";


    requestPermission(Manifest.permission.RECORD_AUDIO,
            RECORD_REQUEST_CODE);
}
```

67.12 Testing the Application

Compile and run the application on an Android device containing a microphone, allow the requested permissions and touch the Record button. After recording, touch Stop followed by Play, at which point the recorded audio should play back through the device speakers. If running on Android 6.0 or later, note that the app requests permission to use the external storage and to record audio when first launched.

67.13 Summary

The Android SDK provides a number of mechanisms for the implementation of audio recording and playback. This chapter has looked at two of these, in the form of the MediaPlayer and MediaRecorder classes. Having covered the theory of using these techniques, this chapter worked through the creation of an example application designed to record and then play back audio. In the course of working with audio in Android, this chapter also looked at the steps involved in ensuring that the device on which the application is running has a microphone before attempting to record audio. The use of external storage in the form of an SD card was also covered.

68. Working with the Google Maps Android API in Android Studio

When Google decided to introduce a map service many years ago, it is hard to say whether or not they ever anticipated having a version available for integration into mobile applications. When the first web based version of what would eventually be called Google Maps was introduced in 2005, the iPhone had yet to ignite the smartphone revolution and the company that was developing the Android operating system would not be acquired by Google for another six months. Whatever aspirations Google had for the future of Google Maps, it is remarkable to consider that all of the power of Google Maps can now be accessed directly via Android applications using the Google Maps Android API.

This chapter is intended to provide an overview of the Google Maps system and Google Maps Android API. The chapter will provide an overview of the different elements that make up the API, detail the steps necessary to configure a development environment to work with Google Maps and then work through some code examples demonstrating some of the basics of Google Maps Android integration.

68.1 The Elements of the Google Maps Android API

The Google Maps Android API consists of a core set of classes that combine to provide mapping capabilities in Android applications. The key elements of a map are as follows:

- **GoogleMap** – The main class of the Google Maps Android API. This class is responsible for downloading and displaying map tiles and for displaying and responding to map controls. The GoogleMap object is not created directly by the application but is instead created when MapView or MapFragment instances are created. A reference to the GoogleMap object can be obtained within application code via a call to the *getMap()* method of a MapView, MapFragment or SupportMapFragment instance.

- **MapView** - A subclass of the View class, this class provides the view canvas onto which the map is drawn by the GoogleMap object, allowing a map to be placed in the user interface layout of an activity.

- **SupportMapFragment** – A subclass of the Fragment class, this class allows a map to be placed within a Fragment in an Android layout.

- **Marker** – The purpose of the Marker class is to allow locations to be marked on a map. Markers are added to a map by obtaining a reference to the GoogleMap object associated with a map and then making a call to the *addMarker()* method of that object instance. The position of a marker is defined via Longitude and Latitude. Markers can be configured in a number of ways, including specifying a title, text and an icon. Markers may also be made to be "draggable", allowing the user to move the marker to different positions on a map.

- **Shapes** – The drawing of lines and shapes on a map is achieved through the use of the *Polyline*, *Polygon* and *Circle* classes.

- **UiSettings** – The UiSettings class provides a level of control from within an application of which user interface controls appear on a map. Using this class, for example, the application can control whether or not the zoom, current location and compass controls appear on a map. This class can also be used to configure which touch screen gestures are recognized by the map.

- **My Location Layer** – When enabled, the My Location Layer displays a button on the map which, when selected by the user, centers the map on the user's current geographical location. If the user is stationary, this location is represented on the map by a blue marker. If the user is in motion the location is represented by a chevron indicating the user's direction of travel.

The best way to gain familiarity with the Google Maps Android API is to work through an example. The remainder of this chapter will create a simple Google Maps based application while highlighting the key areas of the API.

68.2 Creating the Google Maps Project

Create a new project in Android Studio, entering *MapDemo* into the Application name field and *com.ebookfrenzy* as the Company Domain setting before clicking on the *Next* button.

On the form factors screen, enable the *Phone and Tablet* option and set the minimum SDK setting to API 19: Android 4.4 (KitKat). Continue to proceed through the screens, requesting the creation of a *Google Maps Activity* named *MapDemoActivity* with a corresponding layout named *activity_map_demo* and a title of *Map Demo*.

68.3 Obtaining Your Developer Signature

Before an application can make use of the Google Maps Android API, it must first be registered within the Google APIs Console. Before an application can be registered, however, the developer signature (also referred to as the SHA-1 fingerprint) associated with your development environment must be identified. This is contained in a keystore file located in the *.android* subdirectory of your home directory and may be obtained using the *keytool* utility provided as part of the Java SDK as outlined below. In order to make the process easier, however, Android Studio adds some additional files to the project when the *Google Maps Activity* option is selected during the project creation process. One of these files is named *google_maps_api.xml* and is located in the *app -> res -> values* folder of the project.

Contained within the *google_maps_api.xml* file is a link to the Google Developer console. Copy and paste this link into a browser window. Once loaded, a page similar to the following will appear:

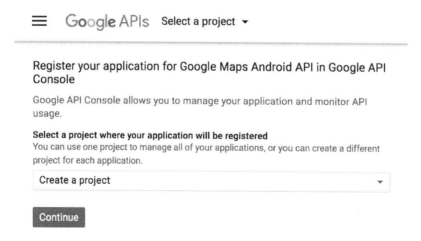

Figure 68-1

Verify that the menu is set to *Create a new project* before clicking on the *Continue* button. Once the API has been enabled, click on the *Create API Key* button. After a short delay, the new project will be created and a panel will appear (Figure 68-2) providing the API key for the application.

API key created

Use this key in your application by passing it with the **key=API_KEY** parameter.

Your API key

AIzaSyCFjcw5pqbjCub5ENTcF2h`

⚠ Restrict your key to prevent unauthorized use in production.

CLOSE   RESTRICT KEY

Figure 68-2

Copy this key, return to Android Studio and paste the API key into the *YOUR_KEY_HERE* section of the file:

```
<string name="google_maps_key"
templateMergeStrategy="preserve" translatable="false">YOUR_KEY_HERE</string>
```

68.4 Testing the Application

Perform a test run of the application to verify that the API key is correctly configured. Assuming that the configuration is correct, the application will run and display a map on the screen.

In the event that a map is not displayed, check the following areas:

- If the application is running on an emulator, make sure that the emulator is running a version of Android that includes the Google APIs. The current operating system can be changed for an AVD configuration by selecting the *Tools -> Android -> AVD Manager* menu option, clicking on the pencil icon in the *Actions* column of the AVD followed by the *Change...* button next to the current Android version. Within the system image dialog, select a target which includes the Google APIs.

- Check the Logcat output for any areas relating to authentication problems with regard to the Google Maps API. This usually means the API key was entered incorrectly or that the application package name does not match that specified when the API key was generated.

- Verify within the Google API Console that the *Google Maps Android API* has been enabled in the Services panel.

68.5 Understanding Geocoding and Reverse Geocoding

It is impossible to talk about maps and geographical locations without first covering the subject of Geocoding. Geocoding can best be described as the process of converting a textual based geographical location (such as a street address) into geographical coordinates expressed in terms of longitude and latitude.

Geocoding can be achieved using the Android Geocoder class. An instance of the Geocoder class can, for example, be passed a string representing a location such as a city name, street address or airport code. The Geocoder will attempt to find a match for the location and return a list of Address objects that potentially match the location string, ranked in order with the closest match at position 0 in the list. A variety of information can then be extracted from the Address objects, including the longitude and latitude of the potential matches.

The following code, for example, requests the location of the National Air and Space Museum in Washington, D.C.:

```
import java.io.IOException;
import java.util.List;
```

```
import android.location.Address;
import android.location.Geocoder;
   .

   .

   .

double latitude;
double longitude;

List<Address> geocodeMatches = null;

try {
        geocodeMatches =
            new Geocoder(this).getFromLocationName(
                "600 Independence Ave SW, Washington, DC 20560", 1);
    } catch (IOException e) {
            // TODO Auto-generated catch block
            e.printStackTrace();
}

if (!geocodeMatches.isEmpty())
{
        latitude = geocodeMatches.get(0).getLatitude();
        longitude = geocodeMatches.get(0).getLongitude();
}
```

Note that the value of 1 is passed through as the second argument to the *getFromLocationName()* method. This simply tells the Geocoder to return only one result in the array. Given the specific nature of the address provided, there should only be one potential match. For more vague location names, however, it may be necessary to request more potential matches and allow the user to choose the correct one.

The above code is an example of *forward-geocoding* in that coordinates are calculated based on a text location description. *Reverse-geocoding*, as the name suggests, involves the translation of geographical coordinates into a human readable address string. Consider, for example, the following code:

```
import java.io.IOException;
import java.util.List;

import android.location.Address;
import android.location.Geocoder;
   .

   .

   .

List<Address> geocodeMatches = null;
String Address1;
String Address2;
String State;
String Zipcode;
String Country;
```

```
try {
        geocodeMatches =
            new Geocoder(this).getFromLocation(38.8874245, -77.0200729, 1);
} catch (IOException e) {
        // TODO Auto-generated catch block
        e.printStackTrace();
}

if (!geocodeMatches.isEmpty())
{
        Address1 = geocodeMatches.get(0).getAddressLine(0);
        Address2 = geocodeMatches.get(0).getAddressLine(1);
        State = geocodeMatches.get(0).getAdminArea();
        Zipcode = geocodeMatches.get(0).getPostalCode();
        Country = geocodeMatches.get(0).getCountryName();
}
```

In this case the Geocoder object is initialized with latitude and longitude values via the *getFromLocation()* method. Once again, only a single matching result is requested. The text based address information is then extracted from the resulting Address object.

It should be noted that the geocoding is not actually performed on the Android device, but rather on a server to which the device connects when a translation is required and the results subsequently returned when the translation is complete. As such, geocoding can only take place when the device has an active internet connection.

68.6 Adding a Map to an Application

The simplest way to add a map to an application is to specify it in the user interface layout XML file for an activity. The following example layout file shows the SupportMapFragment instance added to the *activity_map_demo.xml* file created by Android Studio:

```
<fragment xmlns:android="http://schemas.android.com/apk/res/android"
    xmlns:tools="http://schemas.android.com/tools"
    android:layout_width="match_parent"
    android:layout_height="match_parent"
    android:id="@+id/map"
    tools:context=".MapDemoActivity"
    android:name="com.google.android.gms.maps.SupportMapFragment"/>
```

68.7 Requesting Current Location Permission

As outlined in the chapter entitled *"Making Runtime Permission Requests in Android"*, certain permissions are categorized as being dangerous and require special handing for Android 6.0 or later. One such permission gives applications the ability to identify the user's current location. By default, Android Studio has placed a location permission request within the *AndroidManifest.xml*. Locate this file located under *app -> manifests* in the Project tool window and locate the following permission line:

```
<uses-permission
        android:name="android.permission.ACCESS_FINE_LOCATION" />
```

This will ensure that the app is given the opportunity to provide permission for the app to obtain location information at the point that the app is installed on older versions of Android, but to fully support Android 6.0 or later, the app must also specifically request this permission at runtime. To achieve this, some code needs to be added to the *MapDemoActivity.java* file.

Begin by adding some import directives and a constant to act as the permission request code:

```
package com.ebookfrenzy.mapdemo;
.
.
import android.support.v4.content.ContextCompat;
import android.support.v4.app.ActivityCompat;
import android.Manifest;
import android.widget.Toast;
import android.content.pm.PackageManager;
.
.
public class MapDemoActivity extends FragmentActivity implements
OnMapReadyCallback {

    private static final int LOCATION_REQUEST_CODE = 101;
    private GoogleMap mMap;
.
.
}
```

Next, a method needs to be added to the class to request a specified permission from the user. Remaining within the *MapDemoActivity.java* class file, implement this method as follows:

```
protected void requestPermission(String permissionType,
                                 int requestCode) {

    ActivityCompat.requestPermissions(this,
            new String[]{permissionType}, requestCode
    );
}
```

When the user has responded to the permission request, the *onRequestPermissionsResult()* method will be called on the activity. Remaining in the *MapDemoActivity.java* file, implement this method now so that it reads as follows:

```
@Override
public void onRequestPermissionsResult(int requestCode,
                String permissions[], int[] grantResults) {

    switch (requestCode) {
        case LOCATION_REQUEST_CODE: {

            if (grantResults.length == 0
                    || grantResults[0] !=
                    PackageManager.PERMISSION_GRANTED) {
```

```
            Toast.makeText(this,
                "Unable to show location - permission required",
                        Toast.LENGTH_LONG).show();
        } else {

            SupportMapFragment mapFragment =
                (SupportMapFragment) getSupportFragmentManager()
                        .findFragmentById(R.id.map);
            mapFragment.getMapAsync(this);
        }
    }
}
}
```

If permission has not been granted by the user, the app displays a message indicating that the current location cannot be displayed. If, on the other hand, permission was granted, the map is refreshed to provide an opportunity for the location marker to be displayed.

68.8 Displaying the User's Current Location

Once the appropriate permission has been granted, the user's current location may be displayed on the map by obtaining a reference to the GoogleMap object associated with the displayed map and calling the *setMyLocationEnabled()* method of that instance, passing through a value of *true*.

When the map is ready to display, the *onMapReady()* method of the activity is called. This method will also be called when the map is refreshed within the *onRequestPermissionsResult()* method above. By default, Android Studio has implemented this method and added some code to orient the map over Australia with a marker positioned over the city of Sidney. Locate and edit the *onMapReady()* method in the *MapDemoActivity.java* file to remove this template code and to add code to check the location permission has been granted before enabling display of the user's current location. If permission has not been granted, a request is made to the user via a call to the previously added *requestPermission()* method:

```
@Override
public void onMapReady(GoogleMap googleMap) {
    mMap = googleMap;

    // Add a marker in Sydney and move the camera
    LatLng sydney = new LatLng(-34, 151);
    mMap.addMarker(new MarkerOptions().position(sydney).title("Marker in
Sydney"));
    mMap.moveCamera(CameraUpdateFactory.newLatLng(sydney));

    if (mMap != null) {
        int permission = ContextCompat.checkSelfPermission(this,
                Manifest.permission.ACCESS_FINE_LOCATION);

        if (permission == PackageManager.PERMISSION_GRANTED) {
            mMap.setMyLocationEnabled(true);
        } else {
                requestPermission(
```

```
        Manifest.permission.ACCESS_FINE_LOCATION,
            LOCATION_REQUEST_CODE);
        }
    }
}
```

When the app is now run, the dialog shown in Figure 68-3 will appear requesting location permission. If permission is granted, a blue dot will appear on the map indicating the current location of the device.

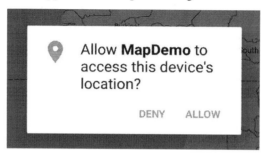

Figure 68-3

68.9 Changing the Map Type

The type of map displayed can be modified dynamically by making a call to the *setMapType()* method of the corresponding GoogleMap object, passing through one of the following values:

· **GoogleMap.MAP_TYPE_NONE** – An empty grid with no mapping tiles displayed.

· **GoogleMap.MAP_TYPE_NORMAL** – The standard view consisting of the classic road map.

· **GoogleMap.MAP_TYPE_SATELLITE** – Displays the satellite imagery of the map region.

· **GoogleMap.MAP_TYPE_HYBRID** – Displays satellite imagery with the road maps superimposed.

· **GoogleMap.MAP_TYPE_TERRAIN** – Displays topographical information such as contour lines and colors.

The following code change to the *onMapReady()* method, for example, switches a map to Satellite mode:

```
.
.
if (mMap != null) {
    int permission = ContextCompat.checkSelfPermission(
            this, Manifest.permission.ACCESS_FINE_LOCATION);

    if (permission == PackageManager.PERMISSION_GRANTED) {
        mMap.setMyLocationEnabled(true);
    } else {
        requestPermission(Manifest.permission.ACCESS_FINE_LOCATION,
                LOCATION_REQUEST_CODE);
    }
    mMap.setMapType(GoogleMap.MAP_TYPE_SATELLITE);
}
.
.
```

Alternatively, the map type may be specified in the XML layout file in which the map is embedded using the *map:mapType* property together with a value of *none, normal, hybrid, satellite* or *terrain*. For example:

```
<?xml version="1.0" encoding="utf-8"?>
<fragment xmlns:android="http://schemas.android.com/apk/res/android"
          xmlns:map="http://schemas.android.com/apk/res-auto"
          android:id="@+id/map"
          android:layout_width="match_parent"
          android:layout_height="match_parent"
          map:mapType="hybrid"
          android:name="com.google.android.gms.maps.SupportMapFragment"/>
```

68.10 Displaying Map Controls to the User

The Google Maps Android API provides a number of controls that may be optionally displayed to the user consisting of zoom in and out buttons, a "my location" button and a compass.

Whether or not the zoom and compass controls are displayed may be controlled either programmatically or within the map element in XML layout resources. In order to configure the controls programmatically, a reference to the UiSettings object associated with the GoogleMap object must be obtained:

```
import com.google.android.gms.maps.UiSettings;
    .
    .
    .
UiSettings mapSettings;
mapSettings = mMap.getUiSettings();
```

The zoom controls are enabled and disabled via the calls to the *setZoomControlsEnabled()* method of the UiSettings object. For example:

```
mapSettings.setZoomControlsEnabled(true);
```

Alternatively, the *map:uiZoomControls* property may be set within the map element of the XML resource file:

```
map:uiZoomControls="false"
```

The compass may be displayed either via a call to the *setCompassEnabled()* method of the UiSettings instance, or through XML resources using the *map:uiCompass* property. Note the compass icon only appears when the map camera is tilted or rotated away from the default orientation.

The "My Location" button will only appear when *My Location* mode is enabled as outlined earlier in this chapter. The button may be prevented from appearing even when in this mode via a call to the *setMyLocationButtonEnabled()* method of the UiSettings instance.

68.11 Handling Map Gesture Interaction

The Google Maps Android API is capable of responding to a number of different user interactions. These interactions can be used to change the area of the map displayed, the zoom level and even the angle of view (such that a 3D representation of the map area is displayed for certain cities).

68.11.1 Map Zooming Gestures

Support for gestures relating to zooming in and out of a map may be enabled or disabled using the *setZoomGesturesEnabled()* method of the UiSettings object associated with the GoogleMap instance. For example, the following code disables zoom gestures for our example map:

```
UiSettings mapSettings;
mapSettings = map.getUiSettings();
mapSettings.setZoomGesturesEnabled(false);
```

The same result can be achieved within an XML resource file by setting the *map:uiZoomGestures* property to true or false.

When enabled, zooming will occur when the user makes pinching gestures on the screen. Similarly, a double tap will zoom in while a two finger tap will zoom out. One finger zooming gestures, on the other hand, are performed by tapping twice but not releasing the second tap and then sliding the finger up and down on the screen to zoom in and out respectively.

68.11.2 Map Scrolling/Panning Gestures

A scrolling, or panning gesture allows the user to move around the map by dragging the map around the screen with a single finger motion. Scrolling gestures may be enabled within code via a call to the *setScrollGesturesEnabled()* method of the UiSettings instance:

```
UiSettings mapSettings;
mapSettings = mMap.getUiSettings();
mapSettings.setScrollGesturesEnabled(true);
```

Alternatively, scrolling on a map instance may be enabled in an XML resource layout file using the *map:uiScrollGestures* property.

68.11.3 Map Tilt Gestures

Tilt gestures allow the user to tilt the angle of projection of the map by placing two fingers on the screen and moving them up and down to adjust the tilt angle. Tilt gestures may be enabled or disabled via a call to the *setTiltGesturesEnabled()* method of the UiSettings instance, for example:

```
UiSettings mapSettings;
mapSettings = mMap.getUiSettings();
mapSettings.setTiltGesturesEnabled(true);
```

Tilt gestures may also be enabled and disabled using the *map:uiTiltGestures* property in an XML layout resource file.

68.11.4 Map Rotation Gestures

By placing two fingers on the screen and rotating them in a circular motion, the user may rotate the orientation of a map when map rotation gestures are enabled. This gesture support is enabled and disabled in code via a call to the *setRotateGesturesEnabled()* method of the UiSettings instance, for example:

```
UiSettings mapSettings;
mapSettings = mMap.getUiSettings();
mapSettings.setRotateGesturesEnabled(true);
```

Rotation gestures may also be enabled or disabled using the *map:uiRotateGestures* property in an XML layout resource file.

68.12 Creating Map Markers

Markers are used to notify the user of locations on a map and take the form of either a standard or custom icon. Markers may also include a title and optional text (referred to as a snippet) and may be configured such that they can be dragged to different locations on the map by the user. When tapped by the user an *info window* will appear displaying additional information about the marker location.

Markers are represented by instances of the Marker class and are added to a map via a call to the *addMarker()* method of the corresponding GoogleMap object. Passed through as an argument to this method is a MarkerOptions class instance containing the various options required for the marker such as the title and snippet text. The location of a marker is defined by specifying latitude and longitude values, also included as part of the MarkerOptions instance. For example, the following code adds a marker including a title, snippet and a position to a specific location on the map:

```
import com.google.android.gms.maps.model.Marker;
import com.google.android.gms.maps.model.LatLng;
import com.google.android.gms.maps.model.MarkerOptions;
.
.
.
LatLng position = new LatLng(38.8874245, -77.0200729);
Marker museum = mMap.addMarker(new MarkerOptions()
                .position(position)
                .title("Museum")
                .snippet("National Air and Space Museum"));
```

When executed, the above code will mark the location specified which, when tapped, will display an info window containing the title and snippet as shown in Figure 68-4:

Figure 68-4

68.13 Controlling the Map Camera

Because Android device screens are flat and the world is a sphere, the Google Maps Android API uses the Mercator projection to represent the earth on a flat surface. The default view of the map is presented to the user as though through a *camera* suspended above the map and pointing directly down at the map. The Google Maps Android API allows the *target, zoom, bearing* and *tilt* of this camera to be changed in real-time from within the application:

- **Target** – The location of the center of the map within the device display specified in terms of longitude and latitude.

- **Zoom** – The zoom level of the camera specified in levels. Increasing the zoom level by 1.0 doubles the width of the amount of the map displayed.

- **Tilt** – The viewing angle of the camera specified as a position on an arc spanning directly over the center of the viewable map area measured in degrees from the top of the arc (this being the nadir of the arc where the camera points directly down to the map).

- **Bearing** – The orientation of the map in degrees measured in a clockwise direction from North.

Camera changes are made by creating an instance of the CameraUpdate class with the appropriate settings. CameraUpdate instances are created by making method calls to the *CameraUpdateFactory* class. Once a CameraUpdate instance has been created, it is applied to the map via a call to the *moveCamera()* method of the GoogleMap instance. To obtain a smooth animated effect as the camera changes, the *animateCamera()* method may be called instead of *moveCamera()*.

A summary of CameraUpdateFactory methods is as follows:

- **CameraUpdateFactory.zoomIn()** – Provides a CameraUpdate instance zoomed in by one level.

- **CameraUpdateFactory.zoomOut()** - Provides a CameraUpdate instance zoomed out by one level.

- **CameraUpdateFactory.zoomTo(float)** - Generates a CameraUpdate instance that changes the zoom level to the specified value.

- **CameraUpdateFactory.zoomBy(float)** – Provides a CameraUpdate instance with a zoom level increased or decreased by the specified amount.

- **CameraUpdateFactory.zoomBy(float, Point)** - Creates a CameraUpdate instance that increases or decreases the zoom level by the specified value.

- **CameraUpdateFactory.newLatLng(LatLng)** - Creates a CameraUpdate instance that changes the camera's target latitude and longitude.

- **CameraUpdateFactory.newLatLngZoom(LatLng, float)** - Generates a CameraUpdate instance that changes the camera's latitude, longitude and zoom.

- **CameraUpdateFactory.newCameraPosition(CameraPosition)** - Returns a CameraUpdate instance that moves the camera to the specified position. A CameraPosition instance can be obtained using CameraPosition. Builder().

The following code, for example, zooms in the camera by one level using animation:

```
mMap.animateCamera(CameraUpdateFactory.zoomIn());
```

The following code, on the other hand, moves the camera to a new location and adjusts the zoom level to 10 without animation:

```
private static final LatLng position =
        new LatLng(38.8874245, -77.0200729);


mMap.moveCamera(CameraUpdateFactory.newLatLngZoom(position, 10));
```

Finally, the next code example uses *CameraPosition.Builder()* to create a CameraPosition object with changes to the target, zoom, bearing and tilt. This change is then applied to the camera using animation:

```
import com.google.android.gms.maps.model.CameraPosition;
import com.google.android.gms.maps.CameraUpdateFactory;
.
.
CameraPosition cameraPosition = new CameraPosition.Builder()
    .target(position)
    .zoom(50)
    .bearing(70)
    .tilt(25)
    .build();
mMap.animateCamera(CameraUpdateFactory.newCameraPosition(
                        cameraPosition));
```

68.14 Summary

This chapter has provided an overview of the key classes and methods that make up the Google Maps Android API and outlined the steps involved in preparing both the development environment and an application project to make use of the API.

69. Printing with the Android Printing Framework

With the introduction of the Android 4.4 KitKat release, it became possible to print content from within Android applications. While subsequent chapters will explore in more detail the options for adding printing support to your own applications, this chapter will focus on the various printing options now available in Android and the steps involved in enabling those options. Having covered these initial topics, the chapter will then provide an overview of the various printing features that are available to Android developers in terms of building printing support into applications.

69.1 The Android Printing Architecture

Printing in Android 4.4 and later is provided by the Printing framework. In basic terms, this framework consists of a Print Manager and a number of print service plugins. It is the responsibility of the Print Manager to handle the print requests from applications on the device and to interact with the print service plugins that are installed on the device, thereby ensuring that print requests are fulfilled. By default, many Android devices have print service plugins installed to enable printing using the Google Cloud Print and Google Drive services. Print Services Plugin for other printer types, if not already installed, may also be obtained from the Google Play store. Print Service Plugins are currently available for HP, Epson, Samsung and Canon printers and plugins from other printer manufactures will most likely be released in the near future though the Google Cloud Print service plugin can also be used to print from an Android device to just about any printer type and model. For the purposes of this book, we will use the HP Print Services Plugin as a reference example.

69.2 The Print Service Plugins

The purpose of the Print Service plugins is to enable applications to print to compatible printers that are visible to the Android device via a local area wireless network or Bluetooth. Print Service plugins are currently available for a wide range of printer brands including HP, Samsung, Brother, Canon, Lexmark and Xerox.

The presence of the Print Service Plugin on an Android device can be verified by loading the Google Play app and performing a search for "Print Services Plugin". Once the plugin is listed in the Play Store, and in the event that the plugin is not already installed, it can be installed by selecting the *Install* button. Figure 69-1, for example, shows the HP Print Service plugin within Google Play.

The Print Services plugins will automatically detect compatible HP printers on the network to which the Android device is currently connected and list them as options when printing from an application.

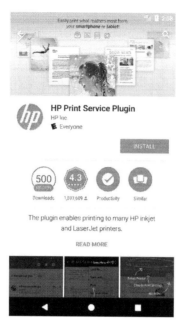

Figure 69-1

69.3 Google Cloud Print

Google Cloud Print is a service provided by Google that enables you to print content onto your own printer over the web from anywhere with internet connectivity. Google Cloud Print supports a wide range of devices and printer models in the form of both *Cloud Ready* and *Classic* printers. A Cloud Ready printer has technology built-in that enables printing via the web. Manufacturers that provide cloud ready printers include Brother, Canon, Dell, Epson, HP, Kodak and Samsung. To identify if your printer is both cloud ready and supported by Google Cloud Print, review the list of printers at the following URL:

https://www.google.com/cloudprint/learn/printers.html

In the case of classic, non-Cloud Ready printers, Google Cloud Print provides support for cloud printing through the installation of software on the computer system to which the classic printer is connected (either directly or over a home or office network).

To set up Google Cloud Print, visit the following web page and login using the same Google account ID that you use when logging in to your Android devices:

https://www.google.com/cloudprint/learn/index.html

Once printers have been added to your Google Cloud Print account, they will be listed as printer destination options when you print from within Android applications on your devices.

69.4 Printing to Google Drive

In addition to supporting physical printers, it is also possible to save printed output to your Google Drive account. When printing from a device, select the *Save to Google Drive* option in the printing panel. The content to be printed will then be converted to a PDF file and saved to the Google Drive cloud-based storage associated with the currently active Google Account ID on the device.

69.5 Save as PDF

The final printing option provided by Android allows the printed content to be saved locally as a PDF file on the Android device. Once selected, this option will request a name for the PDF file and a location on the device into which the document is to be saved.

Both the Save as PDF and Google Drive options can be invaluable in terms of saving paper when testing the printing functionality of your own Android applications.

69.6 Printing from Android Devices

Google recommends that applications which provide the ability to print content do so by placing the print option in the Overflow menu (a topic covered in some detail in the chapter entitled *"Creating and Managing Overflow Menus on Android"*). A number of applications bundled with Android now include "Print…" menu options. Figure 69-2, for example, shows the Print option accessed by selecting the "Share…" option in the Overflow menu of the Chrome browser application:

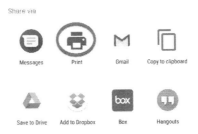

Figure 69-2

Once the print option has been selected from within an application, the standard Android print screen will appear showing a preview of the content to be printed as illustrated in Figure 69-3:

Figure 69-3

Tapping the panel along the top of the screen will display the full range of printing options:

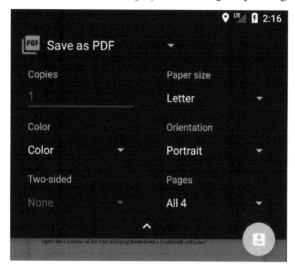

Figure 69-4

The Android print panel provides the usual printing options such as paper size, color, orientation and number of copies. Other print destination options may be accessed by tapping on the current printer or PDF output selection.

69.7 Options for Building Print Support into Android Apps

The Printing framework introduced into the Android 4.4 SDK provides a number of options for incorporating print support into Android applications. These options can be categorized as follows:

69.7.1 Image Printing

As the name suggests, this option allows image printing to be incorporated into Android applications. When adding this feature to an application, the first step is to create a new instance of the PrintHelper class:

```
PrintHelper imagePrinter = new PrintHelper(context);
```

Next, the scale mode for the printed image may be specified via a call to the *setScaleMode()* method of the PrintHelper instance. Options are as follows:

- **SCALE_MODE_FIT** – The image will be scaled to fit within the paper size without any cropping or changes to aspect ratio. This will typically result in white space appearing in one dimension.

- **SCALE_MODE_FILL** – The image will be scaled to fill the paper size with cropping performed where necessary to avoid the appearance of white space in the printed output.

In the absence of a scale mode setting, the system will default to SCALE_MODE_FILL. The following code, for example, sets scale to fit mode on the previously declared PrintHelper instance:

```
imagePrinter.setScaleMode(PrintHelper.SCALE_MODE_FIT);
```

Similarly, the color mode may also be configured to indicate whether the print output is to be in color or black and white. This is achieved by passing one of the following options through to the *setColorMode()* method of the PrintHelper instance:

- **COLOR_MODE_COLOR** – Indicates that the image is to be printed in color.

- **COLOR_MODE_MONOCHROME** – Indicates that the image is to be printed in black and white.

The printing framework will default to color printing unless the monochrome option is specified as follows:

```
imagePrinter.setColorMode(PrintHelper.COLOR_MODE_MONOCHROME);
```

All that is required to complete the printing operation is an image to be printed and a call to the *printBitmap()* method of the PrintHelper instance, passing through a string representing the name to be assigned to the print job and a reference to the image (in the form of either a Bitmap object or a Uri reference to the image):

```
Bitmap bitmap = BitmapFactory.decodeResource(getResources(),
            R.drawable.oceanscene);
imagePrinter.printBitmap("My Test Print Job", bitmap);
```

Once the print job has been started, the Printing framework will display the print dialog and handle both the subsequent interaction with the user and the printing of the image on the user-selected print destination.

69.7.2 Creating and Printing HTML Content

The Android Printing framework also provides an easy way to print HTML based content from within an application. This content can either be in the form of HTML content referenced by the URL of a page hosted on a web site, or HTML content that is dynamically created within the application.

To enable HTML printing, the WebView class has been extended in Android 4.4 to include support for printing with minimal coding requirements.

When dynamically creating HTML content (as opposed to loading and printing an existing web page) the process involves the creation of a WebView object and associating with it a WebViewClient instance. The web view client is then configured to start a print job when the HTML has finished being loaded into the WebView. With the web view client configured, the HTML is then loaded into the WebView, at which point the print process is triggered.

Consider, for example, the following code:

```
public void printContent()
{
        WebView webView = new WebView(this);
        webView.setWebViewClient(new WebViewClient() {

            public boolean shouldOverrideUrlLoading(WebView view,
                    String url)
            {
                return false;
            }

            @Override
            public void onPageFinished(WebView view, String url) {
                    createWebPrintJob(view);
                    myWebView = null;
                }
        });

        String htmlDocument =
```

```
                    "<html><body><h1>Android Print Test</h1><p>"
             + "This is some sample content.</p></body></html>";


        webView.loadDataWithBaseURL(null, htmlDocument,
                    "text/HTML", "UTF-8", null);


        myWebView = webView;
}
```

The code in this method begins by declaring a variable named *myWebView* in which will be stored a reference to the WebView instance created in the method. Within the *printContent()* method, an instance of the WebView class is created to which a WebViewClient instance is then assigned.

The WebViewClient assigned to the web view object is configured to indicate that loading of the HTML content is to be handled by the WebView instance (by returning *false* from the *shouldOverrideUrlLoading()*) method. More importantly, an *onPageFinished()* handler method is declared and implemented to call a method named *createWebPrintJob()*. The *onPageFinished()* callback method will be called automatically when all of the HTML content has been loaded into the web view. This ensures that the print job is not started until the content is ready, thereby ensuring that all of the content is printed.

Next, a string is created containing some HTML to serve as the content. This is then loaded into the web view. Once the HTML is loaded, the *onPageFinished()* method will trigger. Finally, the method stores a reference to the web view object. Without this vital step, there is a significant risk that the Java runtime system will assume that the application no longer needs the web view object and will discard it to free up memory (a concept referred to in Java terminology as *garbage collection*) resulting in the print job terminating prior to completion.

All that remains in this example is to implement the *createWebPrintJob()* method as follows:

```
private void createWebPrintJob(WebView webView) {

        PrintManager printManager = (PrintManager) this
                    .getSystemService(Context.PRINT_SERVICE);

        PrintDocumentAdapter printAdapter =
                    webView.createPrintDocumentAdapter("MyDocument");
        String jobName = getString(R.string.app_name) + " Document";

        PrintJob printJob = printManager.print(jobName, printAdapter,
                    new PrintAttributes.Builder().build());
}
```

This method simply obtains a reference to the PrintManager service and instructs the web view instance to create a print adapter. A new string is created to store the name of the print job (which in this is case based on the name of the application and the word "Document").

Finally, the print job is started by calling the *print()* method of the print manager, passing through the job name, print adapter and a set of default print attributes. If required, the print attributes could be customized to specify resolution (dots per inch), margin and color options.

69.7.3 Printing a Web Page

The steps involved in printing a web page are similar to those outlined above, with the exception that the web view is passed the URL of the web page to be printed in place of the dynamically created HTML, for example:

```
webView.loadUrl("http://developer.android.com/google/index.html");
```

It is also important to note that the WebViewClient configuration is only necessary if a web page is to automatically print as soon as it has loaded. If the printing is to be initiated by the user selecting a menu option after the page has loaded, only the code in the *createWebPrintJob()* method outlined above need be included in the application code. The next chapter, entitled *"An Android HTML and Web Content Printing Example"*, will demonstrate just such a scenario.

69.7.4 Printing a Custom Document

While the HTML and web printing features introduced by the Printing framework provide an easy path to printing content from within an Android application, it is clear that these options will be overly simplistic for more advanced printing requirements. For more complex printing tasks, the Printing framework also provides custom document printing support. This allows content in the form of text and graphics to be drawn onto a canvas and then printed.

Unlike HTML and image printing, which can be implemented with relative ease, custom document printing is a more complex, multi-stage process which will be outlined in the *"A Guide to Android Custom Document Printing"* chapter of this book. These steps can be summarized as follows:

- Connect to the Android Print Manager

- Create a Custom Print Adapter sub-classed from the PrintDocumentAdapter class

- Create a PdfDocument instance to represent the document pages

- Obtain a reference to the pages of the PdfDocument instance, each of which has associated with it a Canvas instance

- Draw the content on the page canvases

- Notify the print framework that the document is ready to print

The custom print adapter outlined in the above steps needs to implement a number of methods which will be called upon by the Android system to perform specific tasks during the printing process. The most important of these are the *onLayout()* method which is responsible for re-arranging the document layout in response to the user changing settings such as paper size or page orientation, and the *onWrite()* method which is responsible for rendering the pages to be printed. This topic will be covered in detail in the chapter entitled *"A Guide to Android Custom Document Printing"*.

69.8 Summary

The Android 4.4 KitKat release introduced the ability to print content from Android devices. Print output can be directed to suitably configured printers, a local PDF file or to the cloud via Google Drive. From the perspective of the Android application developer, these capabilities are available for use in applications by making use of the Printing framework. By far the easiest printing options to implement are those involving content in the form of images and HTML. More advanced printing may, however, be implemented using the custom document printing features of the framework.

70. An Android HTML and Web Content Printing Example

As outlined in the previous chapter, entitled *"An Android HTML and Web Content Printing Example"*, the Android Printing framework can be used to print both web pages and dynamically created HTML content. While there is much similarity in these two approaches to printing, there are also some subtle differences that need to be taken into consideration. This chapter will work through the creation of two example applications in order to bring some clarity to these two printing options.

70.1 Creating the HTML Printing Example Application

Begin this example by launching the Android Studio environment and creating a new project, entering *HTMLPrint* into the Application name field and *ebookfrenzy.com* as the Company Domain setting before clicking on the *Next* button.

On the form factors screen, enable the *Phone and Tablet* option and set the minimum SDK setting to API 21: Android 5.0 (Lollipop). Continue to proceed through the screens, requesting the creation of an Empty Activity named *HTMLPrintActivity* with a corresponding layout named *activity_html_print*.

70.2 Printing Dynamic HTML Content

The first stage of this tutorial is to add code to the project to create some HTML content and send it to the Printing framework in the form of a print job.

Begin by locating the *HTMLPrintActivity.java* file (located in the Project tool window under *app -> java -> com. ebookfrenzy.htmlprint*) and loading it into the editing panel. Once loaded, modify the code so that it reads as outlined in the following listing:

```
package com.ebookfrenzy.htmlprint;

import android.support.v7.app.AppCompatActivity;
import android.os.Bundle;
import android.webkit.WebView;
import android.webkit.WebViewClient;
import android.webkit.WebResourceRequest;
import android.print.PrintAttributes;
import android.print.PrintDocumentAdapter;
import android.print.PrintManager;
import android.content.Context;

public class HTMLPrintActivity extends AppCompatActivity {

    private WebView myWebView;

    @Override
```

```
protected void onCreate(Bundle savedInstanceState) {
    super.onCreate(savedInstanceState);
    setContentView(R.layout.activity_htmlprint);

    printWebView();
}


private void printWebView() {

    WebView webView = new WebView(this);
    webView.setWebViewClient(new WebViewClient() {

        public boolean shouldOverrideUrlLoading(WebView view,
                            WebResourceRequest request)
        {
            return false;
        }

        @Override
        public void onPageFinished(WebView view, String url)
        {
            createWebPrintJob(view);
            myWebView = null;
        }
    });

    String htmlDocument =
        "<html><body><h1>Android Print Test</h1><p>"
        + "This is some sample content.</p></body></html>";

    webView.loadDataWithBaseURL(null, htmlDocument,
            "text/HTML", "UTF-8", null);

    myWebView = webView;
}
}
```

The code changes begin by declaring a variable named *myWebView* in which will be stored a reference to the WebView instance used for the printing operation. Within the *onCreate()* method, an instance of the WebView class is created to which a WebViewClient instance is then assigned.

The WebViewClient assigned to the web view object is configured to indicate that loading of the HTML content is to be handled by the WebView instance (by returning *false* from the *shouldOverrideUrlLoading()* method). More importantly, an *onPageFinished()* handler method is declared and implemented to call a method named *createWebPrintJob()*. The *onPageFinished()* method will be called automatically when all of the HTML content has been loaded into the web view. As outlined in the previous chapter, this step is necessary when printing dynamically created HTML content to ensure that the print job is not started until the content has fully loaded into the WebView.

Next, a String object is created containing some HTML to serve as the content and subsequently loaded into the web view. Once the HTML is loaded, the *onPageFinished()* callback method will trigger. Finally, the method stores a reference to the web view object in the previously declared *myWebView* variable. Without this vital step, there is a significant risk that the Java runtime system will assume that the application no longer needs the web view object and will discard it to free up memory resulting in the print job terminating before completion.

All that remains in this example is to implement the *createWebPrintJob()* method which is currently configured to be called by the *onPageFinished()* callback method. Remaining within the *HTMLPrintActivity.java* file, therefore, implement this method so that it reads as follows:

```
private void createWebPrintJob(WebView webView) {

        PrintManager printManager = (PrintManager) this
                .getSystemService(Context.PRINT_SERVICE);

        PrintDocumentAdapter printAdapter =
                webView.createPrintDocumentAdapter("MyDocument");

        String jobName = getString(R.string.app_name) + " Print Test";

        printManager.print(jobName, printAdapter,
                new PrintAttributes.Builder().build());
}
```

This method obtains a reference to the PrintManager service and instructs the web view instance to create a print adapter. A new string is created to store the name of the print job (in this case based on the name of the application and the word "Print Test").

Finally, the print job is started by calling the *print()* method of the print manager, passing through the job name, print adapter and a set of default print attributes.

Compile and run the application on a device or emulator running Android 5.0 or later. Once launched, the standard Android printing page should appear as illustrated in Figure 70-1.

Figure 70-1

Print to a physical printer if you have one configured, save to Google Drive or, alternatively, select the option to save to a PDF file. Once the print job has been initiated, check the generated output on your chosen destination. Note that when using the Save to PDF option, the system will request a name and location for the PDF file. The *Downloads* folder makes a good option, the contents of which can be viewed by selecting the *Downloads* icon (renamed *Files* on Android 8) located amongst the other app icons on the device.

70.3 Creating the Web Page Printing Example

The second example application to be created in this chapter will provide the user with an Overflow menu option to print the web page currently displayed within a WebView instance. Create a new project in Android Studio, entering *WebPrint* into the Application name field and *ebookfrenzy.com* as the Company Domain setting before clicking on the *Next* button.

On the form factors screen, enable the *Phone and Tablet* option and set the minimum SDK setting to API 21: Android 5.0 (Lollipop). Continue to proceed through the screens, requesting the creation of a Basic Activity (since we will be making use of the context menu provided by the Basic Activity template) named *WebPrintActivity* with the remaining properties set to the default values.

70.4 Removing the Floating Action Button

Selecting the Basic Activity template provided a context menu and a floating action button. Since the floating action button is not required by the app it can be removed before proceeding. Load the *activity_web_print.xml* layout file into the Layout Editor, select the floating action button and tap the keyboard *Delete* key to remove the object from the layout. Edit the *WebPrintActivity.java* file and remove the floating action button code from the onCreate method as follows:

```
@Override
protected void onCreate(Bundle savedInstanceState) {
```

```
super.onCreate(savedInstanceState);
setContentView(R.layout.activity_web_print);
Toolbar toolbar = (Toolbar) findViewById(R.id.toolbar);
setSupportActionBar(toolbar);

FloatingActionButton fab =
        (FloatingActionButton) findViewById(R.id.fab);
fab.setOnClickListener(new View.OnClickListener() {
        @Override
        public void onClick(View view) {
            Snackbar.make(view, "Replace with your own action",
                    Snackbar.LENGTH_LONG)
                    .setAction("Action", null).show();
        }
    });
}
```

70.5 Designing the User Interface Layout

Load the *content_web_print.xml* layout resource file into the Layout Editor tool if it has not already been loaded and, in Design mode, select and delete the "Hello World!" TextView object. From the *Containers* section of the palette, drag and drop a WebView object onto the center of the device screen layout. Using the Attributes tool window, change the layout_width and layout_height properties of the WebView to *match_constraint* so that it fills the entire layout canvas as outlined in Figure 70-2:

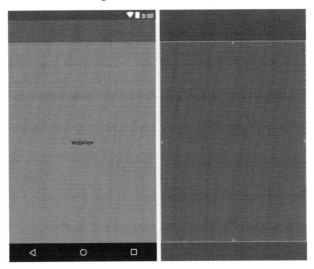

Figure 70-2

Select the newly added WebView instance and change the ID of the view to *myWebView*.

Before proceeding to the next step of this tutorial, an additional permission needs to be added to the project to enable the WebView object to access the internet and download a web page for printing. Add this permission by locating the *AndroidManifest.xml* file in the Project tool window and double-clicking on it to load it into the editing panel. Once loaded, edit the XML content to add the appropriate permission line as shown in the following listing:

```xml
<?xml version="1.0" encoding="utf-8"?>
<manifest xmlns:android="http://schemas.android.com/apk/res/android"
    package="com.ebookfrenzy.webprint" >

    <uses-permission android:name="android.permission.INTERNET" />

    <application
        android:allowBackup="true"
        android:icon="@mipmap/ic_launcher"
        android:label="@string/app_name"
        android:supportsRtl="true"
        android:theme="@style/AppTheme" >
        <activity
            android:name=".WebPrintActivity"
            android:label="@string/app_name"
            android:theme="@style/AppTheme.NoActionBar" >
            <intent-filter>
                <action android:name="android.intent.action.MAIN" />

                <category android:name=
                        "android.intent.category.LAUNCHER" />
            </intent-filter>
        </activity>
    </application>

</manifest>
```

70.6 Loading the Web Page into the WebView

Before the web page can be printed, it needs to be loaded into the WebView instance. For the purposes of this tutorial, this will be performed by a call to the *loadUrl()* method of the WebView instance, which will be placed in a method named *configureWebView()* and called from within the *onCreate()* method of the WebPrintActivity class. Edit the *WebPrintActivity.java* file, therefore, and modify it as follows:

```java
package com.ebookfrenzy.webprint;

import android.os.Bundle;
import android.support.v7.app.AppCompatActivity;
import android.support.v7.widget.Toolbar;
import android.view.Menu;
import android.view.MenuItem;
import android.webkit.WebView;
import android.webkit.WebViewClient;
import android.webkit.WebResourceRequest;

public class WebPrintActivity extends AppCompatActivity {

    private WebView myWebView;
```

```
@Override
protected void onCreate(Bundle savedInstanceState) {
    super.onCreate(savedInstanceState);
    setContentView(R.layout.activity_web_print);
    Toolbar toolbar = (Toolbar) findViewById(R.id.toolbar);
    setSupportActionBar(toolbar);

    configureWebView();
}


private void configureWebView() {

    myWebView = (WebView) findViewById(R.id.myWebView);
    myWebView.setWebViewClient(new WebViewClient(){
        @Override
        public boolean shouldOverrideUrlLoading(
                WebView view, WebResourceRequest request) {
            return super.shouldOverrideUrlLoading(
                    view, request);
        }
    });
    myWebView.getSettings().setJavaScriptEnabled(true);
    myWebView.loadUrl(
            "https://developer.android.com/google/index.html");


}
.
.
}
```

70.7 Adding the Print Menu Option

The option to print the web page will now be added to the Overflow menu using the techniques outlined in the chapter entitled *"Creating and Managing Overflow Menus on Android"*.

The first requirement is a string resource with which to label the menu option. Within the Project tool window, locate the *app -> res -> values -> strings.xml* file, double-click on it to load it into the editor and modify it to add a new string resource:

```
<resources>
    <string name="app_name">WebPrint</string>
    <string name="action_settings">Settings</string>
    <string name="print_string">Print</string>
</resources>
```

Next, load the *app -> res -> menu -> menu_web_print.xml* file into the menu editor, switch to Text mode and replace the *Settings* menu option with the print option:

```
<menu xmlns:android="http://schemas.android.com/apk/res/android"
```

```
        xmlns:tools="http://schemas.android.com/tools"
        tools:context="com.ebookfrenzy.webprint.WebPrintActivity" >
        <item android:id="@+id/action_settings"
            android:title="@string/action_settings"
            android:orderInCategory="100"
            app:showAsAction="never" />


    <item
        android:id="@+id/action_print"
        android:orderInCategory="100"
        app:showAsAction="never"
        android:title="@string/print_string"/>
```

```
</menu>
```

All that remains in terms of configuring the menu option is to modify the *onOptionsItemSelected()* handler method within the *WebPrintActivity.java* file:

```
@Override
public boolean onOptionsItemSelected(MenuItem item) {
    int id = item.getItemId();
    if (id == R.id.action_print) {
        createWebPrintJob(myWebView);
        return true;
    }
    return super.onOptionsItemSelected(item);
}
```

With the *onOptionsItemSelected()* method implemented, the activity will call a method named *createWebPrintJob()* when the print menu option is selected from the overflow menu. The implementation of this method is identical to that used in the previous HTMLPrint project and may now be added to the *WebPrintActivity.java* file such that it reads as follows:

```
package com.ebookfrenzy.webprint;


import android.os.Bundle;
import android.support.v7.app.AppCompatActivity;
import android.support.v7.widget.Toolbar;
import android.view.Menu;
import android.view.MenuItem;
import android.webkit.WebView;
import android.webkit.WebViewClient;
import android.webkit.WebResourceRequest;
import android.print.PrintAttributes;
import android.print.PrintDocumentAdapter;
import android.print.PrintManager;
import android.content.Context;


public class WebPrintActivity extends AppCompatActivity {
```

```
    private WebView myWebView;
.
.
    private void createWebPrintJob(WebView webView) {

        PrintManager printManager = (PrintManager) this
                .getSystemService(Context.PRINT_SERVICE);

        PrintDocumentAdapter printAdapter =
                webView.createPrintDocumentAdapter("MyDocument");

        String jobName = getString(R.string.app_name) +
                " Print Test";

        printManager.print(jobName, printAdapter,
                new PrintAttributes.Builder().build());
    }
.
.
.
}
```

With the code changes complete, run the application on a physical Android device or emulator running Android version 5.0 or later. Once successfully launched, the WebView should be visible with the designated web page loaded. Once the page has loaded, select the Print option from the Overflow menu (Figure 70-3) and use the resulting print panel to print the web page to a suitable destination.

Figure 70-3

70.8 Summary

The Android Printing framework includes extensions to the WebView class that make it possible to print HTML based content from within an Android application. This content can be in the form of HTML created dynamically within the application at runtime, or a pre-existing web page loaded into a WebView instance. In the case of dynamically created HTML, it is important to use a WebViewClient instance to ensure that printing does not start until the HTML has been fully loaded into the WebView.

71. A Guide to Android Custom Document Printing

As we have seen in the preceding chapters, the Android Printing framework makes it relatively easy to build printing support into applications as long as the content is in the form of an image or HTML markup. More advanced printing requirements can be met by making use of the custom document printing feature of the Printing framework.

71.1 An Overview of Android Custom Document Printing

In simplistic terms, custom document printing uses canvases to represent the pages of the document to be printed. The application draws the content to be printed onto these canvases in the form of shapes, colors, text and images. In actual fact, the canvases are represented by instances of the Android Canvas class, thereby providing access to a rich selection of drawing options. Once all the pages have been drawn, the document is then printed.

While this sounds simple enough, there are actually a number of steps that need to be performed to make this happen, which can be summarized as follows:

- Implement a custom print adapter sub-classed from the PrintDocumentAdapter class

- Obtain a reference to the Print Manager Service

- Create an instance of the PdfDocument class in which to store the document pages

- Add pages to the PdfDocument in the form of PdfDocument.Page instances

- Obtain references to the Canvas objects associated with the document pages

- Draw content onto the canvases

- Write the PDF document to a destination output stream provided by the Printing framework

- Notify the Printing framework that the document is ready to print

In this chapter, an overview of these steps will be provided, followed by a detailed tutorial designed to demonstrate the implementation of custom document printing within Android applications.

71.1.1 Custom Print Adapters

The role of the print adapter is to provide the Printing framework with the content to be printed, and to ensure that it is formatted correctly for the user's chosen preferences (taking into consideration factors such as paper size and page orientation).

When printing HTML and images, much of this work is performed by the print adapters provided as part of the Android Printing framework and designed for these specific printing tasks. When printing a web page, for example, a print adapter is created for us when a call is made to the *createPrintDocumentAdapter()* method of an instance of the WebView class.

In the case of custom document printing, however, it is the responsibility of the application developer to design the print adapter and implement the code to draw and format the content in preparation for printing.

Custom print adapters are created by sub-classing the PrintDocumentAdapter class and overriding a set of callback methods within that class which will be called by the Printing framework at various stages in the print process. These callback methods can be summarized as follows:

- **onStart()** – This method is called when the printing process begins and is provided so that the application code has an opportunity to perform any necessary tasks in preparation for creating the print job. Implementation of this method within the PrintDocumentAdapter sub-class is optional.

- **onLayout()** – This callback method is called after the call to the *onStart()* method and then again each time the user makes changes to the print settings (such as changing the orientation, paper size or color settings). This method should adapt the content and layout where necessary to accommodate these changes. Once these changes are completed, the method must return the number of pages to be printed. Implementation of the *onLayout()* method within the PrintDocumentAdapter sub-class is mandatory.

- **onWrite()** – This method is called after each call to *onLayout()* and is responsible for rendering the content on the canvases of the pages to be printed. Amongst other arguments, this method is passed a file descriptor to which the resulting PDF document must be written once rendering is complete. A call is then made to the *onWriteFinished()* callback method passing through an argument containing information about the page ranges to be printed. Implementation of the *onWrite()* method within the PrintDocumentAdapter sub-class is mandatory.

- **onFinish()** – An optional method which, if implemented, is called once by the Printing framework when the printing process is completed, thereby providing the application the opportunity to perform any clean-up operations that may be necessary.

71.2 Preparing the Custom Document Printing Project

Launch the Android Studio environment and create a new project, entering *CustomPrint* into the Application name field and *ebookfrenzy.com* as the Company Domain setting before clicking on the *Next* button.

On the form factors screen, enable the *Phone and Tablet* option and set the minimum SDK setting to API 21: Android 5.0 (Lollipop). Continue to proceed through the screens, requesting the creation of an Empty Activity named *CustomPrintActivity* with a corresponding layout resource file named *activity_custom_print*.

Load the *activity_custom_print.xml* layout file into the Layout Editor tool and, in Design mode, select and delete the "Hello World!" TextView object. Drag and drop a Button view from the Form Widgets section of the palette and position it in the center of the layout view. With the Button view selected, change the text property to "Print Document" and extract the string to a new string. On completion, the user interface layout should match that shown in Figure 71-1:

Figure 71-1

When the button is selected within the application it will be required to call a method to initiate the document printing process. Remaining within the Attributes tool window, set the *onClick* property to call a method named *printDocument*.

71.3 Creating the Custom Print Adapter

Most of the work involved in printing a custom document from within an Android application involves the implementation of the custom print adapter. This example will require a print adapter with the *onLayout()* and *onWrite()* callback methods implemented. Within the *CustomPrintActivity.java* file, add the template for this new class so that it reads as follows:

```
package com.ebookfrenzy.customprint;

import android.support.v7.app.AppCompatActivity;
import android.os.Bundle;
import android.os.CancellationSignal;
import android.os.ParcelFileDescriptor;
import android.print.PageRange;
import android.print.PrintAttributes;
import android.print.PrintDocumentAdapter;
import android.content.Context;

public class CustomPrintActivity extends AppCompatActivity {

    public class MyPrintDocumentAdapter extends PrintDocumentAdapter
    {
        Context context;

        public MyPrintDocumentAdapter(Context context)
```

```
    {
        this.context = context;
    }


    @Override
    public void onLayout(PrintAttributes oldAttributes,
                         PrintAttributes newAttributes,
                         CancellationSignal cancellationSignal,
                         LayoutResultCallback callback,
                         Bundle metadata) {

    }


    @Override
    public void onWrite(final PageRange[] pageRanges,
                        final ParcelFileDescriptor destination,
                        final CancellationSignal
                              cancellationSignal,
                        final WriteResultCallback callback) {

    }


}
.
.
.
}
```

As the new class currently stands, it contains a constructor method which will be called when a new instance of the class is created. The constructor takes as an argument the context of the calling activity which is then stored so that it can be referenced later in the two callback methods.

With the outline of the class established, the next step is to begin implementing the two callback methods, beginning with *onLayout()*.

71.4 Implementing the onLayout() Callback Method

Remaining within the *CustomPrintActivity.java* file, begin by adding some import directives that will be required by the code in the *onLayout()* method:

```
package com.ebookfrenzy.customprint;
.
.
.
import android.print.PrintDocumentInfo;
import android.print.pdf.PrintedPdfDocument;
import android.graphics.pdf.PdfDocument;

public class CustomPrintActivity extends AppCompatActivity {
.
.
}
```

Next, modify the MyPrintDocumentAdapter class to declare variables to be used within the *onLayout()* method:

```
public class MyPrintDocumentAdapter extends PrintDocumentAdapter
{
        Context context;
        private int pageHeight;
        private int pageWidth;
        public PdfDocument myPdfDocument;
        public int totalpages = 4;

        .

        .

}
```

Note that for the purposes of this example, a four page document is going to be printed. In more complex situations, the application will most likely need to dynamically calculate the number of pages to be printed based on the quantity and layout of the content in relation to the user's paper size and page orientation selections.

With the variables declared, implement the *onLayout()* method as outlined in the following code listing:

```
@Override
public void onLayout(PrintAttributes oldAttributes,
                     PrintAttributes newAttributes,
                     CancellationSignal cancellationSignal,
                     LayoutResultCallback callback,
                     Bundle metadata) {

    myPdfDocument = new PrintedPdfDocument(context, newAttributes);

    pageHeight =
         newAttributes.getMediaSize().getHeightMils()/1000 * 72;
    pageWidth =
         newAttributes.getMediaSize().getWidthMils()/1000 * 72;

    if (cancellationSignal.isCanceled() ) {
         callback.onLayoutCancelled();
         return;
    }

    if (totalpages > 0) {
       PrintDocumentInfo.Builder builder = new PrintDocumentInfo
             .Builder("print_output.pdf").setContentType(
                 PrintDocumentInfo.CONTENT_TYPE_DOCUMENT)
             .setPageCount(totalpages);

       PrintDocumentInfo info = builder.build();
       callback.onLayoutFinished(info, true);
    } else {
       callback.onLayoutFailed("Page count is zero.");
```

```
    }
}
```

Clearly this method is performing quite a few tasks, each of which requires some detailed explanation.

To begin with, a new PDF document is created in the form of a PdfDocument class instance. One of the arguments passed into the *onLayout()* method when it is called by the Printing framework is an object of type PrintAttributes containing details about the paper size, resolution and color settings selected by the user for the print output. These settings are used when creating the PDF document, along with the context of the activity previously stored for us by our constructor method:

```
myPdfDocument = new PrintedPdfDocument(context, newAttributes);
```

The method then uses the PrintAttributes object to extract the height and width values for the document pages. These dimensions are stored in the object in the form of thousandths of an inch. Since the methods that will use these values later in this example work in units of 1/72 of an inch these numbers are converted before they are stored:

```
pageHeight = newAttributes.getMediaSize().getHeightMils()/1000 * 72;
pageWidth = newAttributes.getMediaSize().getWidthMils()/1000 * 72;
```

Although this example does not make use of the user's color selection, this property can be obtained via a call to the *getColorMode()* method of the PrintAttributes object which will return a value of either COLOR_MODE_COLOR or COLOR_MODE_MONOCHROME.

When the *onLayout()* method is called, it is passed an object of type *LayoutResultCallback*. This object provides a way for the method to communicate status information back to the Printing framework via a set of methods. The *onLayout()* method, for example, will be called in the event that the user cancels the print process. The fact that the process has been cancelled is indicated via a setting within the CancellationSignal argument. In the event that a cancellation is detected, the *onLayout()* method must call the *onLayoutCancelled()* method of the *LayoutResultCallback* object to notify the Print framework that the cancellation request was received and that the layout task has been cancelled:

```
if (cancellationSignal.isCanceled() ) {
        callback.onLayoutCancelled();
        return;
}
```

When the layout work is complete, the method is required to call the *onLayoutFinished()* method of the *LayoutResultCallback* object, passing through two arguments. The first argument takes the form of a PrintDocumentInfo object containing information about the document to be printed. This information consists of the name to be used for the PDF document, the type of content (in this case a document rather than an image) and the page count. The second argument is a Boolean value indicating whether or not the layout has changed since the last call made to the *onLayout()* method:

```
if (totalpages > 0) {
        PrintDocumentInfo.Builder builder = new PrintDocumentInfo
                .Builder("print_output.pdf")
                .setContentType(
                    PrintDocumentInfo.CONTENT_TYPE_DOCUMENT)
                .setPageCount(totalpages);

        PrintDocumentInfo info = builder.build();
```

```
        callback.onLayoutFinished(info, true);
} else {
        callback.onLayoutFailed("Page count is zero.");
}
```

In the event that the page count is zero, the code reports this failure to the Printing framework via a call to the *onLayoutFailed()* method of the *LayoutResultCallback* object.

The call to the *onLayoutFinished()* method notifies the Printing framework that the layout work is complete, thereby triggering a call to the *onWrite()* method.

71.5 Implementing the onWrite() Callback Method

The *onWrite()* callback method is responsible for rendering the pages of the document and then notifying the Printing framework that the document is ready to be printed. When completed, the *onWrite()* method reads as follows:

```
package com.ebookfrenzy.customprint;

import java.io.FileOutputStream;
import java.io.IOException;
.
.
import android.graphics.pdf.PdfDocument.PageInfo;
.
.
@Override
public void onWrite(final PageRange[] pageRanges,
                    final ParcelFileDescriptor destination,
                    final CancellationSignal cancellationSignal,
                    final WriteResultCallback callback) {

    for (int i = 0; i < totalpages; i++) {
        if (pageInRange(pageRanges, i))
            {
            PageInfo newPage = new PageInfo.Builder(pageWidth,
                pageHeight, i).create();

            PdfDocument.Page page =
                myPdfDocument.startPage(newPage);

            if (cancellationSignal.isCanceled()) {
                callback.onWriteCancelled();
                myPdfDocument.close();
                myPdfDocument = null;
                return;
            }
            drawPage(page, i);
            myPdfDocument.finishPage(page);
```

```
                }
        }


        try {
                myPdfDocument.writeTo(new FileOutputStream(
                                destination.getFileDescriptor()));
        } catch (IOException e) {
                callback.onWriteFailed(e.toString());
                return;
        } finally {
                myPdfDocument.close();
                myPdfDocument = null;
        }


        callback.onWriteFinished(pageRanges);
}
```

The *onWrite()* method starts by looping through each of the pages in the document. It is important to take into consideration, however, that the user may not have requested that all of the pages that make up the document be printed. In actual fact, the Printing framework user interface panel provides the option to specify that specific pages, or ranges of pages be printed. Figure 71-2, for example, shows the print panel configured to print pages 1-4, pages 8 and 9 and pages 11-13 of a document.

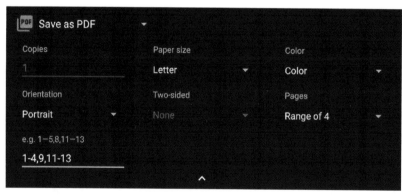

Figure 71-2

When writing the pages to the PDF document, the *onWrite()* method must take steps to ensure that only those pages specified by the user are printed. To make this possible, the Printing framework passes through as an argument an array of PageRange objects indicating the ranges of pages to be printed. In the above *onWrite()* implementation, a method named *pagesInRange()* is called for each page to verify that the page is within the specified ranges. The code for the *pagesInRange()* method will be implemented later in this chapter.

```
for (int i = 0; i < totalpages; i++) {
        if (pageInRange(pageRanges, i))
        {
```

For each page that is within any specified ranges, a new PdfDocument.Page object is created. When creating a new page, the height and width values previously stored by the *onLayout()* method are passed through as arguments so that the page size matches the print options selected by the user:

```
PageInfo newPage = new PageInfo.Builder(pageWidth, pageHeight, i).create();

PdfDocument.Page page = myPdfDocument.startPage(newPage);
```

As with the *onLayout()* method, the *onWrite()* method is required to respond to cancellation requests. In this case, the code notifies the Printing framework that the cancellation has been performed, before closing and de-referencing the myPdfDocument variable:

```
if (cancellationSignal.isCanceled()) {
        callback.onWriteCancelled();
        myPdfDocument.close();
        myPdfDocument = null;
        return;
}
```

As long as the print process has not been cancelled, the method then calls a method to draw the content on the current page before calling the *finishedPage()* method on the myPdfDocument object.

```
drawPage(page, i);
myPdfDocument.finishPage(page);
```

The *drawPage()* method is responsible for drawing the content onto the page and will be implemented once the *onWrite()* method is complete.

When the required number of pages have been added to the PDF document, the document is then written to the *destination* stream using the file descriptor which was passed through as an argument to the *onWrite()* method. If, for any reason, the write operation fails, the method notifies the framework by calling the *onWriteFailed()* method of the *WriteResultCallback* object (also passed as an argument to the *onWrite()* method).

```
try {
        myPdfDocument.writeTo(new FileOutputStream(
                destination.getFileDescriptor()));
} catch (IOException e) {
                callback.onWriteFailed(e.toString());
                return;
} finally {
                myPdfDocument.close();
                myPdfDocument = null;
}
```

Finally, the *onWriteFinish()* method of the *WriteResultsCallback* object is called to notify the Printing framework that the document is ready to be printed.

71.6 Checking a Page is in Range

As previously outlined, when the *onWrite()* method is called it is passed an array of PageRange objects indicating the ranges of pages within the document that are to be printed. The PageRange class is designed to store the start and end pages of a page range which, in turn, may be accessed via the *getStart()* and *getEnd()* methods of the class.

When the *onWrite()* method was implemented in the previous section, a call was made to a method named *pageInRange()*, which takes as arguments an array of PageRange objects and a page number. The role of the *pageInRange()* method is to identify whether the specified page number is within the ranges specified and may be implemented within the MyPrintDocumentAdapter class in the *CustomPrintActivity.java* class as follows:

```
public class MyPrintDocumentAdapter extends PrintDocumentAdapter {
   .
   .
   .

       private boolean pageInRange(PageRange[] pageRanges, int page)
       {
               for (int i = 0; i<pageRanges.length; i++)
               {
                       if ((page >= pageRanges[i].getStart()) &&
                                        (page <= pageRanges[i].getEnd()))
                               return true;
               }
               return false;
       }
   .
   .
}
```

71.7 Drawing the Content on the Page Canvas

We have now reached the point where some code needs to be written to draw the content on the pages so that they are ready for printing. The content that gets drawn is completely application specific and limited only by what can be achieved using the Android Canvas class. For the purposes of this example, however, some simple text and graphics will be drawn on the canvas.

The *onWrite()* method has been designed to call a method named *drawPage()* which takes as arguments the PdfDocument.Page object representing the current page and an integer representing the page number. Within the *CustomPrintActivity.java* file this method should now be implemented as follows:

```
package com.ebookfrenzy.customprint;
   .
   .

import android.graphics.Canvas;
import android.graphics.Color;
import android.graphics.Paint;

public class CustomPrintActivity extends AppCompatActivity {
   .
   .

       public class MyPrintDocumentAdapter extends
                                       PrintDocumentAdapter
       {
   .
   .

               private void drawPage(PdfDocument.Page page,
                               int pagenumber) {
                       Canvas canvas = page.getCanvas();

                       pagenumber++; // Make sure page numbers start at 1
```

```
                        int titleBaseLine = 72;
                        int leftMargin = 54;

                        Paint paint = new Paint();
                        paint.setColor(Color.BLACK);
                        paint.setTextSize(40);
                        canvas.drawText(
                            "Test Print Document Page " + pagenumber,
                                                    leftMargin,
                                                    titleBaseLine,
                                                    paint);

                        paint.setTextSize(14);
                        canvas.drawText("This is some test content to verify that
custom document printing works", leftMargin, titleBaseLine + 35, paint);

                        if (pagenumber % 2 == 0)
                                    paint.setColor(Color.RED);
                        else
                                paint.setColor(Color.GREEN);

                        PageInfo pageInfo = page.getInfo();


                        canvas.drawCircle(pageInfo.getPageWidth()/2,
                                        pageInfo.getPageHeight()/2,
                                        150,
                                        paint);
                }
        .
        .
}
```

Page numbering within the code starts at 0. Since documents traditionally start at page 1, the method begins by incrementing the stored page number. A reference to the Canvas object associated with the page is then obtained and some margin and baseline values declared:

```
Canvas canvas = page.getCanvas();

pagenumber++;

int titleBaseLine = 72;
int leftMargin = 54;
```

Next, the code creates Paint and Color objects to be used for drawing, sets a text size and draws the page title text, including the current page number:

```
Paint paint = new Paint();
```

```
paint.setColor(Color.BLACK);
paint.setTextSize(40);

canvas.drawText("Test Print Document Page " + pagenumber,
                                      leftMargin,
                                      titleBaseLine,
                                      paint);
```

The text size is then reduced and some body text drawn beneath the title:

```
paint.setTextSize(14);

canvas.drawText("This is some test content to verify that custom document
printing works", leftMargin, titleBaseLine + 35, paint);
```

The last task performed by this method involves drawing a circle (red on even numbered pages and green on odd). Having ascertained whether the page is odd or even, the method obtains the height and width of the page before using this information to position the circle in the center of the page:

```
if (pagenumber % 2 == 0)
        paint.setColor(Color.RED);
else
        paint.setColor(Color.GREEN);

PageInfo pageInfo = page.getInfo();

canvas.drawCircle(pageInfo.getPageWidth()/2,
                  pageInfo.getPageHeight()/2,
                  150, paint);
```

Having drawn on the canvas, the method returns control to the *onWrite()* method.

With the completion of the *drawPage()* method, the MyPrintDocumentAdapter class is now finished.

71.8 Starting the Print Job

When the "Print Document" button is touched by the user, the *printDocument()* onClick event handler method will be called. All that now remains before testing can commence, therefore, is to add this method to the *CustomPrintActivity.java* file, taking particular care to ensure that it is placed outside of the MyPrintDocumentAdapter class:

```
package com.ebookfrenzy.customprint;
.
.
.
import android.print.PrintManager;
import android.view.View;

public class CustomPrintActivity extends AppCompatActivity {

        public void printDocument(View view)
        {
```

```
PrintManager printManager = (PrintManager) this
        .getSystemService(Context.PRINT_SERVICE);

String jobName = this.getString(R.string.app_name) +
            " Document";

printManager.print(jobName, new
        MyPrintDocumentAdapter(this),
        null);
    }
    .
    .
    .
}
```

This method obtains a reference to the Print Manager service running on the device before creating a new String object to serve as the job name for the print task. Finally the *print()* method of the Print Manager is called to start the print job, passing through the job name and an instance of our custom print document adapter class.

71.9 Testing the Application

Compile and run the application on an Android device or emulator that is running Android 4.4 or later. When the application has loaded, touch the "Print Document" button to initiate the print job and select a suitable target for the output (the Save to PDF option is a useful option for avoiding wasting paper and printer ink).

Check the printed output which should consist of 4 pages including text and graphics. Figure 71-3, for example, shows the four pages of the document viewed as a PDF file ready to be saved on the device.

Experiment with other print configuration options such as changing the paper size, orientation and pages settings within the print panel. Each setting change should be reflected in the printed output, indicating that the custom print document adapter is functioning correctly.

Figure 71-3

71.10 Summary

Although more complex to implement than the Android Printing framework HTML and image printing options, custom document printing provides considerable flexibility in terms of printing complex content from within an Android application. The majority of the work involved in implementing custom document printing involves the creation of a custom Print Adapter class such that it not only draws the content on the document pages, but also responds correctly as changes are made by the user to print settings such as the page size and range of pages to be printed.

72. An Introduction to Android App Links

As technology evolves, the traditional distinction between web and mobile content is beginning to blur. One area where this is particularly true is the growing popularity of progressive web apps, where web apps look and behave much like traditional mobile apps.

Another trend involves making the content within mobile apps discoverable within web search and via URL links. In the context of Android app development, the App Links and Instant Apps features are designed specifically to make it easier for users to both discover and access content that is stored within an Android app even if the user does not have the app installed.

In this and the following chapter, the topic of Android App Links will be covered. Once App Links have been explained, the chapter entitled *"An Introduction to Android Instant Apps"* will begin coverage of Android Instant Apps.

72.1 An Overview of Android App Links

An app link is a standard HTTP URL intended to serve as an easy way to link directly to a particular place in your app from an external source such as a website or app. App links (also referred to as *deep links*) are used primarily to encourage users to engage with an app and to allow users to share app content. App links also provide the foundation on which Instant Apps are built.

App link implementation is a multi-step process that involves the addition of intent filters to the project manifest, the implementation of link handling code within the associated app activities and the use of digital assets files to associate app and web-based content.

These steps can either be performed manually by making changes within the project, or automatically using the Android Studio App Links Assistant.

The remainder of this chapter will outline app links implementation in terms of the changes that need to be made to a project. The next chapter (*"An Android Studio App Links Tutorial"*) will demonstrate the use of the App Links Assistant to achieve the same results.

72.2 App Link Intent Filters

An app link URL needs to be mapped to a specific activity within an app project. This is achieved by adding intent filters to the project's *AndroidManifest.xml* file designed to launch an activity in response to an *android.intent.action.VIEW* action. The intent filters are declared within the element for the activity to be launched and must contain the data outlining the scheme, host and path of the app link URL. The following manifest fragment, for example, declares an intent filter to launch an activity named MyActivity when an app link matching *http://www.example.com/welcome* is detected:

```
<activity android:name="com.ebookfrenzy.myapp.MyActivity">

    <intent-filter>
        <action android:name="android.intent.action.VIEW" />
```

```
            <category android:name="android.intent.category.DEFAULT" />
            <category android:name="android.intent.category.BROWSABLE" />

            <data
                android:scheme="http"
                android:host="www.example.com"
                android:pathPrefix="/welcome" />
        </intent-filter>
</activity>
```

The order in which ambiguous intent filters are handled can be specified using the *order* property of the intent filter tag as follows:

```
<application>
    <activity android:name=" com.ebookfrenzy.myapp.MyActivity">
        <intent-filter android:order="1">
            .
            .
```

The intent filter will cause the app link to launch the correct activity, but code still needs to be implemented within the target activity to handle the intent appropriately.

72.3 Handling App Link Intents

In most cases, the launched activity will need to gain access to the app link URL and to take specific action based on the way in which the URL is structured. Continuing from the above example, the activity will most likely display different content when launched via a URL containing a path of */welcome/newuser* than one with the path set to */welcome/existinguser*.

When the activity is launched by the link, it is passed an intent object containing data about the action which launched the activity including a Uri object containing the app link URL. Within the initialization stages of the activity, code can be added to extract this data as follows:

```
Intent appLinkIntent = getIntent();
String appLinkAction = appLinkIntent.getAction();
Uri appLinkData = appLinkIntent.getData();
```

Having obtained the Uri for the app link, the various components that make up the URL path can be used to make decisions about the actions to be performed within the activity. In the following code example, the last component of the URL is used to identify whether content should be displayed for a new or existing user:

```
String userType = appLinkData.getLastPathSegment();

if (userType.equals("newuser")) {
    // display new user content
} else {
    // display existing user content
}
```

72.4 Associating the App with a Website

By default, Android will provide the user with a range of options for handling an app link using the panel shown in Figure 72-1. This will usually consist of the Chrome browser and the target app.

Open with AppLinking

JUST ONCE   ALWAYS

Use a different app

Chrome

Figure 72-1

To prevent this from happening the app link URL needs to be associated with the website on which the app link is based. This is achieved by creating a Digital Assets Link file named *assetlinks.json* and installing it within the website's *.well-known* folder. Note that digital asset linking is only possible for websites that are https based.

A digital asset link file comprises a *relation* statement granting permission for a target app to be launched using the web site's link URLs and a target statement declaring the companion app package name and SHA-256 certificate fingerprint for that project. A typical asset link file might, for example, read as follows:

```
[{
    "relation": ["delegate_permission/common.handle_all_urls"],
    "target" : { "namespace": "android_app",
      "package_name": "<app package name here>",
              "sha256_cert_fingerprints": ["<app certificate here>"] }
}]
```

The *assetlinks.json* file can contain multiple digital asset links, potentially allowing a single web site to be associated with more than one companion app.

72.5 Summary

Android App Links allow app activities to be launched via URL links both from external websites and other apps. App links are implemented using a combination of intent filters within the project manifest file and intent handling code within the launched activity. It is also possible, through the use of a Digital Assets Link file, to associate the domain name used in an app link with the corresponding website. Once the association has been established, Android no longer needs to ask the user to select the target app when an app link is used.

73. An Android Studio App Links Tutorial

The goal of this chapter is to provide a practical demonstration of both Android app links and the Android Studio App Link Assistant.

This chapter will add app linking support to an existing Android app, allowing an activity to be launched via an app link URL. In addition to launching the activity, the content displayed will be specified within the path of the URL.

73.1 About the Example App

The project used in this chapter is named AppLinking and is a basic app designed to allow users to find out information about landmarks in London. The app uses a SQLite database accessed through a standard Android content provider class. The app is provided with an existing database containing a set of records for some popular tourist attractions in London. In addition to the existing database entries, the app also lets the user add and delete landmark descriptions.

In its current form, the app allows the existing records to be searched and new records to be added and deleted.

The project consists of two activities named AppLinkingActivity and LandmarkActivity. AppLinkingActivity is the main activity launched at app startup. This activity allows the user to enter search criteria and to add additional records to the database. When a search locates a matching record, LandmarkActivity launches and displays the information for the related landmark.

The goal of this chapter is to enhance the app to add support for app linking so that URLs can be used to display specific landmark records within the app.

73.2 The Database Schema

The data for the example app is contained within a file named *landmarks.db* located in the *app -> assets -> databases* folder of the project hierarchy. The database contains a single table named *locations*, the structure of which is outlined in Table 73-4:

Column	Type	Description
_id	String	The primary index, this column contains string values that uniquely identify the landmarks in the database.
Title	String	The name of the landmark (e.g. London Bridge).
description	String	A description of the landmark.
personal	Boolean	Indicates whether the record is personal or public. This value is set to true for all records added by the user. Existing records provided with the database are set to false.

Table 73-4

73.3 Loading and Running the Project

The project is contained within the *AppLinking* folder of the sample source code download archive located at the following URL:

http://www.ebookfrenzy.com/print/androidstudio30/index.php

Having located the folder, open it within Android Studio and run the app on an device or emulator. Once the app is launched, the screen illustrated in Figure 73-1 below will appear:

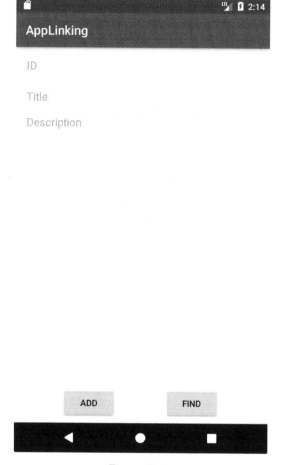

Figure 73-1

As currently implemented, landmarks are located using the ID for the location. The default database configuration currently contains two records referenced by the IDs "londonbridge" and "toweroflondon". Test the search feature by entering *londonbridge* into the ID field and clicking the *Find* button. When a matching record is found, the second activity (LandmarkActivity) is launched and passed information about the record to be displayed. This information takes the form of extra data added to the Intent object. This information is used by LandmarkActivity to extract the record from the database and display it to the user using the screen shown in Figure 73-2.

London Bridge

Throughout history, a number of bridges named London Bridge have spanned the River Thames between the City of London and Southwark, in central London. The current crossing, which opened to traffic in 1973, is a box girder bridge built from concrete and steel. This replaced a 19th-century stone-arched bridge, which in turn superseded a 600-year-old medieval structure. This was preceded by a succession of timber bridges, the first built by the Roman founders of London. (Wikipedia)

Figure 73-2

73.4 Adding the URL Mapping

Now that the app has been loaded into Android Studio and tested, the project is ready for the addition of app link support. The objective is for the LandmarkActivity screen to launch and display information in response to an app link click. This is achieved by mapping a URL to LandmarkActivity. For this example, the format of the URL will be as follows:

```
http://<website domain>/landmarks/<landmarkId>
```

When all of the steps have been completed, the following URL should, for example, cause the app to display information for the Tower of London:

```
http://www.yourdomain.com/landmarks/toweroflondon
```

To add a URL mapping to the project, begin by opening the App Links Assistant using the *Tools -> App Links Assistant* menu option. Once open, the assistant should appear as shown in Figure 73-3:

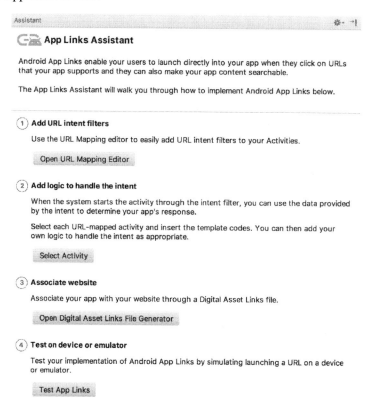

Figure 73-3

Click on the *Open URL Mapping Editor* button to begin mapping a URL to an activity. Within the mapping screen, click on the '+' button (highlighted in Figure 73-4) to add a new URL:

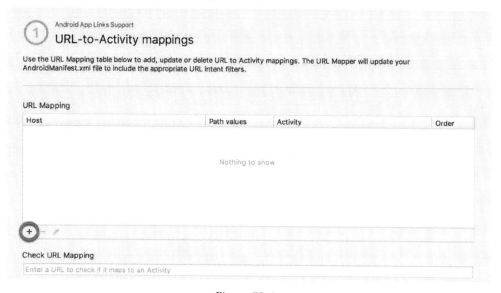

Figure 73-4

In the Host field of the *Add URL Mapping* dialog, enter either the domain name for your website or *http://www. example.com* if you do not have one.

The Path field (marked A in Figure 73-5 below) is where the path component of the URL is declared. The path must be prefixed with / so enter */landmarks* into this field.

The Path menu (B) provides the following three path matching options:

- **path** – The URL must match the path component of the URL exactly in order to launch the activity. If the path is set to /landmarks, for example, *http://www.example.com/landmarks* will be considered a match. A URL of *http://www.example.com/landmarks/londonbridge*, however, will not be considered a match.

- **pathPrefix** – The specified path is only considered as the prefix. Additional path components may be included after the */landmarks* component (for example http://www.example.com/landmarks/londonbridge will still be considered a match).

- **pathPattern** – Allows the path to be specified using pattern matching in the form of basic regular expressions and wildcards, for example *landmarks/*/[l-L]ondon/**

Since the path in this example is a prefix to the landmark ID component, select the *pathPrefix* menu option.

Finally, use the Activity menu (C) to select LandmarkActivity as the activity to be launched in response to the app link:

Figure 73-5

After completing the settings in the dialog, click on the *OK* button to commit the changes. Check that the URL is correctly formatted and assigned to the appropriate activity by entering the following URL into the *Check URL Mapping* field of the mapping screen (where *<your domain>* is set to the domain specified in the Host field above) :

```
http://<your domain>/landmarks/toweroflondon
```

If the mapping is configured correctly, LandmarkActivity will be listed as the mapped activity:

Check URL Mapping

http://www.example.com/landmarks/toweroflondon

This URL maps to com.ebookfrenzy.applinking.LandmarkActivity (app)

Add as a test URL

Figure 73-6

The latest version of Android requires that App Links be declared for both HTTP and HTTPS protocols, even if only one is being used. Before proceeding to the next step, therefore, repeat the above steps to add the HTTPS version of the URL to the list.

The next step will also be performed in the URL mapping screen of the App Links Assistant, so leave the screen selected.

73.5 Adding the Intent Filter

As explained in the previous chapter, an intent filter is needed to allow the target activity to be launched in response to an app link click. In fact, when the URL mapping was added, the intent filter was automatically added to the project manifest file. With the URL mapping selected in the App Links Assistant URL mapping list, scroll down the screen until the intent filter Preview section comes into view. The preview should contain the modified AndroidManifest.xml file with the newly added intent filters included:

Preview

```
        </activity>
        <activity android:name="com.ebookfrenzy.applinking.LandmarkActivity">
            <intent-filter>
                <action android:name="android.intent.action.VIEW" />

                <category android:name="android.intent.category.DEFAULT" />
                <category android:name="android.intent.category.BROWSABLE" />

                <data
                    android:scheme="http"
                    android:host="www.example.com"
                    android:pathPrefix="/landmarks" />
            </intent-filter>
        </activity>
```

Open AndroidManfest.xml

Figure 73-7

73.6 Adding Intent Handling Code

The steps taken so far ensure that the correct activity is launched in response to an appropriately formatted app link URL. The next step is to handle the intent within the LandmarkActivity class so that the correct record is extracted from the database and displayed to the user. Before making any changes to the code within the *LandmarkActivity.java* file, it is worthwhile reviewing some areas of the existing code. Open the *LandmarkActivity.java* file in the code editor and locate the *onCreate()* and *handleIntent()* methods which should currently read as follows:

```java
@Override
protected void onCreate(Bundle savedInstanceState) {
    super.onCreate(savedInstanceState);
    setContentView(R.layout.activity_landmark);

    titleText = (TextView) findViewById(R.id.titleText);
```

```
    descriptionText = (TextView) findViewById(R.id.descriptionText);
    deleteButton = (Button) findViewById(R.id.deleteButton);

    handleIntent(getIntent());
}

private void handleIntent(Intent intent) {
    String landmarkId =
        intent.getStringExtra(AppLinkingActivity.LANDMARK_ID);
    displayLandmark(landmarkId);
}
```

In its current form, the code is expecting to find the landmark ID within the extra data of the Intent bundle. Since the activity can now also be launched by an app link, this code needs to be changed to handle both scenarios. Begin by deleting the call to *handleIntent()* in the *onCreate()* method:

```
@Override
protected void onCreate(Bundle savedInstanceState) {
    super.onCreate(savedInstanceState);
    setContentView(R.layout.activity_landmark);

    titleText = (TextView) findViewById(R.id.titleText);
    descriptionText = (TextView) findViewById(R.id.descriptionText);
    deleteButton = (Button) findViewById(R.id.deleteButton);

    handleIntent(getIntent());
}
```

To add the initial app link intent handling code, return to the App Links Assistant panel and click on the *Select Activity* button listed under step 2. Within the activity selection dialog, select the LandmarkActivity entry before clicking on the *Insert Code* button:

Figure 73-8

Return to the *LandmarkActivity.java* file and note that the following code has been inserted into the *onCreate()*

method:

```
// ATTENTION: This was auto-generated to handle app links.
Intent appLinkIntent = getIntent();
String appLinkAction = appLinkIntent.getAction();
Uri appLinkData = appLinkIntent.getData();
```

This code accesses the Intent object and extracts both the Action string and Uri. If the activity launch is the result of an app link, the action string will be set to *android.intent.action.VIEW* which matches the action declared in the intent filter added to the manifest file. If, on the other hand, the activity was launched by the standard intent launching code in the *findLandmark()* method of the main activity, the action string will be null. By checking the value assigned to the action string, code can be written to identify the way in which the activity was launched and take appropriate action:

```
.
.
import android.net.Uri;
.
.
@Override
protected void onCreate(Bundle savedInstanceState) {
    super.onCreate(savedInstanceState);
    setContentView(R.layout.activity_landmark);
.
.
.

    // ATTENTION: This was auto-generated to handle app links.
    Intent appLinkIntent = getIntent();
    String appLinkAction = appLinkIntent.getAction();
    Uri appLinkData = appLinkIntent.getData();

    String landmarkId = appLinkData.getLastPathSegment();

    if (landmarkId != null) {
        displayLandmark(landmarkId);
    }
}
```

All that remains is to add some additional code to the method to identify the last component in the app link URL path, and to use that as the landmark ID when querying the database:

```
@Override
protected void onCreate(Bundle savedInstanceState) {
    super.onCreate(savedInstanceState);
    setContentView(R.layout.activity_landmark);

    titleText = (TextView) findViewById(R.id.titleText);
    descriptionText = (TextView) findViewById(R.id.descriptionText);
    deleteButton = (Button) findViewById(R.id.deleteButton);
```

```
// ATTENTION: This was auto-generated to handle app links.
Intent appLinkIntent = getIntent();
String appLinkAction = appLinkIntent.getAction();
Uri appLinkData = appLinkIntent.getData();

if (appLinkAction != null) {

    if (appLinkAction.equals("android.intent.action.VIEW")) {
        String landmarkId = appLinkData.getLastPathSegment();

        if (landmarkId != null) {
            Log.i(TAG, "landmarkId = " + landmarkId);
            displayLandmark(landmarkId);
        }
    }
} else {
    handleIntent(appLinkIntent);
}
}
```

If the action string is not null, a check is made to verify that it is set to *android.intent.action.VIEW* before extracting the last component of the Uri path. This component is then used as the landmark ID when making the database query. If, on the other hand, the action string is null, the existing *handleIntent()* method is called to extract the ID from the intent data.

An alternative option to identifying the way in which the activity has been launched is to modify the *findLandmark()* method located in the *AppLinkingActivity.java* so that it also triggers the launch using a View intent action:

```
public void findLandmark(View view) {

    if (!idText.getText().equals("")) {
        Landmark landmark =
                dbHandler.findLandmark(idText.getText().toString());

        if (landmark != null) {
            Uri uri = Uri.parse("http://<your_domain>/landmarks/"
                                            + landmark.getID());
            Intent intent = new Intent(Intent.ACTION_VIEW, uri);
            startActivity(intent);
        } else {
            titleText.setText("No Match");
        }
    }
}
```

This technique has the advantage that code does not need to be written to identify how the activity was launched, but also has the disadvantage that it may trigger the activity selection panel illustrated in Figure 73-10 below unless the app link is associated with a web site.

73.7 Testing the App Link

Test that the intent handling works by returning to the App Links Assistant panel and clicking on the *Test App Links* button. When prompted for a URL to test, enter the URL (using the domain referenced in the app link mapping) for the londonbridge landmark ID before clicking on the *Run Test* button:

Figure 73-9

Select a suitable device or emulator as the deployment target and verify that the landmark screen appears populated with the London Bridge information. Before the activity appears, it is likely that Android will display a panel (Figure 73-10) within which a choice needs to be made as to how the app link is to be handled:

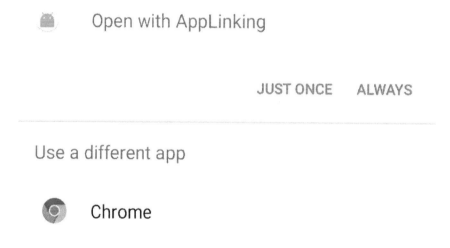

Figure 73-10

Until the app link has been associated with a web site, Android will display this selection panel every time the activity is launched using a View intent action unless the user selects the *Always* option.

73.8 Associating an App Link with a Web Site

As outlined in the previous chapter, an app link may be associated with a web site by creating a Digital Asset Links file and installing it on the web site. Although the steps to generate this file will be covered in this chapter, it will only be possible to test these instructions using your own app (with a unique application ID) and if you have access to an https based web server onto which the assets file can be installed.

To generate the Digital Asset Links file, display the App Links Assistant and click on the *Open Digital Asset Links File Generator* button. This will display the panel shown in Figure 73-11:

Figure 73-11

Enter the URL of the site onto which the assets file is to be uploaded and verify that the application ID matches the package name. Choose either a keystore file containing the SHA signing key for your project, or use the menu to select either the release or debug signing configuration as used by Android Studio, keeping in mind that the debug key will need to be replaced by the release key before you publish your app to the Google Play store.

If your app uses either Google Sign-In or other supported sign-in providers to authenticate users together with Google's Smart Lock feature for storing passwords, selecting the *Support sharing credentials between app and website* option will allow users to store sign-in credentials for use when signing in on both platforms.

Once the assets file has been configured, click on the *Generate Digital Asset Link File* button to preview and save the file:

Figure 73-12

Once the file has been saved, upload it to the path specified beneath the preview panel in the above figure and click on the *Link and Verify* button to complete the process.

After the Digital Assets Link file has been linked and verified, Android should no longer display the selection panel before launching the landmark activity.

73.9 Summary

This chapter has worked through a tutorial designed to demonstrate the steps involved in implementing App Link support within an Android app project. Areas covered in this chapter include the use of the App Link Assistant in Android Studio, App Link URL mapping, intent filters, handling website association using Digital Asset File entries and App Link testing.

74. An Introduction to Android Instant Apps

The previous chapters covered Android App Links and explained how these links can be used to make the content of Android apps easier to discover and share with other users. App links alone, however, are only part of the solution. A significant limitation of app links is that an app link only works if the user already has the corresponding app installed on the Android device. This shortcoming is addressed by combining app links with the Android Instant App feature.

This chapter will provide an overview of Android Instant apps in terms of what they are and how they work. The following chapters will demonstrate how to implement Instant App support in both new and existing Android Studio projects.

74.1 An Overview of Android Instant Apps

A traditional Android app (also referred to as an *installed app*) consists of an APK file containing all of the various components that make up the app including classes, resource files and images. When development on the app is completed, the APK file is published to the Google Play store where prospective users can find and install the app onto their devices.

When an app makes use of Instant Apps, that app is divided into one or more *feature modules*, each of which is contained within a separate *feature APK* file. Each feature consists of a specific area of functionality within the app, typically involving one or more Activity instances. The individual feature APKs are then bundled into an *instant app APK* which is then uploaded to the Google Play Developer Console.

The features within an app are assigned App Links which can be used to launch the feature. When the link is clicked or used in an intent launch, Google Play matches the URL with the feature module, downloads only the required feature APK files and launches the entry point activity as specified in the APK manifest file. This allows the user to quickly gain access to a particular app feature without having to manually go to the Google Play store and install the entire app. The user simply clicks the link and Android Instant Apps handles the rest.

Consider a hotel booking app that displays detailed hotel descriptions. A user with the app installed can send an app link to a friend to display information about a particular hotel. If the app supports Instant Apps and the friend does not already have the app installed, clicking the link will automatically download the APK file for the hotel detail feature of the app and launch it on the device.

To avoid cluttering devices with Instant App features, Android will typically remove infrequently used feature modules installed on a device.

74.2 Instant App Feature Modules

To support Instant Apps, a project needs to be divided into separate feature modules. A feature should contain at least one activity and represent a logical, standalone subset of the app's functionality. A feature module can, in fact, be thought of as a sharable library containing the code for a specific app feature.

All projects must contain one *base feature module*. If an app only consists of one feature, then the base feature module will contain all of the app's functionality. If an app has multiple features, each feature will have its own feature module in addition to the base module. In multi-feature apps, the base feature will typically contain one feature together with any resources that need to be shared with the requested feature module. When an instant app feature is requested, the base feature module is always downloaded in addition to the requested feature. This ensures that any shared resources are available for the requested feature module.

74.3 Instant App Project Structure

An Android Studio project needs to conform to a specific structure if it is to support instant apps. In fact, the project needs to be able to support both traditional installed apps and instant apps. This project structure consists of both an *app module* and an *instant app* module. The app module is responsible for building the standard installable APK file that is installed when the user taps the Install button in the Google Play store. The instant app module, on the other hand is responsible for generating each of the individual feature APK files.

Both the app module and the instant app module are essentially containers for the feature modules that make up the app functionality. This ensures that the same code base is used for both installed and instant app variants. The build files for both modules simply declare the necessary feature modules as dependencies. Figure 74-1, for example, shows the structure for a simple multi-feature project:

Figure 74-1

74.4 The Application and Feature Build Plugins

When a project is built, the build system uses the settings in the Gradle files for the app and instant app modules to decide how the output is to be structured. The *build.gradle* file for the app module will make use of the standard *com.android.application* plugin to build the single installable APK file, including in that file the feature modules declared in the dependencies section:

```
apply plugin: 'com.android.application'

android {
    compileSdkVersion 26
    buildToolsVersion "26.0.0"
```

.

```
.
dependencies {
    implementation project(':myappbase')
    implementation project(':myappdetail')
}
```

The *build.gradle* file for the instant app module, on the other hand, will use the *com.android.instantapp* plugin to build separate feature APK files for the features referenced in the dependencies section. Note that feature dependencies are referenced using *implementation project()* declarations:

```
apply plugin: 'com.android.instantapp'

dependencies {
    implementation project(':myappbase')
    implementation project(':myappfeature')
}
```

Each of the non-base feature modules that make up the app will also have a *build.gradle* file that uses the *com.android.feature* plugin, for example:

```
apply plugin: 'com.android.feature'

android {
    compileSdkVersion 26
    buildToolsVersion "26.0.0"
.
.

.
dependencies {
    implementation project(':myappbase')
}
```

The *build.gradle* file for the base feature module is a special case and must include a *baseFeature true* declaration. The file must also use the *feature project()* declaration for any feature module dependencies together with an *application project()* entry referencing the installed app module, for example:

```
apply plugin: 'com.android.feature'

android {

    baseFeature true

    compileSdkVersion 26
    buildToolsVersion "26.0.0"
.
.

.
dependencies {
    implementation fileTree(dir: 'libs', include: ['*.jar'])
.
```

```
    application project(':myappapk')
    feature project(':myappfeature')
}
```

74.5 Installing the Instant Apps Development SDK

Before working with Instant Apps in Android Studio, the Instant App must be installed. In preparation for the chapters that follows, launch Android Studio and select the *Configure -> SDK Manager* menu option (or use the *Tools -> Android -> SDK Manager* option if a project is already open).

Within the SDK manager screen, select the *SDK Tools* option and locate and enable the *Instant Apps Development SDK* entry:

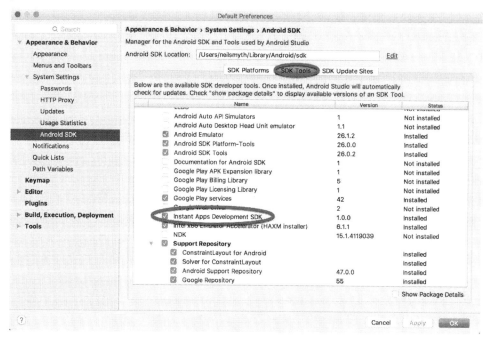

Figure 74-2

With the SDK selected, click on the OK button to perform the installation.

74.6 Summary

Android Instant Apps combine with Android App Links to provide an easy way for users to share and discover the content and features of apps. Instant apps are broken up into separate feature modules which can be launched using app links. When a link is selected, if the app is not already installed on the user's device, the code for the app feature is downloaded by Google Play onto the device and launched. This allows app features to be run on demand without the need to manually install the entire app through the Google Play app.

Each app project must include an app module to contain the standard installable APK file and an instant app module for generating the separate feature APKs. Both the app and instant app modules serve as containers for the feature modules that make up the app. An app must contain at least one feature module and may also contain additional modules for other features.

With the basics of instant apps covered, the next chapter will explain how to add instant app support to a new Android Studio project.

75. An Android Instant App Tutorial

The previous chapter has introduced Android Instant Apps and provided an overview of how these are structured and implemented. Instant Apps can be created as part of a new Android Studio project, or added retroactively to an existing project. This chapter will focus on including instant app support in a new project. The chapters that follow will outline how to add instant app support to an existing project.

75.1 Creating the Instant App Project

Launch Android Studio, select the option to create a new project and name the project *InstantAppDemo* before clicking on the *Next* button. On the subsequent screen, select the *Phone and Tablet* option and change the SDK setting to *API 23: Android 6.0 (Marshmallow)*. Before clicking the Next button, enable the *Include Android Instant App support* option as highlighted in Figure 75-1 below:

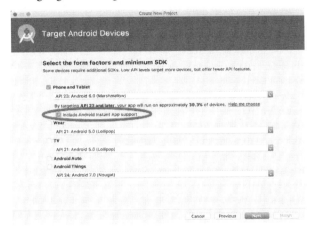

Figure 75-1

Click *Next* and, on the instant app customization screen, name the feature *myfeature*:

Figure 75-2

On the next screen, select the *Empty Activity* template before proceeding to the final screen. Since the Instant App option was selected, the activity configuration screen will provide fields within which to specify an app link for this activity. Specify *example.com* as the *Instant App URL Host*, select the *Path* option from the *Instant App URL Route Type* and enter */home* as the route URL. Name the activity *InstantAppActivity* and the layout *activity_instant_app* before clicking on the *Finish* button to create the new project.

75.2 Reviewing the Project

Based on the selections made, Android Studio has actually completed all of the work necessary to support both installed and instant app builds of the project. All that would be required to complete the app is to implement the functionality in the main activity and to add other feature modules if needed (the latter topic will be covered in the chapter entitled *"Creating Multi-Feature Instant Apps"*).

Before testing the app, it is worthwhile taking some time to review the way in which the project has been structured. At this point, the project structure within the Project Tool window should match that shown in Figure 75-3:

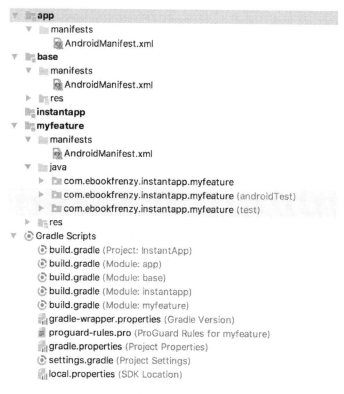

Figure 75-3

The project now consists of an installed app module (*app*), and instant app module (*instantapp*), a base feature module (*base*) and an additional feature module (*myfeature*). Each of these modules has associated with it a *build.gradle* file that defines how the module is to be built and the other modules on which it is dependent. The *build.gradle (Module: app)* file, for example, uses the *com.android.application* plugin to build the installed app version of the project and declares both the *base* and *myfeature* modules as dependencies:

```
apply plugin: 'com.android.application'
```

.

.

```
dependencies {
    implementation project(':myfeature')
    implementation project(':base')
}
```

The Gradle build file for the *instantapp* module also declares the *base* and *myfeature* modules as dependencies, but this time the *com.android.instantapp* plugin is used to build the instant app version of the project:

```
apply plugin: 'com.android.instantapp'

dependencies {
    implementation project(':myfeature')
    implementation project(':base')
}
```

A review of the build file for the *base* module will reveal the use of the *com.android.feature* plugin, a declaration that this is the base class and the *app* and *myfeature* dependencies:

```
apply plugin: 'com.android.feature'

android {
    compileSdkVersion 26
    baseFeature true
    .
    .
    .
}

dependencies {
    application project(':app')
    feature project(':myfeature')
    api 'com.android.support:appcompat-v7:26.0.0'
    api 'com.android.support.constraint:constraint-layout:1.0.2'
}
```

The *myfeature* module contains both the layout and class file for the main activity. Although not necessary for the purposes of this tutorial, any change to the activity would be made within these module files.

In addition to the build files and module structure, Android Studio has also placed the appropriate intent filter for the app link to the *AndroidManifest.xml* file belonging to the *instantapp* module.

75.3 Testing the Installable App

Test the installable app by selecting the *app* entry in the toolbar run configuration selection menu as shown in Figure 75-4 and then clicking on the run button:

Figure 75-4

Select a suitable deployment target and verify that the APK installs and the app launches.

75.4 Testing the Instant App

Before the instant app can be tested, the installed app must first be removed from the device or emulator being used for testing. Launch the Settings app and navigate to the *Apps & notifications* screen. Click on the *App info* link, locate and select the *InstantAppDemo* app then click on the *Uninstall* button.

Once the installed app has been removed, return to Android Studio and select the *instantapp* module in the run configuration menu. Before running the app, open the menu once again and select the *Edit configurations...* option. In the *Run/Debug Configurations* dialog, note that Android Studio has automatically configured the module to launch using the previously declared app link URL:

Figure 75-5

Close the configuration dialog and click on the run button to launch the instant app. As the app is launching the following output will appear in the Run Tool window confirming the instant app is being launched:

```
07/19 10:38:27: Launching instantapp
Side loading instant app.
Launching deeplink: https://example.com/home.

$ adb shell setprop log.tag.AppIndexApi VERBOSE
$ adb shell am start -a android.intent.action.VIEW -c android.intent.category.
BROWSABLE -d https://example.com/home
```

Aside from the different output, the instant app feature should launch just as it did for the installable app.

A review of the installed app on the device within the Settings app will now display the app icon with a lightning bolt to indicate that this is an instant app:

InstantAppDemo
1.53 MB

Figure 75-6

75.5 Reviewing the Instant App APK Files

The previous chapter explained that the installable app APK file contains the basic components that make up an app. To see this in practical terms, select the Android Studio *Build -> Analyze APK...* menu option and navigate to, select and open the *InstantApp -> app -> build -> outputs -> apk -> debug -> app-debug.apk* file. Once selected, the APK Analyzer panel will open and display the content of the APK file. As shown in Figure 75-7 below, this file contains the class dex files and the associated resources for the entire app:

com.ebookfrenzy.instantappdemo (version 1.0)

Raw File Size: **464.2 KB**, Download Size: **289.7 KB**

Compare with previous APK...

File	Raw File Size	Download Size	% of Total Download ...
res	191.5 KB	185.2 KB	66.1%
resources.arsc	185.9 KB	46.5 KB	16.6%
META-INF	19.7 KB	18.5 KB	6.6%
classes6.dex	13.8 KB	13.1 KB	4.7%
classes2.dex	8 KB	7.6 KB	2.7%
classes5.dex	3.2 KB	3.1 KB	1.1%
classes3.dex	2.6 KB	2.5 KB	0.9%
classes4.dex	2.4 KB	2.3 KB	0.8%
AndroidManifest.xml	1.1 KB	1.1 KB	0.4%
classes.dex	429 B	407 B	0.1%

Figure 75-7

Repeat this step, this time navigating to the *InstantApp -> instantapp -> build -> outputs -> apk -> debug -> instantapp-debug.zip* file. Note that this file contains two APK files, one for the base module and the other for the myfeature module, each containing its own dex and resource files:

com.ebookfrenzy.instantapp (version 1.0)

Raw File Size: **1.2 MB**, Download Size: **1.2 MB**

Compare with previous APK...

File	Raw File Size	Download Size	% of Total Download...
base-debug.apk	1.4 MB	1.1 MB	99.7%
classes.dex	989.8 KB	908.9 KB	77.9%
res	195.1 KB	188.7 KB	16.2%
resources.arsc	184.8 KB	46.3 KB	4%
META-INF	19.2 KB	18 KB	1.5%
AndroidManifest.xml	1011 B	1011 B	0.1%
myfeature-debug.apk	4.4 KB	3.7 KB	0.3%
META-INF	1.3 KB	1.2 KB	0.1%
classes.dex	1.1 KB	1.1 KB	0.1%
AndroidManifest.xml	821 B	821 B	0.1%
res	393 B	393 B	0%
resources.arsc	864 B	193 B	0%

Figure 75-8

75.6 Summary

This chapter has outlined the steps to creating a new Android Studio project including Android Instant App support. As revealed in this chapter, much of the work involved in structuring the project to build both installable and instant apps is performed automatically by Android Studio. Having created the example app, this chapter also outlined how to test instant apps and demonstrated the use of the APK Analyzer to review the difference between the APK files for installable and instant app projects.

76. Adapting an Android Studio Project for Instants Apps

In addition to being able to include Instant Apps support in a new project, it is also important to be able to convert an existing Android Studio project to provide instant app installation and launch capabilities.

In this chapter, the AppLinking project completed in the chapter entitled (*"An Android Studio App Links Tutorial"*) will be modified to add instant apps support.

76.1 Getting Started

As previously outlined, the objective of this chapter is to take the existing AppLinking project and modify it to support instant apps. The completed project will consist of an instant app module, a base feature module containing the main activity, and a second feature module containing the landmark detail activity. The app link already configured within the project will be used to install and launch one of these instant app feature modules. A second app link will be added during this tutorial for the other feature module.

Begin by launching Android Studio and opening the completed AppLinking project. If you have not yet completed this project, refer to the *"An Android Studio App Links Tutorial"* chapter, or load the completed version of the app from the *AppLinking_completed* folder of the code samples download available from the following URL:

http://www.ebookfrenzy.com/print/androidstudio30/index.php

Creating the Base Feature Module

The project currently contains an application module named *app* which uses the *com.android.application* build plugin. This module will serve as the base feature module for the modified project, so needs to be given a more descriptive name. Within the project tool window, right-click on the *app* entry and select the *Refactor -> Rename...* option from the menu. In the Rename Module dialog, change the module name to *applinkingbase* before clicking on the *OK* button.

Although the module has been renamed, it is still configured as an application. To resolve this, edit the applinkingbase *build.gradle* file (*Gradle Scripts -> build.gradle (Module: applinkingbase)*) and change the plugin declaration to reference *com.android.feature* instead of *com.android.application*. Since this is no longer an application module, it also no longer makes sense to have an application Id assigned, so also remove this declaration from the build file. Finally, the build file needs to be declared as the base feature module for the project:

```
apply plugin: 'com.android.feature'
.
.
android {
    baseFeature true
    compileSdkVersion 26
    buildToolsVersion "26.0.2"
    defaultConfig {
        applicationId "com.ebookfrenzy.applinking"
```

```
        minSdkVersion 25
        targetSdkVersion 26
        versionCode 1
        versionName "1.0"
        testInstrumentationRunner
                "android.support.test.runner.AndroidJUnitRunner"
    }
    .
    .
    .
```

The next step is to add an application module to the project that will allow the app to continue to support the standard APK app installation mechanism in addition to supporting instant app installations.

76.2 Adding the Application APK Module

At this stage we have a base feature module containing all of the code for the project. The project will still need to be able to generate standard application-type APK files during the build process. This can be achieved by adding an app module to the project and configuring it to contain the *applinkingbase* feature module. To add the new module, select the Android Studio *File -> New Module...* menu option and select the *Phone and Tablet* option from the selection panel (Figure 76-1). Once selected, click on the *Next* button to proceed:

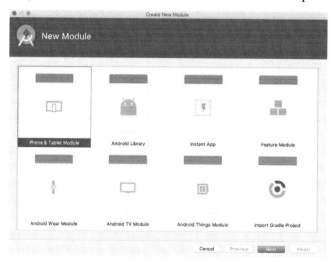

Figure 76-1

On the next screen, set the application/library name to *AppLinking APK* and the module name to *applinkingapk*. Set the minimum SDK to *API 25: Android 7.1.1 Nougat* before clicking on the *Next* button:

Figure 76-2

Since this module is simply a container within which the base feature module will be referenced, it does not need to have any activities of its own. On the final screen, therefore, select the *Add No Activity* option before clicking on the *Finish* button.

When Android Studio generates the new application module, a number of default dependencies will have been added to the module's *build.gradle* file. Since the only dependency that the module actually has is the base feature module, the default dependencies need to be removed from the *build.gradle (applinkingapk)* file and replaced with a reference to the *applinkingbase* module:

```
apply plugin: 'com.android.application'


android {

.

.

.

dependencies {
    implementation project(':applinkingbase')
}
```

Note that since *applinkingapk* is an application module, the build file correctly applies the *com.android. application* plugin.

At this point in the chapter, the original application module has been converted to a base feature module and a new application module has been added and configured to contain the base module. Check that the applinkingapk application module compiles and runs without any problems by selecting it in the toolbar run target menu and clicking on the run button:

Figure 76-3

Verify that the app launches and functions as expected. Assuming that the app still works, it is time to begin adding instant app support.

76.3 Adding an Instant App Module

The project now has a base feature module and an application module used for creating a standard APK for the project. The next step is to add an instant app module to the project. Begin by selecting the Android Studio *File -> New Module…* menu option and selecting the *Instant App* option in the selection panel:

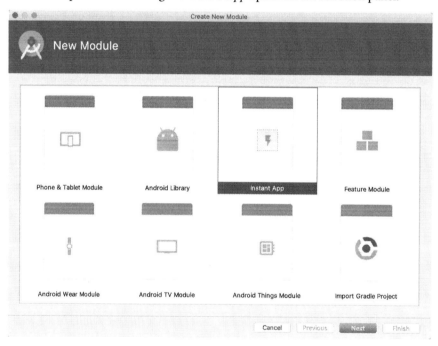

Figure 76-4

Click on the *Next* button, name the module *applinkinginstantapp* and click on the *Finish* button. As with the applinkingapk module, the only dependency for the instant app module is the base feature module. Edit the *build.gradle (applinkinginstantapp)* file and modify it as follows to add this dependency:

```
apply plugin: 'com.android.instantapp'

dependencies {
    implementation project(":applinkingbase")
}
```

Now that the instant app module has been declared, the project is ready to be tested as an instant app. Before proceeding, however, the current standard (i.e. non-instant app APK) for the project must be removed from the device or emulator on which testing is being performed. Launch the Settings app, navigate to the list of installed apps and select and uninstall the *AppLinking APK* app.

76.4 Testing the Instant App

Within the Android Studio toolbar, select *applinkinginstantapp* from the run menu as shown in Figure 76-5:

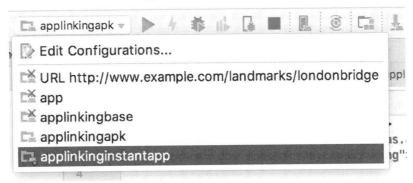

Figure 76-5

Display the menu again, this time selecting the *Edit Configurations…* option. In the launch options section of the configuration dialog, configure a launch URL containing the londonbridge landmark path as illustrated in Figure 76-6:

Figure 76-6

Click on the *Apply* button followed by the *OK* button to commit the change, then launch the instant app using the run button. After the build completes, the instant app will be installed and launched using the URL and display the landmark activity populated with London Bridge information.

On the device or emulator, open the Settings app and navigate to the list of installed apps. The AppLinking app icon will now include a lightning bolt indicating that this is an instant app:

AppIndexing
3.88 MB

Figure 76-7

76.5 Summary

This chapter has outlined how to modify an existing Android Studio app project to add Instant App support. This involved converting the existing app to the base feature module and then creating and configuring both the app and instant app modules, both of which have the base feature module as a dependency. The app was then tested using the previously configured app link. The next chapter will continue with the same project, this time converting it to a multi-feature project.

77. Creating Multi-Feature Instant Apps

The previous chapter took a project designed only for deployment via app installation and modified it to include instant app support. This chapter will take the same project and separate the landmark detail activity into a second feature module to create a multi-feature app project.

77.1 Adding the Second App Link

As currently configured, only the landmark activity is able to be launched using an app link. An app link now also needs to be set up for the main activity. Display the App Link Assistant (*Tools -> App Links Assistant*) and add a new link for (http://www.example.com/home) configured to launch AppLinkingActivity as illustrated in Figure 77-1 below:

Figure 77-1

Repeat this step to add an entry for the URL using the HTTPS protocol.

Edit the *applinkinginstantapp* run configuration once again, change the launch URL to *http://www.example.com/home* and then run the instant app. When the app launches, the AppLinkingActivity screen should appear.

77.2 Creating a Second Feature Module

The final step in this chapter is to extract the LandmarkActivity class from the base module and place it in a separate feature module.

Begin by selecting the *File -> New Module…* menu option and clicking on the Feature Module option:

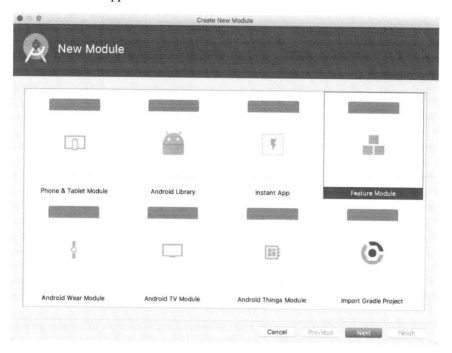

Figure 77-2

Click *Next* and, on the module configuration screen, change the library name to *AppLinking Landmark*, the module name to *applinkinglandmark* and the package name to *com.example.applinkinglandmark*:

Figure 77-3

Click on the *Next* button, select the *Add No Activity* option and click on *Finish*. After the new module has been created, edit the *build.gradle (Module: applinkinglandmark)* file and replace the default dependencies with a reference to the base feature module:

```
apply plugin: 'com.android.feature'

.

.

.

dependencies {
    implementation project(':applinkingbase')
}
```

Now that the landmark activity is no longer going to be in the base module, the new landmark feature module needs to be added as a dependency to both the instant app and app modules. Begin by editing the *build.gradle (Module: applinkingapk)* file and adding the landmark module dependency:

```
dependencies {
    implementation project(':applinkingbase')
    implementation project(':applinkinglandmark')
}
```

Repeat the above step, this time within the *build.gradle (Module: applinkinginstantapp)* file.

Finally, edit the *build.gradle (Module: applinkingbase)* file and add the new module to the existing list of dependencies if it has not already been added by Android Studio, together with the application project directive:

```
dependencies {
    implementation fileTree(dir: 'libs', include: ['*.jar'])

.

.

.

    application project(":applinkingapk")
    feature project(":applinkinglandmark")
}
```

77.3 Moving the Landmark Activity to the New Feature Module

With the preparation work complete, the LandmarkActivity class is ready to be moved from the base feature module to the new feature module. This will require the creation of an *activity* folder within the landmark module. Locate the *com.example.applinkinglandmark* folder in the Project tool window (located under *applinkinglandmark -> java*), right-click on it and select the *New -> Package...* menu option:

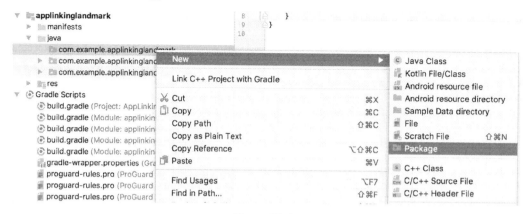

Figure 77-4

In the new package dialog, enter *activity* and click on *OK*.

Locate the *LandmarkActivity.java* file (located under *applinkingbase -> java -> com.ebookfrenzy.applinking*), right-click on it and select the *Cut* menu option. Move back to the newly added *activity* entry within the landmark module and right-click again, this time selecting the *Paste* menu option. When the Move dialog appears, click the *Refactor* button and, in the *Problems Detected* dialog, click on the *Continue* button. Finally, if the *Find Refactoring Preview* panel appears, click on the *Do Refactor* button to relocate the class.

On completion of these steps, the project tree should match that shown in Figure 77-5 below:

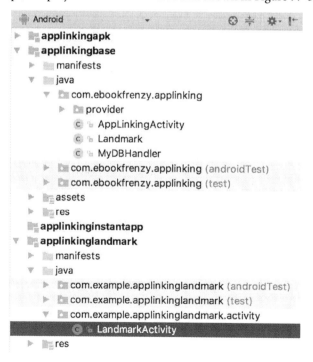

Figure 77-5

The final task to complete the relocation of the activity from the base module to the landmark module is to move the references from the base manifest file to the landmark module manifest.

First, edit the *applinkingbase -> manifests -> AndroidManifest.xml* file and copy the following section of the file:

```
<application
        android:allowBackup="true"
        android:icon="@mipmap/ic_launcher"
        android:label="@string/app_name"
        android:roundIcon="@mipmap/ic_launcher_round"
        android:supportsRtl="true"
        android:theme="@style/AppTheme">
```

Open the *applinkinglandmark -> manifests -> AndroidManifest.xml* file and place the above content into the file so that it reads as follows:

```
<manifest xmlns:android="http://schemas.android.com/apk/res/android"
    package="com.example.applinkinglandmark">


    <application
        android:allowBackup="true"
        android:icon="@mipmap/ic_launcher"
        android:label="@string/app_name"
        android:roundIcon="@mipmap/ic_launcher_round"
        android:supportsRtl="true"
        android:theme="@style/AppTheme">


    </application>


</manifest>
```

Next, cut the following LandmarkActivity element so that it is removed from the *applinkingbase* manifest file and paste it within the application element of the *applinkinglandmark* manifest file:

```
<activity android:name=
"com.ebookfrenzy.applinking.com.example.applinkinglandmark.activity.
LandmarkActivity">

    <intent-filter>
        <action android:name="android.intent.action.VIEW" />

        <category android:name="android.intent.category.DEFAULT" />
        <category android:name="android.intent.category.BROWSABLE" />

        <data
            android:scheme="http"
            android:host="www.example.com"
            android:pathPrefix="/landmarks" />
    </intent-filter>
    <intent-filter>
        <action android:name="android.intent.action.VIEW" />
```

```
        <category android:name="android.intent.category.DEFAULT" />
        <category android:name="android.intent.category.BROWSABLE" />

            <data
                android:scheme="https"
                android:host="www.example.com"
                android:pathPrefix="/landmarks" />
        </intent-filter>
</activity>
```

Remaining within the *applinkinglandmark* manifest file, edit the activity name declaration so that it refers to the new location:

```
<activity android:name=
    "com.example.applinkinglandmark.activity.LandmarkActivity">
```

Select the *Build -> Rebuild Project* menu and wait for the build to complete. The compilation may fail with the following error:

```
Error:(41, 50) error: cannot find symbol class LandmarkActivity
```

If this error occurs, edit the *AppLinkingActivity.java* file and locate the *findLandmark()* method. If the method reads as follows then an additional change is required:

```
public void findLandmark(View view) {

    if (!idText.getText().equals("")) {
        Landmark landmark =
            dbHandler.findLandmark(idText.getText().toString());

        if (landmark != null) {
            Intent intent = new Intent(this, LandmarkActivity.class);
            String landmarkid = idText.getText().toString();
            intent.putExtra(LANDMARK_ID, landmarkid);
            startActivity(intent);
        } else {
            titleText.setText("No Match");
        }
    }
}
```

The problem here is that the code is specifically launching the LandmarkActivity which now resides in a different feature module. In fact, LandmarkActivity is now contained in an entirely separate instant app APK file. Within the AppLinking project folder, the path to the base feature module APK file containing the AppLinkingActivity class is as follows:

applinking-base/build/outputs/apk/feature/debug/applinking-base-debug.apk

The APK file path for the applinkinglandmark feature module containing the LandmarkActivity class, on the other hand, is as follows:

applinkinglandmark/build/outputs/apk/feature/debug/applinkinglandmark-debug.apk

To resolve this issue, the AppLinkingActivity class will need to launch the LandmarkActivity using an App Link as follows, relying on the Instant Apps system to install and launch the landmark instant app APK:

```
.
.
import android.net.Uri;
.
.
public void findLandmark(View view) {

    if (!idText.getText().equals("")) {
        Landmark landmark =
                dbHandler.findLandmark(idText.getText().toString());

        if (landmark != null) {
            Uri uri = Uri.parse("http://example.com/landmarks/" +
                                    landmark.getID());
            Intent intent = new Intent(Intent.ACTION_VIEW, uri);
            startActivity(intent);
        } else {
            titleText.setText("No Match");
        }
    }
}
```

After making this change, rebuild the project and check that the project now builds without error.

77.4 Testing the Multi-Feature Project

Edit the run configuration for the applinkinginstantapp module and set the launch URL to the following:

http://www.example.com/landmarks/londonbridge

When the instant app module is launched, the landmark module should load, launch and display the correct landmark information. Repeat this step, this time with the URL set to the following:

http://www.example.com/home

This time, the APK for the base feature module will install and launch, displaying the AppLinkingActivity screen.

Note that entering a landmark ID and clicking on the *Find* button opens the Chrome browser and loads the http://www.example.com web page instead of launching LandmarkActivity. Once the App Links used by the project have been associated with a web site and the app uploaded to the Google Play console, clicking the *Find* button will install and launch the LandmarkActivity correctly.

77.5 Summary

This chapter has outlined the creation of a multi-feature app project by making modifications to an existing app. The process involved the creation of a new feature module, changes to the build and manifest files and the relocation of an activity from the base feature module to the new module. The chapter also demonstrated the problems that arise when an attempt is made to launch an activity that resides in a different feature module using a standard intent. This problem was resolved by launching the activity using the app link URL.

78. A Guide to the Android Studio Profiler

Introduced in Android Studio 3.0, the Android Profiler provides a way to monitor CPU, networking and memory metrics of an app in realtime as it is running on a device or emulator. This serves as an invaluable tool for performing tasks such as identifying performance bottlenecks in an app, checking that the app makes appropriate use of memory resources and ensuring that the app does not use excessive networking data bandwidth. This chapter will provide a guided tour of the Android Profiler so that you can begin to use it to monitor the behavior and performance of your own apps.

78.1 Accessing the Android Profiler

The Android Profiler appears in a tool window which may be launched either using the *View -> Tool Windows -> Android Profiler* menu option or via any of the usual toolbar options available for displaying Android Studio Tool windows. Once displayed, the Profiler Tool window will appear as illustrated in Figure 78-1:

Figure 78-1

In the above figure, no processes have been detected on any connected devices or currently running emulators. To see profiling information, an app will need to be launched. Before doing that, however, it may be necessary to configure the project to enable advanced profiling information to be collected.

78.2 Enabling Advanced Profiling

If the app is built using an SDK older than API 26, it will be necessary to build the app with some additional monitoring code inserted during compilation in order to be able to monitor all of the metrics supported by the Android Profiler. To enable advanced profiling, begin by editing the build configuration settings for the build target using the menu in the Android Studio toolbar shown in Figure 78-2:

Figure 78-2

Within the Run/Debug configuration dialog, select the *Profiling* tab and enable the *Enable advanced profiling* option before clicking on the *Apply* and *OK* buttons.

78.3 The Android Profiler Tool Window

Once an app is running it can be selected from the device and app selection menus (marked A and B in Figure 78-3) within the Android Profiling tool window to begin monitoring activity.

Figure 78-3

The window will continue to scroll with the latest metrics unless it is paused using the *Live* button (C). Clicking on the button a second time will jump to the current time and resume scrolling. Horizontal scrolling is available for manually moving back and forth within the recorded time-line.

The top row of the window (D) is the *event time-line* and displays changes to the status of the app's activities together with other events such as the user touching the screen, typing text or changing the device orientation. The bottom time-line (E) charts the elapsed time since the app was launched.

The remaining timelines show realtime data for CPU, memory and network usage. Hovering the mouse pointer over any point in the time-line (without clicking) will display additional information similar to that shown in Figure 78-4.

Figure 78-4

Clicking within the CPU, memory or networking timelines will display the corresponding profiler window, each of which will be explored in the remainder of this chapter.

78.4 The CPU Profiler

When displayed, the CPU Profiler window will appear as shown in Figure 78-5. As with the main window, the data is displayed in realtime including the event time-line (A) and a scrolling graph showing CPU usage (B) in realtime for both the current app and a combined total for all other processes on the device:

Figure 78-5

Located beneath the graph is a list of all of the threads associated with the current app (C). Referred to as the *thread activity timelime,* this also takes the form of a scrolling time-line displaying the status of each thread as represented by colored blocks (green for active, yellow for active but waiting for a disk or network I/O operation to complete or gray if the thread is currently sleeping).

The CPU Profiler supports two types of method tracing (in other words profiling individual methods within the running app). The current tracing type, either sampled or instrumented, is selected using the menu marked D. The two tracing types can be summarized as follows:

- **Sampled** – Captures the method call stack at frequent intervals to collect tracing data. While less invasive than instrumented tracing, sampled tracing can miss method calls if they occur during the intervals between captures. Snapshot frequency may be changed by selecting the *Edit configurations…* button within the type selection menu and creating new custom trace types.

- **Instrumented** – Traces the beginning and ending of all method calls performed within the running app. This has the advantage that no method calls are missed during profiling, but may impact app performance due to the overhead of tracing all method calls, resulting in misleading performance data.

Method tracing does not begin until the record button (E) is clicked and continues until the recording is stopped. Once recording completes, the Profiler tool window will display the method trace in *top down* format as shown in Figure 78-6 including information execution timings for the methods.

The trace results may be viewed in Top Down, Bottom Up, Call Chart and Flame Chart modes, each of which can be summarized as follows:

- **Top Down** – Displays the methods called during the trace period in a hierarchical format. Selecting a method will unfold the next level of the hierarchy and display any methods called by that method:

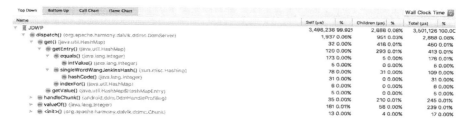

Figure 78-6

- **Bottom Up** – Displays an inverted hierarchical list of methods called during the trace period. Selecting a method displays the list of methods that called the selected method:

Figure 78-7

- **Call Chart** – Provides a graphical representation of the method trace list where the horizontal axis represents the start, end and duration of the method calls. In the vertical axis, each row represents methods called by the method above. Methods contained within the app are colored green, API methods orange and third-party methods appear in blue:

Figure 78-8

- **Flame Chart** – Provides an inverted graphical representation method trace list where each method is sized on the horizontal axis based on the amount of time the method was executing relative to other methods. Wider entries within the chart represent methods that used the most execution time relative to the other methods making it easy to identify which methods are taking the most time to complete. Note that method calls that have matching call stacks (in other words situations where the method was called repeatedly as the result of the same sequence of preceding method calls) are combined in this view to provide an overall representation of the method's performance during the trace period:

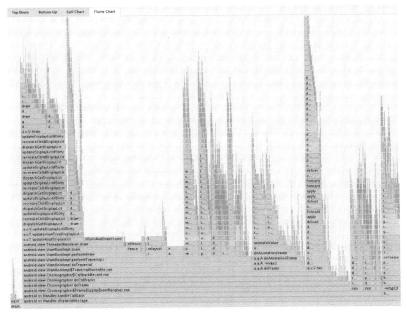

Figure 78-9

Right-clicking on a method entry in any of the above views provides the option to open the source code for the method in a code editing window.

78.5 Memory Profiler

The memory profiler is displayed when the memory time-line is clicked within the main Android Profiler Tool window and appears as shown in Figure 78-10:

Figure 78-10

The memory time-line shows memory allocations relative to the scale on the right-hand side of the time-line for a range of different categories as indicated by the color key. The dashed line (E) represents the number of objects allocated for the app relative to the scale on the left-hand side of the time-line graph.

The trash can icons (F) indicate *garbage collection* events. A garbage collection event occurs when the Android runtime decides that an object residing in memory is no longer needed and automatically removes it to free memory.

In addition to the usual timelines, the window includes buttons to force garbage collection events (A) and to capture a heap dump (B).

A heap dump (Figure 78-11) lists all of the objects within the app that were using memory at the time the dump was performed showing the number of instances of the object in the heap (allocation count), the size of all instances of the object (shallow size) and the total amount of memory being held by the Android runtime system for those objects (retained size).

Class Name	Alloc Count	Shallow Size	Retained Size
app heap	36980	2137679	42702496
FinalizerReference *(java.lang.ref)*	2080	74880	39670920
byte[]	209	289717	289717
long[]	1244	220248	220248
Class *(java.lang)*	248	39833	210178
ProviderList *(sun.security.jca)*	1	17	163357
ProviderConfig[] *(sun.security.jca)*	1	28	153324
int[]	1941	149308	149308
Object[] *(java.lang)*	2364	116676	147161
char[]	3059	130378	130378
String *(java.lang)*	2705	43280	96348
Configuration *(android.content.res)*	897	87009	87231
SolverVariable[] *(android.support.constraint.solver)*	34	70176	70176
ArrayList *(java.util)*	2014	40280	62903
ContentFrameLayout *(android.support.v7.widget)*	17	10540	41873
ConstraintLayout *(android.support.constraint)*	17	10268	40306
View[] *(android.view)*	170	8160	39499
Rect *(android.graphics)*	1627	36648	36648
AppCompatButton *(android.support.v7.widget)*	17	12376	26254
ArrayMap *(android.util)*	935	23376	25813

Figure 78-11

Double clicking on an object in the heap list will display the Instance View panel (marked A in Figure 78-12) displaying a list of instances of the object within the app. Selecting an instance from the list will display the References panel (B) listing where the object is reference. Figure 78-12, for example shows that a String instance has been selected and is listed as being referenced by a variable named *myString* located in the MainActivity class of the app:

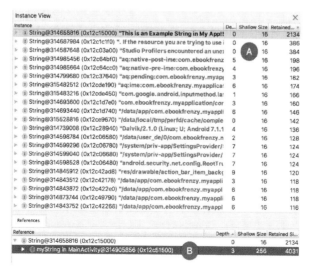

Figure 78-12

Right-clicking on the reference would provide the option to go to the MainActivity class in the heap list, or jump to the source code for that class.

The *Record memory allocations* button (marked C in Figure 78-10 above) will record memory allocations until the button is clicked a second time to stop recording. Once recording is stopped, a list of memory allocations will appear showing allocation count and shallow size values for each class as shown in Figure 78-13:

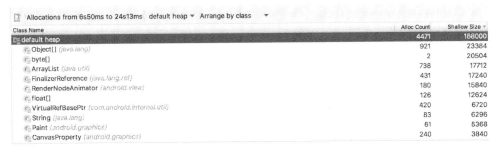

Figure 78-13

Selecting a class from the list will display the Instance View panel listing instances of that class. When an instance is selected, the Call Stack panel will populate with the method trace information for the instance. In Figure 78-14, for example, the Call Stack panel indicates that a String object instance was allocated in a method named *myMethod* located in the MainActivity class which was, in turn, triggered by an *onClick* event in the main thread:

Figure 78-14

78.6 Network Profiler

The Network Profiler is the least complex of the tools provided by the Android Profiler. When selected the Network tool window appears as shown in Figure 78-15:

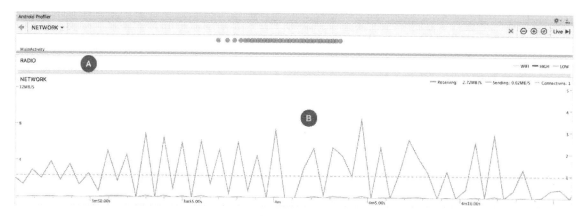

Figure 78-15

In common with the other profiler windows, the Network Profiler window includes an event time-line. The Radio time-line (marked A in Figure 78-15) shows the power status of the radio relative to the Wi-Fi connection if one is available.

The time-line graph (B) includes sent and received data and a count of the number of current connections. At time of writing, the Network Profiler is only able to monitor network activity performed as a result of HttpURLConnection and OkHttp based connections.

To view information about the files sent or received, click and drag on the time-line to select a period of time. On completing the selection, the panel labeled A in Figure 78-16 will appear listing the files. Selecting a file from the list will display the detail panel (B) from which additional information is available including response, header and call stack information:

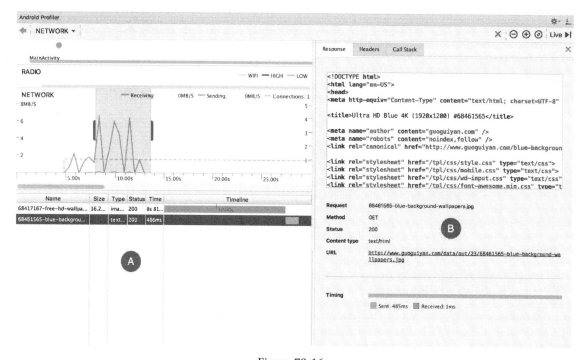

Figure 78-16

78.7 Summary

The Android Profiler monitors the CPU, memory and network resource usage of apps in realtime providing a visual environment in which to locate memory leaks, performance problems and the excessive or inefficient transmission of data over network connections. Consisting of four different profiler views, the Android Profile allows detailed metrics to be monitored, recorded and analyzed.

79. An Android Fingerprint Authentication Tutorial

Fingerprint authentication uses the touch sensor built into many Android devices to identify the user and provide access to both the device and application functionality such as in-app payment options. The implementation of fingerprint authentication is a multi-step process which can, at first, seem overwhelming. When broken down into individual steps, however, the process becomes much less complex. In basic terms, fingerprint authentication is primarily a matter of encryption involving a key, a cipher to perform the encryption and a fingerprint manager to handle the authentication process.

This chapter provides both an overview of fingerprint authentication and a detailed, step by step tutorial that demonstrates a practical approach to implementation.

79.1 An Overview of Fingerprint Authentication

There are essentially 10 steps to implementing fingerprint authentication within an Android app. These steps can be summarized as follows:

Request fingerprint authentication permission within the project Manifest file.

1. Verify that the lock screen of the device on which the app is running is protected by a PIN, pattern or password (fingerprints can only be registered on devices on which the lock screen has been secured).

2. Verify that at least one fingerprint has been registered on the device.

3. Create an instance of the FingerprintManager class.

4. Use a Keystore instance to gain access to the Android Keystore container. This is a storage area used for the secure storage of cryptographic keys on Android devices.

5. Generate an encryption key using the KeyGenerator class and store it in the Keystore container.

6. Initialize an instance of the Cipher class using the key generated in step 5.

7. Use the Cipher instance to create a CryptoObject and assign it to the FingerprintManager instance created in step 4.

8. Call the *authenticate* method of the FingerprintManager instance.

9. Implement methods to handle the callbacks triggered by the authentication process. Provide access to the protected content or functionality on completion of a successful authentication.

Each of the above steps will be covered in greater detail throughout the tutorial outlined in the remainder of this chapter.

79.2 Creating the Fingerprint Authentication Project

Begin this example by launching the Android Studio environment and creating a new project, entering *FingerprintDemo* into the Application name field and *ebookfrenzy.com* as the Company Domain setting before clicking on the *Next* button.

On the form factors screen, enable the *Phone and Tablet* option and set the minimum SDK setting to API 23: Android 6.0 (Marshmallow). Continue through the setup screens, requesting the creation of an Empty Activity named *FingerprintDemoActivity* with a corresponding layout named *activity_fingerprint_demo*.

79.3 Configuring Device Fingerprint Authentication

Fingerprint authentication is only available on devices containing a touch sensor and on which the appropriate configuration steps have been taken to secure the device and enroll at least one fingerprint. For steps on configuring an emulator session to test fingerprint authentication, refer to the chapter entitled *"Using and Configuring the Android Studio AVD Emulator"*.

To configure fingerprint authentication on a physical device begin by opening the Settings app and selecting the *Security & Location* option. Within the Security settings screen, select the *Fingerprint* option. On the resulting information screen click on the *Next* button to proceed to the Fingerprint setup screen. Before fingerprint security can be enabled a backup screen unlocking method (such as a PIN number) must be configured. If the lock screen is not already secured and follow the steps to configure either PIN, pattern or password security.

With the lock screen secured, proceed to the fingerprint detection screen and touch the sensor when prompted to do so (Figure 79-1), repeating the process to add additional fingerprints if required.

Figure 79-1

79.4 Adding the Fingerprint Permission to the Manifest File

Fingerprint authentication requires that the app request the *USE_FINGERPRINT* permission within the project manifest file. Within the Android Studio Project tool window locate and edit the *app -> manifests -> AndroidManifest.xml* file to add the permission request as follows:

```xml
<?xml version="1.0" encoding="utf-8"?>
<manifest xmlns:android="http://schemas.android.com/apk/res/android"
    package="com.ebookfrenzy.fingerprintdemo1">

    <uses-permission
```

```
android:name="android.permission.USE_FINGERPRINT" />
```

79.5 Adding the Fingerprint Icon

Google provides a standard icon (Figure 79-2) which should be displayed whenever an app requests authentication from a user.

Figure 79-2

A copy of this icon is included in the *project_icons* folder of the sample code download available from the following URL:

http://www.ebookfrenzy.com/print/androidstudio30/index.php

Open the filesystem navigator for your operating system, select the *ic_fp_40px.png* image file and press Ctrl-C (Cmd-C on macOS) to copy the file. Return to Android Studio, right-click on the *app -> res -> drawable* folder and select the *Paste* menu option to add a copy of the image file to the project. When the Copy dialog appears, click on the *OK* button to use the default settings.

79.6 Designing the User Interface

In the interests of keeping the example as simple as possible, the only elements within the user interface will be a TextView and an ImageView. Locate and select the *activity_fingerprint_demo.xml* layout resource file to load it into the Layout Editor tool.

Delete the sample TextView object, drag and drop an ImageView object from the *Images* category of the palette and position it in the center of the layout canvas.

After the ImageView widget has been placed within the layout, the *Resources* dialog will appear. From the left-hand panel of the dialog select the *Drawable* option. Within the main panel, enter *ic_fp* into the search box as illustrated in Figure 79-3 to locate the fingerprint icon. Select the icon from the dialog and click on *OK* to assign it to the ImageView object. Resize the ImageView instance if necessary.

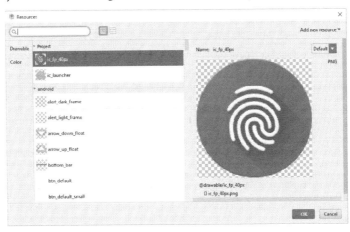

Figure 79-3

Locate the TextView widget from the palette and drag and drop it so that it is positioned in the horizontal center of the layout and beneath the bottom edge of the ImageView object. Using the Attributes tool window, change the text property to "Touch Sensor" and increase the font size to 24sp. Finally, extract the string to a resource named *touch_sensor*.

On completion of the above steps the layout should match that shown in Figure 79-4:

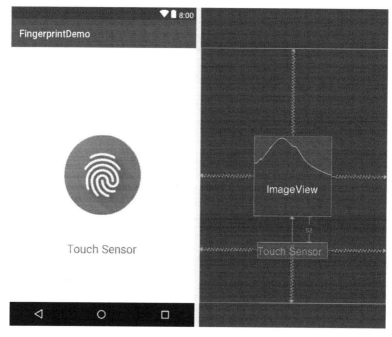

Figure 79-4

79.7 Accessing the Keyguard and Fingerprint Manager Services

Fingerprint authentication makes use of two system services in the form of the KeyguardManager and the FingerprintManager. Edit the *onCreate* method located in the *FingerprintDemoActivity.java* file to obtain references to these two services as follows:

```
package com.ebookfrenzy.fingerprintdemo;

import android.support.v7.app.AppCompatActivity;
import android.os.Bundle;
import android.app.KeyguardManager;
import android.hardware.fingerprint.FingerprintManager;

public class FingerprintDemoActivity extends AppCompatActivity {

    private FingerprintManager fingerprintManager;
    private KeyguardManager keyguardManager;

    @Override
    protected void onCreate(Bundle savedInstanceState) {
        super.onCreate(savedInstanceState);
```

```
        setContentView(R.layout.activity_fingerprint_demo);


        if (getManagers()) {


        }
    }


    private Boolean getManagers() {
        keyguardManager =
                (KeyguardManager) getSystemService(KEYGUARD_SERVICE);
        fingerprintManager =
                (FingerprintManager)
                    getSystemService(FINGERPRINT_SERVICE);
    }
}
```

79.8 Checking the Security Settings

Earlier in this chapter steps were taken to configure the lock screen and register fingerprints on the device or emulator on which the app is going to be tested. It is important, however, to include defensive code in the app to make sure that these requirements have been met before attempting to seek fingerprint authentication. These steps will be performed within the *onCreate* method residing in the *FingerprintDemoActivity.java* file, making use of the Keyguard and Fingerprint manager services. Note that code has also been added to verify that the USE_FINGERPRINT permission has been configured for the app:

```
.
.

import android.widget.Toast;
import android.Manifest;
import android.content.pm.PackageManager;
import android.support.v4.app.ActivityCompat;


public class FingerprintDemoActivity extends AppCompatActivity {

    private FingerprintManager fingerprintManager;
    private KeyguardManager keyguardManager;

.

.

    private Boolean getManagers() {

        keyguardManager =
                (KeyguardManager) getSystemService(KEYGUARD_SERVICE);
        fingerprintManager =
                (FingerprintManager)
                    getSystemService(FINGERPRINT_SERVICE);

        if (!keyguardManager.isKeyguardSecure()) {
```

```
            Toast.makeText(this,
                    "Lock screen security not enabled in Settings",
                    Toast.LENGTH_LONG).show();
            return false;
        }

        if (ActivityCompat.checkSelfPermission(this,
                Manifest.permission.USE_FINGERPRINT) !=
                PackageManager.PERMISSION_GRANTED) {
            Toast.makeText(this,
                    "Fingerprint authentication permission not enabled",
                    Toast.LENGTH_LONG).show();

            return false;
        }

        if (!fingerprintManager.hasEnrolledFingerprints()) {

            // This happens when no fingerprints are registered.
            Toast.makeText(this,
                    "Register at least one fingerprint in Settings",
                    Toast.LENGTH_LONG).show();
            return false;
        }
        return true;
    }
.
.
.
}
```

The above code changes begin by using the Keyguard manager to verify that a backup screen unlocking method has been configured (in other words a PIN or other authentication method can be used as an alternative to fingerprint authentication to unlock the screen). In the event that the lock screen is not secured the code reports the problem to the user and returns from the method.

The fingerprint manager is then used to verify that at least one fingerprint has been registered on the device, once again reporting the problem and returning from the method if necessary.

79.9 Accessing the Android Keystore and KeyGenerator

Part of the fingerprint authentication process involves the generation of an encryption key which is then stored securely on the device using the Android Keystore system. Before the key can be generated and stored, the app must first gain access to the Keystore. A new method named *generateKey* will now be implemented within the *FingerprintDemoActivity.java* file to perform the key generation and storage tasks. Initially, only the code to access the Keystore will be added as follows:

```
.
.
.
import java.security.KeyStore;
```

```
public class FingerprintDemoActivity extends AppCompatActivity {

    private FingerprintManager fingerprintManager;
    private KeyguardManager keyguardManager;
    private KeyStore keyStore;

    .

    .

    .

    protected void generateKey() {
        try {
            keyStore = KeyStore.getInstance("AndroidKeyStore");
        } catch (Exception e) {
            e.printStackTrace();
        }
    }
}
```

A reference to the Keystore is obtained by calling the *getInstance* method of the Keystore class and passing through the identifier of the standard Android keystore container ("AndroidKeyStore"). The next step in the tutorial will be to generate a key using the KeyGenerator service. Before generating this key, code needs to be added to obtain a reference to an instance of the KeyGenerator, passing through as arguments the type of key to be generated and the name of the Keystore container into which the key is to be saved:

```
.

.

import android.security.keystore.KeyProperties;

import java.security.KeyStore;
import java.security.NoSuchAlgorithmException;
import java.security.NoSuchProviderException;

import javax.crypto.KeyGenerator;

public class FingerprintDemoActivity extends AppCompatActivity {

    private FingerprintManager fingerprintManager;
    private KeyguardManager keyguardManager;
    private KeyStore keyStore;
    private KeyGenerator keyGenerator;

    protected void generateKey() {
        try {
            keyStore = KeyStore.getInstance("AndroidKeyStore");
        } catch (Exception e) {
            e.printStackTrace();
        }
```

```
        try {
            keyGenerator = KeyGenerator.getInstance(
                            KeyProperties.KEY_ALGORITHM_AES,
                            "AndroidKeyStore");
        } catch (NoSuchAlgorithmException |
                                NoSuchProviderException e) {
            throw new RuntimeException(
                    "Failed to get KeyGenerator instance", e);
        }
    }
}
```

79.10 Generating the Key

Now that we have a reference to the Android Keystore container and a KeyGenerator instance, the next step is to generate the key that will be used to create a cipher for the encryption process. Remaining within the *FingerprintDemoActivity.java* file, add this new code as follows:

```
.
.
import android.security.keystore.KeyGenParameterSpec;
.
.
import java.security.cert.CertificateException;
import java.security.InvalidAlgorithmParameterException;
import java.io.IOException;
.
.
public class FingerprintDemoActivity extends AppCompatActivity {

    private static final String KEY_NAME = "example_key";
.
.
    protected void generateKey() {
        try {
            keyStore = KeyStore.getInstance("AndroidKeyStore");
        } catch (Exception e) {
            e.printStackTrace();
        }

        try {
            keyGenerator = KeyGenerator.getInstance(
                            KeyProperties.KEY_ALGORITHM_AES,
                            "AndroidKeyStore");
        } catch (NoSuchAlgorithmException |
                                NoSuchProviderException e) {
            throw new RuntimeException(
```

```
                                "Failed to get KeyGenerator instance", e);
        }


        try {
            keyStore.load(null);
            keyGenerator.init(new
                KeyGenParameterSpec.Builder(KEY_NAME,
                    KeyProperties.PURPOSE_ENCRYPT |
                    KeyProperties.PURPOSE_DECRYPT)
                    .setBlockModes(KeyProperties.BLOCK_MODE_CBC)
                    .setUserAuthenticationRequired(true)
                    .setEncryptionPaddings(
                        KeyProperties.ENCRYPTION_PADDING_PKCS7)
                            .build());
            keyGenerator.generateKey();
        } catch (NoSuchAlgorithmException |
                InvalidAlgorithmParameterException
                | CertificateException | IOException e) {
            throw new RuntimeException(e);
        }
    }
}
```

The above changes require some explanation. After importing a number of additional modules the code declares a string variable representing the name (in this case "example_key") that will be used when storing the key in the Keystore container.

Next, the keystore container is loaded and the KeyGenerator initialized. This initialization process makes use of the KeyGenParameterSpec.Builder class to specify the type of key being generated. This includes referencing the key name, configuring the key such that it can be used for both encryption and decryption, and setting various encryption parameters. The *setUserAuthenticationRequired* method call configures the key such that the user is required to authorize every use of the key with a fingerprint authentication. Once the KeyGenerator has been configured, it is then used to generate the key via a call to the *generateKey* method of the instance.

79.11 Initializing the Cipher

Now that the key has been generated the next step is to initialize the cipher that will be used to create the encrypted FingerprintManager.CryptoObject instance. This CryptoObject will, in turn, be used during the fingerprint authentication process. Cipher configuration involves obtaining a Cipher instance and initializing it with the key stored in the Keystore container. Add a new method named *cipherInit* to the *FingerprintDemoActivity.java* file to perform these tasks:

.

```
import android.security.keystore.KeyPermanentlyInvalidatedException;
```

.

.

```
import java.security.InvalidKeyException;
import java.security.KeyStoreException;
```

```
import java.security.UnrecoverableKeyException;
.
.
.
import javax.crypto.NoSuchPaddingException;
import javax.crypto.SecretKey;
import javax.crypto.Cipher;

public class FingerprintDemoActivity extends AppCompatActivity {
.
.

    private Cipher cipher;
.
.
.

    public boolean cipherInit() {
        try {
            cipher = Cipher.getInstance(
                    KeyProperties.KEY_ALGORITHM_AES + "/"
                + KeyProperties.BLOCK_MODE_CBC + "/"
                + KeyProperties.ENCRYPTION_PADDING_PKCS7);
        } catch (NoSuchAlgorithmException |
                        NoSuchPaddingException e) {
            throw new RuntimeException("Failed to get Cipher", e);
        }

        try {
            keyStore.load(null);
            SecretKey key = (SecretKey) keyStore.getKey(KEY_NAME,
                                              null);
            cipher.init(Cipher.ENCRYPT_MODE, key);
            return true;
        } catch (KeyPermanentlyInvalidatedException e) {
            return false;
        } catch (KeyStoreException | CertificateException
                    | UnrecoverableKeyException | IOException
                | NoSuchAlgorithmException | InvalidKeyException e) {
            throw new RuntimeException("Failed to init Cipher", e);
        }
    }
}
```

The *getInstance* method of the Cipher class is called to obtain a Cipher instance which is subsequently configured with the properties required for fingerprint authentication. The previously generated key is then extracted from the Keystore container and used to initialize the Cipher instance. Errors are handled accordingly and a true or false result returned based on the success or otherwise of the cipher initialization process.

Work is now complete on both the *generateKey* and *cipherInit* methods. The next step is to modify the *onCreate* method to call these methods and, in the event of a successful cipher initialization, create a CryptoObject instance.

79.12 Creating the CryptoObject Instance

Remaining within the *FingerprintDemoActivity.java* file, modify the *onCreate* method to call the two newly created methods and generate the CryptoObject as follows:

```java
public class FingerprintDemoActivity extends AppCompatActivity {

    private static final String KEY_NAME = "example_key";
    private FingerprintManager fingerprintManager;
    private KeyguardManager keyguardManager;
    private KeyStore keyStore;
    private KeyGenerator keyGenerator;
    private Cipher cipher;
    private FingerprintManager.CryptoObject cryptoObject;

    @Override
    protected void onCreate(Bundle savedInstanceState) {
        super.onCreate(savedInstanceState);
        setContentView(R.layout.activity_fingerprint_demo);

        if (getManagers()) {
            generateKey();

            if (cipherInit()) {
                cryptoObject =
                        new FingerprintManager.CryptoObject(cipher);
            }

        }
    }

    .
    .
    .
}
```

The final task in the project is to implement a new class to handle the actual fingerprint authentication.

79.13 Implementing the Fingerprint Authentication Handler Class

So far in this chapter most of the work has involved preparing for the fingerprint authentication in terms of the key, cipher and crypto object. The actual authentication is triggered via a call to the *authenticate* method of the FingerprintManager instance. This method call, however, will trigger one of a number of callback events depending on the success or failure of the authentication. Both the *authenticate* method call and the callback handler methods need to be implemented in a class that extends the FingerprintManager.AuthenticationCallback class. Such a class now needs to be added to the project.

Navigate to the *app -> java -> com.ebookfrenzy.fingerprintdemo* entry within the Android Studio Project tool window and right-click on it. From the resulting menu, select the *New -> Java Class* option to display the Create

New Class dialog. Name the class *FingerprintHandler* and click on the *OK* button to create the class.

Edit the new class file so that it extends FingerprintManager.AuthenticationCallback, imports some additional modules and implements a constructor that will allow the application context to be passed through when an instance of the class is created (the context will be used in the callback methods to notify the user of the authentication status):

```
package com.ebookfrenzy.fingerprintdemo;


import android.Manifest;
import android.content.Context;
import android.content.pm.PackageManager;
import android.hardware.fingerprint.FingerprintManager;
import android.os.CancellationSignal;
import android.support.v4.app.ActivityCompat;
import android.widget.Toast;


public class FingerprintHandler extends
                FingerprintManager.AuthenticationCallback {

    private CancellationSignal cancellationSignal;
    private Context appContext;

    public FingerprintHandler(Context context) {
        appContext = context;
    }
}
```

Next a method needs to be added which can be called to initiate the fingerprint authentication. When called, this method will need to be passed the FingerprintManager and CryptoObject instances. Name this method *startAuth* and implement it in the *FingerprintHandler.java* class file as follows (note that code has also been added to once again check that fingerprint permission has been granted):

```
public void startAuth(FingerprintManager manager,
        FingerprintManager.CryptoObject cryptoObject) {

    cancellationSignal = new CancellationSignal();

    if (ActivityCompat.checkSelfPermission(appContext,
            Manifest.permission.USE_FINGERPRINT) !=
                    PackageManager.PERMISSION_GRANTED) {
        return;
    }
    manager.authenticate(cryptoObject, cancellationSignal, 0, this, null);
}
```

Next, add the callback handler methods, each of which is implemented to display a toast message indicating the result of the fingerprint authentication:

```
@Override
```

```
public void onAuthenticationError(int errMsgId,
                            CharSequence errString) {

    Toast.makeText(appContext,
            "Authentication error\n" + errString,
            Toast.LENGTH_LONG).show();
}


@Override
public void onAuthenticationHelp(int helpMsgId,
                            CharSequence helpString) {

    Toast.makeText(appContext,
            "Authentication help\n" + helpString,
            Toast.LENGTH_LONG).show();
}


@Override
public void onAuthenticationFailed() {
    Toast.makeText(appContext,
            "Authentication failed.",
            Toast.LENGTH_LONG).show();
}


@Override
public void onAuthenticationSucceeded(
            FingerprintManager.AuthenticationResult result) {

    Toast.makeText(appContext,
            "Authentication succeeded.",
            Toast.LENGTH_LONG).show();
}
```

The final task before testing the project is to modify the *onCreate* method so that it creates a new instance of the FingerprintHandler class and calls the *startAuth* method. Edit the *FingerprintDemoActivity.java* file and modify the end of the *onCreate* method so that it reads as follows:

```
@Override
protected void onCreate(Bundle savedInstanceState) {
    super.onCreate(savedInstanceState);
    setContentView(R.layout.activity_fingerprint);

    .
    .
    .

    if (cipherInit()) {
        cryptoObject = new FingerprintManager.CryptoObject(cipher);
        FingerprintHandler helper = new FingerprintHandler(this);
        helper.startAuth(fingerprintManager, cryptoObject);
    }
```

}

79.14 Testing the Project

With the project now complete run the app on a physical Android device or emulator session. Once running, either touch the fingerprint sensor or use the extended controls panel within the emulator to simulate a fingerprint touch as outlined the chapter entitled *"Using and Configuring the Android Studio AVD Emulator"*. Assuming a registered fingerprint is detected a toast message will appear indicating a successful authentication as shown in Figure 79-5:

Touch Sensor
Authentication succeeded.

Figure 79-5

Stop the running app and relaunch it, this time using an unregistered fingerprint to attempt the authentication. This time a toast message should appear indicating that the authentication failed.

79.15 Summary

Fingerprint authentication within Android is a multi-step process that can initially appear to be complex. When broken down into individual steps, however, the process becomes clearer. Fingerprint authentication involves the use of keys, ciphers and key storage combined with the features of the FingerprintManager class. This chapter has provided an introduction to these steps and worked through the creation of an example application project intended to show the practical implementation of fingerprint authentication within Android.

80. Handling Different Android Devices and Displays

Before being made available for purchase on the Google Play App Store, an application must first be submitted to the portal for review and approval. One of the most important steps to take before submitting an application is to decide which Android device models the application is intended to support and, more importantly, that the application runs without issue on those devices.

This chapter will cover some of the areas to consider when making sure that an application runs on the widest possible range of Android devices.

80.1 Handling Different Device Displays

Android devices come in a variety of different screen sizes and resolutions. The ideal solution is to design the user interface of your application so that it appears correctly on the widest possible range of devices. The best way to achieve this is to design the user interface using layout managers that do not rely on absolute positioning (i.e. specific X and Y coordinates) such as the ConstraintLayout so that views are positioned relative to both the size of the display and each other.

Similarly, avoid using specific width and height properties wherever possible. When such properties are unavoidable, always use *density-independent (dp)* values as these are automatically scaled to match the device display at application runtime.

Having designed the user interface, be sure to test it on each device on which it is intended to be supported. In the absence of the physical device hardware, use the emulator templates, wherever possible, to test on the widest possible range of devices.

In the event that it is not possible to design the user interface such that a single design will work on all Android devices, another option is to provide a different layout for each display.

80.2 Creating a Layout for each Display Size

The ideal solution to the multiple display problem is to design user interface layouts that adapt to the display size of the device on which the application is running. This, for example, has the advantage of having only one layout to manage when modifying the application. Inevitably, however, there will be situations where this ideal is unachievable given the vast difference in screen size between a phone and a tablet. Another option is to provide different layouts, each tailored to a specific display category. This involves identifying the *smallest width* qualifier value of each display and creating an XML layout file for each one. The smallest width value of a display indicates the minimum width of that display measured in dp units.

Display-specific layouts are implemented by creating additional sub-directories under the *res* directory of a project. The naming convention for these folders is:

layout-<*smallest-width*>

For example, layout resource folders for a range of devices might be configured as follows:

- *res/layout* – The default layout file

- *res/layout-sw200dp*

- *res/layout-sw600dp*

- *res/layout-sw800dp*

Alternatively, more general categories can be created by targeting *small*, *normal*, *large* and *xlarge* displays:

- *res/layout* – The default layout file

- *res/layout-small*

- *res/layout-normal*

- *res/layout-large*

- *res/layout-xlarge*

- *res/layout-land*

Each folder must, in turn, contain a copy of the layout XML file adapted for the corresponding display, all of which must have matching file names. Once implemented, the Android runtime system will automatically select the correct layout file to display to the user to match the device display.

80.3 Creating Layout Variants in Android Studio

Android Studio makes it easy to add additional layout size variants using the *Orientation* button located in the Layout Editor toolbar as highlighted in Figure 80-1:

Figure 80-1

When selected, the menu provides options to create either a preconfigured landscape (res/layout-land) or xlarge (res/layout-xlarge) variants. Alternatively, the *Create Other...* menu option may be used to create variants for other sizes. To create a custom variant, select the *Size* qualifier in the *Select Resource Directory* dialog, click on the button displaying the '>>' character sequence and then make a selection from the *Screen size* drop-down menu:

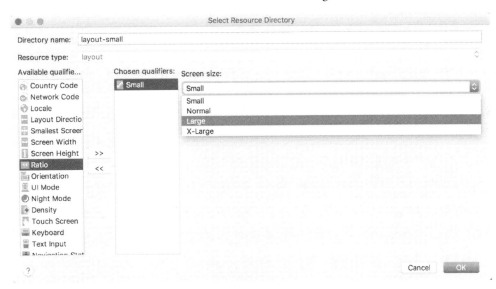

Figure 80-2

At any time during the layout design process, use the Orientation menu to switch to one of the different variants to see how the user interface will appear when running on a device with the corresponding screen size:

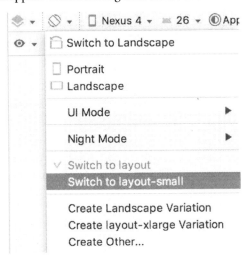

Figure 80-3

80.4 Providing Different Images

User interface layouts are not the only area of concern when adapting an application for different screen densities, dimensions and aspect ratios. Another area to pay attention to is that of images. An image that appears correctly scaled on a large tablet screen, for example, might not appear correctly scaled on a smaller phone based device. As with layouts, however, multiple sets of images can be bundled with the application, each tailored to a specific display. This can once again be achieved by referencing the smallest width value. In this case, *drawable* folders need to be created in the *res* directory. For example:

- *res/drawable* – The default image folder

- *res/drawable-sw200dp*

- *res/drawable-sw600dp*

- *res/drawable-sw800dp*

Having created the folders, simply place the display specific versions of the images into the corresponding folder, using the same name for each of the images.

Alternatively, the images may be categorized into broader display densities using the following directories based on the pixel density of the display:

- *res/drawable-ldpi* - Images for low density screens (approx. 120 dpi)

- *res/drawable-mdpi* – Images for medium-density screens (approx. 160 dpi)

- *res/drawable-hdpi* – Images for high-density screens (approx. 240 dpi)

- *res/drawable-xhdpi* – Images for extra high-density screens (approx. 320 dpi)

- *res/drawable-*tvdpi – Images for displays between medium and high density (approx. 213 dpi)

- *res/drawable-nodpi* – Images that must not be scaled by the system

80.5 Checking for Hardware Support

By now, it should be apparent that not all Android devices were created equal. An application that makes use of specific hardware features (such as a microphone or camera) should include code to gracefully handle the absence of that hardware. This typically involves performing a check to find out if the hardware feature is missing, and subsequently reporting to the user that the corresponding application functionality will not be available.

The following method can be used to check for the presence of a microphone:

```
protected boolean hasMicrophone() {
            return getPackageManager().hasSystemFeature(
            PackageManager.FEATURE_MICROPHONE);
}
```

Similarly, the following method is useful for checking for the presence of a front facing camera:

```
private boolean hasCamera() {
        return getPackageManager().hasSystemFeature(
            PackageManager.FEATURE_CAMERA_FRONT)
}
```

80.6 Providing Device Specific Application Binaries

Even with the best of intentions, there will inevitably be situations where it is not possible to target all Android devices within a single application (though Google certainly encourages developers to target as many devices as possible within a single application binary package). In this situation, the application submission process allows multiple application binaries to be uploaded for a single application. Each binary is then configured to indicate to Google the devices with which the binary is configured to work. When a user subsequently purchases the application, Google ensures that the correct binary is downloaded for the user's device.

It is also important to be aware that it may not always make sense to try to provide support for every Android device model. There is little point, for example, in making an application that relies heavily on a specific hardware feature available on devices that lack that specific hardware. These requirements can be defined using Google Play Filters as outlined at:

http://developer.android.com/google/play/filters.html

80.7 Summary

There is more to completing an Android application than making sure it works on a single device model. Before an application is submitted to the Google Play Developer Console, it should first be tested on as wide a range of display sizes as possible. This includes making sure that the user interface layouts and images scale correctly for each display variation and taking steps to ensure that the application gracefully handles the absence of certain hardware features. It is also possible to submit to the developer console a different application binary for specific Android models, or to state that a particular application simply does not support certain Android devices.

81. Signing and Preparing an Android Application for Release

Once the development work on an Android application is complete and it has been tested on a wide range of Android devices, the next step is to prepare the application for submission to the Google Play App Store. Before submission can take place, however, the application must be packaged for release and signed with a private key. This chapter will work through the steps involved in obtaining a private key and preparing the application package for release.

81.1 The Release Preparation Process

Up until this point in the book, we have been building application projects in a mode suitable for testing and debugging. Building an application package for release to customers via the Google Play store, on the other hand, requires that some additional steps be taken. The first requirement is that the application be compiled in *release mode* instead of *debug mode*. Secondly, the application must be signed with a private key that uniquely identifies you as the application's developer. Finally, the application package must be *aligned*. This is simply a process by which some data files in the application package are formatted with a certain byte alignment to improve performance.

While each of these tasks can be performed outside of the Android Studio environment, the procedures can more easily be performed using the Android Studio build mechanism as outlined in the remainder of this chapter.

81.2 Register for a Google Play Developer Console Account

The first step in the application submission process is to create a Google Play Developer Console account. To do so, navigate to *https://play.google.com/apps/publish/signup/* and follow the instructions to complete the registration process. Note that there is a one-time $25 fee to register. Once an application goes on sale, Google will keep 30% of all revenues associated with the application.

Once the account has been created, the next step is to gather together information about the application. In order to bring your application to market, the following information will be required:

- **Title** – The title of the application.

- **Short Description** - Up to 80 words describing the application.

- **Full Description** – Up to 4000 words describing the application.

- **Screenshots** – Up to 8 screenshots of your application running (a minimum of two is required). Google recommends submitting screenshots of the application running on a 7" or 10" tablet.

- **Language** – The language of the application (the default is US English).

- **Promotional Text** – The text that will be used when your application appears in special promotional features within the Google Play environment.

- **Application Type** – Whether your application is considered to be a *game* or an *application*.

- **Category** – The category that best describes your application (for example finance, health and fitness, education, sports, etc.).

- **Locations** – The geographical locations into which you wish your application to be made available for purchase.

- **Contact Details** – Methods by which users may contact you for support relating to the application. Options include web, email and phone.

- **Pricing & Distribution** – Information about the price of the application and the geographical locations where it is to be marketed and sold.

Having collected the above information, click on the *Create Application* button within the Google Play Console to begin the creation process.

81.3 Configuring the App in the Console

When the Create Application button is first clicked, the *Store listing* screen will appear as shown in Figure 81-1 below. The screen may also be accessed by selecting the *Store listing* option (marked A) in the navigation panel. Once all of the requirements have been met for the Store listing screen, both the *Content rating* (B) and *Pricing & distribution* (C) screens must also be completed:

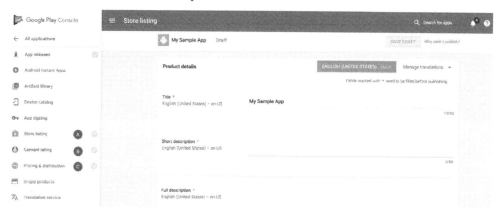

Figure 81-1

Once the app entry has been fully configured, the next step is to upload a release APK for the app.

81.4 Enabling Google Play App Signing

Up until recently, release APKs were signed with a release app signing key from within Android Studio and then uploaded to the Google Play console. While this option is still available, the recommended way to upload APK files is to now use a process referred to as *Google Play App Signing*. For a newly created app, this involves opting in to Google Play App Signing and then generating an *upload key* that is used to sign the release APK file within Android Studio. When the release APK file generated by Android Studio is uploaded, the Google Play console removes the upload key and then signs the file with an app signing key that is stored securely within the Google Play servers. For existing apps, some additional steps are required to enable Google Play Signing and will be covered at the end of this chapter.

Within the Google Play console, select the newly added app entry from the dashboard and select the *App releases* option from the left-hand navigation panel. On the App releases screen, select either the Alpha, Beta or Production management button to upload an APK file for testing or production release (depending on where you are in the app development process):

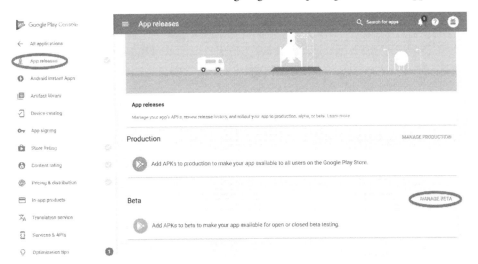

Figure 81-2

On the subsequent screen, click on the *Create Release* button to display the settings screen shown in Figure 81-3:

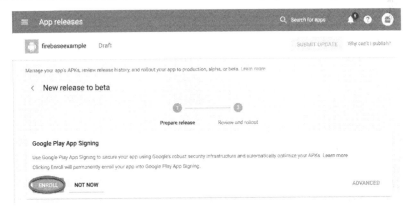

Figure 81-3

To enroll the app in Google Play App Signing, click on the *Enroll* button highlighted in the above figure. This will generate an app signing certificate for the app which will be secured within the Google Play servers.

The next step is to generate the *upload* key from within Android Studio. This is performed as part of the process of generating a signed release APK file for the app and begins with switching the project from *debug* to *release* build mode.

81.5 Changing the Build Variant

The first step in the process of generating a signed application APK file involves changing the build variant for the project from debug to release. This is achieved using the *Build Variants* tool window which can be accessed from the tool window quick access menu (located in the bottom left-hand corner of the Android Studio main window as shown in Figure 81-4).

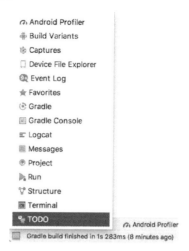

Figure 81-4

Once the Build Variants tool window is displayed, change the Build Variant settings for all the modules listed from *debug* to *release*:

Figure 81-5

The project is now configured to build in release mode. The next step is to configure signing key information for use when generating the signed application package.

81.6 Enabling ProGuard

When generating an application package, the option is available to use ProGuard during the package creation process. ProGuard performs a series of optimization and verification tasks that result in smaller and more efficient byte code. In order to use ProGuard, it is necessary to enable this feature within the Project Structure settings prior to generating the APK file.

The steps to enable ProGuard are as follows:

1. Display the Project Structure dialog (*File -> Project Structure*).

2. Select the "app" module in the far left panel.

3. Select the "Build Types" tab in the main panel and the "release" entry from the middle panel.

4. Change the "Minify Enabled" option from "false" to "true" and click on *OK*.

5. Follow the steps to create a keystore file and build the release APK file.

With the project configured for release building, the next step is to create a keystore file containing the upload key.

81.7 Creating a Keystore File

To create a keystore file, select the *Build -> Generate Signed APK...* menu option to display the Generate Signed APK Wizard dialog as shown in Figure 81-6:

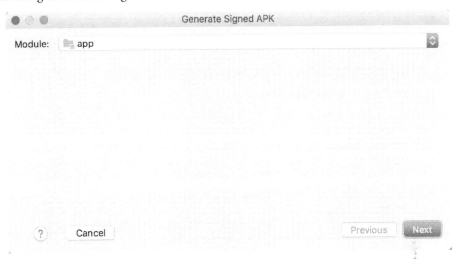

Figure 81-6

Select the module to be generated before clicking on the *Next* button to proceed to the key store selection screen:

Figure 81-7

In the event that you have an existing release keystore file, click on the *Choose existing...* button and navigate to and select the file. In the event that you have yet to create a keystore file, click on the *Create new...* button to display the *New Key Store* dialog (Figure 81-8). Click on the button to the right of the Key store path field and navigate to a suitable location on your file system, enter a name for the keystore file (for example, *release. keystore.jks*) and click on the OK button.

The New Key Store dialog is divided into two sections. The top section relates to the keystore file. In this section, enter a strong password with which to protect the keystore file into both the *Password* and *Confirm* fields. The lower section of the dialog relates to the upload key that will be stored in the key store file.

Figure 81-8

Within the *Certificate* section of the New Key Store dialog, enter the following details:

- An alias by which the key will be referenced. This can be any sequence of characters, though only the first 8 are used by the system.

- A suitably strong password to protect the key.

- The number of years for which the key is to be valid (Google recommends a duration in excess of 25 years).

In addition, information must be provided for at least one of the remaining fields (for example, your first and last name, or organization name).

Figure 81-9

Once the information has been entered, click on the *OK* button to proceed with the package creation.

81.8 Creating the Application APK File

The next task to be performed is to instruct Android Studio to build the application APK package file in release mode and then sign it with the newly created private key. At this point the *Generate Signed APK Wizard* dialog should still be displayed with the keystore path, passwords and key alias fields populated with information:

Figure 81-10

Assuming that the settings are correct, click on the *Next* button to proceed to the APK generation screen (Figure 81-11). Within this screen, review the *Destination APK path:* setting to verify that the location into which the APK file will be generated is acceptable. In the event that another location is preferred, click on the button to the right of the text field and navigate to the desired file system location.

Figure 81-11

Two signature options are provided for selection within the APK generation dialog. Select both the V1 (Jar Signature) and V2 (Full APK Signature). This provides additional security to protect the APK from malicious alteration together with faster app installation times. If problems occur when using the V2 option, repeat the generation process using only the V1 option.

The Gradle system will now compile the application in release mode. Once the build is complete, a dialog will appear providing the option to open the folder containing the APK file in an explorer window, or to load the file into the APK Analyzer:

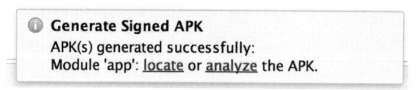

Figure 81-12

At this point the application is ready to be submitted to the Google Play store. Click on the *locate* link to open a filesystem browser window. The file should be named *app-release.apk* and be located in the *app/release* subdirectory of the project folder.

The private key generated as part of this process should be used when signing and releasing future applications and, as such, should be kept in a safe place and securely backed up.

The final step in the process of bringing an Android application to market involves submitting it to the Google Play Developer Console. Once submitted, the application will be available for download from the Google Play App Store.

81.9 Uploading New APK Versions to the Google Play Developer Console

Once the app profile has been created, select the *App Releases* option in the left-hand navigation panel and click on the Alpha, Beta or Production *Manage* button, depending on what stage your app is at:

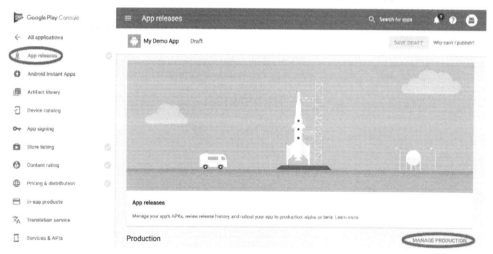

Figure 81-13

Within the Production management screen, click on the *Create Release* button and, on the subsequent screen, click on the *Upload APK* button:

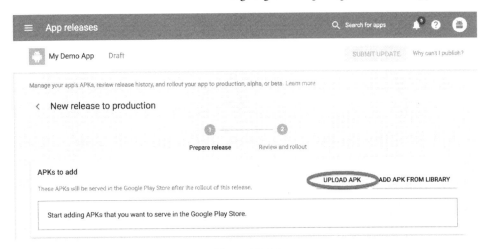

Figure 81-14

Navigate to the APK file generated earlier in this chapter and select and upload it to the Google Play console. Once the file has been uploaded, review the settings and then click on the *Review* button. Assuming that all of the information settings are correct, start the production process by clicking on the *Start Rollout* button. If the rollout button is disabled, click on the *Why can't I publish?* link next to the *Save Draft* button in the top right-hand corner of the screen. This will provide a list of settings that need to be completed before the app can be published for release or testing.

81.10 Managing Testers

If the app is still in the Alpha or Beta testing phase, a list of authorized testers may be specified by selecting the app from within the Google Play console, clicking on *App releases* in the navigation panel, selecting the Manage button for either the Alpha or Beta release and unfolding the *Manage testers* section of the release screen as shown in Figure 81-15:

< Alpha   CREATE RELEASE

Manage testers   Closed Alpha Testing ⌃

Choose how to run your testing program. Learn more   **DISABLE ALPHA TESTING**

Choose a testing method   Closed Alpha Testing ▾

Users   **CREATE LIST**

After you create a list, you can reuse the list for Closed Testing with any of your published apps.

Active List name	Number of users	
☑ Alpha Testers	1 tester	Edit

Feedback Channel ⓘ   Email address or URL

Opt-In URL   https://play.google.com/apps/testing/com.ebookfrenzy.inappbilling3

Share this opt-in link with your testers.

SAVE

Figure 81-15

Signing and Preparing an Android Application for Release

The following options are available for Alpha and Beta app testing:

- **Closed Testing** – Testing is only available for designated users identified by email address or membership in Google Groups and Google+ communities.

- **Open Testing** – The app is made available to all users within the Google Play Store. Users are provided with a mechanism to provide feedback to you during testing. The total number of testers may also be specified (though the number cannot be less than 1000 users).

To configure testing, select the type of testing to be performed and fill in the maximum number of users for open testing, or the list of users for closed testing and save the settings. The opt-in URL can be provided to the test users and used to accept the testing invitation and download the app from the Google Play Store.

81.11 Uploading Instant App APK Files

The process for uploading Instant App APK files is similar to that for a standard app. From within the Google Play console, select the app from the dashboard followed by the *Android Instant Apps* option in the navigation panel as shown in Figure 81-16:

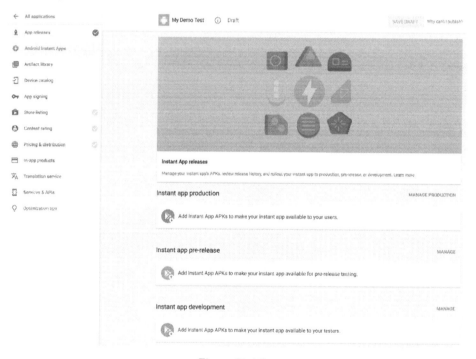

Figure 81-16

Select the option to upload APKs for development, pre-release or testing purposes. If the APKs are to be uploaded for development or pre-release testing, use the *Manage testers* section of the subsequent screen to enter a list of Gmail email addresses for the users that will be testing the app, then click on the Save button followed by the *Create Release* button:

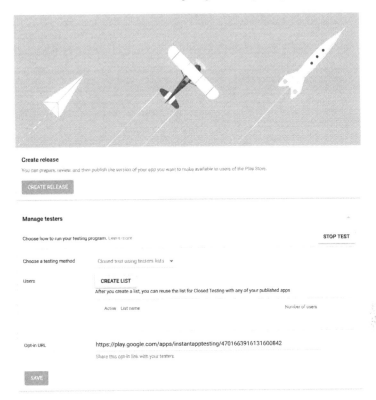

Figure 81-17

Return to Android Studio and follow the previous steps to build the Instant App module of the project using release mode and to generate signed versions of the Instant App APK files. When the build is complete, the Instant App APK files will be packaged in a ZIP file within the *<module name>/release* folder of the project directory. This file may be uploaded to the console without first extracting the separate APK files.

81.12 Uploading New APK Revisions

The first APK file uploaded for your application will invariably have a version code of 1. If an attempt is made to upload another APK file with the same version code number, the console will reject the file with the following error:

```
You need to use a different version code for your APK because you already have
one with version code 1.
```

To resolve this problem, the version code embedded into the APK file needs to be increased. This is performed in the *module* level *build.gradle* file of the project, shown highlighted in Figure 81-18:

Figure 81-18

By default, this file will typically read as follows:

```
apply plugin: 'com.android.application'

android {
    compileSdkVersion 26
    buildToolsVersion "26.0.2"
    defaultConfig {
        applicationId "com.ebookfrenzy.demoapp"
        minSdkVersion 14
        targetSdkVersion 26
        versionCode 1
        versionName "1.0"
        testInstrumentationRunner "android.support.test.runner.
AndroidJUnitRunner"
    }
    buildTypes {
        release {
            minifyEnabled false
            proguardFiles getDefaultProguardFile('proguard-android.
txt'), 'proguard-rules.pro'
        }
    }
}

dependencies {
    implementation fileTree(dir: 'libs', include: ['*.jar'])
    implementation 'com.android.support:appcompat-v7:26.0.2'
    implementation 'com.android.support.constraint:constraint-layout:1.0.2'
    implementation 'com.android.support:design:26.0.2'
    testImplementation 'junit:junit:4.12'
    androidTestImplementation('com.android.support.test.espresso:espresso-
core:3.0.1', {
```

```
        exclude group: 'com.android.support', module: 'support-annotations'
    })
}
```

To change the version code, simply change the number declared next to *versionCode*. To also change the version number displayed to users of your application, change the *versionName* string. For example:

```
versionCode 2
versionName "2.0"
```

Having made these changes, rebuild the APK file and perform the upload again.

81.13 Analyzing the APK File

Android Studio provides the ability to analyze the content of an APK file. This can be useful, for example, when attempting to find out why the APK file is larger than expected or to review the class structure of the application's dex file.

To analyze an APK file, select the Android Studio *Build -> Analyze APK...* menu option and navigate to and choose the APK file to be reviewed. Once loaded into the tool, information will be displayed about the raw and download size of the package together with a listing of the file structure of the package as illustrated in Figure 81-19:

Figure 81-19

Selecting the *classes.dex* file will display the class structure of the file in the lower panel. Within this panel, details of the individual classes may be explored down to the level of the methods within a class:

Class	Defined Methods	Referenced Methods	Size
android	16727	21813	2.3 MB
java		503	12 KB
com	24	28	36.3 KB
org		18	434 B
float[]		1	20 B
int[]		1	20 B
long[]		1	20 B

This dex file defines **2142** classes with **16751** methods, and references **22365** methods.

Figure 81-20

Similarly, selecting a resource or image file within the file list will display the file content within the lower panel. The size differences between two APK files may be reviewed by clicking on the *Compare with previous APK...* button and selecting a second APK file.

81.14 Enabling Google Play Signing for an Existing App

To enable Google Play Signing for an app already registered within the Google Play console, begin by selecting that app from the list of apps in the console dashboard. Once selected, click on the *App signing* link in the left-hand navigation panel as shown in Figure 81-21:

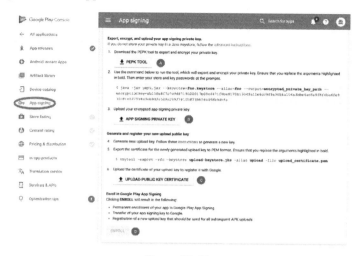

Figure 81-21

The first step is to click on the button to download the *PEPK Tool* (A) which will be used to encrypt the app signing key for the project. Once downloaded, copy it to the directory containing your existing keystore file and run the following command where (*<your app signing key file>* and *<your alias>* are replaced by the name of your keystore file and the corresponding alias key respectively):

```
java -jar pepk.jar --keystore=<your app signing key file> --alias=<your alias> --o
utput=encrypted_private_key_path --encryptionkey=<your app signing key>
```

Enter the keystore and key passwords when prompted, then check that a file named *encrypted_private_key_path* has been generated. This file contains your app signing key encrypted for uploading to the Google Play Store. Return to the Google Play console, click on the *App Signing Key* button (B) and upload the *encrypted_private_key_path* file.

Next, follow the steps outlined earlier in this chapter to generate the upload key and store it in a new keystore file. In a terminal or command-prompt window, change directory to the location of the upload keystore file and run the following command to convert the keystroke into a PEM certificate format file:

```
keytool -export -rfc -keystore <your upload key file> -alias <your alias> -file upl
oad_certificate.pem
```

With the file generated, click on the *Upload Public Key Certificate* button (C) in the Google Play console and upload the PEM certificate file.

Finally, enroll the app in Google Play Signing by clicking on the *Enroll* button (D). Once the app is enrolled, the new upload keystore file must be used whenever the signed APK file is generated within Android Studio.

81.15 Summary

Once an app project is either complete, or ready for user testing, it can be uploaded to the Google Play console and published for production, alpha or beta testing. Before the app can be uploaded, an app entry must be created within the console including information about the app together with screenshots to be used within the Play Store. A release APK file is then generated and signed with an upload key from within Android Studio. After the APK file has been uploaded, Google Play removes the upload key and replaces it with the securely stored app signing key and the app is ready to be published.

The content of an APK file can be reviewed at any time by loading it into the Android Studio APK Analyzer tool.

Chapter 82

82. An Overview of Gradle in Android Studio

Up until this point it has, for the most part, been taken for granted that Android Studio will take the necessary steps to compile and run the application projects that have been created. Android Studio has been achieving this in the background using a system known as *Gradle*.

It is now time to look at how Gradle is used to compile and package together the various elements of an application project and to begin exploring how to configure this system when more advanced requirements are needed in terms of building projects in Android Studio.

82.1 An Overview of Gradle

Gradle is an automated build toolkit that allows the way in which projects are built to be configured and managed through a set of build configuration files. This includes defining how a project is to be built, what dependencies need to be fulfilled for the project to build successfully and what the end result (or results) of the build process should be.

The strength of Gradle lies in the flexibility that it provides to the developer. The Gradle system is a self-contained, command-line based environment that can be integrated into other environments through the use of plug-ins. In the case of Android Studio, Gradle integration is provided through the appropriately named Android Studio Plug-in.

Although the Android Studio Plug-in allows Gradle tasks to be initiated and managed from within Android Studio, the Gradle command-line wrapper can still be used to build Android Studio based projects, including on systems on which Android Studio is not installed.

The configuration rules to build a project are declared in Gradle build files and scripts based on the Groovy programming language.

82.2 Gradle and Android Studio

Gradle brings a number of powerful features to building Android application projects. Some of the key features are as follows:

82.2.1 Sensible Defaults

Gradle implements a concept referred to as *convention over configuration*. This simply means that Gradle has a pre-defined set of sensible default configuration settings that will be used unless they are overridden by settings in the build files. This means that builds can be performed with the minimum of configuration required by the developer. Changes to the build files are only needed when the default configuration does not meet your build needs.

82.2.2 Dependencies

Another key area of Gradle functionality is that of dependencies. Consider, for example, a module within an Android Studio project which triggers an intent to load another module in the project. The first module has, in effect, a dependency on the second module since the application will fail to build if the second module cannot be located and launched at runtime. This dependency can be declared in the Gradle build file for the first module so that the second module is included in the application build, or an error flagged in the event the second module cannot be found or built. Other examples of dependencies are libraries and JAR files on which the project depends in order to compile and run.

Gradle dependencies can be categorized as *local* or *remote*. A local dependency references an item that is present on the local file system of the computer system on which the build is being performed. A remote dependency refers to an item that is present on a remote server (typically referred to as a *repository*).

Remote dependencies are handled for Android Studio projects using another project management tool named *Maven*. If a remote dependency is declared in a Gradle build file using Maven syntax then the dependency will be downloaded automatically from the designated repository and included in the build process. The following dependency declaration, for example, causes the AppCompat library to be added to the project from the Google repository:

```
implementation 'com.android.support:appcompat-v7:26.0.2'
```

82.2.3 Build Variants

In addition to dependencies, Gradle also provides *build variant* support for Android Studio projects. This allows multiple variations of an application to be built from a single project. Android runs on many different devices encompassing a range of processor types and screen sizes. In order to target as wide a range of device types and sizes as possible it will often be necessary to build a number of different variants of an application (for example, one with a user interface for phones and another for tablet sized screens). Through the use of Gradle, this is now possible in Android Studio.

82.2.4 Manifest Entries

Each Android Studio project has associated with it an AndroidManifest.xml file containing configuration details about the application. A number of manifest entries can be specified in Gradle build files which are then auto-generated into the manifest file when the project is built. This capability is complementary to the build variants feature, allowing elements such as the application version number, application ID and SDK version information to be configured differently for each build variant.

82.2.5 APK Signing

The chapter entitled *"Signing and Preparing an Android Application for Release"* covered the creation of a signed release APK file using the Android Studio environment. It is also possible to include the signing information entered through the Android Studio user interface within a Gradle build file so that signed APK files can be generated from the command-line.

82.2.6 ProGuard Support

ProGuard is a tool included with Android Studio that optimizes, shrinks and obfuscates Java byte code to make it more efficient and harder to reverse engineer (the method by which the logic of an application can be identified by others through analysis of the compiled Java byte code). The Gradle build files provide the ability to control whether or not ProGuard is run on your application when it is built.

82.3 The Top-level Gradle Build File

A completed Android Studio project contains everything needed to build an Android application and consists of modules, libraries, manifest files and Gradle build files.

Each project contains one top-level Gradle build file. This file is listed as *build.gradle (Project: <project name>)* and can be found in the project tool window as highlighted in Figure 82-1:

Figure 82-1

By default, the contents of the top level Gradle build file read as follows:

```
// Top-level build file where you can add configuration options common to all sub-
projects/modules.

buildscript {

    repositories {
        google()
        jcenter()
    }
    dependencies {
        classpath 'com.android.tools.build:gradle:3.0.0'


        // NOTE: Do not place your application dependencies here; they belong
        // in the individual module build.gradle files
    }
}


allprojects {
    repositories {
        google()
        jcenter()
    }
}

task clean(type: Delete) {
    delete rootProject.buildDir
}
```

As it stands all the file does is declare that remote libraries are to be obtained using the jcenter repository and that builds are dependent on the Android plugin for Gradle. In most situations it is not necessary to make any changes to this build file.

82.4 Module Level Gradle Build Files

An Android Studio application project is made up of one or more modules. Take, for example, a hypothetical application project named GradleDemo which contains two modules named Module1 and Module2 respectively. In this scenario, each of the modules will require its own Gradle build file. In terms of the project structure, these would be located as follows:

- Module1/build.gradle

- Module2/build.gradle

By default, the Module1 build.gradle file would resemble that of the following listing:

```
apply plugin: 'com.android.application'

android {
    compileSdkVersion 26
    buildToolsVersion "26.0.0"
    defaultConfig {
        applicationId "com.ebookfrenzy.module1"
        minSdkVersion 19
        targetSdkVersion 26
        versionCode 3
        versionName "1.0"
        testInstrumentationRunner "android.support.test.runner.
AndroidJUnitRunner"
    }
    buildTypes {
        release {
            minifyEnabled false
            proguardFiles getDefaultProguardFile('proguard-android.
txt'), 'proguard-rules.pro'
        }
    }
}

dependencies {
    implementation fileTree(dir: 'libs', include: ['*.jar'])
    implementation 'com.android.support:appcompat-v7:26.0.2'
    implementation 'com.android.support.constraint:constraint-layout:1.0.2'
    testImplementation 'junit:junit:4.12'
    androidTestImplementation 'com.android.support.test:runner:1.0.0'
    androidTestImplementation 'com.android.support.test.espresso:espresso-
core:3.0.0'
}
```

As is evident from the file content, the build file begins by declaring the use of the Gradle Android application plug-in:

```
apply plugin: 'com.android.application'
```

The *android* section of the file then states the version of both the SDK and the Android Build Tools that are to be used when building Module1.

```
android {
    compileSdkVersion 26
    buildToolsVersion "26.0.0"
```

The items declared in the defaultConfig section define elements that are to be generated into the module's *AndroidManifest.xml* file during the build. These settings, which may be modified in the build file, are taken from the settings entered within Android Studio when the module was first created:

```
defaultConfig {
    applicationId "com.ebookfrenzy.module1"
    minSdkVersion 19
    targetSdkVersion 26
    versionCode 1
    versionName "1.0"
}
```

The buildTypes section contains instructions on whether and how to run ProGuard on the APK file when a release version of the application is built:

```
buildTypes {
    release {
        runProguard false
        proguardFiles getDefaultProguardFile('proguard-android.txt'),
                    'proguard-rules.pro'
    }
}
```

As currently configured, ProGuard will not be run when Module1 is built. To enable ProGuard, the *runProguard* entry needs to be changed from *false* to *true*. The *proguard-rules.pro* file can be found in the module directory of the project. Changes made to this file override the default settings in the *proguard-android.txt* file which is located on the Android SDK installation directory under *sdk/tools/proguard*.

Since no debug buildType is declared in this file, the defaults will be used (built without ProGuard, signed with a debug key and with debug symbols enabled).

An additional section, entitled *productFlavors* may also be included in the module build file to enable multiple build variants to be created.

Finally, the dependencies section lists any local and remote dependencies on which the module is dependent. The first dependency reads as follows:

```
implementation fileTree(dir: 'libs', include: ['*.jar'])
```

This is a standard line that tells the Gradle system that any JAR file located in the module's lib sub-directory is to be included in the project build. If, for example, a JAR file named myclasses.jar was present in the GradleDemo/Module1/lib folder of the project, that JAR file would be treated as a module dependency and included in the build process.

The last dependency lines in the above example file designate that the Android Support and Design libraries need to be included from the Android Repository:

```
implementation 'com.android.support:appcompat-v7:26.0.0'
implementation 'com.android.support:design:26.0.0'
```

Note that the dependency declaration can include version numbers to indicate which version of the library should be included.

82.5 Configuring Signing Settings in the Build File

The *"Signing and Preparing an Android Application for Release"* chapter of this book covered the steps involved in setting up keys and generating a signed release APK file using the Android Studio user interface. These settings may also be declared within a *signingSettings* section of the build.gradle file. For example:

```
apply plugin: 'android'

android {
    compileSdkVersion 26
    buildToolsVersion "26.0.0"

    defaultConfig {
        applicationId "com.ebookfrenzy.gradledemo.module1"
        minSdkVersion 19
        targetSdkVersion 26
        versionCode 1
        versionName "1.0"
    }

    signingConfigs {
        release {
            storeFile file("keystore.release")
            storePassword "your keystore password here"
            keyAlias "your key alias here"
            keyPassword "your key password here"
        }
    }
    buildTypes {
    .

    .

    .

}
```

The above example embeds the key password information directly into the build file. Alternatives to this approach are to extract these values from system environment variables:

```
signingConfigs {
    release {
        storeFile file("keystore.release")
        storePassword System.getenv("KEYSTOREPASSWD")
        keyAlias "your key alias here"
```

```
        keyPassword System.getenv("KEYPASSWD")
    }
}
```

Yet another approach is to configure the build file so that Gradle prompts for the passwords to be entered during the build process:

```
signingConfigs {
    release {
        storeFile file("keystore.release")
        storePassword System.console().readLine
                ("\nEnter Keystore password: ")
        keyAlias "your key alias here"
        keyPassword System.console().readLIne("\nEnter Key password: ")
    }
}
```

82.6 Running Gradle Tasks from the Command-line

Each Android Studio project contains a Gradle wrapper tool for the purpose of allowing Gradle tasks to be invoked from the command line. This tool is located in the root directory of each project folder. While this wrapper is executable on Windows systems, it needs to have execute permission enabled on Linux and macOS before it can be used. To enable execute permission, open a terminal window, change directory to the project folder for which the wrapper is needed and execute the following command:

```
chmod +x gradlew
```

Once the file has execute permissions, the location of the file will either need to be added to your $PATH environment variable, or the name prefixed by ./ in order to run. For example:

```
./gradlew tasks
```

Gradle views project building in terms of number of different tasks. A full listing of tasks that are available for the current project can be obtained by running the following command from within the project directory (remembering to prefix the command with a ./ if running in macOS or Linux):

```
gradlew tasks
```

To build a debug release of the project suitable for device or emulator testing, use the assembleDebug option:

```
gradlew assembleDebug
```

Alternatively, to build a release version of the application:

```
gradlew assembleRelease
```

82.7 Summary

For the most part, Android Studio performs application builds in the background without any intervention from the developer. This build process is handled using the Gradle system, an automated build toolkit designed to allow the ways in which projects are built to be configured and managed through a set of build configuration files. While the default behavior of Gradle is adequate for many basic project build requirements, the need to configure the build process is inevitable with more complex projects. This chapter has provided an overview of the Gradle build system and configuration files within the context of an Android Studio project.

Index

Index

Index

Index

Index

Index

Index

Index

T

Index

X

Ready for Kotlin?

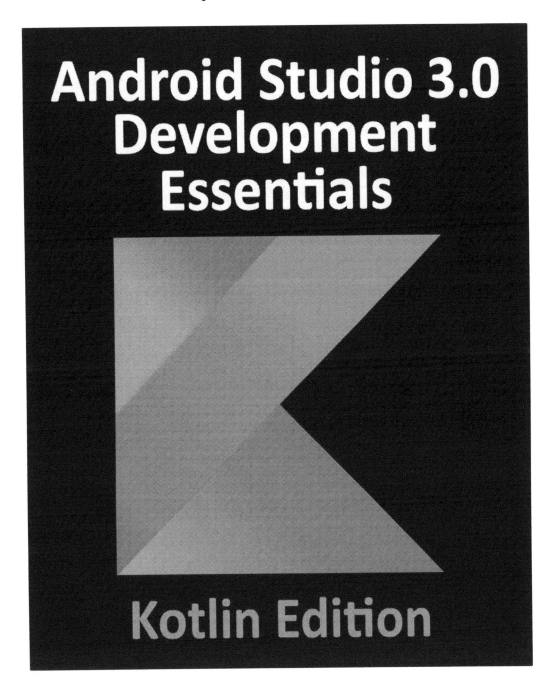

Learn more at *https://goo.gl/Q6usd4*

Also Available

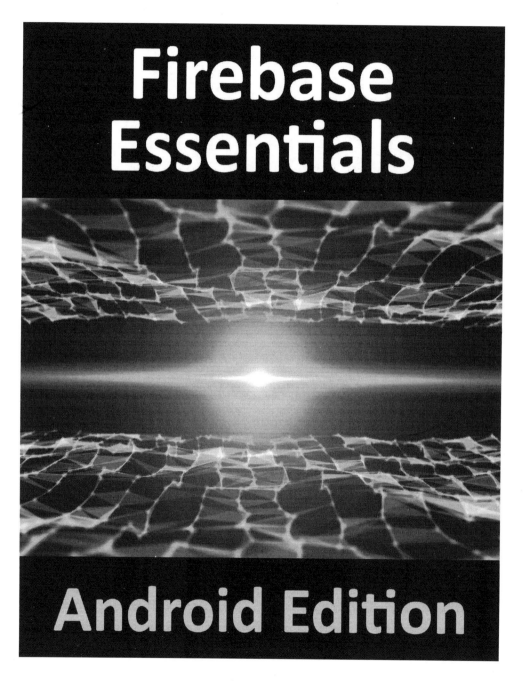

Firebase Essentials

Android Edition

Learn more at *https://goo.gl/5F381e*